HEATING, COOLING, LIGHTING

THIRD EDITION

HEATING, COOLING, LIGHTING:

Sustainable Design
Methods for Architects

Norbert Lechner

WILEY

John Wiley & Sons, Inc.

Published by John Wiley & Sons, Inc., Hoboken, New Jersey
Published simultaneously in Canada

For general information about our other products and services, please contact our Customer Care Department
within the United States at (800) 762-2974, outside the United States at (317) 572-3993 or fax (317) 572-4002.

Wiley also publishes its books in a variety of electronic formats. Some content that appears in print may not be
available in electronic books. For more information about Wiley products, visit our web site at www.wiley.com.

Library of Congress Cataloging-in-Publication Data:

Lechner, Norbert.
    Heating, cooling, lighting : design methods for architects / Norbert Lechner. —3rd ed.
        p. cm.
    Includes bibliographical references and index.
    ISBN 978-0-470-04809-2 (cloth)
        1. Heating.   2. Air conditioning.   3. Lighting.   I. Title.
    TH7222.L33   2008
    697—dc22   2008027971

Printed in the United States of America

10 9 8 7 6 5 4

This book is dedicated to a more sustainable and just world and to the idea that human beings can reverse global warming.

CONTENTS

FOREWORD TO THE FIRST EDITION

Professor Lechner's book differs from most of its predecessors in several important respects: (1) he deals with the heating, cooling, and lighting of buildings, not as discrete and isolated problems, but in the holistic sense of being integral parts of the larger task of environmental manipulation; (2) he deals with the subjects not merely from the engineer's limited commitment to mechanical and economic efficiency but from the much broader viewpoint of human comfort and physical and psychic well being; (3) he deals with these problems in relation to the central paradox of architecture—how to provide a stable, predetermined internal environment in an external environment that is in constant flux across time and space; and finally, (4) he approaches all aspects of this complex subject from a truly cultural—as opposed to a narrowly technological—perspective.

This attitude toward contemporary technology is by no means hostile. On the contrary, Professor Lechner handles it competently and comprehensively. But he never loses sight of the fact that the task of providing a truly satisfactory enclosure for human activity is that one must view the *building as a whole*. He points out, quite correctly, that until the last century or so, the manipulation of environmental factors was, of necessity, an architectural problem. It was the building itself—and only incidentally any meager mechanical equipment that the period happened to afford—that provided habitable space. To illustrate this point, he makes continuous and illuminating analysis to both high-style and vernacular traditions, to show how sagaciously the problems of climate control were tackled by earlier, prescientific, premechanized societies.

This is no easy-to-read copybook for those designers seeking shortcuts to glitzy postmodern architecture. On the contrary, it is a closely reasoned, carefully constructed guide for architects (young *and* old) who are seeking an escape route from the energy-wasteful, socially destructive cul-de-sac into which the practices of the past several decades have led us. Nor is it a Luddite critique of modern technology; to the contrary, it is a wise and civilized explication of how we must employ technical and scientific knowledge if we in the architectural field are to do our bit toward avoiding environmental disaster.

JAMES MARSTON FITCH
Hon. AIA, Hon. FRIBA
In memory of James Marston Fitch, architect,
historian, professor, preservationist, and
architectural theorist, 1909–2000.

FOREWORD TO THE THIRD EDITION

The words written by James Marston Fitch in 1991 in the Foreword to the First Edition are still valid, but the stakes are now much higher. Because the fate of the planet is at stake, it is no longer just a question of us following a particular architectural philosophy. Buildings consume about half of all energy produced in the United States and around the world. Building operations alone are responsible for 43 percent of total U.S. greenhouse gas emissions. To avert dangerous climate change, building design must transform, as exemplified by the internationally supported 2030 Challenge. Professor Lechner's book clearly illustrates how to achieve the energy consumption reduction targets called for by the 2030 Challenge. The book illustrates the many energy-saving strategies available to designers. It provides the information needed during the early phases of the design process, when a building's energy consumption patterns are defined. By using many of the strategies presented in this book, much of the energy consumed to heat, light, and cool buildings can be reduced dramatically.

Professor Lechner's book is also an important resource for those architects who are concerned about the aesthetic aspects of sustainability. He convincingly explains and demonstrates how lessons learned from vernacular architecture can be combined with the best of modern ideas to create very low impact, yet beautifully designed and humane architecture. Since carbon neutral buildings can be fully powered by renewable resources, a future of low-impact buildings is not only necessary but also possible.

EDWARD MAZRIA, AIA

PREFACE

IN THIS COMPLETELY REWORKED THIRD EDITION, the goal of previous editions remains: to provide the appropriate knowledge at the level of complexity needed at the schematic design stage. In the years since the first edition was published, we have moved from a shortage of information to a flood because of the Internet. This book will aid the designer because it presents the information in a concise, logical, accessible, and useful arrangement.

Since heating, cooling, and lighting are accomplished by adding energy to or removing it from a building, and since the consumption of energy is causing global warming, it is vital for architects to design low-energy, sustainable buildings. Although sustainability deals with many issues, the energy issues are the most critical. Thus, an additional goal of this book is to provide architects with the skills and knowledge needed to create low-energy and low-carbon-emission buildings.

Although every chapter has been improved and updated, the greatest change from the previous two editions is the use of Systeme International (SI) units in addition to the inch-pound (I-P) units. Also, Appendix M (conversion factors from I-P to SI) has been added. Chapter 15 (The Thermal Envelope) has been completely revised and greatly expanded, and Appendix L (Tables of R-values) has been added to support that chapter. New developments such as green roofs, cool roofing, cool towers, vacuum insulation, heat bridges, and light-emitting diode (LED) lighting have been added where appropriate in the book.

Because solar-responsive design is such an important part of sustainable design, sun angle information is now given for the whole planet rather than just for the United States. Appendix C gives altitude and azimuth angles in numerical form to greatly simplify the use of these angles. Also, the information and sources on heliodons has been expanded to make it easier to obtain this most useful tool for achieving solar-responsive design.

Because of the increasing interest in natural ventilation, the instructions for building and using a water table are included in Appendix N. A water table is used for modeling air flow through or around buildings. The appendix in the second edition that has listed schools that provide opportunities in energy-conscious design now provides a Web address, because the author has helped set up a Web page that will be continuously updated and expanded.

This book focuses on the schematic design stage, where the key decisions are made. The graph below points out how the earliest decisions have the greatest impact on a project. A building's cost and environmental impact are established mainly at the schematic design stage. The most basic decisions of size, orientation, and form often have the greatest impact on the resources required both during construction and during operation. Thus, designs for sustainable buildings are achieved primarily by the earliest decisions in the design process rather than by add-ons and engineering decisions made after the architectural design of the building has been essentially completed.

The information in this book is presented to support the three-tier approach to sustainable design of the heating, cooling, and lighting of buildings. The first tier is load avoidance. Here the need for heating, cooling, and lighting is minimized by the design of the building itself. The second tier consists of using natural energies as much as is practical. This tier is also accomplished mainly by the design of the building itself. The third and last tier uses mechanical and electrical equipment to satisfy the needs not provided for by the first two tiers.

With the knowledge and information presented in this book, the first two tiers can provide most of the thermal and lighting requirements of a building. As a consequence, the mechanical and electrical equipment of the third tier will be substantially smaller and will use much less energy than is typical now, thereby resulting in more sustainable buildings. Since tiers one and two are the domain of the architect, the role of the engineer at the third tier is to provide only the heating, cooling, and lighting that the architect could not.

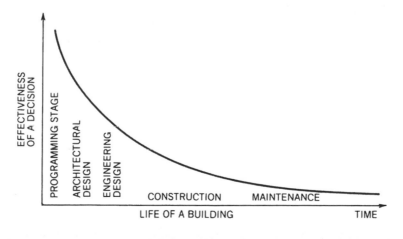

ACKNOWLEDGMENTS

For the third edition, I would like to thank especially Joe Aplin for his excellent work on the new and revised drawings. I also greatly appreciate the thoughtful and thorough reviews of Chapter 16 by mechanical engineers Dennis J. Wessel, P.E., LEED A.P., of Karpinski Engineering, and Fiona Cousins, P.E., LEED A.P., of ARUP Engineers. The typing and proofreading were done by my son, Walden Lechner, of Manuscript Services. And again, I want to thank my wife, Prof. Judith Lechner, whose support and love are invaluable for me.

NORBERT LECHNER
Prof. Emeritus and Architect
Auburn University

HEATING,
COOLING,
LIGHTING

CHAPTER 1

HEATING, COOLING, AND LIGHTING AS FORM-GIVERS IN ARCHITECTURE

Two essential qualities of architecture [commodity and delight], handed down from Vitruvius, can be attained more fully when they are seen as continuous, rather than separated, virtues.

... In general, however, this creative melding of qualities [commodity and delight] is most likely to occur when the architect is not preoccupied either with form-making or with problem-solving, but can view the experience of the building as an integrated whole....

John Morris Dixon
Editor of Progressive Architecture, 1990

All design projects should engage the environment in a way that dramatically reduces or eliminates the need for fossil fuel.

The 2010 Imperative,
Edward Mazria, AIA,
Founder of Architecture 2030

1.1 INTRODUCTION

Architecture has been called journalism in stone, since it has always reflected the culture, climate, and resources of the time and place. Eventually, as new forces emerged, architecture moved to its next stage. During the Renaissance, for example, the main influence was the rediscovery of the classical world. What is the predominant influence on architecture today?

The story that is now shaping the future of architecture is sustainability. There are few people left today who are not in favor of creating a sustainable world or who would claim that we are living in a sustainable world. Since building impacts the environment more than any other human activity, architects have both the responsibility and the opportunity to lead us to a sustainable future.

Sustainable architecture can be achieved by using "the best of the old and the best of the new." By using modern science, technology, and ideas of aesthetics combined with traditional ideas that responded to human needs, regionalism, and climate, a new architecture is being created. Such architecture will be richer than contemporary architecture, which gives no clue to where a building is located. Much contemporary architecture looks the same in New York, Paris, New Delhi, or Tokyo. Furthermore, this de facto "international" architecture is equally inappropriate wherever it is built since it is not sustainable.

Sustainability covers many issues, but none is as important as energy. More than any other factor, the energy consumption of buildings is destroying the planet as we know it. Buildings use about 48 percent of all the energy consumed, with 40 percent for the operation of buildings and 8 percent for the construction of buildings (Fig. 1.1a). This energy is mostly derived from fossil sources that produce the carbon dioxide that is the main cause of global warming. We must replace these polluting sources with clean, renewable energy

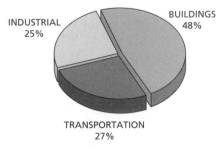

U.S. ENERGY CONSUMPTION

Figure 1.1a Buildings are the main cause of global warming because they use about 48 percent of all energy. Of that 48 percent, about 40 percent is for operating the buildings (heating, cooling, lighting, computers, etc.) and about 8 percent is for their construction (creating materials transportation, and erection). (Courtesy Architecture 2030.)

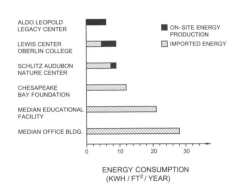

ENERGY CONSUMPTION
(KWH / FT² / YEAR)

Figure 1.1b The good news is that buildings do not have to use climate-changing fossil fuels. Over the years, we have learned how to design buildings so energy efficient that we can now build zero-energy buildings. The small amount of energy that they still need can be supplied by renewable sources such as photovoltaics on the roof.

sources such as wind, solar energy, and biomass, or we must increase the efficiency of our building stock so that it uses less energy, or we must do both. Of course, we need to do both, but decreasing the energy consumption of buildings is both quicker and less expensive. Furthermore, the design of energy-responsive buildings will yield a new aesthetic that can replace both the blandness of most modern buildings and the unimaginative copying of previous styles.

Is it really possible for architecture to seriously address the problem of global warming? The answer is an unambiguous yes, both because present buildings are so wasteful of energy and because we know how to design and build buildings that use 80 percent less energy than the standard new building. Presently, there are architects around the world designing "zero-energy buildings." Such buildings are designed to use as little energy as possible, with the small remaining load being met by renewable energy such as photovoltaics (Fig. 1.1b). We have the *know-how* (see Sidebox 1.1); all we need is the *will*.

SIDEBOX 1.1

Characteristics of a Zero-Energy House

- Superinsulated walls, roof, and floor
- Airtight construction with a heat recovery unit for ventilation
- High-performance, properly oriented windows
- Windows fully shaded in summer
- Passive solar heating
- Active solar domestic hot water
- High-efficiency appliances
- High-efficiency electric lighting
- High-efficiency heating and cooling system (e.g., earth-coupled heat pump)
- Photovoltaics on roof that produce the small amount of electricity still needed

This book was written to help the architect design sustainable buildings that use very little energy. It presents rules of thumb, guidelines, and examples that are drawn from the best of the old and the best of the new. Traditional architecture, which used little if any energy, is presented for ideas and inspiration. Folk or indigenous buildings usually responded to their climate, their locality, and their culture, as the next section shows.

1.2 VERNACULAR AND REGIONAL ARCHITECTURE

One of the main reasons for regional differences in architecture is the response to climate. If we look at buildings in hot and humid climates, in hot and dry climates, and in cold climates, we find that they are quite different from one another.

In hot and dry climates, one usually finds massive walls used for their time-lag effect. Since the sun is very intense, small windows will adequately light the interiors. The windows are also small because during the daytime the hot outdoor air makes ventilation largely undesirable. The exterior surface colors are usually very light to minimize the absorption of solar radiation. Interior surfaces are also light to help diffuse the sunlight entering through the small windows (Fig. 1.2a).

Since there is usually little rain, roofs can be flat and, consequently, are available as additional living and sleeping areas during summer nights. Outdoor areas cool quickly after the sun sets because of the rapid radiation to the clear night sky. Thus, roofs are more comfortable than the interiors, which are still quite warm from the daytime heat stored in the massive construction.

Even community planning responds to climate. In hot and dry climates, buildings are often closely clustered for the shade they offer one another and the public spaces between them.

In hot and humid climates, we find a very different kind of building. Although temperatures are lower, the high humidity creates great discomfort. The main relief comes from moving air across the skin to increase the rate of evaporative cooling. Although the water vapor in the air weakens the sun, direct solar radiation is still very undesirable. The typical antebellum house (see Fig. 1.2b) responds to the humid climate by its use of many large windows, large overhangs, shutters, light-colored walls, and high ceilings. The large windows maximize ventilation, while the overhangs and shutters protect from both solar radiation and rain. The light-colored walls minimize heat gain.

Since in humid climates nighttime temperatures are not much lower than daytime temperatures, massive construction is not an advantage. Buildings are, therefore, usually made of lightweight wood construction. High ceilings permit larger windows and allow the air to stratify. As a result, people inhabit the lower and cooler air layers. Vertical ventilation through roof monitors or high windows not only increases ventilation but also exhausts the hottest air layers first. For this reason, high gabled roofs without ceilings are popular in many parts of the world that have hot and humid climates (Fig. 1.2c).

Buildings are sited as far apart as possible for maximum access to the cooling breezes. In some humid regions of the Middle East, wind scoops are used to further increase the natural ventilation through the building (Fig. 1.2d).

In mild but very overcast climates, like the Pacific Northwest, buildings open up to capture all the daylight possible. In this kind of climate, the use of bay windows is quite common (Fig. 1.2e).

And finally, in a predominantly cold climate, we see a very different kind of architecture. In such a climate, the emphasis is on heat retention. Buildings, like the local animals, tend to be very compact to minimize the surface-area-to-volume ratio. Windows are few because they are weak points in the thermal envelope. Since the thermal resistance of the walls is very important, wood rather than stone is usually used (Fig. 1.2f). Because hot air rises, ceilings are kept very low (often below 7 feet). Trees and landforms are used to protect against the cold winter winds. In spite of the desire for views and daylight, windows are often sacrificed for the overpowering need to conserve heat.

Figure 1.2a Massive construction, small windows, and light colors are typical in hot and dry climates, as in this Yemeni village. It is also common, in such climates, to find flat roofs and buildings huddled together for mutual shading. (Drawing by Richard Millman.)

Figure 1.2b In hot and humid climates, natural ventilation from shaded windows is the key to thermal comfort. This Charleston, South Carolina, house uses covered porches and balconies to shade the windows, as well as to create cool outdoor living spaces. The white color and roof monitor are also important in minimizing summer overheating.

Figure 1.2c In hot and humid climates, such as Sumatra, Indonesia, native buildings are often raised on stilts and have high roofs with open gables to maximize natural ventilation.

Figure 1.2d When additional ventilation is desired, wind scoops can be used, as on this reconstructed historical dwelling in Dubai. Also note the open weave of the walls to further increase natural ventilation. (Photograph by Richard Millman.)

Figure 1.2e Bay windows are used to capture as much light as possible in a mild but very overcast climate such as that found in Eureka, California.

Figure 1.2f In cold climates, compactness, thick wooden walls, and a severe limit on window area were the traditional ways to stay warm. In very cold climates, the fireplace was located either on the inside of the exterior wall or in the center of the building.

1.3 FORMAL ARCHITECTURE

Not only vernacular structures but also buildings designed by the most sophisticated architects have responded to the need for environmental control. After all, the Greek portico is simply a feature to protect against the rain and sun (Fig. 1.3a). The perennial popularity of classical architecture is based not only on aesthetic but also on practical grounds. There is hardly a better way to shade windows, walls, and porches than with large overhangs supported by colonnades or arcades (Fig. 1.3b).

The Roman basilicas consisted of large high-ceilinged spaces that were very comfortable is hot climates during the summer. Clerestory windows were used to bring daylight into these central spaces. Both the trussed roof and groin-vaulted basilicas became prototypes for Christian churches (Fig. 1.3c).

One of the Gothic builders' main goals was to maximize the window area for a large fire-resistant hall. By means of an inspired structural system, they sent an abundance of daylight through stained glass (Fig. 1.3d).

The need for heating, cooling, and lighting has also affected the work of the twentieth-century masters, such as Frank Lloyd Wright. The Marin County Court House emphasizes the importance of shading and daylighting. To give most offices access to daylight, the building consists of linear elements separated by a glass-covered atrium (Fig. 1.3e). The outside windows are shaded from the direct sun by an arcade-like overhang (Fig. 1.3f). Since the arches are not structural, Frank Lloyd Wright shows them hanging from the building.

Modern architecture prided itself on its foundation of logic. "Form follows function" was seen as much

Figure 1.3a The classical portico has its functional roots in the sun- and rain-protected entrance of the early Greek megaron. (Maison Carée, Nimes, France.)

Figure 1.3b The classical revival style was especially popular in the South because it was very suitable for hot climates.

Figure 1.3c Roman basilicas and the Christian churches based on them used clerestory windows to light the large interior spaces. The Thermae of Diocletian, Rome (302 A.D.), was converted by Michelangelo into the church of Saint Maria Degli Angeli. (Photograph by Clark Lundell.)

more sensible than "form follows some arbitrary historical style." However, "function" was usually interpreted as referring to structure or building circulation. Rarely did it refer to low energy usage, which was seen as a minor issue at best but usually was not considered at all. Although that belief was never logical, it is clearly wrong today since energy is the number one issue facing the earth.

One exception was Le Corbusier, who also felt strongly that the building should be effective in heating, cooling, and lighting itself. His development of the "brise soleil" will be discussed in some detail later. A feature found in a number of his buildings is the **parasol roof**, an umbrella-like structure covering the whole building. A good example of this concept is the "Maison d'Homme," which Le Corbusier designed in glass and painted steel (Fig. 1.3g).

Today, with no predominant style guiding architects, revivalism is common. The buildings in Fig. 1.3h use the classical portico for shading. Such historical adaptations can be more climate responsive than the "international style," which often ignores the local climate. Buildings in cold climates can continue to benefit from compactness, and buildings in hot and dry climates still benefit from massive walls and light exterior surfaces. Looking to the past in one's locality will lead to the development of a new and sustainable regional style.

1.4 THE ARCHITECTURAL APPROACH

The sustainable design of heating, cooling, and lighting buildings can be accomplished in three tiers (Fig. 1.4). The first tier is the architectural design of the building itself to minimize heat loss in the winter, to minimize heat gain in the summer, and to use light efficiently. Poor decisions at this point can easily double or triple the size of the mechanical equipment and energy eventually needed. On the other hand, making

Figure 1.3d Daylight was given a mystical quality as it passed through the large stained-glass windows of the Gothic cathedral. (Photograph by Clark Lundell.)

Figure 1.3e In the linear central atrium of the Marin County House, F.L. Wright used white surfaces to reflect light down to the lower levels. The offices facing the atrium have all-glass walls.

Figure 1.3f The exterior windows of the Marin County Court House are protected from direct sun by an arcade-like exterior corridor.

Figure 1.3g The "Maison d'Homme" in Zurich, Switzerland, demonstrates well the concept of the parasol roof. The building is now called "Centre le Corbusier." (Photograph by William Gwinn.)

Figure 1.3h These postmodern buildings promote the concept of "regionalism" in that they reflect a previous and appropriate style of the hot and humid Southeast.

the right design choices in tier one can reduce the energy consumption of buildings as much as 60 percent.

The second tier involves the use of natural energies through such methods as passive heating, cooling, and daylighting systems. The proper decisions at this point can reduce the energy consumption another 20 percent. Thus, the strategies in tiers one and two, which are both purely architectural, can reduce the energy consumption of buildings up to 80 percent. Tier 3 consists of designing the mechanical equipment to be as efficient as possible. That effort could reduce energy consumption another 8 percent. Thus, only 12 percent as much energy is needed as in a conventional building. That small amount of energy can be derived from renewable sources both on and off site. Table 1.4 shows some of the design topics that are typical at each of the three tiers.

The heating, cooling, and lighting design of buildings always involves all three tiers, whether consciously considered or not. Unfortunately, in the recent past, minimal demands were placed on the building itself to affect the indoor environment. It was assumed that it was primarily the engineers at the third tier who

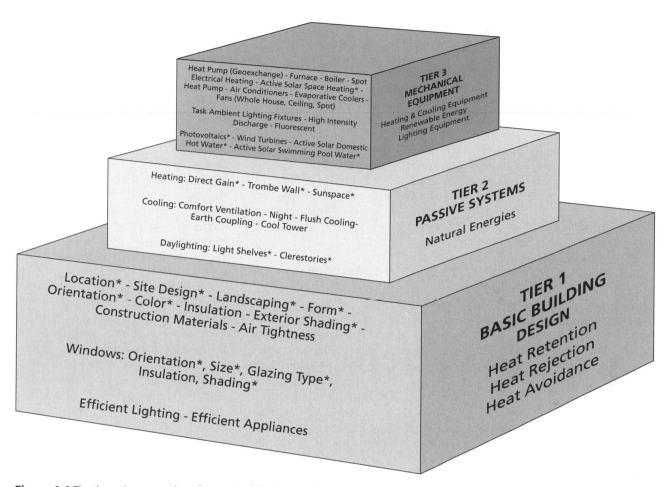

Heat Pump (Geoexchange) - Furnace - Boiler - Spot
Electrical Heating - Active Solar Space Heating* -
Heat Pump - Air Conditioners - Evaporative Coolers -
Fans (Whole House, Ceiling, Spot)

Task Ambient Lighting Fixtures - High Intensity
Discharge - Fluorescent

Photovoltaics* - Wind Turbines - Active Solar Domestic
Hot Water* - Active Solar Swimming Pool Water*

**TIER 3
MECHANICAL
EQUIPMENT**
Heating & Cooling Equipment
Renewable Energy
Lighting Equipment

Heating: Direct Gain* - Trombe Wall* - Sunspace*

Cooling: Comfort Ventilation - Night - Flush Cooling-
Earth Coupling - Cool Tower

Daylighting: Light Shelves* - Clerestories*

**TIER 2
PASSIVE SYSTEMS**
Natural Energies

Location* - Site Design* - Landscaping* - Form* -
Orientation* - Color* - Insulation - Exterior Shading* -
Construction Materials - Air Tightness

Windows: Orientation*, Size*, Glazing Type*,
Insulation, Shading*

Efficient Lighting - Efficient Appliances

**TIER 1
BASIC BUILDING
DESIGN**
Heat Retention
Heat Rejection
Heat Avoidance

Figure 1.4 The three-tier approach to the sustainability design of heating, cooling, and lighting is shown. Tiers one and two are the domain of the architect, and proper design decisions at these two levels can reduce the energy consumption of buildings as much as 80 percent. All items with an asterisk are part of solar-responsive design. This image can be downloaded for free and used as a poster. It is available at www.cadc.auburn.edu/sun-emulator.

Table 1.4 The Three-Tier Design Approach

	Heating	Cooling	Lighting
Tier 1	*Conservation*	*Heat avoidance*	*Daylight*
Basic Building Design	1. Surface-to-volume ratio 2. Insulation 3. Infiltration	1. Shading 2. Exterior colors 3. Insulation 4. Mass	1. Windows 2. Glazing type 3. Interior finishes
Tier 2	*Passive solar*	*Passive cooling*	*Daylighting*
Natural Energies and Passive Techniques	1. Direct gain 2. Trombe wall 3. Sunspace	1. Evaporative cooling 2. Night-flush cooling 3. Comfort ventilation	1. Skylights 2. Clerestories 3. Light shelves
Tier 3	*Heating equipment*	*Cooling equipment*	*Electric light*
Mechanical and Electrical Equipment	1. Furnace 2. Boiler 3. Ducts/Pipes 4. Fuels	1. Refrigeration machine 2. Ducts 3. Geo-exchange	1. Lamps 2. Fixtures 3. Location of fixtures

were responsible for the environmental control of the building. Thus, architects, who were often indifferent to the heating, cooling, and lighting needs of buildings, sometimes designed buildings that were at odds with their environment. For example, buildings with large glazed areas were designed for very hot or very cold climates. The engineers were then forced to design giant, energy-guzzling heating and cooling plants to maintain thermal comfort. Ironically, these mostly glass buildings had their electric lights on during the day, when daylight was abundant, because they were not designed to gather quality daylighting. The size of the mechanical equipment can be seen as an indicator of the architect's success, or lack thereof, in using the building itself to control the indoor environment.

In some climates, it is possible to reduce the mechanical equipment to zero. For example, Amory Lovins designed his home/office for the Rocky Mountain Institute in Snowmass, Colorado, where it is very cold in the winter and quite hot in the summer, to have no heating or cooling system at all. He used the strategies of tiers one and two to accomplish most of the heating and cooling, and he used photovoltaics and active solar for any energy still needed.

When it is consciously recognized that each of these tiers is an integral part of the heating, cooling, and lighting design process, the buildings are improved in several ways. The buildings are often less expensive because of reduced mechanical-equipment and energy needs. They are usually also more comfortable because the mechanical equipment does not have to fight such giant thermal loads. Furthermore, the buildings are often more interesting because some of the money that is normally spent on the mechanical equipment is spent instead on the architectural elements. Unlike hidden mechanical equipment, features, such as shading devices, are a very visible part of the exterior aesthetic—thus the name of this chapter is "Heating, Cooling, and Lighting as Form-Givers in Architecture."

1.5 DYNAMIC VERSUS STATIC BUILDINGS

Contemporary buildings are essentially static with a few dynamic parts, such as the mechanical equipment, doors, and sometimes operable windows. On the other hand, smart, sustainable buildings adapt to their changing environments. This change can occur continuously over a day as, for example, a movable shading device that extends when it is sunny and retracts when it is cloudy. Alternatively, the change could be on an annual basis, whereby a shading device is extended during the summer and retracted in the winter, much like a

deciduous tree. The dynamic aspect can be modest, as in movable shading devices, or it can be dramatic, as when the whole building rotates to track the sun (Figs. 9.16b to 9.16d). Not only will dynamic buildings perform much better than static buildings, but they also will provide an exciting aesthetic, the **aesthetic of change**. Numerous examples of dynamic buildings are included throughout the book, but most will be found in the chapters on shading, passive cooling, and daylighting.

1.6 PASSIVE SURVIVABILITY

We should design buildings not only to sustain the planet but also to sustain us during an emergency. For example, houses on stilts had a better chance to survive the storm-surge of Hurricane Katrina than the typical houses built close to the ground.

We rely on our buildings' mechanical systems and imported energy supplies to keep us warm in the winter, cool in the summer, and out of the dark all year. Yet, in January 1998, an ice storm in eastern Canada left 4 million people without power for weeks during the height of the winter. Heat waves in the United States and Europe are becoming more severe and frequent. Is it wise to rely on mechanical equipment and uninterrupted energy supplies? Alex Wilson of the *Environmental Building News* suggests that building design should include a new mandate: **passive survivability**.

Fortunately, a sustainable building will also have more passive survivability than a conventional building. The strategies mentioned in this book, such as higher levels of insulation, passive solar, passive cooling, and daylighting, all increase the passive survivability of a building.

1.7 ENERGY AND ARCHITECTURE

The heating, cooling, and lighting of buildings are accomplished by either adding or removing energy.

Consequently, this book is about the manipulation and use of energy. In the 1960s, the consumption of energy was considered a trivial concern. For example, buildings were sometimes designed without light switches because it was believed that it was more economical to leave the lights on—continuously. Also, the most popular air-conditioning equipment for larger buildings was the "terminal reheat system," in which the air was first cooled to the lowest level needed by any space, then reheated as necessary to satisfy the other spaces. The double use of energy was not considered an important issue.

Buildings now use about 40 percent of all the energy consumed in the United States (Fig. 1.1a). To construct them takes another 8 percent of all the energy. Clearly, then, the building industry has a major responsibility in the energy picture of this planet. Architects have both the responsibility and the opportunity to design in an energy-conserving manner.

The responsibility is all the greater because of the effective life of the product. Automobiles last only about ten years, and so any mistakes will not burden society too long. Most buildings, however, have a useful life of at least fifty years. The consequences of design decisions now will be with us for a long time.

Unfortunately, the phrase **energy conservation** has negative connotations. It makes one think of shortages and discomfort. Yet architecture that conserves energy can be comfortable, sustainable, humane, and aesthetically pleasing. It can also be less expensive than conventional architecture. Operating costs are reduced because of lower energy bills, and first costs are often reduced because of the smaller amount of heating and cooling equipment that is required. To avoid the negative connotations, the more positive and flexible phrases **energy-efficient design** or **energy-conscious design** have been adopted to describe a concern for energy conservation in architecture. Energy-conscious design yields buildings that minimize the need for expensive, polluting, and nonrenewable energy. Because of the benefit to planet Earth, such design is now called **sustainable, green** or **low carbon**.

Because of global warming, it is now widely recognized that reducing the energy appetite of buildings is the number one green issue. For example, in 2007 the U.S. Green Building Council (USGBC) increased the energy requirements for LEED (Leadership in Energy and Environmental Design) certification. As Fig. 1.7 illustrates, the energy issues are a very large subset of all of the sustainability issues. Figure 1.7 also demonstrates that the solar issues are a surprisingly large subset of the energy issues. One reason for this is that "solar" refers to many strategies: photovoltaics (solar cells), active solar (hot water), passive solar (space heating), daylighting, and shading. Although shading is the reverse of collecting solar energy, it is one of the most important solar design strategies, because it can save large amounts of air-conditioning energy at low cost.

In describing "The Next Industrial Revolution," William McDonough and Michael Braungart say that it is based on three basic principles:

1. *Waste equals food*—Everything must be produced in such a manner that, when its useful life is over, it becomes a healthy source of raw materials to produce new things.
2. *Respect diversity*—Designs for everything will respect the regional, cultural, and materials of a place.
3. *Use solar energy*—All energy sources must be nonpolluting and renewable, and buildings must be solar responsive.

Thus, we see again how solar energy and solar responsive design will play a critical role in any thoughtful plan for a sustainable future.

Besides the sustainability rating system mentioned above (i.e., LEED), in the United States and Canada there is also Green Globes,™ which was developed by the Green Building Initiative (GBI). Other systems are used in other parts of the world, and two important components of all of these rating systems are energy efficiency and the use of solar energy.

Another method for encouraging sustainable design is to give awards. Every year the American Institute of Architecture Committee on the Environment (AIA/COTE) announces the "Top Ten" from all the submissions of sustainable design. Energy responsiveness is an important criterion.

Since global warming is by far the most critical issue of sustainability, the organization **Architecture 2030** was formed to reduce the greenhouse gas emissions of buildings to zero by the year 2030. The organization asks architects and building groups to implement the 2030 Challenge, which requires that buildings reduce their greenhouse gas emissions by 50 percent by the year 2010 and then incrementally reduce it further until the emissions are zero in 2030. Among the numerous groups that have signed on are the American Institute of Architects (AIA), the U.S. Green Building Council (USGBC) which operates Leadership in Energy and Environmental Design (LEED), the U.S. Conference of Mayors, the U.S. government for its own buildings, and numerous foreign groups.

The target dates of the **2030 Challenge** are based on the scientific evidence for how much time we have before humans lose control of climate change brought about by our greenhouse gas emissions. To accomplish these real and necessary targets, building design must incorporate as many energy-saving strategies as possible. Most of the required architectural strategies are covered in this book.

1.8 ARCHITECTURE AND HEATING, COOLING, AND LIGHTING

The following design considerations have an impact on both the appearance and the heating, cooling, and lighting of a building: form, orientation, compactness (surface-area-to-volume ratio), size and location of windows, and the nature of the building materials. Thus, when architects start to design the appearance of a building, they simultaneously start the design of the heating, cooling, and lighting. Because of this inseparable relationship between architectural features and the heating, cooling, and lighting of buildings, we can say that the environmental controls are **form-givers** in architecture.

It is not just tiers one and two that have aesthetic impact. The mechanical

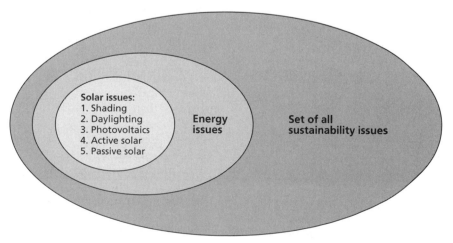

Figure 1.7 Sustainable design includes a very large set of issues, and the energy issues are a large subset thereof. The solar issues are a much larger subset of the energy issues than most people realize. This image can be downloaded for free and used as a poster. It is available at www.cadc.auburn.edu/sun-emulator.

equipment required for heating and cooling is often quite bulky, and because it requires access to outside air, it is frequently visible on the exterior. The lighting equipment, although less bulky, is even more visible. Thus, even tier three is interconnected with the architectural aesthetics, and, as such, must be considered at the earliest stages of the design process.

1.9 CONCLUSION

The heating, cooling, and lighting of buildings are accomplished not just by mechanical equipment, but mostly by the design of the building itself. The design decisions that affect these environmental controls have, for the most part, a strong effect on the form and aesthetics of buildings.

Thus, through design, architects have the opportunity to simultaneously satisfy their need for aesthetic expression and to efficiently heat, cool, and light buildings. Only through architectural design can buildings be heated, cooled, and lit in a sustainable way. The next chapter explains the nature of sustainability in more detail.

KEY IDEAS OF CHAPTER 1

1. Both vernacular and formal architecture were traditionally designed to respond to the heating, cooling, and lighting needs of buildings.
2. Borrowing appropriate regional design solutions from the past (e.g., the classical portico for shade) can help in creating sustainable buildings.
3. In the twentieth century, only the engineers, with their mechanical and electrical equipment, responded to the environmental needs of buildings. Architects provided these needs in the past, and they can again be important players in the future.
4. The heating, cooling, and lighting needs of buildings can be designed by the three-tier approach:

   TIER ONE: the basic design of the building form and fabric (by the architect)
   TIER TWO: the design of passive systems (mostly by the architect)
   TIER THREE: the design of the mechanical and electrical equipment (by the engineer).
5. Buildings use about 40 percent of all the energy consumed in the United States. Their construction takes another 8 percent.
6. Currently, the dynamic mechanical equipment responds to the continually changing heating, cooling, and lighting needs of a building. There are both functional and aesthetic benefits when the building itself is more responsive to the environment (e.g., movable shading devices). Buildings should be dynamic rather than static.
7. Sustainable buildings also provide "passive survivability" in case of power outages or high fuel costs.
8. Because of global warming, it is imperative that buildings use less energy and achieve zero greenhouse gas emissions by 2030.
9. There is great aesthetic potential in energy-conscious architecture.

Resources

FURTHER READING

See the Bibliography in the back of the book for full citations.

Banham, R. *The Architecture of the Well-Tempered Environment.*
Brown, G. Z., and M. DeKay. *Sun, Wind, and Light: Architectural Design Strategies.*
Duly, C. *The Houses of Mankind.*
Fathy, H. *Natural Energy and Vernacular Architecture: Principles and Examples with Reference to Hot Arid Climates.*
Fitch, J. M. *The Architecture of the American People.*
Fitch, J. M. *Shelter: Models of Native Ingenuity.*
Fitch, J. M., and W. Bobenhausen. *American Building: The Environmental Forces That Shape It.*

Heschong, L. *Thermal Delight in Architecture.*
Konya, A. *Design Primer for Hot Climates.*
Lovins, Amory, et al. *Winning the Oil Endgame.* www.oilendgame.com.
Lovins, Amory. "More Profit with Less Carbon."
McDonough, W., and M. Braungart. *The Next Industrial Revolution.*
Nabokov, P., and R. Easton. *Native American Architecture.*
Olgyay, V. *Design with Climate: Bioclimatic Approach to Architectural Regionalism.*
Rapoport, A. *House Form and Culture.*
Rudofsky, B. *Architecture without Architects: A Short Introduction to Non-Pedigreed Architecture.*
Rudofsky, B. *The Prodigious Builders: Notes Toward a Natural History of Architecture.*

Stein, R. G. *Architecture and Energy: Conserving Energy Through Rational Design.*
Susanka, Sarah. *The Not So Big House: A Blueprint for the Way We Really Live.*
Taylor, J. S. *Commonsense Architecture: A Cross-Cultural Survey of Practical Design Principles.*

PAPERS

Knowles, R. "On Being the Right Size," www.rcf.usc.edu/~rknowles.
Knowles, R. "Rhythm and Ritual," www.rcf.usc.edu/~rknowles.
Knowles, R. "The Rituals of Place," www.rcf.usc.edu/~rknowles.

ORGANIZATIONS

Architecture 2030 www.Architecture2030.org.
Rocky Mountain Institute www.rmi.org.

SUSTAINABLE DESIGN

Sustainable development is development that meets the needs of the present without compromising the ability of future generations to meet their own needs.
***The United Nations World Commission on Environment and Development,
the Brundtland Report, 1987***

As we peer into society's future, we—you and I, and our government—must avoid the impulse to live only for today, plundering, for our own ease and convenience, the precious resources of tomorrow. We cannot mortgage the material assets of our grandchildren without risking the loss also of their political and spiritual heritage. We want democracy to survive for all generations to come, not to become the insolvent phantom of tomorrow.
President Dwight D. Eisenhower's Farewell Address, 1961

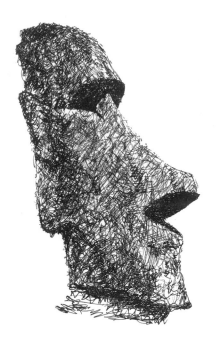

Figure 2.1 The mysterious stone heads of Easter Island. (Drawn by Ethan Lechner)

2.1 EASTER ISLAND: LEARNING FROM THE PAST

Easter Island has long mystified archaeologists. When the tiny remote island, 2,000 miles (3,200 km) from the nearest continent, was "discovered" on Easter day in 1722, about 200 mammoth stone statues, some more than 30 feet tall and weighing more than 80 tons, stood on the island [Fig. 2.1].

The island was a biological wasteland. Except for introduced rats and chickens, there were no animal species higher than insects and only a few dozen plant species—mostly grasses and ferns—and nothing more than 10 feet in height. There was no obvious way that the island's 2,000 or so inhabitants could have transported and hoisted the huge statues.

Based on an analysis of ancient pollen, researchers have now established that Easter Island was a very different place when the Polynesians first arrived around 400 A.D. In fact, it was a subtropical paradise, rich in biodiversity. The Easter Island palm grew more than 80 feet tall and would have been ideal for carving into canoes for fishing, as well as equipment for erecting statues. In addition to the rich plant life, there were at least twenty-five species of nesting birds.

We now believe that Easter Islanders exploited their resources to the point that they exterminated all species of higher animals and many species of plants. The island's ecosystem might have been destroyed in a cascading fashion; as certain birds were eliminated, for example, trees dependent on those birds for pollination could no longer reproduce. Denuded of forests, the land eroded, carrying nutrients out to sea.

Researchers believe that the island population had grown to a peak of 20,000 that lived in a highly organized structure. But as food (or the ability to get it) became scarce, this structure broke down into warring tribal factions. By 1722, the island's population had dropped to 2,000.

Why didn't the Easter Islanders see what was happening? Jared Diamond, in the August 1995, *Discover* magazine, suggests that the collapse happened "not with a bang but a whimper." Their means of making boats, rope, and log rollers disappeared over decades or even generations and either they didn't see what was happening or couldn't do anything about it.

Will humanity as a whole do better with planet Earth than the Polynesian settlers did with their Easter Island paradise? Many politicians and talk-show hosts claim that there are no limits to growth—that environmental doomsayers are wrong. But Easter Island shows us that limits are real. Let's not wait until it is too late to come to grips with these limits.

Shortened by permission from Alex Wilson, editor and publisher, *Environmental Building News (EBN).* * The full article appeared in *EBN*, Volume 4, Number 5, September–October 1995.

Environmental Building News is a monthly newsletter for architects and builders committed to improving the sustainability of buildings and the built environment (see Appendix K for the address).

2.2 SUSTAINABLE DESIGN

In the long run, sustainable design is not an option but a necessity. Earth, with 6.7 billion people, is rapidly approaching the same level of stress that 20,000 people caused to Easter Island. We are literally covering planet Earth with people (see Fig 2.2a). We are depleting our land and water resources; we are destroying biodiversity; we are polluting the land, water, and air; and we are changing the climate, with potentially catastrophic results.

In the short term, it *seems* that we do not have to practice sustainable design, but that is true only if we ignore the future. We are using up resources and polluting the planet without regard to the needs of our children and our children's children (Fig. 2.2b).

The World Congress of Architects in Chicago in June 1993, said:

> Sustainability means meeting the needs of the current generation without compromising the ability of future generations to meet their own needs. A sustainable society restores, preserves, and enhances nature and culture for the benefit of all life present and future; a diverse and healthy environment is intrinsically valuable and essential to a healthy society; today's society is seriously degrading the environment and is not sustainable.

Figure 2.2a Nighttime lights of the world as viewed from satellites clearly show how people are filling up the planet. (From NASA.)

Figure 2.2b Where mountain once stood, a colossal hole now exists. Human beings are literally moving mountains to feed their appetite for resources. For a sense of scale, note the trains on the terraces on the far side. The tunnel at the bottom of this open-pit copper mine in Utah is for the trains to take the ore to smelters beyond the mountains.

Many ways exist to describe sustainable design. One approach urges using the four Rs:

REDUCE
REUSE
RECYCLE
REGENERATE

This book will focus on the first R, **reduce.** Although the word "reduce" might evoke images of deprivation, it applies primarily to the reduction of waste and extravagance. For example, American houses have more than doubled in size since 1950, and since families are now smaller, the increase in size per person is about 2.8. Is that really necessary? Are Americans happier today than in 1950? Are "starter castles" and "McMansions" the route to happiness? The book *The Not So Big House*, written by the architect Sarah Susanka, was a national best seller. Many people have discovered that bigger is not better much of the time.

Besides reducing their size, we can also reduce the energy appetite of our buildings. Consider how inefficient a conventionally built home is, when a demonstration home in Lakeland, Florida, wastes 80 percent less energy (FSEC, 1998). Proven techniques in the areas of heating, cooling, and lighting can easily reduce energy use in commercial buildings by 50 percent, and with a little effort 80 percent reductions are possible. We have the knowledge, tools, and materials to cut energy use tremendously by designing more efficient buildings. One of the most advanced examples is the Lovins' home/office in Snowmass, CO, which is a zero-energy building. Although the primary focus of this book is "reduce" by design, the building industry can also make use of the other three sustainability techniques, which will be briefly discussed in the next section.

2.3 REUSE, RECYCLE, AND REGENERATE BY DESIGN

Figure 2.3a shows a sight that is much too common: a building being demolished. Instead, it should probably be renovated and **reused**.

Even if the building in Fig. 2.3a could not be saved, it could still be **recycled**. By a process of deconstruction, it could be taken apart, and its component

parts could be either recycled (concrete, steel, lumber, etc.) or reused (windows, doors, bricks, etc.). Instead, most buildings end up as landfill, with their resources and embodied energy (see Section 3.23) completely lost.

The fourth R, **regenerate**, deals with the fact that much of the Earth has already been degraded and needs to be restored. Since little is known about how to restore the earth, the Center for Regenerative Studies was established at Cal Poly Pomona through the pioneering work of John T. Lyle (see Fig. 2.3b). Participating students from Cal Poly Pomona reside on-site to learn and investigate how to live a sustainable and regenerative lifestyle. Both the landscape and the architecture of the Center— for instance, the use of fruit-bearing plants as shading elements—were carefully designed to demonstrate and explore green techniques (Fig. 2.3c).

2.4 THE GREEN MOVEMENT

The issues related to sustainability are so all-encompassing that many feel that a different word should be used.

The word **green** is often used because its connotations are flexible and it symbolizes nature, which truly is sustainable. For the same reason, many use the word **ecological**. Still others prefer the phrase **environmentally responsible**. The words might be different, but the goals are the same.

The world community is becoming increasingly aware of the seriousness of our situation, and many important steps have been taken. The most successful so far has been the Montreal Protocol of 1987, through which the world agreed to rapidly phase out chlorofluorocarbons, which are depleting the ozone layer, thereby exposing the planet to more harmful ultraviolet radiation. Because the danger was clear and imminent, the world's resolve was swift and decisive.

Other important gatherings have addressed the need for environmental reform. In 1992, the largest gathering of world leaders in history met at the Earth Summit in Rio de Janeiro to endorse the principle of sustainable development. The American Institute of Architects has set up the Committee on the Environment (COTE) to help

Figure 2.3a Buildings marked for demolition should be either reused through renovation or recycled through the process of deconstruction.

Figure 2.3b The Center for Regenerative Studies at Cal Poly Pomona was established to teach and explore how to restore the planet. The buildings are all oriented to the south, with few if any windows facing east or west. The roofs also face south to support active solar hot water collectors and future photovoltaic panels.

Figure 2.3c The Center for Regenerative Studies. (Photo by Walter Grondzik.)

architects understand the problems and the responses needed for creating a sustainable world. In 1997, representatives of many countries met in Kyoto, Japan, to agree on concrete measures to address global warming. Some countries, like Germany, have decided to make sustainability a national goal for several reasons: it is the moral action that they owe to the children of the world, for their national security, and for economic reasons.

2.5 POPULATION AND SUSTAINABILITY

As of 2007, the population of the Earth was 6.7 billion. There are various estimates on the rate of population growth, as seen in Fig. 2.5a. It is appropriate to ask how many people the earth can hold. The answer to that question depends on the response to further questions. Is the capacity of the earth to be sustainable, and what is to be the standard of living?

The sustainable population or **carrying capacity** of the Earth might already have been exceeded. Global warming is one indicator that we have exceeded the Earth's carrying capacity.

Also, Fig. 2.5b shows that although the world's production of grain keeps increasing, it is not keeping up with population growth.

Paul Ehrlich and John Holden proposed the following relationship:

$$I = P \times A \times T$$

where

I = environmental impact
P = population
A = affluence per person
T = technology

This relationship clearly shows that the greater the population, the greater the impact on the environment. It also shows that the more affluent a society, the greater the impact on the environment. For example, a family that lives in a 2500 ft² (225 m²) house affects the environment far more than a family that lives in a 1000 ft² (90 m²) house. Thus, it should be noted that for a given impact on the environment, the greater the population, the lower must be the affluence. Consequently, the higher a standard of living we want, the greater is the need to stop population growth.

Technology also has a great impact on the environment. A person today will have a much greater impact on the environment than a person a couple of centuries ago did, when there were no automobiles, air travel, air conditioning, endless electrical appliances, abundant electrical lighting, etc. So far, most technology has had a negative impact on the environment. We can change that situation, and this book shows how to use technology that is more benign. Although not the purpose of this book, it must be recognized that sustainability cannot be achieved only by good technology; it requires us to change our values so that a high quality of life is not equated with consumption. We also need to understand that trying

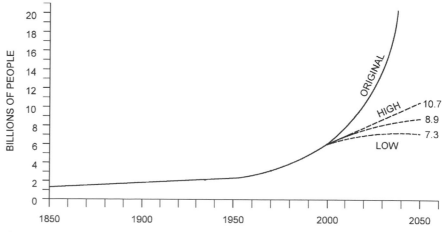

Figure 2.5a Various population projections are given since actual growth is impossible to predict with certainty. (After "World Population Prospects: The 1998 Revision," United Nations, December 1998.)

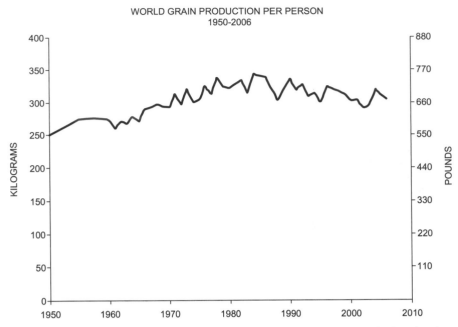

WORLD GRAIN PRODUCTION PER PERSON
1950-2006

Figure 2.5b One indication that the world has reached its carrying capacity is the fact that the world's grain production per person has been decreasing since about 1985. (U.S. Department of Agriculture; United Nations.)

Let us look to nature for guidance on what kind of growth we want. Most living things grow until they mature. In nature, unlimited growth is seen as pathological. As the environmental writer Edward Abbey noted: "Growth for the sake of growth is the ideology of the cancer cell." Nature suggests that growth should continue until a state of maturity is reached, whereupon the focus should be on improving the quality and not the quantity.

A steady growth *rate* does not result in steady growth. This misconception is a major reason for our inability to plan properly for the future. For example, if the world population continues growing at its 1.9 percent rate (a small rate?) from 1975, it will grow to a size where there will be one person for every square meter (approximately a square yard) of dry land on Earth in only 550 years (Bartlett, 1978). This is an example of the power of exponential growth.

to create a high standard of living for the inhabitants of the world without population control "is as though one attempted to build a 100 story skyscraper from good materials, but one forgot to put in a foundation" (Bartlett, 1997).

2.6 GROWTH

As we have seen, the growth of both population and affluence place great stress on the planet. There are environmental impacts from the growing use of petroleum, wood, concrete, water, and just about everything else.

How is it, then, that we generally think positively about growth? Most politicians get elected by promising growth. Most communities think that 5 percent annual growth is a great idea, but do they realize that with steady 5 percent growth per year, the community will double in size every fourteen years? The **doubling time** for any fixed growth rate is easy to determine. See Sidebox 2.6.

Growth is popular for several reasons: many people make a good living based on growth, we generally think bigger is better, and we don't fully understand the long-term consequences of growth.

2.7 EXPONENTIAL GROWTH

Since this book is about heating, cooling, and lighting, let us look at the growth of energy consumption over the last 10,000 years (Fig. 2.7). As in all exponential curves, growth is very slow for a very long time. Then, all of a sudden, growth becomes very rapid and then almost instantly out of control. Because the implications of exponential growth are almost sinister, it is important to take a closer look at this concept.

We have a very good intuitive feel for straight-line relationships. We know that if it takes one minute to fill one bucket of water, it will take five minutes to fill five such buckets. We do not, however, have that kind of intuitive understanding of nonlinear (exponential) relationships. Yet, some of the most important developments facing humankind involve exponential relationships. Population, resource depletion, and energy consumption are all growing at an exponential rate, and their graphs look very much like Figure 2.7.

SIDEBOX 2.6

To determine the doubling time for any fixed rate of growth, use the following equation:

$$T_2 = 70/G$$

where:

T_2 = doubling time
G = growth rate in percent

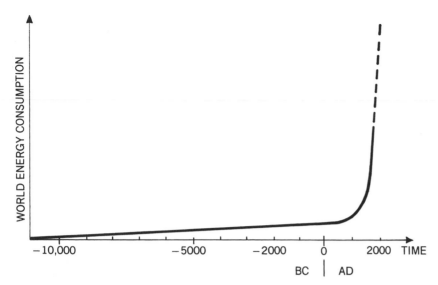

Figure 2.7 The exponential growth in world energy consumption and population growth are very similar.

2.8 THE AMOEBA ANALOGY*

Suppose a single-celled amoeba splits in two once every minute. The growth rate of this amoeba would be exponential, as Fig. 2.8a illustrates. If we graph this growth, it yields the exponential curve seen in Fig. 2.8b. Now let us also suppose that we have a certain size bottle (a resource) that would take the reproducing amoeba ten hours to fill. In other words, if we put one amoeba into the bottle and it splits every minute, then in ten hours the bottle will be full of amoebas, and all the space will be used up.

*Based on the work of Albert A. Bartlett (Bartlett, 1978).

Question: How long will it take for the amoeba to use up only 3 percent of the bottle?

A. 18 minutes (3 percent of 10 hours)
B. about one hour
C. about 5 hours
D. about 8 hours
E. 9 hours and 55 minutes

Since the amoeba doubles every minute, let us work backward from the end.

Time	Percentage of bottle used up	
10:00	100 percent	
9:59	50 percent	
9:58	25 percent	
9:57	12 percent	
9:56	6 percent	
9:55	3 percent	Answer

For the amoeba, the space in the bottle is a valuable resource. Do you think the average amoeba would have listened to a doomsayer who at nine hours and fifty-five minutes predicted that the end of the "bottle space" was almost upon them? Certainly not—they would have laughed. Since only 3 percent of the precious resource is used up, there is plenty of time left before the end.

Of course, some enterprising amoeba went out and searched for more bottles. If they found three more bottles, then they increased their resource to 400 percent of the original. Obviously, that was a way to solve their shortage problem. Or was it?

Question: How much additional time was bought by the 400 percent increase?

Answer: Since the amoeba doubles every minute, the following table tells the sad tale.

Time	Percent of the bottle filled
10:00	100 percent
10:01	200 percent
10:02	400 percent

The amoeba gained only two more minutes by finding three more bottles. Obviously, it is hopeless to try to supply the resources necessary to maintain exponential growth at its later stages. What, then, is the solution?

In nature, there is no such thing as limitless exponential growth. For example, the growth of the amoeba actually follows an **S curve**. Although

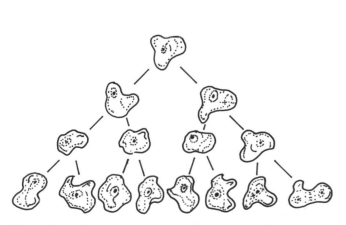

Figure 2.8a The exponential growth of an amoeba colony.

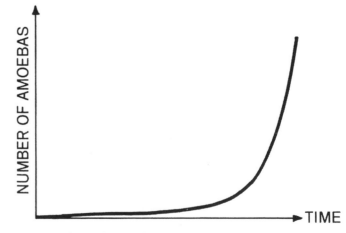

Figure 2.8b The theoretical exponential growth of an amoeba colony.

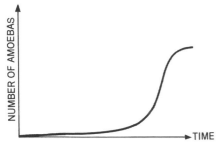

Figure 2.8c The actual growth of an amoeba colony.

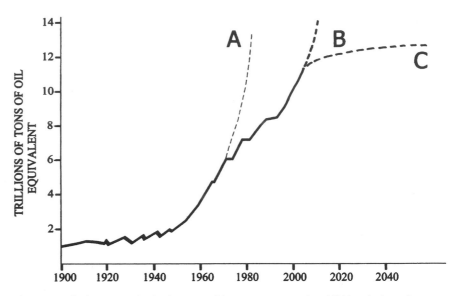

Figure 2.8d Alternate paths for future world energy consumption: (A) historical trend not followed because of the 1973 energy crisis; (B) trend if old wasteful habits return; (C) trend if conservation and efficiency continue to guide our policies. (After: "State of the World, 1999," International Energy agency, 2006.)

growth starts at an exponential rate, it quickly levels off, as seen in Fig. 2.8c. The amoebas not only run out of food, but also poison themselves with their excretions. Since humans are not above nature, they cannot support exponential growth very long either. If people do not control their growth willingly, nature will take over and reduce growth by such timeless measures as pollution, shortages, famine, disease, and war.

Until 1973, the growth of energy consumption followed the exponential curve A in Fig. 2.8d. Then, with the beginning of the energy crisis of 1973, energy consumption followed an S-shaped curve. Initially the shortages and later the implementation of efficiency strategies dramatically reduced energy consumption growth. Our attitude to the growth of energy consumption will determine whether we will follow another dangerous exponential curve B or a more sensible growth pattern, such as that indicated by curve C.

2.9 SUPPLY VERSUS EFFICIENCY

The laws of exponential growth make it quite clear that we can match energy production with demand only if we limit the growth of demand. In addition, it turns out that efficiency (conservation) is more attractive than increasing the supply from both an economic and an environmental point of view. The Harvard Business School published a major report called *Energy Future* (Stobaugh and Yerkin, 1979), which clearly presented the economic

advantages of conservation (efficiency). The report concluded that conservation combined with the use of solar energy is the best solution to our energy problem. In the following discussion of energy sources, it will become clear that almost every other source of energy involves severe environmental costs.

The economic advantage of efficiency is demonstrated by the following example. The Tennessee Valley Authority (TVA) was faced with an impending shortage of electrical energy required for the economic growth of the valley. The first inclination was to build new electric generating plants. Instead, a creative analysis showed that efficiency would be significantly less expensive. The TVA loaned its customers the money required to insulate their homes. Although the customers had to repay the loans, their monthly bills were lower than before, because the reduced energy bills more than compensated for the increase due to loan payments. As a consequence of reduced consumption due to efficiency, the TVA had surplus low-cost electricity to sell, the customers paid less to keep their homes warm, and everyone had a better environment because no new power plants had to be built.

Efficiency is a strategy where everyone wins. And as Amory Lovins, a hero of the planet, says, "If a building is not efficient, it is not beautiful."

2.10 SUSTAINABLE-DESIGN ISSUES

Creating a sustainable green building involves all aspects of design, which is more than one book can discuss in detail. There is, however, an important subset of issues that is discussed here, namely, energy (Fig. 1.7).

Heating, cooling, and lighting are all accomplished by moving energy into or out of a building. As mentioned in the previous chapter, buildings use about 48 percent of all the energy consumed in the United States. Because of global warming, air pollution, and energy-resource depletion, the energy subset of all the sustainability issues is probably the most urgent to address.

The highly regarded *Environmental Building News* had printed a list of what it believes are the eleven most important sustainable design issues. They are reproduced below. Note that the first issue is "**Save Energy**: Design and build energy-efficient buildings." Although this book covers only some of the issues, the whole list is reproduced.

Priority List for Sustainable Building*

1. **Save Energy:** Design and build energy-efficient buildings.
2. **Recycle Buildings:** Utilize existing buildings and infrastructure instead of developing open space.
3. **Create Community:** Design communities to reduce dependence on automobiles and to foster a sense of community.
4. **Reduce Material Use:** Optimize design to make use of smaller spaces and utilize materials efficiently.
5. **Protect and Enhance the Site:** Preserve or restore local ecosystems and biodiversity.
6. **Select Low-Impact Materials:** Specify low-environmental-impact, resource-efficient materials.
7. **Maximize Longevity:** Design for durability and adaptability.
8. **Save Water:** Design buildings and landscapes that are water-efficient.
9. **Make the Buildings Healthy:** Provide a safe and comfortable indoor environment.
10. **Minimize Construction and Demolition Waste:** Return, reuse, and recycle job-site waste, and practice environmentalism in your business.
11. **"Green Up" Your Business:** Minimize the environmental impact of your own business practices, and spread the word.

2.11 CLIMATE CHANGE

It has been previously mentioned that energy issues are related to global warming. The 2007 report of the Intergovernmental Panel on Climate Change (IPCC) states that the warming of the climate is unequivocal and most of it is caused by human-created greenhouse gases. It also states that before the end of this century (1) the Earth's temperature will rise between 2 and 11.5°F (1.1 and 6.4°C), (2) there will be more and greater droughts, heat waves, cyclones, and heavy rainfall, and (3) sea

*Reprinted by permission from the *Environmental Building News*. See the September–October 1995 issue for a more thorough discussion of these issues.

levels will rise from 7 to 23 in. (18 to 59 cm) unless there are rapid, dynamic changes in ice flow, in which case the increase could be much greater.

The cause of the global warming is no mystery when we look at the increase of the **greenhouse** gas carbon dioxide over the same time period (see Fig. 2.11a, lower graph). Humanity is also heating the planet by producing methane, nitrous oxide, and some other minor greenhouse gases. Most of the heating, however, is due to the carbon dioxide produced from burning the fossil fuels coal, oil, and natural gas. The greenhouse effect

will be explained in the next section.

Small increases in global temperatures can have serious effects besides deadly hotter summers. Precipitation patterns will change, with a corresponding disruption in agriculture; some of the world's poorest and most heavily populated regions will be losers. There will be more droughts in some areas and floods in others. Diseases that thrive in warmer climates, such as malaria, will spread over more of the globe, and species extinction will have a further negative impact on the present ecology. And perhaps most important, there will be

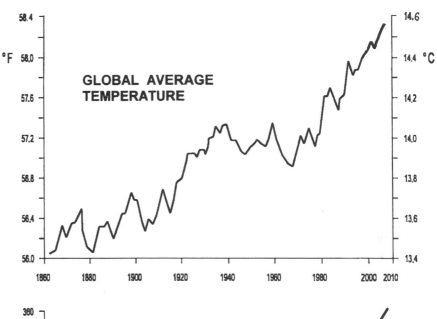

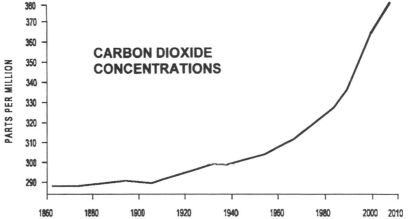

Figure 2.11a The upper graph represents the increase of the global average temperature, and the lower graph represents the increase of carbon dioxide during the same time period. (Sources: temperature data from Goddard Institute for Space Studies; carbon dioxide data from Scripps Institution of Oceanography, updated 2007.)

a rise in the sea level.

Although the IPCC's latest prediction of sea level rise is only 7 to 23 in. (18 to 59 cm), they qualified that prediction by saying it is based on the present pattern. The IPCC's report does not describe worst-case scenarios (e.g., the seas could rise 240 ft [80 m]) but rather the most likely pattern as extrapolated from present trends.

When important decisions are made about the future, we must base them not only on likelihood but also on the severity of outcomes. For example, few people play Russian roulette, where a person spins the cylinder of a revolver loaded with only one bullet, aims the muzzle at his head, and pulls the trigger (Fig 2.11c). Although the probability of dying is only a low one in six (17 percent), sane people don't play because the outcome is a disaster. Similarly, we should not play Russian roulette with the planet, which we are clearly doing (Fig. 2.11d).

A major reason for uncertainty about climate change is that the climate may experience one or more tipping points. For example, a tower that starts leaning will continue to lean slowly until it reaches it **tipping point**, when it will suddenly fall (Fig. 2.11e). We know of several potential tipping points in global warming. One of these is the melting of the permafrost found in northern Canada, Alaska, and Russia. Huge amounts of organic material will decompose, giving off both carbon dioxide and methane, which is twenty-one times a more powerful greenhouse gas than carbon dioxide. Thus, a faster warming planet melts permafrost faster, which creates more greenhouse gases, and so on.

Another potential tipping point is the rather sudden change of ocean currents such as the Gulf Stream, which in particular would put Europe into a mini ice age. Also, as the arctic ice melts, the reflectivity of the surface changes from 90 percent (ice) to 10 percent (land and water).

We must heed the warnings of hurricane Katrina, major planetary heat waves, and unusual worldwide flooding, taking action immediately to minimize the severity of global warming. As the eminent physicist Albert A. Bartlett said, "We must recognize that it is not acceptable to base our national [planetary] future on the motto, 'When in doubt, gamble' " (Bartlett, 1978).

One of the main reasons for inaction is the mistaken belief that fighting global warming hurts the economy. The opposite is true. A major report in 2006 for the United Kingdom by Sir Nicholas Stern, a former chief economist with the World Bank, states that unless we act soon, global warming will cause a worldwide economic depression. Furthermore, countries like Germany, which have made sustainability a national goal, are thriving economically. Their economy will be

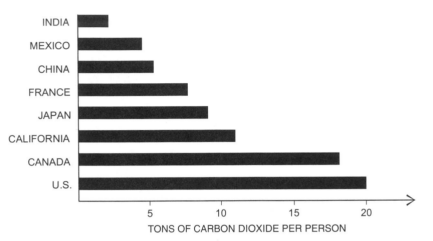

Figure 2.11b The United States emits more carbon dioxide per person than most other nations of the world. These 2002 statistics have not changed much for the United States and most other nations. A major exception is China, for which 2007 statistics were available and are shown. Note that the United States still emits about four times more carbon dioxide per person than does China. (*Sources*: ORNL and Wikipedia)

Figure 2.11c Russian roulette is unpopular not because of the odds but because the stakes are too high.

Figure 2.11e Many phenomena exhibit a tipping effect whereby change is gradual until a point of instability occurs. Global warming could well be such a phenomenon.

Figure 2.11d This generation has no right to play Russian roulette with the planet. It is immoral!

booming when the world comes to them to buy sustainable technology.

Because of our tremendous appetite for energy, Americans produce more carbon dioxide per person than just about any other nation (Fig. 2.11b). Furthermore, because we have a long history of industrialization and because we have a large population, the United States has produced about 30 percent

of all the carbon dioxide in the atmosphere, which is by far the largest amount of any country (see Table 2.11). Reducing our dependence on the carbon-dioxide-producing fossil fuels has more benefits than just reducing global warming. In the short run, it will reduce our dependency on foreign oil, and in the long run, it will prepare us for the day when fossil fuels are finally used up.

2.12 THE GLOBAL GREENHOUSE

The greenhouse gases in the atmosphere act as a one-way radiation trap. They allow most of the solar radiation to pass through to reach the earth's surface, which when heated radiates increased amounts of heat back into space. The greenhouse gases, however, block the escape of much of this outgoing heat radiation (see Fig. 2.12).

Table 2.11 Cumulative Carbon Dioxide Emissions, 1900–2002*	
Country	**Percent of World**
United States	29.3
Russia	8.1
China	7.8
Germany	7.3
United Kingdom	6.3
Japan	4.1
France	2.9
India	2.2
Australia	1.1
Mexico	1.0
South Korea	0.8
Iran	0.6
Indonesia	0.5
Pakistan	0.2
Developed countries	76
Developing countries	24

Source: World Resource Institute

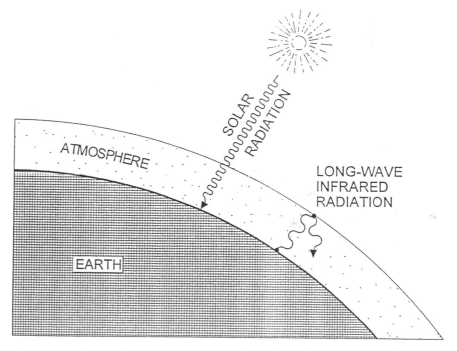

Figure 2.12 The atmosphere acts as a horticultural greenhouse by allowing most of the solar radiation to enter but blocks part of the long-wave infrared radiation from leaving the planet.

The present average temperature is the result of the existing level of water vapor and other greenhouse gases mentioned above. As a result of these gases, the earth is about 60°F (35°C) warmer than it would be without these gases. When more greenhouse gases are added to the atmosphere, the equilibrium temperature increases and the earth gets warmer.

2.13 THE OZONE HOLE

The ozone hole is another example of a critical undesired change to the atmosphere. The air conditioning of buildings has led indirectly to a hole in the ozone layer that protects the earth from most of the sun's harmful ultraviolet radiation (Fig. 2.13). The chlorofluorocarbon (CFC) molecules that were invented to provide a safe, inert refrigerant for air conditioners have turned out to have a tragic flaw, inertness, which ironically was considered their major virtue. When these molecules escape from air conditioners or are released as propellants in spray cans, they survive to slowly migrate to the upper atmosphere, which contains ozone. There, the CFCs deplete the protective ozone layer for an estimated fifty years before they themselves are destroyed. Consequently, the problems will be with us long after we eliminate all CFCs on the surface.

The 1987 Montreal Protocol, which the United States wholeheartedly supports, requires countries to phase out the production of CFCs. Although this is a classic example of how technological solutions can be the source of new problems, it is also a good example of how world cooperation based on sound science can respond quickly to a serious problem.

Regretfully, international cooperation has not succeeded as well in controlling greenhouse emissions. Progress is slow for various reasons, one of which is the shortsighted policies of some fossil-fuel and transportation industries.

2.14 EFFICIENCY

To fight global warming, we must understand what our energy options are. The next few sections will describe the pros and cons of each energy source available to us. However, it must be clearly understood that by far the most important option is efficiency, which is the easiest, quickest, and least expensive way to fight global warming. Efficiency is the "low-hanging fruit" (Fig. 2.14).

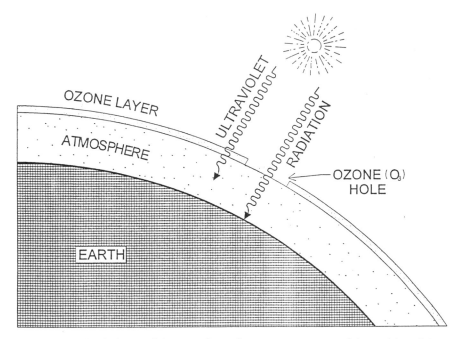

Figure 2.13 The depletion of the ozone layer allows greater amounts of the sun's harmful ultraviolet radiation to reach the Earth's surface.

Figure 2.14 Efficiency is the low-hanging fruit. We should not put all our effort in going after the high fruits (Photovoltaic, wind, hydrogen, etc.) until we have picked the low-hanging fruits (orientation, insulation, shading, etc.).

For example, optimized window design can reduce energy consumption and carbon dioxide production by over 40 percent. Although such a window system will cost more initially, it will not only reduce energy costs for the life of the building, but will also reduce the first cost of the air-conditioning system.

As stated before, the purpose of this book is to help the architect create energy-responsive buildings that are both efficient and beautiful.

2.15 ENERGY SOURCES

Which energy sources are available to power our buildings, and which are sustainable? We can divide all of the sources into the two main categories: renewable and nonrenewable:

I. Renewable
   A. Solar
   B. Wind
   C. Biomass
   D. Hydroelectric
   E. Geothermal

II. Nonrenewable
   A. Fossil fuels
      1. Oil
      2. Natural gas
      3. Coal
   B. Nuclear
      1. Fission
      2. Fusion?

Figure 2.15 shows that we are using mostly nonrenewable energy sources. This is an unfortunate situation because not only are we using up these sources, but they are the very ones causing pollution and global warming. We must switch as quickly as possible from nonrenewable to renewable sources. Before we look at each source in terms of its ability to power building sustainably, let's look at a brief example of the history of energy use in buildings.

2.16 ANCIENT GREECE: A HISTORICAL EXAMPLE

The role of energy in buildings was largely ignored in recent history until the energy crisis of 1973, when some of the leading members of the Organization of Petroleum Exporting Countries (OPEC) suddenly raised prices and set up an embargo on oil exports to the United States. The resulting energy shortages made us realize how dependent we were (and still are) on unreliable energy sources. We began thinking about how we use energy in buildings.

Before the energy crisis, a discussion of ancient Greek architecture would not have even mentioned the word "energy." The ancient Greeks, however, became aware of energy issues as the beautiful, rugged land on which they built their monuments became scarred and eroded by the clearing of trees to heat their buildings. The philosopher Plato said of his country: "All the richer and softer parts have fallen away and the mere skeleton of the land remains."

The ancient Greeks responded to the problem partly by using solar energy. Socrates, another philosopher, thought that this was important enough to compel him to explain this method of designing buildings. According to Xenophon, Socrates said: "In houses that look toward the south, the sun penetrates the portico in winter, while in summer the path of the sun is right over our heads and above the roof so that there is shade" (see Fig. 2.16). Socrates continued talking about a house that has a two-story section: "The section of the house facing south must be built lower than the northern section in order not to cut off the winter sun" (Butti and Perdin, 1980).

2.17 NONRENEWABLE ENERGY SOURCES

When we use nonrenewable energy sources, we are much like the heir living it up on an inheritance with no thought of tomorrow until one day he or she finds that the bank account is empty. Two major categories of nonrenewable energy sources exist: fossil fuels and nuclear energy.

Fossil Fuels

For hundreds of millions of years, green plants trapped solar energy by the process of photosynthesis. The accumulation and transformation of these plants into solid, liquid, and gaseous states produced what we call the **fossil fuels**: coal, oil, and gas. When we burn these, we are actually using the solar energy that was stored hundreds of millions of years ago. Because of the extremely long time required to convert living plants into fossil fuels, in effect they are depletable or nonrenewable energy sources. The fossil-fuel age started around 1850 and will last at most a few centuries more. The finite nature of the fossil fuel age is clearly illustrated by Fig. 2.17a.

Most air pollution and smog are a result of the burning of fossil fuels (see Fig. 2.17b). The use of fossil fuels also

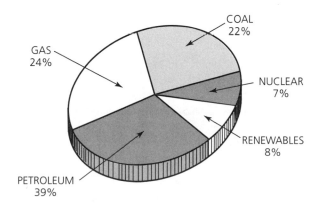

Figure 2.15 Energy consumption by source in the United States. Note that 92 percent is from nonrenewable sources.

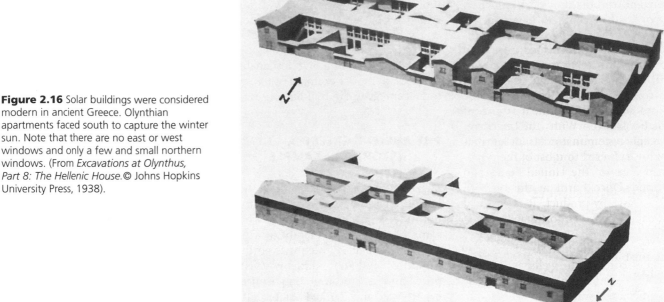

Figure 2.16 Solar buildings were considered modern in ancient Greece. Olynthian apartments faced south to capture the winter sun. Note that there are no east or west windows and only a few and small northern windows. (From *Excavations at Olynthus, Part 8: The Hellenic House.*© Johns Hopkins University Press, 1938).

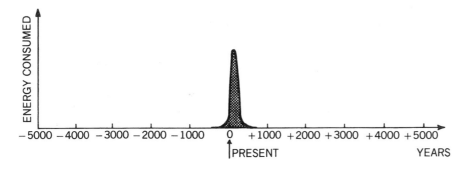

Figure 2.17a The age of fossil fuels in the longer span of human history. (After Hubbert.)

Figure 2.17b Air pollution covering New York City is not like this every day. Often the pollution is blown away to Connecticut or New Jersey.

causes acid rain and, most important of all, global warming.

Natural Gas

Natural gas, which is composed primarily of methane, is a convenient source of energy. Except for the global-warming carbon dioxide it produces when burnt, it is a clean energy source. With the extensive pipeline system that exists, natural gas can be delivered to most of the populated areas of the United States and Europe. Once burnt at the oil well as a waste by-product, it is in great demand today. Unfortunately, most of the easily obtained gas is already out of the ground. Most of the new sources come from wells as deep as 15,000 ft (4,500 m) and even these supplies are limited. Gas will, therefore, be a much more expensive fuel in the future. Since gas is also a valuable raw material for fertilizer and other chemicals, it will soon be too valuable to burn. We are importing natural gas in the form of **liquefied natural gas** (LNG). To maintain the gas in liquid form, it is shipped in tankers at −260°F [−162°C]. There is some concern about safety because if such a tanker exploded and ignited in a busy harbor, the devastation would be similar to that caused by a small nuclear bomb.

Oil

The most useful and important energy source today is oil. But the world supply is limited and will be mostly depleted by the end of this century. Our domestic supply will run out even sooner. The United States is already importing more than 60 percent of its oil. Since oil is also important in making lubricants, plastics, and other chemicals, it, like natural gas, will soon become too valuable to burn.

Long before we run out of oil, its price will rise. Research has shown that the demand becomes greater than the supply when half of the resource has been extracted. This is

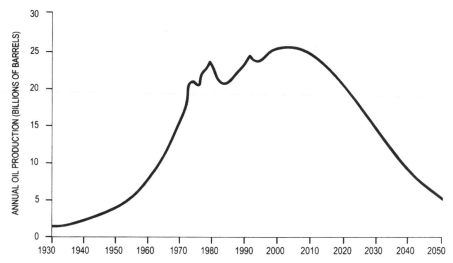

Figure 2.17c The price of oil is expected to increase significantly after production peaks, which is expected somewhere between 2010 and 2020. (After Campbell and Laherrère, 1998.)

Figure 2.17d Oil platforms for drilling underwater are very expensive; therefore, the oil extracted there is also more expensive.

also the point where peak production occurs. The best estimate for the peaking of world oil production is sometime during the second decade of this century, although some experts say that it is happening now (Fig. 2.17c). Demand will exceed production for several reasons. Since much of the easily obtainable oil has already been pumped out of the ground, we are now forced to either drill deeper, underwater (Fig. 2.17d) or in almost inaccessible places, such as the north slope of Alaska. We are also forced to use lower grades of petroleum, which either increase refinery costs or increase air pollution.

Unconventional sources of oil, such as oil shale and coal liquefaction, are not economically viable at present and will be very expensive if and when used.

Because the cost of oil has risen high enough, tar sands are now being mined for oil. Besides the high monetary cost, there is also a very high cost to the environment. An area the size of Florida is being devastated in Alberta, Canada. In addition, huge amounts of energy and water are needed to extract the oil from the tar sands.

Most important, however, is that no matter where the oil comes from, burning it produces carbon dioxide and global warming.

Coal

By far the most abundant fossil fuel we have is coal. Although there is enough coal in the United States to last for well over 100 years, significant problems are associated with its use. The difficulties start with the mining. Deep mining is dangerous to miners in two ways. First, there is the ever-present danger of explosions and mine cave-ins. Second, in the long run there is the danger of severe respiratory ailments due to the coal dust. If the coal is close enough to the surface, strip mining might be preferred. Less dangerous to people, strip mining is quite harmful to the land. Reclamation is possible but expensive. Much of the strip mining will occur in the western United States, where the water necessary for reclamation is a very scarce resource.

Additional difficulties result because coal is not convenient to transport, handle, or use. Since coal is a rather dirty fuel to burn and a major cause of acid rain, its use will be restricted to large burners, where expensive equipment can be installed to reduce air pollution. Even if coal were burned "cleanly," it would still continue to produce carbon dioxide and global warming.

To overcome some of the negative impacts, the coal industry has developed a technology called the "integrated gasification combined cycle" (IGCC). With this technology the smokestack will release far fewer pollutants such as mercury (toxic metal), sulfur dioxide (acid rain), nitrogen oxides (smog), and soot. In theory, this technology would also allow the capture of carbon dioxide in order to sequester it underground. However, this technology is new and expensive, and large-scale sequestering of carbon dioxide is an unproven idea.

All of these difficulties add up to make coal an inconvenient, expensive, and risky source of energy. Although plentiful, it is not the answer to our energy problems.

Nuclear Fission

In fission, certain heavy atoms, such as uranium-235, are split into two middle-size atoms and in the process also give off neutrons and an incredible amount of energy (Fig. 2.17e). During the 1950s it was widely believed that electricity produced from nuclear energy would be too cheap to meter.

Even with huge governmental subsidies because of nuclear energy's defense potential, this dream has not become a reality. In fact, just the opposite has happened. Nuclear energy has become one of the most expensive and least desirable ways to produce electricity. One important factor in the decline of nuclear power is that the public is now hesitant to accept the risks. Nuclear-power accident, such as the one that took place at Chernobyl in the Soviet Union in 1986, spread deadly radiation over a large area. The nuclear accident at Three Mile Island, Pennsylvania, in 1979 might have been just as serious if the very expensive containment vessel had not been built. More than twenty years later, the reactor is still entombed, with a billion-dollar cleanup bill. The safety features needed to prevent accidents have made the plants uneconomical. Even with all the safety features, the risks are still not zero, as Fig. 2.17f shows.

Another problem facing the nuclear power industry is the shortage of uranium-235, which is very rare and will be depleted soon. The main hope was to use the much more plentiful U-238 isotope by turning it into a fuel. This requires the construction of breeder reactors that turn U-238 into the fissionable element **plutonium**. Plutonium, appropriately named for the god of the underworld, is a horrendous material. It is extremely toxic and ideal for making atomic bombs.

To get the nuclear fuel necessary, both enrichment and reprocessing plants are required. Such plants are an ideal source of nuclear bomb material for terrorists and unreliable countries. We must remember that countries change governments and that a country we trust today may be our enemy in the future.

The overall efficiency of the power plants has not been as high as had

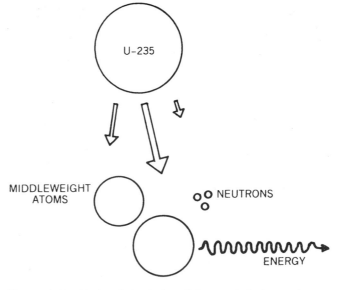

Figure 2.17e Nuclear fission is the splitting apart of a heavy atom.

Figure 2.17f Take this quiz: This sign refers to what kind of power plant? (A) Photovoltaic, (B) wind, (C) biomass, (D) nuclear. (Courtesy Southern Nuclear).

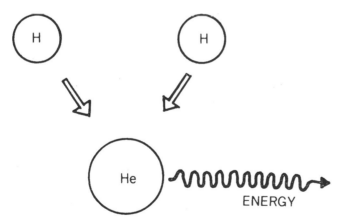

Figure 2.17g Nuclear fusion consists of the union of very light atoms. For example, the fusion of two hydrogen atoms yields an atom of helium as well as a great deal of extra energy.

been hoped. The initial cost of a nuclear power plant is high, the operating efficiency is low, and the problem of disposing of radioactive nuclear waste has still not been solved.

Since uranium is a rare element, huge mines creating mountains of radioactive waste are needed. Nuclear power plants also need huge amounts of cooling water. Those plants that are located on rivers either use or heat up the river. In 2003, during a heat wave/drought, France had to restrict some of its nuclear power plants because they were overheating the rivers that cooled them.

Lately, the nuclear power industry has argued that new technology is foolproof. However, they want the government to pass a law exempting them from all liability. Why is that necessary if their new systems are foolproof?

Thus, there are many excellent reasons not to go with the nuclear option besides the fact that it is much more expensive than renewable energy. As the very reputable business magazine *The Economist* said in its May 19, 2001, issue: "Nuclear power, once claimed to be too cheap to meter, is now too costly to matter."

Nuclear Fusion

When two light atoms fuse to create a heavier atom, energy is released by the process called **fusion** (Fig. 2.17g). This is the same process that occurs in the sun and stars. It is quite unlike **fission**, a process through which atoms decay by coming apart.

Fusion has many potential advantages over fission. Fusion uses hydrogen, the most plentiful material in the universe, as its fuel. It produces much less radioactive waste than fission. It is also an inherently much safer process because fusion is self-extinguishing, while fission is self-exciting, when something goes wrong.

All the advantages, however, do not change the fact that a fusion power plant does not yet exist, and we have no guarantee that we can ever make fusion work economically. Even the optimists do not expect fusion to supply significant amounts of power anytime soon.

Considering the shortcomings, perhaps the best nuclear power plant is the one 93 million miles away—the sun. It is ready to supply us with all the energy we need right now.

2.18 RENEWABLE ENERGY SOURCES

The following sources all share the very important assets of being renewable and of not contributing to global warming. Solar, wind, hydroelectric, energy, and biomass are renewable because they are all variations of solar energy. Of the renewable energy sources, only geothermal energy does not depend on the sun.

Solar Energy

The term **solar energy** refers to the use of solar radiation in a number of different ways. The building-integrated solar collection methods are all discussed at some depth in this book:

- Passive solar energy (Chapter 7)
- Photovoltaics and active solar energy (Chapter 8)
- Daylighting (Chapter 13)

The word "solar" is also used for special applications, such as solar thermal energy, which are used for the generation of electricity. A very successful approach has been the **parabolic trough** solar power plant. Several such plants produce electricity economically in the United States and some other countries. In a solar **central receiver** system, a large array of tracking flat mirrors reflects sunlight onto a collector mounted on a tower. Also, there is the **dish system**, where a parabaloid reflector focuses the sun on the collector located in each dish. An important advantage of dish systems is that they can be built in much smaller units than the central receiver system.

In one year, the amount of solar energy that reaches the surface of the earth is 10,000 times greater than all the energy of all kinds that humanity uses in that period. Why, then, aren't we using solar energy? This question can be explained only partly by the technical problems involved. These technical problems stem from the diffuseness, intermittent availability, and uneven distribution of solar energy.

Many solutions to the technical problems exist, but they all add to the costs of what would otherwise be a free energy source. However, the clever techniques developed for using solar energy have reduced the collection and storage costs to the point where some forms of solar energy are economical in most situations.

The nontechnical problems facing the acceptance of solar energy are primarily a result of people's beliefs that it is unconventional, looks bad, does not work, is futuristic, etc. On the contrary, in most applications, such as daylighting or the use of sun spaces, solar energy can add special delight to architecture. Interesting aesthetic forms are a natural product of solar design (see Fig. 11.6e). Solar energy promises not only to increase the nation's energy supply and reduce global warming, but also to enrich its architecture.

Besides being renewable, solar energy has other important advantages. It is exceedingly kind to the environment. No air, water, land, or thermal pollution results. Solar energy is also very safe to use. It is a decentralized source of energy available to everyone everywhere. With its use, individuals are less dependent on brittle or monopolistic centralized energy sources, and countries are secure from energy embargoes. China, Germany, Japan, and Switzerland have embarked on ambitious solar programs in order to become more energy-independent, while the United States is depending more and more on foreign oil, already importing more than 60 percent.

Photovoltaic Energy

If one were to imagine the ideal energy source, it might well be photovoltaic (PV) cells. They are often made of the most common material on earth—silicon. They produce the most flexible and valuable form of energy—electricity. They are very reliable—no moving parts. They do not pollute in any way—no noise, no smoke, no radiation. And they draw on an inexhaustible source of energy—the sun.

Over the last twenty years, the cost of PV electricity has been declining steadily, and it is in the process of becoming competitive with conventional electricity. PV electricity is already competitive for installations that are far from the existing power grid, and during peak demand times when electricity is very expensive.

The greatest potential lies with **building-integrated photovoltaics** (BIPV) both for our energy future and for architecture. For more information about PV see Chapter 8.

Wind Energy

The ancient Persians used wind power to pump water. Windmills first came to Europe in the twelfth century. They were successfully used over the centuries for such tasks as grinding wheat and pumping water. More than 6 million windmills and wind turbines have been used in the United States over the last 150 years (Fig. 2.18a). Windmills were used primarily to pump water on farms and ranches (Fig. 2.18b). Wind turbines also produced electricity for remote areas before rural electrification in the 1930s.

Today, wind turbines are having a revival because they can produce clean, renewable energy at the same cost as conventional energy. Where wind is plentiful and electricity is expensive, wind power is often the least expensive source of energy. All over the world, giant wind turbines and wind farms are generating electricity for the power grid (Fig. 2.18c). Wind electricity could easily supply 20 percent of U.S. needs.

Small wind turbines can be an excellent source of electricity for individual buildings where the wind resource is sufficient, which is a function of both velocity and duration. Color plate 22 shows where favorable wind conditions can be found in the United States. Of course, local conditions are critical, and a local survey should be made for obstacles or especially favorable conditions. Mountaintops, mountain passes, and shorelines are often good locations in all parts of the country. For economic reasons, minimum annual average wind speeds of 9 mph (14 kph), or 4 meters per second (m/s), are needed. See the end of the chapter for information on wind-resource availability.

Since the power output of a wind turbine is proportional to the *cube* of the wind speed (see Sidebox 2.18),

Figure 2.18a This windmill in Colonial Williamsburg, Virginia, was used to grind wheat.

Figure 2.18b Windmills still pump water on some ranches and farms, and small modern wind turbines produce electricity for individual homes.

a windy site is critical, and there is a great incentive to raise the turbine as high into the air as possible to reach higher wind speeds. Most often, wind machines are supported on towers, some as high as 400 ft (125 m). Wind turbines come in all sizes, but even the small ones should be mounted at least 40 ft (12 m) above the ground in order to catch enough wind. One exception

is the building, integrated wind turbine that makes use of the high-velocity wind found at the leading edge of a flat-roofed building (Fig. 2.18d).

The power output of a wind turbine is also proportional to the square of the length of the rotor blades (Fig. 2.18e). A 6.6-ft (2 m)-diameter rotor is enough to power a television, while a 66-ft (20 m)-diameter rotor

can generate enough electricity for 500 Americans or 1000 Europeans.

The intermittent nature of wind power is not a serious problem, since other energy sources can supply the electricity to the grid when there is not enough wind. Although wind's intermittent nature must be accounted for, it is, nevertheless, one of the best renewable energy sources.

In the case of wind turbines dedicated to one or more buildings, any power produced that is not needed can be sold to the grid, and when there is no wind, power can be purchased from the grid. This is the same situation that occurs with building-dedicated PV systems.

In stand-alone systems, a large battery is needed. It has been found, however, that **hybrid systems**, in which wind power is combined with PV cells, are very efficient because they complement each other. In winter, there is less sun but more wind, while in summer, the PV cells generate more electricity than the wind turbine. Similarly, on stormy days, there is less sun but more wind.

SIDEBOX 2.18

The power produced by a wind machine is proportional to the cube of the wind speed and the square of the rotor radius,

Where

$$P \approx V^3 \times D^2$$
P = power output
V = air speed
D = rotor diameter

For example, the power output will be 8 (2^3) times as large if the wind speed doubles. Stated another way, a 12.6 mph wind will yield twice the power of a 10-mph wind.

Also, if the rotor diameter is doubled (2^2), the power output will be four times as large.

Figure 2.18c Utility size wind farm in Oklahoma.

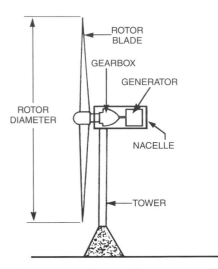

Figure 2.18e The essential components of a wind turbine. (Drawing from DOE/CE-0359P.)

Figure 2.18d Small wind turbines can be used to capture the high-velocity wind generated by buildings at the edge of a flat roof. (Courtesy AeroVironment Inc., Monrovia, CA [www.AVinc.com])

Although some wind farms are spread over large areas of land, the land can still be used for crops and grazing. This is not the case for hydropower, where the land behind the dam is flooded and lost. Also, wind farms require only about one-fifth the amount of land that hydropower needs.

There is also some concern about the aesthetic impact because, by their very nature, wind machines must be high in the air. There have been few complaints about actual installations, and the author believes there is inherent beauty in a device that produces renewable, nonpolluting energy.

Biomass Energy

Photosynthesis stores solar energy for later use. This is how plants solve the problems of diffuseness and intermittent availability, which are associated with solar energy. This stored energy can be turned into heat or electricity, or converted into such fuels as methane gas, alcohol, and hydrogen. Because **biomass** is renewable and carbon neutral, and because with modern technology its use is relatively pollution-free, it is an attractive energy source. Two major sources of biomass exist: (1) plants grown specifically for their energy content and (2) organic waste from agriculture, industry, or consumers (garbage).

Thus, wind turbines and PV cells are frequently used together, as shown in Fig. 8.5c. Also, see Sections 8.5 and 8.6 for a discussion of typical electrical systems.

Small wind turbines do make some noise, but most people do not find the noise very objectionable, and wind machines are being designed to be less noisy. Especially in certain locations, wind machines have killed some birds. Although this is a concern, it is a minor problem when compared with about 57 million birds that are killed each year in collisions with cars and another 97 million birds that die in collisions with plate-glass windows.

Some types of biomass can be converted into **biofuels**, while the rest is burned to create electricity. There are three major types of biofuels: (1) ethanol alcohol, (2) biodiesel, and (3) methane.

Because **ethanol alcohol** is presently made from sugars or carbohydrates, large-scale use will compete with food production, and on a worldwide basis there is no food to spare. Consequently, alcohol made from cellulose is a better source. Plants like switchgrass, which can grow on land too poor for food production, would be ideal sources of cellulose. Unfortunately, at this point, creating alcohol from cellulose is a process still being perfected.

Biodiesel can use oil wastes from restaurants, but when made from other plants it again competes with food or causes ecological damage. Thus, biodiesel is good but limited in its use.

Methane, the main component of natural gas, is an excellent biofuel when made from the decay of waste materials on farms, ranches, or landfills (Fig. 2.18f). Not only is it a very valuable fuel, but its collection and combustion prevent its addition to the atmosphere, where it acts as a greenhouse gas twenty-one times more powerful than carbon dioxide.

We must be careful about turning biomass into energy, because decomposed biomass is food for new plants (Fig. 2.18g). As William McDonough, architect, author, and former dean of the School of Architecture at the University of Virginia, said, "Waste is food."

Burning biomass instead of fossil fuels can reduce the problem of global warming because biomass is **carbon-neutral**. When growing, plants remove the same amount of carbon dioxide from the atmosphere that is returned when the biomass is burned. Thus, over time, there is no net change in the carbon dioxide content of the atmosphere.

Wood used to heat houses is an example of biomass energy. Large-scale burning of wood in fireplaces or stoves, however, is not desirable

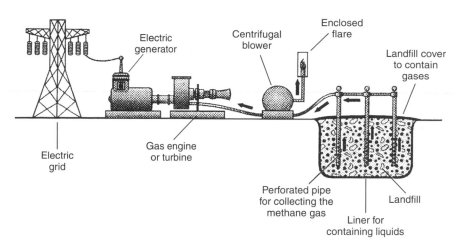

Figure 2.18f Landfill gas can be collected to generate electricity. (Fact Sheet No. 16, Texas State Energy Conservation Office.)

Figure 2.18g Saving biomass to replenish the soil makes sense at both the macro and micro level. This sign was found in a residential development outside of Houston, Texas.

because of the low efficiency and large amount of air pollution produced. Fireplaces are *very* inefficient (see Section 16.2), and wood stoves are still polluting.

Biomass is a desirable source of energy, but it is limited in magnitude because plants are needed to produce food and other products, such as lumber. Furthermore, using all biomass for energy will deprive the soil of decaying material that is needed for the next generation of plants.

Hydroelectric Energy

The use of water power, also called **hydropower** or **hydroelectricity**, has an ancient history: watermills were already popular in the Roman Empire. The

overshot wheel (Fig. 2.18h) was found to be the most efficient, but it required at least a 10-ft (3 m) fall (head) of the water. When there was little vertical fall in the water but sufficient flow, an **undershot wheel** (Fig. 2.18i) was found to be best. Today, compact turbines are driven by water delivered in pipes.

The power available from a stream is a function of both head and flow. **Head** is the pressure developed by the vertical fall of the water, often expressed in pounds per square inch (kilopascals). **Flow** is the amount of water that passes a given point in a given time as, for example, ft³ per minute (liters per second). The flow is the result of both the cross section and velocity of a stream or river.

Since power output is directly proportional to both head and flow, different combinations of head and flow will work equally well. For example, a very small hydropower plant can be designed to work equally with 20 ft of head and a flow of 100 ft³ per minute (6 m and 48 l/s), or 40 ft of head and a flow of 50 ft³ per minute (12 m and 24 l/s).

Today, water power is used almost exclusively to generate electricity. The main expense is often the dam that is required to generate the head and store water to maintain an even flow (Fig. 2.18j). One advantage of hydropower over some other renewable sources is the relative ease of storing energy. The main disadvantage of hydroelectricity is that large areas of land must be flooded to create the storage lakes. This land is most frequently prime agricultural land and is often highly populated. Another disadvantage is the disturbance of the local ecology, for example, where fish cannot reach their spawning grounds. For this reason, many existing dams in the United States are being demolished.

Figure 2.18k illustrates a simple, small-scale hydroelectric system. The dam generates the required head, stores water, and diverts water into the pipe leading to the turbine located at a lower elevation. Modern turbines have high rotational speeds (rpm) so that they can efficiently drive electric generators.

All but the smallest systems require dams, which are both expensive and environmentally questionable. Very small systems are known as "micro-hydropower" and can use the run of the river without a dam. The site must still have an elevation change of at least 3 ft (1 m) in order to generate the minimum head required. Of course, the more head (elevation change), the better.

About 5 percent of the energy in the United States is supplied by falling water. At present, we are using about one-third of the total

Figure 2.18h An overshot waterwheel is best used where river water can be diverted high enough to be dropped onto the waterwheel. The waterwheel shown is in Korea.

Figure 2.18i An undershot waterwheel uses the flow of the river for power. This Cambodian waterwheel is used to lift river water for irrigation.

Figure 2.18j Hydroelectric dams produce pressure (head), and some also store water and, therefore, energy for later use.

hydroelectric resource available. Full use of this resource is not possible because some of the best sites remaining are too valuable to lose. For example, it would be hard to find anyone who would want to flood the Grand Canyon or Yosemite Valley behind hydroelectric dams. Most Americans now see our scenic rivers and valleys as great resources to be protected.

Hydroelectric energy will continue to be a reliable but limited source for our national energy needs.

Marine Energy

The four types of marine power sources are (1) tidal power, (2) wave power, (3) ocean current power, and (4) ocean thermal energy conversion.

Tidal power has been used for centuries with great success. Because it is most efficient where bays have small openings to the sea, its application is limited. **Wave power** is more widely distributed but more difficult to harness. **Ocean current power** is very much like wind power except that water turbines are used. Like wind, it is available only in certain locations. **Ocean thermal energy conversion** (OTEC) uses the large temperature difference between the deep ocean and its surface to generate power. All of the marine energy sources except tidal power are still in their experimental and development stages.

Geothermal Energy

The term **geothermal** has been used to describe two quite different energy systems: (1) the extraction of heat originating deep in the earth and (2) the use of the ground just below the surface as a source of heat in the winter and a **heat sink** in the summer. To eliminate confusion, the second system is now usually called by the much more descriptive name **geoexchange**.

Geothermal energy is available where sufficient heat is brought near the surface by conduction, bulges of magma, or circulation of ground water to great depths (Fig. 2.18l). In a few places, like Yellowstone National Park, hot water and steam bring the heat right to the surface. Other such sites, like the geysers in northern California and the Hatchobaru power station in Japan (Fig. 2.18m), use this heat to generate electricity. In some places like Iceland, geothermal energy is also used to heat buildings. Although surface sites are few in number, there is a tremendous resource of hot rock energy at depths of 5 to 10 mi (8 to 16 km) By drilling two holes, water can be pumped down one hole to the hot rock layers where it is heated, and then the hot water and/or steam can be returned through the second hole to drive a turbine or heat buildings. In the city of Boise, Idaho, a geothermal system

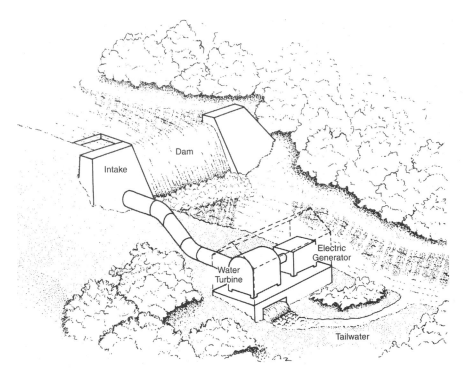

Figure 2.18k A simple, small-scale hydroelectric system. The dam can be eliminated with a **run-of-river** system in a fast-flowing stream or river by placing propeller-driven generators in the flow of water. (From *Building Control Systems* by Vaughn Bradshaw. 2nd edition. © John Wiley & Sons, Inc., 1993.)

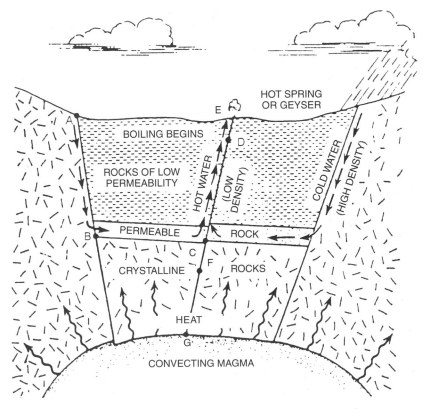

Figure 2.18l At present, the primary source of geothermal energy comes from water circulating deep into the Earth. (From "Sourcebook on the Production of Electricity from Geothermal Energy," U.S. Department of Energy.)

heats over 360 buildings including the state capitol. The United States has enough geothermal resources (Color Plate 19) to meet 6 percent of its 2025 energy needs.

Geo-Exchange

The low-grade thermal energy at the normal temperature of shallow ground can be extracted by a heat pump to heat buildings or domestic hot water (heat pumps are explained in Section 16.19). This same heat pump can use the ground as a heat sink in the summer. Since the ground is warmer than the air in winter and cooler than the air in summer, a **ground-source heat pump** is much more efficient than normal **air-source heat pumps.** Also, since electricity is used to pump heat and not create it, a geo-exchange heat pump is three to four times more efficient than resistance electric heating.

The use of geo-exchange heat pumps can significantly reduce our consumption of energy and the corresponding emission of pollution and greenhouse gases. Reductions of 40 percent over air-source heat pumps and reductions of 70 percent compared to electric-resistance heating and standard air-conditioning equipment are feasible. See Chapter 16 for a more detailed discussion of this excellent system.

2.19 HYDROGEN

Although hydrogen is *not* a source of energy, it might play an important role in a sustainable economy. Hydrogen is the ideal nonpolluting fuel because when it is burned, only water is produced. It does not contribute to global warming.

Hydrogen is abundant, but all of it is locked up in compounds, such as water (H_2O). The closest place to mine free hydrogen is the planet Jupiter. Until we can go there, we will have to manufacture it here on earth. To produce free hydrogen, energy is needed to break the chemical bonds. Although several methods exist for

Figure 2.18m The Hatchobaru geothermal power station in Japan. (Courtesy of Kyushu Electric Power Co., Inc.)

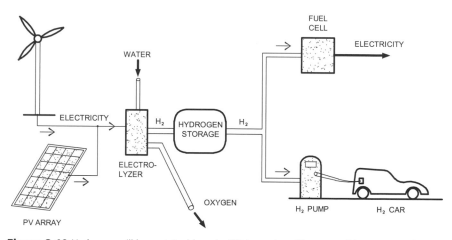

Figure 2.19 Hydrogen will be sustainable only, if it is produced by renewable energy such as PV and wind. It can be used both as a fuel for our vehicles and for fuel cells that power and heat our buildings.

producing hydrogen, the process must use renewable energy sources to produce a truly clean, sustainable fuel. Hydrogen can be separated from natural gas, coal, or other hydrocarbons by a process called **reformation**, but this source of hydrogen is not sustainable.

Hydrogen can also be created by living organism in ponds, but the most practical source is electrolysis with electricity generated by wind and PV.

Hydrogen is a good match for the intermittent sources of solar and wind, whose main weakness is energy storage. Whenever excess electricity is produced, it can be used to produce hydrogen from water by electrolysis (Fig. 2.19). The hydrogen can then be used to generate pollution-free electricity in fuel cells, which are explained in Section 3.22. It can also be used to power automobile engines.

The efficient and economical storage of hydrogen remains a technical problem, however. High-pressure tanks are heavy and expensive. To store hydrogen as a liquid, one must cool it to $-423°F$ ($-253°C$). A more efficient solution might be to store the hydrogen in chemical compounds called **hydrides.** More research is needed to make hydrogen the fuel of choice.

Hydrogen has the potential to become a clean, renewable fuel to power our cars and buildings, but since it is not a source of energy, we must still develop the renewable energy sources described above.

2.20 CONCLUSION

> If we are looking for insurance against want and oppression, we will find it only in our neighbors' prosperity and goodwill and, beyond, that, in the good health of our worldly places, our homelands. If we were sincerely looking for a place of safety, for real security and success, then we would begin to turn to our communities—and not the communities simply of our human neighbors, but also of the water, earth, and air, the plants and animals, all the creatures with whom our local life is shared.
> —*Wendell Berry, Author*

We are not achieving safety by the way we use energy. We are damaging the environment, changing the climate, and using up our nonrenewable energy sources at a phenomenal rate (Fig. 2.20a). Our present course is not sustainable.

Since buildings use almost one-half of all the energy consumed and almost three-quarters of all the electricity, the building-design community has both the responsibility and the opportunity to make major changes in energy use. The amount of energy a building consumes is mainly a function of its design.

Since the energy crisis of 1973, many fine buildings have shown us that buildings can be both energy-efficient and aesthetically successful. As Bob Berkebile, one of our most environmentally responsive architects, has said, "If a building makes animals or people or the planet sick, it's not beautiful and it's not good design" (Wylie, 1994).

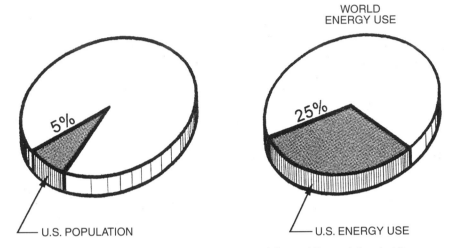

Figure 2.20a The United States has about 5 percent of the world's population, but it consumes about 25 percent of the world's energy.

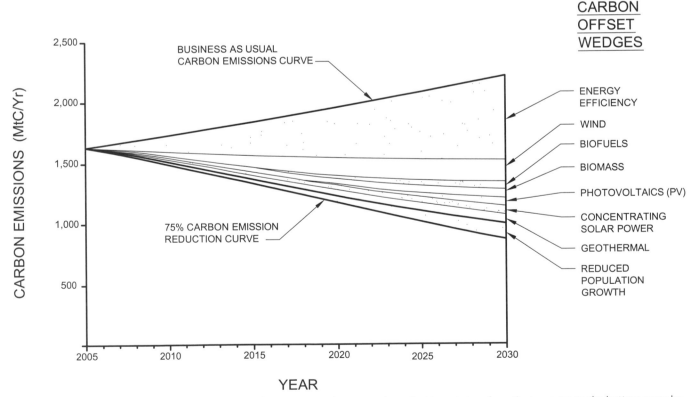

Figure 2.20b To prevent a global warming catastrophe, we must reduce our carbon dioxide emissions from the top curve to the bottom curve by reducing our dependence on fossil energy. By using all of the renewable energy, wedges and especially the efficiency wedge, we can accomplish this most important planetary goal. This graph is based on the work of "stabilization wedges" by Pacala and Socolow (Pacala 2004).

We in the United States have a special obligation because we use 25 percent of the world's energy and produce 22 percent of the carbon dioxide, but have only 5 percent of the world's population (Fig. 2.20a). As mentioned before, each American produces more carbon dioxide than the citizen of any other country (the only exceptions are citizens of tiny oil-rich countries like Qatar). We also have been producing carbon dioxide for a long time, so that as a country we are responsible for 29 percent of all the man-made carbon dioxide in the atmosphere (see again Table 2.11). We also have the wealth and resources to lead the way. As a leader in research and technology, we can create and share the technical tools for creating a sustainable world.

Some people incorrectly assume that nothing can be done about global warming. However, the renewable energies mentioned above, together with efficiency, can radically reduce greenhouse gasses and lead us to a sustainable world (Fig. 2.20b).

The existence of comfortable modern zero-energy buildings proves that there is much we can do in the building sector. The other large user of energy is transportation. Although not the topic of this book, it is inspiring to know that huge savings are possible in automobiles as well. Presently, less than 1 percent of the gasoline energy is used to move the driver. Over 99 percent is lost in waste heat and in moving the vehicle mass. That is a lot of inefficiency that can be reduced. For example, in the near future,

it will be possible to build SUVs that get 65 miles per gallon (mpg) (26 kml) and be safer as well (Amory Lovins, RMI).

The following chapters present the information and design tools needed to create aesthetic, energy-conscious buildings. The goal is to *reduce* the amount of energy that buildings need using the three-tier approach: design of the building itself, use of passive systems, and finally, efficient mechanical systems.

Since heating, cooling, and lighting are consequences of energy manipulation, it is important to understand certain principles of energy. The next chapter reviews some of the basic concepts and introduces other important relationships between energy and objects.

KEY IDEAS OF CHAPTER 2

1. We are squandering the earth's riches, destroying the environment, and changing the climate without regard to the needs of future generations.
2. Sustainability can be achieved by implementing the four Rs: reduce, reuse, recycle, and regenerate.
3. Sustainable design is also known as green, ecological, and environmentally responsible design.
4. The greater the population, the more difficult it is to achieve sustainability.
5. The greater the affluence, the more difficult it is to achieve sustainability.
6. Limitless growth is the enemy of sustainability.

7. Because many important phenomena, such as energy consumption, are exhibiting exponential growth, and because people do not have a good understanding of the implications of exponential growth, improper decisions are being made about the future.
8. Sustainability can be achieved only if we design and build energy-efficient buildings.
9. The massive use of fossil fuels is causing global warming and climate change.
10. At present, most of our energy comes from nonrenewable and polluting energy sources, such as coal, oil, gas, and nuclear energy.

11. Efficiency is the best, quickest, and most cost-effective way to reduce our dependence on fossil and nuclear energy.
12. We must switch to renewable, nonpolluting energy sources such as solar, wind, biomass, hydropower, and geothermal energy.
13. Geo-exchange heat pumps have great potential for energy conservation.
14. Although not a source of energy, hydrogen has the potential to be the clean fuel of the future.
15. As architect Bob Berkabile said, "If a building makes animals or people or the planet sick, it's not beautiful and it's not good design."

References

Bartlett, A. "Forgotten Fundamentals of the Energy Crisis." *American Journal of Physics*, September, 1978, 46–54.

Barlett, A. "Reflections on Sustainability, Population Growth, and the Environment—Revisited." *Renewable Resources Journal*. Winter, 1997, 6–23.

Butti, K., and J. Perdin. *A Golden Thread*. New York: Van Nostrand Reinhold, 1980.

Campbell, C., and J. Laherrère. "The End of Cheap Oil." *Scientific American*, March 1998, 278–281.

FSEC. "Air-Conditioning Use Cut by 80 Percent in Lakeland Research Home, Cocoa, FI." *Solar Collector*, June–July 1998, 23–28.

Hubbert, K. M. *American Journal of Physics*, vol. 49, no. 11, 1981.

McDonough, W., and M. Braungart. "The Next Industrial Revolution." *The Atlantic Monthly*, October 1998, 82–92.

Pacala, S., and Socolow, R. "Stabilization Wedges: Solving the Climate Problem for the Next 50 Years with . . ." *Science* 13, August 2004: 968–972.

Stobaugh, R., and D. Yerkin. *Energy Future—Report of the Energy Project at the Harvard Business School*. New York: Random House, 1979.

Wylie, A. "Form with a Function." *America West Airlines Magazine*, April 1994, 57–61.

World Resource Institute www.wri.org Search: "Searchable Database" for "CO_2 Emissions: Cumulative CO_2 emissions, 1900–2002."

Resources

FURTHER READING

(See the Bibliography in the back of the book for full citations.)

American Wind Energy Association. *Permitting Small Wind Turbines: A Handbook.*

Barnett, D. L., and W. D. Browning. *A Primer on Sustainable Building.*

Barlett, A. A. "Reflections on Sustainability, Population Growth, and the Environment—Revisited."

Campbell, C. J., and J. H. Leherrère. "The End of Cheap Oil."

Commoner, B. *The Politics of Energy.*

Crosbie, M. J. *Green Architecture: A Guide to Sustainable Design.*

Crowther, R. *Ecologic Architecture. Environmental Building News.* See Appendix K.

Ehrlich, P. R., and A. H. Ehrlich. *The Population Explosion.*

Gelbspan, R. *The Heat Is On: The High Stakes Battle Over Earth's Threatened Climate.*

Gore, A. *An Inconvenient Truth.*

Hawken, P. *The Ecology of Commerce: A Declaration of Sustainability.*

Hawken, P., A. Lovins, and L. H. Lovins. *Natural Capitalism: Creating the Next Industrial Revolution.*

Lovins, A. B. *Soft Energy Paths.*

Lovins, Amory, B. "More Profit with Less Carbon."

Lovins, A. B., and L. H. Lovins. *Brittle Power: Energy Strategy for National Security.*

Lovins, Amory, B., et al. *Winning the Oil Endgame.*

Lyle, J. T. *Regenerative Design for Sustainable Development.*

Susanka, S., *The Not So Big House.*

Scheer, H. *A Solar Manifesto: The Need for a Total Solar Energy Supply—And How to Achieve It.*

Singh, M. *The Timeless Energy of the Sun for Life and Peace with Nature.*

Wilson, E. O. "Is Humanity Suicidal? We're Flirting with the Extinction of Our Species." *New York Times Magazine.*

VIDEOS

(See Appendix K for full citations and ordering information.)

Affluenza. KCTS Television *Arithmetic, Population, and Energy.* Dr. Albert A. Barlett. 65 minutes.

An Inconvenient Truth. Al Gore.

Keeping the Earth: Religious and Scientific Perspectives on the Environment. 27 minutes.

World Population. ZPG.

ORGANIZATIONS

(See Appendix K for full citations and ordering information.)

American Hydrogen Association (E-mail): aha@getnet.com www.clean-air.org

American Solar Energy Society www.csn.net.solar/factbase.htm National group for renewable-energy education.

CREST—Center for Renewable Energy and Sustainable Technology www.crest.org Comprehensive educational source for renewables.

Rocky Mountain Institute www.rmi.org An excellent source of objective energy information.

National Renewable Energy Laboratory www.nrel.gov Good source for detailed information on renewables.

Union of Concerned Scientists www.ucsusa.org

WIND INFORMATION

Wind energy data can be obtained from:

American Wind Energy Association (AWEA) 122 C Street, NW, 4th Floor, Washington, DC 20001 (202) 383-2500 Fax (202) 383-2505 www.econet.org/awea

National Climatic Data Center 151 Patton Avenue, Room 120, Ashville, NC 28801 (704) 271-4800 Fax (704) 271-4876 E-mail orders@ncdc.noaa.gov www.ncdc.noaa.gov

Wind Energy Resource Atlas of the U.S. Battelle Pacific Northwest Laboratories. Available from the American Wind Energy Association (see above) or the National Technical Information Service (see Appendix K).

CHAPTER

BASIC PRINCIPLES | 3

If we are anything, we must be a democracy of the intellect. We must not perish by the distance between people and government, between people and power. . . . And that distance can only be conflated, can only be closed, if knowledge sits in the homes and heads of people with no ambition to control others, and not up in the isolated seats of power.

J. Bronowski
The Ascent of Man, *1973*

3.1 INTRODUCTION

The heating, cooling, and lighting of buildings are accomplished by adding or removing energy. A good basic understanding of the physics of energy and its related principles is a prerequisite for much of the material in the following chapters. Consequently, this chapter is devoted to both a review of some rather well-known concepts and an introduction to some less familiar ideas such as mean radiant temperature, time lag, the insulating effect of mass, and embodied energy.

3.2 HEAT

Energy comes in many forms, and most of these are used in buildings. Much of this book, however, is concerned with energy in the form of heat, which exists in three different forms:

1. **Sensible heat**—can be measured with a thermometer
2. **Latent heat**—the change of state or phase change of a material
3. **Radiant heat**—a form of electromagnetic radiation

3.3 SENSIBLE HEAT

The random motion of molecules is a form of energy called **sensible heat.** An object whose molecules have a larger random motion is said to be hotter and to contain more heat (see Fig. 3.3a). Because this type of heat can be measured by a thermometer and felt by our skin, it is called sensible heat. If the two objects in Fig. 3.3a are brought into contact, some of the more intense random motion of the object on the left will be transferred to the object on the right by the heat-flow mechanism called **conduction.** The molecules must be close to each other in order to collide. Since in air the molecules are far apart, air is not a good conductor of heat. A vacuum allows no conduction at all.

Temperature is a measure of the intensity of the random motion of

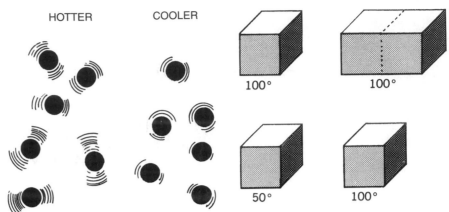

HOTTER   COOLER

Figure 3.3a Sensible heat is the random motion of molecules, and temperature is a measure of the intensity of that motion.

Figure 3.3b The amount of sensible heat is a function of both temperature and mass. In each case, the blocks on the right have twice as much sensible heat content as the blocks on the left.

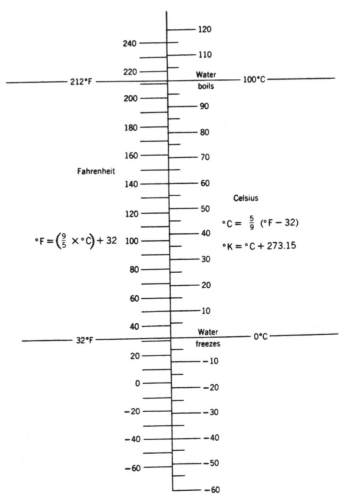

$$°F = \left(\frac{9}{5} \times °C\right) + 32$$

$$°C = \frac{5}{9} \ (°F - 32)$$

$$°K = °C + 273.15$$

Figure 3.3c Conversion: Fahrenheit–Celsius degrees. (From *Mechanical and Electrical Equipment for Buildings*, 9th edition, Stein and Reynolds, © 2000 John Wiley & Sons, Inc.)

Table 3.3 Units of Heat and Temperature		
	I–P System*	SI System
Heat	British thermal unit (Btu)	joule (J) or calorie (cal)
Heat flow	Btu/hour (Btu/h)	watt (W) or joule/second (J/s)
Temperature	Fahrenheit (°F)	Celsius (°C)

*I-P = inch-pound.

molecules. We cannot determine the heat content of an object just by knowing its temperature. For example, in Fig. 3.3b (top), we see two blocks of a certain material that are both at the same temperature. Yet the block on the right will contain twice the heat because it has twice the mass.

The mass alone cannot determine the heat content either. In Fig. 3.3b (bottom), we see two blocks of the same size, yet one block has more heat content because it has a higher temperature. Thus, sensible heat content is a function of both mass and temperature. It is also a function of heat capacity, which is discussed in Section 3.15.

In the United States, we still use the Fahrenheit (°F) scale for temperature and the British thermal unit (Btu) as our unit of heat. The rest of the world, including Great Britain, uses the Systeme International (SI) where temperature is measured in Celsius (°C) and heat in the unit called the "joule" or "calorie." (See Table 3.3 and Fig. 3.3c).

3.4 LATENT HEAT

By adding 1 (Btu) of heat to a pound of water, its temperature is raised 1°F (4.2J/g/°C). It takes, however, 144 Btu to change a pound of ice into a pound of water and about 1000 Btu to change a pound of water into a pound of steam (Fig. 3.4). It takes very large amounts of energy to break the bonds between the molecules when a change of state occurs. "**Heat of fusion**" is required to melt a solid and "**heat of vaporization**" is required to change a liquid into a gas. Notice also that the water is no hotter than the ice and the steam is no hotter than the

water, even though a large amount of heat is added. This heat energy, which is very real but cannot be measured by a thermometer, is called "latent heat." In melting ice or boiling water, sensible heat is changed into latent heat, and when steam condenses and water freezes, the latent heat is turned back into sensible heat.

Latent heat is a compact and convenient form for storing and transferring heat. However, since the melting and boiling points of water are not always suitable, we use other materials called "refrigerants," which have the melting and boiling temperatures necessary for refrigeration machines.

3.5 EVAPORATIVE COOLING

When sweat evaporates from the skin, a large amount of heat is required. This heat of vaporization is drawn from the skin, which is cooled in the process. The sensible heat in the skin is turned into the latent heat of the water vapor.

As water evaporates, the air next to the skin becomes humid and eventually even saturated. The moisture in the air will then inhibit further evaporation. Thus, either air motion to remove this moist air or very dry air is required to make **evaporative cooling** efficient (Fig. 3.5).

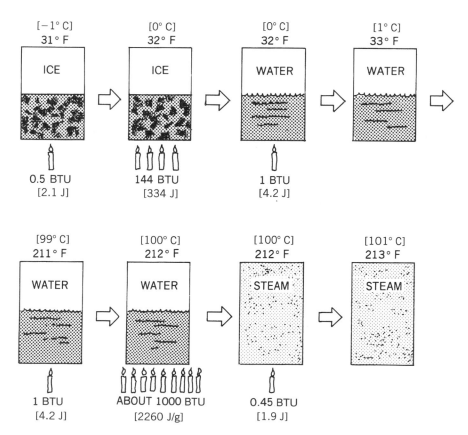

Figure 3.4 Latent heat is the large amount of energy required to change the state of a material (phase change), and it cannot be measured by a thermometer. The values given here are for 1 pound (1 gram) of water, ice, or steam.

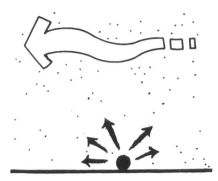

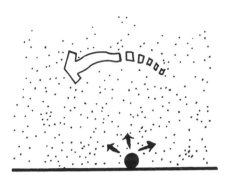

Figure 3.5 The rate of evaporative cooling is a function of both humidity and air movement. Evaporation is rapid when the humidity is low and air movement is high. Evaporation is slow when the humidity is high and air movement is low.

Buildings can also be cooled by evaporation. Water sprayed on the roof can dramatically reduce its temperature. In dry climates, air entering buildings can be cooled with water sprays. Such techniques will be described in Chapter 10.

3.6 CONVECTION

As a gas or liquid acquires heat by conduction, the fluid expands and becomes less dense. It will then rise by floating on top of denser and cooler fluid, as seen in Fig. 3.6a. The resulting currents transfer heat by the mechanism called **natural convection**. This heat-transfer mechanism is very much dependent on gravity and, therefore, heat never convects down. Since we are surrounded by air, natural convection is a very important heat-transfer mechanism.

When there is no air motion due to the wind or a fan, natural convection

currents tend to create layers that are at different temperatures. In rooms, hot air collects near the ceiling and cold air near the floor (Fig. 3.6b). This **stratification** can be an asset in the summer and a liability in the winter. Strategies to deal with this phenomenon will be discussed throughout this book. A similar situation occurs in still lakes where surface water is much warmer than deep water (Fig. 3.6b).

A different type of convection occurs when the air is moved by a

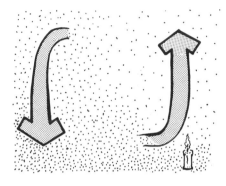

Figure 3.6a Natural-convection currents result from differences in temperature.

fan or by the wind, or when water is moved by a pump (Fig. 3.6c). When a fluid (gas or liquid) is circulated between hotter and cooler areas, heat will be transferred by the mechanism known as **forced convection**.

3.7 TRANSPORT

In the eighteenth and nineteenth centuries, it was common to use warming pans to preheat beds. The typical warming pan, as shown in Fig. 3.7, was about 12 in. (30 cm) in diameter and about 4 in. (10 cm) deep, and it had a long wooden handle. It was filled with hot embers from the fireplace, carried to the bedrooms, and passed between the sheets to remove the chill. In the early twentieth century, it was common to use hot-water bottles for the same purpose. This transfer of heat by moving material is called **transport**. Because of its convenience, forced convection is much more popular today for moving heat around a building than is transport.

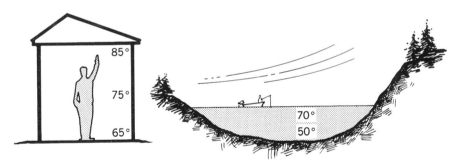

Figure 3.6b Stratification results from natural convection unless other forces are present to mix the air or water.

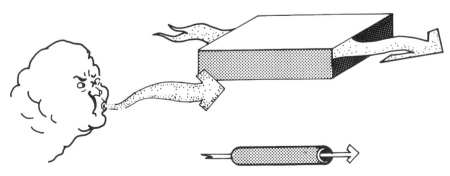

Figure 3.6c Forced convection is caused by wind, fans, or pumps.

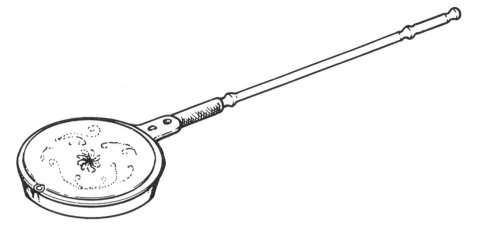

Figure 3.7 Warming pans and hot-water bottles were popular in the past to transport heat from the fireplace or stove to cold beds.

Figure 3.8 One cubic foot (1 L) of water can store or transfer the same amount of heat as over 3000 ft³ (3,000 L) of air.

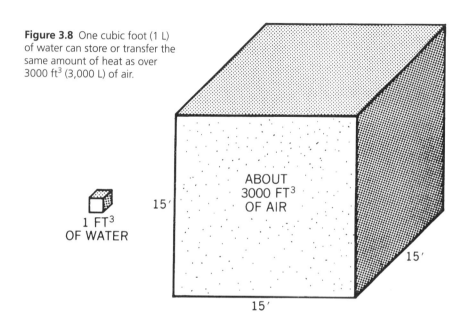

1 FT³ OF WATER

ABOUT 3000 FT³ OF AIR

15′ 15′ 15′

3.8 ENERGY-TRANSFER MEDIUMS

In both the heating and cooling of buildings, a major design decision is the choice of the energy-transfer medium. The most common alternatives are air and water. It is, therefore, very valuable to understand the relative heat-transfer capacity of these two materials. Because air has both much lower density and much less specific heat than water, much more of it is required to store or transfer heat. To store or transfer equal amounts of heat, we need a volume of air about 3000 times greater than that of water (Fig. 3.8).

3.9 RADIATION

The third form of heat is radiant heat. All parts of the **electromagnetic spectrum** transfer radiant energy. All bodies facing an air space or a vacuum emit and absorb radiant energy continuously. Hot bodies lose heat by radiation because they emit more energy than they absorb (Fig. 3.9a). Objects at room temperature radiate in the infrared region of the electromagnetic spectrum, while objects hot enough to glow radiate in the visible part of the spectrum. Thus, the wavelength or frequency of the radiation emitted is a function of the temperature of the object.

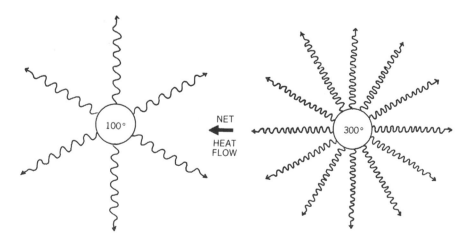

100°   NET HEAT FLOW   300°

Figure 3.9a Although all objects absorb and emit radiant energy, there will be a net radiant flow from warmer to cooler objects.

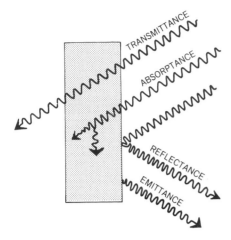

Figure 3.9b Four different types of interaction are possible between energy and matter.

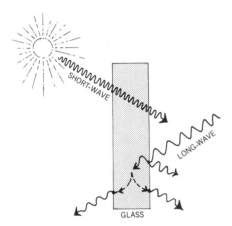

Figure 3.9c The type of interaction depends not only on the nature of the material but also on the wavelength of the radiation.

Since radiation is not affected by gravity, a body will radiate down as much as up. Radiation is, however, affected by the nature of the material with which it interacts and especially the surface of the material. The four possible interactions, as illustrated in Fig. 3.9b, are as follows:

1. **Transmittance**—the situation in which radiation passes through the material.
2. **Absorptance**—the situation in which radiation is converted into sensible heat within the material.
3. **Reflectance**—the situation in which radiation is reflected off the surface.

4. **Emittance**—the situation in which radiation is given off by the surface, thereby reducing the sensible heat content of the object. Polished metal surfaces have low emittance, while most other materials have high emittance.

The type of interaction that will occur is a function not only of the material but also of the wavelength of the radiation. For example, glass interacts very differently with **solar radiation** (short-wave) than with thermal radiation (long-wave infrared), as shown in Fig. 3.9c. Glass is mostly transparent to short-wave radiation and opaque to long-wave radiation. The long-wave radiation is mostly absorbed, thereby heating up the glass. Much of the absorbed radiation is then reradiated from the glass inward and outward. The net effect is that some of the long-wave radiation is blocked by the glass. The greenhouse effect, explained below, is partly due to this property of glass and most plastics used for glazing. Polyethelene is the major exception, since it is transparent to infrared radiation.

3.10 GREENHOUSE EFFECT

The concept of the **greenhouse effect** is vital for understanding both solar energy and climate change. The greenhouse effect is due to the fact that the type of interaction that occurs between a material and radiant energy depends on the wavelength of that radiation.

Figure 3.10a illustrates the basic concept of the greenhouse effect. The short-wave solar radiation is able to pass easily through the glass, whereupon it is absorbed by indoor objects. As these objects warm up, they increase their emission of radiation in the long-wave portion of the electromagnetic spectrum. Since glass is opaque to this radiation, much of the energy is trapped. The glass has created, in effect, a heat trap and the indoor temperature begins to rise.

To better understand this very important concept, let us look at the

Figure 3.10a The greenhouse effect is partly a consequence of the fact that glazing transmits short-wave but blocks long-wave radiation.

vertically aligned graphs in Fig. 3.10b. First, look at the top graph, which describes the behavior of glass with respect to radiation. The percentage transmission is given as a function of the wavelength of the radiation. Notice that glass has a very high transmission for radiation between 0.3 and 3 μm (millionth of a meter) and zero transmission for radiation above and below that "window."

The bottom graph of Figure 3.10b shows the wavelengths of the radiation reaching the Earth. It consists of about 5 percent **ultraviolet** (UV), about 45 percent visible light, and about 50 percent **solar infrared** (IR). The bottom graph also shows the wavelengths of radiation emitted by objects at room temperature, which are also part of the infrared spectrum. To distinguish these from the solar infrared, they are called **long-wave infrared** and, consequently, the solar infrared is also called **short-wave infrared**.

The graphs together show that the part of the electromagnetic spectrum for which glass is transparent corresponds to solar radiation, and the part for which glass is opaque corresponds to the long-wave infrared **heat radiation** given off by objects at room temperature. The solar radiation enters through the glass and is absorbed by objects in the room. These objects heat up and then increase their reradiation in the long-wave infrared part of the spectrum. Since glass is opaque

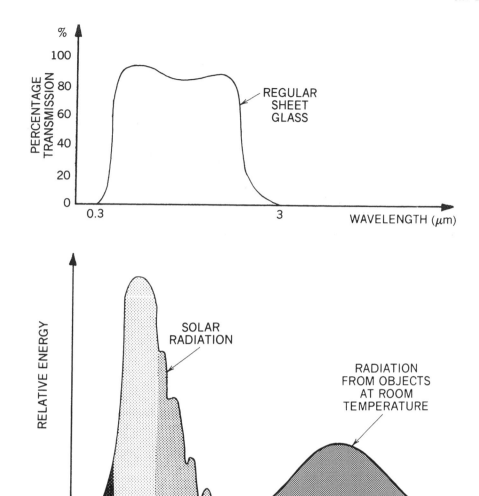

Figure 3.10b Note that these two graphs are aligned vertically. Thus, the top graph shows that glass transmits about 90 percent of both the visible and short-wave infrared portions of sunlight. It also shows that glass does not transmit any of the long-wave infrared radiation emitted by objects at room temperature.

3.11 EQUILIBRIUM TEMPERATURE OF A SURFACE

Understanding the heating, cooling, and lighting of buildings requires a fair amount of knowledge of the behavior of radiant energy. For example, what is the best color for a solar collector, and what is the best color for a roof to reject solar heat in the summer? Figure 3.11 illustrates how surfaces of different colors and finishes interact with radiant energy. To understand why a black metal plate will get much warmer in the sun than a white metal plate, we must remember that materials vary in the way they emit and absorb radiant energy. The balance between absorptance and emittance determines how hot the plate will get, the **equilibrium temperature**. Black has a much higher equilibrium temperature than white because it has a much higher absorptance factor. However, black is not the ideal collector of radiant energy because of its high emissivity. Its equilibrium temperature is suppressed because it reradiates much of the energy it has absorbed.

To increase efficiency in solar collectors, a type of **selective surface** was developed. These finishes have the same high absorptance as black but are stingier in emitting radiation. Thus, their equilibrium temperature is very high.

White is the best color to minimize heat gain in the summer because it is not only a poor absorber but also a good emitter of any energy that is absorbed. Thus, white does not like to collect heat, and a very low equilibrium temperature results. This low surface temperature minimizes the heat gain to the material below the surface.

Polished-metal surfaces, such as shiny aluminum, can be used as radiant barriers because they neither absorb nor emit radiation readily. For this reason, aluminum foil is sometimes used in buildings as a radiant barrier. However, the equilibrium temperature of a polished-metal surface is higher than that of a white surface because the metal does not emit whatever it has absorbed. Although both

to this radiation, much of the energy is trapped and the room heats up. This is one of the mechanisms of the greenhouse effect. The other major mechanism of the greenhouse effect is the obvious fact that the glazing stops the convective loss of hot air. These mechanisms form a very effective heat trap.

Note that glass changes from 0 to about 80 percent transmission in the ultraviolet part of the spectrum. Thus, the longer wavelengths of UV pass through the glass, while the shorter UV, which cause sunburn, do not. The longer UV radiation contributes to both solar heating and the fading of colors.

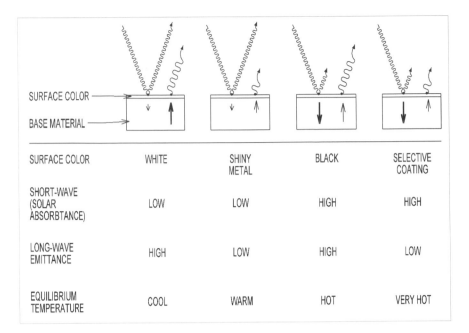

Figure 3.11 The equilibrium temperature is a consequence of both the absorptance and the emittance characteristics of a material. If these colors were the finishes of automobiles, it would be easy to predict which would be hotter and which cooler.

SURFACE COLOR	WHITE	SHINY METAL	BLACK	SELECTIVE COATING
SHORT-WAVE (SOLAR ABSORBTANCE)	LOW	LOW	HIGH	HIGH
LONG-WAVE EMITTANCE	HIGH	LOW	HIGH	LOW
EQUILIBRIUM TEMPERATURE	COOL	WARM	HOT	VERY HOT

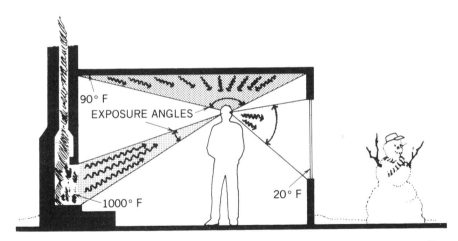

Figure 3.12 The mean radiant temperature (MRT) at any point is a result of the combined effect of a surface's temperature and angle of exposure.

white and polished metals reflect about the same percentage of sunlight, white is a much better emitter of heat radiation and so will be cooler in the sun than a polished-metal surface.

3.12 MEAN RADIANT TEMPERATURE

To determine if a certain body will be a net gainer or loser of radiant energy, we must consider both the temperature and the exposure angle of all objects that are in view of the body in question. The **mean radiant temperature (MRT)** describes the radiant environment for a point in space. For example, the radiant effect on one's face by a fireplace (Fig. 3.12) is quite high because the fire's temperature at about 1000°F (540°C) more than compensates for the small angle of exposure. A radiant ceiling can have just as much of a warming effect but with a much lower temperature (90°F)

(32°C) because its large area creates a large exposure angle. The radiant effect can also be negative, as in the case of a person standing in front of a cold window.

Walking toward the fire (Fig. 3.12) would increase the MRT, while walking toward the cold window would reduce it because the relative size of the exposure angles would change. Many a "cold draft" near large windows in winter is actually a misinterpretation of a low MRT. The significant effect MRT has on thermal comfort is further explained in the next chapter. See Sidebox 3.12.

3.13 HEAT FLOW

Heat flows naturally from a higher temperature to a lower temperature but not necessarily from more heat to less heat. To better understand this, we can consider a water analogy. In this analogy, the height between different levels of water represents the temperature difference between two heat sources and the volume of water represents the amount of heat.

Since both reservoirs are at the same level, as shown in Fig. 3.13 (top), there is no flow. The fact that there is more water (heat) on one side than the other is of no consequence.

If, however, the levels of the reservoirs are not the same, then flow occurs, as indicated in Fig. 3.13 (bottom). Notice that this occurs even when the amount of water (heat) is less on the higher side. Just as water will flow only down, so heat will flow only from a higher temperature to a lower temperature.

To get the water to a higher level, some kind of pump is required. Heat, likewise, can be raised to a higher temperature only by some kind of "heat pump," which works against the natural flow. Refrigeration machines, the essential devices in air conditioners and freezers, pump heat from a lower to a higher temperature. They will be explained in some detail in Chapter 16.

Mean Radiant Temperature

MRT is the weighted-average radiant temperature of a point in space, and it varies from point to point. The most precise calculation would use solid angles, but for simplicity, the following two-dimensional version in plan or section is often used:

$$MRT_A = \frac{\Sigma T \cdot \Theta}{360} = \frac{T_1 \cdot \Theta_1 + T_2 \cdot \Theta_2 + T_3 \cdot \Theta_3 + \ldots}{360°}$$

where

MRT_A = mean radiant temperature for point A
T = temperature of a surface
Θ = exposure angle of a surface from the point being considered

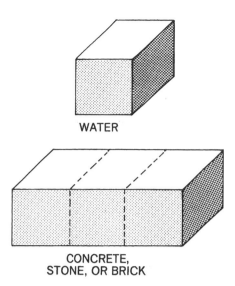

Figure 3.15 If the container of water and the concrete block are at the same temperature, they will contain the same amount of sensible heat. Because it takes only one-third as much water to hold the same amount of heat as concrete, water has three times the volumetric heat capacity of concrete.

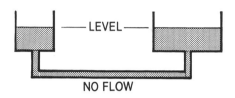

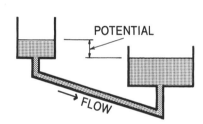

Figure 3.13 A water analogy shows how temperature, not heat content, determines heat flow.

In the I–P system heat flow is measured in Btu per hour (Btu/h). For example, the heat loss from a building is measured in Btu/h, and the rating of a furnace, which describes the rate at which heat is delivered, is also given in Btu/h. In the SI system, heat flow is described by watts (W), which are equal to joules per second (J/s) (see Table 3.3).

3.14 HEAT SINK

It is easy to see how transporting hot water to a room also supplies heat to the room. It is not so obvious, however, to see how supplying chilled water cools the room. Are we supplying

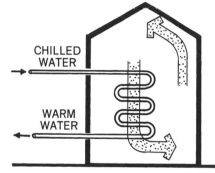

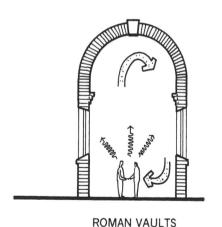

ROMAN VAULTS

Figure 3.14 The cooling effect of a heat sink can result from a cold fluid or from the mass of the building itself.

"coolth"? This imaginary concept only confuses and should not be used. A correct and very useful concept is that of a **heat sink**. In Fig. 3.14 (top) the room is cooled by the chilled water that is acting as a heat sink. The chilled water soaks up heat and gets warmer while the room gets cooler.

Often the massive structure of a building acts as a heat sink. Many massive buildings feel comfortably cool on hot summer days, as in Fig. 3.14 (bottom). During the night, these buildings give up their heat by convection to the cool night air and by radiation to the cold sky—thus recharging their heat sink capability for the next day. However, in very humid regions the high nighttime temperatures prevent effective recharging of the heat sink; consequently, massive buildings are not helpful.

3.15 HEAT CAPACITY

The amount of heat required to raise the temperature of a material 1°F (1°C) is called the **heat capacity** of that material. The heat capacity of different materials varies widely, but in general, heavier materials have a higher heat capacity. Water is an exception in that it has the highest heat capacity even though it is a middleweight material (Fig. 3.15). In architecture we are usually more interested in the heat capacity per volume than in the heat capacity per weight, which is more commonly known as **specific heat**.

Also note again the dramatic difference in heat capacity between air and water, as shown in Fig. 3.8. This clearly indicates why water is used so often to store or move heat. See Table 7.17A for the heat capacity of various common materials.

3.16 THERMAL RESISTANCE

The opposition of materials and air spaces to the flow of heat by conduction, convection, and radiation is called **thermal resistance**. By knowing the resistance of a material, we can predict how much heat will flow through it and can compare materials with each other. The thermal resistance of building materials is largely a function of the number and size of air spaces that they contain. For example, 1 in. (1 cm) of wood has the same thermal resistance as 12 in. (12 cm) of concrete mainly because of the air spaces created by the cells in the wood (Fig. 3.16). However, this is true only under steady-state conditions, where the temperature across a material remains constant for a long period of time. Under certain dynamic temperature

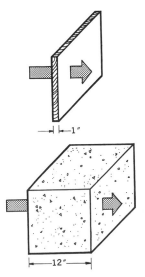

Figure 3.16 The heat flow is equal through the two materials because the thermal resistance of wood is twelve times as great as that of concrete.

conditions, 12 in. (12 cm) of concrete can appear to have more resistance to heat flow than 1 in. (1 cm) of wood. To understand this, we must consider the concept of time lag, explained in Section 3.18. Because the units of thermal resistance are complex and hard to remember, technical literature frequently gives the thermal resistance in terms of R-value (see Sidebox 3.16).

3.17 HEAT-FLOW COEFFICIENT

Much of the technical literature describes the thermal characteristics of wall or roof systems in terms of the heat-flow coefficient U rather than the total thermal resistance. Because the heat-flow coefficient is a measure of heat flow (conductance), it is the reciprocal of thermal resistance (see Sidebox 3.17).

3.18 TIME LAG

Consider what happens when two walls with **equal thermal resistance**, 12 in. (12 cm) of concrete or 1 in. (1 cm) of wood, are first exposed to

a temperature difference. Although these two walls have the same thermal resistance, they do not have the same heat capacity. Although wood and concrete have about the same volumetric heat capacity (i.e., for equal volumes), 12 in. (12 cm) of concrete will have twelve times the heat capacity of 1 in. (1 cm) of wood.

Let's say that the temperature is 100°F (43°C) on one side and 50°F (10°C) on the other side of both the concrete and the wooden walls. Heat will flow through both walls, but the initial heat to enter will be used to raise the temperature of each material. Only after the walls have substantially warmed up can heat exit the other side. This delay in heat conduction is very short for the 1 in. (1 cm) wooden wall because of its low heat capacity, while it is much longer for the concrete wall with its high heat capacity. This delayed heat-flow phenomenon is known as **time lag**.

This concept can be understood more easily by means of a water analogy in which pipe friction represents thermal resistance and an in-line storage tank represents the thermal capacity

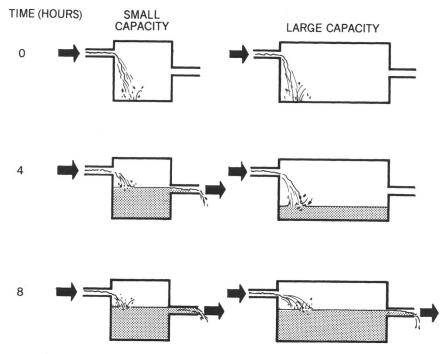

Figure 3.18 This water analogy of time lag illustrates how high capacity delays the passage of water under dynamic conditions. Similarly, high heat capacity delays the transmission of heat under dynamic conditions. This example is similar to heat flow through either 1 in. (1 cm) of wood (small capacity) or 12 in. (12 cm) of concrete (high capacity).

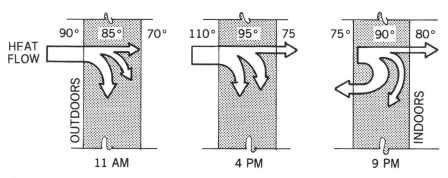

Figure 3.19 The insulating effect of mass is most pronounced in hot and dry climates in the summer. The same wall is shown at three different times of the day.

concrete house in the desert on a summer day. A wall of this building is shown at three different times of day (Fig. 3.19). At 11 A.M. the indoor temperature is lower than the outdoor temperature and heat will flow inward. However, most of this heat is diverted to raising the temperature of the wall.

At 4 P.M. the outdoor temperature is very high. Although some heat is now reaching the indoors, much heat is still being diverted to further raising the temperature of the wall.

However, at 9 P.M. the outside temperature has declined enough to be below the indoor temperature and especially the wall temperature. Now most of the heat that was stored in the wall is flowing outward without ever reaching the interior of the house. In this situation, the time lag of the massive material "insulated" the building from the high outdoor temperatures. It is important to note that the benefits of time lag occur only if the outdoor temperature fluctuates. Also, the larger the daily temperature swing, the greater the insulating effect of the mass. Thus, this insulating effect of mass is most beneficial in hot and dry climates during the summer. This effect is not very helpful in cold climates where the temperature remains consistently below the indoor temperature, and it is only slightly helpful in humid climates, where the daily temperature range is small. In *very* humid climates, the thermal mass can be a liability and should be avoided if the building is naturally ventilated.

of a material (Fig. 3.18). The small tank represents 1 in. (1 cm) of wood (small heat capacity) and the large tank represents 12 in. (12 cm) of concrete (large heat capacity). After four hours, water (heat) is flowing through the pipe with the low capacity but not through the system with the high capacity. Thus, high-capacity materials have a greater time lag than low-capacity materials. Also note that the time lag ends when the storage tank

is full. Under steady-state conditions there is no time lag.

3.19 INSULATING EFFECT OF MASS

If the temperature difference across a massive material fluctuates in certain specific ways, then the massive material will act as if it had high thermal resistance. Let us consider a massive

3.20 ENERGY CONVERSION

The First Law of Thermodynamics states that energy can be neither created nor destroyed, only changed in form. But while energy is never lost, the Second Law of Thermodynamics states that its ability to do work can decline. For example, high-temperature steam can generate electricity with a steam turbine, while the same amount of heat in the form of

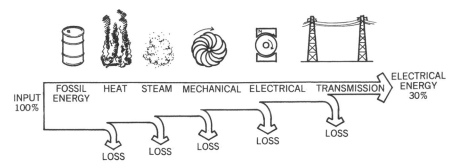

Figure 3.20 In the conversion of fossil fuel into electricity, about 70 percent of the original energy is lost.

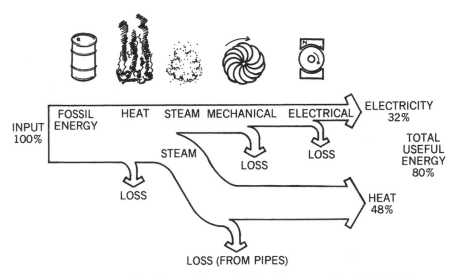

Figure 3.21a Because combined-heat-and-power (CHP) systems generate electricity at the building site, they are able to utilize much of the heat normally wasted at the power plant, and they eliminate the transmission losses.

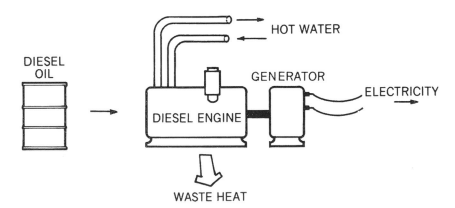

Figure 3.21b Packaged CHP units are self-contained and easily integrated into a building. Other fuels, such as natural gas and biodiesel, can also be used.

Figure 3.20 shows the conversion of a fossil fuel into electricity. The low efficiency (approximately 30 percent) is a consequence of the large number of conversions required. Thus, electrical energy should not be used when a better alternative is available. For example, heating directly with fossil fuels can be more than 80 percent efficient. It is important, however, to note that this example does not argue for the use of fossil fuels, either at the power plant or in the home. As the rest of the book explains, there are better ways to heat, cool, and light our buildings.

3.21 COMBINED HEAT AND POWER

Combined heat and power (CHP), also known as **cogeneration**, can greatly reduce the energy losses in producing electricity. Through the generation of electricity at the building site, efficiencies of up to 85 percent are possible. Heat, normally wasted at the central power plant, can be used for domestic hot-water or space heating (Fig. 3.21a). Also, overland electrical-transmission losses are almost completely eliminated. Compact and fairly maintenance-free packaged CHP units are commercially available for all sizes of buildings (Fig. 3.21b). More than 40,000 units have been installed in Japenese houses.

3.22 FUEL CELLS

CHP can be even more efficient if a **fuel cell** is used to generate the electricity. Because fuel cells are safe, clean, noiseless, low-maintenance, and compact, they can be placed in any building. Thus, there are no transmission losses, and the waste heat can be used (Fig. 3.22).

Fuel cells are powered with hydrogen that combines with oxygen in the air to form water, electricity, and heat. No emissions pollute the air or cause global warming. No flue is needed.

A green high-rise building, 4 Times Square in New York City, uses two

warm water cannot perform this task. Electricity is a very high-grade, valuable energy form, and to use it to purposely generate low-grade heat is a terrible waste. Sunlight is another

high-grade energy source. It should be used to day light a building before it turns into heat.

Whenever energy is converted into a different form, there will be a loss.

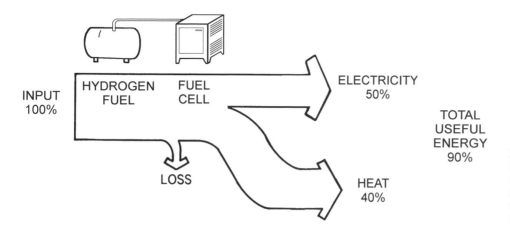

Figure 3.22 Because fuel cells use hydrogen to directly generate electricity and useful heat right inside buildings, about 90 percent of the original energy can be utilized. Fuel cells run off of nonpolluting hydrogen.

fuel cells, located on the fourth floor, to generate a significant portion of the electrical load. Since natural gas is used to create the hydrogen, some carbon dioxide is produced. However, much less carbon dioxide is produced than in conventional buildings because of the high efficiency of the fuel cells.

It is very important to note that hydrogen is *not* a source of energy but rather a way to store energy. Hydrogen has to be made by means of energy intensive processes such as **electrolysis**, in which electricity splits the water molecule into hydrogen and oxygen. Fuel cells have their greatest potential to create sustainable buildings when fueled with hydrogen made from renewable sources of energy, such as wind or solar energy.

3.23 EMBODIED ENERGY

Most discussions of energy and buildings are concerned with the use and operation of a building. It is now recognized that it can take large quantities of energy to construct a building. This **embodied energy** is a result of both the construction machinery and the energy required to make and transport the materials. For example, aluminum embodies four times as much energy as steel and about twelve times as much as wood. The embodied energy in a modern office building is about the same as the amount

Figure 3.23 A large amount of embodied energy can be saved when existing buildings are reused. (From a poster, copyright 1980 by the National Trust for Historic Preservation.)

of energy the building will consume in fifteen years.

Much of the embodied energy can be saved when we recycle old buildings. Thus, conservation of energy is another good argument for adaptive reuse and historic preservation (Fig. 3.23).

3.24 CONCLUSION

The basic principles described in this chapter will be applied throughout this book. Many of these ideas will make more sense when their applications are mentioned in later chapters. It will often prove useful to refer back to these explanations, although more detailed explanations will be given when appropriate. Special concepts, such as those related to lighting, will be explained when needed.

KEY IDEAS OF CHAPTER 3

1. Sensible heat is the type of heat that can be measured with a thermometer. Dry air has only sensible heat.
2. Heat energy absorbed or given off as a material changes phase is called "latent heat." It is also called "heat of vaporization" and "heat of fusion," and it cannot be measured with a thermometer. Air has latent heat when it has water vapor.
3. Heat is transferred by conduction, convection, radiation, and transport.
4. Stratification of temperatures results from natural convection.
5. Water can hold about 3000 times as much heat as an equal volume of air. Therefore, we say that water has a much greater heat capacity than air.
6. Matter and energy interact in four ways:
   a. Transmittance
   b. Absorptance
   c. Reflectance
   d. Emittance

7. The greenhouse effect traps heat by allowing most short-wave radiation to be admitted while blocking most long-wave radiation from leaving.
8. The equilibrium temperature of an object sitting in the sun is a result of the relative absorptance and emittance characteristics of the exposed surface.
9. The mean radiant temperature (MRT) describes the radiant environment. An object will simultaneously gain radiation from hotter objects and lose radiation to cooler objects.
10. A cooler object is a potential heat sink. Chilled water or a massive building cooled overnight can act as a heat sink to cool the interior of a building.
11. Thermal resistance is a measure of a material's resistance to heat flow by the mechanisms of conduction, convection, and radiation.
12. Time lag is the phenomenon describing the delay of heat flow through a material. Massive materials have more time lag than light materials.

13. Under certain dynamic temperature conditions, the time lag of massive materials can resist heat flow.
14. The Second Law of Thermodynamics tells us that usable energy is lost every time energy is converted from one form to another. As a consequence, heating a home directly with gas can be 90 percent efficient, while heating with resistance electricity, which was generated by gas, is only 30 percent efficient.
15. Fuel cells have the potential to efficiently generate electricity and supply useful heat as a by-product inside buildings with little or no pollution. But hydrogen must be made, and, therefore, is not a source of energy. Hydrogen made from renewable sources of energy will be sustainable.
16. The energy needed to construct a building is the embodied energy of that building. When buildings are demolished, this embodied energy is lost.

THERMAL COMFORT

Thermal Comfort—that condition of mind which expresses satisfaction
with the thermal environment.
ASHRAE Standard 55-66

4.1 BIOLOGICAL MACHINE

The human being is a biological machine that burns food as a fuel and generates heat as a by-product. This metabolic process is very similar to what happens in an automobile, where gasoline is the fuel and heat is also a significant by-product (Fig. 4.1a). Both types of machines must be able to dissipate the waste heat in order to prevent overheating (Fig. 4.1b). All of the heat-flow mechanisms mentioned in Chapter 3 are employed to maintain the optimum temperature.

All warm-blooded animals, and humans in particular, require a very constant temperature. The **hypothalmus**, a part of our brain, regulates our bodies to maintain an interior temperature of about 98.6°F (37°C), and any small deviation creates severe stress. Only 10 to 15 degrees higher or 20 degrees lower can cause death. Our bodies have several mechanisms to regulate heat flow to guarantee that the heat loss equals the heat generated and that thermal equilibrium will be about 98.6°F (37°C).

Some heat is lost by exhaling warm, moist air from the lungs, but most of the body's heat flow is through the skin. The skin regulates heat flow partly by controlling the amount of blood flowing through it. In summer the skin is flushed with blood to increase the heat loss, while in winter little blood is allowed to circulate near the surface and the skin becomes an insulator. The skin temperature will, therefore, be much lower in winter than in summer. Skin surface temperatures can vary over 50°F (27°C) in response to the ambient temperature. The skin also contains sweat glands that control body heat loss by evaporation.

Hair is another important device to control the rate of heat loss. Although we no longer have much fur, we still have the muscles that could make our fur stand upright for extra thermal insulation. When we get gooseflesh, we see a vestige of the old mechanism. After some days of exposure, the body can acclimatize to very

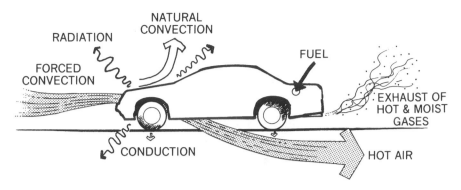

Figure 4.1a Methods of dissipating waste heat from an automobile.

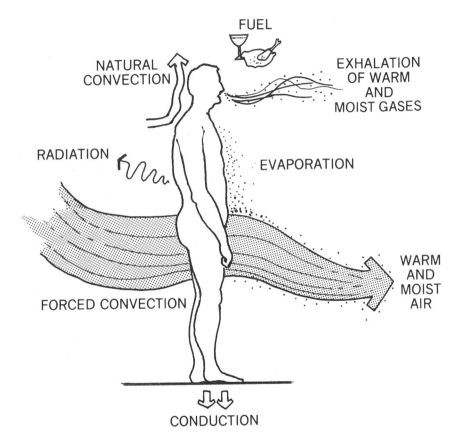

Figure 4.1b Methods of dissipating waste heat from a biological machine.

high or low temperatures. Changing the total amount of blood is one important mechanism, with more blood produced under warmer conditions. Excessive heat loss is called **hypothermia**, while insufficient heat loss is **hyperthermia**.

The graph in Fig. 4.1c shows how the effectiveness of our heat loss mechanisms varies with the ambient temperature. Curve 1 represents the heat generated by a person at rest as the ambient temperature changes. Curve 2

represents the heat lost by conduction, convection, and radiation. Since the heat loss by these mechanisms depends on the temperature difference, it is not surprising that heat loss decreases as ambient temperature increases. When the ambient temperature reaches the body temperature of 98.6°F (37°C), no heat loss can occur by conduction, convection, and radiation. Fortunately, another heat-loss mechanism is not affected by the ambient temperature. Heat loss by evaporation actually

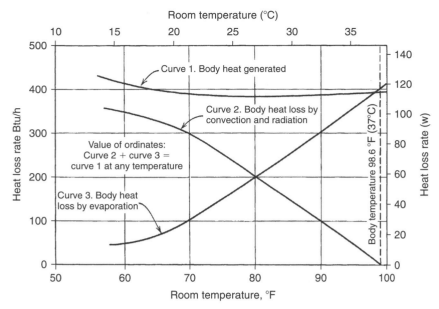

Figure 4.1c The way heat is lost from a body depends on the ambient temperature. This chart assumes the person is at rest and that the relative humidity is 45 percent. (From *Mechanical and Electrical Equipment for Buildings,* 9th edition, Stein and Reynolds, © 2000 John Wiley & Sons, Inc.)

works better at higher temperatures. Curve 3 (Fig. 4.1c) represents the heat lost by evaporation as the ambient temperature changes with the relative humidity fixed at 45 percent.

Although the nerve endings in our skin cannot sense humidity very well, they can sense wetness, which is often related to high RH. The nerve endings also do not sense temperature

but rather heat flow. Thus metal, with its high conductivity, will feel cooler than wood at the same temperature.

4.2 THERMAL BARRIERS

If we could all live in the Garden of Eden, it would be easy for our body mechanisms to control heat flow. The real world, however, places our bodies under almost constant thermal stress. Any barrier as thin as the skin will have great difficulty maintaining a constant temperature in a widely changing environment. Consequently, additional barriers are needed to achieve thermal comfort. Clothing, though it acts as an extra skin, is not always sufficient for thermal comfort. Buildings provide a milder environment for the clothed human being. In the drafty buildings of previous ages, still more barriers were needed. The canopy bed was one solution (Fig. 4.2a). In modern buildings we come close to re-creating the thermal aspects of the Garden of Eden.

Figure 4.2a The concept of multiple barriers is very appropriate for thermal comfort. Three barriers are shown: clothing, canopy bed, and building. (From *Mansions of England in Olden Time* by Joseph Nash.)

Figure 4.2b The geodesic dome of the U.S. Pavilion, Expo 67, Montreal, protects the interior structures from extreme temperatures, sun, wind, and rain.

This concept of progressive barriers promises to be continued. There was a serious suggestion, for example, to enclose the new capital of Alaska in a pneumatic membrane structure and thereby greatly reduce the thermal stress on the building's inside. Pneumatic structures are ideal for this purpose because they can enclose very large areas at reasonable cost. The U.S. Pavilion for Expo 67 in Montreal, Canada, used a different structural system for the same purpose. Figure 4.2b shows the geodesic dome that created a microclimate within which thermally fragile structures were built. Vents and shades were used to control this microclimate (see Fig. 9.16a).

More modest but quite common are the sheltered streets of our modern enclosed shopping malls, which had their beginnings in such projects as the Galleria Vittorio Emanuele in Milan, Italy, completed in 1877 (Fig. 4.2c). The Crystal Palace, built for the Great Exhibition of 1851 in London (Fig. 4.2d), was the ancestor of both the Galleria and the modern Expo pavilion mentioned above. With an area of 770,000 ft² (71,500 m²), it created a new microclimate in a large section of Hyde Park.

Figure 4.2c The Galleria Vittorio Emanuele, Milan, Italy, completed 1877, protects both the street and buildings. (Photograph by Clark Lundell.)

Figure 4.2d The Crystal Palace, built for the Great Exhibition of 1851, created a benign microclimate in Hyde Park, London. (Victoria and Albert Museum, London.)

4.3 METABOLIC RATE

To maintain vital thermal equilibrium, our bodies must lose heat at the same rate at which the metabolic rate produces it. This heat production is partly a function of outside temperature but mostly a function of activity. A very active person generates heat at a rate more than eight times that of a reclining person. Table 4.3 shows the heat production related to various activities. For a better intuitive understanding, the equivalent heat production in terms of 100-watt lamps is also shown.

Table 4.3 Body Heat Production as a Function of Activity

	Activity	Heat Produced (Btu/h)		Watts
	Sleeping	340		100
	Light work	680		200
	Walking	1020		300
	Jogging	2720		800

Notes:
1. The numbers given are approximate.
2. 1w = 3,412 Btu/h.

4.4 THERMAL CONDITIONS OF THE ENVIRONMENT

To create thermal comfort, we must understand not only the heat dissipation mechanisms of the human body but also the four environmental conditions that allow the heat to be lost.

These four conditions are:

1. Air temperature (°F) (°C)
2. Humidity
3. Air movement (feet/minute) (m/s)
4. Mean radiant temperature (MRT)

All of these conditions affect the body simultaneously. Let us first examine how each of these conditions by itself affects the rate of heat loss in human beings.

1. *Air temperature* The air temperature will determine the rate at which heat is lost to the air, mostly by convection. Above 98.6°F (37°C), the heat flow reverses and the body will gain heat from the air. The comfort range for most people (80 percent) extends from 68°F (20°C) in winter to 78°F (25°C) in summer. The range is this large mostly because warmer clothing is worn in the winter.
2. *Relative humidity* Evaporation of skin moisture is largely a function of air humidity. Dry air can readily absorb the moisture from the skin, and the resulting rapid evaporation will effectively cool the body. On the other hand, when the relative humidity (RH) reaches 100 percent, the air is holding all the water vapor it can and cooling by evaporation stops. For comfort the RH should be above 20 percent all year, below 60 percent in the summer, and below 80 percent in the winter. These boundaries are not very precise, but at very low humidity levels there will be complaints of dry noses, mouths, eyes, and skin and increases in respiratory illnesses. Static electricity and shrinkage of wood are also problems caused by low humidities.

High humidity not only reduces the evaporative cooling rate, but also encourages the formation of skin moisture (sweat), which the body senses as uncomfortable. Furthermore, mildew growth is frequently a serious problem when the humidity is high.

3. *Air movement* Air movement affects the heat-loss rate by both convection and evaporation. Consequently, air velocity has a very pronounced effect on heat loss. In the summer, it is a great asset and in the winter a liability. The comfortable range is from about 20 to about 60 feet/minute (fpm) (0.1 to 0.3 m/s). From about 60 to about 200 fpm (0.3 to 1 m/s), air motion is noticeable but acceptable depending on the activity being performed. Above 200 fpm (2 mph) (3.2 k/h), the air motion can be slightly unpleasant and disruptive (e.g., papers are blown around). A **draft** is an undesirable local cooling of the human body by air movement, and it is a serious thermal comfort problem. See Table 10.8 for a more detailed description of how air velocity affects comfort. Air motion is also required to prevent excessive stratification, which tends to make heads warmer and feet colder—exactly the opposite of what is comfortable.

In cold climates, **windchill factors** are often given on weather reports because they better describe the severity of the cold than is possible with temperatures alone. The windchill factor is equal to the still-air temperature that would have the same cooling effect on a human being as does the combined effect of the actual temperature and wind speed.

Although air movement from a breeze is usually desirable in the summer, it is not in very hot and dry climates. If the air is above 98.6°F (37°C), it will heat the skin by convection while it

cools by evaporation. The higher the temperature, the less the total cooling effect.

4. *Mean radiant temperature* When the MRT differs greatly from the air temperature, its effect must be considered. For example, when you sit in front of a south-facing window on a sunny day in the winter, you might actually feel too warm, even though the air temperature is a comfortable 75°F (24°C). This is because the sun's rays raised the MRT to a level too high for comfort. As soon as the sun sets, however, you will probably feel cold even though the air temperature in the room is still 75°F (24°C). This time the cold window glass lowered the MRT too far, and you experience a net radiant loss. It is important to realize that the skin and clothing temperature is not 98.6°F (37°C) but varies greatly with the ambient temperature. To help visualize the radiant exchange, assume the skin temperature to be about 80°F (27°C). In general, the goal is to maintain the MRT close to the ambient air temperature. In a well-insulated and shaded building, the MRT will be close to that of the indoor air temperature.

The psychrometric chart described in the next section is a powerful tool for understanding how the combination of temperature and humidity affects comfort.

4.5 THE PSYCHROMETRIC CHART

A useful and convenient way to understand some of the interrelationships of the thermal conditions of the environment is by means of the psychrometric chart (Fig. 4.5a). The horizontal axis describes the temperature of the air, the vertical axis describes the actual amount of water vapor in the air, called **humidity ratio** or **specific humidity**, and the curved lines describe the **relative humidity (RH)**. The diagram has two boundaries that are absolute limits. The bottom edge describes air that is completely dry (0 percent RH), and the upper curved boundary describes air that is completely saturated with water vapor (100 percent RH). The upper boundary is curved because as air gets warmer, it can hold more water vapor. Even if we know how much water vapor is already in the air, we cannot predict how much more it can hold unless we also know the temperature of the air. The RH is affected by changes in either the amount of moisture in the air or the temperature of the air.

Every point on the psychrometric chart represents a sample of air at a particular temperature and moisture level (Fig. 4.5a). Moving vertically up on the chart indicates that moisture is being added to that air sample (see Fig. 4.5b), while a downward motion on the chart represents water vapor removal (dehumidification). Movement to the right indicates that the air sample is being heated, and movement to the left indicates cooling of the air. Thus, if a sample of air at 80°F (27°C) and 40 percent RH (point A) is cooled to 60°F (15°C), the point representing the air sample will move horizontally to the left on the psychrometric chart to point B (Fig. 4.5c). Its RH, however, has increased to about 78 percent even though there was no change in the moisture content of the air (i.e., no vertical movement on the chart). The RH increased because cool air can hold less moisture than warm air, and the existing moisture level is now a larger percentage of what air can hold at that cooler temperature.

On the other hand, if the air at point A is heated to 100°F (38°C) (point C in Fig. 4.5d), then its relative humidity will be about 22 percent. The RH changed because warm air can hold more moisture than cool air, and the existing moisture level is now a smaller percentage of what the air can hold at that higher temperature.

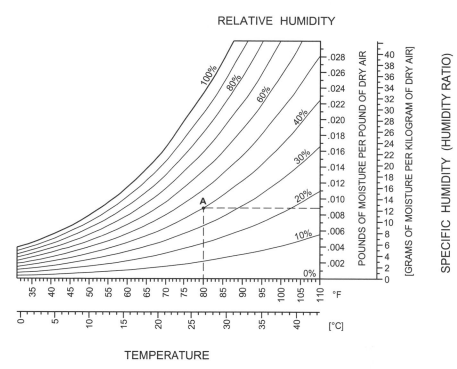

Figure 4.5a Each point on the psychrometric chart represents the properties of a sample of air at a particular temperature and moisture level. At point A, for example, the air sample has a temperature of 80°F (27°C), an RH of 40 percent, and an actual moisture content of about 0.009 lb of water per pound of dry air (14 g of water per kilogram of dry air).

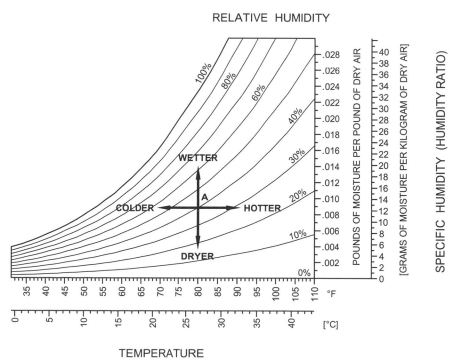

Figure 4.5b Changes in the temperature or moisture of a sample of air are represented by movement on the psychrometric chart.

RELATIVE HUMIDITY

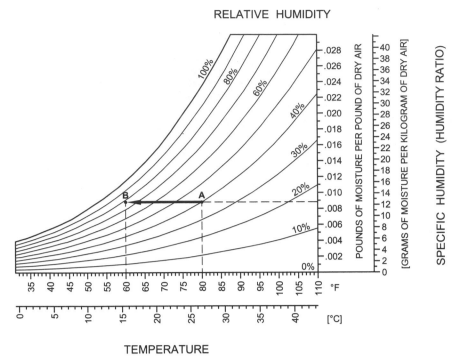

TEMPERATURE

Figure 4.5c If an air sample is cooled, its RH will increase even though there was no change in moisture content.

RELATIVE HUMIDITY

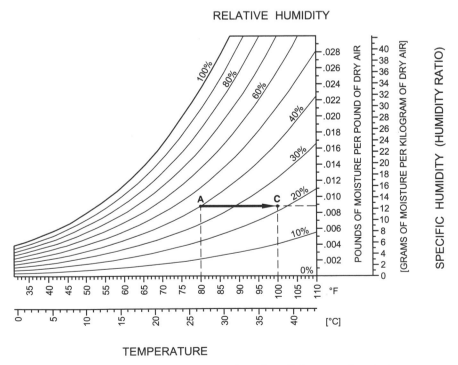

TEMPERATURE

Figure 4.5d If an air sample is heated, its relative humidity will drop even though there was no change in moisture content.

4.6 DEW POINT AND WET-BULB TEMPERATURES

What would happen to air that is at 80°F (27°C) and 40 percent RH if it were cooled to 53°F (12°C)? Look at point A in Fig. 4.6a. As the air is cooled, the RH keeps increasing until it is 100 percent at about 53°F (12°C) (point D). This is a special condition called the **dew point temperature (DPT).** At this point the air is fully saturated (100 percent RH) and cannot hold any more moisture. Any cooling beyond this point results in condensation where some of the water comes out of solution in the air. This phenomenon is also seen in rain, snow, fog, hoarfrost, and the "sweating" of a cold glass of water.

If the above sample of air is cooled beyond 53°F (12°C) to 40°F (4°C), it will reach point E on the psychrometric chart (Fig. 4.6a). Although its RH is still 100 percent, its specific humidity (humidity ratio) has decreased. Note the downward movement on the psychrometric chart from a humidity ratio of about 0.009 to about 0.0055 lb of water per pound of dry air (12 to 8 g/kg). Consequently, about 0.0035 lb of water per pound of dry air (4 g/kg) was removed from the air when it was cooled from 80°F (27°C) to 40°F (4°C). We can say that the air was **dehumidified**.

The DPT is also an indication of how much moisture is in the air at any temperature. The higher the DPT, the more moisture. Thus, the DPT can be used to describe the actual amount of moisture in the air. Weather reports often give the DPT to describe the moisture content of the air.

Another way to describe the amount of moisture in an air sample is by giving its **web-bulb temperature.** The wet-bulb temperature is determined by slinging two thermometers side by side through the air. One thermometer has its bulb covered with a wet sock. If this **sling psychrometer** is slung around in dry air, the temperature of the wet-bulb thermometer will drop significantly below the temperature of the dry-bulb thermometer

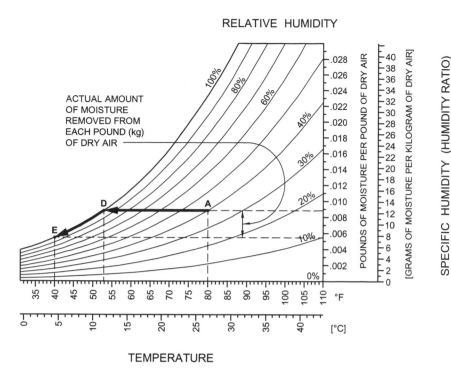

Figure 4.6a When an air sample is cooled sufficiently, its RH increases until is reaches 100 percent, which is also called the "saturation" or "dew point." Any cooling beyond this point results in moisture condensing out of the air.

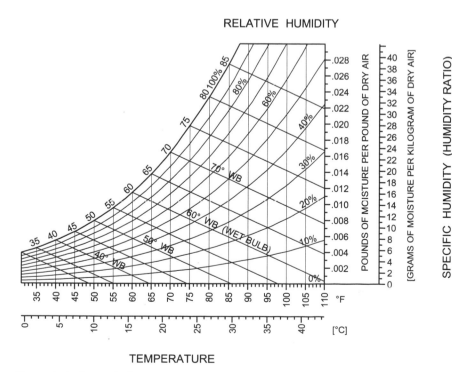

Figure 4.6b The wet-bulb temperature can be measured with a sling psychrometer. It is an indicator of the RH, the actual moisture content, and the heat content of the air.

because of the large evaporation of water. Similarly, if the air is humid, the wet-bulb temperature will drop only a little. And, of course, if the air is at 100 percent RH, no evaporation will take place, and the wet-bulb and dry-bulb temperatures will be the same. Figure 4.6b shows how at 100 percent RH, the wet-bulb temperatures (slanted lines) and the dry-bulb temperatures (vertical lines) are the same.

4.7 HEAT CONTENT OF AIR

The psychrometric chart can also be used to describe the sensible-, latent-, and total-heat content of an air sample. The total-heat or **enthalpy** (sensible plus latent heat) scale is a standard part of the psychrometric chart and is shown in Fig. 4.7a. Note that an upward movement on the chart increases not only the moisture content but also the latent-heat content. This is not a surprise if you remember that water vapor is a form of latent heat. Also, note that a movement to the right increases not only temperature but also the sensible-heat content of an air sample. This also is not a surprise because temperature is an indicator of sensible-heat content.

Figure 4.7b shows air that is being both heated and humidified. Thus, when the air reaches point F, it has both more sensible and more latent heat than it had at point A. The total increase in Btus per pound of dry air (kJ/kg) can be read directly from the enthalpy scale.

In Fig. 4.7c, we see a sample of air that is being cooled by the evaporation of water. If the air is humidified to 80 percent RH, the moisture content will increase and the temperature will decrease. Since the loss of sensible heat equals the gain in latent heat, the total-heat content is the same for point G as it was for point A. Note that there is no change on the total-heat scale. A change in the air that does not result in a change of total-heat content is called an **adiabatic change.** This is an important and common phenomenon since this

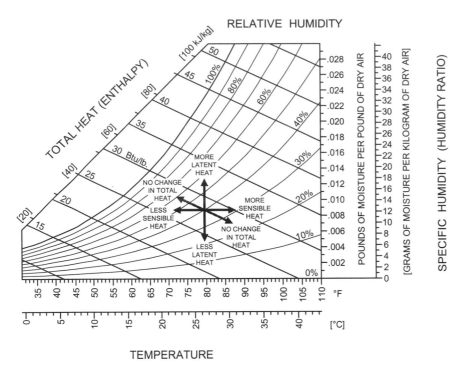

Figure 4.7a The psychrometric chart also presents information on the heat content of a sample of air. Heat is gained by either an increase in temperature (sensible heat) or an increase in moisture (latent heat) or both.

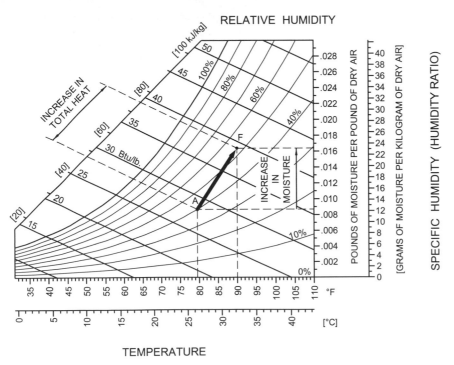

Figure 4.7b Heating and humidifying an air sample increases both its sensible heat and its latent heat. The total-heat gain can be read directly from the enthalpy scale.

is what happens in evaporative cooling, in which the evaporation of water converts sensible heat to latent heat and the total-heat content remains the same. Thus, although the air becomes cooler, it also becomes more humid. It is equally true that when water vapor condenses into water, the temperature rises, since latent heat is being converted to an equal amount of sensible heat.

4.8 THERMAL COMFORT

Thermal comfort occurs when body temperatures are held within narrow ranges, skin moisture is low, and the body's effort of temperature regulation is minimized (after ASHRAE, 1997). Certain combinations of air temperature, RH, air motion, and MRT will result in what most people consider thermal comfort. When these combinations of air temperature and RH are plotted on a psychrometric chart, they define an area known as the **comfort zone** (Fig. 4.8a). Since the psychrometric chart relates only temperature and humidity, the other two factors (air motion and MRT) are held fixed. The MRT is assumed to be near the air temperature, and the air motion is assumed to be modest.

It is important to note that the given boundaries of the comfort zone are not absolute, because thermal comfort also varies with culture, time of year, health, the amount of fat an individual carries, the amount of clothing worn, and, most important, physical activity. The American Society for Heating, Refrigerating and Air Conditioning Engineers (ASHRAE) defines thermal comfort as "that condition of mind which expresses satisfaction with the thermal environment." While conditions required for thermal comfort vary from person to person, the comfort zone should be the goal of the thermal design of a building because it defines those conditions that 80 percent of people in our society find comfortable. A more detailed look at the comfort zone shows that it consits of both a

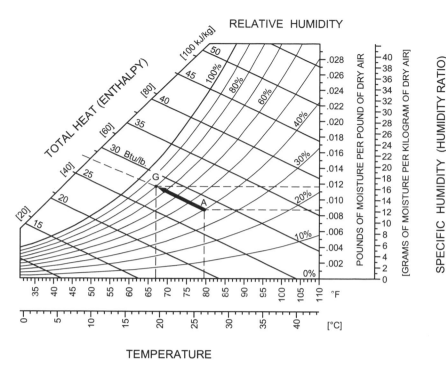

Figure 4.7c In evaporative cooling, the increase in latent heat equals the decrease in sensible heat. An adiabatic change is a change in which the total-heat content of the air remains constant.

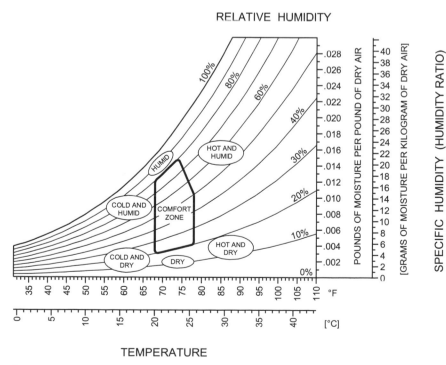

Figure 4.8a The comfort zone and various types of discomfort outside that zone are shown on this psychrometric chart.

summer and winter zone (Fig. 4.8b). For the sake of simplicity, this book continues to use the traditional zone, with the caveat that the left side of the zone is more appropriate for winter and the right side for summer.

Whenever possible, additional controls should be made available for the occupants of a building so that they can create the thermal conditions that are just right for them. Portable fans and heaters, numerous thermostats, and operable windows are devices people can use to fine-tune their environment. Mechanical equipment systems are now commercially available that allow individual thermal control at each work station.

The chart in Fig. 4.8a also indicates the type of discomfort one experiences outside of the comfort zone. These discomfort zones correspond to different climates. For example, the American Southwest has a summer climate that is hot and dry, found on the lower right of the psychrometric chart (Fig. 4.8a). Unfortunately, very few climates have a sizable portion of the year in the comfort zone.

The following discussion shows how the comfort zone shifts when certain variables that had been held constant are allowed to change.

4.9 SHIFTING OF THE COMFORT ZONE

The comfort zone will shift on the psychrometric chart if we change some of the assumptions made above. In Fig. 4.9a the shift of the comfort zone is due to an increase in the MRT. Cooler air temperatures are required to compensate for the increased heating from radiation. Likewise, a low MRT would have to be offset by an increase in the air temperature. For example, a room with a large expanse of glass must be kept warmer in the winter and cooler in the summer than a room with a more modest window area. The large window area creates a high MRT in the summer and a low MRT in the winter. For every 3-degree increase or decrease in MRT, the air temperature

RELATIVE HUMIDITY

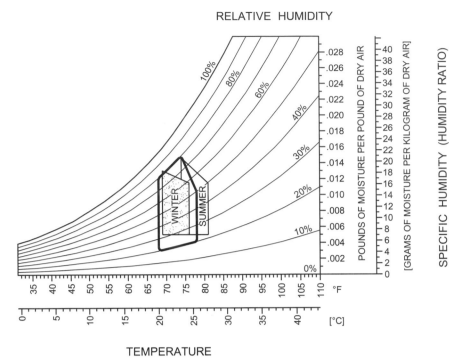

Figure 4.8b A more detailed look at the comfort zone shows that it actually consists of two slightly overlapping zones. (After *ASHRAE Handbook of Fundamentals*, 1997.)

RELATIVE HUMIDITY

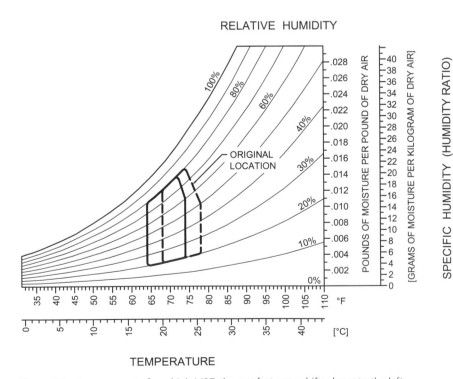

Figure 4.9a To compensate for a high MRT, the comfort zone shifts down to the left.

must be adjusted 2 degrees in the opposite direction. Window shading (Chapter 9) and better-insulated windows (Chapter 15) can have tremendous effects on the MRT.

In Fig. 4.9b the shift of the comfort zone is due to increased air velocity. The cooling effect of the air motion is offset by an increase in the air temperature. We usually make use of this relationship in the reverse situation. When the air temperature is too high for comfort, we often use air motion (i.e., open a window or turn on a fan) to raise the comfort zone so that it includes the higher air temperature. Every increase of 15 fpm (0.8 m/s) of air speed results in a 1-degree drop in the comfort zone. Chapter 10 will explain how air movement can be used for passive cooling.

There is also a shift of the comfort zone due to physical activity. Cooler temperatures are required to help the body dissipate the increased production of heat. Gymnasiums, for example, should always be kept significantly cooler than classrooms. Thus, the comfort zone shifts down to the left when physical activity is increased (Fig. 4.9c).

4.10 CLOTHING AND COMFORT

Unfortunately, an architect cannot specify the clothing to be worn by the occupants of his or her building. Too often, fashion, status, and tradition in clothing work against thermal comfort. In some extremely hot climates women were—in a few places still are—required to wear black veils and robes that completely cover their bodies. Unfortunately, some of our own customs are almost as inappropriate. A three-piece suit with a necktie can get quite hot in the summer. A miniskirt in the winter is just as unsuitable. Clothing styles should be seasonal indoors as well as outdoors so that our heating and cooling systems can work less hard. We could save millions of barrels of oil if men wore three-piece suits only in the

RELATIVE HUMIDITY

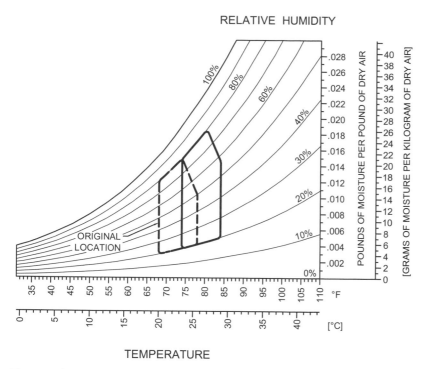

Figure 4.9b To compensate for high air velocity, the comfort zone shifts up to the right.

RELATIVE HUMIDITY

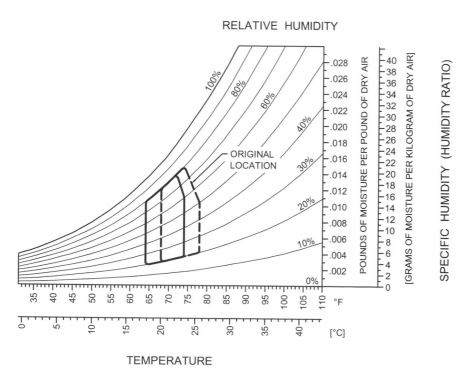

Figure 4.9c To compensate for an increase in physical activity, the comfort zone shifts down to the left.

winter and women wore miniskirts only in summer. Note to fashion designers: You can help fight global warming.

The insulating properties of clothing have been quantified in the unit of thermal resistance called the **clo**. In winter, a high clo value is achieved by clothing that creates many air spaces, either by multiple layers or by a porous weave. If wind is present, then an outer layer that is fairly airtight but permeable to water vapor is required.

In summer a very low clo value is, of course, required. Since it is even more important in the summer than in the winter that moisture can pass through the clothing, a very permeable fabric should be used. Cotton is especially good because it acts as a wick to transfer moisture from the skin to the air. Although wool is not as good as cotton in absorbing moisture, it is still much better than some man-made materials. Also, loose billowing clothing will promote the dissipation of both sensible and latent (water-vapor) heat by a little forced convection.

4.11 STRATEGIES

Much of the rest of this book discusses the various strategies that have been developed to create thermal comfort in our buildings. The version of the psychrometric chart shown in Fig. 4.11 is called the **building bioclimatic chart** because it integrates architectural strategies with human comfort needs. If you compare this chart with Fig. 4.8a, you will see the relationship between strategies and discomfort (climate) conditions more clearly. For example, the strategy of evaporative cooling (the lower-right area in Fig. 4.11) corresponds with the hot and dry discomfort zone (the lower-right area in Fig. 4.8a). The diagram shows that internal heat gains from sources such as machines, people, and lights are sufficient to heat the building in slightly cool conditions.

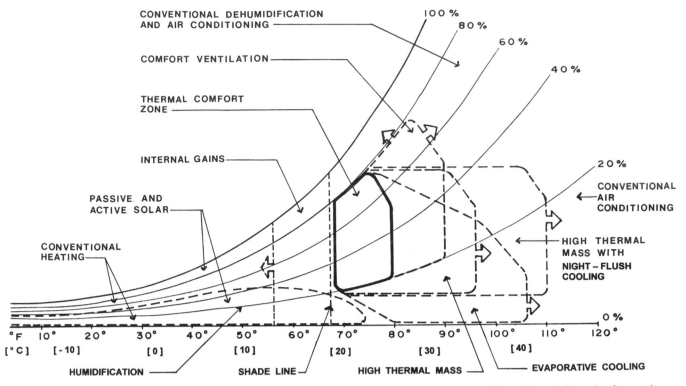

CONVENTIONAL DEHUMIDIFICATION
AND AIR CONDITIONING
100 %
80 %
60 %
COMFORT VENTILATION
40 %
THERMAL COMFORT
ZONE
INTERNAL GAINS
PASSIVE AND
ACTIVE SOLAR
20 %
CONVENTIONAL
AIR
CONDITIONING
HIGH THERMAL
MASS WITH
NIGHT – FLUSH
COOLING
CONVENTIONAL
HEATING
0 %
°F   10°   20°   30°   40°   50°   60°   70°   80°   90°   100°   110°   120°
[°C]   [-10]   [0]   [10]   [20]   [30]   [40]
HUMIDIFICATION   SHADE LINE   HIGH THERMAL MASS   EVAPORATIVE COOLING

Figure 4.11 This building bioclimatic chart is a summary of design strategies as a function of ambient conditions (climate). (From *Psychrometric-Bioclimatic Chart*, copyright by Baruch Givoni and Murray Milne.)

Also, when the climate conditions are to the right of the **shade line**, the sun should be prevented from entering the windows. This line, as well as all the boundaries of the various zones shown in the diagram, are not precisely fixed but should be considered as fuzzy limits.

4.12 CONCLUSION

One of the primary functions of buildings is to help create thermal comfort. By understanding human comfort needs and the four conditions of the environment that affect comfort (i.e., temperature, RH, air speed, and MRT), the architect can better design buildings that are comfortable, yet use a minimum of mechanical equipment and little energy. Because climate determines many of the specific architectural strategies that should be used, it is discussed in the next chapter.

KEY IDEAS OF CHAPTER 4

1. For thermal comfort, the body must eliminate waste heat by means of conduction, convection, radiation, and evaporation.
2. The amount of waste heat produced is mostly a function of the physical activity being performed.
3. Four factors of the environment together determine how easily the body can eject the waste heat. Their comfort ranges are:
   a) Air temperature: 68° to 78°F (20° to 25°C)
   b) Relative humidity: 20 to 80 percent in the winter and 20 to 60 percent in the summer

   c) Air velocity: 20 to 60 fpm (0.1 to 0.3 m/s)
   d) MRT (near air temperature)
4. Certain combinations of these four factors result in what is called "thermal comfort," which can be represented by the comfort zone on various charts such as the psychrometric chart.
5. When one or more of the four factors of the environment is somewhat outside the comfort range, the remaining factors can be adjusted up or down to compensate, thereby restoring thermal comfort.

6. The psychrometric chart describes the combined effect of temperature and its coincident humidity.
7. A certain set of temperatures and coincident humidities is called the "comfort zone" on the psychrometric chart.
8. The building-bioclimatic chart shows which architectural design strategies are appropriate for different climates, as determined by temperatures and their coincident humidities.

Resources

FURTHER READING

(See the Bibliography in the back of the book for full citations.)

ASHRAE Handbook of Fundamentals.
Bradshaw, V. *The Building Environment: Active and Passive Control Systems,* 3rd ed.

Flynn, J. E., et al. *Architectural Interior Systems: Lighting, Acoustics. Air Conditioning,* 3rd ed.
Givoni, B. *Man, Climate and Architecture,* 2nd ed.
Giovni, B. *Climate Considerations in Building and Urban Design.*
Stein, B., J. Reynolds, W. T. Grondzik, and A. G. Kwok. *Mechanical and Electrical Equipment for Buildings,* 10th ed. A general resource.

ORGANIZATIONS

(See Appendix K for full citations.)

American Society of Heating, Refrigerating, and Air-Conditioning Engineers (ASHRAE).

CLIMATE | 5

The earth provides enough to satisfy every man's need, but not
enough to satisfy every man's greed.
Mahatma Gandhi

We must begin by taking note of the countries and climates in which homes are to be
built if our designs for them are to be correct. One type of house seems appropriate for
Egypt, another for Spain . . . one still different for Rome. . . . It is obvious that design
for homes ought to conform to diversities of climate.
The Ten Books on Architecture
Vitruvius
Architect, first century B.C.

5.1 INTRODUCTION

As the quote by Vitruvius on the previous page indicates, designing buildings in harmony with their climates is an age-old idea. To design in conformity with climate, the designer needs to understand the microclimate of the site, since all climatic experience of both people and buildings is at this level. In some cases, the microclimate can be quite different from the larger climate. If Mark Twain were alive today, he would never have said, "Everyone talks about the weather but no one does anything about it." It is now easy to see how man changes the microclimate by such acts as replacing farmland and forest with the hard and massive materials of cities, irrigating a desert and making it a humid area, and constructing high-rise buildings to form windy canyons. Unfortunately, these changes in the microclimate are rarely beneficial, since they are usually done without concern for the consequences.

Most serious, however, are the changes we are making to the macroclimate. As was discussed more fully in Chapter 2, global warming and climate change are caused by the large-scale burning of fossil fuels, which is increasing the amount of carbon dioxide in the air. Carbon dioxide, like water vapor, is transparent to solar energy but not to the long-wave radiation emitted by the earth's surface. Thus, the ground and atmosphere are heated by the phenomenon known as the **greenhouse effect**. The heating of the earth will create very undesirable changes in the world's climates.

It is too late to stop climate change from starting, but we still have the opportunity to limit the degree of change. Indeed, we have the duty to do everything possible to minimize the amount of change. Climate-responsive buildings are gentle on the climate because they use less energy. However, to design them, we first need to understand the basics of climate.

5.2 CLIMATE

The climate, or average weather, is primarily a function of the sun. The world "climate" comes from the Greek *klima*, which means the slope of the earth in respect to the sun. The Greeks realized that climate is largely a function of sun angles (latitude) and, therefore, they divided the world into the tropic, temperate, and arctic zones.

The atmosphere is a giant heat machine fueled by the sun. Since the atmosphere is largely transparent to solar energy, the main heating of the air occurs at the earth's surface (Fig. 5.2a). As the air is heated, it rises and creates a low-pressure area at ground level. Since the surface of the earth is not heated equally, there will be both relatively low- and high-pressure areas with wind as a consequence.

A global north–south flow of air is generated because the equator is heated more than the poles (Fig. 5.2b). This global flow is modified by both the changes in season and the rotation of the earth (Fig. 5.2c) Another major

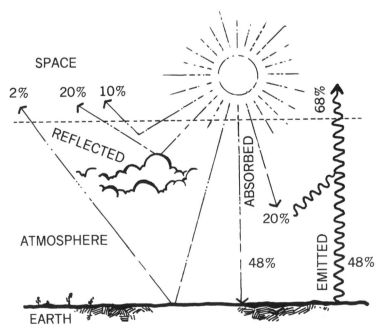

Figure 5.2a The atmosphere is heated mainly by contact with the solar-heated ground. On an annual basis, the energy absorbed by the earth equals the energy radiated back into space. In the summer there is a gain, in the winter an equal loss. This was true until about 100 years ago, when human-caused global warming started.

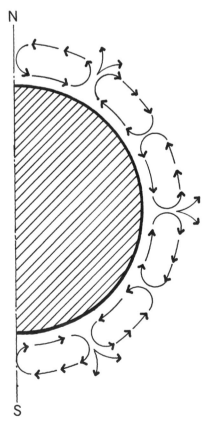

Figure 5.2b Because the earth is heated more at the equator than at the poles, giant global convection currents are generated.

Figure 5.2c The rotation of the Earth deflects the north–south air currents by an effect known as the "Coriolis force." (From *Wind Power for Farms, Homes and Small Industry*, by the U.S. Department of Energy, 1978.)

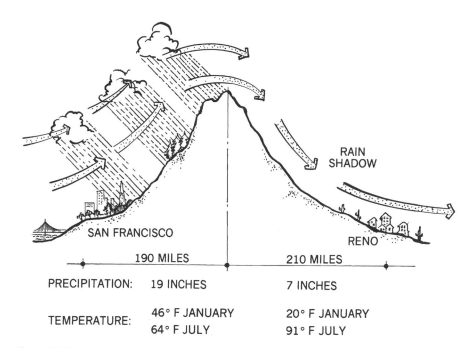

	190 MILES	210 MILES
PRECIPITATION:	19 INCHES	7 INCHES
TEMPERATURE:	46° F JANUARY	20° F JANUARY
	64° F JULY	91° F JULY

Figure 5.2d In certain cases, mountain ranges cause rapid changes from relatively wet and cool to hot and dry climates. (From *American Buildings: 2: The Environmental Forces That Shape It* by James Marston Fitch, copyright James Marston Fitch, 1972.)

factor affecting winds and, therefore, climate is the uneven distribution of landmasses on the globe. Because of its higher heat capacity, water does not heat up or cool down as fast as the land. Thus, temperature changes over water tend to be more moderate than over land, and the farther inland one gets from large bodies of water, the more extreme are the temperatures. For example, the annual temperature range on the island of Key West, Florida, is about 24°F (13°C), while the annual temperature range inland at San Antonio, Texas, only slightly farther north, is about 56°F (31°C). These water-land temperature differences also create pressure differences that drive the winds.

Mountain ranges not only block or divert winds but also have a major effect on the moisture content of the air. A good example of this important climatic phenomenon is the American West. Over the Pacific Ocean solar radiation evaporates water, and the air becomes quite humid. The westerlies blow this moist air overland, where it is forced up over the north–south mountain ranges (Fig. 5.2d). As the air rises, it cools at a rate of about 3.6°F (2°C) for every 1000 ft (300 m). When the temperature drops, the relative humidity (RH) increases until it reaches 100 percent, the saturation point. Any additional cooling will cause moisture to condense in the form of clouds, rain, or snow. On the far side of the mountains, the now drier air falls and, consequently, heats up again.

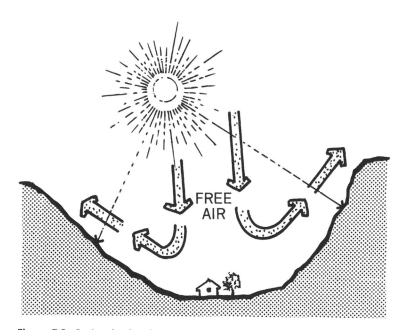

Figure 5.2e During the day, the air moves up the mountainsides.

As the temperature increases, the RH decreases and a rainshadow is created. Thus, a mountain ridge can be a sharp border between a cool, wet climate and a hot, dry climate.

Mountains also create local winds that vary from day to night. During the day, the air next to the mountain surface heats up faster than free air at the same height. Thus, warm air moves up along the slopes during the day (Fig. 5.2e). At night, the process is reversed: the air moves down the slopes because the mountain surface

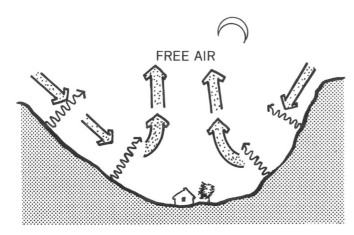

FREE AIR

Figure 5.2f At night, the land cools rapidly by radiation and the air currents move down the mountainsides.

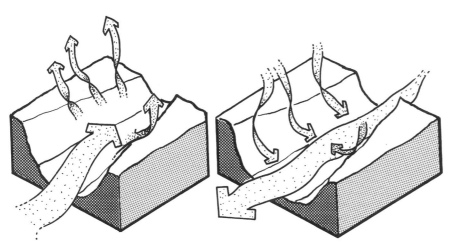

Figure 5.2g The effects described in Figs. 5.2e and 5.2f are greatly magnified in narrow-sloping valleys. During the day, strong winds blow up the valley; at night, the winds reverse. (After "Sun, Wind, and Light," 2nd ed., by Brown, G. Z., and De Kazo, M., John Wiley & Sons.)

Figure 5.2h The temperature differences between land and water create sea breezes during the day and land breezes at night.

cools by radiation more quickly than the free air (Fig. 5.2f). In narrow valleys, this phenomenon can create very strong winds up along the valley floor during the day and down the valley at night (Fig. 5.2g).

A similar day–night reversal of winds occurs near large bodies of water. The large heat capacity of water prevents it from heating or cooling as fast as land. Thus, during the day the air is hotter over land than over water. The resultant pressure differences generate sea breezes (Fig. 5.2h). At night, the temperatures and air flows reverse. In the late afternoon and early morning, when the land and sea are at the same temperature, there is no breeze. Furthermore, at night the breezes are weaker than during the day because the temperature differences between land and water are smaller.

The amount of moisture in the air has a pronounced effect on the ambient temperature. In dry climates, there is little moisture to block the intense solar radiation from reaching the ground, and, thus, summer daytime temperatures are very high—over 100°F (38°C). Also, at night there is little moisture to block the outgoing long-wave radiation; consequently, nights are cool and the **diurnal temperature range** is high—more than 30°F (17°C) (Fig. 5.2i). On the other hand, in humid and especially cloudy regions, the moisture blocks some solar radiation to make summer daytime temperatures much more moderate—below 90°F (32°C). At night, the outgoing long-wave radiation is also blocked by the moisture, and consequently, temperatures do not drop much (Fig. 5.2j). The diurnal temperature range is, therefore, small—below 20°F (11°C). It should be noted that water has a much stronger blocking effect on radiation when it is in the form of droplets (clouds) than in the form of a gas (humidity).

The various forces in the atmosphere interact to form a large set of diverse climates. Later in the chapter there will be a description of seventeen different climate regions found in the United States and Canada.

5.3 MICROCLIMATE

For a number of reasons, the local climate can be quite different from the climate region in which it is found. If buildings are to relate properly to their environment, they must be designed for the microclimate in which they exist. The following factors are mainly responsible for making the microclimate deviate from the macroclimate.

1. *Elevation above sea level:* The steeper the slope of the land, the faster the temperature will drop with an increase in elevation. The limit, of course, is a vertical ascent, which will produce a cooling rate of about 3.6°F (2°C) per 1000 ft (300 m).

2. *Form of land:* South-facing slopes are warmer than north-facing slopes because they receive much more solar radiation (Fig. 5.3a). For this reason, ski slopes are usually found on the north slopes of mountains, while vineyards are located on the south slopes (Fig. 5.3b). South slopes are also protected from the cold winter winds that usually come from the north. West slopes are warmer than east slopes because the period of high solar radiation

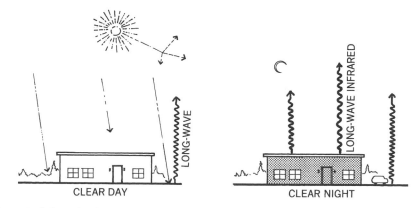

Figure 5.2i Since dry climates have little moisture to block radiation, daytime temperatures are high and night temperatures are low. The diurnal temperature range is, therefore, large.

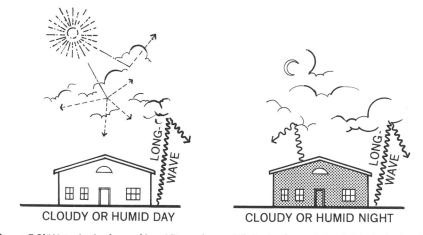

Figure 5.2j Water in the form of humidity and especially in the form of clouds blocks both solar and long-wave radiation. Thus, in humid or cloudy climates, daytime temperatures are not as high and nighttime temperatures are not as low as in hot and dry climates. The diurnal range is, therefore, small.

Figure 5.3a The north side (south slope) of this east–west road in Maryland is several weeks further into spring than the south side (north slope), where the snow melts much more slowly.

Figure 5.3b South-facing slopes can receive more than 100 times as much solar radiation as north-facing slopes.

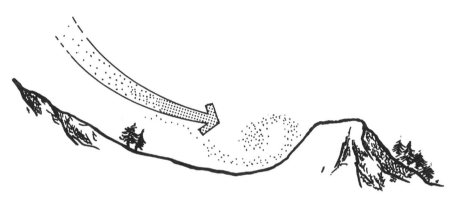

Figure 5.3c Since cool air is heavier than warm air, it drains into low-lying areas, forming pools of cold air.

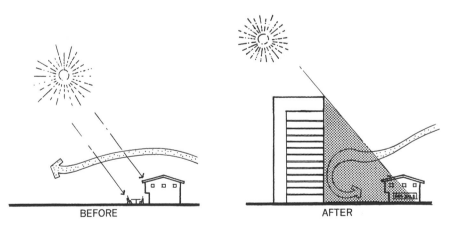

Figure 5.3d A delightfully sunny and wind-protected southern exposure can be turned into a cold, windy microclimate by the construction of a large building to the south.

corresponds with the high ambient air temperatures of the afternoon. Low areas tend to collect pools of cold, heavy air (Fig. 5.3c). If the air is also moist, fog will frequently form. The fog, in turn, reflects the solar radiation, so that these areas remain cool longer in the morning.

3. *Size, shape, and proximity of bodies of water:* As mentioned before, large bodies of water have a significant moderating effect on temperature, they generate the daily alternating land and sea breezes, and they increase the humidity.

4. *Soil types:* The heat capacity, color, and water content of soil can have a significant effect on the microclimate. Evaporation from the soil cools the air above the ground. Light-colored sand can reflect large amounts of sunlight, thereby reducing the heating of the soil, and thus of the air, but at the same time it greatly increases the radiation load on people or buildings. Because of their high heat capacity, rocks can absorb heat during the day and then release it at night. The cliff dwellings of the Southwest benefited greatly from this effect (see Fig. 10.21).

5. *Vegetation:* By means of shading and transpiration plants can significantly reduce air and ground temperatures. They also increase the humidity, whether or not it is already too high. Evapotranspiration is the combined effect of evaporation from soil and transpiration from plants. In a hot, humid climate, the ideal situation is to have a high canopy of trees for shade but no low plants that could block the breeze. The stagnant air from low trees and shrubs enables the humidity to build up to undesirably high levels. In cold climates, plants can reduce the cooling effect of the wind. Vegetation can also reduce noise and clean the air of dust and certain other pollutants.

6. *Manmade structures:* Buildings streets, and parking lots, because of their number, size, mass, and color, have a very significant effect on the microclimate. The shade of buildings can create a cold north-like orientation on what was previously a warm southern exposure (Fig. 5.3d). On the other hand, buildings can create shade from the hot summer sun and block the cold winter winds. Large areas of pavement, especially dark-colored

SKETCH OF AN URBAN HEAT-ISLAND PROFILE

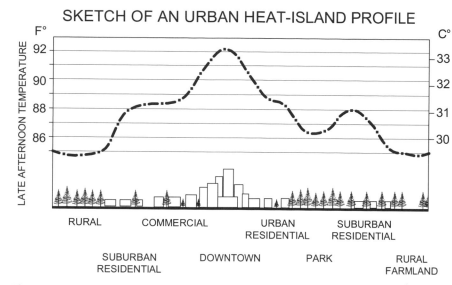

RURAL   COMMERCIAL   URBAN RESIDENTIAL   SUBURBAN RESIDENTIAL

SUBURBAN RESIDENTIAL   DOWNTOWN   PARK   RURAL FARMLAND

Figure 5.3e A sketch of a typical urban heat-island profile. This profile of a hypothetical metropolitan area shows temperature changes correlated to the density of development and trees. (Reproduced from *Cooling Our Communities: A Guidebook on Tree Planting and Light-Colored Surfacing*, LBL-31587, published by Lawrence Berkeley National Laboratory, 1992.)

asphalt, can generate temperatures as high as 140°F (60°C). The heated air then migrates to over-heat adjacent areas as well.

In large cities, the combined effect of all the man-made structures results in a climate significantly different from that of the surrounding country-side. The **annual mean** temperature will usually be about 1.5°F (0.8°C) warmer, while the winter minimum temperature may be about 3°F (1.7°C) higher. In summer, cities can be 7°F (4°C) warmer than rural areas and are, therefore, often known as **heat islands** (Fig. 5.3e). Solar radiation, however, will be about 20 percent lower due to the air pollution, and the RH will be about 6 percent less because of the reduced amount of evapotranspira-tion. Although the overall wind speed is about 25 percent lower, very high local wind speeds often occur in the urban canyons.

5.4 CLIMATIC ANOMALIES

Radical variations in the climate of a region are possible under certain conditions. One of the most famous climate anomalies is found in Lugano, Switzerland. Although Lugano has the same latitude as Quebec (47°), the climates are as different as if Lugano were 1500 miles (2400 km) farther south.

This unusually warm climate in a northern region is largely a result of the unique geography of the area. Lugano is located where the southern slope of the Alps meets a large lake (Fig. 5.4). It is thus fully exposed to both the direct winter sun and that reflected off the lake. The water also

has a moderating effect on sudden temperature changes. The Alps pro-tect the area from cold and wet winter winds. Those winds that do get across the Alps are dried and heated, just as are the winds crossing the Sierra Nevadas in California (Fig. 5.2d). And, lastly, the climate in Lugano is so unusually warm because of the low elevation of the land. Meanwhile, cold alpine climates are only a few miles away up in the mountains.

Less dramatic variations in the microclimates of a region are quite common. It is not unusual to find in rather flat country that two areas only a few miles apart have temperature differences as great as 30°F (17°C). Suburban areas are often more than 7°F (4°C) cooler during the day and more than 10°F (5.6°C) cooler at night than urban areas. Even a distance of only 100 ft (30 m) can make a signifi-cant difference. The author has noted very dramatic temperature differences on his half-acre lot. Consequently, he relaxes in one part of the garden in the summer and in a different part in the cooler seasons.

Very localized variations in the microclimate are especially obvious in the spring. When the snow melts, it does so in irregular patches. The warm areas are also the first to see the green growth of spring. Areas only a few feet apart might be two or more weeks apart in temperature. These variations are not hard to understand

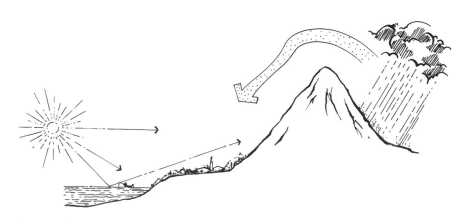

Figure 5.4 The combination of a low elevation, south-facing slopes, high mountains to the north, and a large lake to the south creates a subtropical climate in Lugano, Switzerland, even though it is as far north as Quebec.

when one considers the fact that in New York on December 21 a south wall receives 108 times as much solar radiation as a north wall. A designer must not only know the climate of the region but also the specific microclimate of the building site.

Since buildings designed for their climate will use less energy, they will also reduce the amount of global warming. Although climate-responsive design has always been the appropriate design approach, it is fast becoming the mandatory approach.

5.5 CLIMATE REGIONS OF THE UNITED STATES

No book could ever describe all of the microclimates found in the United States. Designers must, therefore, use the best available published data and modify it to fit their specific site. The United States government collects and publishes extensive weather and climatic data. See the end of this chapter for information about some of these resources. However, since the information is usually not arranged in a convenient form for architects to use, some appropriate climate data in a useful graphic format is included in this book.

When the United States is divided into only a few climate regions, the information is too general to be very useful. On the other hand, when too much information is presented, it often becomes inaccessible. As a compromise, this book divides the United States and Canada into seventeen climate regions (Fig. 5.5). This subdivision system and much of the climatic information are based on material from the book *Regional Guidelines for Building Passive Energy Conserving Homes* produced by the AIA/Research Corporation.

The remainder of this chapter describes these seventeen climate regions. Included with the climate data for each region is a set of specific climate-related design priorities appropriate for envelope-dominated buildings, such as homes and small institutional and commercial buildings. Specific design strategies that respond to those climatic design priorities are given at the end of the chapter (see Section 5.9).

Some words of caution are very important here. The following climatic data should be used only as a starting point. As much as possible, corrections should be made to account for local microclimates. For building sites near the border between regions, the climatic data for the

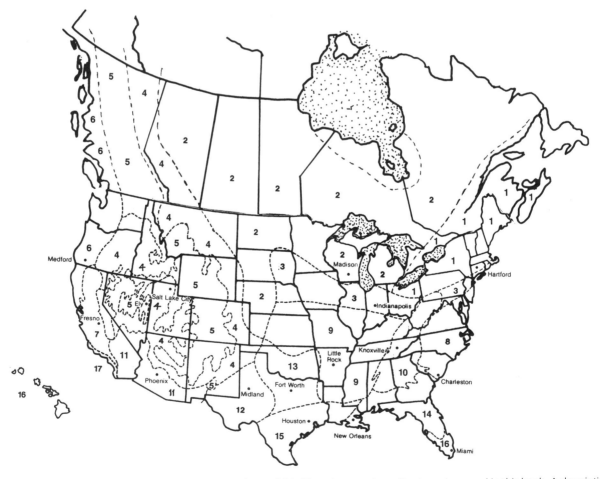

Figure 5.5 This map shows how the United States and Canada are divided into the seventeen climate regions used in this book. A description of each climate region can be found in the Climate Data Tables that follow.

two regions should be interpolated. The borders should be considered as fuzzy lines rather than the sharp lines shown in Fig. 5.5.

Because of the Web, it is now possible to easily obtain climate information about more specific locations. In the United States, look at www.cdc.noaa.gov/usclimate and www.wcc.nrcs.usda.gov/climate. In Canada, see www.climate.weatheroffice.ec.gc.ca. For the rest of the world, see www.world-climate.com

5.6 EXPLANATIONS OF THE CLIMATIC DATA TABLES

Each of the seventeen climatic regions is described by a **climatic data table** consisting of two facing pages (Fig. 5.6a), and each part marked with a circled uppercase letter is described below.

(A) *Sketch:* The drawing is a representative example of a traditional residential building appropriate for that particular climate region.

(B) *Climate Region:* The climate of the region is represented by the climatic data for the reference city. The darkened portion of the map represents the particular region for which the data are given.

(C) *The Climate:* This section of the Climate Data Table provides a verbal description of the climate.

(D) *The Building Bioclimatic Chart:* This chart defines the climate in relationship to thermal comfort and the design strategies required to create thermal comfort. See Section 4.11 for an explanation of the building bioclimatic chart.

The climate of the particular region is presented on this chart by means of straight lines, each of which represents the temperature and humidity conditions for one month of the year. Each line is generated by plotting the monthly normal daily maximum and minimum temperatures with their corresponding RH values. The line connecting these two points is assumed to represent the typical temperature and humidity conditions of that month (Fig. 5.6b). The twelve monthly lines represent the annual climate of that region.

This method of presenting the climate has several advantages. It graphically defines in one diagram both temperature and humidity for each month of the year. This is important because thermal comfort is a function of their combined effect. It shows

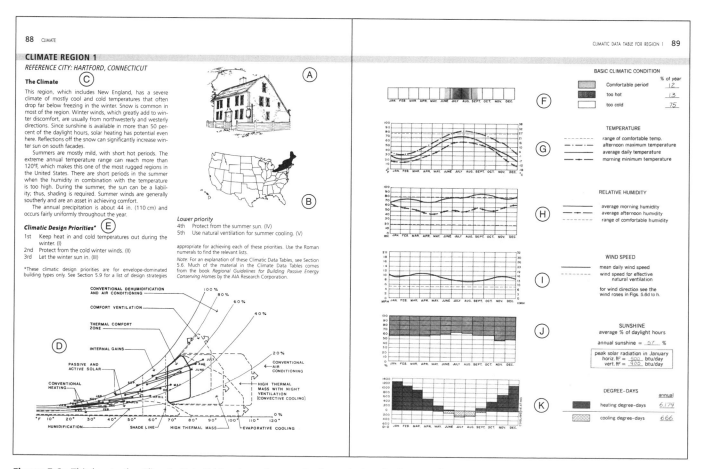

Figure 5.6a This key to the Climatic Data Tables shows how each climate is described on two facing pages.

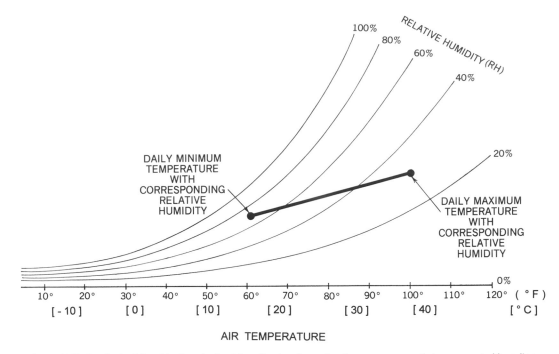

Figure 5.6b On the building bioclimatic chart the climate of a region for any one month is represented by a line.

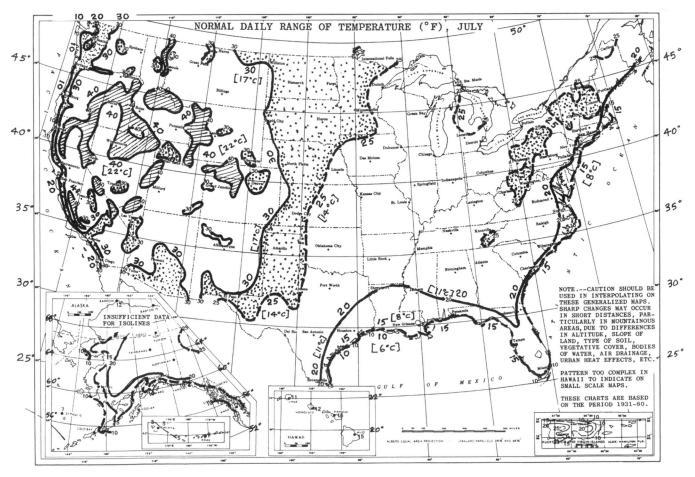

Figure 5.6c July normal daily temperature ranges. (From *Climate Atlas of the U.S.,* National Oceanic and Atmospheric Administration (NOAA) 1983.)

how severe or mild the climate is by the relationship of the twelve lines to the comfort zone. It also shows which design strategies are appropriate for the particular climate. For example, the chart for Climate 7 (Fresno, California) indicates a hot and dry summer climate for which evaporative cooling is an appropriate strategy.

(E) *Climatic Design Priorities:* For each climate, a set of design priorities is given for "envelope-dominated buildings," such as residences and small office buildings. "Internally dominated buildings," such as large office buildings, are less affected by climate and have much smaller heating and much greater cooling needs. They usually also have a greater need for daylighting. Consequently, these priorities are not directly applicable for internally dominated building types.

The priorities are listed in descending order of importance. The designer should start with the first priority and include as many of the rest as possible. Note that the words "summer" and "winter" are used to refer to the overheated and underheated periods of the year and not necessarily to the calendar months.

(F) *Basic Climate Condition:* This chart shows the periods of the year when the combined effect of temperature and humidity makes the climate either too hot, too cold, or just comfortable. The chart offers a quick answer to the question of what the main thrust of the building design should be: whether the design should respond to a climate that is mainly too hot, too cold, both too hot and too cold, or mostly comfortable.

(G) *Temperature:* The temperatures given are averages over many years. Although occasional temperatures are much higher and lower than the averages shown, most designs are based on normal rather than unusual conditions. The vertical distance between the afternoon maximum and morning minimum temperatures represents the diurnal (daily) temperature range. The horizontal dashed lines define the comfort zone.

Daily temperature ranges can also be obtained from the map of Fig. 5.6c. These values are critical in choosing the appropriate passive cooling techniques explained in Chapter 10.

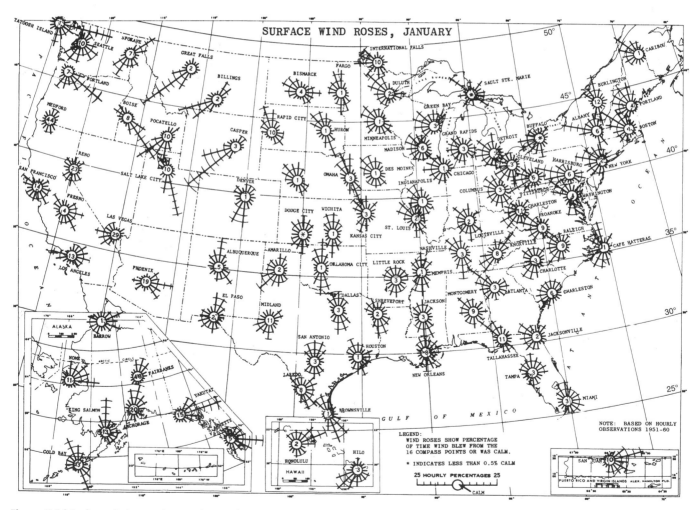

Figure 5.6d Surface wind roses, January. (From *Climate Atlas of the U.S.,* National Oceanic and Atmospheric Administration (NOAA), 1983.)

(H) *Humidity:* Even when the absolute moisture in the air remains fairly constant throughout the day, the RH will vary inversely with the temperature. Since hot air can hold more moisture than cold air, the RH will generally be lowest during the afternoons, when the temperatures are highest. Likewise, early in the morning, when temperatures are lowest, the RH will be at its highest.

The horizontal dashed lines define the comfort range for RH. However, even humidity levels within the comfort zone can be excessive if the coincident temperature is high enough. Thus, the building bioclimatic chart is a better indicator of thermal comfort than this chart.

(I) *Wind:* This chart shows the mean daily wind speeds in an open field at the reference city. The dashed line indicates the minimum wind speed required for effective natural ventilation in humid climates.

For wind direction, see the wind roses shown on maps of the United States in Figs. 5.6d, 5.6e, 5.6f, and 5.6g. A wind rose shows the percentage of time the wind blows from the sixteen compass points or the air is calm. Each notch represents 5 percent of the time, and the number in the center circle represents the percentage of time there was no wind (calm). Maps of wind roses are included here for four critical months: the coldest (January), the

hottest (July), and two transitional months (April and October).

The Web is now an excellent source of climate information. Figure 5.6h is an example of a wind rose for Chicago downloaded from the site address given in the figure. These types of wind roses give not only the direction of the wind but also the wind speed and how often that occurs in percentage terms.

It is extremely important to note that local wind direction and speed can be very different from those at the weather station. All wind charts should, therefore, be used with great care.

(J) *Sunshine:* This chart shows the percentage of the daylight hours of

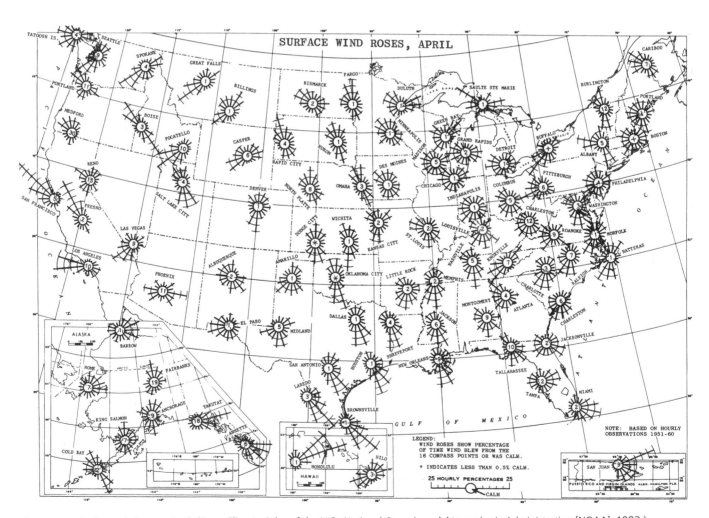

Figure 5.6e Surface wind roses, April. (From *Climate Atlas of the U.S.,* National Oceanic and Atmospheric Administration [NOAA], 1983.)

Table 5.6 Hours of Daylight Per Day*			
	Latitude		
Month	*30°N*	*40°N*	*50°N*
January	10:25	9:39	8:33
February	11:09	10:43	10:07
March	11:58	11:55	11:51
April	12:53	13:15	13:45
May	13:39	14:23	15:24
June	14:04	15:00	16:21
July	13:54	14:45	15:57
August	13:14	13:46	14:30
September	12:22	12:28	12:39
October	11:28	12:28	12:39
November	10:39	9:59	9:04
December	10:14	9:21	8:06

*Values given are for the fifteenth day of each month.

each month that the sun is shining. This data is useful for solar heating, shading, and daylighting design. The charts show that direct sunlight is plentiful in all climates. Since there are about 4460 hours of daylight in a year, the percentages in the charts indicate that there are more than 2000 hours of sunshine even in the cloudiest climate. Thus, direct sunshine is a major design consideration in all climates.

To determine the average number of sunshine hours for a representative day for any month, multiply the percentage of sunshine from the chart by the number of daylight hours in Table 5.6. Since the number of daylight hours varies with

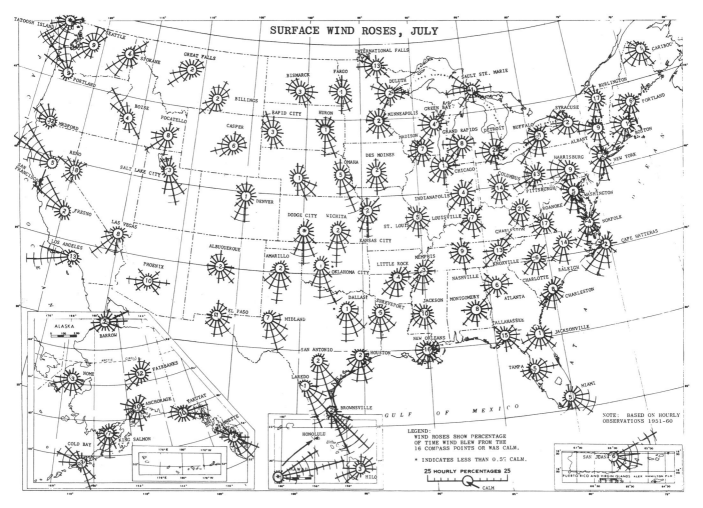

Figure 5.6f Surface wind roses, July (From *Climate Atlas of the U.S.*, National Oceanic and Atmospheric Administration [NOAA], 1983.)

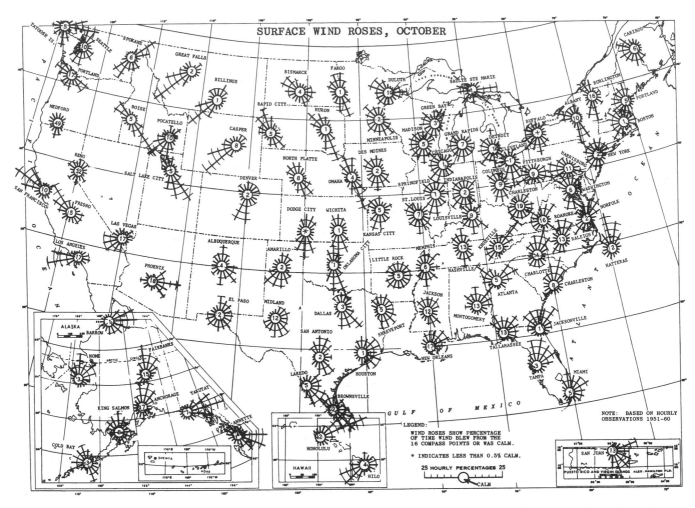

Figure 5.6g Surface wind roses, October. (From *Climate Atlas of the U.S.,* National Oceanic and Atmospheric Administration [NOAA], 1983.)

latitude, the table contains values for 30°, 40°, and 50° north latitude.

The annual percentage of sunshine is also given at the right of the chart. Along with the data on sunshine, some solar-radiation data is also given (enclosed in rectangle). This data can give a quick estimate of the peak amount of solar heating that can be expected during one day in January on either a horizontal or vertical square foot.

(K) *Degree-Days:* Degree-days are a good indicator of the severity of winter and summer. Although the concept was developed to predict the amount of heating fuel required,

it is now also used to predict the amount of cooling energy required. The **degree-days** shown here are for the typical base of 65°F (18°C). The difference between the average temperature of a particular day and 65°F (18°C) is the number of degree-days for that day. The chart shows the total number of degree-days for each month with heating degree-days above the zero line and cooling degree-days below. Thus, it is easy to determine visually both the length and depth of the heating and cooling periods and the relative size of each period. The yearly totals are given in numerical form.

Degree-Day Rules of Thumb

Heating Degree-Days (HDDs)

1. Areas with more than 5500 HDDs per year are characterized by long, cold winters.
2. Areas with fewer than 2000 HDDs per year are characterized by very mild winters.

Cooling Degree-Days (CDDs)

1. Areas with more than 1500 CDDs per year are characterized by long, hot summers and substantial cooling requirements.

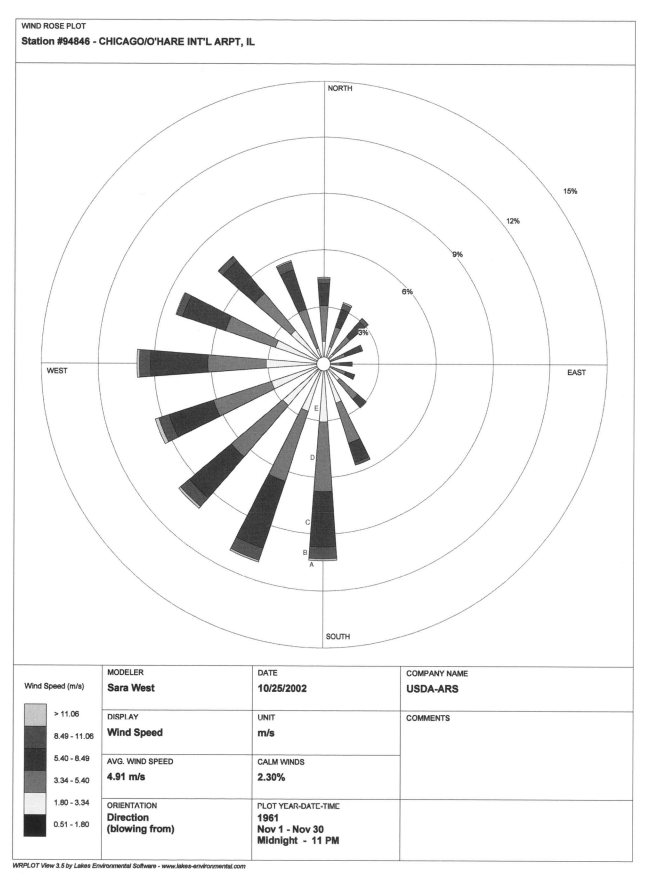

WRPLOT View 3.5 by Lakes Environmental Software - www.lakes-environmental.com

Figure 5.6h This wind rose shows the direction and frequency of various wind speeds in Chicago in November. It shows that the wind comes from the south a little more than 10 percent of the time. It also shows that the wind speed is 12–19 mph (5.40–8.49 m/s) about 3 percent of the time (truncated sector "C"). Note that because the actual wind roses are in color, the wind speed is easy to read from the legend. To change wind speed from m/s to mph, multiply by 2.237. Wind roses for most U.S. cities can be found at www.wcc.nrcs.usda.gov/climate/windrose.html.

Precipitation: Annual Climatology (1971–2000)

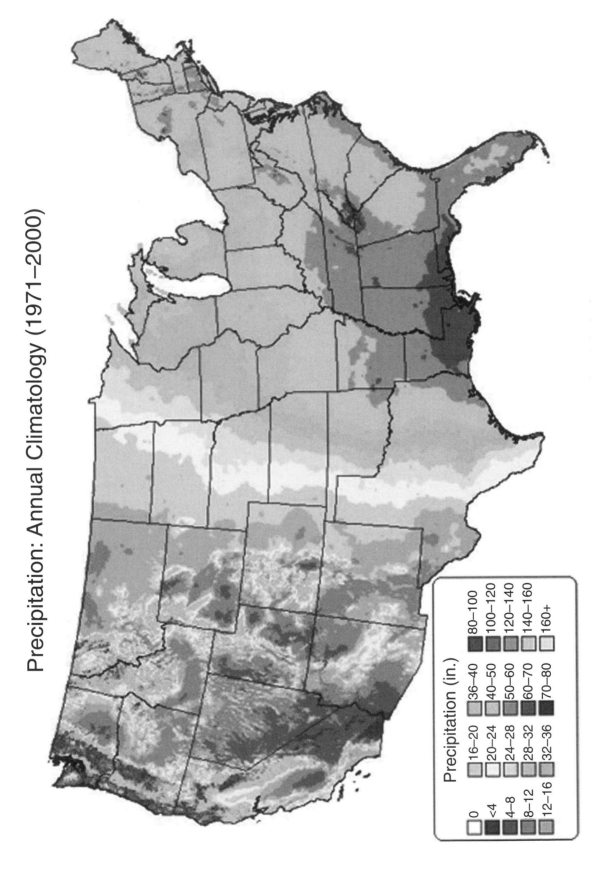

Precipitation (in.)

0	16–20	36–40	80–100
<4	20–24	40–50	100–120
4–8	24–28	50–60	120–140
8–12	28–32	60–70	140–160
12–16	32–36	70–80	160+

Figure 5.7 This map of average annual precipitation is available in color at www.wcc.nrcs.usda.gov/climate/prism.html.

2. Areas with fewer than 500 CDDs per year are characterized by mild summers and little need for mechanical cooling.

5.7 ADDITIONAL CLIMATE INFORMATION

Additional excellent climate information is available on the Internet. For example, the average annual precipitation for the United States is shown in Fig. 5.7. This and many other U.S. climate maps are available at www.wcc.nrcs.usda.gov/images/usprism.

Detailed climate information for each county in the United States is available by following these steps:

1. Go to www.wcc.nrcs.usda.gov/climate/prism.html.
2. Click on "Climate Reports."
3. Click on "Map Based Climate Information Retrieval."
4. Click on the state in which the county is located.
5. On the map of the state, click on the county for which the climate information is desired.

See page 129 for more sources of climate information

5.8 CLIMATE INFORMATION FOR OTHER COUNTRIES

Unfortunately, this book cannot provide climate information for the whole world. Besides locally available and Web-based information, climate information for many countries can be inferred from similar climates in the United States. Because of its size and location on the planet, the United States has many of the climates that exist on Earth.

To use the seventeen U.S. climate regions presented in this chapter when SI units are desired, use the following conversion factors:

1. Temperature—use the conversion scale of Fig. 3.3c to change °F to °C.
2. Wind speed—multiply mph by 1.6 to get kph or multiply mph by 0.447 to get m/s.
3. Peak solar radiation—multiply the BTU/day $\times$ ft^2 by 7.29 to get watt-hours/day $\times$ m^2.
4. Heating degree-days—multiply HDD (°F) by 0.56 to get HDD (°C).

CLIMATE REGION 1

REFERENCE CITY: HARTFORD, CONNECTICUT

The Climate

This region, which includes New England, has a severe climate of mostly cool and cold temperatures that often drop far below freezing in the winter. Snow is common in most of the region. Winter winds, which greatly add to winter discomfort, are usually from northwesterly and westerly directions. Since sunshine is available in more than 50 percent of the daylight hours, solar heating has potential even here. Reflections off the snow can significantly increase winter sun on south facades.

Summers are mostly mild, with short hot periods. The extreme annual temperature range can reach more than 120°F, which makes this one of the most rugged regions in the United States. There are short periods in the summer when the humidity in combination with the temperature is too high. During the summer, the sun can be a liability; thus, shading is required. Summer winds are generally southerly and are an asset in achieving comfort.

The annual precipitation is about 44 in. (110 cm) and occurs fairly uniformly throughout the year.

Climatic Design Priorities*

1st   Keep heat in and cold temperatures out during the winter. (I)
2nd Protect from the cold winter winds. (II)
3rd   Let the winter sun in. (III)

*These climatic design priorities are for envelope-dominated building types only. See Section 5.9 for a list of design strategies

Lower priority

4th   Protect from the summer sun. (IV)
5th   Use natural ventilation for summer cooling. (V)

appropriate for achieving each of these priorities. Use the Roman numerals to find the relevant lists.

Note: For an explanation of these Climatic Data Tables, see Section 5.6. Much of the material in the Climate Data Tables comes from the book *Regional Guidelines for Building Passive Energy Conserving Homes* by the AIA Research Corporation.

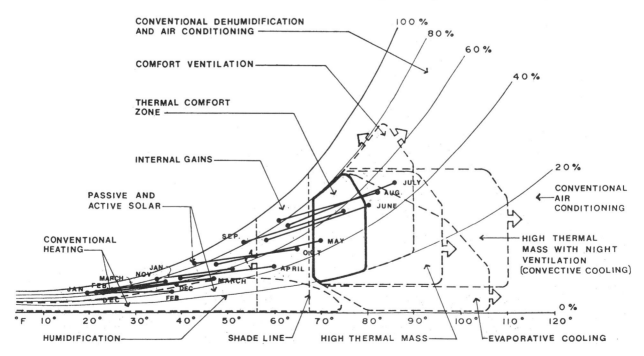

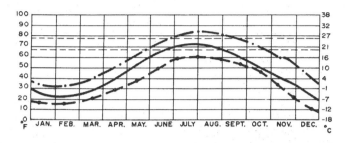

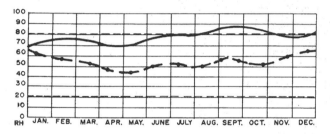

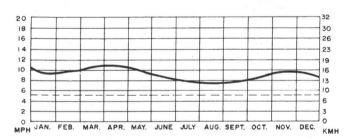

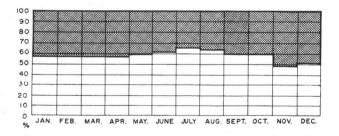

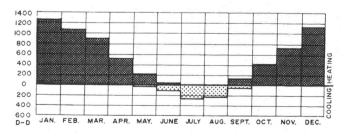

BASIC CLIMATIC CONDITION

		% of year
	Comfortable period	12
	too hot	13
	too cold	75

TEMPERATURE

- - - - - - - range of comfortable temp.
- · - · - · - afternoon maximum temperature
———————— average daily temperature
———•———•——— morning minimum temperature

RELATIVE HUMIDITY

———————— average morning humidity
——•——•—— average afternoon humidity
- - - - - - - range of comfortable humidity

WIND SPEED

———————— mean daily wind speed
- - - - - - - wind speed for effective
        natural ventilation

for wind direction see the
wind roses in Figs. 5.6d to h.

SUNSHINE
average % of daylight hours

annual sunshine = 57 %

peak solar radiation in January
horiz. ft² = 500 btu/day
vert. ft² = 900 btu/day

DEGREE-DAYS

		annual
	heating degree-days	6,174
	cooling degree-days	666

CLIMATE REGION 2

REFERENCE CITY: MADISON, WISCONSIN

The Climate

The climate of the northern plains is similar to that of region I but is even more severe because this inland region is far from the moderating effect of the oceans. The main concern is with the winter low temperatures, which are often combined with fairly high wind speeds.

Although summers are very hot, they are less of a concern because they are short. The sun is an asset in the winter and a liability in the summer.

The annual precipitation of about 31 in. (78 cm) occurs throughout the year, but summer months receive over twice as much as winter months.

*Climatic Design Priorities**

1st   Keep heat in and cold temperatures out in the winter. (I)
2nd   Protect from the cold winter winds. (II)
3rd   Let the winter sun in. (III)

*These climatic design priorities are for envelope-dominated building types only. See Section 5.9 for a list of design strategies appropriate for achieving each of these priorities. Use the Roman numerals to find the relevant lists.

Note: For an explanation of these Climatic Data Tables, see Section 5.6. Much of the material in the Climate Data Tables comes from the book *Regional Guidelines for Building Passive Energy Conserving Homes*, by the AIA Research Corporation.

Lower priority

4th   Use thermal mass to reduce day-to-night temperature swings in the summer. (VII)
5th   Protect from the summer sun. (IV)
6th   Use natural ventilation for summer cooling. (V)

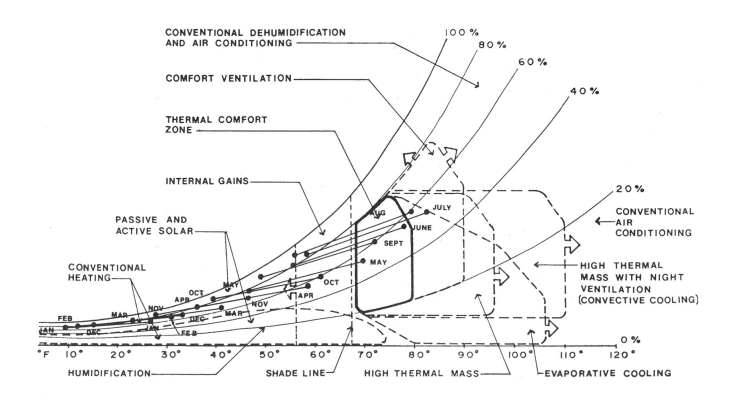

BASIC CLIMATIC CONDITION

		% of year
	Comfortable period	12
	too hot	12
	too cold	76

TEMPERATURE

- - - - - - -   range of comfortable temp.
- · - · - · -   afternoon maximum temperature
————————   average daily temperature
—•—•—•—   morning minimum temperature

RELATIVE HUMIDITY

————————   average morning humidity
—•—•—•—   average afternoon humidity
- - - - - - -   range of comfortable humidity

WIND SPEED

————————   mean daily wind speed
- - - - - - -   wind speed for effective natural ventilation

for wind direction see the wind roses in Figs. 5.6d to h

SUNSHINE
average % of daylight hours

annual sunshine = 54 %

peak solar radiation in January
horiz. ft² = 600 btu/day
vert. ft² = 1100 btu/day

DEGREE-DAYS

		annual
	heating degree-days	7,642
	cooling degree-days	467

CLIMATE REGION 3

REFERENCE CITY: INDIANAPOLIS, INDIANA

The Climate

This climate of the Midwest is similar to that of regions 1 and 2, but it is somewhat milder in winter. Cold winds, however, are still an important concern. The mean annual snowfall ranges from 12 to 60 in. (30–150 cm). There is some potential for solar energy in the winter since the sun shines more than 40 percent of the daylight hours.

Significant cooling loads are common since high summer temperatures often coincide with high humidity. Winds are an asset during the summer.

The annual precipitation is about 39 in. (98 cm) and occurs fairly uniformly throughout the year.

Climatic Design Priorities*

1st   Keep heat in and cold temperatures out in the winter. (I)
2nd   Protect from the cold winter winds. (II)
3rd   Let the winter sun in. (III)

*These climatic design priorities are for envelope-dominated building types only. See Section 5.9 for a list of design strategies appropriate for achieving each of these priorities. Use the Roman numerals to find the relevant lists.

Note: For an explanation of these Climatic Data Tables, see Section 5.6. Much of the material in the Climate Data Tables comes from the book *Regional Guidelines for Building Passive Energy Conserving Homes* by the AIA Research Corporation.

Lower priority

4th   Keep hot temperatures out during the summer. (VIII)
5th   Protect from the summer sun. (IV)
6th   Use natural ventilation for summer cooling. (V)

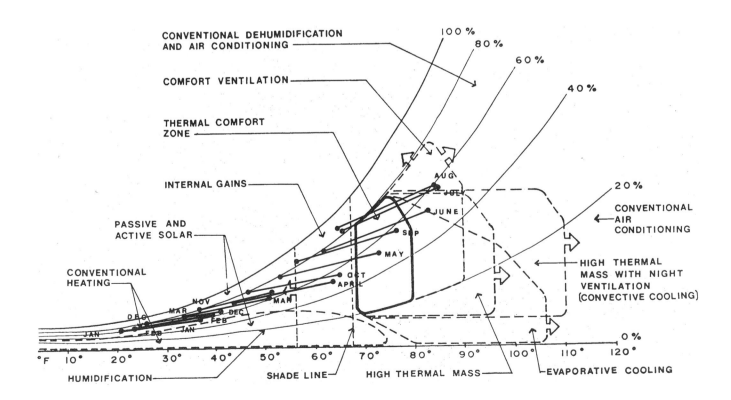

JAN. FEB. MAR. APR. MAY. JUNE JULY AUG. SEPT. OCT. NOV. DEC.

BASIC CLIMATIC CONDITION

		% of year
	Comfortable period	14
	too hot	20
	too cold	66

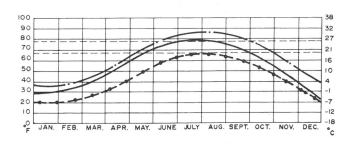

TEMPERATURE

– – – – – –	range of comfortable temp.
– · – · – · –	afternoon maximum temperature
———————	average daily temperature
—•——•——•—	morning minimum temperature

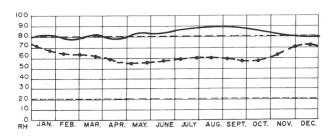

RELATIVE HUMIDITY

———————	average morning humidity
—•——•——•—	average afternoon humidity
– – – – – –	range of comfortable humidity

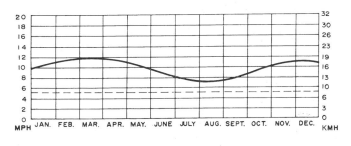

WIND SPEED

———————	mean daily wind speed
– – – – – –	wind speed for effective natural ventilation

for wind direction see the
wind roses in Figs. 5.6d to h

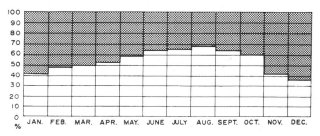

SUNSHINE
average % of daylight hours

annual sunshine = __55__ %

peak solar radiation in January
horiz. ft² = __500__ btu/day
vert. ft² = __800__ btu/day

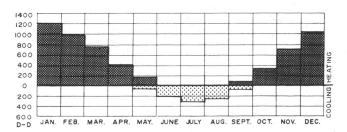

DEGREE-DAYS

		annual
	heating degree-days	5,650
	cooling degree-days	988

CLIMATE REGION 4
REFERENCE CITY: SALT LAKE CITY, UTAH

The Climate

This is the climate of the Great Plains, intermountain basin, and plateaus. It is a semiarid climate with cold, windy winters and warm, dry summers. Winters are very cold, with frequent but short storms alternating with sunny periods.

Summer temperatures are high, but the humidity is low. Thus, the diurnal temperature range is high and summer nights are generally cool. There is much potential for both passive heating and cooling.

The annual precipitation is about 15 in. (38 cm) and occurs fairly uniformly throughout the year, but spring is the wettest season.

*Climatic Design Priorities**

1st Keep the heat in and the cold temperatures out during the winter. (I)
2nd Let the winter sun in. (III)
3rd Protect from the cold winter winds. (II)

*These climatic design priorities are for envelope-dominated building types only. See Section 5.9 for a list of design strategies appropriate for achieving each of these priorities. Use the Roman numerals to find the relevant lists.

Note: For an explanation of these Climatic Data Tables, see Section 5.6. Much of the material in the Climate Data Tables comes from the book *Regional Guidelines for Building Passive Energy Conserving Homes* by the AIA Research Corporation.

Lower priority

4th Use thermal mass to reduce day-to-night temperature swings in the summer. (VII)
5th Protect from the summer sun. (IV)
6th Use evaporative cooling in the summer. (IX)
7th Use natural ventilation for summer cooling. (V)

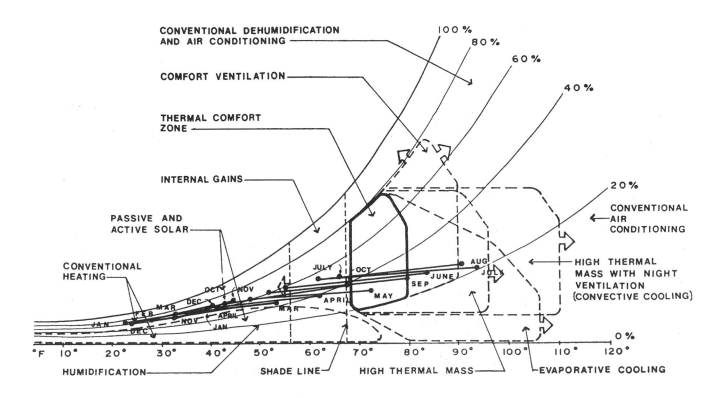

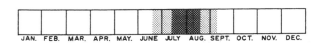

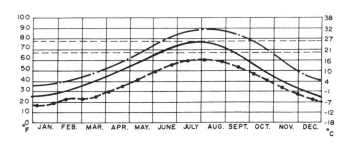

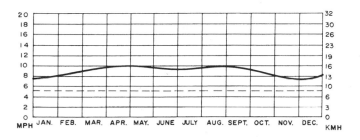

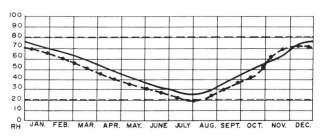

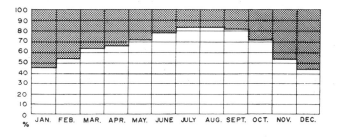

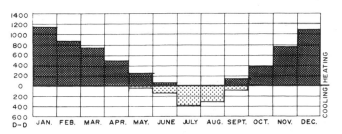

BASIC CLIMATIC CONDITION

		% of year
	Comfortable period	12
	too hot	11
	too cold	77

TEMPERATURE

- - - - - - - range of comfortable temp.
— · — · — · — afternoon maximum temperature
—————— average daily temperature
—•—•—•— morning minimum temperature

RELATIVE HUMIDITY

—————— average morning humidity
—•—•—•— average afternoon humidity
- - - - - - - range of comfortable humidity

WIND SPEED

—————— mean daily wind speed
- - - - - - - wind speed for effective
              natural ventilation

for wind direction see the
wind roses in Figs. 5.6d to h.

SUNSHINE
average % of daylight hours

annual sunshine = _66_ %

peak solar radiation in January
horiz. ft² = _700_ btu/day
vert. ft² = _1100_ btu/day

DEGREE-DAYS

		annual
	heating degree-days	5,802
	cooling degree-days	981

CLIMATE REGION 5

REFERENCE CITY: ELY, NEVADA

The Climate

This is a high, mountainous, and semiarid region above 7000 ft (2100 m) in southern latitudes and above 6000 ft (1800 m) in northern latitudes. It is a mostly cool and cold climate. Snow is plentiful and may remain on the ground for more than half the year. The temperature and, thus, the snow cover vary tremendously with the slope orientation and elevation. Heating is required most of the year. Fortunately, sunshine is available more than 60 percent of the winter daylight hours.

Summer temperatures are modest, and comfort is easily achieved by natural ventilation. Summer nights are quite cool because of the high diurnal temperature range.

The annual precipitation is about 9 in. (23 cm) and occurs fairly uniformly throughout the year.

*Climatic Design Priorities**

1st   Keep the heat in and the cold air out during the winter. (I)
2nd   Let the winter sun in. (III)
3rd   Protect from the cold winter winds. (II)
4th   Use thermal mass to reduce day-to-night temperature swings in the summer. (VII)

*These climatic design priorities are for envelope-dominated building types only. See Section 5.9 for a list of design strategies appropriate for achieving each of these priorities. Use the Roman numerals to find the relevant lists.

Note: For an explanation of these Climatic Data Tables, see Section 5.6. Much of the material in the Climate Data Tables comes from the book *Regional Guidelines for Building Passive Energy Conserving Homes* by the AIA Research Corporation.

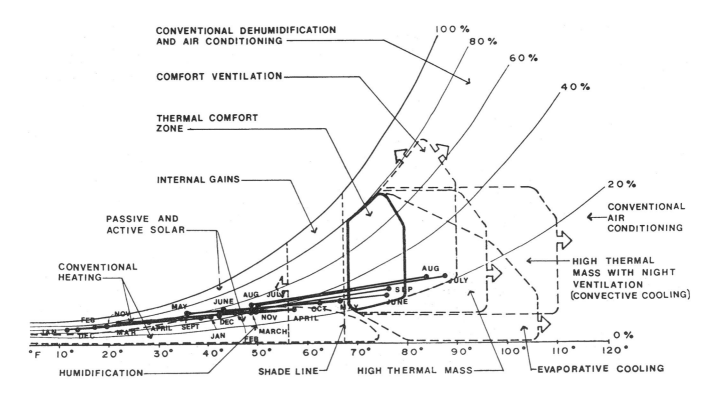

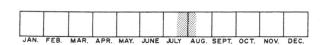

JAN. FEB. MAR. APR. MAY. JUNE JULY AUG. SEPT. OCT. NOV. DEC.

BASIC CLIMATIC CONDITION

		% of year
Comfortable period		8
too hot		0
too cold		92

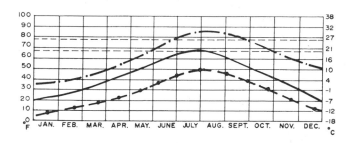

TEMPERATURE

– – – – – range of comfortable temp.

– · – · – afternoon maximum temperature

———— average daily temperature

—•—•— morning minimum temperature

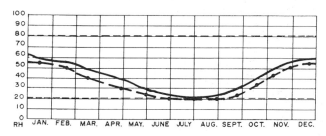

RELATIVE HUMIDITY

———— average morning humidity

—·—·— average afternoon humidity

– – – – – range of comfortable humidity

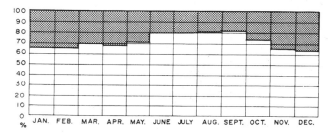

WIND SPEED

———— mean daily wind speed

– – – – – wind speed for effective
natural ventilation

for wind direction see the
wind roses in Figs. 5.6d to h.

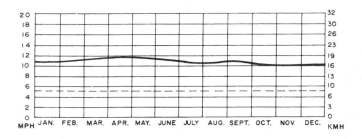

SUNSHINE
average % of daylight hours

annual sunshine = __73__ %

peak solar radiation in January
horiz. ft² = __900__ btu/day
vert. ft² = __1600__ btu/day

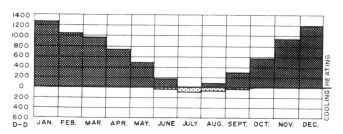

DEGREE-DAYS

		annual
heating degree-days		7,700
cooling degree-days		192

CLIMATE REGION 6

REFERENCE CITY: MEDFORD, OREGON

The Climate

The northern California, Oregon, and Washington coastal region has a very mild climate. In winter the temperatures are cool and rain is common. Although the skies are frequently overcast, solar heating is still possible because of the small heating load created by the mild climate. The high RH is not a significant problem because it does not coincide with high summer temperatures.

The region has a large variation in microclimates because of changes in both elevation and distance from the coast. In some areas the winter winds are a significant problem. A designer should, therefore, obtain additional local weather data.

The annual precipitation is about 20 in. (50 cm) but most of it occurs in the winter months. The summers are quite dry and sunny.

*Climatic Design Priorities**

1st   Keep the heat in and the cold temperatures out during the winter. (I)
2nd   Let the winter sun in (mostly diffused sun because of the clouds). (III)
3rd   Protect from the cold winter winds. (II)

*These climatic design priorities are for envelope-dominated building types only. See Section 5.9 for a list of design strategies appropriate for achieving each of these priorities. Use the Roman numerals to find the relevant lists.

Note: For an explanation of these Climatic Data Tables, see Section 5.6. Much of the material in the Climate Data Tables comes from the book *Regional Guidelines for Building Passive Energy Conserving Homes* by the AIA Research Corporation.

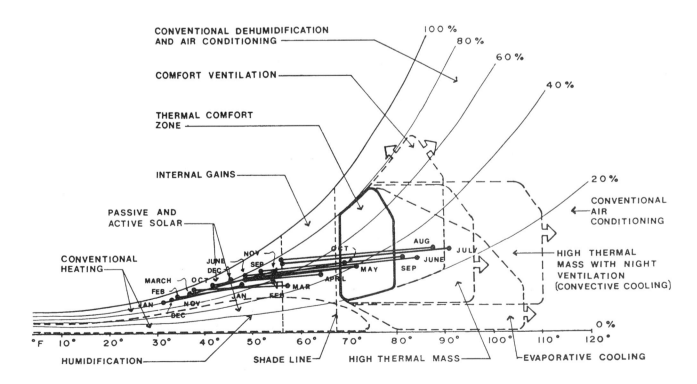

BASIC CLIMATIC CONDITION

		% of year
▦	Comfortable period	13
▩	too hot	8
☐	too cold	79

JAN.	FEB.	MAR.	APR.	MAY.	JUNE	JULY	AUG.	SEPT.	OCT.	NOV.	DEC.

TEMPERATURE

- – – – – – range of comfortable temp.
- – · – · – afternoon maximum temperature
- ——— average daily temperature
- —•—•— morning minimum temperature

RELATIVE HUMIDITY

- ——— average morning humidity
- —•—•— average afternoon humidity
- – – – – – range of comfortable humidity

WIND SPEED

- ——— mean daily wind speed
- – – – – – wind speed for effective natural ventilation

for wind direction see the wind roses in Figs. 5.6d to h.

SUNSHINE
average % of daylight hours

annual sunshine = 47 %

peak solar radiation in January
horiz. ft² = 300 btu/day
vert. ft² = 550 btu/day

DEGREE-DAYS

		annual
▦	heating degree-days	4,798
▦	cooling degree-days	645

CLIMATE REGION 7

REFERENCE CITY: FRESNO, CALIFORNIA

The Climate

This region includes California's Central Valley and parts of the central coast. Winters are moderately cold, with most of the annual rain of about 11 in. (28 cm) falling during that period. Winter sunshine, nevertheless, is plentiful.

Summers are hot and dry. The low humidity causes a large diurnal temperature range; consequently, summer nights are cool. Rain is rare during the summer months.

Since spring and fall are very comfortable, and much of the rest of the year is not very uncomfortable, outdoor living is very popular in this region.

Because of the varying distances to the ocean, significant changes in microclimate exist. Near the coast the temperatures are more moderate in both winter and summer. Neither winter nor summer dominates the climate of this region.

*Climatic Design Priorities**

1st Keep the heat in and cold temperatures out during the winter. (I)
2nd Keep hot temperatures out during the summer. (VIII)
3rd Let the winter sun in. (III)
4th Protect from the summer sun. (IV)
5th Use thermal mass to reduce day-to-night temperature swings during the summer. (VII)
6th Use natural ventilation for cooling in the spring and fall. (V)
7th Use evaporative cooling in the summer. (IX)
8th Protect from the cold winter winds. (II)

*These climatic design priorities are for envelope-dominated building types only. See Section 5.9 for a list of design strategies appropriate for achieving each of these priorities. Use the Roman numerals to find the relevant lists.

Note: For an explanation of these Climatic Data Tables, see Section 5.6. Much of the material in the Climate Data Tables comes from the book *Regional Guidelines for Building Passive Energy Conserving Homes* by the AIA Research Corporation.

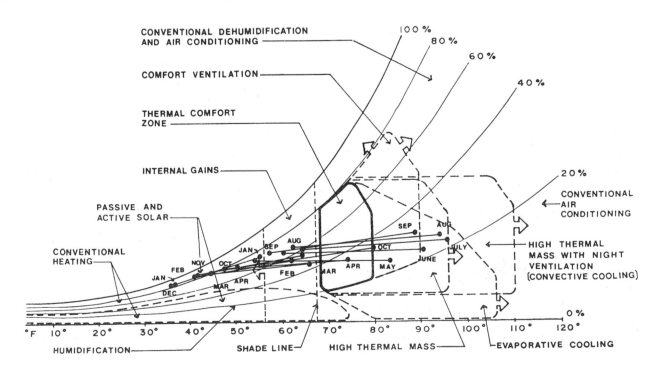

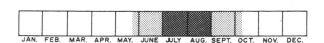

BASIC CLIMATIC CONDITION

		% of year
	Comfortable period	21
	too hot	17
	too cold	62

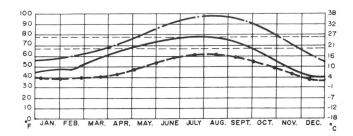

TEMPERATURE

– – – – –   range of comfortable temp.
– · – · –   afternoon maximum temperature
———   average daily temperature
–•– •–   morning minimum temperature

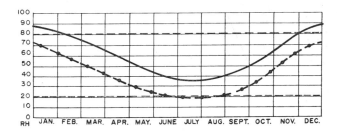

RELATIVE HUMIDITY

———   average morning humidity
–•–•–   average afternoon humidity
– – – – –   range of comfortable humidity

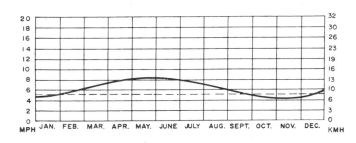

WIND SPEED

———   mean daily wind speed
– – – – –   wind speed for effective natural ventilation

for wind direction see the wind roses in Figs. 5.6d to h.

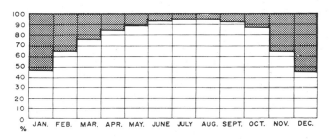

SUNSHINE
average % of daylight hours

annual sunshine = 78 %

peak solar radiation in January
horiz. ft² = 600 btu/day
vert. ft² = 1050 btu/day

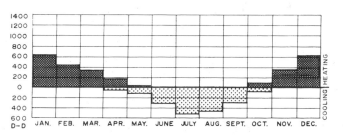

DEGREE-DAYS

		annual
	heating degree-days	2,647
	cooling degree-days	1,769

CLIMATE REGION 8

REFERENCE CITY: CHARLESTON, SOUTH CAROLINA

The Climate

This mid-Atlantic-coast climate is relatively temperate, with four distinct seasons. Although summers are very hot and humid and winters are somewhat cold, spring and fall are generally quite pleasant. Summer winds are an important asset in this hot and humid climate.

The annual precipitation is about 47 in. (118 cm) and occurs fairly uniformly throughout the year. Summer, however, is the wettest season, with thunderstorms common during that period. Tropical storms are an occasional possibility.

*Climatic Design Priorities**

1st   Keep the heat in and the cold temperatures out during the winter. (I)
2nd   Use natural ventilation for summer cooling. (V)
3rd   Let the winter sun in. (III)
4th   Protect from the summer sun. (IV)

Lower priority

5th   Protect from the cold winter winds. (II)
6th   Avoid creating additional humidity during the summer. (X)

*These climatic design priorities are for envelope-dominated building types only. See Section 5.9 for a list of design strategies appropriate for achieving each of these priorities. Use the Roman numerals to find the relevant lists.

Note: For an explanation of these Climatic Data Tables, see Section 5.6. Much of the material in the Climate Data Tables comes from the book *Regional Guidelines for Building Passive Energy Conserving Homes* by the AIA Research Corporation.

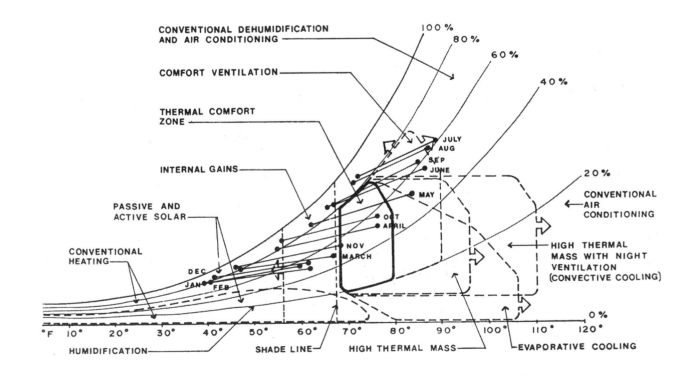

BASIC CLIMATIC CONDITION

		% of year
▨	Comfortable period	12
▨	too hot	42
☐	too cold	46

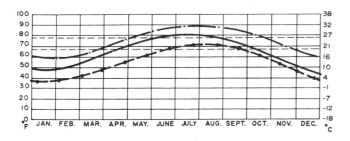

TEMPERATURE

- – – – – – – range of comfortable temp.
- – · – · – afternoon maximum temperature
- ————— average daily temperature
- —•—•— morning minimum temperature

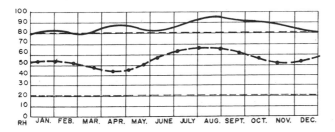

RELATIVE HUMIDITY

- ————— average morning humidity
- —•—•— average afternoon humidity
- – – – – – range of comfortable humidity

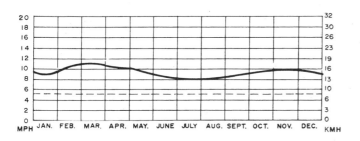

WIND SPEED

- ————— mean daily wind speed
- – – – – – wind speed for effective natural ventilation

for wind direction see the wind roses in Figs. 5.6d to h.

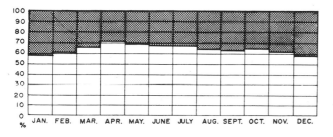

SUNSHINE
average % of daylight hours

annual sunshine = 65 %

peak solar radiation in January
horiz. ft² = 900 btu/day
vert. ft² = 1300 btu/day

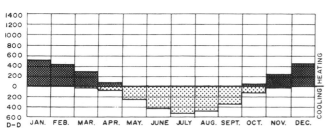

DEGREE-DAYS

		annual
▨	heating degree-days	1,868
▨	cooling degree-days	2,304

CLIMATE REGION 9

REFERENCE CITY: LITTLE ROCK, ARKANSAS

The Climate

The climate of the Mississippi Valley is similar to that of region 8, except that it is slightly more severe in both summer and winter due to the distance from the oceans. Winters are quite cold, with chilling winds from the northwest. Summers are hot and humid, with winds often from the southwest.

The annual precipitation is about 49 in. (123 cm) and occurs fairly uniformly throughout the year.

*Climatic Design Priorities**

1st Keep the heat in and cold temperatures out during the winter. (I)
2nd Let the winter sun in. (II)
3rd Use natural ventilation for summer cooling. (V)
4th Protect from the cold winter winds. (II)
5th Protect from the summer sun. (IV)
6th Avoid creating additional humidity during the summers. (X)

*These climatic design priorities are for envelope-dominated building types only. See Section 5.9 for a list of design strategies appropriate for achieving each of these priorities. Use the Roman numerals to find the relevant lists.

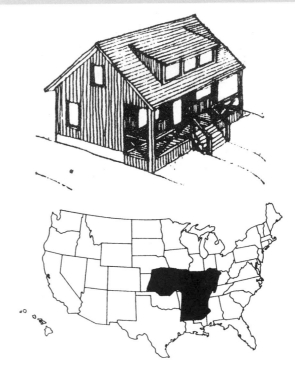

Note: For an explanation of these Climatic Data Tables, see Section 5.6. Much of the material in the Climate Data Tables comes from the book *Regional Guidelines for Building Passive Energy Conserving Homes* by the AIA Research Corporation.

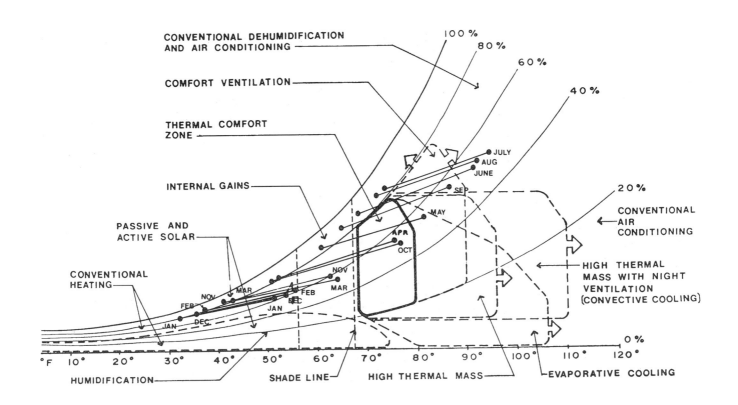

BASIC CLIMATIC CONDITION

		% of year
▒	Comfortable period	13
▓	too hot	35
☐	too cold	52

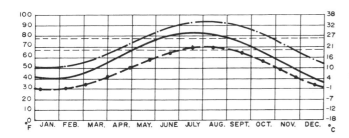

TEMPERATURE

- – – – – – range of comfortable temp.
- –·–·–·– afternoon maximum temperature
- ————— average daily temperature
- —•—•— morning minimum temperature

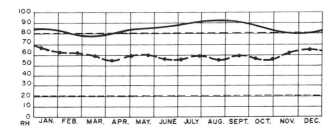

RELATIVE HUMIDITY

- ————— average morning humidity
- —•—•— average afternoon humidity
- – – – – – range of comfortable humidity

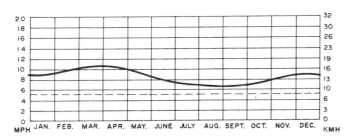

WIND SPEED

- ————— mean daily wind speed
- – – – – – wind speed for effective natural ventilation

for wind direction see the wind roses in Figs. 5.6d to h.

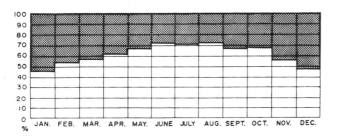

SUNSHINE
average % of daylight hours

annual sunshine = 62 %

peak solar radiation in January
horiz. ft² = 600 btu/day
vert. ft² = 900 btu/day

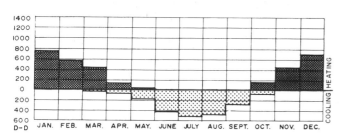

DEGREE-DAYS

		annual
▒	heating degree-days	3,152
░	cooling degree-days	2,045

CLIMATE REGION 10

REFERENCE CITY: KNOXVILLE, TENNESSEE

The Climate

The climate of Appalachia is relatively temperate, with a long and pleasant spring and fall. Winters are quite cool, with a significant chilling effect from the wind. Temperatures are somewhat cooler at the northern end of this region. Snow is also more common at the northern end, although it occurs fairly frequently at higher elevations at the southern end of the region.

Summers are hot and somewhat humid. However, the humidity is low enough to allow a fair amount of night cooling; thus, the diurnal temperature range is fairly high. There is also a fair amount of wind available for cooling in the summer.

The annual precipitation is about 47 in. (118 cm) and occurs rather uniformly throughout the year.

*Climatic Design Priorities**

1st Keep the heat in and the cold temperatures out in the winter. (I)
2nd Use natural ventilation for summer cooling. (V)
3rd Let the winter sun in. (III)
4th Protect from the summer sun. (IV)
5th Protect from the cold winter winds. (II)
6th Avoid creating additional humidity during the summer. (X)

*These climatic design priorities are for envelope-dominated building types only. See Section 5.9 for a list of design strategies appropriate for achieving each of these priorities. Use the Roman numerals to find the relevant lists.

Note: For an explanation of these Climatic Data Tables, see Section 5.6. Much of the material in the Climate Data Tables comes from the book *Regional Guidelines for Building Passive Energy Conserving Homes* by the AIA Research Corporation.

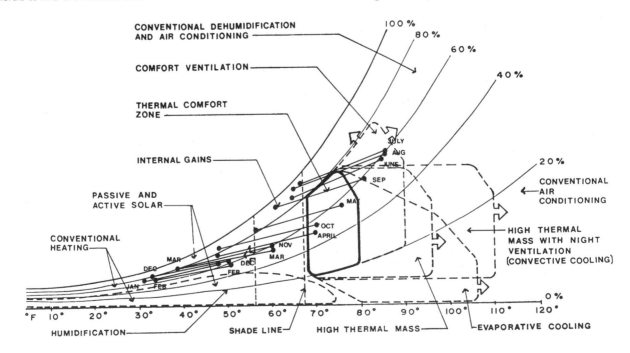

JAN. FEB. MAR. APR. MAY. JUNE JULY AUG. SEPT. OCT. NOV. DEC.

BASIC CLIMATIC CONDITION

		% of year
	Comfortable period	16
	too hot	28
	too cold	56

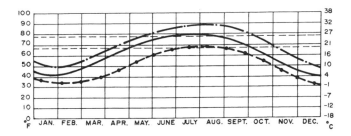

TEMPERATURE

- – – – – range of comfortable temp.
- – · – · – afternoon maximum temperature
- ——— average daily temperature
- —•—•— morning minimum temperature

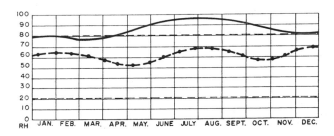

RELATIVE HUMIDITY

- ——— average morning humidity
- —•—•— average afternoon humidity
- – – – – range of comfortable humidity

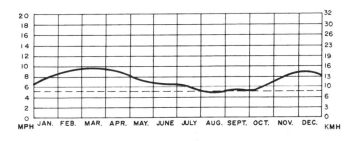

WIND SPEED

- ——— mean daily wind speed
- – – – – wind speed for effective natural ventilation

for wind direction see the wind roses in Figs. 5.6d to h.

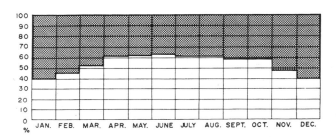

SUNSHINE
average % of daylight hours

annual sunshine = 55 %

peak solar radiation in January
horiz. ft² = 600 btu/day
vert. ft² = 800 btu/day

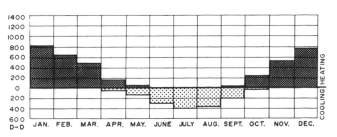

DEGREE-DAYS

		annual
	heating degree-days	3,658
	cooling degree-days	1,449

CLIMATE REGION 11

REFERENCE CITY: PHOENIX, ARIZONA

The Climate

The climate of the Southwest desert regions is characterized by extremely hot and dry summers and moderately cold winters. The skies are clear most of the year, with annual sunshine of about 85 percent.

Since summers are extremely hot and dry, the diurnal temperature range is very large; consequently, nights are quite cool. The humidity is below the comfort range much of the year. Summer overheating is the main concern for the designer.

The annual precipitation of about 7 in. (18 cm) is quite low and occurs throughout the year. April, May, and June are the driest months, while August is the wettest, with 1 in. (2.5 cm) of rain.

*Climatic Design Priorities**

1st   Keep hot temperatures out during the summer. (VIII)
2nd   Protect from the summer sun. (IV)
3rd   Use evaporative cooling in the summer. (IX)
4th   Use thermal mass to reduce day-to-night temperature swings during the summer. (VII)

Lower priority

5th   Keep the heat in and the cool temperatures out during the winter. (I)
6th   Let the winter sun in. (III)
7th   Use natural ventilation to cool in the spring and fall. (VI)

* These climatic design priorities are for envelope-dominated building types only. See Section 5.9 for a specific list of design strategies appropriate for achieving each of these priorities. Use the Roman numerals to find the relevant lists.

Note: For an explanation of these Climatic Data Tables, see Section 5.6. Much of the material in the Climate Data Tables comes from the book *Regional Guidelines for Building Passive Energy Conserving Homes* by the AIA Research Corporation.

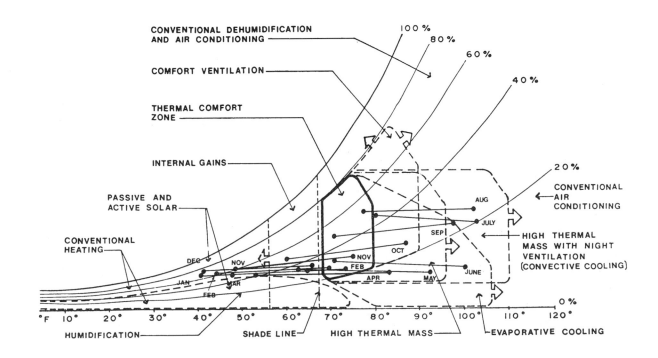

BASIC CLIMATIC CONDITION

		% of year
▨	Comfortable period	15
▨	too hot	37
☐	too cold	48

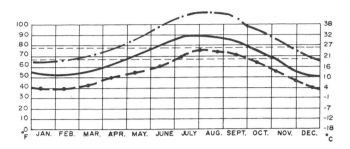

TEMPERATURE

– – – – –	range of comfortable temp.
– · – · –	afternoon maximum temperature
———	average daily temperature
—•—•—	morning minimum temperature

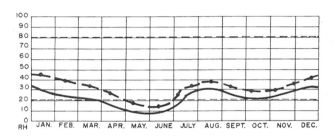

RELATIVE HUMIDITY

———	average morning humidity
—•—•—	average afternoon humidity
– – – –	range of comfortable humidity

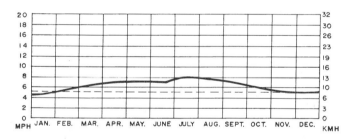

WIND SPEED

| ——— | mean daily wind speed |
| – – – – | wind speed for effective natural ventilation |

for wind direction see the wind roses in Figs. 5.6d to h.

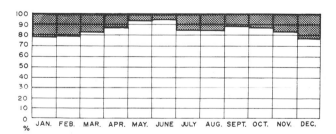

SUNSHINE
average % of daylight hours

annual sunshine = _85_ %

peak solar radiation in January
horiz. ft² = _1200_ btu/day
vert. ft² = _1600_ btu/day

DEGREE-DAYS

		annual
▨	heating degree-days	1,442
▨	cooling degree-days	3,746

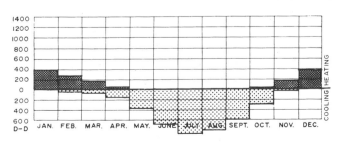

CLIMATE REGION 12

REFERENCE CITY: MIDLAND, TEXAS

The Climate

This area of west Texas and southeast New Mexico has an arid climate of hot summers and cool winters. Plentiful sunshine, more than 60 percent in the winter, can supply ample solar heating. The low humidity in summer facilitates the effective use of evaporative cooling. Thus, in this region, climatic design can have a very beneficial impact on thermal comfort.

The annual precipitation is about 14 in., (35 cm) and although it occurs throughout the year, most of it falls during the summer months.

*Climatic Design Priorities**

1st   Use evaporative cooling in summer. (IX)
2nd   Let the winter sun in. (III)
3rd   Protect from the summer sun. (IV)
4th   Keep the heat in and the cool temperatures out during the winter. (I)
5th   Keep hot temperatures out during the summer. (VIII)
6th   Protect from the cold winter winds. (II)
7th   Use natural ventilation for summer cooling. (V)
8th   Use thermal mass to reduce day-to-night temperature swings during the summer. (VII).

*These climatic design priorities are for envelope-dominated building types only. See Section 5.9 for a list of design strategies appropriate for achieving each of these priorities. Use the Roman numerals to find the relevant lists.

Note: For an explanation of these Climatic Data Tables, see Section 5.6. Much of the material in the Climate Data Tables comes from the book *Regional Guidelines for Building Passive Energy Conserving Homes* by the AIA Research Corporation.

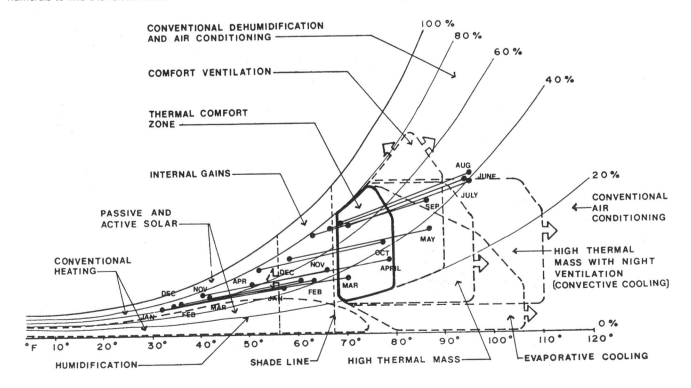

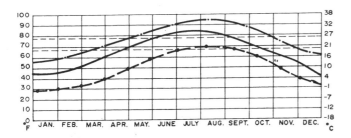

BASIC CLIMATIC CONDITION

		% of year
▨	Comfortable period	19
■	too hot	26
☐	too cold	55

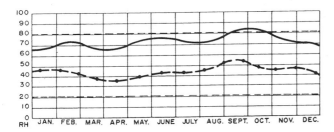

TEMPERATURE

– – – – –　range of comfortable temp.

–·–·–·–　afternoon maximum temperature

————　average daily temperature

–•–•–	morning minimum temperature

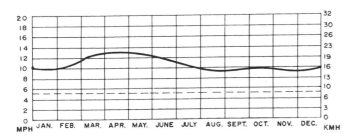

RELATIVE HUMIDITY

————　average morning humidity

–•–•–	average afternoon humidity

– – – – –	range of comfortable humidity

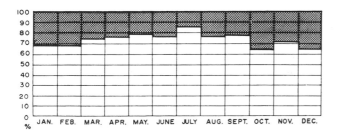

WIND SPEED

————　mean daily wind speed

– – – – –	wind speed for effective natural ventilation

for wind direction see the wind roses in Figs. 5.6d to h.

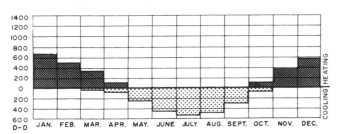

SUNSHINE
average % of daylight hours

annual sunshine = 74 %

peak solar radiation in January
horiz. ft² = 1100 btu/day
vert. ft² = 1450 btu/day

DEGREE-DAYS

		annual
■	heating degree-days	2658
▨	cooling degree-days	2,126

CLIMATE REGION 13

REFERENCE CITY: FORT WORTH, TEXAS

The Climate

This area of Oklahoma and north Texas has cold winters and hot summers. Cold winds come from the north and northeast. There is a significant amount of sunshine available for winter solar heating.

During part of the summer, the high temperatures and fairly high humidity combine to create uncomfortable conditions. During other times in the summer, the humidity drops sufficiently to enable evaporative cooling to work. There are also ample summer winds for natural ventilation.

During the drier parts of the summer and especially during spring and fall, the diurnal temperature range is large enough to encourage the use of thermal mass. The annual precipitation is about 29 in. (73 cm), and it occurs fairly uniformly throughout the year.

Climatic Design Priorities*

1st   Use natural ventilation for cooling in spring and fall. (V)
2nd   Let the winter sun in. (III)
3rd   Protect from the summer sun. (IV)
4th   Protect from the cold winter winds. (II)

Lower priority

5th   Use thermal mass to reduce day-to-night temperature swings during the summer. (VII)

*These climatic design priorities are for envelope-dominated building types only. See Section 5.9 for a list of design strategies appropriate for achieving each of these priorities. Use the Roman numerals to find the relevant lists.

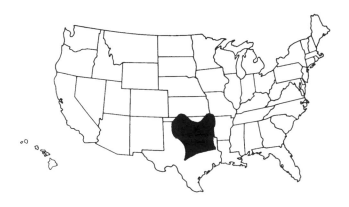

Note: For an explanation of these Climatic Data Tables, see Section 5.6. Much of the material in the Climate Data Tables comes from the book *Regional Guidelines for Building Passive Energy Conserving Homes* by the AIA Research Corporation.

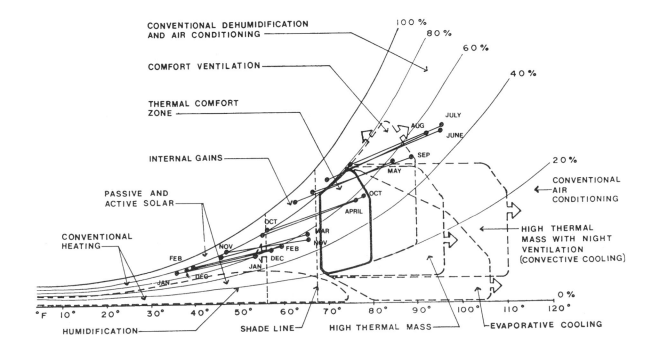

BASIC CLIMATIC CONDITION

		% of year
	Comfortable period	14
	too hot	39
	too cold	47

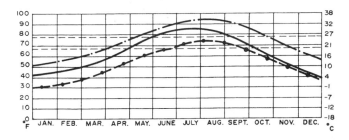

TEMPERATURE

- - - - - - - range of comfortable temp.
- · - · - · - afternoon maximum temperature
——————— average daily temperature
——•——•—— morning minimum temperature

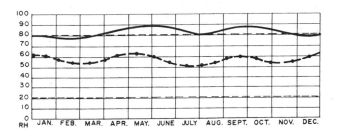

RELATIVE HUMIDITY

——————— average morning humidity
——•——•—— average afternoon humidity
- - - - - - - range of comfortable humidity

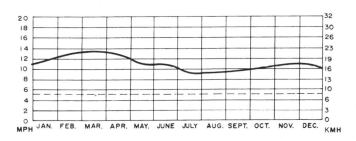

WIND SPEED

——————— mean daily wind speed
- - - - - - - wind speed for effective
              natural ventilation

for wind direction see the
wind roses in Figs. 5.6d to h.

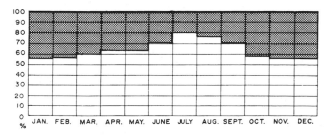

SUNSHINE
average % of daylight hours

annual sunshine = 64 %

peak solar radiation in January
horiz. ft² = 900 btu/day
vert. ft² = 1200 btu/day

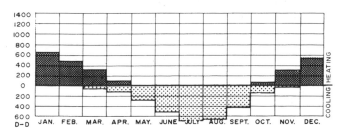

DEGREE-DAYS

		annual
	heating degree-days	2,407
	cooling degree-days	2,809

CLIMATE REGION 14

REFERENCE CITY: NEW ORLEANS, LOUISIANA

The Climate

This Gulf Coast region has cool but short winters. Summers, on the other hand, are hot, very humid, and long. The flat, damp ground and frequent rains create a very humid climate. Besides creating thermal discomfort, the high humidity causes mildew problems. Much of the region has reliable sea breezes, which are strongest during the day, weaker at night, and nonexistent during the morning and evening when the wind reverses direction.

The annual precipitation is quite high at 60 in. (150 cm), and it occurs fairly uniformly throughout the year.

*Climatic Design Priorities**

1st   Allow natural ventilation to both cool and remove excess moisture in the summer. (VI)
2nd   Protect from the summer sun. (IV)
3rd   Avoid creating additional humidity during the summer. (X)

Lower priority

4th   Let the winter sun in. (III)
5th   Protect from the cold winter winds. (II)

*These climatic design priorities are for envelope-dominated building types only. See Section 5.9 for a list of design strategies appropriate for achieving each of these priorities. Use the Roman numerals to find the relevant lists.

Note: For an explanation of these Climatic Data Tables, see Section 5.6. Much of the material in the Climate Data Tables comes from the book *Regional Guidelines for Building Passive Energy Conserving Homes* by the AIA Research Corporation.

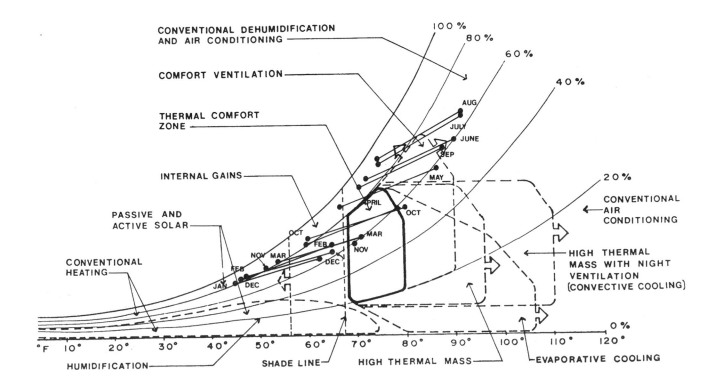

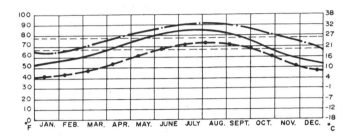

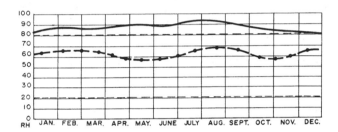

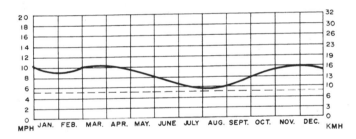

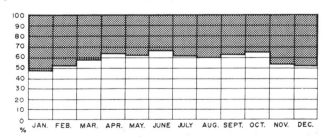

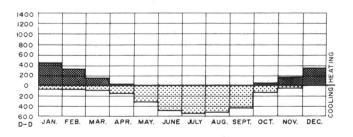

BASIC CLIMATIC CONDITION

		% of year
	Comfortable period	12
	too hot	52
	too cold	36

TEMPERATURE

– – – – – range of comfortable temp.

– · – · – afternoon maximum temperature

———— average daily temperature

—•—•— morning minimum temperature

RELATIVE HUMIDITY

———— average morning humidity

—•—•— average afternoon humidity

– – – – – range of comfortable humidity

WIND SPEED

———— mean daily wind speed

– – – – – wind speed for effective
natural ventilation

for wind direction see the
wind roses in Figs. 5.6d to h.

SUNSHINE
average % of daylight hours

annual sunshine = 59 %

peak solar radiation in January
horiz. ft² = 800 btu/day
vert. ft² = 1250 btu/day

DEGREE-DAYS

		annual
	heating degree-days	1,490
	cooling degree-days	2,686

CLIMATE REGION 15

REFERENCE CITY: HOUSTON, TEXAS

The Climate

This part of the Gulf Coast is similar to region 14 except that the summers are more severe. Very high temperatures and humidity levels make this a very uncomfortable summer climate. The high humidity and clouds prevent the temperature from dropping much at night. Thus, the diurnal temperature range is quite small. Fortunately, frequent coastal breezes exist in the summer.

Winters are short and mild. Ample sunshine can supply most of the winter heating demands, but the main concern for the designer is summer overheating.

The annual precipitation is about 45 in. (113 cm) and occurs fairly uniformly throughout the year.

*Climatic Design Priorities**

1st Keep hot temperatures out during the summer. (VIII)
2nd Allow natural ventilation to both cool and remove excess moisture in the summer. (VI)
3rd Protect from the summer sun. (IV)
4th Avoid creating additional humidity during the summer. (X)

Lower priority

5th Protect from the cold winter winds. (II)
6th Let the winter sun in. (III)
7th Keep the heat in and the cool temperatures out during the winter. (I)

*These climatic design priorities are for envelope-dominated building types only. See Section 5.9 for a list of design strategies appropriate for achieving each of these priorities. Use the Roman numerals to find the relevant lists.

Note: For an explanation of these Climatic Data Tables, see Section 5.6. Much of the material in the Climate Data Tables comes from the book *Regional Guidelines for Building Passive Energy Conserving Homes* by the AIA Research Corporation.

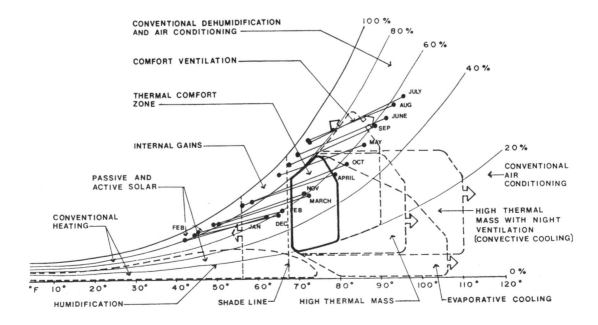

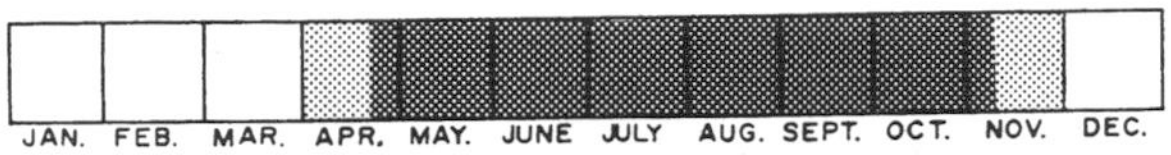

JAN. FEB. MAR. APR. MAY. JUNE JULY AUG. SEPT. OCT. NOV. DEC.

BASIC CLIMATIC CONDITION

	% of year
Comfortable period	11
too hot	54
too cold	35

100
90
80
70
60
50
40
30
20
10
0
°F
38
32
27
21
16
10
4
-1
-7
-12
-18
°C
JAN. FEB. MAR. APR. MAY. JUNE JULY AUG. SEPT. OCT. NOV. DEC.

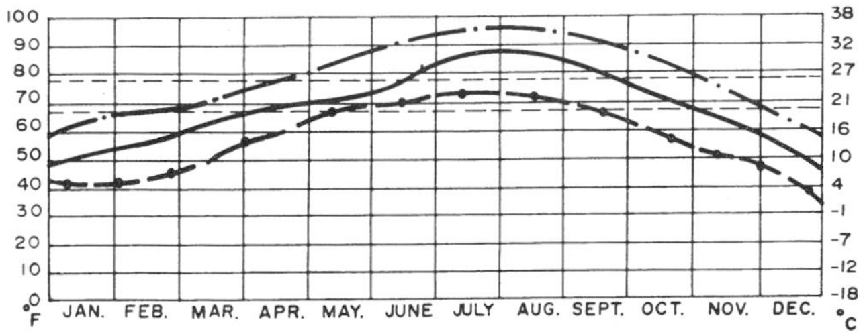

TEMPERATURE

range of comfortable temp.
afternoon maximum temperature
average daily temperature
morning minimum temperature

100
90
80
70
60
50
40
30
20
10
0
RH
JAN. FEB. MAR. APR. MAY. JUNE JULY AUG. SEPT. OCT. NOV. DEC.

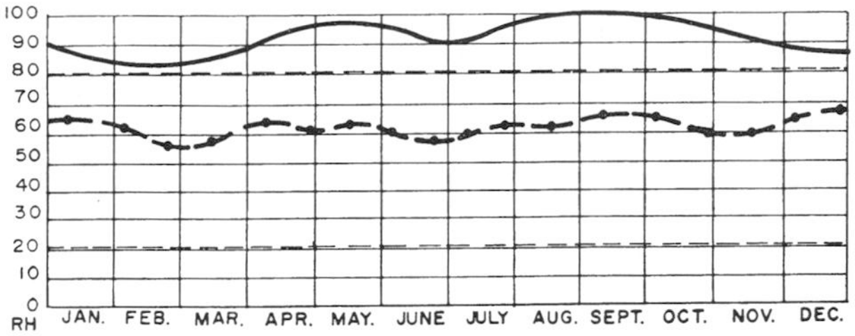

RELATIVE HUMIDITY

average morning humidity
average afternoon humidity
range of comfortable humidity

20
18
16
14
12
10
8
6
4
2
0
MPH
32
30
26
23
19
16
13
10
6
3
0
KMH
JAN. FEB. MAR. APR. MAY. JUNE JULY AUG. SEPT. OCT. NOV. DEC.

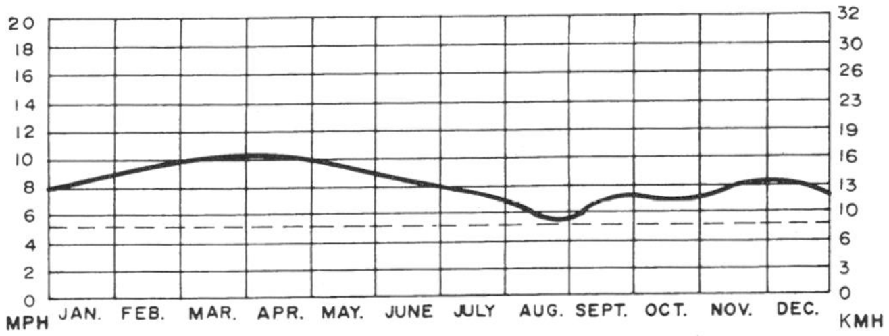

WIND SPEED

mean daily wind speed
wind speed for effective natural ventilation

for wind direction see the wind roses in Figs. 5.6d to h.

100
90
80
70
60
50
40
30
20
10
0
%
JAN. FEB. MAR. APR. MAY. JUNE JULY AUG. SEPT. OCT. NOV. DEC.

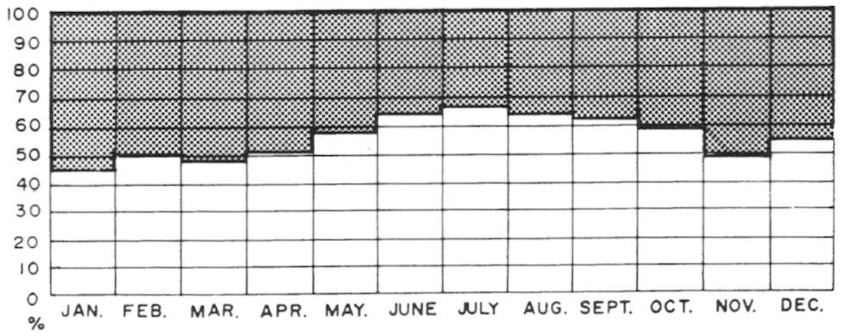

SUNSHINE

average % of daylight hours

annual sunshine = 56 %

peak solar radiation in January
horiz. ft² = 1050 btu/day
vert. ft² = 1300 btu/day

1400
1200
1000
800
600
400
200
0
200
400
600
D-D
HEATING
COOLING
JAN. FEB. MAR. APR. MAY. JUNE JULY AUG. SEPT. OCT. NOV. DEC.

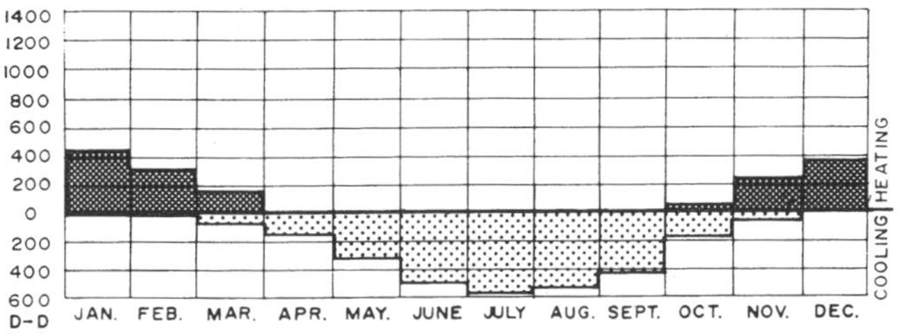

DEGREE-DAYS

	annual
heating degree-days	1,549
cooling degree-days	2,761

CLIMATE REGION 16

REFERENCE CITY: MIAMI, FLORIDA

The Climate

The climate of southern Florida has long, hot summers and no winters. When the slightly high temperatures are combined with high humidity, uncomfortable summers are the result. However, in spring, fall, and winter, the climate is quite pleasant. Ocean winds add significantly to year-round comfort.

The annual precipitation is quite high at about 58 in., (145 cm) and much of the rain falls during the summer months.

Climatic Design Priorities*

1st Open the building to the outdoors since temperatures are comfortable much of the year. (XI)
2nd Protect from the summer sun. (IV)
3rd Allow natural ventilation to both cool and remove excess moisture most of the year. (VI)
4th Avoid creating additional humidity. (X)

Lower priority

5th Keep the hot temperatures out during the summer. (VIII)
6th Keep the heat in and the cool temperatures out during the winter. (I)

*These climatic design priorities are for envelope-dominated building types only. See Section 5.9 for a list of design strategies appropriate for achieving each of these priorities. Use the Roman numerals to find the relevant lists.

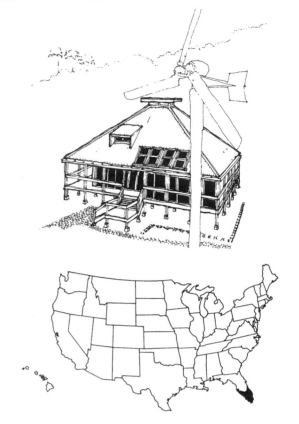

Note: For an explanation of these Climatic Data Tables, see Section 5.6. Much of the material in the Climate Data Tables comes from the book *Regional Guidelines for Building Passive Energy Conserving Homes* by the AIA Research Corporation.

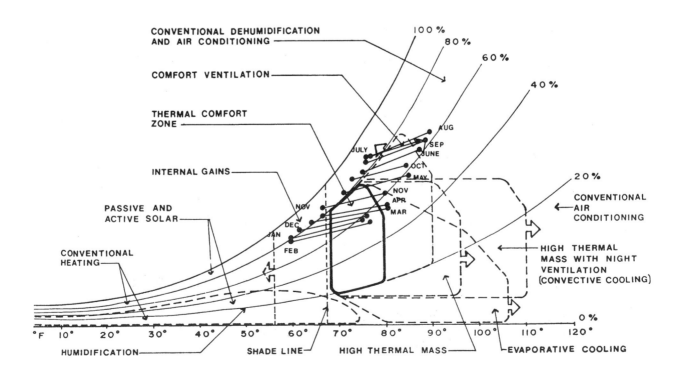

JAN. FEB. MAR. APR. MAY. JUNE JULY AUG. SEPT. OCT. NOV. DEC.

BASIC CLIMATIC CONDITION

		% of year
	Comfortable period	20
	too hot	69
	too cold	11

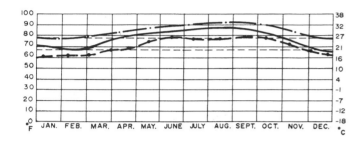

TEMPERATURE

– – – – –	range of comfortable temp.
– · – · – · –	afternoon maximum temperature
—————	average daily temperature
– •– •–	morning minimum temperature

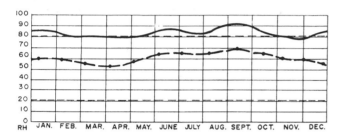

RELATIVE HUMIDITY

—————	average morning humidity
– •– •–	average afternoon humidity
– – – – –	range of comfortable humidity

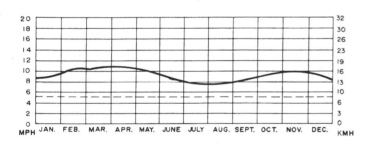

WIND SPEED

—————	mean daily wind speed
– – – – –	wind speed for effective natural ventilation

for wind direction see the wind roses in Figs. 5.6d to h.

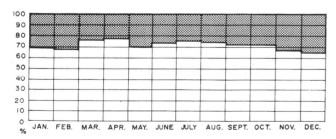

SUNSHINE
average % of daylight hours

annual sunshine = 72 %

peak solar radiation in January
horiz. ft² = 1300 btu/day
vert. ft² = 1450 btu/day

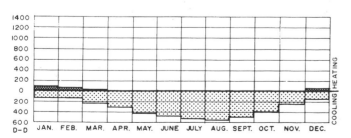

DEGREE-DAYS

annual

		annual
	heating degree-days	199
	cooling degree-days	4,095

CLIMATE REGION 17

REFERENCE CITY: LOS ANGELES, CALIFORNIA

The Climate

The semiarid climate of Southern California is very mild because of the almost constant cool winds from the ocean. Although these onshore winds bring high humidity, comfort is maintained because of the low temperatures.

Occasionally when the wind reverses, hot desert air enters the region. Because this air is dry, comfort is still maintained. There is a sharp increase in temperature and a decrease in humidity as one leaves the coast. Thus, a large variation in the local microclimates exists.

Winter temperatures are very moderate, and little heating is required. Although the annual precipitation of about 15 in. (38 cm) is not very low, the rain falls mainly in the winter. Since there is almost no rain during the summer, few plants can grow year-round without irrigation. Since sunshine is plentiful all year, solar heating, especially for hot water, is very advantageous.

Climatic Design Priorities*

1st Open the building to the outdoors since temperatures are comfortable most of the year. (XI)
2nd Protect from the summer sun. (IV)
3rd Let the winter sun in. (III)
4th Use natural ventilation for summer cooling. (V)
5th Use thermal mass to reduce day-to-night temperature swings in the summer. (VII)

*These climatic design priorities are for envelope-dominated building types only. See Section 5.9 for a list of design strategies appropriate for achieving each of these priorities. Use the Roman numerals to find the relevant lists.

Note: For an explanation of these Climatic Data Tables, see Section 5.6. Much of the material in the Climate Data Tables comes from the book *Regional Guidelines for Building Passive Energy Conserving Homes* by the AIA Research Corporation.

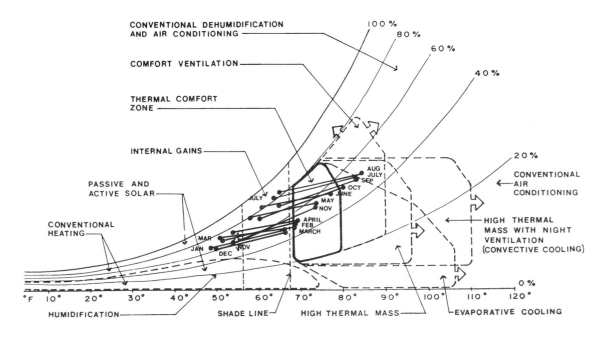

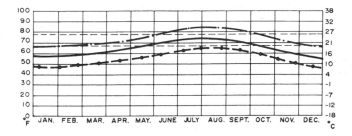

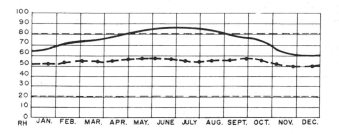

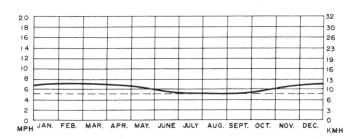

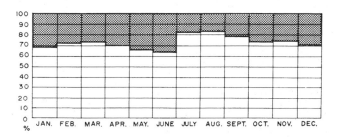

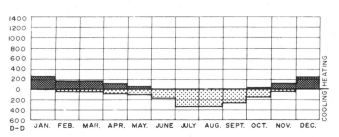

BASIC CLIMATIC CONDITION

		% of year
▨	Comfortable period	64
▨	too hot	8
☐	too cold	28

TEMPERATURE

- — — — — range of comfortable temp.
- —·—·—·— afternoon maximum temperature
- ———————— average daily temperature
- —•—•—•— morning minimum temperature

RELATIVE HUMIDITY

- ———————— average morning humidity
- —•—•—•— average afternoon humidity
- — — — — range of comfortable humidity

WIND SPEED

- ———————— mean daily wind speed
- — — — — wind speed for effective
  natural ventilation

for wind direction see the
wind roses in Figs. 5.6d to h.

SUNSHINE
average % of daylight hours

annual sunshine = 73 %

peak solar radiation in January
horiz. ft² = 900 btu/day
vert. ft² = 1200 btu/day

DEGREE-DAYS

		annual
▨	heating degree-days	1,204
▨	cooling degree-days	1,339

5.9 DESIGN STRATEGIES

The following climate-related design strategies are appropriate ways of achieving the design priorities listed in the Climatic Data Tables (above). More detailed information is found in the chapters shown in parentheses.

Winter

I. *Keep the heat in and the cold temperatures out during the winter.* (Fig. 5.9a).
   a. Avoid building on cold northern slopes. (Chapter 11)
   b. Build on the middle of slopes to avoid both the pools of cold air at the bottom and the high winds at the top of hills. (Chapter 11)
   c. Use a compact design with a minimum surface-area-to-volume ratio. For example, use two- instead of one-story buildings. (Chapter 15)
   d. Build attached or clustered buildings to minimize the number of exposed walls. (Chapter 15)
   e. Use earth sheltering in the form of underground or bermed structures. (Chapter 15)
   f. Place buffer spaces that have lower temperature requirements (closets, storage rooms, stairs, garages, gymnasiums, heavy work areas, etc.) along the north wall. Place a sun-space buffer room on the south wall. (Chapters 7 and 15)
   g. Use temperature zoning by both space and time since some spaces can be kept cooler than others at all times or at certain times. For example, bedrooms can be kept cooler during the day, and living rooms can be kept cooler at night when everyone is asleep. (Chapter 16)
   h. Minimize the window area on all orientations except south. (Chapters 7 and 15)
   i. Use double or triple glazing, low-e coatings, and movable insulation on windows. (Chapter 15)
   j. Use plentiful insulation in walls, on roofs, under floors, over crawl spaces, on foundation walls, and around slab edges. (Chapter 15)
   k. Insulation should be a continuous envelope to prevent heat bridges. Avoid structural elements that are exposed on the exterior, since they pierce the insulation. Avoid fireplaces and other masonry elements that penetrate the insulation layer. (Chapter 15)
   l. Place doors on fireplaces to prevent heated room air from escaping through the chimney. Supply fireplaces and stoves with outdoor combustion air. (Chapter 16)

II. *Protect from the cold winter winds* (Fig. 5.9b).
   a. Avoid windy locations, such as hilltops. (Chapter 11)
   b. Use evergreen vegetation to create windbreaks. (Chapter 11)
   c. Use garden walls to protect the building and especially entrances from cold winds. (Chapter 11)
   d. In very windy areas, keep buildings close to the ground (one story).
   e. Use compact designs to minimize the surface area exposed to the wind. (Chapter 15)
   f. Use streamlined shapes with rounded corners to both deflect the wind and minimize the surface-area-to-volume ratio.
   g. Cluster buildings for mutual wind protection. (Chapter 11)
   h. Use long sloping roofs, as in the New England saltbox houses, to deflect the wind over the building and to create sheltered zones on the sunny side.
   i. Place garages and other utility spaces on the winter windward side. This is usually the north, northwest, and northeast side of the building.
   j. Use sun spaces and glazed-in porches as windbreaks.
   k. Use earth sheltering or build in hollows. Also, the wind can be deflected by earth berms

Figure 5.9a Use attached buildings to reduce the exposed wall area. Use compact building forms and two-story plans. Use at least double glazing. Always use low-e glazing, and consider using movable night insulation. (Drawings from *Regional Guidelines for Building Passive Energy Conserving Homes* by the AIA Research Corporation.)

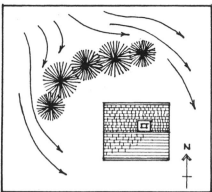
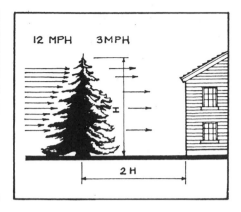

Figure 5.9b Build in wind-protected areas such as the side of a hill. Plant or build barriers against the wind. Evergreen trees are effective wind barriers. (Drawings from *Regional Guidelines for Building Passive Energy Conserving Homes* by the AIA Research Corporation.)

built against the wall or by constructing protective earth banks a short distance from the building. (Chapters 11 and 15)

l. Minimize openings, especially on the side facing the winter winds, and place the main entry on the leeward side. (Chapter 15)

m. Use storm windows, storm doors, air locks (vestibules), and revolving doors to minimize infiltration. (Chapter 15)

n. Close all attic and crawl-space vents, but see Chapter 15 for precautions against the hazards of water vapor and radon gas.

o. Use tight construction, caulking, and weather stripping to minimize infiltration. Use high-quality operable windows and doors. (Chapter 15)

p. Place outdoor courtyards on the south side of the building. (Chapter 11)

q. In winter, even windows in freestanding garden walls should be closed to protect the enclosure from cold winds.

r. In snow country, use snow fences and windscreens to keep snow from blocking entries and south-facing windows.

III. *Let the winter sun in (covered in Chapter 7 unless noted otherwise)* (Fig. 5.9c).

a. Build on south, southeast, or southwest slopes. (Chapter 11)

b. Check for solar access that might be blocked by landforms, vegetation, and man-made structures. (Chapter 11)

c. Avoid trees on the south side of the building. (Chapter 11)

d. Use only deciduous trees on the southeast and southwest sides.

e. Also, use deciduous trees on the east and west sides if winter is very long.

f. The long axis of the building should run east–west.

g. Most windows should face south.

h. Use south-facing clerestories and dormers instead of skylights.

i. Place spaces that benefit the most from solar heating along the south wall. Spaces that benefit the least should be along the north wall (e.g., storage rooms, garages). (Chapter 15)

j. Use an open floor plan to enable sun and sun-warmed

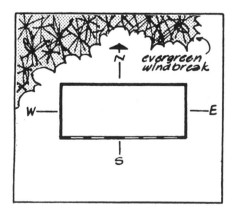

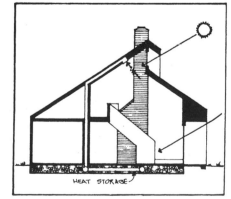

Figure 5.9c Orient building with the long side facing south. Avoid trees or other structures on the south side. Place most windows on the south facade. Use mainly vertical glazing. Use south-facing clerestory windows or dormers to bring the sun farther into the interior. (Drawings from *Regional Guidelines for Building Passive Energy Conserving Homes* by the AIA Research Corporation.)

air to penetrate throughout the building.

k. Use direct-gain, Trombe walls, and sunspaces for effective passive solar heating.

l. Use thermal mass on the interior to absorb and store solar radiation.

m. Use light-colored patios, pavements, or land surfaces to reflect additional sunlight through windows.

n. Use specular reflectors (polished aluminum) to reflect additional sunlight through windows.

o. Use active solar collectors for domestic hot water, swimming-pool heating, space heating, and process heat for industry. (Chapter 8)

p. If there is little or no summer overheating, use dark colors on exterior walls (especially the south wall).

q. Create sunny but wind-protected outdoor spaces on the south side of the building. (Chapter 11)

Summer

IV. *Protect from the summer sun (covered in Chapter 9 unless noted otherwise)* (Fig. 5.9d).

a. Avoid building on east and especially west slopes. North slopes are best if solar heating is not required in the winter, while south slopes are best if solar heating is desirable in the winter. (Chapter 11)

b. Use plants for shading. Evergreen trees can be used on the east, west, and north sides of a building. Deciduous plants are most appropriate for shading the southeast, the southwest, and the roof. Unless carefully placed, deciduous plants on the south side of a building might do more harm in the winter than good in the summer. The exception is a very hot climate with a very mild winter. (Chapter 11)

c. Avoid light-colored ground covers around the building to minimize reflected light entering windows unless daylighting is an important strategy. Living ground covers are best because they do not heat the air while they absorb solar radiation.

d. Have neighboring buildings shade each other. Tall buildings with narrow alleys between them work best. (Chapter 11)

e. Avoid reflections from adjacent structures that have white walls and/or reflective glazing.

f. Build attached houses or clusters to minimize the number of exposed walls. (Chapter 15)

g. Use free-standing or wing walls to shade the east, west, and north walls.

h. Use the form of the building to shade itself (e.g., cantilever floors, balconies, courtyards).

i. Avoid east and especially west windows if at all possible. Minimize the size and number of any east and west windows that are necessary. Project windows on east and west facades so that they face in a northerly or southerly direction.

j. Use only vertical glazing. Any horizontal or sloped glazing (skylights) should be shaded on the outside during the summer. Only skylights on steep northern roofs do not require exterior shading.

k. Use exterior shading devices on all windows except north windows in cool climates.

l. Shade not only windows but also east and especially west walls. In very hot climates, also shade the south wall.

m. Use a double or second roof (ice house roof), with the space between the roofs well ventilated. Use a parasol roof.

n. Use shaded outdoor spaces, such as porches and carports,

Figure 5.9d Orient the short side of the building to the east and west and avoid windows on these facades if possible. Use overhangs, balconies, and porches to shade both windows and walls. Use large overhanging roofs and porticoes to shade both windows and walls. (Drawings from *Regional Guidelines for Building Passive Energy Conserving Homes* by the AIA Research Corporation.)

to protect the south, east, and especially west facades.

o. Use open rather than solid shading devices to prevent trapping hot air next to the windows.

p. Use vines on trellises for shading. (Chapters 9 and 11)

q. Use movable shading devices that can retract to allow full winter sun penetration and more daylight on cloudy summer days.

r. Use highly reflective building surface (white is best). The roof and west wall are the most critical.

s. Use interior shading devices in addition to exterior shading devices.

t. Use "selective glazing" to reduce heat gain but still allow views and daylighting.

u. Place outdoor courtyards, which are intended for summer use, on the north side of the building. The east side is the next best choice. (Chapter 11)

V. *Use natural ventilation for summer cooling (covered in Chapter 10 unless noted otherwise)* (Fig. 5.9e).

a. Night ventilation that is used to cool the building in preparation for the next day is called "night flush cooling" and is described under priority VII below.

b. Natural ventilation that cools people by passing air over their skin is called "comfort ventilation."

c. Site and orient the building to capture the prevailing winds. (Chapters 10 and 11)

d. Direct and channel winds toward the building by means of landscaping and landforms. (Chapter 11)

e. Keep buildings far enough apart to allow full access to the desirable winds. (Chapter 11)

f. In mild climates where winters are not very cold and summer temperatures are not extremely high, use a noncompact shape for maximum cross-ventilation.

g. Elevate the main living space since wind velocity increases with the height above ground.

h. Use high ceilings, two-story spaces, and open stairwells for vertical air movement and for the benefits of stratification.

i. Provide cross-ventilation by using large windows on both the windward and leeward sides of the building.

j. Use fin walls to direct air through the windows.

k. Use a combination of high and low openings to take advantage of the stack effect.

l. Use roof openings to vent both the attic and the whole building. Use openings, such as monitors, cupolas, dormers,

roof turrets, ridge vents, gable vents, and soffit vents.

m. Use porches to create cool outdoor spaces and to protect open windows from sun and rain.

n. Use a double or parasol roof with sufficient clearance to allow the wind to ventilate the hot air collecting between the two roofs. (Chapter 9)

o. Use high-quality operable windows with good seals to allow summer ventilation while preventing winter infiltration. (Chapter 15)

p. Use an open floor plan for maximum air flow. Minimize the use of partitions.

q. Keep transoms and doors open between rooms.

r. Use a solar chimney to move air vertically through a building on calm, sunny days.

s. Use operable windows or movable panels in garden walls to maximize the summer ventilation of a site while allowing protection against the winter winds.

VI. *Allow natural ventilation to both cool and remove excess moisture in the summer (covered in Chapter 10 unless otherwise noted).* (Fig. 5.9f)

a. All the strategies from priority V above also apply here.

b. Elevate the main living floor above the high humidity found near the ground.

Figure 5.9e Provide many large but shaded windows for ventilation. Provide both high and low openings. Provide large openings to vent attic spaces. (Drawings from *Regional Guidelines for Building Passive Energy Conserving Homes* by the AIA Research Corporation.)

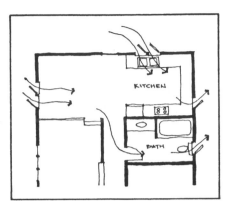

Figure 5.9f Raise the building above the moisture at ground level and ventilate under the building. Allow natural ventilation to carry away moisture from kitchens, bathrooms, and laundry rooms. Avoid dense landscaping near ground level, but a high canopy of trees is good. (Drawings from *Regional Guidelines for Building Passive Energy Conserving Homes* by the AIA Research Corporation.)

c. Use plants sparsely. Minimize low trees, shrubbery, and ground covers to enable air to circulate through the site to remove moisture. Use only trees that have a high canopy. (Chapter 11)

d. Avoid deep basements that cannot be ventilated well.

VII. *Use thermal mass to reduce day-to-night temperature swings in the summer (covered in Chapter 10 unless noted otherwise).* (Fig. 5.9g)

a. This cooling strategy is also known as "night flush cooling" because the thermal mass is usually cooled with night ventilation. See Chapter 10 for a description of this strategy.

b. Use massive construction materials since they have a high heat capacity. Use materials such as brick, concrete, stone, and adobe. (Chapter 15)

c. Place insulation on the outside of the thermal mass. (Chapter 15)

d. If massive materials are also to be used on the outside, sandwich the insulation between the inside and outside walls. (Chapter 15)

e. Use earth or rock in direct contact with the uninsulated walls. (Chapters 10 and 15)

f. Keep daytime hot air out of the building by closing all openings.

g. Open the building at night to allow cool air to enter. Use the strategies of natural ventilation, listed above in priority V, to maximize the night cooling of the thermal mass.

h. Use water as a thermal mass because of its very high heat capacity. Use containers that maximize heat transfer into and out of the water. (Chapter 7)

i. Use radiant or evaporative cooling for additional temperature drop in the thermal mass at night.

j. Use mechanical equipment at night when it is most efficient to create a heat sink. By cooling the building at night, the cool thermal mass can soak up heat the next day. (Chapter 16)

k. Use earth sheltering to maximize the benefits of mass. (Chapters 10 and 15)

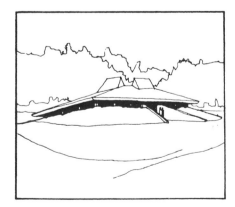

Figure 5.9g Use thermal mass to reduce the impact of high temperatures. Use the thermal mass of the earth. Use berms or sloping sites for earth-sheltered buildings. (Drawings from *Regional Guidelines for Building Passive Energy Conserving Homes* by the AIA Research Corporation.)

  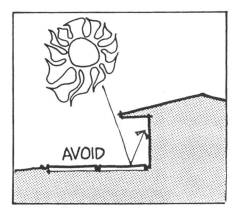

Figure 5.9h Use compact, well-insulated, and white-painted buildings. Use attached housing units to minimize the exposed wall area. Have buildings shade each other. Avoid reflecting sun into windows. (Drawings from *Regional Guidelines for Building Passive Energy Conserving Homes* by the AIA Research Corporation.)

VIII. *Keep hot temperatures out during the summer* (Fig. 5.9h).
  a. Use compact designs to minimize the surface-area-to-volume ratio. (Chapter 15)
  b. Build attached houses to minimize the number of exposed walls. (Chapters 11 and 15)
  c. Use vegetation and shade structures to maintain cool ambient air around the building and to prevent reflecting sunlight into the windows. (Chapter 11)
  d. Use earth sheltering in the form of underground or bermed structures. (Chapter 15)
  e. Use plenty of insulation in the building envelope. (Chapter 15)
  f. Use few and small windows to keep heat out.

  g. Use exterior window shutters. In hot climates use double glazing, and in very hot climates also use movable insulation over windows during the day when a space is unoccupied (e.g., a bedroom). (Chapter 15)
  h. Isolate sources of heat in a separate room, wing, or building (e.g., kitchen).
  i. Zone building so that certain spaces are cooled only while occupied. (Chapter 16)
  j. Use light-colored roofs and walls to reflect the sun's heat.

IX. *Use evaporative cooling in the summer (covered in Chapter 10 unless otherwise noted)* (Fig. 5.9i).
  a. Locate pools or fountains in the building, in a courtyard, or in the path of incoming winds.

  b. Use transpiration by plants to cool the air both indoors and outdoors.
  c. Spray water on roof, walls, and patios to cool these surfaces.
  d. Pass incoming air through a curtain of water or a wet fabric.
  e. Use a roof pond or another "indirect evaporative cooling" system.
  f. Use an "evaporative cooler." This simple and inexpensive mechanical device uses very little electrical energy.

X. *Avoid creating additional humidity during the summer* (Fig 5.9j).
  a. Do not use evaporative cooling strategies in humid climates.
  b. Use underground or drip rather than spray irrigation.
  c. Avoid pools and fountains.

  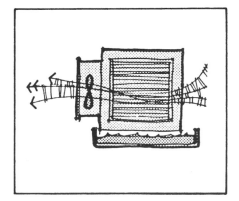

Figure 5.9i Use fountains, pools, and plants for evaporative cooling. Use courtyards to prevent cooled air from blowing away. Use energy-conserving evaporative coolers. (Drawings from *Regional Guidelines for Building Passive Energy Conserving Homes* by the AIA Research Corporation.)

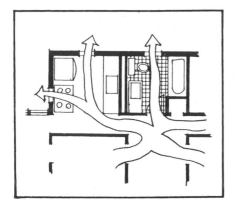

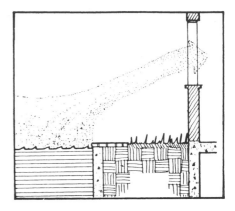

Figure 5.9j Use exhaust fans to remove excess moisture from kitchens, bathrooms, and laundry rooms. In humid climates, minimize indoor plants, and keep them out of direct sunlight to reduce transpiration. Avoid pools, fountains, and plants in the landscape. Minimize interior partitions, and provide many openings in the exterior walls. (Drawings from *Regional Guidelines for Building Passive Energy Conserving Homes* by the AIA Research Corporation.)

d. Keep the area around the building dry by providing the proper drainage of land. Channel runoff water from the roof and paved areas away from the site.

e. Use permeable paving materials to prevent puddles on the surface.

f. Minimize plants, especially indoors. Use plants that add little water to the air by transpiration. Such plants are usually native to dry climates. Use trees that have a high canopy.

g. Shade plants and pools of water both indoors and out because the heat of the sun greatly increases the rate of transpiration and evaporation.

h. Use exhaust fans in kitchens, bathrooms, laundry rooms, etc., to remove excess moisture.

XI. *Open the building to the outdoors since temperatures are comfortable much of the year* (Fig. 5.9k).

a. Create outdoor spaces with different orientations for use at different times of the year. For example, use outdoor spaces on the south side in the winter and on the north side in the summer.

b. Create outdoor living areas that are sheltered from the hot summer sun and cool winter winds.

c. Use noncompact building designs for maximum contact with the outdoors. Use an articulated building with many extensions or wings to create outdoor living spaces.

d. Use large areas of operable windows, doors, and even movable walls to increase contact with the outdoors.

e. Create pavilion-like buildings that have few interior partitions and minimal exterior walls.

Figure 5.9k Use operable and movable wall panels. Create sheltered outdoor spaces with various orientations for use at different times of day and year. (Drawings from *Regional Guidelines for Building Passive Energy Conserving Homes* by the AIA Research Corporation.)

KEY IDEAS OF CHAPTER 5

1. Because of water vapor and clouds in hot and humid climates, daytime temperatures are lower and nighttime temperatures are higher. Thus, the diurnal temperature range is small.

2. Because of lack of water in the air, hot and dry climates have high daytime temperatures and low nighttime temperatures. Thus, the diurnal temperature range is large.

3. Because of such features as elevation, form of land, large bodies of water, soil types, vegetation, and man-made objects, the microclimate can be significantly different from the regional climate.

4. The direction of the wind is given by wind roses.

5. The building bioclimatic chart is an excellent tool for understanding a climate in terms of temperatures and the coincident RH.

6. The sunshine chart indicates the relative importance of direct sunshine for shading, solar heating, and daylighting for each climate region.

7. The degree-days chart is an excellent tool for determining the depth and severity (heating and cooling loads) of winter and summer.

8. Design priorities are given for each of the seventeen climate regions detailed in this chapter. Design strategies or techniques for addressing the priorities are given at the end of the chapter.

Acknowledgment

Much of the material in this chapter was taken from the book *Regional Guidelines for Building Passive Energy Conserving Homes* by the AIA Research Corporation.

Resources

FURTHER READING

(See the Bibliography in the back of the book for full citations.)

AIA Research Corporation. *Regional Guidelines for Building Passive Energy Conserving Homes.*

ASHRAE Handbook. Fundamentals. Compatative Climatic Data for the United States.

Fitch, J. M., with W. Bobenhausen. *American Building: The Environmental Forces That Shape It.*

National Oceanic and Atmospheric Administration (NOAA). *Climate Atlas of the United States.*

Olgyay, V. *Design with Climate: A Bioclimatic Approach to Architectural Regionalism.*

Ruffner, J. A., and F. E. Bair. *The Weather Almanac.*

Stein, B., and J. Reynolds. *Mechanical and Electrical Equipment for Buildings,* 10th ed.

Watson, D., and K. Labs. *Climatic Design: Energy-Efficient Building Principles and Practices.*

WEB RESOURCES—UNITED STATES

Climate Atlas of the United States, published in 1968 and reprinted in 1983 by the National Oceanic and Atmospheric Administration (NOAA), National Climate Data Center (NCDC) (contains maps of the United States showing contour lines for various climate conditions) www.wrcc.dri.edu/climmaps

National Climatic Data Center of the United States www.ncdc.noaa.gov

National Resources Conservation Service (NRCS) www.wcc.nrcs.usda.gov www.wcc.nrcs.usda.gov/climate/prism.html

- Climate information by county
- Digital maps of precipitation
- Wind roses

USA Climate, created by Sustainable By Design www.susdesign.com/usa climate

WEB RESOURCES—WORLD

Canadian climate—National Climate Data and Information Archive (excellent source for climate of cities all over Canada) www.climate.weatheroffice.ec.gc.ca

World Climate—limited climate information for cities all over the world www.worldclimate.com

SOLAR GEOMETRY

6

It is the mission of modern architecture to concern itself with the sun.

Le Corbusier
from a letter to Sert.

6.1 INTRODUCTION

People used to worship the sun as a god; they understood how much life depended on sunshine. However, with the rapid growth of science and technology, humankind came to believe that all problems could be solved by high technology and that it was no longer necessary to live in harmony with nature. An architectural example of this attitude is the construction of an all-glass building in the desert, which can be kept habitable only by means of huge energy-guzzling air-conditioning plants.

The looming crisis of global warming must persuade us to reconsider our relationships with nature and technology. There is a deepening conviction that progress will come mainly from technology that is in harmony with nature. The fast-growing interest in sustainable or green design illustrates this shift in attitude. In architecture, this point of view is represented by buildings that let the sun shine in during the winter and are shaded from the sun in the summer (see Fig. 6.1).

This approach to architecture requires that the designer have a good understanding of the natural world. Central to this understanding is the relationship of the sun to the earth. This chapter discusses solar radiation and solar geometry.

6.2 THE SUN

The sun is a huge fusion reactor in which light atoms are fused into heavier atoms, and in the process energy is released. This reaction can occur only in the interior of the sun, where the necessary temperature of 25,000,000°F (14,000,000°C) exists. The solar radiation reaching earth, however, is emitted from the sun's surface, which is much cooler (Fig. 6.2a). Solar radiation is, therefore, the kind of radiation that a body having a temperature of about 10,000°F (5,500°C) emits. The amount and composition of solar radiation reaching the outer edge of the earth's atmosphere are quite unvarying and are called the **solar constant.** The amount and composition of the radiation reaching the earth's surface, however, vary widely with sun angles, elevation, and the composition of the atmosphere (Fig. 6.2b).

6.3 ELLIPTICAL ORBIT

The orbit of the earth is not a circle but an ellipse, so that the distance between the earth and the sun varies as the earth revolves around the sun (Fig. 6.3). The distance varies about 3.3 percent, and this results in a small

Figure 6.1 Part of the year the sun is our friend, and part of the year it is our enemy. (Drawing by Le Corbusier from Le Corbusier: *Oevre Complete, 1938–1944*, Vol. 4, by W. Boesiger, 7th ed. Verlag fuer Architektur Artemis © 1977.)

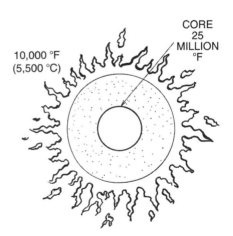

Figure 6.2a The surface temperature of the sun determines the type of radiation emitted.

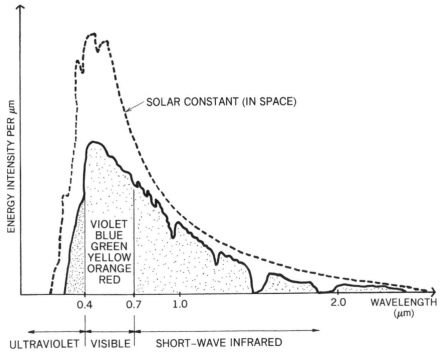

Figure 6.2b The solar spectrum at the earth's surface consists of about 47 percent visible, 48 percent short-wave infrared, and about 5 percent ultraviolet radiation.

annual variation in the intensity of solar radiation.

Does this explain why it is cooler in January than in July? No, because we are actually closer to the sun in January than July. In fact, this variation in distance from the sun slightly reduces the severity of winters and summers in the northern hemisphere. What then is the cause of the seasons?

Since the sun is very far away and since it lies in the plane of the earth's orbit, solar radiation striking the earth is always parallel to this plane (Fig. 6.3). While the earth revolves around the sun, it also spins around its own north–south axis. Since this axis is not perpendicular to the orbital plane but is tilted 23.5° off the normal to this plane, and since the orientation in space of this axis of rotation remains fixed as the earth revolves around the sun, the angle at which the sun's rays hit the earth continuously changes throughout the year. This tilt of 23.5° is the cause of the seasons and has major implications for solar design.

6.4 TILT OF THE EARTH'S AXIS

Because the tilt of the earth's axis is fixed, the Northern Hemisphere faces the sun in June and the Southern Hemisphere faces the sun in December (Fig. 6.4a). The extreme conditions occur on June 21, when the North Pole is pointing most nearly toward the sun, and on December 21, when the North Pole is pointing farthest away from the sun.

Notice that on June 21, the sun's rays are perpendicular to the earth's surface along the Tropic of Cancer, which is, not by coincidence, at latitude 23.5°N (Fig. 6.4b). No part of the earth north of the Tropic of Cancer ever has the sun directly overhead. It is also the longest day in the Northern Hemisphere, and is called the **summer solstice.** Furthermore on that day, all of the earth north of the Arctic Circle will have twenty-four hours of sunlight.

Six months later, on December 21, at the opposite end of the earth's orbit

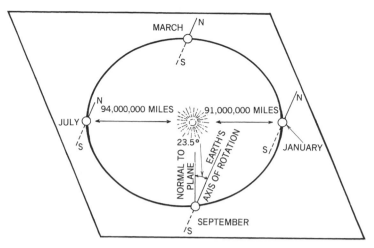

Figure 6.3 The earth's axis of rotation is tilted to the plane of the elliptical orbit. The distance to the sun is 3,000,000 miles (4,800,000 km) closer in January than in July.

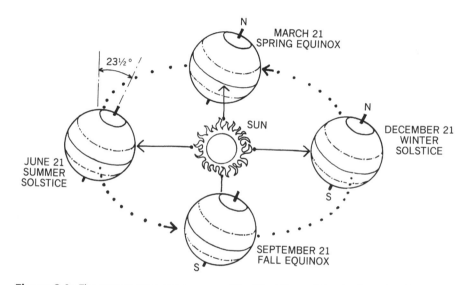

Figure 6.4a The seasons are a consequence of the tilt of the earth's axis of rotation. (From *Solar Dwelling Design Concepts* by AIA Research Corporation, U.S. Dept. Housing and Urban Development, 1976. HUD-PDR-154(4).)

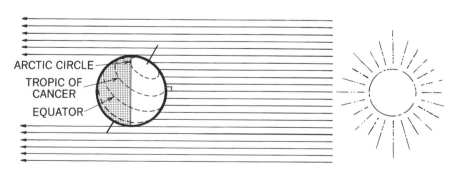

Figure 6.4b During the summer solstice (June 21), the sun is directly overhead on the Tropic of Cancer, which is 23.5°N latitude.

Figure 6.4c During the winter solstice (December 21), the sun is directly overhead on the Tropic of Capricorn, which is 23.5°S latitude.

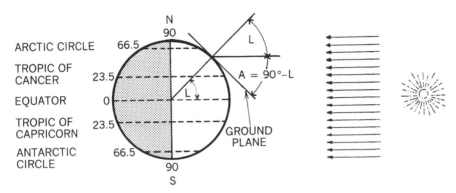

Figure 6.5a On the equinox, the sun's altitude (A) at solar noon at any place on earth is equal to 90° minus the latitude (L).

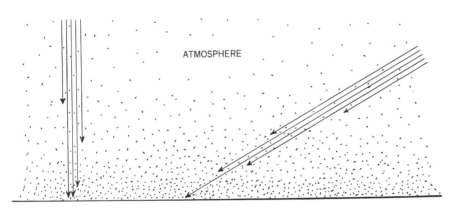

Figure 6.5b The altitude angle determines how much of the solar radiation will be absorbed by the atmosphere.

around the sun, the North Pole points so far away from the sun that now all of the earth above the Arctic Circle experiences twenty-four hours of darkness (Fig. 6.4c). In the Northern Hemisphere, this is the day with the longest night and is also known as the **winter solstice**. On this day, the sun is perpendicular to the Southern Hemisphere along the Tropic of Capricorn, which, of course, is at latitude 23.5° south. Meanwhile, the sun's rays that do fall on the Northern Hemisphere do so at much lower sun angles (altitude angles) than those striking the Southern Hemisphere.

Halfway between the longest and shortest days of the year is the day of equal nighttime and daytime hours. This situation occurs twice a year, on March and September 21, and is known as the spring and fall **equinox** (Fig. 6.4a). On these days the sun is directly overhead on the equator.

6.5 CONSEQUENCES OF THE ALTITUDE ANGLE

The vertical angle at which the sun's rays strike the earth is called the **altitude angle** and is a function of the geographic latitude, time of year, and time of day. In Fig. 6.5a we see how the altitude angle is derived from these three factors. The simplest situation occurs at 12 noon on the equinox, when the sun's rays are perpendicular to the earth at the equator (Fig. 6.5a). To find the altitude angle of the sun at any latitude, draw the ground plane tangent to the earth at that latitude. By simple geometric principles, it can be shown that the altitude angle is equal to 90° minus the latitude. There are two important consequences of this altitude angle on climate and the seasons.

The first effect of the altitude angle is illustrated by Fig. 6.5b, which indicates that at low angles the sun's rays pass through more of the atmosphere. Consequently, the radiation reaching the surface will be weaker and more modified in composition. The extreme case occurs at sunset, when the radiation is red and weak enough to be looked at. This is because of the selective absorption, reflection, and refraction of solar radiation in the atmosphere.

The second effect of the altitude angle is illustrated in the diagram of the **cosine law** (Fig. 6.5c). This law says that a given beam of sunlight will illuminate a larger area as the sun gets lower in the sky. As the given sunbeam is spread over larger areas, the sunlight on each square unit of land naturally gets weaker. The amount of sunlight that a surface receives changes with the cosine of the angle between the sun's rays and the normal to the surface.

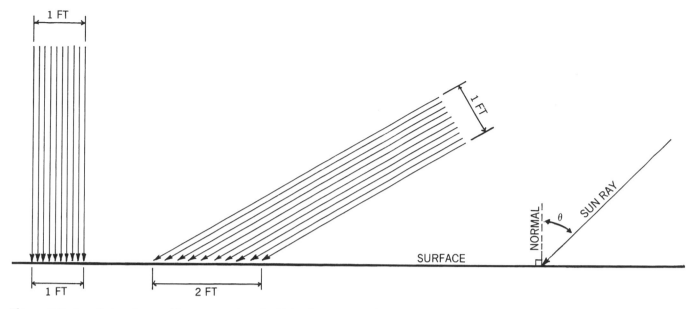

Figure 6.5c A vertical sunbeam with a cross section of 1 ft² (1 m²) will heat 1 ft² (1 m²) of land. At a certain low-altitude angle, however, that same 1 ft² (1 m²) sunbeam will heat 2 ft² (2 m²) of land. Consequently, each square foot (m²) of land receives only half the solar heating. Thus, as the altitude angle decreases, so does the heating of the land. This phenomenon is called the "cosine law," because the radiation received by a surface is a function of the cosine of angle Θ measured from the normal to the surface.

6.6 WINTER

Now we can understand what causes winter. The temperature of the air, as well as that of the land, is mainly a result of the amount of solar radiation absorbed by the land. The air is mainly heated or cooled by its contact with the earth. The reasons for less radiation falling on the ground in the winter are the following.

Most important is the fact that there are far fewer hours of daylight in the winter. The exact number is a function of latitude (see Table 5.6). As was mentioned earlier, there is no sunlight above the Arctic Circle on December 21, and at 40° latitude, for example, there are almost six fewer hours of daylight on December 21 than on June 21.

The second reason for reduced heating of the earth is the cosine law. On December 21, the solar radiation falling on a square foot (square meter) of land is significantly less than that on June 21.

Lastly, the lower sun angles increase the amount of atmosphere the sun must pass through and, therefore, there

is again less radiation reaching each square foot (square meter) of land.

6.7 THE SUN REVOLVES AROUND THE EARTH!

Despite threats of torture and death, Galileo and Copernicus spoke up and convinced the world that the earth revolves around the sun. Nevertheless, I would like to suggest, for nonreligious reasons, that we again assume that the sun revolves around the earth or at least that the sun revolves around the building in question. For the moment, this assumption makes it infinitely more convenient to understand sun angles. To make things even more convenient, let us also assume a sky dome (Fig. 6.11b), where a large clear plastic hemisphere is placed over the building site in question.

6.8 SKY DOME

In Fig. 6.8a we see an imaginary **sky dome** placed over the building site. We are interested only in the sun rays

that penetrate the sky dome on their way to the building at the center. The points where these sun rays penetrate the sky dome every hour are marked. When all the points for one day are connected, we get a line on the sky dome called the **sun path** for that day. Figure 6.8a shows the highest sun path of the year (summer solstice), the lowest sun path (winter solstice), and the middle sun paths (equinoxes). Note that the sun enters the sky dome only between the sun paths of the summer and winter solstices. Since the solar radiation is quite weak in the early and late hours of the day, the part of the sky dome through which the most powerful sun rays enter is called the **solar window.** Figure 6.8b shows the conventional solar window, which is assumed to begin at 9 A.M. and end at 3 P.M. Ideally, no trees, buildings, or other obstacles should block the sun rays entering through the solar window during those months when solar energy is desired. Space heating requires solar access only during the winter months (the lower portion of the solar window), while domestic hot-water heating and photovoltaics (PV)

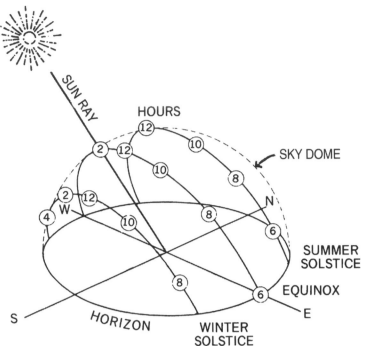

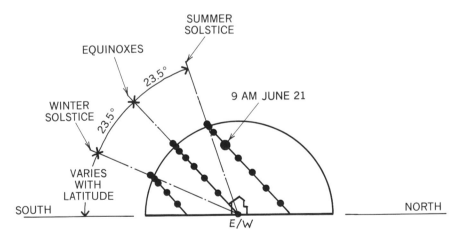

Figure 6.8a The sky dome and the three sun paths of June 21, September/March 21, and December 21 are shown. (From *Architectural Graphic Standards*, Ramsey/Sleeper 8th ed. John R. Hoke, ed. copyright John Wiley, 1988.)

Figure 6.8c An east elevation of the sky dome is shown. The east–west axis is the point at the center of the sky dome. It is also where the sun rises and sets on the equinoxes. [From *Solar Dwelling Design Concepts* by AIA Research Corporation. U.S. Dept. Housing and Urban Development, 1976. HUD-PDR-154(4).]

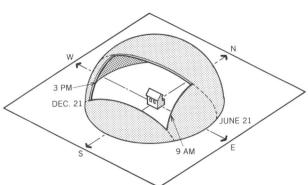

Figure 6.8b The part of the sky dome between the December 21 and June 21 sun paths is called the "solar window." Most radiation in the winter is received between 9 A.M. and 3 P.M.

The sun's motion is completely symmetrical about a north–south axis. Notice in the diagram that the sun moves 23.5° on either side of the equinoxes because of the tilt of the earth's axis of rotation. The total vertical travel between winter and summer is, therefore, 47°. The actual altitude angles, however, depend on the latitude.

6.9 DETERMINING ALTITUDE AND AZIMUTH ANGLES

By far the easiest way to work with the compound angle of sun rays is to use component angles. The most useful components are the altitude angle, which is measured in a vertical plane, and the **azimuth angle,** which is measured in a horizontal plane.

In Fig. 6.9a we see a sun ray enter the sky dome at 2 P.M. on the equinox. The horizontal projection of this sun ray lies in the ground plane. The vertical angle from this projection to the sun ray is called the **altitude.** It tells us how high the sun is in the sky. The horizontal angle, which is measured from south on a north–south line, is called the **azimuth.**

It is important to understand that the above discussions on sun angles refer only to direct radiation. Water and dust particles scatter the solar radiation (Fig. 6.9b), so that on cloudy, humid, or dusty days the diffuse

require solar access for the whole year (whole solar window).

An east elevation of the sky dome is illustrated in Fig. 6.8c. The sun paths for the summer solstice (June 21), equinoxes (March 21 and September 21), and winter solstice (December 21) are shown in edge view. The afternoon part of the sun path is directly behind the morning part. The mark for 3 P.M. is, therefore, directly behind the 9 A.M. mark labeled in the diagram.

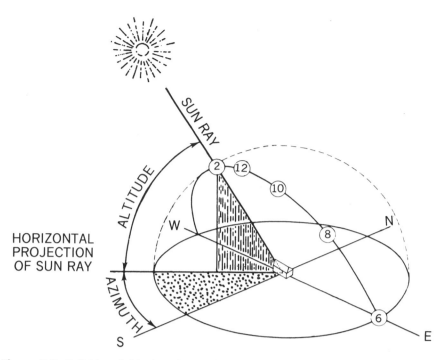

Figure 6.9a Definition of altitude and azimuth angles. (From *Architectural Graphic Standards*, Ramsey/Sleeper 8th ed. John R. Hoke, ed. copyright John Wiley, 1988).

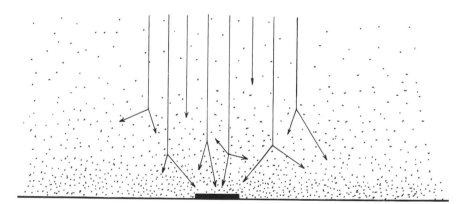

Figure 6.9b Diffuse radiation.

radiation becomes the dominant form of solar energy.

6.10 SOLAR TIME

At 12 noon **solar time**, the sun is always due south. However, the sun is not due south at 12 noon **clock time** because solar time varies from clock time. There are three reasons for this. The first is the common use of **daylight saving time**. The second

is the deviation in longitude of the building site from the standard longitude of the time zone. The third reason is a consequence of the fact that the earth's speed in its orbit around the sun changes during the year. The amount of correction, therefore, depends on the time of year. Changing solar time to clock time or vice versa is quite complicated, and fortunately, the conversion is almost never necessary since our goal is simply to collect the sun rays when it is too cold and to

reject the sun rays when it is too hot, or our goal is to collect as much sun as possible for generating hot water or electricity. Therefore, the conversion is not explained in this book, and all references to time are in solar time. The author can think of only one situation where knowing the clock time of certain sun angles is important in architecture. The situation, very rare today, is designing a temple to the sun where a beam of sunlight hits the altar at a particular clock time in order to evoke some magic.

6.11 HORIZONTAL SUN-PATH DIAGRAMS

Although altitude and azimuth angles can be readily obtained from tables, it is more informative to obtain the information from sun-path diagrams. In Fig. 6.11a we again see the sky dome, but this time it has a grid of altitude and azimuth lines drawn on it, just as a globe of the earth has latitude and longitude lines. Just as there are maps of the world that are usually either cylindrical or polar projections, there are vertical or horizontal projections of the sky dome (Fig. 6.11a). Notice how the grids project on the horizontal and vertical planes.

The sky dome shown in Fig. 6.11b has an azimuth grid, an altitude grid, and the sun paths for each month of the year for 32°N latitude. When the sun paths are plotted on a horizontal projection of the sky dome, we get a sun-path diagram such as the one shown in Fig. 6.11c. In these diagrams, the sun path of day 21 of each month is labeled by a Roman numeral (e.g., XII = December). The hours of the day are labeled along the sun path of June (VI). The concentric rings describe the altitude, and the radial lines define azimuth. The sun-path diagram for 36°N latitude is shown in Fig. 6.11c. Additional sun-path diagrams, at 4° latitude intervals, are found in Appendix A.

Example: Find the altitude and azimuth of the sun in Memphis, Tennessee, on

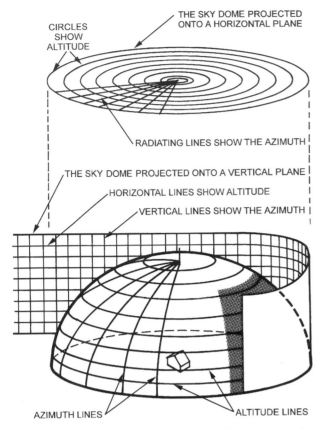

Figure 6.11a Derivation of the horizontal and vertical sun-path diagrams.

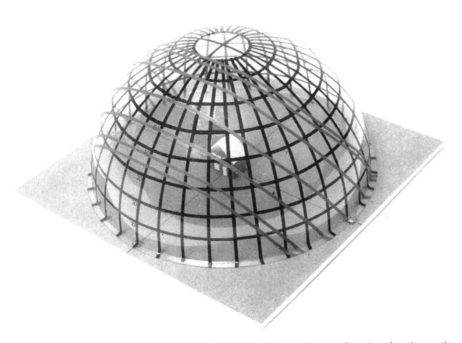

Figure 6.11b A model of the sky dome. The sun paths for the twenty-first day of each month are shown. Only seven paths are needed for twelve months because of symmetry (i.e., May 21 has the same path as July 21).

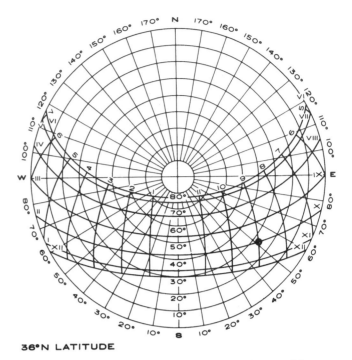

36°N LATITUDE

Figure 6.11c Horizontal sun-path diagram. A complete set of these diagrams is found in Appendix A. (From *Architectural Graphic Standards*. Ramsey/Sleeper 8th ed. John R. Hoke, ed. copyright John Wiley, 1988.)

February 21 at 9 A.M., and then draw the sunbeams representing the sun at this time on a plan and section.

Step 1. From a map of the United States, find the latitude of Memphis (see Fig. 5.6d). Since it is at about 35° latitude, use the sun-path diagram for 36°N latitude (found in Appendix A and Fig. 6.11c).

Step 2. On this sun-path diagram, find the intersection of the sun path for February 21 (curve II) and the 9 A.M. line. This point represents the location where the sun ray penetrates the sky dome. The intersection is shown as a heavy dot in Fig. 6.11c.

Step 3. From the concentric circles, the altitude is found to be about 27°.

Step 4. From the radial lines, the azimuth is found to be about 51° east of south.

Step 5. On a plan of the building, use the azimuth angle to draw the left- and rightmost sun rays through the east and south windows (Fig. 6.11d).

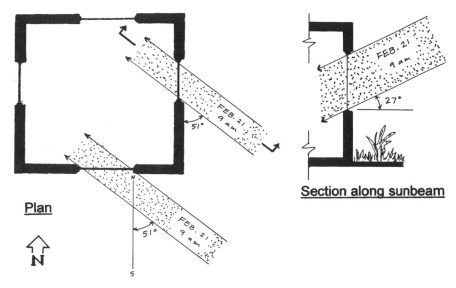

Step 6. On a section through the east window, use the altitude angle to draw the top- and bottommost sun rays (Fig. 6.11d).

Step 7. Shade in the area between the extreme sun rays at each window to create the sunbeams representing both the direction and magnitude of the sunbeams entering these windows (Fig. 6.11d).

Figure 6.11d The azimuth angle measured from a north–south line is used to draw the sunbeam in plan. The altitude angle is used to draw the sunbeam in section. To prevent graphical distortion, the section is cut along the sunbeam, as can be seen from the section marks on the east window in plan.

6.12 VERTICAL SUN-PATH DIAGRAMS

Figure 6.11a also shows how a vertical projection of the sky dome is developed. Notice that the apex point of the sky dome is projected as a line. Consequently, severe distortions occur at high altitudes. In Fig. 6.12a, we see a vertical sun-path diagram for 36°N latitude.

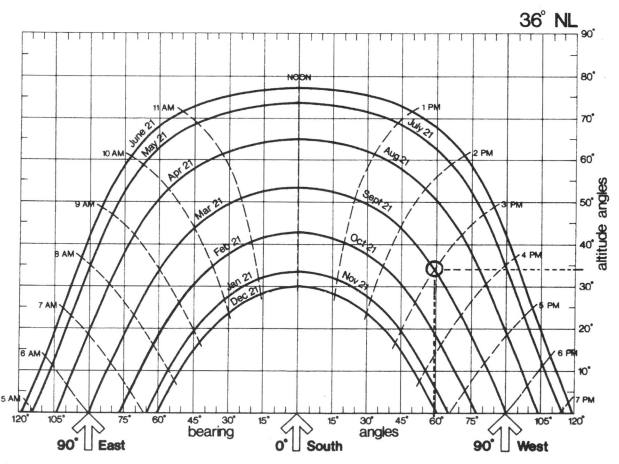

Figure 6.12a Vertical sun-path diagram. A complete set of these diagrams is found in Appendix B. (Reprinted from *The Passive Solar Energy Book*, copyright E. Mazria, 1979, by permission.)

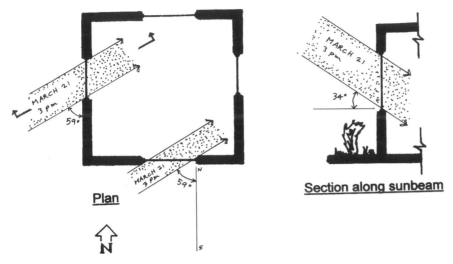

Figure 6.12b Azimuth angles are used to draw sunbeams in plan, and altitude angles are used in section. To prevent graphical distortion, the section is cut along the sunbeam, as can be seen on the west window in plan.

Altitude and azimuth angles are found in a manner similar to that used in the horizontal sun-path diagrams. Appendix B has vertical sun-path diagrams at 4-degree intervals.

Example: Find the altitude and azimuth of a sun ray in Albuquerque, New Mexico, on March 21 at 3 P.M. and then draw the sunbeams representing the sun at this time on a plan and section.

Step 1. From Appendix B, choose the sun-path diagram that is within 2° of the place in question. Since Albuquerque is at 35°N latitude, use the sun path for 36°N.

Step 2. Find the intersection of the curves for March 21 and 3 P.M. (see the circle in Fig. 6.12a).

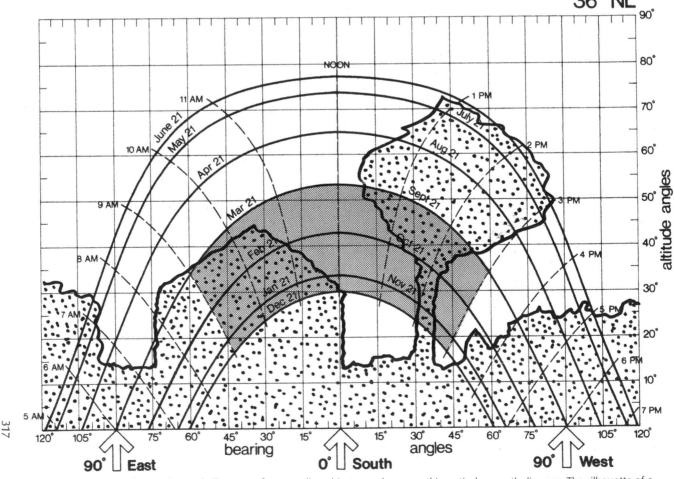

Figure 6.12c The winter solar window and silhouette of surrounding objects are shown on this vertical sun path diagram. The silhouette of a specific location was hand-drawn by means of a site-evaluation tool described in Section 6.14. (Sun path diagram from *The Passive Solar Energy Book,* copyright E. Mazria, 1979, reprinted by permission.)

Step 3. From the horizontal scale, the azimuth is found to be about 59° *west* of south.

Step 4. From the vertical scale, the altitude is found to be about 34° above the horizontal.

Step 5. On a plan of the building, use the azimuth angle to draw the left- and rightmost sun rays through the west and south windows (Fig. 6.12b).

Step 6. On a section through the west window, use the altitude angle to draw the bottom- and topmost sun ray (Fig. 6.12b).

Step 7. Shade in the area between the extreme sun rays at each window to create the sunbeams (Fig. 6.12b).

Besides being a source of sun-angle data, all sun-path diagrams are very helpful in creating a mental model of the sun's motion across the sky. The diagrams can also be used for visualizing and documenting the solar window and any obstacles that might be blocking it. The finely shaded area of Fig. 6.12c is the winter solar window from 9 A.M. to 3 P.M. The roughly shaded area along the bottom represents the silhouette of trees and buildings surrounding a particular site. Notice that one building and one tree are partially blocking the solar window during the critical winter months. The easiest and quickest way to generate such a horizon profile is to use the site-evaluation tools described in Section 6.14.

Although sun-path diagrams are invaluable for understanding solar geometry, sometimes it is easier to get the altitude and azimuth angles from a table. Thus, Appendix C provides a table of altitude and azimuth angles for every 4° of latitude from the equator to the poles.

6.13 SUN-PATH MODELS

Three-dimensional models of the sun-path diagrams are especially helpful in understanding the complex geometry of sun angles (Fig. 6.13). For simplicity only the sun paths for June 21, March/September 21, and December 21 are shown. These models can help a designer better visualize how the sun will relate to a building located at the center of the sun-path model.

The various models illustrate how sun paths vary with latitude. Models are shown for the special latitudes of the Equator at 0°, the Tropic of Cancer at 23.5° (the model is for 24°), the Arctic Circle at 66.5° (the model

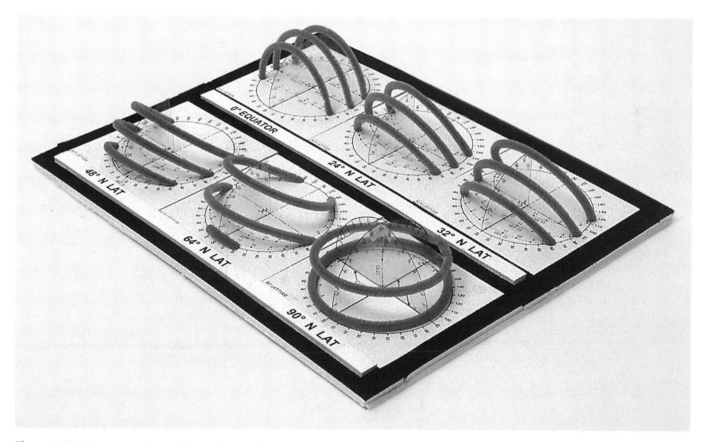

Figure 6.13 Various sun-path models are shown to illustrate how sun angles vary with latitude. In each case, the highest sunpath is for June 21, the middle for March/September 21, and the lowest for December 21. Thus, the sun paths for all other months would be located between the highest and lowest sun paths.

is for 64°), and the North Pole at 90°. Appendix F presents complete instructions and a set of charts required to create a sun-path model at 4° intervals of latitude. It is worthwhile to spend the fifteen minutes required to make one of these sun-path models. The model can be placed on the corner of the designer's table to be a reminder of where the sun is at different times of the day and year.

6.14 SOLAR SITE-EVALUATIONS TOOLS

A solar building on a site that does not have access to the sun is a total disaster. Fortunately, there are good tools available for analyzing a site in regard to solar access. Appendix H presents information on how to buy or build your own low-cost site-evaluation tool similar to the one shown in Fig. 6.14.

As Fig. 6.14 illustrates, the site is viewed through the device in such a manner that the sun-path diagrams are superimposed on an image of the site. It is then immediately clear to what extent the solar window is blocked.

The Solar Pathfinder™, ASSET, and the Sun Eye™ are commercially available site-evaluation tools. See Appendix H for more information about solar site-evaluation tools.

One serious drawback of any site-evaluation tool is that it indicates the solar access only for the spot where the tool is used. It cannot easily determine the solar access for the roof of a proposed multistory building. There is, however, a solution to this problem. A scale model of the site analyzed with a heliodon is an excellent method of evaluating the site for solar access. The scale model can then also be used for the design and presentation stages of the building project.

6.15 HELIODONS

To simulate shade, shadows, sun penetration, and solar access on a scale model, a device called a **heliodon** is used. A heliodon simulates the relationship between the sun and a building. The three variables that affect this relationship are latitude, time of year, and time of day. Every heliodon has a light source, an artificial ground plane, and three adjustments so that the light will strike the ground plane at the proper angle corresponding to the latitude, time of year, and time of day desired. In the heliodon shown in Fig. 6.15a, we can see the light moving on a circular track to stimulate time of day. The track slides forward and back to simulate time of year, and it is tilted to simulate the latitude.

Heliodons are excellent tools for creating solar-responsive designs. Because of the compound angles created by sunrays, graphical tools are awkward and/or misleading. Experience has shown that although computer models are powerful, physical models are still better. It is well known that a picture is worth a thousand words, but it is less well known that a model is worth a thousand pictures. Physical modeling is very easy to understand, infinitely flexible, and inexpensive once you have a heliodon, and some heliodons are very inexpensive.

As powerful and flexible tools, heliodons have many uses in both teaching and design. Heliodons are excellent tools for teaching both solar geometry and specific design strategies like overhangs and fins for shading. In the design process they have several functions:

1. Site analysis for determining solar access
2. Design of the building form
3. Design of specific features such as shading devices
4. Analysis of alternative designs
5. Presentation either live or through photographs or videos

Because heliodons are such powerful tools, the author believes that

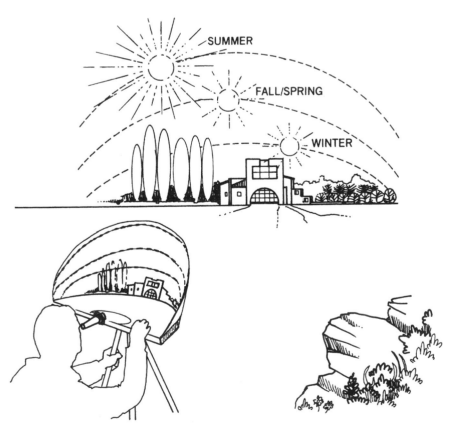

Figure 6.14 The vertical sun-path diagram is used as part of a solar-site evaluation tool. South is always straight ahead when using this tool.

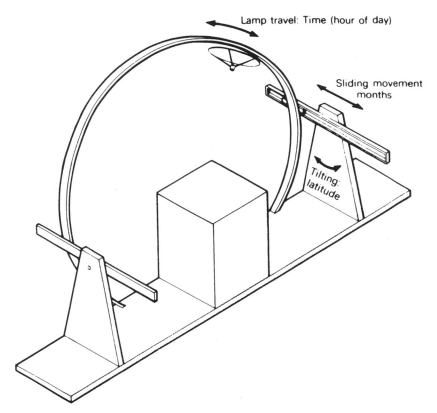

Figure 6.15a This type of heliodon ("solarscope B") was developed by Szokolay. (From *Environmental Science Handbook for Architects and Builders* by S. V. Szokolay, copyright John Wiley, 1980.)

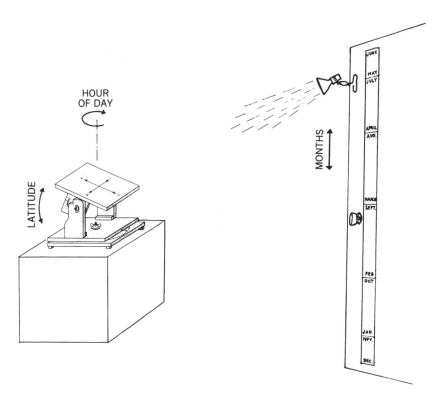

Figure 6.15b This tabletop heliodon is a practical and appropriate tool for every architect, planner, developer, and landscape architect.

every architecture firm and every architecture school should have at least one. For this reason, Appendix I gives information on how to build or where to buy a heliodon. Since there are many kinds of heliodons, the advantages and disadvantages of the major ones are discussed below.

The tabletop heliodon shown in Fig. 6.15b consists of a model stand, which rests on a table, and a clip-on lamp, which is supported by the edge of an ordinary door. The adjustment for time of year is made by moving the light up or down along the door edge. The model stand is tilted for the latitude and rotated about a vertical axis for the time-of-day adjustment.

This heliodon is very easy and inexpensive to construct (about 30 dollars). Another virtue of this heliodon is that even though it can accommodate large models, it is lightweight and compact, making it easy to store or to carry. Because of the many virtues of this type of heliodon, complete instructions for its use and construction are included in Appendix I.

This heliodon, unlike the ones described later, can be taken outdoors and used with the parallel light from the sun. Consequently, the use of sundials for model testing is explained next.

6.16 SUNDIALS FOR MODEL TESTING

The least expensive way to test models for shading, solar access, and daylighting is to use a sundial (Fig. 6.16). Instead of using a sundial, the conventional way to determine time from the position of the sun, the sundial is rotated and tilted until the desired analysis time and date are achieved from the actual position of the sun at the time of testing. Thus, a sundial would be mounted on a model so that its south and that of the model align. The model along with the sundial is then rotated and tilted until the shadow of the gnomon points to the time and day to be analyzed. Instructions for making sundials for

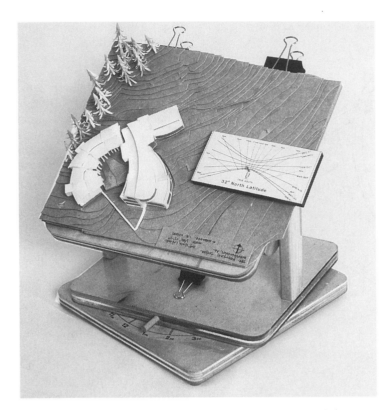

Figure 6.16 Sundials can be used to test models either under sunlight or a remote electric light source.

various latitudes can be found in Appendix E. The tabletop heliodon can be used to hold the model at the appropriate orientation and tilt. See the "Alternate Mode of Use of the Heliodon" in Section I.4 of Appendix I for instructions on how to use the sundial in conjunction with the heliodon.

Sundials have important advantages and disadvantages in regard to testing physical models. When one uses the sun as a source of light, great accuracy can be achieved in modeling shadows and sunbeams. However, this mode of testing is limited to daytime on sunny days, which are not common in some climates and some times of the year. A slightly less accurate but sometimes more practical use of the sundial is in conjunction with an electric light source, such as a slide projector at the end of a corridor. The farther the light source is from the model, the more parallel are the light rays.

The author believes that sundials are great for making accurate photographs

Figure 6.17a The Sun Simulator heliodon was developed by the author at Auburn University, Alabama.

of finished designs and for studying daylight models outdoors, while conceptually clear heliodons are better during the design process for understanding solar access and shading.

6.17 CONCEPTUALLY CLEAR HELIODONS

Two new types of heliodons have been developed by the author at Auburn University. They are three-dimensional models of the solar window, with each month's sun path represented by an arch. Thus, even before any lights are turned on, the heliodons are powerful tools to teach solar geometry. Because the ground plane (model) is always horizontal, these heliodons simulate our everyday experience of the sun revolving over a building site. They make solar geometry so simple that even a child can understand it. Because of this clarity, they are called "conceptually clear heliodons."

The first conceptually clear heliodon to be developed was the "Sun Simulator" (Fig. 6.17a). It was built for the latitude of Auburn (32°) and is about 15 ft (4.5 m) in diameter so that large models can be tested in front of a whole class. Because of the annual symmetry, all twelve months can be simulated with only seven arches, as can be seen on any sun-path diagram. There is one light for each hour of the day that can be conveniently switched on to make model testing very easy. To increase the range of latitudes that can be simulated, the model table can be tilted up to 5° each way. Conceptual clarity is not lost if the model is tilted only a few degrees. This adjustment allows the testing of models from as far south as Miami to as far north as San Francisco. Complete CAD drawings are available for free from the author to build such a heliodon for any latitude (see Appendix I).

The "Sun Emulator" heliodon was developed by the author for those schools and architectural firms that don't have room or the resources to build their own heliodon (Fig. 6.17b). The Sun Emulator was designed to be completely assembled at the factory, and it is as large as possible while still fitting through a 3 ft (0.9 m) door. It can simulate any latitude from the equator to the poles and still have the model's ground plane completely horizontal. Because the lights are only 3 ft (0.9 m) from the center of the table, models need to be small for accuracy. For more information about the Sun Emulator, see Appendix I.

6.18 CONCLUSION

The concepts presented in this chapter on the relationship between the sun and the earth are fundamental for an understanding of much of this book. The chapters on passive solar energy, shading, passive cooling, and daylighting depend heavily on the information presented here.

Because solar geometry is very complicated, the author highly recommends a heliodon for every architect, planner, and developer, as well as for schools of architecture and science museums. There is an appropriate model and price for every situation.

Figure 6.17b The Sun Emulator heliodon was developed for those architecture schools and firms that do not have the room for a permanently fixed heliodon such as the Sun Simulator. The conceptually clear Sun Emulator is completely assembled at the factory and, when stored, requires a floor area of only 3 × 6 ft (1 × 2 m).

KEY IDEAS OF CHAPTER 6

1. Solar radiation reaching the earth's surface consists of about 47 percent visible, 48 percent short-wave infrared (heat), and about 5 percent ultraviolet radiation.
2. Winter is the result of a shorter number of daylight hours, the filtering effect of lower sun angles, and the cosine law.
3. The sun is 47° higher in the sky in the summer than in the winter.
4. Sun angles are defined by altitude and azimuth angles. The altitude is measured from the horizontal and the azimuth from south.
5. The solar window is that part of the sky dome through which the sun shines.
6. Sun-path diagrams present both the pattern of the sun's motion across the sky and specific sun-angle data.
7. Sun-path models and sundials are simple tools for achieving solar-responsive architecture.
8. The solar access to a site can be determined by "site evaluation tools."
9. A heliodon is a powerful tool for achieving solar-responsive architecture.

Resources

HELIODONS

For more information on how to build or purchase a heliodon, see Appendix I.

FURTHER READING

(See the Bibliography in the back of the book for full citations.)

Anderson, B. *Solar Energy*.
Bennett, R. *Sun Angles for Design*.
Knowles, R. L. *Ritual House*.
Mazria, E. *The Passive Solar Energy Book*.
Stein, B., J. S. Reynolds, W. T., Grondzik, and A. G. Kwok. *Mechanical and Electrical Equipment for Buildings*.

PAPERS

Knowles, R. L. "Rhythm and Ritual," www-rcf.usc.edu/~rknowles
Knowles, R. L. "On Being the Right Size," www-rcf.usc.edu/~rknowles

PASSIVE SOLAR

7

The useful practice of the "Ancients" should be employed on the site so that loggias should be filled with winter sun, but shaded in the summer.

Leone Battista Alberti
from his treatise **De Re Aedificatoria,** *1452,*
the first modern work on architecture,
which influenced the development of
the Renaissance architectural style.

Orientation is 80 percent of passive solar design.

Doug Balcomb,
solar scientist

7.1 HISTORY

Although the ancient Greeks used the sun to heat their homes, the benefits were modest because much of the captured heat escaped again through the open windows. The efficient and practical Romans first solved this problem by using glass in their windows sometime around 50 A.D. The glass created an efficient heat trap by what we now call the **greenhouse effect**. The idea worked so well that the Romans found a variety of uses for it.

The upper classes often added a sunroom (heliocaminus) to their villas. Greenhouses produced fruits and vegetables year-round. The later, more modern version of the Roman baths usually faced the winter sunset (south-west) when the solar heat was most needed. Solar heating was important enough that Roman architects, such as Vitruvius, wrote about it in their books.

With the fall of Rome, the use of solar energy declined, and Europe entered the Dark Ages. During the Renaissance, architects such as Palladio read and appreciated the advice of the Roman architect Vitruvius. Palladio utilized such classical principles as placing summer rooms on the north side and winter rooms on the south side of a building. Unfortunately, northern Europe copied the style but not the principles that guided Palladio.

The seventeenth century in northern Europe saw a revival of solar heating, but not for people. Exotic plants from newly discovered lands, and the appetite of a sizable upper class for oranges and other warm-climate fruits, created a need for greenhouses (Fig. 7.1a). With the invention of better glass-making techniques, the eighteenth century became known as the "age of the greenhouse." Eventually, those greenhouses that were attached to the main building became known as **conservatories** (see Fig. 7.1b). These, like our modern **sunspaces,** were used for growing plants, added space to the living area, and helped heat the main house in the winter. This use of the sun, however, was reserved for the rich.

The idea of solar heating for everyone did not start in Europe until the 1920s. In Germany, housing projects were designed to take advantage of the sun. Walter Gropius of the Bauhaus was a leading supporter of this new movement. The research and accumulated experience with solar design then slowly made its way across the Atlantic with men like Gropius and Marcel Breuer.

7.2 SOLAR IN AMERICA

Passive solar design also has Native American roots. Many of the early Native American settlements in the Southwest show a remarkable understanding of passive solar principles. One of the most interesting is Pueblo Bonito (Fig. 7.2a), where the housing in the south-facing semicircular village stepped up to give each home full access to the sun and the massive construction stored the heat for nighttime use.

Figure 7.1a The orangery on the grounds of the royal palace in Prague, the Czech Republic, has an all-glass south facade and an opaque roof, which are typical of the greenhouses that became popular in the eighteenth century.

Figure 7.1b Conservatories supplied plants, heat, and extra living space for the upper classes in nineteenth-century Europe. Conservatory of Princess Mathilde Bonaparte, Paris, about 1869. (From *Uber Land und Meer, Allgemeine Illustrierte Zeitung*, 1868.)

Figure 7.2a Pueblo Bonito, Chaco Canyon, New Mexico, built about 1000 A.D., is an example of an indigenous American solar village. (From *Houses and House-Life of the American Aborigines* by Lewis Morgan [contributions to *North American Ethnology*. Vol. 4], U.S. Department of the Interior/U.S. G.P.O., 1881.)

Some of the colonial buildings in New England also show an appreciation of good orientation. The saltbox, as shown in Fig. 7.2b, had a two-story wall with numerous windows facing south to catch the winter sun. The one-story north wall had few windows and a long roof to deflect the cold winter winds.

Aside from these early examples, the heating of homes with the sun made slow progress until the 1930s, when a number of different American architects started to explore the potential of solar heating. One of the leaders was George Fred Keck, who built many successful solar homes (Fig. 7.2c). The pioneering work of these American architects, the influence of the immigrant Europeans, and the memory of the wartime fuel shortages made solar heating very popular during the initial housing boom at the end of World War II. But the slightly higher initial cost of solar homes and the continually falling price of fuels resulted in public indifference to solar heating by the late 1950s.

7.3 SOLAR HEMICYCLE

One of the most interesting solar homes built during this time was the Jacobs II House (Fig. 7.3a), designed by Frank Lloyd Wright. Figure 7.3b shows a floor plan of this house, which Wright called a **solar hemicycle.** As usual, Wright was ahead of his time, because this building would in many ways make a fine passive home by present-day standards. For example, most of the glazing faces the winter sun but is well shaded from the summer sun by a 6-ft (1.8 m) overhang (Fig. 7.3c). Plenty of thermal mass, in the form of stone walls and a concrete floor slab, stores heat for the night and prevents overheating during the day (Fig. 7.3d). The building is insulated to reduce heat loss, and an earth berm protects the northern side. The exposed stone walls are cavity walls filled with vermiculite insulation. Windows on opposite sides of the building allow cross-ventilation during the summer.

Like most of Wright's work, the design of this house is very well

Figure 7.2b The New England saltbox faced the sun and turned its back to the cold northern winds. (From *Regional Guidelines for Building Passive Energy Conserving Homes*, by AIA. Research Corporation, U.S. G.P.O., 1980.)

Figure 7.2c One of the first modern solar houses in America. Architect, George Fred Keck, Chicago, 1940s. (Courtesy of Libby-Owens-Ford Co.)

Figure 7.3a The Jacobs II House, Architect, Frank Lloyd Wright, Madison, Wisconsin, circa 1948. (Photograph by Ezra Stoller © Esto.)

Figure 7.3d Interior view of the Jacobs II House. (Photograph by Ezra Stoller © Esto).

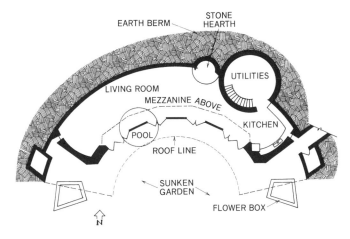

Figure 7.3b Plan of the Jacobs II house.

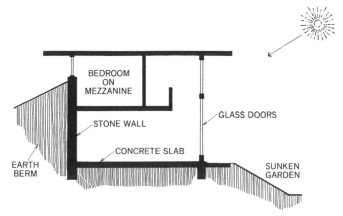

Figure 7.3c Section of the Jacobs II house.

integrated. For example, the curved walls not only create a sheltered patio, but also very effectively resist the pressure of the earth berm, just as a curved dam resists the pressure of the water behind it. The abundant irregularly laid stone walls supply the thermal mass while relating the interior to the natural environment of the building site. Successfully integrating the psychological and functional demands seems to produce the best architecture. This is what the truly great architects have in common.

7.4 LATEST REDISCOVERY OF PASSIVE SOLAR

From the late 1950s until the mid-1970s, it was widely assumed that active solar systems, with their mechanical gadgets, had the greatest potential for harnessing the sun. Slowly, however, it was realized that using active collectors for space heating would add significantly to the first costs of a home, while passive solar heating could be achieved with little or no additional first costs. It also became apparent that passive solar systems had lower maintainance and higher reliability.

Possibly the greatest advantage of passive solar is that it usually results in a more pleasant indoor environment, while active collectors only supply heat. The Human Services Field Office in Taos, New Mexico, is a pleasant place to work because of the abundance of sunlight that enters, especially in the winter (Fig. 7.4a). A sawtooth arrangement on the east and west walls enables the windows on those facades to also face south. There are also continuous clerestory windows across the whole roof so that even interior rooms have access to the sun. Black-painted water drums just inside the clerestory windows store heat for nighttime use, while insulated shutters reduce the heat loss.

Much of the renewed interest in passive solar occurred in New Mexico not only because of the plentiful sun, but also because of the presence of a community of people who were willing to experiment with a different lifestyle. An example is the idealistic developer Wayne Nichols, who built many solar houses, including the well-known Balcomb House, described later. As so often happens, successful experiments in alternate lifestyles are later adopted by the mainstream culture. Passive solar is now being accepted by the established culture because it has proved to be a very good idea.

Passive solar heating is also gaining popularity in other countries. Successful passive solar houses are even being built in climates with almost constant clouds and gloomy weather, such as northern Germany at a latitude of 54°. This is the same latitude as that of southern Alaska (Fig. 7.4b). The success of passive buildings in so many different climates is a good indication of the validity of this approach to design.

Passive solar also provides security from power interruptions and the possibility of extremely high energy costs. With so many benefits, passive solar should be a fundamental part of every building design.

Figure 7.4a The Human Services Field Office, Taos, New Mexico (1979), has all of its windows facing 20° east of south to take advantage of the winter morning sun. The clerestory windows, which cover the whole roof, supply both daylight and solar heat.

Figure 7.4b Integrated passive and hybrid solar multiple housing, Berlin, 1988. (Courtesy of and copyright Institute fur Bau-, Umwelt- und Solar Forschung.)

7.5 PASSIVE SOLAR

"Passive solar" refers to a system that collects, stores, and redistributes solar energy without the use of fans, pumps, or complex controllers. It functions by relying on the integrated approach to building design, where the basic building elements, such as windows, walls, and floors, have as many different functions as possible. For example, the walls not only hold up the roof and keep out the weather but also act as heat-storage and heat-radiating elements. In this way, the various components of a building simultaneously satisfy architectural, structural, and energy requirements.

Every passive solar heating system has at least two elements: a collector consisting of south-facing glazing and an energy-storage element that usually consists of thermal mass, such as rock or water.

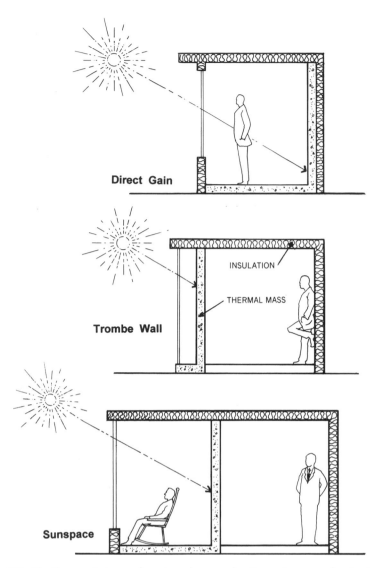

Figure 7.5a The three main types of passive solar space-heating systems are: direct gain, Trombe wall, and sunspace.

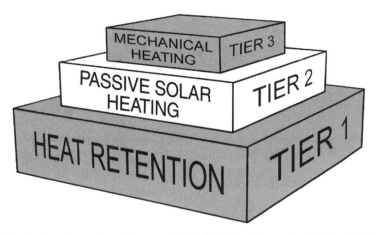

Figure 7.5b Passive solar heating is the second tier of the three-tier approach to sustainable design. The first tier is heat retention.

Depending on the relationship of these two elements, there are several possible types of passive solar systems. Figure 7.5a illustrates the three main concepts:

1. Direct gain
2. Trombe wall
3. Sunspace

Each of these popular space-heating concepts will be discussed in more detail. The chapter will conclude with a discussion of a few less common passive space-heating systems.

Passive solar is part of the rational design accomplished through the three-tier design approach (Fig. 7.5b). The first tier consists of minimizing heat loss through the building envelope by proper insulation, orientation, and surface-area-to-volume ratios. The better the architect designs the thermal barrier, the less heating will be required. The second tier, which consists of harvesting the sun's energy by passive means, is explained in this chapter. The mechanical equipment and fossil energy of the third tier are needed only to supply the small amount of heating not provided by tiers one and two. A passive solar building can provide 60 to 80 percent of the required heating in the United States.

7.6 DIRECT-GAIN SYSTEMS

Every south-facing window creates a **direct-gain system**, while windows facing east, west, and especially north lose more heat than they gain in the winter. The greenhouse effect, described in Chapter 3, acts as a one-way heat valve. It lets the short-wave solar energy enter but blocks the heat from escaping (Fig. 7.6a). The thermal mass inside the building then absorbs this heat, both to prevent daytime overheating and to store it for nighttime use (Fig. 7.6b). The proper ratio of mass to south-facing glazing is critical.

The graph in Fig. 7.6c shows the heating effect of south glazing in a building with the conventional

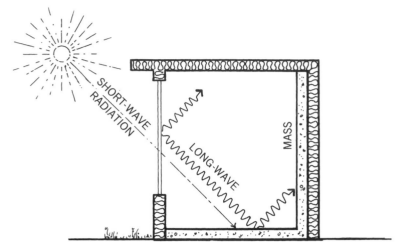

Figure 7.6a The greenhouse effect collects and traps solar radiation during the day.

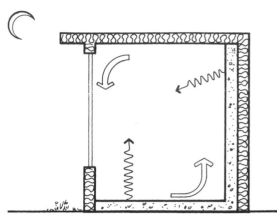

Figure 7.6b The thermal mass stores the heat for nighttime use while preventing overheating during the day.

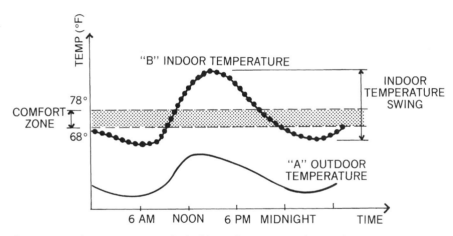

Figure 7.6c A low-mass passive solar building will experience a large indoor temperature swing during a twenty-four-hour period of a winter day. The comfort zone is assumed to be 68° to 78°F (20° to 25°C).

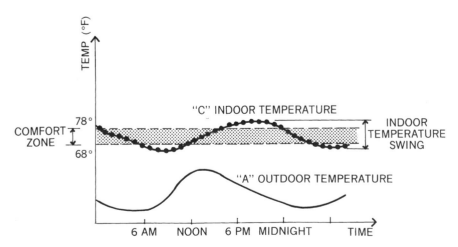

Figure 7.6d A high-mass passive solar building will experience only a small indoor temperature swing during a winter day.

heating turned off. Curve "A" is the outdoor temperature during a typical cold but sunny day. Curve "B" describes the indoor temperature in a direct-gain system with little mass. Notice the large indoor temperature swing from day to night. In the early afternoon, the temperature will be much above the comfort zone, while late at night it will be below the comfort zone. Increasing the area of south glazing will not only raise the curve but also increase the temperature swing. The overheating in the afternoon will then be even worse.

In the graph of Fig. 7.6d, we see the benefits of thermal mass. Although the outdoor temperature is the same as in Fig. 7.6c, the indoor temperature (curve "C") is almost entirely within the comfort zone. The thermal mass has reduced the amplitude of the temperature swing so that little overheating occurs in the afternoon and little overcooling at night. Thus, the designer's goal is to get the right mix of south glazing area and thermal mass so that the indoor temperature fluctuates within the comfort zone.

The ideal and most convenient location for thermal mass is the floor, because it receives the most direct sunlight, and floor heating is the most comfortable type of heating. Thus, in most situations, a concrete floor slab should be used. A modern concrete floor is sustainable, healthy, and beautiful. Rich colors and patterns are possible through the use of colored concrete, stains, or special aggregates near the surface. The concrete can also be hardened and polished to create a very durable, smooth finish. Thus, additional floor coverings that interfere with heat absorption/release are unnecessary.

Since in direct gain the building is the collector, all contents, such as the drywall, furniture, and books, act as thermal mass. However, the contents are usually not sufficient if there is no exposed concrete floor slab, and additional thermal mass must be added. The thermal mass can be masonry, water, or a phase-change material. These alternatives will be discussed in more detail later in this chapter.

Although solar heat can be supplied by convection to the rooms on the north side of a building, it is much better to supply solar radiation directly by means of south-facing clerestory windows, as shown in Fig. 7.6e. Skylights, although not as good as clerestories, can still be used if a reflector is included, as shown in Fig. 7.6f. The same reflector can also shade some of the summer sun if it is moved to the position shown in Fig. 7.6g.

Frank Lloyd Wright's solar hemicycle, described above, is a good example of the direct-gain approach. Although the Urban Villa shown in Fig. 7.6h and as a case study (see Section 17.3) also has a curved, south-facing wall, most direct-gain systems consist of straight walls facing due south or as

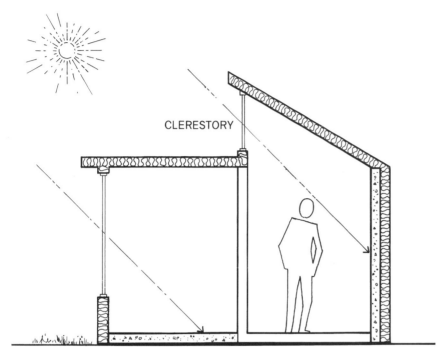

Figure 7.6e Use clerestory windows to bring the solar radiation directly to interior or north-facing rooms.

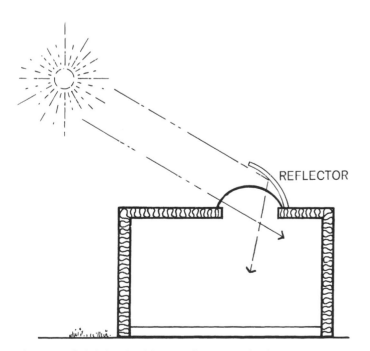

Figure 7.6f Skylights should use a reflector to make them more effective in the winter.

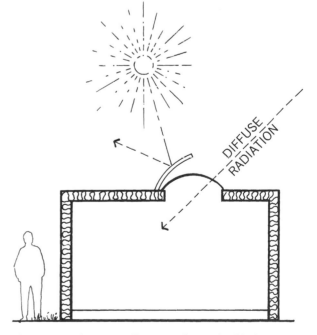

Figure 7.6g The same reflector can be used to block excessive summer sun.

Figure 7.6h The Urban Villa has a large south-facing façade that is 40 percent glass. It minimizes heat loss by using superinsulation, many shared walls, and a compact design. Summer comfort is achieved through ventilation and shading. The building is explained as a case study in Section 17.3. (Photograph from CADDET Technical Brochure No. 64)

Table 7.7A Rules For Estimating Optimum Areas of South-Facing Glazing For Direct-Gain and Trombe Walls				
			Heating Load Contributed by Solar (%)	
Climate Region (see Chapter 5)	Reference City	South Glazing Area as a Percentage of Floor Area*	No Night Insulation	With Night Insulation†
1	Hartford, CT	35	19	64
2	Madison, WI	40	17	74
3	Indianapolis, IN	28	21	60
4	Salt Lake City, UT	26	39	72
5	Ely, NE	23	41	77
6	Medford, OR	24	32	60
7	Fresno, CA	17	46	65
8	Charleston, SC	14	41	59
9	Little Rock, AK	19	38	62
10	Knoxville, TN	18	33	56
11	Phoenix, AZ	12	60	75
12	Midland, TX	18	52	72
13	Fort Worth, TX	17	44	64
14	New Orleans, LA	11	46	61
15	Houston, TX	11	43	59
16	Miami, FL	2	48	54
17	Los Angeles, CA	9	58	72

*Use the floor area of those parts of the building that will receive benefits from solar heating either by direct radiation or by convection from the solar-heated parts of the building.
†High-efficiency windows with an R_{IP} over 4 [R_{SI} over 0.7] can be used instead of night insulation. However, using night insulation in addition to high-performance windows is even better.

close to south as possible. Of all the passive systems, direct gain is the most efficient when energy collection and first costs are the main concerns.

7.7 DESIGN GUIDELINES FOR DIRECT-GAIN SYSTEMS

Area of South Glazing

Use Table 7.7A as a guideline for initial sizing of south-facing glazing. The table is based on the seventeen climate regions described in Chapter 5. The last column shows how much more effective passive heating systems are when night insulation is used over the windows or when high-efficiency windows are used.

Notes on Table 7.7A

1. The table presents *optimum* south-glazing areas.
2. Smaller south-glazing areas than those shown in the table will still supply a significant amount of heat.
3. Larger glazing areas will collect more solar energy.
4. Adequate thermal mass must be supplied (see Table 7.7B).

Table 7.7B Rules for Estimating Required Thermal Mass in Direct-Gain Systems

Thermal Mass	Thickness	Surface Area to Glazing Area
Masonry or concrete exposed to direct solar radiation (Fig. 7.7a)	4–6 in. (10–15 cm)	3
Masonry or concrete exposed to reflected solar radiation (Fig. 7.7b)	2–4 in. (5–10 cm)	6
Water	About 6 in. (15 cm)	About 1/2

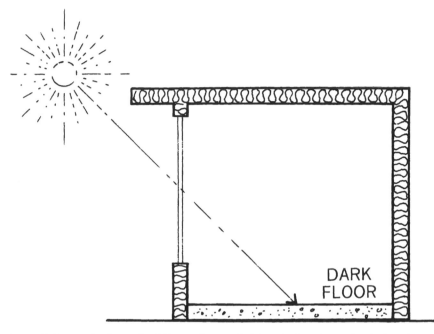

Figure 7.7a Massive floors should be medium to dark in color in order to absorb the solar radiation.

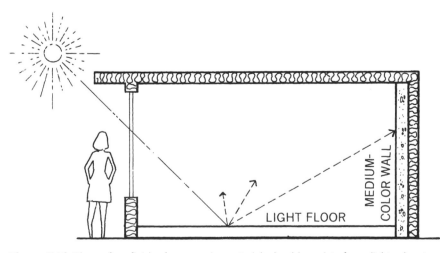

Figure 7.7b The surface finish of nonmassive materials should consist of very light colors to reflect the sun to the darker massive material.

5. Windows should be double-glazed except in very mild climates.
6. High-efficiency windows (($R_{IP} > 4$) [$R_{SI} > 0.7$]) can be used instead of night insulation (see Chapter 15).
7. The building must be well insulated.
8. Unless large amounts of light are desired for daylighting, sunbathing etc., direct-gain glazing areas should not exceed about 20 percent of the floor area. In those cases where more than 20 percent glazing is used, use either Trombe walls or sunspaces to supply the additional glazing area.

Thermal-Mass Sizing

Use Table 7.7B as a guideline for sizing thermal mass for direct-gain systems. Keep in mind that slabs and walls of concrete, brick, or rock should be 4–6 in. (10–15 cm) thick. From a thermal point of view, anything over 6 in. (15 cm) thick is only slightly helpful in a direct-gain system. Also, any thermal mass not receiving either direct or reflected solar radiation is mostly ineffective.

Notes on Table 7.7B

1. A combination of mass directly and indirectly exposed to the sun is quite common.
2. The table specifies minimum mass areas. Additional mass will increase thermal comfort by reducing temperature extremes.
3. Mass surface area is more important than mass thickness.
4. Keep mass as close as possible to the floor for structural as well as thermal reasons.
5. The thermal mass should be medium to dark in color, while surfaces of nonmassive materials should be very light in color to reflect the solar radiation to the darker mass materials (Fig. 7.7b).
6. If the mass is widely distributed in the space, then diffusing glazing or diffusing elements should be used (Fig. 7.7c).
7. For more information on thermal mass, see Section 7.17.

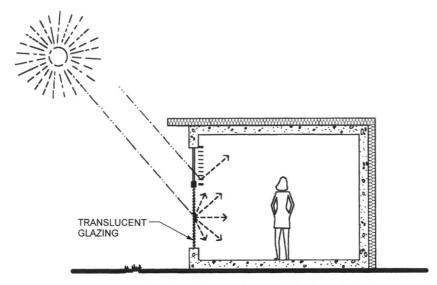

Figure 7.7c Reflected or diffused radiation will distribute the heat more evenly in the space. It is especially useful where ceilings are massive.

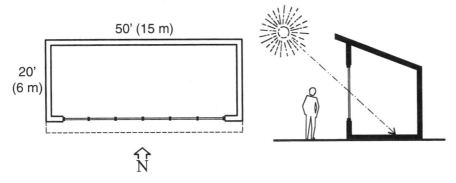

Figure 7.8 The plan and section used in the direct-gain example problem are shown.

7.8 EXAMPLE

*Design a direct-gain system for a 1000 ft²
(90 m²) building in Little Rock, Arkansas,
as shown in Fig. 7.8.*

Procedure:

1. Table 7.7A tells us that if the area of south-facing glazing is 19 percent of the floor area, then we can expect solar energy to supply about 62 percent of the winter heating load (if high-efficiency windows or night insulation is used). Use this recommendation unless there are special reasons to use larger or smaller glazing areas.

2. Thus, the area of south-facing glazing should be about 19 percent × 1000 ft² = 190 ft² (19 percent × 90 m² = 17.1 m²).

3. Table 7.7B tells us that we will need 3 ft² (3 m²) of mass for each square foot (m²) of glazing if the mass is directly exposed to the sun. Thus, 190 ft² × 3 = 570 ft² (17.1 m² × 3 = 51.3 m²) is required. If we use a concrete slab, then we have a slab area of 1000 ft² (90 m²), of which only 570 ft² (51.3 m²) is required for storing heat. The remaining 430 ft² (38.7 m²) will help to reduce the indoor daily temperature swing or it can be covered by carpet if desired.

7.9 TROMBE WALL SYSTEMS

The Trombe wall was named after professor Felix Trombe, who developed this technique in France in 1966. In this passive system, the thermal mass consists of a wall just inside the south-facing glazing (Fig. 7.9a). As before, the greenhouse effect traps the solar radiation. Because the surface of the wall facing the sun is either covered with a selective coating or painted a dark color, it gets quite hot during the day, causing heat to flow into the wall. Since the Trombe wall is quite thick—often about 12 in. (30 cm) thick—and the time lag is quite long, the heat does not reach the interior surface until evening. This time-lag effect of mass was explained in Section 3.18. If there is enough mass, the wall can act as a radiant heater all night long (Fig. 7.9b).

When only the sun's heat and not its light is desired, the Trombe wall is the system of choice. Because this is a rare occurrence, the Trombe wall is ordinarily used in combination with direct gain. The direct-gain part of the system delivers heat early in the day, functional light, views, and the delight of winter sunshine, while the Trombe wall stores heat for nighttime use. The combination of systems prevents the need for excessive light levels, which can cause glare and fading of colors. When one carefully chooses the right combination of systems, great thermal and visual comfort are possible.

Although the Trombe wall is usually made of solid materials, such as concrete, brick, stone, or adobe, it can also be made of containers of water.

Rectangular steel tanks can be fabricated, but most water walls consist of vertical tubes. If steel tubes or tanks are used, they should be painted a dark color on the glazing side and a light color on the room side. Corrosion of the steel tanks can be prevented by adding either rust control additives or sacrificial metal to the water. Often, however, the tubes are made of translucent or transparent plastic to allow some light to pass through (Fig. 7.9c). The water

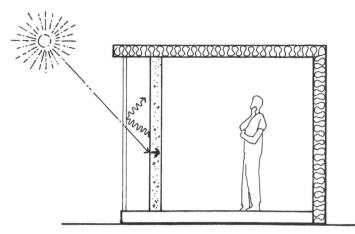

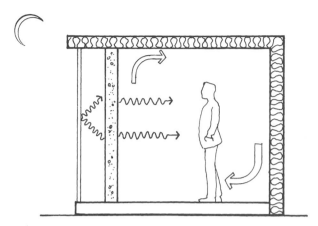

Figure 7.9a The Trombe wall passive-solar heating system collects heat without having light enter the space.

Figure 7.9b Because of the wall's eight- to twelve-hour time lag, most of the heat is released at night.

Figure 7.9c A Trombe wall can consist of vertical tubes filled with water. The tubes can be opaque, translucent, or transparent. (Courtesy of and © Solar Components Corporation.)

can be left clear or tinted any color. Transparent tubes are especially beautiful because of the way they refract the light. Tests have shown that clear water is almost as efficient as tinted water or opaque containers when it comes to storing heat.

As mentioned before, a mix of Trombe walls and direct gain usually yields the best design solution. Although most Trombe walls are full height with punched windows, sometimes they are built as a parapet wall (Fig. 7.9d). An arrangement, as shown in Fig. 7.16b, can increase morning pickup, prevent afternoon overheating, and provide adequate storage through the night.

The Visitor Center at Zion National Park, Utah, uses many passive strategies. South-facing windows provide both daylight and winter heating. The wall below the windows is a Trombe wall characterized by the use of textured glazing (Fig. 7.9e). The windows and Trombe walls are shaded in the summer, and "cool towers" supply cool air, as described in Section 10.13.

The Colorado Rocky Mountain College in Glenwood Springs also uses Trombe walls (Fig. 7.9f). In this high-elevation, cold-mountain climate, day-time heating without excessive light is achieved by the use of high and low vents in the Trombe wall.

The Shelly Ridge Girl Scout Center near Philadelphia, Pennsylvania, is another wonderful example of mixed Trombe wall and direct-gain systems (Fig. 7.9g). Since most scout activities happen during the day and early evening, the Trombe wall was made of brick only 4 in. (10 cm) thick so that the resulting short time lag delivered the heat during the afternoon and early evening. There was plenty of direct gain for early heating and day-lighting (Fig. 7.9h). Because the 4-in. (10 cm) thick Trombe wall was much too high to be stable, a timber grid was used to support the brick and the glazing (Fig. 7.9i). Crank-out awnings were extended in the summer to shade most of the direct-gain windows.

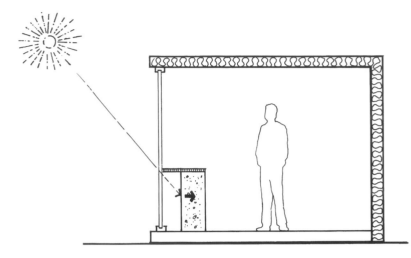

Figure 7.9d A half-height wall allows controlled direct gain for daytime heating and daylighting while also storing heat for the night. Water tanks or tubes could also be used.

Figure 7.9e The Visitor Center at Zion National Park uses Trombe walls, direct gain, and daylighting. The clerestory windows provide high-quality daylighting and direct gain for the north end of the building. Also note the photovoltaic panels on the south-facing roof.

Figure 7.9f Trombe walls with vents provide extra daytime heating without excessive light and glare at the Colorado Rocky Mountain College. Architect: Peter Dobrovolny. (© Robert Benson, photographer)

Figure 7.9g The Shelly Ridge Girl Scout Center near Philadelphia, Pennsylvania, utilizes both direct-gain and Trombe wall passive systems. Glass is used for the direct gain, and translucent Fiberglas panels are used for the Trombe wall. Awnings are extended in the summer to shade the direct-gain windows. (Photograph © Otto Baitz/ESTO.)

Figure 7.9h The direct-gain windows provide daylighting, views, and heat early in the day, while the Trombe wall provides heat in the early evening. (Photograph © Otto Baitz/ESTO.)

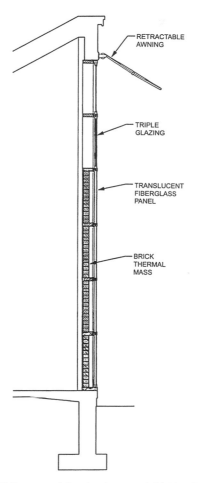

RETRACTABLE AWNING

TRIPLE GLAZING

TRANSLUCENT FIBERGLASS PANEL

BRICK THERMAL MASS

Figure 7.9i Because of the slenderness of this Trombe wall, a wooden frame was used to support both the brick and the window walls. (Courtesy Bohlin Cywinski Jackson Architects.)

161

Summer evenings, however, would be cooler if the Trombe wall were also shaded. A screen hung in front of the glazing during the summer would be especially effective since it would shade the Trombe wall from

direct, diffuse, and reflected radiation (Fig. 7.9j).

The Girl Scouts learned the methods and benefits of passive solar firsthand from using the building. They learned more experiential

lessons from the direct-gain heated lobby (Area #4 in Fig. 7.9k), where a stained-glass gnomon and hour marks embedded in the floor create a sundial.

Some early Trombe walls had indoor vents to supply daytime heat in winter and outdoor vents to prevent summer overheating. It is now clear that these vents do not work well in either summer or winter. Instead, direct gain should supply daytime heat in the winter, and an outside shading device should prevent heat collection in the summer.

From the outside, Trombe walls are sometimes indistinguishable from windows. Under certain lighting conditions, however, the dark wall is visible. If this is undesirable, textured glass can be used both to hide the dark wall and to serve as an aesthetic device to differentiate the Trombe

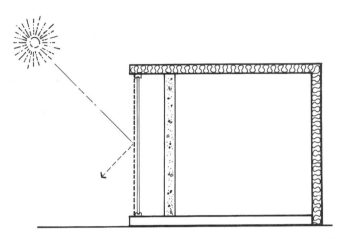

Figure 7.9j In hot climates, a shade screen should be draped over the Trombe wall glazing during the summer.

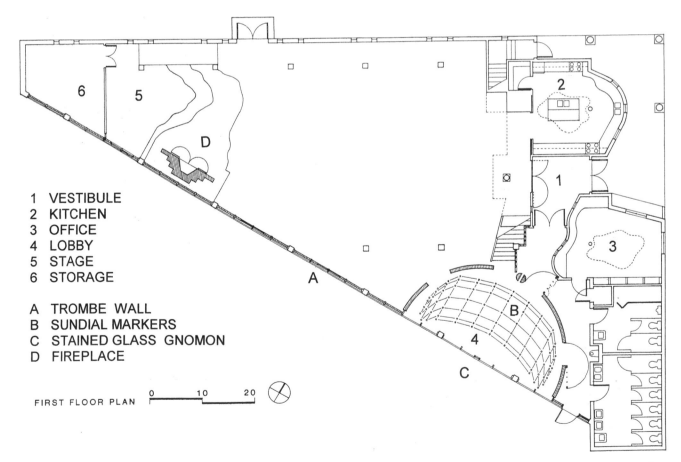

1 VESTIBULE
2 KITCHEN
3 OFFICE
4 LOBBY
5 STAGE
6 STORAGE

A TROMBE WALL
B SUNDIAL MARKERS
C STAINED GLASS GNOMON
D FIREPLACE

FIRST FLOOR PLAN

0   10   20

Figure 7.9k In the lobby (area 4) a stained-glass gnomon projects the time in the room-size sundial embedded in the floor slab. The triangular shape of the buildings makes the south wall the largest of the three walls. (Courtesy Bohlin Cywinski Jackson Architects.)

wall from ordinary windows. Since dark colors are almost as effective as black, some Trombe walls use clear glass to show the dark brick, dark natural stones, water tubes, or another attractive thermal-mass system.

The Trombe wall system is also known as the **thermal-storage wall system**. This author prefers the term "Trombe wall" because not all thermal walls are part of this system—only those that are just inside and parallel to the glazing.

7.10 DESIGN GUIDELINES FOR TROMBE WALL SYSTEMS

Area of South Glazing

Table 7.7A is used for Trombe walls as well as direct-gain systems. The total area of south glazing can be divided between the two systems as the designer wishes.

Thermal-Mass Sizing

The area of south-facing glazing should be matched by an equal area of thermal mass. However, the mass must be much thicker than that in direct-gain systems. The thickness for various materials is shown in Table 7.10. For best results, the mass should be at least 1 in. (2.5 cm) from the glazing. The surface facing the glazing should be covered with a black high-efficiency, "selective" coating if possible, while the surface facing the living space can be any color, including white. If a selective coating is not used, then double glazing is recommended.

7.11 EXAMPLE

Redesign the building in Example 7.8 to be half Trombe wall and half direct gain.

Procedure:

1. Total required south-facing glazing is again obtained from Table 7.7A: 19 percent $\times$ 1000 ft^2 = 190 ft^2 (19 percent $\times$ 90 m^2 = 17.1 m^2).
2. Since half of the glazing will be for direct gain, the Trombe wall will require 50 percent $\times$ 190 ft^2 = 95 ft^2 (0.5 $\times$ 17.1 m^2 = 8.6 m^2).
3. If we use a brick Trombe wall, it will have an area of 95 ft^2 (8.6 m^2) and a thickness of at least 10 in. (25 cm) (from Table 7.10). The slab for direct gain will have an area of 95 ft^2 $\times$ 3 = 285 ft^2 (8.6 m^2 $\times$ 3 = 25.8 m^2) (Table 7.7B).
4. Consider using a Trombe wall 3 ft-high (0.9 m) $\times$ 32 ft long (9.6 m) = 96 ft^2 > 95 ft^2 required (0.9 m $\times$ 9.6 m = 8.6 m^2) as shown in Fig. 7.9d. Do not block the inside of the wall with furniture since it must act as a radiator at night.
5. The window above the wall would also be 3 ft high (0.9 m) $\times$ 32 ft (9.6 m) long = 96 ft^2 > 95 ft^2 required for the direct gain glazing (0.9 m $\times$ 9.6 m = 8.6 m^2).

7.12 SUNSPACES

A sunspace is a room designed to collect heat for the main part of a building, as well as to serve as a secondary living area. This connect is derived from the conservatories popular in the eighteenth and nineteenth centuries.

Until recently, this design element was usually called an "attached greenhouse," but that was a misleading name because growing plants is only an optional function. More appropriate terms were "solarium" or "sunroom," but the term **sunspace** seems to have become most common. Sunspaces are one of the most popular passive systems, not only because of their heating efficiency, but even more so because of the amenities that they offer. Most people find the semi-outdoor aspect of sunspaces extremely attractive. Almost everyone finds it pleasurable to be in a warm, sunny space on a cold winter day.

Sunspaces are considered adjunct living spaces because the temperature is typically allowed to swing widely. On a sunny, cold day, the temperature can go as high as 90°F (32°C) during the day and cool down to 50°F (10°C) just before sunrise. Here we have an efficient solar collector that can also be used as an attractive living space much, but not all, of the time. Consequently, a sunspace must be designed as a separate thermal zone that can be isolated from the rest of the building. Figure 7.12a shows the three ways a sunspace can relate physically to the main building.

In Fig. 7.12b we see a sunspace collecting solar heat during the day. Much of the heat is carried into the main building through doors, windows, or vents. The rest of the captured solar heat is absorbed in the sunspace's thermal mass such as the floor slab and the masonry common wall. At night, as seen in Fig. 7.12c, the doors, windows, and vents are closed to keep the main part of the building warm. The heat stored in the thermal mass keeps the house comfortable and prevents the sunspace from freezing.

Because sunspaces are generally poorly insulated and shaded, they should not be heated or cooled. Mechanical heating and cooling would require so much energy that a sunspace would become a net loser rather than a gainer of energy. Large temperature swings should be

Table 7.10 Rules for Estimating the Required Thickness of a Trombe Wall		
Thermal Mass	Thickness*	Surface Area per Glazing Area Ratio
Adobe (dry earth)	6–10 in. (15–25 cm)	1
Concrete or brick	10–16 in. (20–30 cm)	1
Water†	8 or more in. (20 cm)	1

*Use the thinner thickness for evening heat and the thickner one for all-night heat.
†If tubes are used, they should be at least 10 in. (25 cm) in diameter.
Source: *Solar Age*, May 1979, p. 64.

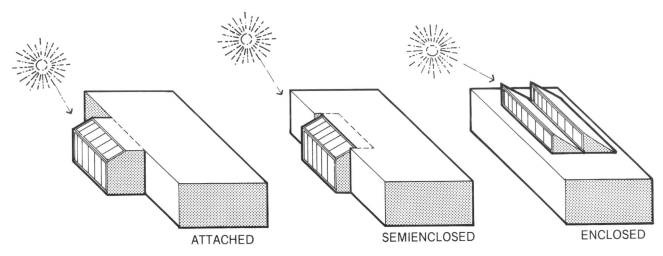

Figure 7.12a Possible relationships of a sunspace to the main building.

ATTACHED   SEMIENCLOSED   ENCLOSED

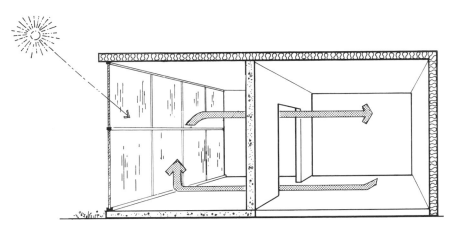

Figure 7.12b During the day, the sunspace collects solar radiation and distributes much of the heat to the rest of the building. Thermal mass stores much of the heat for nighttime use.

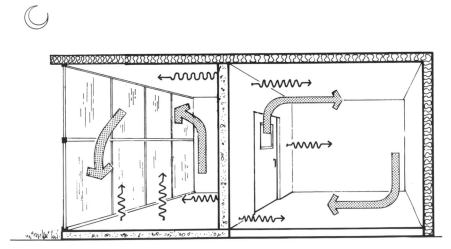

Figure 7.12c At night, the sunspace must be sealed from the main building to keep it from becoming an energy drain on the main building.

expected, and when the temperatures get extreme, the space should be temporarily abandoned. However, a well-designed sunspace is a delight most of the year.

Because sunspaces not only collect heat during the day but also act as a buffer at night, they are used in the BedZED zero-energy development (Fig. 7.12d). The cross section of the buildings was designed to maximize the south orientation and to prevent the shading of the next row of houses to the north (Fig. 7.12e). Since work areas need less heat than homes, office spaces are placed on the north side of each building. The dynamic roof ventilators (wind cowels) are explained in Section 10.6.

7.13 BALCOMB HOUSE

One of the best-known sunspace houses (Fig. 7.13a) belonged to J. Douglas Balcomb, the foremost researcher in passive solar systems. Because it is located in historic Santa Fe, New Mexico, adobe is used for the common wall (Fig. 7.13b). Double doors enable convection currents to heat the house during the day but seal off the sunspace at night (Fig. 7.13c). Also, at night the common adobe wall heats both the house and the sunspace. The sunspace not only contributes about 90 percent of the heating,

Figure 7.12d The Beddington Zero (fossil) Energy Development (BedZED) uses sunspaces to collect heat during the day, act as a buffer at night, and serve as an additional living space most of the time. Architect Bill Dunster, Engineers: ARUP. (Courtesy ARUP)

but it is a delightful place to spend an afternoon.

Another solar heating strategy used here actually makes this a **hybrid** solar building. It is partly **active solar** because fans force the hot air, collecting at the ceiling of the sunspace, to pass through a rock bed below the first-floor slab. This strategy does not contribute much heat, but it does increase the comfort level within the building. Rock beds are rarely used now because of their complexity and expense.

On the roof is a large vent to allow hot air to escape during the overheated periods of summer and fall (Fig. 7.13b). Unfortunately, venting is usually not enough to prevent overheating, and in most climates shading of the glass is of critical importance. Since shading inclined glass is much more complicated than

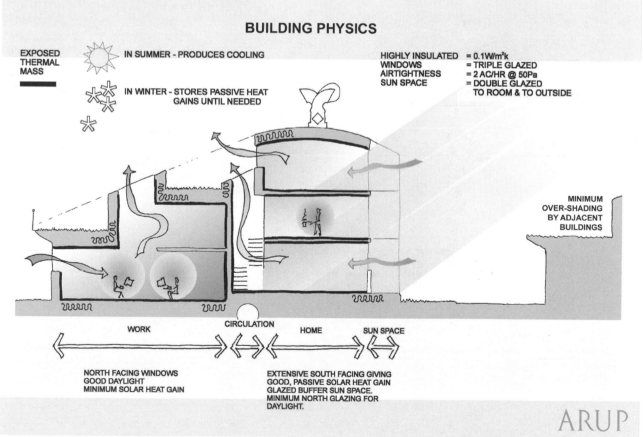

Figure 7.12e This section of BedZED shows the passive solar sunspaces on the south side (to the right) and the cooler work spaces on the north. The shape of the cross section maximizes south exposure for each building while providing solar access to the building to the north. (Courtesy ARUP)

Figure 7.13a One of the first and most interesting sunspace houses is the Balcomb residence in Santa Fe, New Mexico.

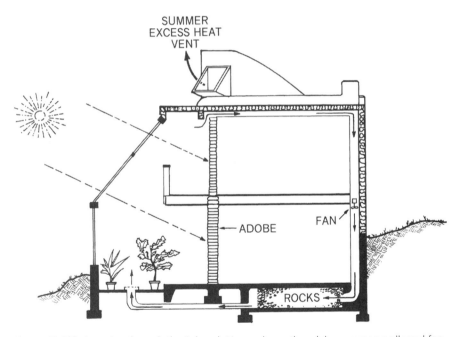

Figure 7.13b A section through the Balcomb House shows the adobe common wall used for storing heat. The sloping south glazing is a problem in the summer and should, therefore, not be used in most climates.

shading vertical glass, the glazing should usually be vertical.

The graph in Fig. 7.13d illustrates the performance of the Balcomb House during three winter days. Such performance is typical of a well-designed sunspace system. Note that the outdoor temperatures were quite cold, with a low of about 18°F (–9°C). The sunspace temperature swing was quite wide, with a low of 58°F (14°C) and a high of 88°F (31°C). The house, on the other hand, was fairly comfortable, with a modest swing of temperatures from a low of about 65°F (18°C) to a high of 74°F (23°C). The graph shows the different character of the two thermal zones. Although the addition of a small amount of auxiliary heating can create complete comfort in the house, the sunspace is always allowed its large temperature swing.

7.14 SUNSPACE DESIGN GUIDELINES

Glazing

To maximize solar heating, the slope of the glazing should be perpendicular to the sun during the coldest time of the year (e.g., January/February). However, from the point of view of safety, water leakage, and, most important, sun shading, vertical glazing is best. Very little if any glazing should be used on the end walls facing east and west. Such glazing is a thermal liability in both winter and summer.

Use Table 7.7A to determine the minimum glazing area desired for the total south facade. Since sunspaces are often sized for other than thermal reasons, the total glazing area might end up much larger than suggested in Table 7.7A. This is acceptable because overheating of sunspaces will have much less of an impact on the main house than overheating from direct-gain or Trombe wall systems. For best results, however, use a movable shading system as described in Section 9.4.

Vent Sizing

To prevent overheating, especially in summer and fall, venting of the sunspace to the outdoors is required, as shown in Fig. 7.14a. The low inlet vent area should be about 8 percent of the south-facing glazing area and the upper exhaust vent should be another 8 percent. Smaller openings will suffice if an exhaust fan is used. The fan should be sized to move about 150 cfm for every 100 ft² of sunspace (70 lps per 9 m²).

To heat the house in the winter, openings in the form of doors,

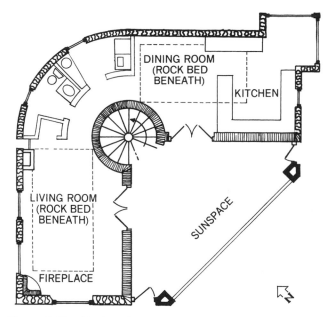

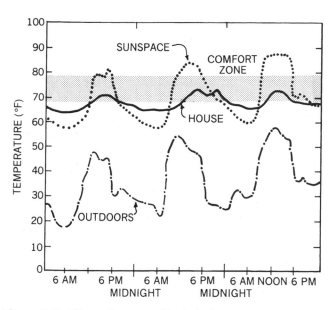

Figure 7.13c This plan of the Balcomb House shows how the building surrounds the sunspace.

Figure 7.13d The performance of both the house and sunspace are shown for three sunny but cold winter days. No auxiliary heating was used during this test.

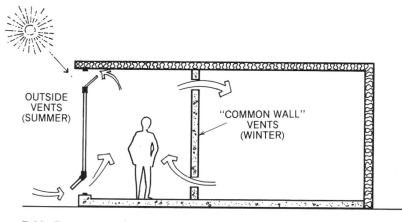

Figure 7.14a To prevent overheating in the summer, the sunspace must be vented to the outdoors. Vents, windows, or doors in the common wall allow daytime winter heat to flow from the sunspace into the main building.

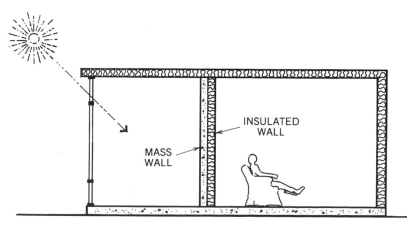

Figure 7.14b In extreme climates, the sunspace should be completely isolated from the main building by an insulated wall.

windows, or vents are required in the common wall between the house and the sunspace. The total area of any combination of these openings must add up to a minimum of 16 percent of the glazing area. Larger openings are better.

Thermal-Mass Sizing

The size of the mass depends on the function of the sunspace. If it is primarily a solar collector, then there should be little mass so that most of the heat ends up in the house. On the other hand, if the sunspace is to be a useful space with a modest temperature swing, then it should have much more mass.

A good solution for temperate climates is a common thermal-storage wall, as shown in Fig. 7.12b. In extremely hot or cold climates, it might be desirable to completely isolate the house from the sunspace. In this case, an insulated, less massive masonry wall might be used, as shown in Fig. 7.14b. When heat is desired, the doors, windows, or vents in the common wall are opened. When the sunspace needs to be isolated from the main building, the openings

Table 7.14 Rules for Estimating The Required Thermal Mass In Sunspace Systems

Thermal Mass	Thickness in Inches (cm)	Surface Area per Glazing area ratio
Masonry common wall (noninsulated)	8 to 12 (20 to 30)	1
Masonry common wall (insulated)*	4 to 6 (10 to 15)	2
Water†	About 12†	About 1/2

*Since this mass is exclusively for the sunspace, some additional mass will be required for the main building.
†Use about 2 gallons of water for each square foot (90 L/m²) of glazing.
Source: *Solar Age*, June 1984, p. 32.

are closed and the insulated wall acts as a thermal barrier. With either type of wall, water or a phase-change material can be efficiently used instead of masonry for thermal storage. For rules in sizing the mass in a sunspace, see Table 7.14.

7.15 COMPARISON OF THE THREE MAIN PASSIVE HEATING SYSTEMS

Table 7.15 compares the three main passive solar heating systems by listing the main advantages and disadvantages of each approach.

7.16 GENERAL CONSIDERATIONS FOR PASSIVE SOLAR SYSTEMS

The following comments refer to all of the above passive systems.

Orientation

"Orientation is 80 percent of passive solar design," says Doug Balcomb, the foremost passive solar scientist. Usually solar glazing should be oriented to the south. In most cases, this orientation gives the best results for both winter heating and summer shading. The graph in Fig. 7.16a illustrates

how the solar radiation transmitted through a vertical south window is maximal in the winter and minimal in the summer. This ideal situation is not true for any other orientation. Note how the curves for horizontal, east–west, and north windows indicate minimal heat collection in the winter and maximal heat collection in the summer. Who would want that? The south orientation is not just better—it is significantly better. In winter, south glazing collects about three times the solar radiation that east or west glazing collects, and in summer, south glazing collects only about one-third the radiation that east or west collects. With shading, the benefits of south glazing are even better.

Since in the real world a due-south orientation is not always possible, it is useful to know that solar glazing will still work well if oriented up to 20° east or west of true south. Even at 45° to true south, passive solar still works fairly well.

There are special conditions, however, when true south is not best. Consider the following examples:

1. Schools, which need heating early in the morning and little heating in late afternoon or at night, should be oriented about 30° to the east.
2. It is sometimes desirable, as in schools, to use a combination of systems, each of which has a different orientation. For example, the solution shown in Fig. 7.16b will give quick heating by direct gain in the morning. In the afternoon, overheating is prevented by having the solar radiation charge the Trombe walls for nighttime use.
3. Areas with morning fog or cloudiness should be oriented west of south.
4. Buildings that are used mainly at night (e.g., some residences where no one is home during the day) should be oriented about 10° west of south.
5. To avoid shading from neighboring buildings, trees, etc., reorient either to the east or west as needed.

Table 7.15 Comparison of Passive Solar Heating Systems

System	Advantages	Disadvantages
Direct gain	Promotes the use of large "picture" windows Least expensive Most efficient Can effectively use clerestories Daylighting and heating can be combined, which makes this system very appropriate for schools, small offices, etc. Very flexible and best when total glazing area is small	Too much light, which can cause glare and fading of colors. Thermal-storage floors must not be covered by carpets Only few and small paintings can be hung on thermal-mass walls Overheating can occur if precautions are not taken Fairly large temperature swings must be tolerated (about 10°F) (6°C)
Trombe wall	Gives high level of thermal comfort Good in conjunction with direct gain to limit lighting levels Medium cost Good for large heating loads	More expensive than direct gain Less glazing will be available for views and daylighting Not good for very cloudy climates
Sunspaces	A very attractive amenity Extra living space Can function as a greenhouse	Most expensive system Least efficient

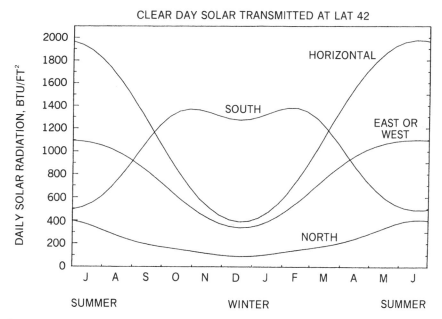

CLEAR DAY SOLAR TRANSMITTED AT LAT 42

Figure 7.16a Vertical south glazing is usually the best choice because it transmits the maximum solar radiation in the winter and the minimum in the summer. (From *Workbook for Workshop on Advanced Passive Solar Design*, by J. Douglas Balcomb and Robert Jones, © J. Douglas Balcomb, 1987.)

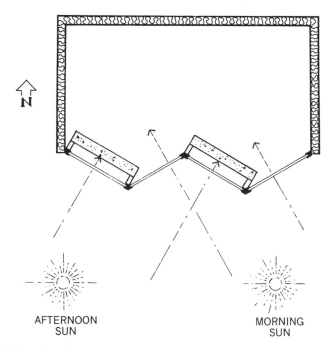

Figure 7.16b Plan view of a combined system of direct gain and Trombe walls to get quick morning heating and to prevent afternoon overheating.

Plan

The plan should be designed to take advantage of the daily cycle of the sun (Fig. 15.5f). Waking up to the morning sun and eating breakfast on a table flooded with sunlight on the east side of a house is both physiologically and psychologically satisfying. Later in the day, relaxing in a sun-filled living or family room on the south or southwest side of the building is a great pleasure. There is growing scientific evidence that supporting our natural circadian rhythms can promote well-being.

Distribute south-facing glazing throughout the building proportionally to the heat loss of each space. Use clerestories to bring a southern exposure to northern rooms (Fig. 7.6e).

Slope of Glazing

Although the optimum collection slope for glazing is sloped, vertical glazing is almost always preferred. Vertical glazing is less expensive, safer, easier to shade on both the exterior and interior, easier to fit with night insulation, and actually collects more heat when snow acts as a reflector.

Shading

Passive solar heating systems can become a liability during the overheated periods of the year if they are not properly shaded, as demonstrated in Fig. 7.16c. Not only should direct sunrays be rejected, but reflected and diffuse radiation should also be blocked. The problem of reflected heat is most acute in hot and dry areas, while that of diffuse radiation is most critical in humid regions.

As Chapter 9 will show, any fixed, south-facing overhang that is deep enough to fully shade a window for the whole overheated period will also shade the window too much during the underheated period. Consequently, movable overhangs such as awnings should be used whenever possible. When that is not possible, as in south-facing porches on balconies, the glazing line should be moved instead (Fig. 7.16d). A full discussion of shading is presented in Chapter 9.

Reflectors

Exterior **specular** (mirror-like) reflectors can increase the solar collection without some of the drawbacks of using larger glazing areas. Both winter

Figure 7.16c To prevent passive solar from becoming a liability in the summer, the Real Goods Solar Living Center shades the large area of glazing with a combination of roof overhangs, an extensive deciduous plant-covered pergola, and movable awnings, which are not visible in this photograph but can be seen in Fig. 17.2f, where this building is described as a case study. (Courtesy van der Ryn Architects, ©Richard Barnes, photographer.)

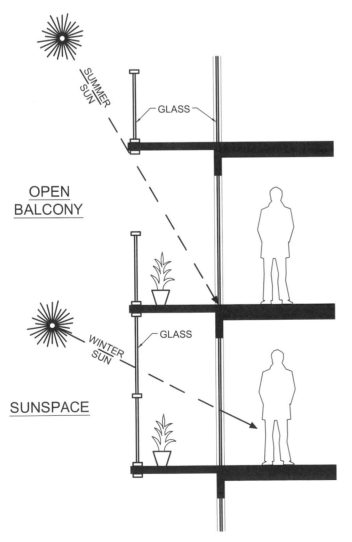

heat loss and summer heat gain can be minimized by using reflectors rather than larger window sizes to increase the solar collection. Specular reflectors can also be very beneficial in daylighting designs, which are discussed in Chapter 13. However, specular reflectors are not inexpensive, and they are quite inefficient when used on narrow windows (Fig. 7.16e).

Since a specular surface reflects light so that the angle of incidence equals the angle of reflectance, the length of the reflector is determined by the ray of sunshine that just clears the head of the window (Fig. 7.16f). For the angle of incidence, use the altitude angle of the sun on January 21 at 12 noon. This angle can be found in Appendix C.

To prevent unwanted collection, the specular reflector should be removed or rotated out of the way in the summer. If the reflector cannot be removed, then it should be at least rotated so that the summer sun is not reflected into the window. The angle of tilt should be at least equal to the latitude (Fig. 7.16g).

Diffusing reflectors (white) are also beneficial, but they must be much larger than specular reflectors because only a small percentage of the

Figure 7.16d Balconies or covered porches that effectively shade windows or glass doors in the summer unfortunately also block much needed sun in the winter. By enclosing the balconies in glazing during the winter, a valuable sunspace can be created.

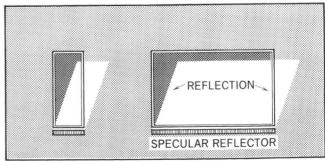

Figure 7.16e Specular reflectors are much less efficient on narrow than on wide windows. The diagram shows how on a south orientation the afternoon sun is reflected toward the east side of the window.

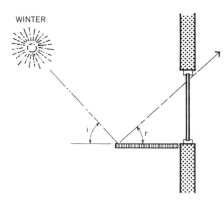

Figure 7.16f The length of a specular reflector is determined by the sunray that just clears the window head.

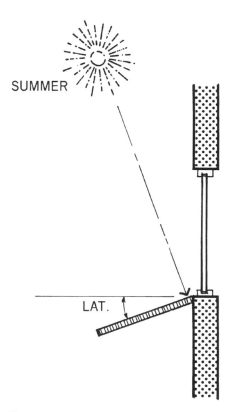

Figure 7.16g When summer sun is not desired, specular reflectors that are not removed should be tilted at least to the angle roughly equal to the latitude

sun is reflected in the direction of the window. Where it exists, snow is ideal because of its large area, seasonal existence, and "low" cost. Although neither light-colored concrete nor gravel has a very high reflectance factor, they can still be beneficial if used in large areas.

Conservation

High-performance windows or night insulation over the solar glazing is recommended highly. In most parts of the country, these strategies can significantly improve the performance of passive heating systems in winter. Night insulation can also be used to reject the sun during summer days. Furthermore, it can offer privacy control and eliminate the "black hole" effect of bare glazing at night. Night insulation is most appropriate for direct-gain systems. It is less practical in sunspaces and Trombe walls, where high-performance windows may be the better choice.

Night insulation can take several forms. Drapes with thermal liners have many advantages but are limited in their thermal resistance. Rigid panels can have high R-values but are complicated to install and use.

High-efficiency windows are becoming increasingly popular because they have no special needs in regard to installation and require no user involvement. However, they do not cancel the need for shading, privacy, or the elimination of the black-hole effect at night. Thus, high-performance windows with modest night insulation may be the best mix for direct-gain windows. These strategies are discussed further in Chapter 15.

7.17 HEAT-STORAGE MATERIALS

The success of passive solar heating and some passive cooling systems depends largely on the proper use of heat-storage materials. When comparing various materials for storing heat in buildings, the architectural designer is mainly interested in the heat capacity in terms of the energy per volume rather than the unit of weight. Table 7.17A shows the large variation in **volumetric heat capacity** among materials.

Air, for example, is almost completely worthless as a heat-storage material because it has so little mass. Insulation, too, can store only insignificant amounts of heat because it

Table 7.17A Heat capacity of Materials by Volume		
	Heat Capacity by Volume*	
Materials	Btu/ft³·°F	kJ/m³·°C
Water	62	4000
Steel	59	3700
Concrete*		
Heavy	30	2000
Light	17	1100
Brick*	25	1500
Wood*		
Oak	20	1200
Pine	15	1000
Redwood	10	700
Insulation	1	60
Air	0.02	1

*Since some building materials vary tremendously, these are only approximate values.

consists mostly of air. Water, on the other hand, is one of the best heat-storage materials, and steel is almost as good. Except for wood, it seems that the heavy materials are good and the light materials are bad for storing heat. Although wood has a high heat capacity because of its water content, it is only slightly suitable for heat storage because it has a low conductance of heat, which prevents the center of a mass of wood from participating efficiently in the storage of heat. Thus, for a material to be a good heat-storage medium, it must have both a high heat capacity and high conductance. For this reason water, steel, brick, and concrete (stone) are some of the best choices.

Water is an excellent heat-storage material not only because it has the highest heat capacity of any material, but also because it has a very high heat-absorption rate. In water, natural convection currents as well as conduction help to move the heat to the interior of the mass (Fig. 7.17a). Because of the somewhat slow conductance of heat in concrete, brick, stone, etc. the thermally effective thickness of these solids is limited. Although concrete, stone, brick, and adobe are not as efficient as water when it comes to

Table 7.17B Comparison of Various Heat-Storage Materials		
Material	**Advantages**	**Disadvantages**
Water	Quite compact Free	A storage container is required and can be expensive Leakage is possible
Concrete (stone)	Very stable Can also serve as wall, floor, etc.	Expensive to buy and install because of weight
Phase-change material	Most compact Can fit into ordinary wood-frame construction	Most expensive Long-term reliability is not yet proven

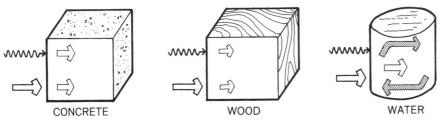

CONCRETE   WOOD   WATER

Figure 7.17a Because the conduction of heat into the interior of a material is critical for heat storage, wood is not good for storing heat, while water is excellent.

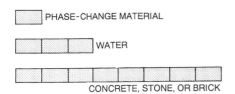

PHASE-CHANGE MATERIAL

WATER

CONCRETE, STONE, OR BRICK

Figure 7.17b Relative volumes required for equal heat storage are shown.

storing heat, they have a number of advantages. They don't leak or freeze, and they usually also serve as the structure. Note that Tables 7.7B and 7.10, which are used to estimate the required thermal mass, give the optimum thickness of the mass. When more heat storage is required, the surface area and not the thickness should be increased.

There are even more efficient materials for storing heat. These are called **phase-change materials** (PCM). They store the energy in the form of latent heat, while the previously mentioned materials store the energy as sensible heat. Since for passive heating the phase change must occur near room temperature, paraffin and the salt hydrates (e.g., calcium chloride hexahydrate and Glauber's salt) are the most promising phase-change materials.

Figure 7.17b shows that to store equal amounts of heat, water requires only one-third the volume of concrete, while phase-change materials require only one-ninth of the volume of concrete. Not only do phase-change materials take up very little space, they also reduce the daily temperature swing. By using the heat of fusion (latent heat), large amounts of heat can be stored at the melting point of the material. Consequently, the materials chosen are those that melt in the comfort range (68°–78°F) (20°–25°C).

The phase-change materials are often embedded in drywall panels in order to create a large surface area, to avoid using additional building space, and to avoid additional labor costs.

See Table 7.17B for a comparison of various heat storage materials.

7.18 OTHER PASSIVE HEATING SYSTEMS

Convective-Loop System (Thermosiphon)

In Fig. 7.18a, we see the basic elements of a convective-loop system. The solar collector generates a hot

fluid (air or water) that rises to the storage area. Meanwhile, the cooler fluid sinks from storage and flows into the collector. This flow by natural convection is also called **thermosiphoning**. At night, the convection currents would reverse if the storage container were not located higher than the collector. The key to success in this system, therefore, is to place the thermal storage at a higher elevation than the collector. Unfortunately, this is usually difficult to do because of the weight of the water or rocks that are the typical storage mediums. Placing such as mass in an elevated position can be quite a problem unless you are lucky enough to have a building site that slopes down steeply to the south.

The Paul Davis House in Corrales, New Mexico, is located on a steep slope so that a hot-air collector can heat a rock bed under the house (Fig. 7.18b). At night, the heat from the rock bed is allowed to flow into the house, while cool air from the house returns to the rock bed. This is also a convective loop and is controlled by a damper. The house is heated during the day by direct gain.

Although strictly speaking this is a passive system, it has more in common with active than with passive solar systems. It is not an integrated approach since both collector and rock storage have only one function. This raises the cost significantly and, therefore, it is not a very popular passive system. A further discussion of related collector and heat storage systems can be found in Chapter 8 under active solar systems.

Roof Ponds

This concept is similar to the Trombe wall except that in this case we have a thermal-storage roof. In this roof-pond system, water is stored in black plastic bags on a metal deck roof, and during a winter day the sun heats the water bags (Fig. 7.18c). The heat is quickly conducted down and radiated from the ceiling into the living space. At night, movable insulation covers

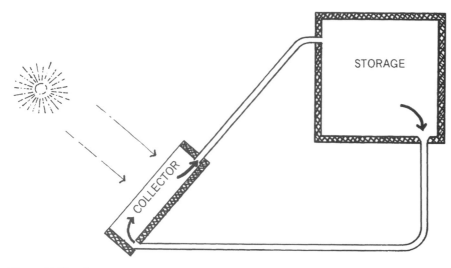

Figure 7.18a The passive convective loop (thermosiphon) system requires the storage to be above the collector.

the water to keep the heat from being lost to the night sky (Fig. 7.18d).

In theory, the roof pond is an attractive system because it not only heats passively in winter but can also give effective passive cooling in the summer. During the overheated part of the year, the insulation covers the house during the day and is removed at night. This passive cooling strategy is explained further in Section 10.11.

Unfortunately, this concept has some serious practical problems. One difficulty is that no one has been able to develop a workable, movable insulation system for the roof. Another problem is the weight of the water and potential water leakage.

And most importantly, because of the cosine law, flat roofs receive less solar radiation than sloped or vertical surfaces in the winter. The higher the latitude, the worse this problem becomes. Therefore, roof ponds are

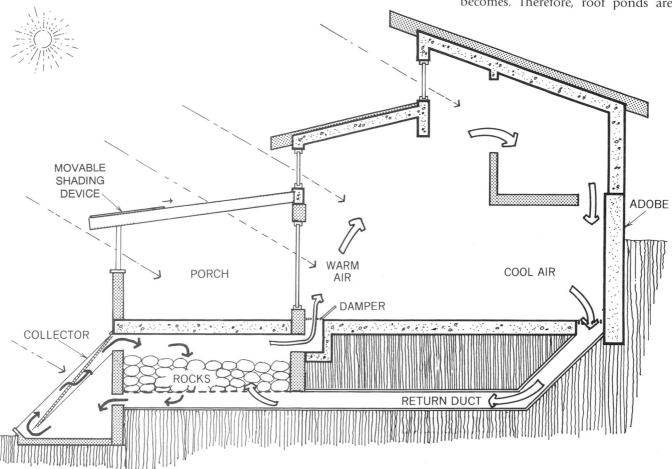

Figure 7.18b A convective loop heats the rock bed in the Davis House, Corrales, New Mexico, designed by Steve Baer.

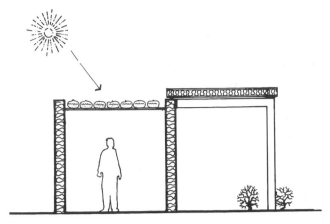

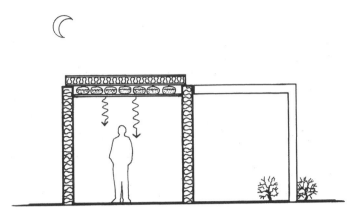

Figure 7.18c During a winter day, the black plastic bags of water are exposed to the sun in the roof-pond system.

Figure 7.18d During a winter night, a rigid insulation panel is slid over the water.

only for latitudes below 30° that have cold winters, as can be found at high elevations.

Roof Radiation Trap

To overcome some of the serious difficulties with roof ponds, Prof. B. Givoni developed the Roof Radiation Trap system. As shown in Fig. 7.18e, the glazing on the roof is tilted to maximize winter collection at any latitude (tilt = latitude + 15°). After passing through the glazing, the solar radiation is absorbed by the black-painted concrete ceiling slab. The building is, thus, heated by radiation from the ceiling. The sloped roof is well insulated, and a movable shutter can reduce heat loss

through the glass at night. This system can also be adapted for summer passive cooling and is described further in Section 10.12.

Lightweight Collecting Walls

The lightweight collecting wall shown in Fig. 7.18f is useful in very cold climates for those types of buildings in which extra heating is required during the day and little heat is required at night. This is typical of many schools, office buildings, and factories. Since there is no special storage mass in this system, all of the solar radiation falling on the collector is used to heat the interior air while the sun is shining.

7.19 CONCLUSION

It has often been said that there is no such thing as a free lunch. However, the benefits of using orientation correctly *are* a free lunch. As stated before, passive solar is 80 percent orientation. Thus, orienting windows to the south yields free energy. The chart in Fig. 7.19 shows that only south windows have a net gain on a cold January day in Salt Lake City, Utah. Merely by moving the windows to the south wall, passive solar heating is achieved—a free lunch (Case 2 in Fig. 7.19). As will be seen in Chapter 9, another free lunch is available in the summer by using orientation correctly.

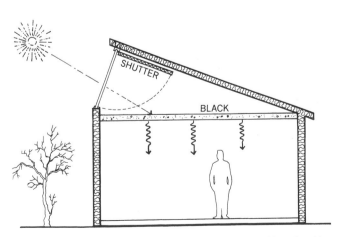

Figure 7.18e The roof radiation trap system developed by Givoni in Israel is shown.

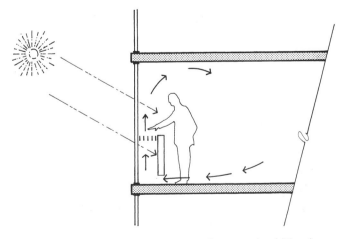

Figure 7.18f A lightweight collecting wall can supply additional daytime heating by natural convention and radiation without the introduction of excessive light.

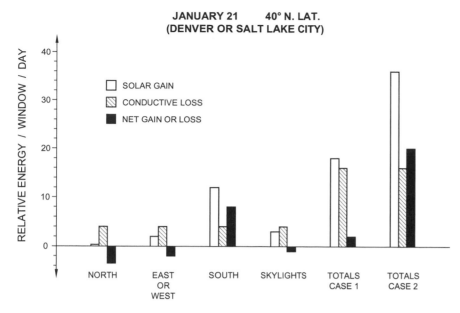

**JANUARY 21   40° N. LAT.
(DENVER OR SALT LAKE CITY)**

- □ SOLAR GAIN
- ▨ CONDUCTIVE LOSS
- ■ NET GAIN OR LOSS

CASE 1: EQUAL WINDOW AREA ON NORTH, EAST (OR WEST),
SOUTH, AND SKYLIGHT.

CASE 2: SAME AMOUNT OF GLAZING AS IN CASE 1,
BUT ALL PLACED ON SOUTH WALL.

NOTE: 1. ALL WINDOWS ARE DOUBLE GLAZED WITH LOW-E.
2. ALL BUT SOUTH WINDOWS HAVE "SELECTIVE LOW-E"
TO REDUCE SOLAR GAIN.

Figure 7.19 The benefits of orientation are made clear from this study of heat gain and heat loss for windows on various walls on a cold winter day. As can be seen, only south windows capture more heat from the sun than they lose in a twenty-four-hour period. Case 2 demonstrates the benefits of placing all the windows on the south wall. Thus, passive solar is 80 percent orientation.

Many factors determine the best choice of a passive heating system. Climate, building type, user preference, and cost are some of the major considerations. Often it is best to use a combination of systems to satisfy the demands of a particular situation. At other times, a variation of only one system will prove best. It is also likely that some good ideas have not yet been developed. It is certain, however, that most buildings that require heating can benefit from some type of passive heating system.

Not only are passive heating systems a vital strategy for sustainability, they also provide passive security when the normal supply of energy is interrupted or becomes too expensive. Pipes and people will never freeze in a passive solar building. Even without backup heating, the temperature will not go below 55°F (13°C) in a cold and sunny climate or below 45°F (7°C) in a cold and cloudy climate.

In urban areas and far northern latitudes, solar access may not be available for passive systems but may still be available high on the roof. In such cases, solar heating can still be achieved by active systems described in the next chapter.

KEY IDEAS OF CHAPTER 7

1. Maximize south-facing glazing because south windows
   a. Collect much more sun during the day than they lose at night
   b. Collect much more sun in the winter than in the summer
2. Passive solar heating consists essentially of south-facing glazing and thermal mass.
3. In a direct-gain system, the more mass receiving direct or reflected solar radiation, the better. The mass should have a large surface area rather than depth.

4. The three main passive solar systems are
   a. Direct gain
   b. Trombe wall
   c. Sunspace
5. Direct-gain systems are the simplest and most economical but result in high light levels.
6. Trombe walls supply heat without light.
7. Sunspaces are delightful living spaces as well as solar heaters.
8. To keep a sunspace from being an energy liability, one must design

it to be a semitemperate living space (i.e., neither mechanically heated nor cooled).
9. Passive systems must be shaded in summer to prevent an asset from becoming a liability.
10. Passive solar is 80 percent orientation.
11. Passive solar provides security against power outages and high energy prices.
12. Passive solar is a vital strategy for sustainability.

Resources

FURTHER READING

(See the Bibliography in the back of the book for full citations.)

Anderson, B. *Solar Energy: Fundamentals in Building Design.*

Anderson, B., and M. Wells. *Passive Solar Energy.*

ASHRAE. *Passive Solar Heating Analysis: A Design Manual.*

Balcomb, J. D. *Passive Solar Buildings.*

Boonstra, C., ed. *Solar Energy in Building Renovation.*

Brown, G. Z., and M. DeKay. *Sun, Wind, and Light: Architectural Design Strategies,* 2nd ed.

Buckley, S. *Sun Up to Sun Down.*

Clegg, P., and D. Watkins. *Sunspaces: New Vistas for Living and Growing.*

Cook, J. *Award Winning Passive Solar House Designs.*

Daniels, K. *The Technology of Ecological Building: Basic Principles and Measures, Examples and Ideas.*

Givoni, B. *Climate Considerations in Building and Urban Design.*

Heinz, T. A. "Frank Lloyd Wright's Jacobs II House."

Hestnes, A. G., R. Hastings, and B. Saxhof, eds. *Solar Energy Houses: Strategies, Technologies, Examples.*

Jones, R. W., and R. D. McFarland. *The Sunspace Primer: A Guide to Passive Solar Heating.*

Kachadorian, J. *The Passive Solar House: Using Solar Design to Heat and Cool Your Home.*

Kohlmaier, G., and B. von Sartory. *Das Glashaus: Ein Bautypus des 19. Jahrhunderts.*

Kwok, Alison G., and Walter T. Grondzik. *The Green Studio Handbook: Environmental Strategies for Schematic Design.*

Los Alamos National Lab. *Passive Solar Heating Analysis: A Design Manual.*

Mazria, E. *The Passive Solar Energy Book.*

Miller, B. *Buildings for a Sustainable America: Case Studies.*

Panchyk, K. *Solar Interior: Energy Efficient Spaces Designed for Comfort.*

Potts, M. *The New Independent Home: People and Houses That Harvest the Sun.*

Singh, M. *The Timeless Energy of the Sun for Life and Peace with Nature.*

Stein, B., J. Reynolds, W. T. Grondzik, and A. G. Kwok. *Mechanical and Electrical Equipment for Buildings,* 10th ed.

Steven Winter Associates. *The Passive Solar Design and Construction Handbook.*

Watson, D. *Designing and Building a Solar House: Your Place in the Sun.*

PERIODICALS

Solar Today

ORGANIZATIONS

(See Appendix K for full citations.)

American Solar Energy Society
www.ases.org

National Group for Renewable Energy Education.

Center for Renewable Energy and Sustainable Technology (CREST)
www.crest.org

Florida Solar Energy Center (FSEC)
www.fsec.org

National Center for Appropriate Technology (NCAT)
www.ncat.org

National Renewable Energy Laboratory (NREL)
www.nrel.gov

Sustainable Buildings Industry Council (SBIC)
www.sbic.org

8

PHOTOVOLTAICS AND ACTIVE SOLAR

In real estate the mantra is:
location
location
location

In solar design the mantra is:
orientation
orientation
orientation

How can it be that the people of Turkey and China can afford solar hot water heaters while Americans can't?
Anonymous

177

8.1 INTRODUCTION

Although, from a distance, photovoltaic (PV) and active solar collectors appear quite similar, they produce distinctly different forms of energy. **PV panels** produce the very high-grade energy of electricity while **active solar panels** produce the low-grade thermal energy of low-temperature heat. Electricity is called a **high-grade energy source** because it can be used to do all kinds of work (generate light, move elevators, etc.), while low-temperature heat can do little more than heat water or a building.

These two systems are discussed in the same chapter because they are often mounted side-by-side on a building, they look similar, and their needs for orientation and tilt are similar. The term "solar panel" should not be used since it can apply equally well to either active solar or PV panels. PV panels are discussed first.

8.2 THE ALMOST IDEAL ENERGY SOURCE

As was mentioned in Chapter 2, the conventional energy sources all have serious drawbacks. What, then, would be the almost-ideal energy source? What are the characteristics of the ideal energy source?

Characteristics of the Ideal Energy Source

1. Sustainable (renewable)
2. Nonpolluting
3. Not dangerous to people or the planet
4. High-grade energy useful for any purpose
5. Silent
6. Supplies power where it is needed (no need to transport energy)
7. Most available at peak demand time, which is frequently a hot, sunny summer day
8. Has the additional benefit of creating the building envelope (i.e., displaces conventional building materials)
9. High reliability
10. No moving parts
11. No maintenance required
12. Modular (can come in any size required)
13. Low operating cost
14. Low initial cost
15. Supplies energy all the time

PV is the only energy source that comes close to having these characteristics. PV meets or exceeds all except the last two characteristics: "low initial costs" and "supplies energy all the time." The fact that PV doesn't generate electricity at night is not as big a problem as it seems because batteries or the power grid can be used to store the electricity. During the day, clouds are not as severe a problem as one might guess either, because PV can use diffused light quite well.

Cloudiness and PV-Output Rules of Thumb*

1. About 80 percent output on partly cloudy days
2. About 50 percent output on hazy/humid days
3. About 30 percent output on extremely overcast days

In places where conventional electricity is either very expensive or unavailable, as on islands or areas remote from the power grid, PV is the economical choice. It is also often less expensive than conventionally produced electricity when peak demand occurs, as is usual, on a hot, sunny day. In the near future, PV will be a competitive source of electricity in most situations.

As more PV is used, its cost will continue to decline through rapid technological improvements and the economics of scale (Fig. 8.2). PV has the potential to become very inexpensive because of its inherent simplicity and the very small amount of material that it requires. At the same time that PV becomes less expensive, it will become more attractive as more people recognize the need for a sustainable, clean energy source that does not produce any greenhouse gases.

Several countries have decided that PV needs to be implemented now. Germany, Switzerland, and Japan all have relatively low solar irradiation, and yet they are using PV widely. In comparison most of the United States and the world has excellent solar irradiation and therefore should also use PV extensively.

8.3 HISTORY OF PV

Becquerel discovered the photoelectric effect in 1839, and Bell Laboratories developed the first crystalline silicon cell in 1954. Little practical progress was made until 1958, when the space program needed an extremely light

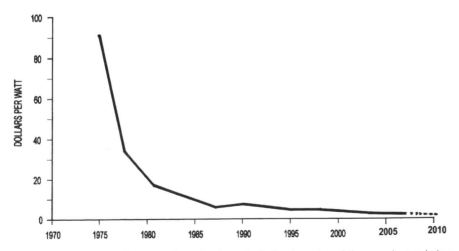

Figure 8.2 PV systems have experienced a dramatic decline in cost, and they are close to being economical (Maycock, 1998 and updated 2007) for most buildings.

*From Tapping into the Sun.

Figure 8.3a The Lord House in Maine is a grid-connected building with half of the roof generating electricity and the other half, hot water. During the day, electricity is sold to the power company, and at night it is bought back. The house is also passively heated and superinsulated. (Courtesy Solar Design Associates, Inc.)

Figure 8.3b The Intercultural Center at Georgetown University is a fine example of building-integrated photovoltaics (BIPV). The south-facing roof is covered with a 300-kilowatt PV array that provides about 50 percent of the building's electrical needs. (Courtesy of © BP Solarex.)

Figure 8.3c Several power companies have set up PV farms to harvest the sun. This energy is most available on hot, sunny summer days, precisely when it is needed to supply electricity for air conditioning. Shown is the 2-megawatt, single-axis-tracking system of the Sacramento Municipal Utility District at Rancho Seco, California. The nuclear power plant, seen in the background, has been shut down. (Courtesy Sacramento Municipal Utility District.)

and reliable source of electricity for its satellites. Although PV proved very reliable, the cost was initially too high for earthbound applications. However, continuing research, development, and mass production have reduced the cost of PV to make it practical not only for locations remote to the power grid but also to supply power to buildings connected to the grid. PV is also widely used in developing countries where villages are often far from the power grid. In the developed world, many individuals, communities, and countries use PV to address the issues of global warming, sustainability, and energy security (see Figs. 8.3a–8.3c).

8.4 THE PV CELL

PV cells, sometimes also known as **solar cells**, are made from materials that convert light directly into electricity. Most use silicon with small amounts of certain impurities added to create an excess of electrons in one layer and a lack of electrons in the other layer. Photons of light create free electrons in one layer, and a conducting strip enables the electrons to flow through an external circuit to reach the layer that lacks electrons (Fig. 8.4a).

Single-crystal silicon cells are the most efficient but also the most expensive. To reduce the cost, polycrystalline and thin-film PV cells have been developed. Thin-film PV is made of amorphous silicon, copper indium diselenide, or cadmium telluride. Although these cells convert sunlight

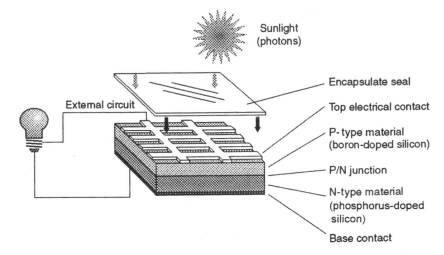

Figure 8.4a A section through a typical PV cell. Photons of light generate free electrons. The metal grid on the top and the metal plate on the bottom allow for the collection and return of the free electrons through an external electric circuit. (Drawing from Fact Sheet No. 11 from State Energy Conservation Office of Texas.)

into electricity at half the efficiency of the single-crystal silicon cells, their lower cost more than compensates whenever collector area is not limited (see Table 8.4). Continuing research is raising the efficiency of all cells, with 41 percent the highest reached in a laboratory so far.

Because most PV cells are small and fragile and produce only a small amount of power, a collection of cells is encased to form modules. Modules come in many sizes, but to make handling easy, they are rarely over 3 ft wide and 5 ft long. Some modules are combined to form panels, which are further combined to form an array (Fig. 8.4b).

Like batteries, when two cells or modules are connected in series, the voltage doubles; when they are connected in parallel, their current doubles. Thus, a sufficient number of cells in the right combination can produce any combination of voltage and current.

SIDEBOX 8.4

The electrical power produced is equal to the product of the current and voltage.

$$W = I \cdot V$$

where

> W = power in watts
> I = current in amperes
> V = voltage in volts

The electrical energy produced is equal to the power times the amount of time that the power is produced.

$$E = W \cdot H$$

where

E = electrical energy in watt-hours
W = power in watts
H = time in hours

Since the number of watt-hours is usually very large, electrical energy is usually measured in kilowatt-hours.

$$E = K \cdot W \cdot H$$

where

> $1\ KW = 1000\ W$

Table 8.4 The Efficiency of PV Cells	
Type of PV Cell	**Efficiency Range (%)**
Single-crystal silicon	16–20
Multicrystal silicon	14–17
Thin film	7–12

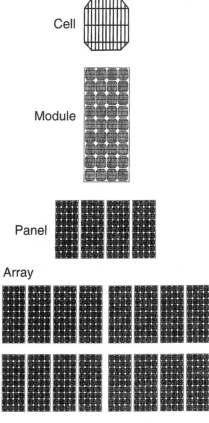

Figure 8.4b Cells combine to form modules, modules form panels, and panels combine to form an array. (From Federal Technology Alert: Photovoltaics.)

Since electrical power is the product of voltage and current, any amount of power can be produced with enough cells (see Sidebox 8.4).

8.5 TYPES OF PV SYSTEMS

Two basic types of PV systems exist for buildings: stand-alone and grid-connected. When connection to a power grid is not possible or not wanted, a stand-alone system is required. In such cases, batteries are needed to supply power at night on overcast days, and when peak power is required. The PV arrays are sized to handle both normal daytime loads and battery charging. The batteries add significantly to the cost and maintenance of the systems.

When PV is used where the power grid exists, batteries are not needed. During a sunny day, excess PV power is sold to the utility, and at night, power is drawn from the grid. In effect, the grid acts as a giant storage battery. This can be an advantage to both the PV owners and many power companies, because the greatest demand on their grid is often on hot, sunny summer days, while at night the power companies have excess capacity that they are eager to sell.

Right now, most people pay the average cost over a day and year for electricity, but with the deregulation of the power industry, time-of-day pricing has become common. The price at peak hours is often so high that PV can compete. Grid connection with PV systems is already possible because the Public Utilities Regulatory Policy Act of 1978 states that utilities are required to buy power from owners of PV systems. **Net-metering laws** in many states require the power companies to buy PV power from individuals at the same rate they charge.

In a grid-connected system, an inverter is required to change the direct current from the PV array to the alternating current (AC) at the correct voltage of the grid (Fig. 8.5a). All appliances in the building are then ordinary AC, 120v (or whatever the baseline voltage is). Note again that batteries are

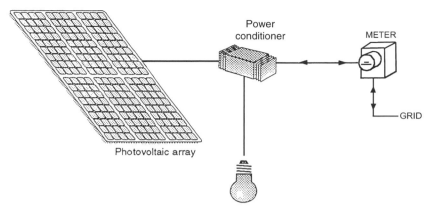

Figure 8.5a A typical grid-connected PV system. On a sunny day, the excess power will flow into the grid and the meter will run backward. The power conditioner contains an inverter to change DC into AC.

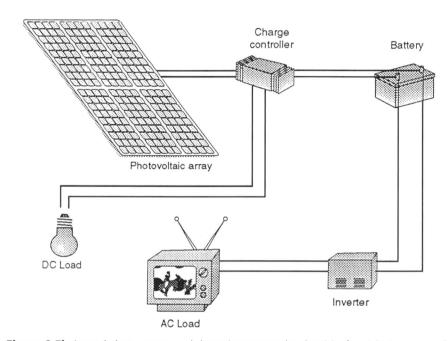

Figure 8.5b A stand-alone system needs batteries to store the electricity for nighttime use and an inverter to change DC to AC current.

not needed, which is a significant saving of both money and maintenance.

In stand-alone systems, the excess electricity produced during the day is stored in batteries for nighttime and dark, cloudy days (Fig. 8.5b). Since inverters are expensive and can consume as much as 20 percent of the power the PV produces, buildings must use as many low-voltage direct-current (DC) appliances in place of standard AC appliances as possible. A small, less expensive inverter can then supply the AC appliances. Also, since PV cells and batteries are expensive, backup

power is preferable over an extra-large PV system for lengthy overcast periods or storms. A hybrid system using wind power is often the ideal complement to PV because not only can the wind blow at night, but also it is usually extra windy during bad weather. Furthermore, in the winter, when there is less solar energy to harvest, it is usually windier than it is in the summer (Fig. 8.5c). Not all regions, however, are suitable for wind power. See the discussion of wind power in Chapter 2.

When a reliable wind source is not available, an engine generator

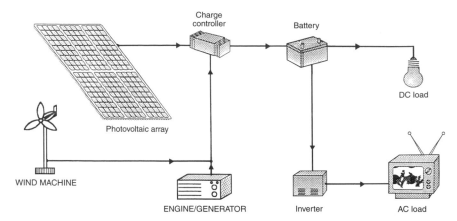

Figure 8.5c Hybrid systems give the most reliable power at the least cost for stand-alone installations.

unit should be used to back up the PV system. It is reasonable to ask: why bother with the PV system at all? Why not just use the engine generator? Many remote installations that previously used only an engine generator are switching to the PV hybrid system because it is more reliable, requires much less maintenance, makes no noise, and needs little fuel, which is always a burden to bring to a remote site. In a well-designed hybrid system, the engine generator will operate only a few times a year, during unusually long cloudy periods.

8.6 BALANCE OF SYSTEM EQUIPMENT

A PV installation consists of the PV array and the **balance of system (BOS) equipment**. Typically, the BOS equipment comprises a charge controller, an inverter (for AC), switches, fuses, wires, etc. For stand-alone systems, the BOS equipment also includes the batteries. A small wall panel is usually sufficient for most of the BOS equipment except for the batteries.

In stand-alone systems, the excess electricity produced when the sun is shining is stored in batteries. Although several different types of batteries are available, many systems use a deep-cycle version of the lead-acid batteries found in cars. For safety and long

life, batteries should be stored in well-ventilated, cool, dry chambers. Batteries need to be vented outdoors because of the hydrogen that is produced during charging. Consequently, they should be stored either indoors next to an outdoor wall or in an insulated shed against the outside wall. A separate structure will work only if the batteries can be kept from getting too warm or too cold; 77°F (25°C) is the optimum temperature.

In the near future, an alternative to batteries might be the use of nonpolluting **fuel cells**. During the day, the sun will provide energy for the production of hydrogen via the electrolysis of water. At night, the fuel cell will generate electricity, and with hydrogen as the fuel, the only by-product will be water.

Commercial fuel cells are now on the market. Many experts are convinced that hydrogen is the fuel of the future, but, of course, hydrogen is not a source of energy: it must be produced, and PV is one sustainable way to produce it.

8.7 BUILDING-INTEGRATED PHOTOVOLTAICS

PV systems can power buildings in a variety of ways, ranging from large-scale remote PV power plants to part of the building fabric. Some utilities are augmenting their electrical capacity

through large, centralized PV farms (Fig. 8.3c), while other power companies are setting up smaller PV fields closer to the electrical users. PV arrays can also be set up on the land adjacent to the building (Fig. 8.7a), placed on the roof (Fig. 8.7b), or integrated into the building envelope (Fig. 8.7c), in which case the phrase **building-integrated photovoltaics (BIPV)** is used. BIPV systems can replace the roofing, siding, curtain wall, glazing, or special elements such as overhangs and canopies.

There are a number of important benefits to using BIPV:

1. The elimination of the cost of transporting electricity to the building, which can be more than 50 percent of the cost of the electricity
2. The elimination of the energy waste of transporting electricity, which can be as much as 25 percent (Fig. 8.7d)
3. The avoidance of using valuable open space to mount the PV array
4. The avoidance of part of the cost of the building envelope by using PV modules instead
5. The avoidance of a support structure since the building structure exists anyway
6. The aesthetic potential of using a new type of cladding material
7. The benefit of generating all or at least a significant portion of the required electricity in an environmentally friendly way

Although at this time PV modules are still expensive, they are no more expensive than some premium architectural cladding. PV is not more expensive, for example, than granite or marble facing. Thus, one can save either all or part of the cost of the PV array by eliminating the cost of the building element being replaced.

PV modules come in many sizes, finishes, and colors. Most silicon cells are a beautiful blue color, with the crystalline structure forming an attractive pattern (Fig. 8.7e). Many thin-film PV modules are dark brown, and some are flexible so that they can

Figure 8.7a An on-site PV array requires a support structure and some open land for solar access. A sun-tracking system is shown. (Courtesy Ecological Design Institute ©.)

Figure 8.7b On existing sloped roofs, the PV is usually placed on the roofing. (Courtesy Sacramento Municipal Utility District.)

Figure 8.7c The BIPV standing seam roofing on this Maryland townhouse (at the center) is almost indistinguishable from conventional, standard seam roofing on the other buildings. (Courtesy United Solar Systems Corp., UNI-solar® Photovoltaic Roofing.)

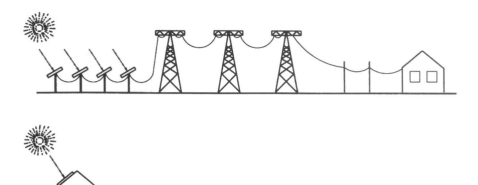

Figure 8.7d Besides displacing part of a building's weathering skin, BIPV eliminates the electrical-transmission losses, which can be as high as 25 percent with the existing power grid.

and ancillary structures such as overhangs, entrance canopies, and shading structures for parking areas. Each of the four parts will be discussed in some detail after a short discussion of the PV characteristics that are important in building integration.

Since the PV modules are fairly dark in color and *must not* be shaded, much heat is produced, which not only degrades the performance of the PV cells but also may heat the building. Thus, cooling the cells is an important concern and will be discussed later. Also important are the orientation and tilt of the PV array, which will be discussed next.

8.8 ORIENTATION AND TILT

The maximum collection of solar radiation occurs when the collector is perpendicular to the direct beam radiation.

be used on curved surfaces (Fig. 8.7f). Cells are now being developed that are gold, violet, or green in color. A variety of semitransparent PV modules can be used as glazing. Cells can be round, semicircular, octagonal, square, or rectangular, and custom modules and panels can be produced for large projects.

There are four major parts of the building envelope into which PV can be integrated: walls, roofs, glazing,

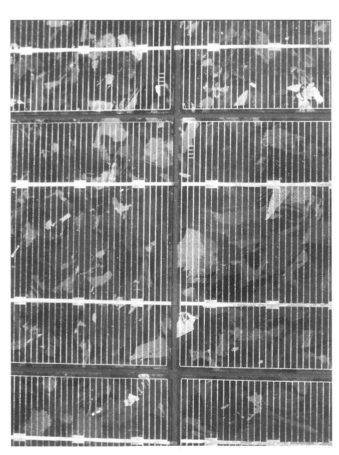

Figure 8.7e PV modules can be very attractive, as shown in this blue pattern of polycrystalline silicon cells.

Figure 8.7f Because thin-film modules are flexible, they are easily integrated into curved architecture.

Since the sun moves both daily and annually, only a two-axis tracking collector can maximize the collection over a year. Tracking collectors, however, excel only in dry climates that have mostly direct-beam radiation, and even there, 10 to 20 percent of the solar radiation is diffuse. In most sunny and humid climates, only about one-half of the solar radiation is direct, while in cloudy climates 80 percent or more of the radiation is diffuse. When PV cells were very expensive, it made good sense to invest in a tracking device in most climates (Fig. 8.7a). Now tracking collectors should be considered only for sunny and dry climates, and even there, the advantages of building integration may be greater than the benefits of tracking.

Even with building integration, orientation and tilt should still be considered. The best tilt for a PV array is primarily a function of the time of year that maximum power is required. Hot climates need the most electricity in the summer for air conditioning, while cold climates need maximum electricity in the winter for lighting- and heating-system pumps and blowers. Use the design guidelines in Section 8.16 for choosing the optimum tilt for the PV.

Usually, the optimal orientation is due south, but there is little loss up to 20° east or 20° west of south. The daily-load profile, however, can influence the orientation. For example, elementary schools that start early in the morning and end in the middle of the afternoon should have the array facing about 30° east of south; in a climate with a morning fog, a southwest orientation would be appropriate. Since peak electrical demand usually occurs on hot, sunny summer afternoons, the PV module could also be facing west.

As PV modules get less expensive, the optimal orientation and tilt will become less important. Already, it makes sense to cover the roof and sometimes the south facade. East and west facades are not far behind because they can produce up to 60 percent

of the optimal south output. Eventually, all orientations except north will be clad with PV.

8.9 ROOFS CLAD WITH PV

Ideally, the roof should have the slope (tilt) described in Fig 8.16, with the PV replacing the roofing (Fig. 8.7c). On flat roofs, a support structure can offer the ideal tilt, but, of course, the benefits of building integration are lost (Fig. 8.9a). A sawtooth clerestory is superior to a flat roof because the north-facing slope can be glazed for daylighting, while the south slope supports the BIPV (Fig. 8.9b). The south-facing PV can also be of the semitransparent kind, so that the clerestories can both collect

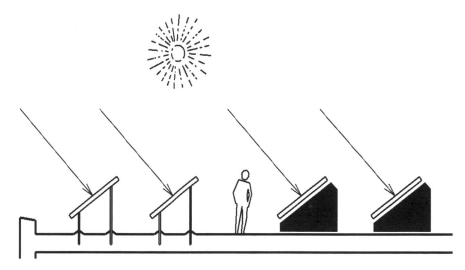

Figure 8.9a Support structures can provide the appropriate tilt for the PV on flat roofs, but they do not provide the benefits of being building integrated. The use of heavy concrete or gravel-filled support structures makes it unnecessary to penetrate the roof membrane.

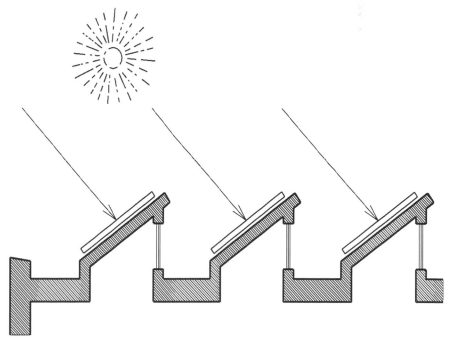

Figure 8.9b Sawtooth clerestories can provide both daylighting and the proper tilt for BIPV.

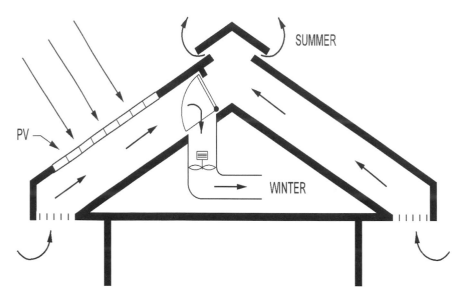

Figure 8.9c Ventilate the underside of the PV in summer to keep the cells from overheating. In winter, this warm air can be used to heat the building.

Figure 8.9d PV shingles are designed to blend in with standard shingles. (Courtesy United States Solar Systems Corp., manufacturing solar roofing under the brand name UNI-solar®.)

south daylight and generate electricity. Also, sloped roofs are easier to waterproof. A flat slope is usually not desirable for the PV because it is too far from the ideal tilt (except near the equator) and because of dirt and snow accumulation. In northern latitudes, a vertical orientation may be best in order to avoid snow accumulations while benefiting from the snow's solar reflection.

If the PV is integrated into the roof, the underside needs to be ventilated to cool it. In winter this waste heat can be collected to heat the building (Fig. 8.9c). For more traditional roofs, PV shingles, slates, and tiles are available. They are used in the conventional manner except that an electrical connection must be made with every unit (Fig. 8.9d).

8.10 FACADES CLAD WITH PV

Not only south but also east and west facades can be clad with PV and still generate a significant amount of electricity. If mullions are used on the exterior, they should be as shallow as possible to prevent shading of the PV (Fig. 8.10a). Use the PV on the upper facade only if the lower areas are shaded, as is common in dense urban areas or sites with many trees (Fig. 8.10b). As with the roof, it is best to leave an airspace behind the PV to cool the panels, and in winter this warm air can be collected to heat the building (Fig. 8.10c).

8.11 GLAZING AND PV

There are two types of PV glazing systems. One is semitransparent, much like tinted glazing (Fig. 8.11a). The other consists of opaque cells mounted on clear glazing, with the spacing of the cells determining the ratio of clear to opaque. This is much like ordinary glazing painted with frets (Fig. 8.11b).

With either type of PV glazing, it is possible to control the amount of light being transmitted. Of course, the more light transmitted the lower the power production. Even with very transparent PV systems, large amounts of power can be produced because of the large amount of glazing in most modern buildings. PV glazing is especially appropriate in clerestories or skylights since these are not designed for view.

Under development is a transparent PV glazing that utilizes only solar infrared radiation to generate electricity. Thus, both cool daylight and electricity are produced by the glazing—just what most office buildings in hot climates need.

Figure 8.10a The APS Building in Fairfield, California, uses thin-film PV integrated into the curtain wall, skylight, and awning. (Courtesy Kiss & Cathcart, architects. © Richard Barnes, photographer.)

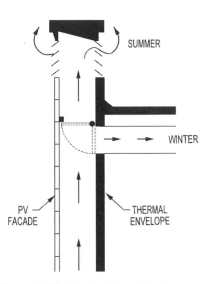

Figure 8.10c This double-wall design enables the air behind the PV to be vented in the summer to cool both the PV and the building. In winter, the hot air can be used to heat the north side of the building.

Figure 8.10b The New York City skyscraper at 4 Times Square uses BIPV spandrel panels only on floors 35 to 48, because the lower floors are shaded too much. (Courtesy Kiss & Cathcart, architects.)

Figure 8.11a Semitransparent PV glazing is used as skylight glazing in the APS factory in Fairfield, California. (Courtesy Kiss & Cathcart, architects. © Richard Barnes, photographer.)

Figure 8.11b Opaque PV cells are mounted on clear glass. The spacing between cells determines the degree of shading. As seen from below, the entranceway canopy of the Aquatic Center at the Georgia Institute of Technology is roofed with a 4.5-kilowatt array of Solarex PowerWall™ MSX-240/AC laminates. With their integrated inverters, these laminates provide grid-synchronized AC power. They use an optional clear Tedlar® backing material that emphasizes the precision of solar cell placement and provides soft, natural lighting under the canopy. (Courtesy of © BP Solarex.)

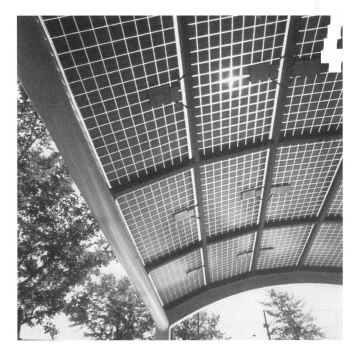

8.12 PV SHADING DEVICES

Shading devices are a very good application for PV because they can be designed to be tilted at the optimum angle (Figs. 8.12a and 8.12b). Shading devices either can be opaque or can use PV glazing with a wide range of transparency.

PV can also be integrated into entrance canopies or freestanding shading structures (Fig. 8.12c). Although at present the shading of automobiles in hot parking lots is usually too expensive, as a combination PV generator and shading structure, its cost becomes more reasonable. As electric cars become more common, these

structures will serve as ideal charging stations (Fig. 8.12d).

8.13 PV: PART OF THE SECOND TIER

It is important to understand that electrical generation by PV is part of the second tier of the three-tier approach

Figure 8.12a This close-up of the Center for Environmental Sciences and Technology Management (CESTM), State University of New York (SUNY), Albany, clearly shows the tilt of the PV shading devices. (Courtesy Kawneer Company, Inc., © Gordon H. Schenck, Jr., 1996, photographer.)

Figure 8.12b Another view of the PV shading devices on the CESTM. (Courtesy Kawneer Company, Inc., © Gordon H. Schenck, Jr., 1996, photographer.)

Figure 8.12c The barrel-vaulted entrance canopy to the Aquatic Center at the Georgia Institute of Technology is made entirely of PV modules. See the underside of this canopy in Fig. 8.11b. (Courtesy and © BP Solarex.)

Figure 8.12d Automobile shading structures covered with PV are also ideal electric car-charging stations. (Courtesy Sacramento Municipal Utility District.)

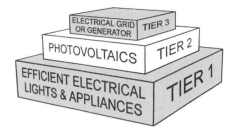

Figure 8.13 As always, the three-tier approach is a logical and sustainable strategy for environmental design.

to environmental design (Fig. 8.13). The first tier consists of utilizing efficient electrical appliances, lighting systems, and air-conditioning systems to minimize the electrical load. The second tier consists of using PV to generate clean, sustainable electricity. The third tier consists of utilizing a generator or an electrical grid to supply the small amount of electrical power and energy still required. This is not only the most sustainable approach, but also usually the most economical.

8.14 SIZING A PV SYSTEM

Grid-connected systems are sized differently from stand-alone systems, and their design will be discussed later. For stand-alone systems, sizing is critical because too large a system is a very expensive waste. As mentioned above, the three-tier approach to design should be utilized to minimize the electrical load. Furthermore, the two very large users of low-grade energy, which are space heating and domestic hot water, should not be supplied by the PV. Passive solar is the first choice for space heating, and active solar is the best choice for domestic hot water. Backup energy for both space heating and domestic hot water could come from gas or wood.

There should be backup power from an engine generator or a reliable source of wind power; otherwise, the PV system would have to be significantly larger in order to store power for extended periods of bad weather. The resultant cost would be unnecessarily high.

Sizing of a Stand-Alone System

The following guidelines are for stand-alone systems with a backup power source occasionally used. Use the rules of thumb presented in Table 8.14 for a first approximation and the calculations in the next section for a more precise estimate.

It is critical to consider winter conditions when designing a PV system in northern regions because the lights are on for many hours, and the PV array sees the sun for few hours. In southern regions, winter design is less critical because there are more hours of daylight. Because summer air conditioning is almost mandatory in southern regions, peak electrical loads usually occur in the summer.

Sizing a Grid-Connected PV System

There is no limit to the desired array area since the grid can use all the power produced at peak times in most areas of the United States. The cost of the array is the main determinant of size. Because the present cost of PV is high, only the orientations that can generate the most power should be used. As PV prices decline, more and more building surfaces will be clad in PV. In homes, the roof area might be all that is needed, but in commercial, institutional, and industrial buildings, the walls, roofs, and glazing will also be put to work generating electricity. Section 8.16 will discuss the efficiency of different orientations. However, since much of the U.S. electrical demand peaks on hot, sunny summer days, most grid-connected PV systems should also peak at that time.

One likely possibility is that the power companies will rent roof space from the user in order to generate the power where it is needed. This will enable the utility to avoid the great expense of upgrading the distribution system. This is already the case with the Sacramento Municipal Utility District (SMUD) in California. More than ninety electric utilities have formed the Utility Photovoltaics Group to promote and sponsor PV installations on or around buildings.

To prevent the future problem of collectors being added at unattractive odd angles, new buildings should be oriented so that their roofs face in a southerly direction close to the optimum tilt. *From now on, all buildings should use or anticipate PV cladding.*

Table 8.14 Approximate Method For Sizing Stand-Alone Systems*		Array Size†		Battery storage‡	
Building Type	**Climate***	**(ft²)**	**(m²)**	**(ft²)**	**(m²)**
Small residence	Mild and sunny	50	4.5	10	0.9
	Cold and cloudy	100	9	20	1.8
	Hot and humid	100	9		
Average residence	Mild and sunny	100	9	20	1.8
	Cold and cloudy	500	45	100	9
	Hot and humid	500	45	100	9
Large residence	Mild and sunny	500	45	100	9
	Cold and cloudy	1,000	90	200	18
	Hot and humid	1,000	90	200	18

*Hot and humid climates need a large array because of the air-conditioner load. In cold and cloudy climates, the large array is due to the combined effect of lighting long winter nights and short cloudy days for generating power.
†The size of the array is very approximate in part because of the large variance in cell efficiency.
‡A space with this floor area will also contain the BOS, which includes the controller, inverter, switches, and circuit breakers.

8.15 FINDING THE PV ARRAY SIZE FOR A STAND-ALONE BUILDING BY THE SHORT CALCULATION METHOD

The size of the PV array depends on the following factors:

1. Amount of electrical energy needed per day (KWH/day)
2. System efficiency—losses in inverters, controllers, etc. (50 percent is typical)
3. Amount of solar radiation available per day (KWH/m²/day)
4. Power produced by the PV module (KW/m²)

Steps for Sizing a PV Array

1. Use Tables 8.15A and 8.15B to determine the electrical load per day in watt-hours per day.

   WH/day = (___)

2. Find the adjusted load by multiplying the WH/day (Step 1) by 1.5 to account for system losses.

   (WH/day) × 1.5 = (___)

3. Determine the solar energy available at the site for one day in terms of "sun-hours" from the map of Fig. 8.15a for winter-peaking loads and Fig. 8.15b for summer-peaking loads.

   sun-hours = (___)

4. To find the required peak-watts (W_p), divide the adjusted load (Step 2) by the sun-hours (Step 3).

$$W_P = \frac{\text{adjusted (WH/day)}}{\text{sun-hours}} = (\_\_\_)$$

5. Find the array size by dividing W_p (Step 4) by

   12 W/ft² for single-crystal silicon cells

   or 10 W/ft² for polycrystalline silicon cells

   or 5 W/ft² for amorphous silicon or thin-film cells

   or 5 W/ft² for PV standing seam roof

   or 2.5 W/ft² for PV shingles.

$$A = \frac{W_P}{W/ft^2} = (\_\_\_)ft^2$$

(For m², multiply ft² by 0.09.)

As might be expected, more efficient cells cost more. Less efficient cells sometimes give more watts per dollar, and the roof area of most residences is more than adequate to use low-efficiency cells and still generate all the power needed, especially if the roof faces south at the appropriate tilt angle.

Example:

Find the array size for a stand-alone residence located in the middle of Pennsylvania (40° latitude). The total load in watt-hours per day is 3000, and the roof is made of a standing-seam PV material facing south at a tilt angle of 55° (latitude plus 15° for winter peaking).

Table 8.15A Worksheet for Determining the Electrical Load

Appliances	Watts*	Number of Hours Used Per Day	Watt-Hours Per Day
Lights			
Refrigerator†			
Washing machine			
Furnace blower			
Air conditioning			
Exhaust fans			
Television			
Computer			
Miscellaneous plug loads			
Other			
		Total Watt-Hours Per Day	___

*Find actual watts from appliances to be used or refer to Table 8.15B.
†Because refrigerators cycle on and off, they typically run about six hours per day.

Table 8.15B Typical Appliance Wattage

Device	Wattage
Incandescent lights* (wattage of lamps)	—
Fluorescent lamps (wattage of lamps plus 10% for ballast)	—
Coffeepot	200
Microwave	1000
Dishwasher	1300
Washing machine	500
Vacuum cleaner	500
Clothes dryer (uses gas)	350
Furnace blower	500
Air conditioner (central)	3000
Ceiling fan	30
Computer and printer	200
Television and videocassette recorder	200
Stereo	20
Refrigerator—conventional	500
Refrigerator—high efficiency	200

*Avoid the use of incandescent lamps and minimize the use of halogen lamps (see Chapter 14).

Step 1. Use the given load: 3000 WH/day.

Step 2. Find the adjusted load by multiplying by 1.5:

3000 (1.5) = 4500 WH/day

Step 3. Determine the sun-hours by using Fig. 8.15a (for this northern location the sun-hours = 2).

Step 4. Find the peak-watts (Wp) by dividing the adjusted load by the sun-hours:

4500/2 = 2250 Wp

Step 5. Since a standing-seam roof is specified, divide Wp by 5 W/ft² to find the area of the array:

2250/5 = 450 ft²
(450 ft² × 0.09 = 40.5 m²)

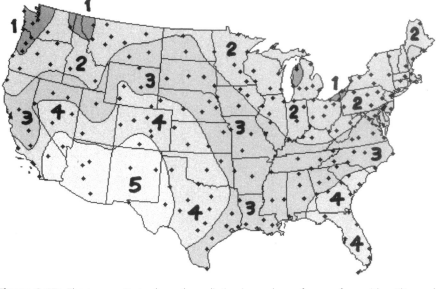

Figure 8.15a The average December solar radiation in sun-hours for a surface with a tilt equal to latitude plus 15°. Because December has the least sunshine, it is usually used for sizing PV systems. (From the National Renewable Energy Laboratory–NREL.)

8.16 DESIGN GUIDELINES

Use the following guidelines to get the full benefits of the PV system sized with the methods described above:

1. Use BIPV to save money and improve the aesthetics.
2. Use the following orientations and slopes in descending order of efficiency (most efficient first).
   a. Southerly orientation tilted at (see Fig. 8.16):
      - latitude for maximum annual energy production
      - latitude − 15° for summer peaking
      - latitude + 15° for winter peaking
   b. South wall
   c. West wall
   d. East wall
3. Make sure the array is shaded as little as possible. Avoid having even a small area of array shaded because of the "Christmas-lights-in-series-syndrome," where if one light goes out, all the lights go out.

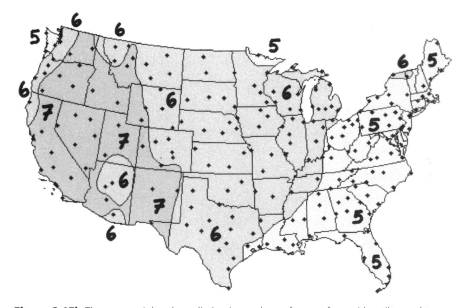

Figure 8.15b The average July solar radiation in sun hours for a surface with a tilt equal to latitude minus 15°. (From the National Renewable Energy Laboratory–NREL.)

Fortunately, solar performance is not degraded too much with some deviation from the optimum tilt and orientation. For example, in most of the United States, there will be only a 10 percent loss if the tilt is anywhere from 15 to 60° and the orientation is within 45° of true south (*Environmental Building* News, 1999).

4. Keep modules cool by venting their backs (cool cells generate more electricity than hot cells), and use this heat in winter.
5. Avoid horizontal arrays since they collect dirt and snow.
6. Mount modules at a steep tilt in snow country so that snow will quickly slide off.

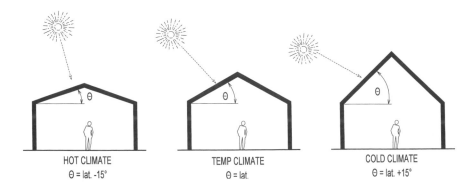

Figure 8.16 This figure shows the recommended tilt angles for PV arrays in order to maximize electricity production as a function of climate

8.17 THE PROMISE OF PV

In architecture, an elegant solution is one that has many benefits besides solving the immediate problem. Thus, a roof would be much more elegant if, besides its traditional function, it also produced all the energy the building needed. If PV replaced all of the roofing, the amount of power produced would be much more than any residence could use. Consequently, each home would be an exporter of energy, and instead of being a burden on the environment, many buildings could become environmental assets.

I remember looking out at the roofscape of New York City from a high building and thinking what a waste these thousands of empty, flat roofs were. Very few roofs were used either for gardens or for cooling-tower supports. Consider the enormous value of this resource, which is about equal to the built land area of the city. If these roofs were covered by PV, the energy would be produced right where it is needed, with minimal transmission losses (Fig. 8.17). If all roofs in the United States were covered with PV, they could produce 35 percent of all the required electricity. With the deregulation of the electric power industry, an entrepreneur could offer a building owner a free, no-maintenance, high-quality roof for the privilege of generating power. What a gigantic amount of clean, renewable power would be generated right where it is needed.

If all roofs and most south walls were covered with PV, most towns and small cities would produce all the electricity they needed. Although large cities, especially with dense clusters of high-rise buildings, could not be energy-independent, they would need to import much less power than at present. All new construction should either have BIPV or be designed to accept PV when the cost has declined further. In such cases, a temporary low-cost weathering skin could be used until building-integrated materials became cost-competitive.

PV applications are not limited to the Sunbelt but are appropriate in almost all climates. In Norway, which is as far north as Alaska, more than 50,000 vacation houses are powered solely by PV systems, and Germany, with its limited solar resource, is presently the leading user of PV in the world.

8.18 THE COST EFFECTIVENESS OF PV AND ACTIVE SOLAR APPLICATIONS

The main competitors of PV for roof space are solar collectors designed to produce hot air or water. Hot air is used primarily for space heating, while hot water can be used for a number of purposes: domestic hot water, space heating, space cooling, swimming-pool heating, and commercial

Figure 8.17 A 360-kilowatt array using Solarex's MSX-120 power modules mounted on the roof of the aquatic center. The installation is located on the campus of Georgia Tech University, Atlanta, the site of the 1996 Summer Olympics. (Courtesy and © BP Solarex.)

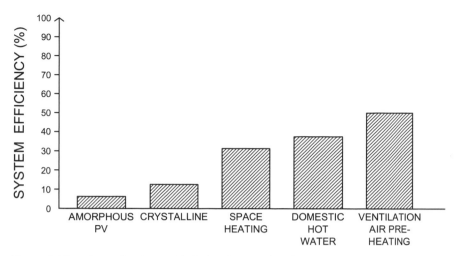

Figure 8.18a It is usually wise to pick the low-hanging fruit first. Passive solar is usually the most cost effective strategy when there is solar access to the windows. This chart shows that "green heat" in the form of air and hot-water solar heating is far more efficient than PV. Solar-heated air and hot water are also more economical.

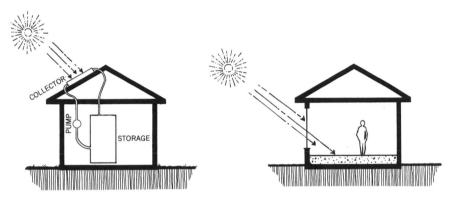

Figure 8.18c Active solar requires specialized mechanical equipment to make it work, while passive solar relies only on the building itself. Passive solar is less expensive in most cases.

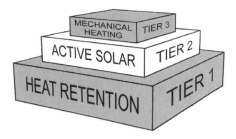

Figure 8.18b A building's hot-air and water needs are best provided by tier two of the three-tier design approach.

hot water. Regarding the present and near-future costs of PV, it is much more economical to create hot air or water directly rather than to use PV electricity (Fig. 8.18a). Also, as was explained in Chapter 3, it is not sensible to convert a high-grade energy, such as electricity, directly into a low-grade energy, such as heat.

The most sustainable way to meet a building's need for hot air and water can be understood by the three-tier design approach (Fig. 8.18b). Tier one consists of minimizing the needs through efficiency. In the second tier, active collectors harvest the sun. Only in the third tier will mechanical systems using nonrenewable energies be called upon to supply the small load that remains after tiers one and two.

The term **active solar** is used to designate mechanical devices whose sole purpose is to collect solar energy in the form of heat and then store it for later use. The working fluid is sometimes air, but usually it is water pumped from the collector to the storage tank. This system is referred to as "active solar" because it has a pump and, more important, because it does just one thing: collect heat. On the other hand, a passive system, as discussed in the previous chapter, uses only the basic building fabric to collect the heat (Fig. 8.18c). Since the building fabric is there anyway, passive solar is free or nearly so. Furthermore, since there are no mechanical parts to break or wear out, passive solar is more reliable and requires little or

no maintenance. Thus, it is generally agreed that passive solar is the best choice for space heating where it will work. It won't work, for example, if only the roof of a building has access to the winter sun. In that case, active solar space heating might be appropriate. Solar access is often a problem in urban areas, in wooded sites (especially if evergreen), and in high latitudes where the very low winter sun in easily blocked. Thus, active solar is sometimes used for space heating, but mostly it is used for heating water for other purposes.

Five different applications exist for hot water in buildings: swimming-pool heating, domestic hot water, commercial/institutional hot water, space heating, and solar cooling. Commercial/institutional hot water is much like domestic hot water. Buildings, such as hospitals, apartment buildings, schools, jails, car washes, nursing homes, health clubs, restaurants, and hotels, all use large quantities of hot water that can be produced economically by an active solar system. See Table 8.18 for the relative cost effectiveness of these different applications.

Why is it so appropriate to use active solar for heating swimming pools? One reason is that pools are heated only in the spring, summer, and fall (to extend the swimming season) when much more solar energy is available than in the winter. Another reason is based on the Laws of Thermodynamics: all solar collectors have the highest efficiency at their lowest operating temperature. Since pool-water temperatures are rather low (about 80°F) (26°C), the efficiency

Table 8.18 Cost Effectiveness of Active Solar Applications

Application	Economical?
Swimming-pool heating	Yes, (two- to three-year payback)
Domestic hot water	Yes (five- to eight-year payback)
Active space heating	Sometimes (rarely in the South, frequently in cold northern climates when passive solar is not possible)
Solar space cooling or dehumidification	Sometimes (long payback period at present)
Process hot water	Usually

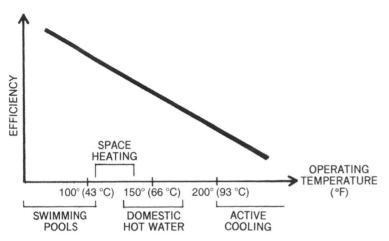

Figure 8.18d The performance of a typical flat-plate solar collector is shown. Although the exact curve varies with the collector type, the efficiency always declines with an increase in the collection temperature. Note how the temperature and application are related.

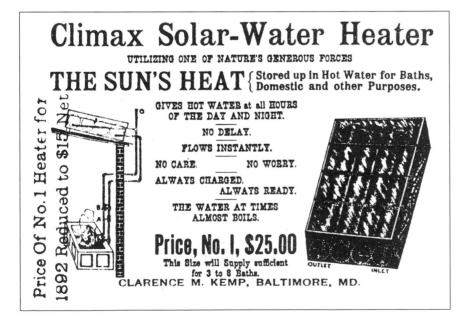

Figure 8.18e This advertisement for a solar hot-water heater appeared in 1892. (From Special Collections, Romaine Collection, University of California, Santa Barbara; cited in *A Golden Thread* by Ken Butti and John Perlin.)

of the solar collectors is very high (Fig. 8.18d). This low-temperature efficiency also applies to two forms of space heating. A radiant floor heating system can make good use of water heated to only 90°F (32°C) and a heat pump can **upgrade** the heat that solar collectors gather. Heat pumps will be explained in Chapter 16.

Domestic hot water is also a good application for active solar but for a different reason. Since domestic hot water is required year-round, the equipment is never idle. This, unfortunately, is not true for space heating. Not only is an active solar space-heating system idle for much of the year, but when it does work in the winter, the supply of solar energy is at its lowest point. Consequently, active systems for space heating are less efficient than they are for domestic hot water or swimming-pool heating. However, an important exception exists. Preheating ventilation air in cold climates can be accomplished very economically with transpired collectors, which will be discussed in Section 8.24.

Limitations on active solar systems are more economic than technical. Where cheap, alternative energy sources are not available, solar energy is popular. Active solar systems are common in many countries—millions of systems are now operating in Europe, Asia, and the Middle East. China is now the largest producer, user, and exporter of active solar systems in the world. As a matter of fact, active solar systems were sold in the United States at the turn of the twentieth century and became quite popular in Florida and Southern California (Fig 8.18e). By 1941, about 60,000 solar hot-water systems existed in the United States. Solar energy declined after that time, not because it did not work but because fossil energy was cheaper and it was no longer fashionable. Because only the poor kept their solar rooftop systems, the public developed a negative image of solar energy.

Because solar swimming-pool heaters are the most cost-effective and simplest of the active solar systems, they are described first.

8.19 ACTIVE SOLAR SWIMMING-POOL HEATING

As mentioned before, solar swimming-pool heaters are very cost-effective because they collect the sun during the part of the year when solar energy is plentiful and because they collect heat at rather low temperatures. At these relatively low temperatures, the collectors are not only very efficient but they can also be rather simple and inexpensive to manufacture (Fig. 8.19a). The rest of the system is also inexpensive because the existing filtration equipment can often be used to circulate the water (Fig. 8.19b). And unlike other active solar heaters, freeze protection is not needed because the systems are not used in the winter.

As with buildings, the first step in heating a pool is to reduce heat loss. Since most of the heat is lost by evaporation, a pool cover is a must. The above discussion refers to outdoor pools. For indoor pools that can be used year-round, active solar systems similar to the kinds used for domestic hot water described below are required.

Rules of Thumb for Sizing Swimming-Pool Collectors*

1. For the hot southern United States, use a collector area equal to 50 percent of the pool area.
2. For the cold northern United States, use a collector area equal to the pool area.
3. For states in the middle, use a collector area equal to 75 percent of the pool area.

8.20 SOLAR HOT-WATER SYSTEMS

Since most buildings need domestic hot water, most active systems use water rather than air as a heat-transfer-and-storage medium. Such water-based

*These values are for orientation within 20° of south and a tilt angle near (latitude −15°). For only fair orientation and tilt, add 25 percent, and for poor orientation and tilt, add a 50 percent additional collector area.

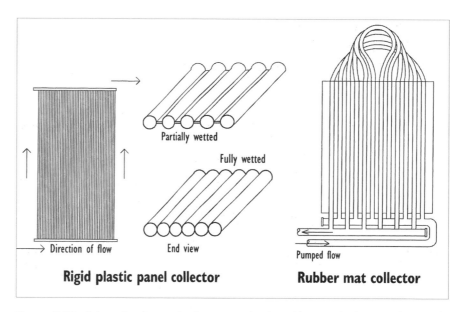

Figure 8.19a Solar swimming-pool collectors are simple and inexpensive because they need neither glass covers nor insulation. Some are made of flexible extruded plastic that can be shipped in a roll. (Courtesy Dan Cuoshi © *Home Energy Magazine*.)

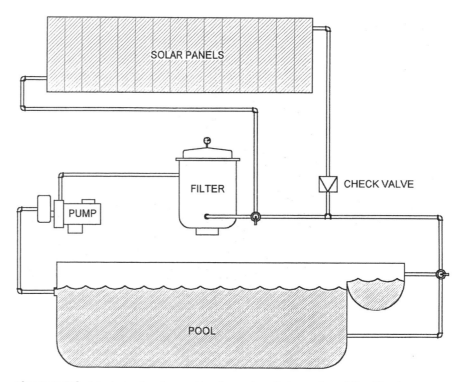

Figure 8.19b A typical swimming-pool heating system that uses the existing filtration equipment to circulate the water is shown. (After Sun Trapper Solar System Inc.)

systems can also be easily used for space heating. Each system must have a collector, heat-transfer fluid, and a storage device. To protect against freezing and boiling, some water systems use a mixture of water and antifreeze. An insulated tank, usually located indoors, stores the hot water. The collector must be more sophisticated than the swimming-pool kind because it has to generate medium-high temperatures (120° to 140°F) [50° to 60°C] even on very cold winter days.

The most common kind of collector used for producing domestic hot water is called a **flat plate collector**, which essentially consists of a metal plate coated with a black **selective surface** to reduce heat loss by reradiation (see Section 3.11). A glass cover creates the greenhouse effect to maximize the energy collected, and insulation is used to reduce heat loss from the back and sides of the collector (Fig. 8.20a). Water is pumped through pipes attached to the hot collector plate, and the heated water is then stored in tanks located inside the building. To prevent contamination of the potable domestic hot water, a heat exchanger is used.

When the controller senses that the water is warmer in the collector than in the storage tank, the pump is activated, and when the sun sets and the collector is cooler than the storage tank, the controller shuts off the pump. In a particular arrangement called a **drain-back system**, the water completely drains into the indoor tank whenever the pump does not operate (Fig. 8.20b). If the pump fails to operate, this safety measure will

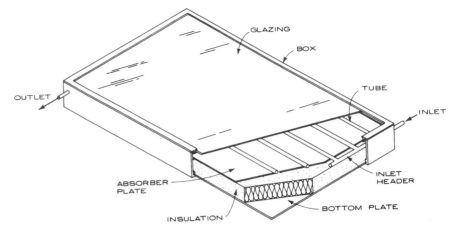

Figure 8.20a A typical flat-plate collector designed to heat a liquid. (From *Architectural Graphic Standards, Ramsey/Sleeper*, 8th ed., John R. Hoke, editor © John Wiley & Sons, Inc., 1988.)

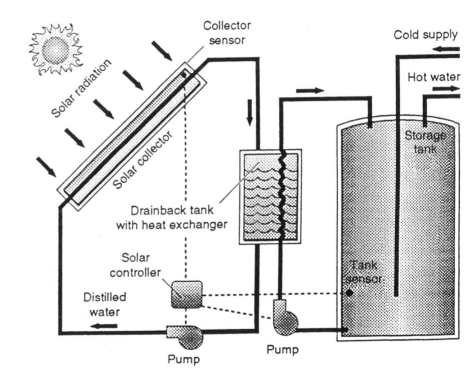

Figure 8.20b The drain-back solar hot-water system is shown. To prevent contamination of the domestic hot water, a double-walled heat exchanger is submerged in the storage tank. A space-heating system can also utilize the hot water in the tank. (From the Texas State Energy Conservation Office, Fact Sheet #10.)

Figure 8.20c Because a concentrating collector uses a parabolic mirror to achieve high temperatures, it must track the sun.

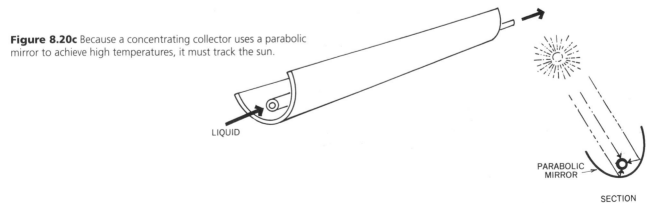

prevent freezing or boiling in the collector without the need for antifreeze. Other arrangements are used, depending on the climate and the particular company that makes the system.

It is not practical to try to design a 100 percent solar system because the supply of sunshine is irregular. It would take a very large solar collector and storage system to supply hot water after a week of cloudy, cold weather. Since such a large system would be completely overdesigned for much of the year, and the overall efficiency would be low. Thus, a 100 percent solar heating system is not economical; the optimum percentage varies with the climate but is usually between 60 and 80 percent.

When very hot water is required, special collectors are used. Either by concentrating the sun or by reducing the heat loss, water can be heated above the boiling point.

The concentrating collectors are more complicated because they must track the sun along one axis (Fig. 8.20c). The vacuum tube collectors are almost universally used in China because they do not need to track the sun, have very high efficiency, and can be mass-produced (Fig. 8.20d). If heat pipes are used inside the evacuated tube, then the tubes must be used in an inclined position (Fig. 8.20e). On the other hand, if water is circulated through the vacuum tubes, they can be used in any position. They have even been used as a balcony railing (Fig. 8.20f). The tubes are 2 to 4 in. (5 to 10 cm) in diameter, and they come in many lengths.

8.21 SOLAR HOT-AIR COLLECTORS

Hot-air collectors are used primarily for space heating. The main disadvantages of air as a collecting fluid are: much fan power is needed because of the low heat capacity of air, the

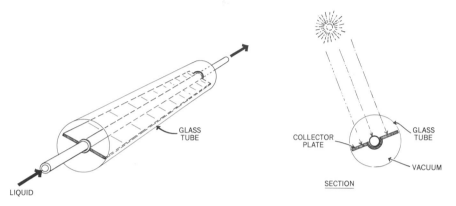

Figure 8.20d A vacuum-tube collector achieves high temperatures by reducing heat loss. All convective and most conductive losses are eliminated by the vacuum, and most radiant losses are eliminated by a selective coating.

Figure 8.20e Vacuum-tube solar collectors can produce very hot water efficiently. They can also be an attractive visual element, as seen in these townhouses in Aspen, Colorado.

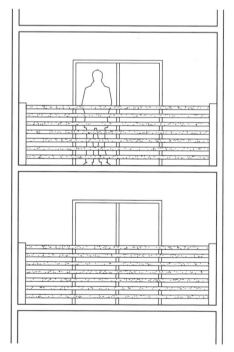

Figure 8.20f In multistory buildings in northern latitudes, the solar collectors can be mounted vertically on south-facing facades. Here vacuum-tube collectors are used as a balcony railing.

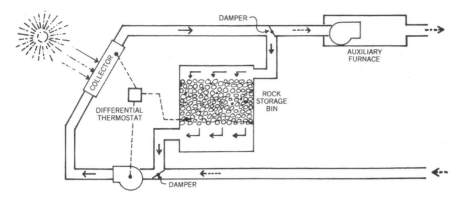

Figure 8.21a A typical solar hot-air system. As shown, the dampers are set for the collection mode. (After *Architectural Graphic Standards*.)

Figure 8.21b One popular active solar system in Japan uses special hot-air collectors to gather the heat and concrete floor slabs to store the heat. The collectors cover the whole roof, but for economic reasons, only the upper third is covered with glass. This system is used in homes, schools, and small community buildings. (After Oku Mura of the OM Solar Association/OM Institute.)

WINTER DAY MODE

collectors and ducts are bulky, it is hard to prevent air leakage, and it is inefficient to heat domestic hot water with the hot air. The advantages are: air doesn't freeze or boil, leaks don't cause damage, and the warm air can be used directly to heat the building. Early systems usually stored the heat in a rock bin (Fig. 8.21a). However, it is usually more economical to use the mass of the building, as in the popular Japanese system described in Figs. 8.21b through 8.21f.

A very simple and cost-effective hot-air system consists of vertical flat-plate collectors attached to the south façade (Fig. 8.21g). Two small holes through the south wall allow a small fan to circulate room air through the collector for daytime heat without additional sunlight entering the space.

8.22 DESIGNING AN ACTIVE SOLAR SYSTEM

Because of the expense of solar equipment, the system must be designed to be as efficient as possible. It is most important to maximize the solar exposure by aiming the collectors at the sun and by minimizing the shading of a collector while it gathers energy from about 9 A.M. to 3 P.M. In most cases, rooftops have the best solar access (Figs. 8.22a and 8.22b). Rooftop mounting also saves land and minimizes the potential for damage that exists with ground-mounted collectors. A study model on a heliodon is the most effective way to check for solar access. See Chapter 11 for a discussion on solar access.

Collector Orientation

Usually it is best to orient solar collectors toward true south. Variations up to 20° east or 20° west are acceptable

Figure 8.21c Winter Day Mode: Fresh outdoor air entering through attic vents is first preheated by the unglazed portion of the metal roof and then fully heated by the more efficient glazed section. The air-handling unit then blows the air under the floor slab to heat the perimeter of the building while it also stores heat in the slab. (After Oku Mura of the OM Solar Association/OM Institute.)

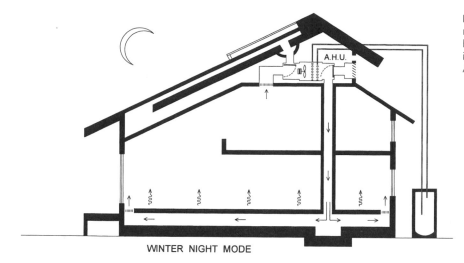

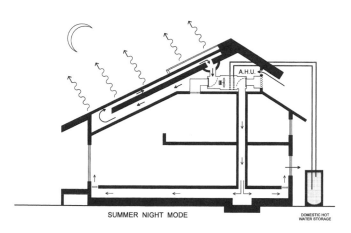

WINTER NIGHT MODE

Figure 8.21d Winter Night Mode: When necessary, an auxiliary heating coil in the air-handling unit supplements the heat stored in the slab. (After Oku Mura of the OM Solar Association/OM Institute.)

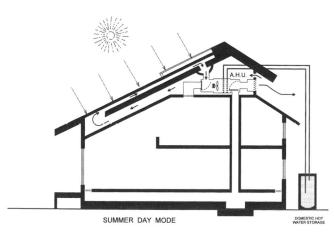

SUMMER NIGHT MODE

DOMESTIC HOT WATER STORAGE

Figure 8.21e Summer Night Mode: Outdoor air is cooled by passing through the metal roof collectors that radiate heat to the night sky. The cooled air then cools the floor slab and interior spaces in preparation for the next hot day. (After Oku Mura of the OM Solar Association/OM Institute.)

SUMMER DAY MODE

DOMESTIC HOT WATER STORAGE

Figure 8.21f Summer Day Mode: As in the winter, outdoor air is passed through the collectors, but now the heat is transferred into a domestic hot-water coil and then exhausted outdoors. In the process, the roof and attic are cooled by the flow of this outdoor air. Note that the attic vents and exhaust louvers from the air-handling unit are widely separated horizontally. (After Oku Mura of the Om Solar Assoc./Om Institute.)

Figure 8.21g Simple and inexpensive hot-air collectors can be added to the south wall of new or existing buildings for additional daytime solar heating. (Courtesy Sun Mate™.)

(Fig. 8.22c). For special conditions, such as a need for morning heat or the prevalence of morning fog, a 20° to 30° shift to the east or west can even be beneficial.

Collector Tilt

The **optimum tilt** of the collectors is a function of latitude and the purpose

of the solar collectors. Figure 8.22d illustrates the tilt angle for different heating applications as a function of latitude and the purpose of the collector. Collectors are most efficient when they are perpendicular to the sunrays. However, with the daily and seasonal motions of the sun, that is possible only with tracking collectors, which, unfortunately, are too complicated

in most circumstances. Thus, the tilt angles given in Fig. 8.22d are the optimum slopes for collectors.

Collector Size

The collector size depends on a number of factors: type of heating (pool water, domestic water, or space heating), amount of heat required, climate, and efficiency of the collector system. Table 8.22A gives the approximate collector areas and storage-tank sizes for domestic hot-water heating, while Table 8.22B gives the approximate sizes of collectors and storage tanks for a combined space-heating and domestic hot-water system. For sizing swimming-pool heating systems, see Section 8.19. In all cases, the collector area should be increased to compensate for a poor tilt angle, a poor orientation, or a partial shading of collectors.

8.23 ACTIVE/PASSIVE SOLAR SYSTEMS

At the end of Chapter 7, it was mentioned that although the convective-loop (thermosiphon) system (Fig. 7.18a) is a passive system because it uses no pumps, it is more closely

Figure 8.22a This add-on to an existing building consists of two flat-plate collectors for domestic hot water. There is also a special low-temperature swimming-pool collector made of flexible plastic that is draped over the roof tiles (upper right.)

Figure 8.22b The active solar collectors are an integral part of this roof design. (Courtesy and © Chromagen-Solar Energy Systems, Israel.)

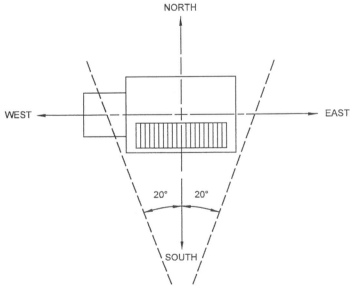

Figure 8.22c Although south is usually the best orientation for collecting solar energy, a deviation of up to 20° is not critical.

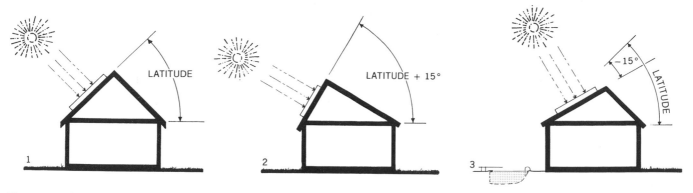

Figure 8.22d The best collector tilt is a function of latitude and the purpose of the collector (1) a collector tilt for domestic hot water; (2) a collector tilt for space heating and for combination space heating and domestic hot water; (3) a collector tilt for heating swimming pools or for solar cooling.

Number of People per Household	Approximate Collector Size (Ft²)† in Regions				Approximate Tank Size			
	A	B	C	D	Gallons	(liters)	ft³	(m³)
1–2	30	40	60	80	60	227	8	0.2
3	40	53	80	107	80	303	11	0.3
4	50	67	100	133	100	379	13	0.4
5	60	80	120	160	120	754	16	0.5
6	70	93	140	187	140	530	19	0.6

Table 8.22A Approximate Sizing of a Solar Domestic Hot-Water System*

*Based on rules of thumb and the map from AAA Solar Service and Supply, Inc., Albuquerque, New Mexico.
† The collector area is also a function of its efficiency. High-efficiency collectors, such as the vacuum-tube type, require a smaller area but cost more, and vice versa. (For m², multiply ft² by 0.09.)

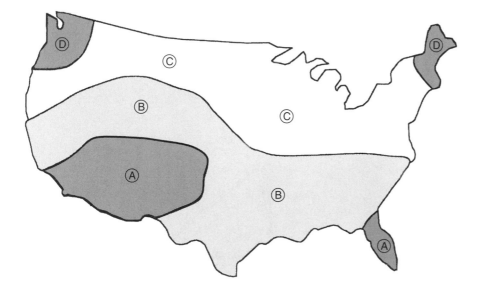

more popular thermosiphon system is called **the integral collector storage (ICS) system** because the storage tank and collector are combined in one unit (Fig. 8.23b). Because these systems have no moving parts and a minimum of plumbing, they are very cost-effective and popular. They are most appropriate in mild to temperate climates because the storage, although well insulated, is outdoors. For thermosiphons to work, the storage tank must be above the collector. Their major disadvantage is aesthetic since they cannot be easily integrated into the roof, while flat-plate collectors can look much like skylights.

8.24 PREHEATING OF VENTILATION AIR

As mentioned earlier, active solar swimming-pool heating is very cost-effective partly because simple, inexpensive collectors that don't use glass covers are sufficient for the low-temperature heat that is collected. Similarly, simple inexpensive solar collectors are sufficient to preheat ventilation air because even a small rise above the winter outdoor air temperature is a benefit.

A simple ventilation preheater can be made by mounting dark metal cladding a few inches in front of a south wall. A ventilation fan moves cold outdoor air across the back of the metal cladding before the air enters the building. Unfortunately,

related to active systems. The first active solar systems at the turn of the twentieth century used this natural-convection technique. Because of their simplicity and low cost, two

different thermosiphon systems are becoming popular for domestic hot water. In one system, called a **batch heater**, the storage tank is also the collector (Fig. 8.23a). The

Table 8.22B Approximate Sizing of a Combined Space-Heating and Domestic Hot-Water System for a 1500 ft² (135 m²) Home

Climate Region	Reference City	Approximate Collector Area (ft²)	(m²)	Approximate Storage Size			
				Water (ft³)	(m³)	Rock Bin* (ft³)	(m³)
1	Hartford, CT	800	72	200	5.7	600	17
2	Madison, WI	750	68	200	5.7	600	17
3	Indianapolis, IN	800	72	200	5.7	600	17
4	Salt Lake City, UT	750	68	200	5.7	600	17
5	Ely, NE	750	68	200	5.7	600	17
6	Medford, OR	500	45	100	2.8	300	8.5
7	Fresno, CA	300	27	70	2	210	6
8	Charleston, SC	500	45	100	2.8	300	8.5
9	Little Rock, AK	500	45	100	2.8	300	8.5
10	Knoxville, TN	500	45	100	2.8	300	8.5
11	Phoenix, AZ	300	27	70	2	210	6
12	Midland, TX	200	18	40	1.1	120	3.4
13	Fort Worth, TX	200	18	40	1.1	120	3.4
14	New Orleans, LA	200	18	40	1.1	120	3.4
15	Houston, TX	200	18	40	1.1	120	3.4
16	Miami, FL	50	5	10	0.3	30	0.8
17	Los Angeles, CA	50	5	0	0	30	0.8

Sizes are approximate and vary with the actual microclimate and the efficiency of specific equipment.
*Rock bin is used with a hot-air system.

this strategy does not capture the warm air film that forms on the front of the dark metal collector. Through the use of perforated cladding, however, heat is collected from both the front and back of the collector, yielding efficiencies as high as 75 percent (Fig. 8.24a). Such transpired solar collectors even save energy at night because the heat lost through the south wall is brought back in by the incoming ventilation air. In summer, the building ventilation system bypasses the solar collector, while the air being heated inside the collector rises by the stack effect and exits through the top perforations. Thus, minimal heat gain results in the summer from the solar collector.

Since the collector is the facade, the collector's appearance is very important. Fortunately, any dark color will work almost as well as black. On sunny days, the air can be heated anywhere from 30° to 50°F (17° to 30°C) above the ambient temperature. Even on cloudy days, the system is still about 25 percent efficient.

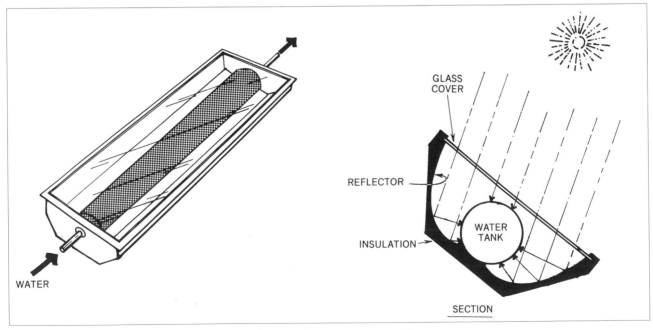

Figure 8.23a In a batch-type hot-water heater, the collector and storage are one and the same.

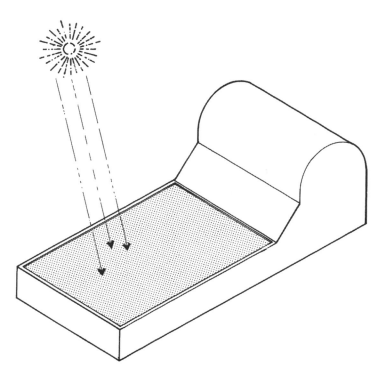

Figure 8.23b In an ICS system, the collector and storage tank are supplied in one package.

Figure 8.24b This Windsor, Ontario, apartment building uses the world's tallest solar collector to preheat ventilation air. (Courtesy Conserval Systems Inc., makers of the Solarwall™ system.)

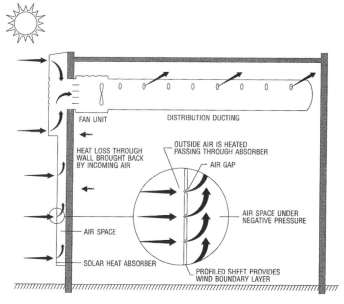

Figure 8.24a An active solar transpired ventilation preheater system is shown. Much greater efficiencies are achieved when metal collectors are perforated. (Courtesy Conserval Systems Inc., makers of the Solarwall™ system.)

All buildings need to bring in outdoor air for health reasons. Because we use materials that give off toxic components, **indoor-air quality (IAQ)** has become an important issue. Small buildings, such as residences, have traditionally relied on infiltration to supply the needed fresh air, while large buildings have relied on a designed ventilation system. Because energy-efficient buildings have a tight envelope, all buildings now need a carefully designed ventilation system, and in winter preheating this fresh air will save a great deal of energy. Figure 8.24b shows a high-rise apartment building that uses an active solar ventilation preheater made of perforated cladding panels. Preheating ventilation air is also appropriate for existing buildings. It is especially useful for buildings with badly deteriorated south facades, for which new cladding might be needed anyway.

The transpired solar collectors are most useful in cold climates, where much ventilation is required (e.g., industrial buildings, hospitals, schools, restaurants), and they are least appropriate in warm climates, where much air conditioning is used. In hot climates, heat exchangers can be used that recover ventilation energy in both summer and winter. Heat exchangers, which are also known as "energy recovery units," will be described in Section 16.18.

8.25 THE FUTURE OF ACTIVE SOLAR

There is no reason why 100 percent of outdoor swimming pools should not be heated with active solar, since the cost of solar energy for this application is easily competitive with fossil energy.

Domestic hot water should also be heated with active solar collectors unless the building has no access to the sun. Heating water is the second largest consumer of energy in homes after space heating and cooling. The term "domestic hot water" refers to all hot water used in homes, restaurants, laundries, schools, and most car washes. However, domestic hot water does not include hot water used for heating buildings.

Passive solar energy should be used for space heating wherever possible. When the walls and windows do not have enough exposure to the winter sun, active solar space heating should be used. In cold climates, solar preheating of ventilation air should also be used.

In hot climates, solar air conditioning should be considered. Absorption refrigeration machines can operate on solar hot water, as described in Section 16.9. The technology has existed for over twenty years, but its high cost has been a problem. New technology, mass production, and rising energy costs may change that situation. There is much potential for solar cooling because the most cooling energy is needed at the same time of year when solar energy is most abundant.

8.26   CONCLUSION

It is now appropriate for every building to collect as much solar radiation as possible, since solar energy is a central pillar of sustainability. The threat of global warming requires us to use the sun in every form possible (Fig. 8.26a). Imagine every roof of a city covered with solar collectors. You don't have to imagine. In Dezhou, China, every roof is covered with active solar collectors to supply the domestic hot water (Fig. 8.26b).

Figure 8.26a The Oxford Solar House, in Oxford, England, demonstrates solar in its many forms. The south-facing roof consists of a mix of passive solar, active solar, and PV panels. The skylight supplies daylight and direct-gain heat, the active solar supplies the domestic hot water, and the PV supplies the electricity. In addition, the south facade uses both direct gain and sun space passive solar. (Photo from Caddet Technical Brochure #84.)

Figure 8.26b This roofscape in Dezhou, China, is an example to the world of what is possible. Not only does every roof have solar collectors, but also the buildings and streets are all aligned for the best solar orientation.

Figure 8.26c When active solar or PV is not considered in the original design, retrofit installations can prove to be very awkward.

To create a sustainable building, first use efficiency to reduce the need for energy. Second, use the passive techniques to further reduce the energy load. Finally, use active solar to supply most of the low-grade heat requirements for domestic hot water and space heating. Then use PV to generate the high-grade energy of electricity to operate all the lights and appliances.

Because of a similarity in appearance and solar-access requirements, active solar and PV can be integrated side-by-side in buildings. In residences, the entire south-facing roof can be used for a combination of active solar and PV panels (Figs. 8.3a and 8.26a). In commercial, institutional, and industrial buildings, the south wall should also be used.

It is most important that all new buildings either utilize these technologies or at the very least allow for them in the future. Thus, buildings should face south and have south-facing roofs at the appropriate tilt angle. Roads should be laid out to accommodate the building's orientation (see Chapter 11). If these steps are not taken, many buildings in the future will have solar collectors at odd angles to the architecture (Fig. 8.26c).

Rather, the use of passive solar, active solar, and PV should generate a new aesthetic. This will be an opportunity to create new forms appropriate for a sustainable world (see again Fig. 8.3b).

Although it is easy to see how passive, active, and PV are various solar building techniques, it is not obvious that shading is also a solar technique. Just like passive and active solar reduce the need for conventional energy in the winter, shading reduces the need for energy in the summer. Thus, rejecting the sun can be as valuable as collecting it. The next chapter is about shading.

KEY IDEAS OF CHAPTER 8

1. Photovoltaic (PV)-generated electricity is an almost ideal energy source. PV converts sunlight directly into electricity.
2. Most of the electricity in the middle of the twenty-first century will probably come from PV.
3. PV should be building-integrated (i.e., PV modules should displace the weathering skin of a building).

4. PV is appropriate not only in the Sunbelt but in every climate.
5. Stand-alone PV systems are best for buildings some distance from the power grid. Such systems require batteries and backup power.
6. Grid-connected PV systems are best for buildings on or near the power grid, which replaces the need for batteries and backup power.

7. Wind power is sometimes a good complement to PV power.
8. A southern orientation and a tilt equal to the latitude maximize the PV output.
9. To match energy supply to demand, the optimum orientation and tilt can be off 15 to 30° from that of the maximum output.

10. PV has the potential to be very inexpensive because little material is used and the assembly is very simple.
11. As PV costs decline because of research and mass production, the optimum tilt and orientation will become less important. Someday, all south-facing roofs, south walls, west walls, east walls, and shading devices will be clad with PV.
12. Transparent PV modules can be used as glazing.
13. Energy-efficient appliances and lighting, as well as passive systems, should be used in conjunction with PV.
14. Use PV to generate the necessary high-grade energy of electricity, and use active solar to generate the low-grade thermal energy needed in buildings.
15. Solar swimming-pool heating is the best and most effective way to extend the swimming season in outdoor pools.
16. The area of most solar collectors for pool heating is approximately equal to the pool area in the North and about half the pool area in the South.
17. Wherever possible, active solar should be used to heat domestic hot water.
18. Active solar space heating should be considered if passive solar heating is not possible.
19. Use radiant floor heating and/or a heat pump in conjunction with the active solar space-heating system.
20. Because solar energy is most available when cooling is required, active solar space cooling has much potential.
21. All south-facing roofs should be covered with a mix of active solar and PV in order to protect the environment, control global warming, and lead society to a sustainable economy.
22. Green solar architecture will produce an exciting new aesthetic in harmony with the world.

References

Environmental Building News, July/August, 1999, p. 13

Maycock, P. "1997 World Cell/Module Shipments," *PV News*, February 1998 (updated 2007).

Tapping into the Sun: Today's Applications of Photovoltaic Technology, U.S. Department of Energy, rev. April 1995.

Resources

FURTHER READING

(See the Bibliography in the back of the book for full citations.)

Kwok, Alison G., and Walter T. Grondzik. *The Green Studio Handbook: Environmental Strategies for Schematic Design.*

Singh, M. *The Timeless Energy of the Sun for Life and Place with Nature.*

PERIODICALS

Environmental Building News
Solar Today

ORGANIZATIONS

(See Appendix K for full citations.)

American Solar Energy Society (ASES)
www.ases.org

Florida Solar Energy Center (FSEC)
www.fsec.ucf.edu

Interstate Renewable Energy Council (IREC)
www.irecusa.org
Good source for information about government incentive programs

International Solar Energy Association (ISES)
www.ises.org

National Renewable Energy Laboratory (NREL)
www.nrel.gov
Good source for detailed information on renewables.

Sandia National Laboratories
www.sandia.gov

Solar Energy Industries Association (SEIA)
www.seia.org
SEIA is the national trade organization of PV and thermal manufacturers and component suppliers.

SHADING AND LIGHT COLORS

Wisdom demands a new orientation of science and technology towards the organic, the
gentle, the non-violent, the elegant and beautiful.

E. F. Schumacher
Small Is Beautiful, 1973

The sun control device has to be on the outside of the building, an element of the facade,
an element of architecture. And because this device is so important a part of our open
architecture, it may develop into as characteristic a form as the Doric column.

Marcel Breuer,
Sun and Shadow

9.1 HISTORY OF SHADING

The prediction by Marcel Breuer on the previous page may yet become a reality because of global warming. Of all the solar strategies, shading may be the most important. The benefits of shading are so great and obvious that we see its application throughout history and across cultures. We see its effect on classical architecture as well as on unrefined vernacular buildings ("architecture without architects").

Many of the larger shading elements had the purpose of shading both the building and an outdoor living space. The porticoes and colonnades of ancient Greek and Roman buildings certainly had this as a major part of their function (see Fig. 9.1a). Greek Revival architecture was so successful in the American South because it offered the much-needed shading, as well as symbolic and aesthetic benefits. In hot and humid regions, large windows are required to maximize natural ventilation, but at the same time, any sunlight that enters through these large windows increases the discomfort. Large overhangs that are supported by columns can resolve this conflict (see Fig. 9.1b). The white color of Greek Revival architecture is also very appropriate for hot climates.

In any good architecture, building elements are usually multifunctional. The fact that the Greek portico also protects against the rain does not negate its importance for solar control. It just makes the concept of a portico all the more valuable in hot and humid regions, where rain is common and the sun is oppressive.

While we need not be as literal as revival architecture, borrowing from the past can be very useful when there are functional as well as aesthetic benefits (Fig. 9.1c). There is a rich supply of historical examples from which to draw. Traditional design features from around the world, while appearing different, often developed in response to the same needs. The Greek portico, mentioned above, is closely related to the porch, verandah (from India), balcony, loggia, gallery, arcade,

Figure 9.1a Ancient Greek architecture made full use of colonnades and porticoes for protection against the elements and especially the sun. Stoa of Attalos II Athens.

Figure 9.1b Greek Revival architecture was especially popular in the South, where it contributed greatly to thermal comfort. The Hermitage, Andrew Jackson's home near Nashville, Tennessee.

Figure 9.1c Postmodernism, with its allusion to classical architecture, can draw on time-tested ideas for thermal comfort, as in the public library for San Juan Capistrano, California, designed by Michael Graves.

Figure 9.1d Loggias supported on arcades and colonnades shielded the large windows necessary for natural ventilation in the hot and humid climate of Venice. Sometimes an open-walled extra floor was added above the top floor to ventilate the heat collecting under the roof.

Figure 9.1e Victorian architecture made much use of the porch and the covered balcony to shade the building and create cool outdoor spaces. Eufaula, Alabama.

colonnade, and engawa (from Japan). See Figs. 9.1a–h).

Chinese, Korean, and Japanese architecture is dominated by the use of large overhangs (Fig. 9.1f). The Japanese made much use of a veranda-like element called the "engawa." This large overhang protected the sliding wall panels that could be opened to maximize access to ventilation, light, and view. When the panels are closed, light enters through a continuous translucent strip window above. Also note how rainwater is led down to a drain by means of a hanging chain (Fig. 9.1g). In the early twentieth century, the Green brothers developed a style appropriate for California by using concepts derived from Japanese architecture (Fig. 9.1h).

Many great architects have understood the importance of shading and used it to create powerful visual statements. Frank Lloyd Wright used shading strategies in most of his buildings. Early in his career, he used large overhangs both to create thermal comfort and to make an aesthetic statement about building on the prairie. In his Robie House (Fig. 9.1i), Wright used large areas of operable glazing to maximize natural ventilation during the hot and humid Chicago summers. He understood, however, that this would do more harm than good unless he shaded the glazing from the sun. The very long cantilevered overhangs not only supply the much-needed shade, but also create strong horizontal lines that reflect the nature of the region. See Fig. 10.8b for a plan view of the Robie House.

Of all architects, Le Corbusier is most closely linked with an aesthetic based on sun shading. It is interesting to note how this came about. In 1932, Le Corbusier designed a multistory building in Paris known as the Cité de Refuge. It was designed with an all-glass south facade so that a maximum amount of sunlight could warm and cheer the residents. In December passive solar worked wonderfully, but in June the building became unbearably hot. As a result of this mistake, Le Corbusier invented the fixed structural sunshade now known as **brise-soleil**

Figure 9.1f Much Asian architecture is dominated by large overhangs. Golden Pavilion, Kyoto, Japan. (Courtesy of Japan National Tourist Organization.)

Figure 9.1g The sliding wall panels can be opened for maximum access to ventilation, light, and view. The engawa or porch is clearly visible in this building in the Japanese Garden of Portland, Oregon.

(sun-breaker). In Fig. 9.1j, we see the building after it was retrofitted with a brise-soleil.

Le Corbusier realized the dual nature of the sun—our friend in the winter and our enemy in the summer. His own artwork says it best (Fig. 6.1). After this realization, shading became a central part of his architecture. For him, the aesthetic opportunities were

Figure 9.1h The Gamble House in Pasadena, (California, 1908, by Green and Green shows the strong influence of Japanese architecture. Note especially the large roof overhangs. (Model by Gary Kamemoto and Robert Takei, University of Southern California.)

Figure 9.1i Large overhangs dominate the design of the Robie House, Chicago, 1909, by Frank Lloyd Wright.

Figure 9.1j Sunshades known as brise-soleil were retrofitted on the Cité de Refuge, Paris, which Le Corbusier designed in 1932 without sunshades. (Photograph by Alan Cook.)

Figure 9.1k The brise-soleil and parasol roof shade the High Court at Chandigarh, India. Evaporation from the reflecting pool helps cool the air.

Figure 9.1l The Maharajah's Palace at Mysore, India, illustrates the extensive shading techniques used in some Indian architecture. (Courtesy of Government of India Tourist Office.)

Figure 9.1m An often-overlooked benefit of the traditional, thick masonry wall was the shading produced from both the vertical and horizontal elements. (Old office building in lower Manhattan.)

Figure 9.1n As this architect's rendering indicates, awnings were considered desirable for both their functional and aesthetic benefits. (From *Country Clubs* by Clifford C. Wendehack.)

9.2 SHADING

Passive solar heating works! It works even better in the summer, because there is much more sun and the outdoor temperature is much higher. Thus, shading is required to prevent passive solar heating in the summer.

Shading is a key strategy for achieving thermal comfort in the summer. Shading, as part of heat avoidance, is tier one of the three-tier design approach to cooling a building (Fig. 9.2a). The second tier consists

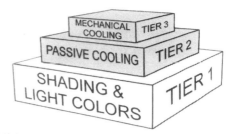

Figure 9.2a The three-tier approach to design is a logical and sustainable method for achieving thermal comfort in the summer.

as important as the protection from the sun. Thus, many of his buildings use sunshading as strong visual element. Some of the best examples come from the Indian city of Chandigarh, where Le Corbusier designed many of the government buildings. The brise-soleil and parasol roof not only shade but also create powerful visual statements in the High Court Building (Fig. 9.1k). The Maharaja's Palace at Mysore has some similarity with the High Court, and it is, therefore, tempting to speculate on how much Le Corbusier was influenced by native Indian architecture (Fig. 9.1l). For another example of the parasol roof, see Fig. 1.3g, and for another example of the brise-soleil see Figs. 10.6cc and dd.

Traditional buildings often provided shading even when it was not a conscious goal. Because windows were usually set back into deep bearing walls or even thick masonry curtain walls, the effect was that of a shallow brise-soleil (Fig. 9.1m).

The recent history of the awning give us insight into how our sense of aesthetics changes. The rendering shown in Fig. 9.1n indicates that awnings were considered a desirable aesthetic object in the first half of the twentieth century. When air conditioning became available, richer people could afford to abandon the use of awnings, while the poor still used them. Consequently, awnings were associated with poor and run-down buildings. Fortunately, the functional and aesthetic benefits of awnings are being rediscovered in the twenty-first century.

Figure 9.2b In the Conoco Headquarters complex in Houston, Texas, Kevin Roche was inspired by the local Texas plantation style with its large overhangs and column-supported porches. The awning-like translucent overhangs are 13 ft deep because they shade two floors, face in all directions of the compass, protect verandas, and block the sky and its strong, diffused radiation in this humid climate. Trellises covered with jasmine and fig ivy protect the first floor, as well as the courtyards where the second-story verandas leave off. In this very hot and wet climate, even the on-grade parking is protected by awning-like Fiberglas sunshades (not shown).

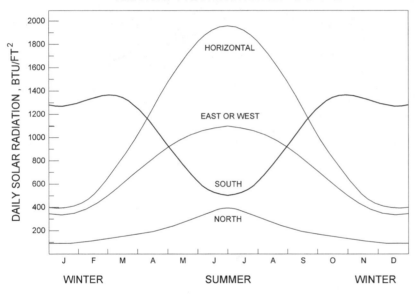

CLEAR DAY SOLAR TRANSMITTED AT LAT. 42

HORIZONTAL

EAST OR WEST

SOUTH

NORTH

DAILY SOLAR RADIATION, BTU/FT^2

WINTER   SUMMER   WINTER

Figure 9.2c All orientations except south receive maximum solar radiation in summer. A skylight receives about four times the solar heating that south windows receive on June 21. (After the *Workbook for Workshop on Advanced Passive Solar Design* by J. Douglas Balcomb and Robert Jones, © J. Douglas Balcomb, 1987.)

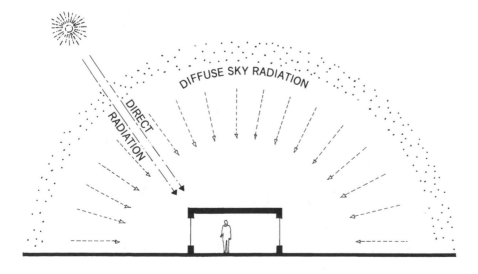

DIFFUSE SKY RADIATION

DIRECT RADIATION

Figure 9.2d In humid, polluted, and dusty regions, the diffuse-sky component is a large part of the total solar load.

of passive cooling, and the third uses mechanical equipment to cool whatever the architectural strategies of tiers one and two could not accomplish.

Although shading of the whole building is beneficial, shading of the windows is crucial. Consequently, most of the following discussion refers to the shading of windows.

Shading is a solar strategy even though it blocks rather than collects solar radiation. Shading requires a better understanding of solar geometry than any of the other solar strategies: passive solar, active solar, PV, and daylighting. Shading may also be the most important solar strategy because most people live in hot climates and they all want air conditioning. Thus, shading may save more energy economically than any other solar strategy. Which window orientations need the most shading in the summer? The graph in Fig. 9.2c shows that on June 21, a skylight (horizontal glazing) collects about four times more solar radiation than a south window. Clearly, then, skylights need very effective shading or, better yet, should be avoided. Figure 9.2c also shows that east or west glazing collects more than two times the solar radiation of south windows. Thus, the shading of east and west windows is also more important than the shading of south windows.

If the graph in Fig. 9.2c looks familiar, it is not surprising, since a variation of it appeared as Fig. 7.16a, which was used to show how much more solar radiation south windows collected than any other orientation in the winter. Thus, south windows are very desirable from both a shading and passive solar heating point of view. Skylights should be avoided because they collect a large amount of solar radiation in the summer and little in the winter. Similarly, east and west windows are not desirable from a heating and cooling point of view.

The total solar load consists of three components: direct, diffuse, and reflected radiation. To prevent passive solar heating when it is not wanted, one must always shade a window

from the direct solar component and often also from the diffuse sky and reflected components. In sunny humid regions, like the Southeast, the diffuse-sky radiation can be very significant (Fig. 9.2b). Sunny areas with much dust or pollution can also create much diffuse radiation (Fig. 9.2d). Reflected radiation, on the other hand, can be a large problem in such areas as the Southwest, where intense sunlight and high-reflectance surfaces often coexist. The problem also occurs in urban areas, where highly reflective surfaces can be quite common. Concrete paving, white walls, and reflective glazing can all reflect intense solar radiation into a window. There are cases where the north facade of a building experiences the solar load of a south orientation because a large building with reflective glazing was built toward the north (Fig. 9.2e).

The type, size, and location of a shading device will, therefore, depend in part on the size of the direct, diffuse, and reflected components of the total solar load. The reflected component is usually best controlled by reducing the reflectivity of the offending surfaces. This is often accomplished by the use of plants. The diffuse-sky component is, however, a much harder problem because radiation comes from a large exposure angle. It is, therefore, usually

controlled by additional indoor shading devices or shading within the glazing. The direct solar component is effectively controlled by exterior shading devices.

The need for shading might seem to conflict with the demand for daylighting. Fortunately, when solar energy is brought into a building in a very controlled manner, it can supply high-quality lighting as well as reduce the heat gain. This is accomplished by allowing just enough light to enter so that the electric lights can be turned off. A more detailed discussion of day-lighting versus shading is found in Section 13.6.

When it is not used for daylighting, solar radiation should be blocked during the overheated period of the year. A residence in the North would experience an overheated period that is only a few months long. That same residence in the South or a large office building in the North could experience overheated periods that are two to three times as long. Thus, the required shading period for any building depends on both the climate and the nature of the building. Shading periods are discussed in Section 9.5. below.

Shading can be accomplished by exterior devices, by glazing, or by indoor shading devices. Although

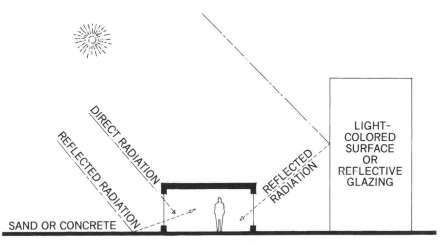

Figure 9.2e In dry regions, the solar load consists mainly of the direct and reflected components. However, large white surfaces and reflective glazing can be a problem in all climates.

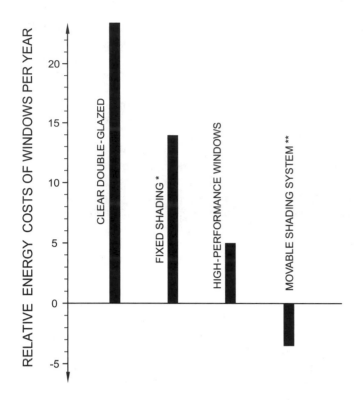

RELATIVE ENERGY COSTS OF WINDOWS PER YEAR

CLEAR DOUBLE-GLAZED

FIXED SHADING *

HIGH-PERFORMANCE WINDOWS

MOVABLE SHADING SYSTEM **

NOTE: ALL WINDOWS ON NORTH, EAST, WEST, AND SOUTH ARE OF EQUAL AREA AND ALL HAVE LOW SHGC GLAZING.

* FIXED 2 ft [0.6 m] OVERHANG ON ALL WINDOWS
** INCLUDES WINTER GAIN THAT WAS BLOCKED BY FIXED SHADING

Figure 9.2f Nonshaded windows are energy guzzlers. Movable shading is by far the best because it allows much more of the winter sun to enter. Thus, windows become energy assets rather than energy liabilities.

indoor shading is almost always movable, exterior shading can also be movable. Figure 9.2f shows the relative energy costs of various shading strategies. The best performers by far are external movable shading devices.

The goal of a shading design is not just to keep the sun out but also to allow as much view as possible. After all, most people agree that the most important function of a window is to provide a view. The shading design guidelines presented here help the designer to preserve the view as much as possible.

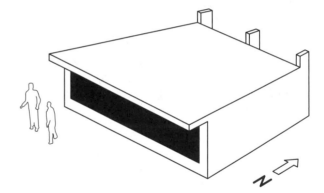

Figure 9.3a Each orientation requires a different shading strategy. From a shading point of view, east and west windows are best avoided.

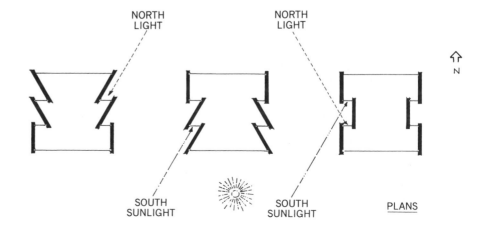

Figure 9.3b These plans illustrate how windows on east and west facades can face either north or south.

NORTH LIGHT

NORTH LIGHT

SOUTH SUNLIGHT

SOUTH SUNLIGHT

PLANS

N

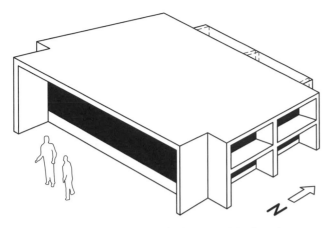

Figure 9.3c Shading is improved when a combination of vertical and horizontal elements is used.

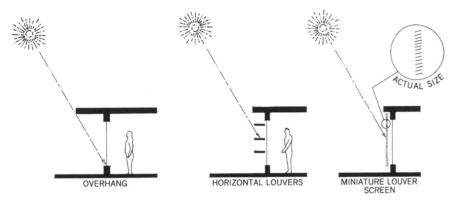

OVERHANG   HORIZONTAL LOUVERS   MINIATURE LOUVER SCREEN

Figure 9.3d Many small elements can create the same shading effect as one large device. However, the view is best with the large overhang.

External shading devices are discussed first and in most detail because they are the most effective barrier against the sun and have the most pronounced effect on the aesthetics of a building.

9.3 FIXED EXTERIOR SHADING DEVICES

As with passive solar systems, orientation is critical with shading. Each orientation requires a different shading strategy. The horizontal overhang on south-facing windows is very effective during the summer because the sun is then high in the sky. Although less effective, the horizontal overhang is also the best on the east, southeast, southwest, and west orientations. In hot climates, north windows also need to be shaded because, during the summer, the sun rises north of east and sets north of west. Since the sun is low in the sky at these times, the horizontal overhang is not effective, and small vertical fins work best on the north facade (Fig. 9.3a).

East- and west-facing windows pose a difficult problem because of the low-altitude angle of the sun in the morning and afternoon. The best solution by far is to avoid using east and especially west windows as much as possible. The next best solution is to have the windows on the east and west facades face north or south, as shown in the plans of Fig. 9.3b. If that is also not possible, then minimize the window area and use horizontal overhangs However, it must be understood that if they are to be very effective, they will severely restrict the view. Even the more effective movable devices described later still severely limit the view.

In some cases, a combination of vertical and horizontal elements can be used, as shown in Fig. 9.3c. When these elements are closely spaced, the system is called an **eggcrate.**

Since the problem of shading is one of blocking the sun at certain angles, many small devices can have the same effect as a few large ones, as shown in Fig. 9.3d. In each case, the ratio of length of overhang to the vertical portion of the window shaded is the same. Screens are available that consist of miniature louvers (about ten per inch) that are very effective in blocking the sun and yet are almost as transparent as insect screens. Medium-sized, vertically stacked overhangs are often used because they are structurally simple yet visually attractive when viewed from outdoors. (Fig. 9.3e).

Remember, view is the highest priority for most windows. A single large horizontal overhang is usually the best choice. Although it obstructs the high sky, the more important horizontal view is unimpeded, while vertical fins are rarely desirable because they block the horizontal view.

Skylights (horizontal glazing systems) create a difficult shading problem because they face the sun most directly during the worst part of the year, summer at noon (Fig. 9.3f). Therefore skylights, like east and west windows, should be avoided. A much better solution for letting year-round daylight and winter sun enter through the roof is the use of clerestory windows (Fig. 9.3g). The vertical glazing in the clerestory can then be shaded by the window techniques explained in this chapter. If domed-type skylights are to be used, consider using shade/reflectors, as illustrated in Fig. 7.6g.

Table 9.3 shows some of the most common fixed external shading devices. They are all variations of either the horizontal overhang, the vertical fin, or the eggcrate, which is a combination of the first two. The louvers and

Figure 9.3e The Samsung headquarters building in Seoul, South Korea, uses green-tinted glass overhangs (louvers) to shade the windows.

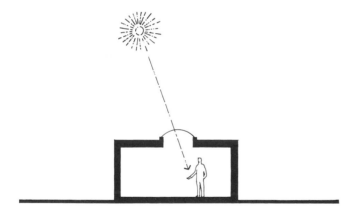

Figure 9.3f Skylights (horizontal glazing) should usually be avoided because they face the summer sun.

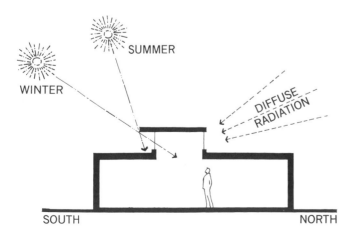

Figure 9.3g Clerestory windows should be used instead of skylights because they allow the sun to enter in a controlled manner.

Table 9.3 Examples of Fixed Shading Devices

		Descriptive Name	Best Orientation*	Comments
I		Overhang Horizontal panel	South, east, west	Traps hot air Can be loaded by snow and wind
II		Overhang Horizontal louvers in horizontal plane	South, east, west	Free air movement Snow or wind load is small Small scale **Best buy!**
III		Overhang Horizontal louvers in vertical plane	South, east, west	Reduces length of overhang View restricted Also available with miniature louvers
IV		Overhang Vertical panel	South, east, west	Free air movement No snow load View restricted
V		Vertical fin	North	Restricts view if used on east and west orientations
VI		Vertical fin slanted	East, West	Slant toward north Restricts view significantly **Not recommended**
VII		Eggcrate	East, west	For very hot climates View very restricted Traps hot air **Not recommended**
VIII		Eggcrate with slanted fins	East, west	Slant toward north View very restricted Traps hot air For very hot climates **Not recommended**

* For temperate climates. In the tropics, north becomes similar to south, and at the equator they are equal.
Source: Architectural Graphic Standards, 8th ed. John R. Hoke, ed. (Wiley, 1988).

fins can be angled for additional solar control. Almost an infinite number of variations are possible, as can be seen by looking at the work of such architects as Le Corbusier, Oscar Niemeyer, Richard Neutra, Paul Rudolph, and E. D. Stone. For examples of the work of these and many other architects, the author highly recommends the book *Solar Control and Shading Devices* by Olgyay and Olgyay.

Fixed rather than movable shading devices are often used because of their simplicity, low cost, and low maintenance. Their effectiveness is limited, however, for several signification reasons, and movable shading devices should be seriously considered.

9.4 MOVABLE SHADING DEVICES

It is not surprising that movable shading devices respond better to the dynamic nature of the environment than do static devices. Since we need shade during the overheated periods and sun during the underheated periods, a shading device must be in phase with the thermal conditions. With a fixed shading device, the period of solar exposure to the window is not a function of temperature but rather of sun position (Fig. 9.4a).

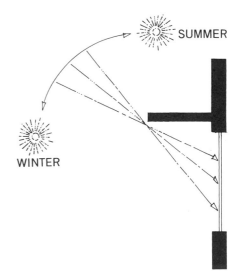

Figure 9.4a With a fixed shading device, the solar exposure of a window is a function of sun position and not of the temperature.

Unfortunately, sun angles and temperature are not in phase for several reasons. For example, daily weather patterns vary widely, especially in spring and fall, when one day might be too hot while the next might be too cold.

However, the most important reason for the discrepancy between sun angles and temperature is that the solar year and thermal year are out of phase. Because of its great mass, the earth heats up slowly in spring and does not reach its maximum summer temperature until one or two months after the day of maximum heating, the summer solstice (June 21). Similarly in the winter, there is a one to two-month time lag in the cooling of the earth. The minimum heating effect from the sun comes on December 21, while the coldest days are in January or February. Figure 9.4b shows the overheated and underheated periods of the year for one of the U.S. climate regions. Note that the overheated period is not symmetrical about June 21. A fixed shading device will shade for equal time periods before and after June 21. For example, April 21 and August 21 will receive the same shade, even though August is significantly hotter.

To get full shading, we might try a fixed shading device (Fig 9.4b), which is sized to provide shade until the end of the overheated period (Oct. 21, in this case). Although we now have shade throughout the entire overheated period, we also shade the windows during part of the underheated period Feb. 21 to March 21. Only a movable shading device, as shown in Fig. 9.4c, can overcome this problem.

The movement of shading devices can be very simple or very complex. An adjustment twice a year can be quite effective, yet simple. Late in spring, at the beginning of the overheated period, the shading device would be manually extended. At the end of the overheated period in late fall, the device would be retracted for full solar exposure (Fig. 9.4d).

Before air conditioning became available, awnings were used to effectively shade windows in the summer.

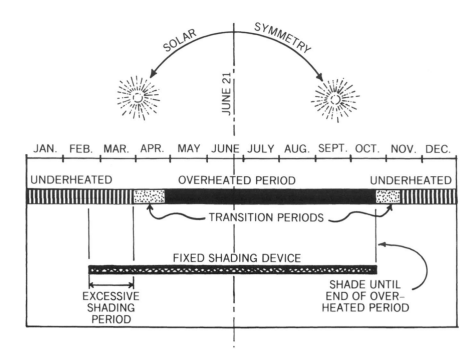

Figure 9.4b The large upper bar defines the annual climate of a particular place. The smaller lower bar defines the time period when a fixed shading device fully shades a window. Note that for a fixed shading device, the shading period is symmetrical about June 21, while the climate is not. Thus, any fixed shading device that is designed to fully shade until the end of the overheated period will also shade the window at the end of the underheated period, when full sun exposure is still needed.

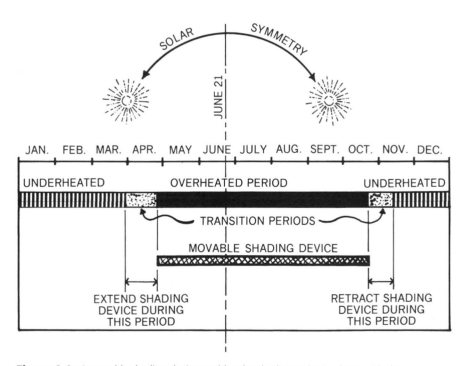

Figure 9.4c A movable shading device enables the shading to be in phase with the thermal year.

Awnings were used on many buildings but were particularly common on luxury buildings, such as major hotels (Fig. 9.4e). In the winter, the awnings were removed to let more sun and light enter the building. Modern awnings are excellent shading devices. They can be durable, attractive, and easily adjustable to meet requirements on a daily and even hourly

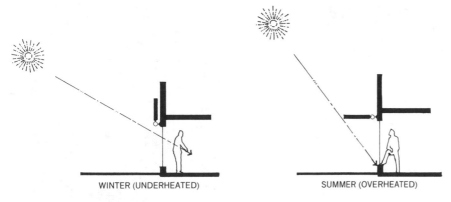

Figure 9.4d A movable shading device with just two simple adjustments per year can function extremely well.

Figure 9.4e Awnings were a common element on many buildings during the first half of the twentieth century. After giving effective shade in the summer, they are removed in order to allow more sun and light to enter the building in the winter.

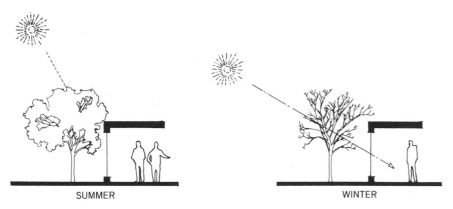

Figure 9.4f The shading from trees depends on the species, pruning, and maturity of the plants. Transmission can be as low as 20 percent in the summer and as high as 70 percent in the winter. Unfortunately, with some trees, winter transmission can be as low as 40 percent.

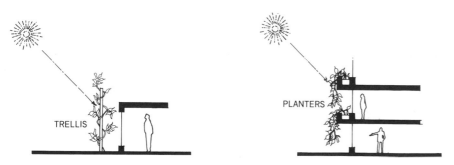

Figure 9.4g Vines can be very effective sunshading devices. Some vines grow as much as 30 ft (9 m) in one year.

The main disadvantage of using plants is the fact that leafless plants still create some shade, some types much more than others (Fig. 9.4f). Thus, trees are not recommended in front of south windows. Other disadvantages include slow growth, limited height, and the possibility of disease destroying the plant. However, vines growing on a trellis or hanging from a planter can overcome many of these problems (Figs. 9.4g and h). Given enough time, vines will grow to great heights (Fig 9.4i). In hot climates,

Figure 9.4h Since trees grow too slowly to help much on multistory buildings, planters can bring the shade plants to each level almost immediately.

basis. Movable shading devices, which adjust to the sun on a daily basis, are often automated, while those that need to be adjusted only twice a year are usually manually operated. Table 9.4 presents a variety of movable shading devices.

In many ways, the best shading devices are the deciduous plants, most of which are in phase with the thermal year because they gain and lose their leaves in response to temperature changes. Other advantages of deciduous plants include low cost, aesthetically pleasing quality, ability to reduce glare, visual privacy, and ability to cool the air by transpiration from the leaves.

Table 9.4 Examples of Movable Shading Devices

		Descriptive Name	Best Orientation	Comments
IX		Overhang Awning	South, east, west	Fully adjustable for annual, daily, or hourly conditions; Traps hot air; Good for view; Can be retracted during storms; **Best buy!**
X		Overhang Rotating horizontal louvers	South, east, west	Will block some view and winter sun
XI		Fin Rotating fins	East, west	Much more effective than fixed fins; Less restricted view than slanted fixed fins
XII		Eggcrate Rotating horizontal louvers	East, west	View very obstructed but less than fixed eggcrate; For very hot climates only; **Not recommended**
XIII		Deciduous plants Trees Vines	East, west southeast, southwest	View restricted but attractive for low-canopy trees; Air cooled; **Highly recommended**
XIV		Exterior roller shade	East, west, southeast, southwest	Very flexible from completely open to completely closed; View is restricted when shade is used; **Provides security**

Figure 9.4i Medium- to dark-colored walls in hot climates benefit greatly from a vine cover.

there is great benefit in shading not only windows but also walls. The darker the wall, the greater the benefit. A study in Miami of a moderately sparse vine 3 in. (7 cm) thick on a west wall resulted in a drop of the wall temperature by 8°F (4.5°C) in the morning and 14°F (8°C) in the afternoon. For examples of vines and trees for shading see Chapter 11. In general, the east and west orientations are the best locations for deciduous plants.

Another very effective movable shading device is the exterior roller shade. The Bateson office building makes very effective use of exterior fabric roller shades (see Fig. 17.6c). A roller shade made of rigid slats is very popular in Europe and is now available here (Fig. 9.4j). It offers security as well as very effective shading. These shading devices are especially appropriate on difficult east and west exposures, where for half a day almost no shading is necessary and for the other half almost full cover is required. Figure 9.4k shows how these roller shades are mounted on or in a building.

It has been said that the great inventions of humankind are fire, the wheel, and the venetian blind. The venetian blind just got better—it can now be used outdoors as well as indoors, and the outdoor venetian blinds allow the same great range

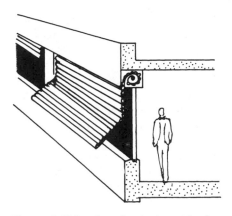

Figure 9.4j Exterior roller shades made of rigid slats not only move in a vertical plane but some can also project out like an awning.

of adjustments as the indoor kind. Unlike most shading devices, venetian blinds are excellent for controlled daylighting. They are widely used on commercial buildings in Germany (Fig. 9.4l).

A similar but less flexible system is to have exterior louvers that only rotate (Fig. 9.4m). Although mechanically simpler than venetian blinds, they will always block the view a little. There is a widely held conviction that since a building should be as low maintenance as possible, movable shading devices are unacceptable.

This is a little like saying that because an automobile should be low maintenance, the wheels should be fixed and not allowed to turn. The author believes that the use of existing technology and careful detailing can produce trouble-free, low-maintenance, movable shading devices.

9.5 SHADING PERIODS OF THE YEAR

Windows need shading during the overheated period of the year, which is a function of both climate and building type. From an energy point of view, buildings can be divided into two main types: **envelope dominated** and **internally dominated**.

The envelope-dominated building is very much affected by the climate because it has a large surface-area-to-volume ratio and because it has

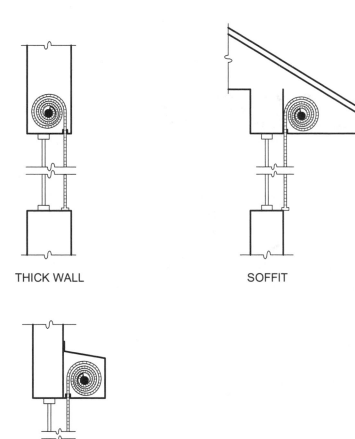

THICK WALL   SOFFIT

RETROFIT

Figure 9.4k Although it is best to integrate exterior roller shades into the design of a new building, they can be added to existing buildings.

Figure 9.4l Exterior venetian blinds have all of the adjustments possible with interior venetian blinds, but they are much more effective in keeping the sun out. They also make an architectural statement on the facade. This building is in Freiburg, Germany.

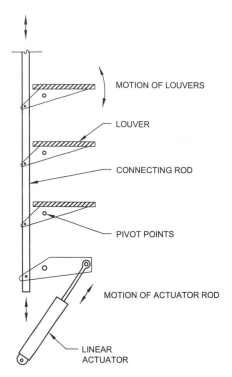

MOTION OF LOUVERS

LOUVER

CONNECTING ROD

PIVOT POINTS

MOTION OF ACTUATOR ROD

LINEAR ACTUATOR

Figure 9.4m Adjustable exterior louvers are effective sun control devices, but they will always obstruct the view somewhat, unlike exterior venetian blinds, which can be drawn up out of the way. Actuators are often used to rotate a whole column or row of movable louvers.

only modest internal heat sources. The internally dominated building, on the other hand, tends to have a small surface-area-to-volume ratio and large internal heat gains from such sources as machines, lights, and people. See Table 9.5A for a comparison of the two types of buildings.

A more precise way to define buildings than by the above two types is the concept of **balance point temperature** (BPT). Buildings do not need heating when the outdoor temperature is only slightly below the comfort zone because there are internal heat sources (lights, people, machines, etc.) and because the skin of the building slows the loss of heat. Thus, the greater the internal heat sources and the more effectively the building skin can retain heat, the lower will be the outdoor temperature before heating will be required. The BPT is that outdoor

temperature below which heating is required. It is a consequence of building design and function, not climate. The BPT for a typical internally dominated building is about 50°F (10°C), and for a typical envelope dominated building it is about 60°F (15°C).

Since the comfort zone has a range of about 10°F (5°C) wide (68° to 78°F) (20° to 25°C), the overheated period of the year starts at about 10°F (5°C) above the BPT of any building. For example, for an internally dominated building (BPT = 50°F [10°C]) the overheated period would start when the average daily outdoor temperature reached about 60°F (15°C). Consequently, the lower the BPT of a particular building, the shorter will be

the underheated period (heating season), and the longer will be its overheated period (cooling season) during which time shading is required.

Table 9.5B shows the over- and underheated periods of the year for internally dominated buildings (BPT = 50°F [10°C]) in each of seventeen climate regions, while Table 9.5C gives the same information for envelope-dominated buildings (BPT = 60°F [15°C]). Note how much shorter the overheated periods are in Table 9.5C compared to Table 9.5B. Also, it is very important to note that the overheated periods are never symmetrical about June 21. As mentioned earlier, the thermal year is always out of phase with the solar year.

Table 9.5A Comparison of Envelope Dominated and Internally Dominated Building Types		
Characteristic	**Envelope Dominated**	**Internally Dominated**
Balance point temperature	60°F (15°C)*	50°F (10°C)
Building form	Spread out	Compact
Surface-area-to-volume ratio	High	Low
Internal heat gain	Low	High
Internal rooms	Very few	Many
Number of exterior walls of typical room	2 to 3	0 to 1
Use of passive solar heating	Yes, except in very hot climates	No, except in very cold climates
Typical examples	Residences, small office buildings, some small schools	Large office and school buildings, auditoriums, theaters, factories

* Superinsulated buildings tend to have a balance point temperature of about 50°F (10°C) even though the other characteristics are those of an envelope-dominated building.

Table 9.5B Overheated and Underheated Periods for Internally Dominated Buildings

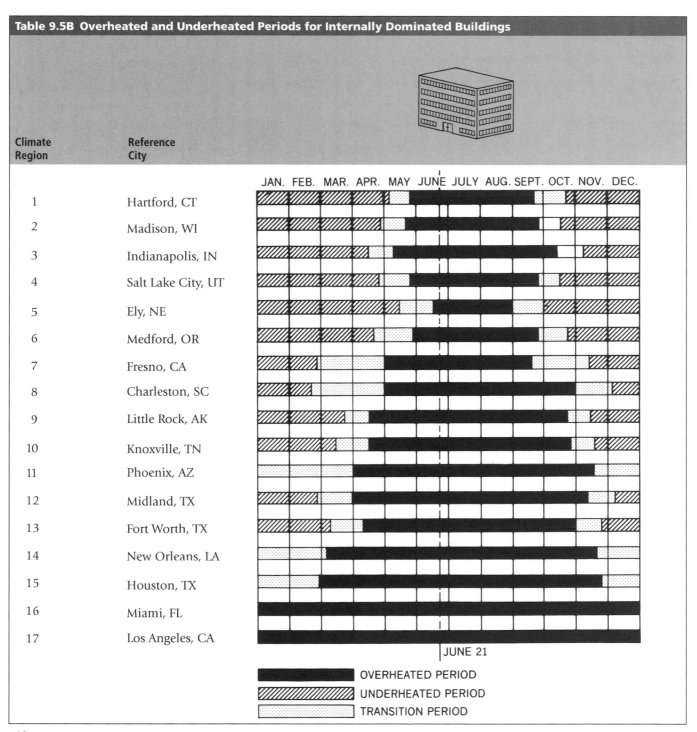

Climate Region	Reference City
1	Hartford, CT
2	Madison, WI
3	Indianapolis, IN
4	Salt Lake City, UT
5	Ely, NE
6	Medford, OR
7	Fresno, CA
8	Charleston, SC
9	Little Rock, AK
10	Knoxville, TN
11	Phoenix, AZ
12	Midland, TX
13	Fort Worth, TX
14	New Orleans, LA
15	Houston, TX
16	Miami, FL
17	Los Angeles, CA

JUNE 21

■ OVERHEATED PERIOD
▨ UNDERHEATED PERIOD
▦ TRANSITION PERIOD

Notes:
This table is for well-constructed, modern, internally dominated buildings (BPT = 50°F [10°C]).
The Overheated period occurs when average daily outdoor temperature is greater than 60°F (15°C).
The Underheated period occurs when average daily outdoor temperature is under 50°F (10°C).

Table 9.5C Overheated and Underheated Periods for Envelope-Dominated Buildings

Climate Region	Reference City	JAN.	FEB.	MAR.	APR.	MAY	JUNE	JULY	AUG.	SEPT.	OCT.	NOV.	DEC.
1	Hartford, CT												
2	Madison, WI												
3	Indianapolis, IN												
4	Salt Lake City, UT												
5	Ely, NE												
6	Medford, OR												
7	Fresno, CA												
8	Charleston, SC												
9	Little Rock, AK												
10	Knoxville, TN												
11	Phoenix, AZ												
12	Midland, TX												
13	Fort Worth, TX												
14	New Orleans, LA												
15	Houston, TX												
16	Miami, FL												
17	Los Angeles, CA												

JUNE 21

■ OVERHEATED PERIOD

▨ UNDERHEATED PERIOD

⬚ TRANSITION PERIOD

Notes:
This table is for well-constructed, modern, envelope-dominated buildings (BPT = 60°F [15°C]).
The Overheated period occurs when average daily outdoor temperature is greater than 70°F (21°C).
The Underheated period occurs when average daily outdoor temperature is under 60°F (15°C).

9.6 HORIZONTAL OVERHANGS

Most shading devices consist of either horizontal overhangs, vertical fins, or a combination of the two. The horizontal overhang and its many variations are the best choice for the south facade. Because they are directionally selective in a desirable way, they can block the sun, which is always above the horizon, while allowing the view, which is mostly of the horizon and below. Horizontal overhangs can also be designed to block the high summer sun while allowing the lower winter sun to enter the window. Although

less effective, they are usually also the best choice for east, southeast, southwest, and west orientations.

Horizontal louvers have a number of advantages over solid overhangs. Horizontal louvers in a horizontal plane reduce structural loads by allowing wind and snow to pass right through. In the summer, they also minimize the collection of hot air next to the windows under the overhang (Fig. 9.6a). Horizontal louvers in a vertical plane (Diagram III in Table 9.3) are appropriate when the projecting distance from the wall must be limited. This could be important if

a building is on or near the property line. Louvers can also be useful when the architecture calls for small-scale elements that creates a richer texture and a more humane scale.

When designing an overhang for the south facade, one must remember that the sun comes from the southeast before noon and from the southwest after noon. Therefore, the sun will outflank any overhang the same width as a window. Narrow windows need either a very wide overhang or vertical fins in addition to the overhang (Fig. 9.6b). Wide strip windows are less affected by this problem, as can be seen in Fig. 9.6c.

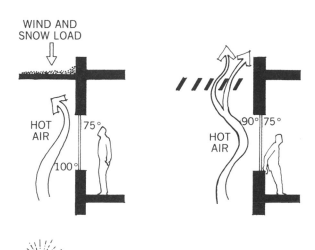

Figure 9.6a Horizontal louvered overhangs both vent hot air and minimize snow and wind loads. Also, their smaller-scale appearance is often desirable.

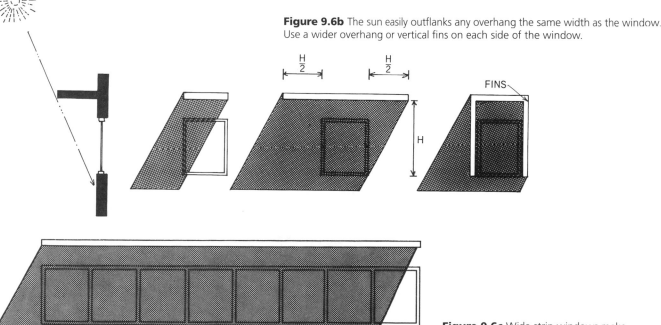

Figure 9.6b The sun easily outflanks any overhang the same width as the window. Use a wider overhang or vertical fins on each side of the window.

Figure 9.6c Wide strip windows make efficient use of the horizontal overhang.

36°N LATITUDE
A.21

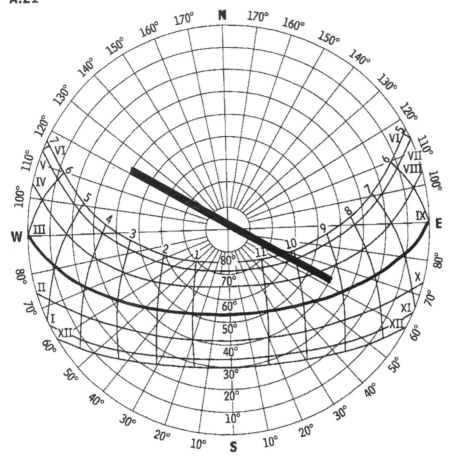

Figure 9.7a Highlight the sun path that represents the end of the overheated period. Draw the window through the center of the diagram.

9.7 DESIGN OF HORIZONTAL OVERHANGS—BASIC METHOD

1. Find the date of the end of the overheated period (i.e., last day that full shading is required) for envelope-dominated and internally dominated buildings from Tables 9.5B and 9.5C.
2. On a horizontal sun-path diagram for the appropriate latitude, darken the sun path that defines the end of the overheated period (Fig. 9.7a).
3. On this sun-path diagram, draw a line representing the orientation of the window through the center point (Fig. 9.7a).

4. Also through the center point, draw the sunray that is perpendicular to the window (Fig. 9.7b).
5. Find the point of intersection between the sunray and the sun path from step 2 above.
6. By means of this point, find the altitude angle and time of day of the sunray.
7. On a section of the window, draw the sunray to the windowsill (Fig. 9.7c).
8. Draw a horizontal overhang that reaches this sunray.*
9. Extend the overhang a minimum distance of $H/2$ on each side of the window if fins are not used.

---

* In order to prevent the sun from outflanking the overhang, it is necessary to extend the

shading device on either side of the window or to add fins on both sides of the window.

EXAMPLE

Problem:

Design a shading device for a window that is facing southwest at an azimuth of 120° (30° north of an east–west line). It is located at 36° N latitude in the city of Knoxville, Tennessee, in an envelope dominated school.

Solution

Step 1. From Table 9.5C, the end of the overheated period is about September 21 (use the closest 21st day of a month).

Step 2. On the horizontal sun-path diagram for 36°, darken the sun path for September 21 (Fig. 9.7a).

Step 3. On this same sun path diagram, draw the window through the center (Fig. 9.7a).

Step 4. Draw a sunray perpendicular to the window through the center of the sun path diagram (Fig. 9.7b).

Step 5. Locate the intersection of the sunray and sun path, from which we can determine the altitude angle and time of day when the sun is perpendicular to the window.

Step 6. Altitude = 49° Time of day = 1:15 P.M.

Step 7. On a section of the window, draw the sunray at an altitude angle of 49° from the windowsill (Fig. 9.7c).

Step 8. Design an overhang that reaches this sunray (Fig. 9.7c). One of many possible solutions is shown.

Step 9. Extend the overhang a distance of $H/2$ on either side of the window, or add vertical fins on both sides, or a combination, as shown in Fig. 9.7d.

36°N LATITUDE

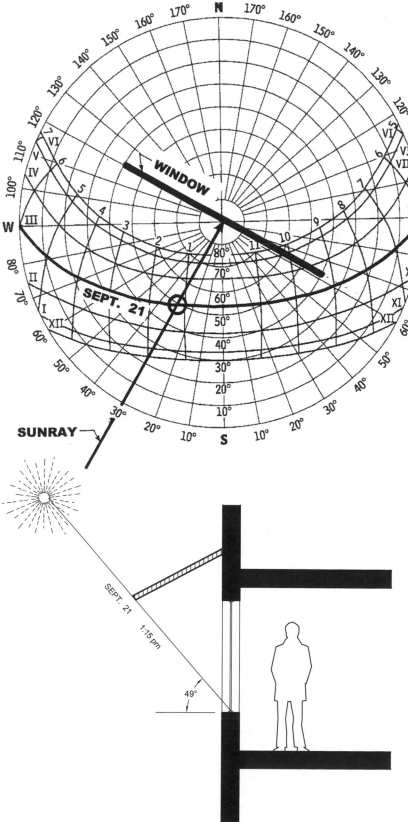

SUNRAY

SEPT. 21

1:15 pm

49°

Figure 9.7b Draw the sunray that is perpendicular to the window at the center of the sun path diagram. The altitude angle of this sunray can be determined from the point that results from the intersection of this sunray and the sun path that represents the end of the overheated period. From this point, it is also possible to determine the time of day when the sun is perpendicular to the window at this time of year.

Figure 9.7c On a section draw the sunray from the windowsill. Any overhang that reaches this sunray will shade the window the whole overheated period of the year.

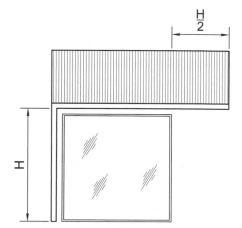

Figure 9.7d To prevent the sun from outflanking the overhang, a vertical fin is used on the west side of the window and an overhang extension is used on the south side. This solution is asymmetric because the solar geometry is asymmetric in relation to this window.

9.8 SHADING DESIGN FOR SOUTH WINDOWS

For south windows, the first step is to decide on either a fixed or movable horizontal overhang. Use the following rules for this purpose.

Rules for Selecting a South-Shading Strategy

1. If shading is the main concern and passive heating is not required, then a fixed overhang may be used.
2. If *both* passive heating and shading are important (long over- and underheated periods), then a movable overhang should be used.

The next step is to choose or design a particular kind of horizontal overhang. Refer to Tables 9.3 and 9.4 for examples of the generic types.

The size, angle, and location of the shading device can be determined by several different methods. The most powerful, flexible, and informative is the use of physical models. This method will be explained in detail in Section 9.18. There are also graphic methods, one of which was explained in the previous section. Finally, there are rules and design guidelines. Because this last method is the quickest and easiest, it is presented here in some detail. It must be noted, however, that this method is always limited in flexibility and application. The author, therefore, strongly recommends the use of physical models in conjunction with the design guidelines described below.

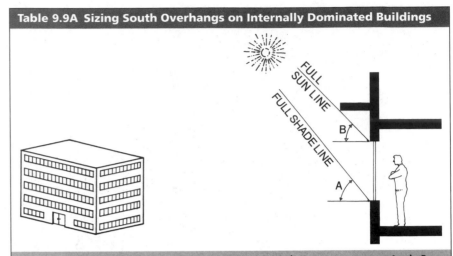

Table 9.9A Sizing South Overhangs on Internally Dominated Buildings

Climate Region	Reference City	Angle A (Full Shade)	Angle B (Full Sun)
1	Hartford, CT	59	54
2	Madison, WI	58	47
3	Indianapolis, IN	53	47
4	Salt Lake City, UT	60	49
5	Ely, NE	69	59
6	Medford, OR	59	45
7	Fresno, CA	55	33
8	Charleston, SC	54	36
9	Little Rock, AK	54	43
10	Knoxville, TN	53	41
11	Phoenix, AZ*	48	NA
12	Midland, TX	52	40
13	Fort Worth, TX	54	41
14	New Orleans, LA*	49	NA
15	Houston, TX*	49	NA
16	Miami, FL*	40	NA
17	Los Angeles, CA*	33	NA

Notes:
This table is for south-facing windows or windows oriented up to 20° off south.
An overhang reaching the full shade line will shade a window for most of the overheated period.
An overhang not projecting beyond the full sun line will allow full solar exposure of a window for most of the underheated period.
* Use a fixed overhang projecting to the full shade line, because passive solar heating is not required in these climates for internally dominated buildings.

9.9 DESIGN GUIDELINES FOR FIXED SOUTH OVERHANGS

As stated in the rules above, a fixed horizontal overhang is most appropriate when passive solar heating is not desired. The goal, then, is to find the length of overhang that will shade the south windows during most of the overheated period.

Figure 9.9a shows the sun angle at the end of the overheated period. Since the sun is higher in the sky during the rest of the overheated period, any overhang that extends to the line shown will fully shade the window for the whole overheated period. This **full shade line** is defined by angle A and is drawn from the windowsill. This angle is given for each climate region in Table 9.9A for internally dominated buildings and in Table 9.9B for envelope-dominated buildings.

Overhangs that are higher on the wall and that extend to the full shade line will still block the direct radiation and yet give a larger view of the sky. However, this would not be desirable in regions with significant diffuse radiation, since both increased overheating and visual glare will result from the increased exposure to the bright sky (Fig. 9.9b). Even the overhang shown in Fig. 9.9a might not

Table 9.9B Sizing South Overhangs on Envelope-Dominated Buildings

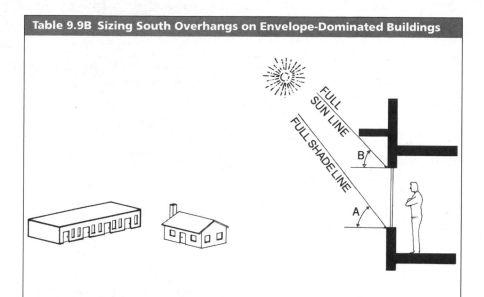

Climate Region	Reference City	Angle A (Full Shade)	Angle B (Full Sun)
1	Hartford, CT	65	59
2	Madison, WI	64	55
3	Indianapolis, IN	63	55
4	Salt Lake City, UT	65	60
5	Ely, NE	72	69
6	Medford, OR	71	61
7	Fresno, CA	64	45
8	Charleston, SC	65	49
9	Little Rock, AK	63	52
10	Knoxville, TN	62	51
11	Phoenix, AZ	56	49
12	Midland, TX	63	50
13	Fort Worth, TX	61	54
14	New Orleans, LA	63	44
15	Houston, TX	60	42
16	Miami, FL*	50	NA
17	Los Angeles, CA	61	43

Notes:
This table is for south-facing windows or windows oriented up to 20° off south.
An overhang reaching the full shade line will shade a window for most of the overheated period.
An overhang not projecting beyond the full sun line will allow full solar exposure of a window for most of the underheated period.
*Use a fixed overhang projecting to the full shade line because passive solar heating is not required in this climate.

Figure 9.9a The full shade line determines the length of overhang required for shade during the overheated period.

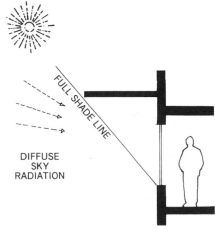

Figure 9.9b Fixed overhangs placed higher on the wall are not desirable in humid climates, because of the large amount of diffuse radiation and glare.

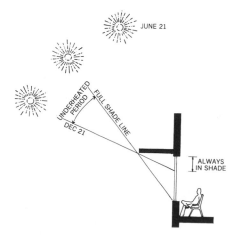

Figure 9.9c A fixed overhang designed to shade a window during the whole overheated period will also shade part of the window during the underheated period.

be sufficient in very humid regions, where over 50 percent of the total radiation can come from the diffuse sky. Rather than increasing the length of the overhang, it might be desirable to use other devices, such as curtains or plants, to block the diffuse radiation from the low sky.

As the sun dips below the full shade line later in the year, the window will gradually receive some solar radiation. However, the upper portion of the window will be in shade even at the winter solstice (Fig. 9.9c). Remember that *any fixed overhang that is very effective in the summer will also block some of the passive heating in the winter.*

Furthermore, an overhang extending to the full shade line can result in a quite dark interior. If daylighting is desired, as is often the case, then the strategies of Chapter 13 should be followed. The techniques described there allow ample light to enter a building while minimizing the overheating effect.

Procedure for Designing Fixed South Overhangs

1. Determine the climate region of the building from Fig. 5.5.
2. Determine angle A from Table 9.9A for internally dominated and from Table 9.9B for envelope-dominated buildings.
3. On a section of the window, draw the full shade line from the windowsill.
4. Any overhang that extends to this line will give full shade during most of the overheated period of the year.
5. Shorter overhangs would still be useful, even though they would shade less of the overheated period.

9.10 DESIGN GUIDELINES FOR MOVABLE SOUTH OVERHANGS

The design of movable overhangs is the same as for fixed overhangs for the overheated period of the year. However, to make effective use of passive solar heating, the overhang must retract to avoid shading the window during the underheated period.

To ensure full-sun exposure of a window during the underheated period (winter), two points must be addressed. The first is to determine at which times of year the overhang must be retracted, and the second is to determine how far it must be retracted.

The simplest and most practical approach to the first question is to extend and retract the shading device

during the spring and fall transition periods. These periods are described in Tables 9.5B and 9.5C. Making the twice-annual changeover could be no more complicated than washing the windows and could be done at the same time.

The sun angle at the *end* of the underheated period (i.e., the last day of the underheated period on which full solar exposure of the window is desired) determines the **full sun line** (Fig. 9.10a). Since the sun is lower than this position during the rest of winter, any overhang short of this line will not block the sun when it is needed. This full sun line is defined by angle B and is drawn from the window's head. The appropriate angle is

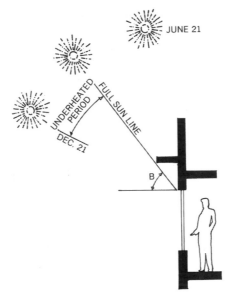

Figure 9.10a The full sun line determines the maximum allowable projection of an overhang during the winter period.

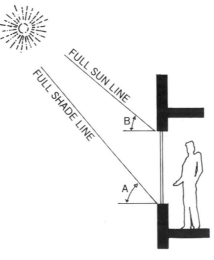

Figure 9.10b A fixed overhang, unlike a movable overhang, will not work well because it cannot both meet the full shade line and stay behind the full sun line.

given for each climate region in Tables 9.9A and 9.9B.

Procedure for Designing Movable South Overhangs

1. Determine the climate region of the building from Fig. 5.5.
2. Determine angles A and B from Table 9.9A for internally dominated buildings and from Table 9.9B for envelope-dominated buildings.
3. On a section of the window, draw the full shade line (angle A) from the windowsill, and draw the full sun line (angle B) from the window head (Fig. 9.10b).
4. A movable overhang will have to extend to the full shade line during the overheated portion of the year and not extend beyond the full sun line during the underheated period of the year. See Fig. 9.10c for two of many possible solutions.
5. The overhang should be extended during the spring transition period and retracted during the fall transition period. The dates for these transition periods can be determined from Table 9.5B for internally dominated and Table 9.5C for envelope-dominated buildings.

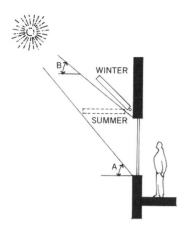

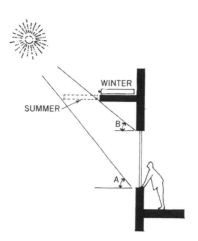

Figure 9.10c Two alternative movable overhangs are shown in both the winter (underheated) and the summer (overheated) positions. Of course, awnings are the most common movable shading device.

9.11 SHADING FOR EAST AND WEST WINDOWS

For the east and west orientations, unlike the south, it is not possible to fully shade the summer sun with a fixed overhang. Fig. 9.11a shows how futile it would be to try to completely shade east or west windows with a horizontal overhang. Although the direct sun rays cannot be shaded at all times with an overhang, it is nevertheless worthwhile to shade the windows part of the time.

Since little winter heating can be expected from east and west windows, shading devices on those orientations can be designed purely on the basis of the summer requirement.

No shading device will fully shade the east or west windows and allow a good view, because the low sun will be part of the view. Since the view is a very high priority for windows, the author believes that a horizontal overhang offers the best combination of view and shade not only for the south, but for east and west as well. However, the horizontal overhangs must be much longer on the east and west than on the south, and they need to be backed up with another shading device such as venetian blinds.

Vertical fins are often presented as the shading devices of choice for east and west. In fact, they shade no better than horizontal overhangs, but they obstruct the view much more. Figure 9.11b illustrates the fact

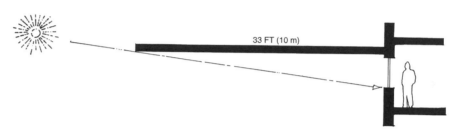

33 FT (10 m)

Figure 9.11a The 33-ft (10 m) overhang needed to shade a 4-ft (1.2 m) window on August 21 at 6 P.M. at 36° N latitude illustrates the futility of trying to fully shade east and west windows with fixed horizontal overhangs.

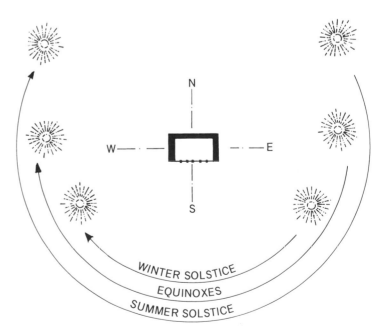

Figure 9.11b This plan view illustrates the sweep of the sun's azimuth angle at different times of the year from sunrise to sunset.

that there is a time every morning and afternoon when the sun shines directly at the east and west facades of a building during the summer six months of the year (March 21 to September 21). Therefore, vertical fins that face directly east or west will allow some sun penetration every day during the worst six months of the year. To minimize this solar penetration, we need to minimize the "exposure angle" (Fig. 9.11c). We can accomplish this by decreasing the spacing of the fins, by making the fins deeper, or both. To be highly effective, the fins must be so deep and so closely spaced that a view through them becomes almost impossible.

Vertical fins can be appropriate either when there is a desire to control the direction of view (e.g., slant fins to the northeast to block the view to the west and southwest) or when the view is of minor importance. In that case, the fins could be slanted either to the south for more winter sun or to the north for more cool daylight or both if the fins are movable.

By moving in response to the daily cycle of the sun, movable fins allow somewhat unobstructed views for most of the day and yet block the sun when necessary. For example, movable fins on a west window would be held in the perpendicular position until the afternoon, when the sun threatened to outflank them (Fig. 9.11d, top). Either at once or gradually, they would then rotate to the position shown in Fig. 9.11d, bottom.

Movable vertical fins can provide both better views and more shade than fixed fins, but still not as much as a movable overhang. Furthermore, since the view is usually the top priority, fins are not recommended on the east and west windows.

Rules for East and West Windows

1. Use as few east and especially west windows as possible.
2. Have windows on east or west facades face north or south, as shown in Fig. 9.3b.

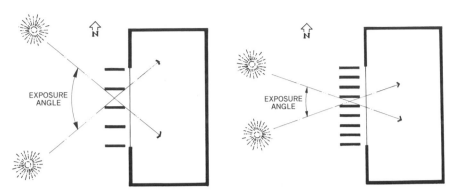

Figure 9.11c A plan view of vertical fins on a west (east) facade illustrates how solar penetration is reduced by moving fins closer together, by making them deeper, or both.

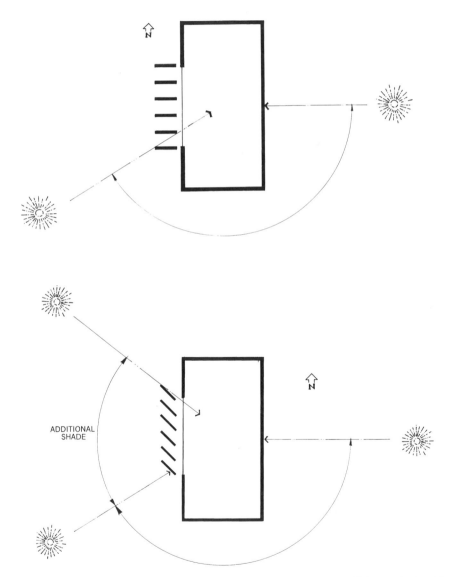

Figure 9.11d Movable fins would be in their maximum open position until the sun is about to enter. At that time, the fins would rotate to block any direct sunlight (bottom).

3. Since views of the ground and horizon are usually important, use a horizontal overhang with a backup movable shading device.
4. Use trees, plant-covered trellises, or hanging plants (Figs. 9.4f–h).
5. If views to the east or west are not very desirable vertical fins can be an alternative. Slant the fins toward the northwest if shading is required most of the year. Slant the fins toward the southwest if winter sun is desired.
6. Use movable shading devices for both better shading and better views.

9.12 DESIGN OF EAST AND WEST HORIZONTAL OVERHANGS

When views to the east and west are desirable, use horizontal overhangs. A long overhang can be reasonably effective and yet give a better view of the landscape than do vertical fins. Although there is a fair amount of time when the sun peeks under an east and west overhang, there are many hours of useful shade. In most cases, horizontal overhangs are better than vertical fins for east and west orientations.

When the sun peeks under overhangs, it is important to have some additional protection in the form of venetian blinds, roller shades, drapes, etc.

Table 9.12 allows the designer to determine the length of overhang needed to shade east and west windows from 8 A.M. to 4 P.M. (solar time) during most of the overheated period. The length of overhang thus determined should be a guide rather than a rigid requirement. Shorter overhangs, although less effective, are still worthwhile.

The absurdly long overhangs required in hot climates, as indicated by Table 9.12, indicate the problem with east and west windows. It is, therefore, worth repeating once more that east and west windows should be avoided if at all possible in hot climates.

Procedure for Designing East and West Fixed Overhangs

1. Determine the climate region from Fig. 5.5.
2. Determine angle C from Table 9.12.
3. On a section of the east or west window, draw the shade line from the windowsill.
4. Any overhang that projects to this line will shade east and west windows from 8 A.M. to 4 P.M. during most of the overheated period. Of course, shorter overhangs would still be useful and longer ones would be even better.

Table 9.12 Sizing East and West Horizontal Fixed Overhangs

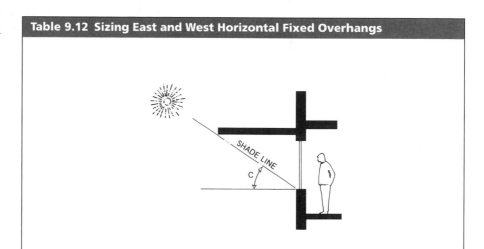

Climate Region	Reference City	Angle C Internally Dominated	Envelope-Dominated
1	Hartford, CT	30	34
2	Madison, WI	30	34
3	Indianapolis, IN	25	32
4	Salt Lake City, UT	30	33
5	Ely, NE	34	36
6	Medford, OR	30	37
7	Fresno, CA	25	30
8	Charleston, SC	23	29
9	Little Rock, AK	24	29
10	Knoxville, TN	23	29
11	Phoenix, AZ	19	24
12	Midland, TX	22	28
13	Fort Worth, TX	23	28
14	New Orleans, LA	19	27
15	Houston, TX	19	25
16	Miami, FL	14	19
17	Los Angeles, CA	9	28

Notes:
Any overhang that extends to the shade line defined by angle C will shade east and west windows from 8 A.M. to 4 P.M. during most of the overheated period. Choose the column for angle C according to the building type (internally or envelope-dominated). The extremely long overhang required in hot climates indicates the problem of shading east and west windows.

9.13 DESIGN OF SLANTED VERTICAL FINS

The following procedure will yield a slanted vertical fin system that will shade east and west windows from direct sun for the whole year between 7 A.M. and 5 P.M. (solar time). Since the sun is fairly low in the sky after 5 P.M., neighboring trees and buildings often provide additional shade for windows on the ground floor.

Procedure for Designing Slanted Vertical Fins

1. Find the latitude of the building site from Fig. 5.6d.
2. From Table 9.13, determine the shade line angle D.
3. On a plan of the east or west window, draw the shade line at angle D from an east–west line (Fig. 9.13, left).
4. Draw slanted vertical fins so that the head of one fin and the tail of the adjacent one both touch the shade line (Fig. 9.13, left). Different solutions are possible by varying the size, spacing, and slant of the fins (Fig. 9.13, right).

Table 9.13	Shade Line Angle for Slanted Vertical Fins*
Latitude	Angle D
24	18
28	15
32	12
36	10
40	9
44	8
48	7

*This table is for vertical fins slanted toward the north on east or west windows. Designs based on this table will provide shade from direct sun for the whole year between 7 A.M. and 5 P.M. (solar time). This table can also be used to design vertical fins on north windows for the same time period.

9.14 DESIGN OF FINS ON NORTH WINDOWS

Buildings with long overheated periods may also require shading of north windows. Because of the sun angles involved, small vertical fins are often sufficient to give full shade from 7 a.m. to 5 p.m. (solar time) (see Figs. 17.8b and c). Figure 9.14 illustrates how the fins are determined by the same angle D used for sizing slanted fins on the east and west.

Procedure for Designing North Fins

1. Find the latitude of the building site from Fig. 5.6d.
2. From Table 9.13, determine the appropriate angle D.
3. On a plan of the north window, draw the shade line at angle D from an east–west line (Fig. 9.14, left).
4. Draw vertical fins to meet this shade line, and note that if intermediate fins are used, all fins will be shorter (Fig. 9.14 right).
5. Remember that fins are required on both the east and west sides of north windows.
6. To prevent the high sun from outflanking the top of the fins, add an overhang as deep as the fins.
7. Below the Tropic of Cancer (23.5° latitude) north windows are increasingly similar to south windows until at the equator they are equal.

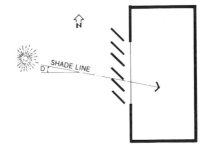
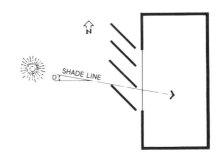

Figure 9.13 The shade line at angle D determines the combination of fin spacing, fin depth, and fin slant on east and west windows. An alternative solution is also shown.

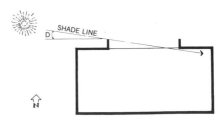
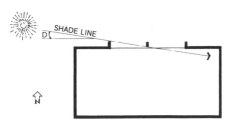

Figure 9.14 The shade line at angle D also determines the vertical-fin design on north windows. An alternative solution is also shown.

9.15 DESIGN GUIDELINES FOR EGGCRATE SHADING DEVICES

Eggcrate shading devices are mainly for east and west windows in *hot* climates and for the additional southeast and southwest orientations in *very hot* climates. An eggcrate is a combination of horizontal overhangs (louvers) and vertical fins. By controlling sun penetration by both the altitude and azimuth angle of the sun, very effective shading of windows can be achieved. The view, however, is usually very obstructed.

The brise-soleil, developed by Le Corbusier, is an eggcrate system with dimensions frequently at the scale of rooms (Figs. 9.1j and k). Since shading is a geometric problem, many small devices are equivalent to a few large ones (see again Fig. 9.3d). Therefore, eggcrates can also be made at the scale of a fine screen. In India these screens were often cut from a single piece of marble (Fig. 9.15a). Today, these screens are most often made of metal (Fig. 9.15b) or masonry units (Fig. 9.15c). The shading effect of eggcrates at different scales is identical, but the view from the inside and the aesthetic appearance from the outside vary greatly.

The designer should first decide on the general appearance of the eggcrate system. The required dimensions of each unit (Fig. 9.15d) are best determined experimentally by means of a heliodon. As far as sun penetration is concerned, the scale of the eggcrate can be changed at any time as long as the ratios of h/d and w/d are kept constant. The use of the heliodon for this purpose will be explained in detail below.

The author does not recommend small-scale eggcrate shading if either a view or light is desired. Use such systems only where ventilation or security is the main objective.

Figure 9.15a This marble screen, carved from a single piece of stone, is actually a miniature eggcrate shading device. The **thickness of the slab** is critical. The same pattern in a flat metal plate would be practically useless as a shading device. (Photograph by Suresh Choudhary.)

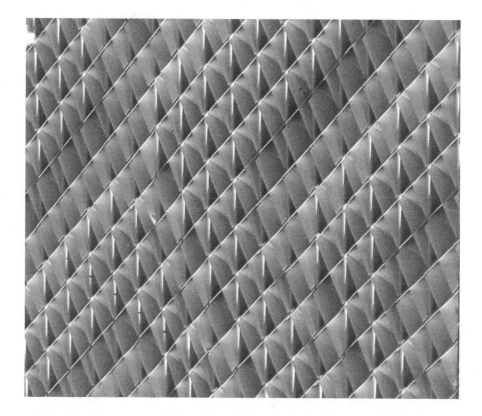

Figure 9.15b An eggcrate shading device made of metal. (Courtesy of Construction Specialties, Inc.)

Figure 9.15c An eggcrate shading device made of masonry units is shown. As with all small-scale eggcrate shading, the view and daylighting are greatly restricted.

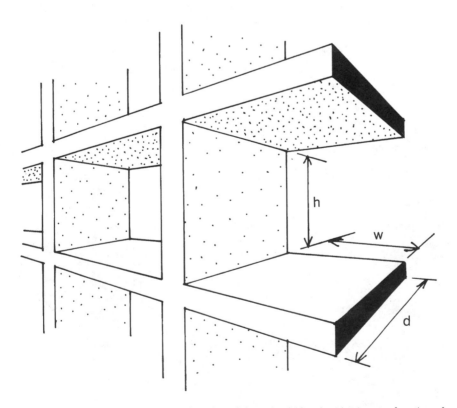

Figure 9.15d The shading effect is a function of the ratios *h/d* and *w/d*. It is not a function of actual size.

9.16 SPECIAL SHADING STRATEGIES

Most external shading devices are variations of the horizontal overhang, vertical fin, or eggcrate. However, some interesting exceptions exist.

The geodesic dome designed by Buckminster Fuller for the U.S. Pavilion, Expo '67, created an artificial climate for the structures within (Fig. 4.2b). To prevent overheating inside the clear plastic dome, the upper panels had vents and special roller shades. Each glazed hexagonal structural unit had six triangular roller shades operated by a servomotor. Figure 9.16a shows these shades in various positions.

A completely different approach is to rotate the building with the changing azimuth of the sun. If this sounds far-fetched, consider the fact that rotating buildings have already been built. To enjoy the beautiful panoramic view of his Connecticut property, Richard Foster built a revolving house (Fig. 9.16b).

A rotating building specifically designed for its solar benefits is the "Heliotrope" built in Freiburg, Germany, by the architect Rolf Disch as his home (Fig 9.16c&d). The building, like a heliotrope flower, tracks the sun. In the winter, the triple-glazed windows face the sun, while in the summer the building exposes its blank insulated wall to the hot sun. The balcony railing consists of a vacuum tube solar hot-water collector. Rotating separately on the roof, the PV array generates much more electricity than the building needs. Thus, the Heliotrope is better than a **zero-energy building**—it is an **energy-plus house.**

A similar but simpler approach would be to have the building stand still but a shade move around it. For example, a barn door hanging from a curved track could follow the sun around a building (Fig. 9.16e). If the barn door were covered with PV cells, you would have a tracking solar collector as well. Or the barn door could be made of darkly tinted glazing so

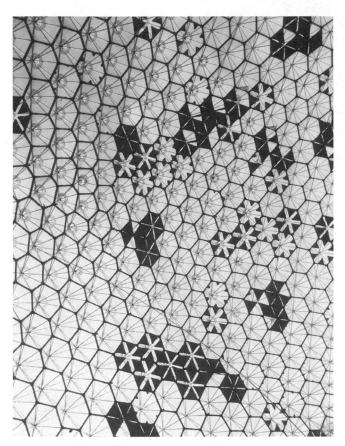

Figure 9.16c Architect Rolf Disch of Freiburg, Germany, has designed his home to track the sun. His "Heliotrope" house rotates to face welcoming windows toward the winter sun and a blank wall to intercept the summer sun. The PV panels on the roof rotate separately to always collect the maximum solar radiation. (Courtesy Architect Rolf Disch.)

Figure 9.16a The U.S. Pavilion, Expo '67, Montreal, Canada, was designed by Buckminster Fuller. This view of the dome from the inside shows the vent holes and triangular roller shades that prevent overheating in the summer.

Figure 9.16b The residence that architect Richard Foster built for himself in Wilton, Connecticut, in 1967 is round and rotates 360° to take full advantage of the panoramic view and passive solar heating. (Courtesy of Richard Foster, architect.)

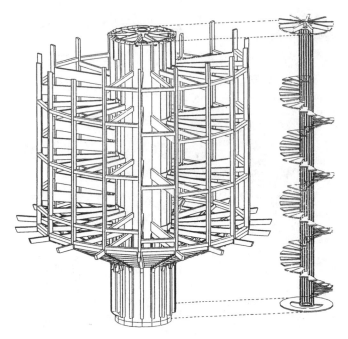

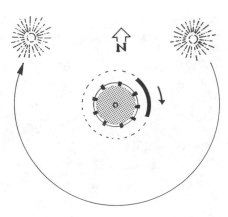

Figure 9.16e A shading panel can rotate around the building in phase with the sun. If the panel is covered with PV, it also acts as a tracking solar collector.

Figure 9.16d A section of the rotating solar house called the Heliotrope. (Courtesy Architect Rolf Disch.)

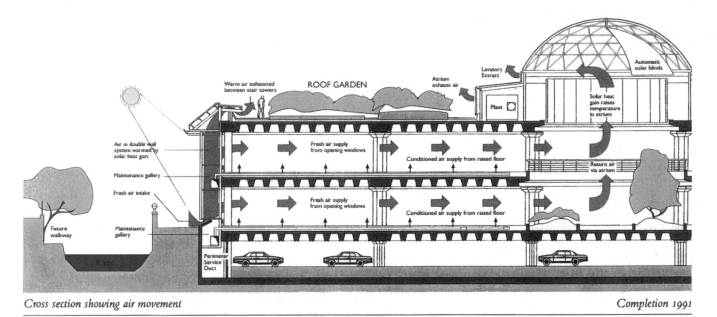

THE MICHAEL LAIRD PARTNERSHIP

Figure 9.16f The Tanfield House in Edinburgh, Scotland, designed by Michael Laird Partners, uses domes to daylight and ventilate the atria. To prevent overheating, triangular solar blinds rotate when needed on indoor tracks to block the sun. (Tanfield House, Edinburgh—Michael Laird Architects.)

that the building always has "sunglasses" facing the sun in the summer.

Instead of sunglasses, the Tanfield House uses a triangular parasol to shade its glass domes. The solar blind is a spherical triangle that moves on an indoor circular track in order to block the sun when appropriate (Fig. 9.16f). The domes are used for daylighting, natural ventilation, and space heating.

The architect of the Indian Heritage Center in New Delhi, India, decided that the best way to shade not only the windows but also the walls and the land between buildings would be to have a shade structure spanning between buildings (Fig. 9.16g). The space-frame supported shading allows wind, rain, and hot air to pass through. The shading

simulates the functional and aesthetic benefits of a very high canopy of trees.

9.17 SHADING OUTDOOR SPACES

Shading of outdoor spaces can be just as important as shading buildings. Open-air amphitheaters and stadiums are a special problem because of their size and need for unobstructed sight-lines. The most popular solution is the use of membrane tension structures, since they can span large distances at relatively low cost. Most often, water-proof membranes are used because they also protect against rain (Fig. 9.17a), but in dry climates, an open-weave fabric might be more appropriate. This is not a new idea, however, for the Romans covered not only their theaters but even their gigantic Colosseum with an awning (Fig. 9.17b). Modern small-scale versions of removable awnings called "toldos" are shown in Figs. 9.17c and d.

Many traditional shading structures were designed to create shade while letting air and rain pass right through. The **pergola**, **trellis**, and **arbor** are examples of such structures (Fig. 9.17e–g). Pergolas without plants must be carefully designed if

Figure 9.17a A membrane tension structure for shading outdoor seating in Snowmass, Colorado, is shown.

Figure 9.17b The Roman Colosseum, which was built about 80 A.D. and seated about 50,000 spectators, was covered with a giant awning for sun protection. (From *L'anfiteatro Flavio Descritto e Deliniato* by Carlo Fontana, Vaillant, 1725.)

Figure 9.17d This winter garden in Washington, DC, is protected from the summer sun by folding awnings also known as toldos. In this special case, the shading is on the indoor side of the glazing.

Figure 9.17c This type of retractable awning suspended from cables is called a toldo. Disneyland, Los Angeles, California.

Figure 9.17e These trellised outdoor reading areas are part of the public library in San Juan Capistrano, California, designed by Michael Graves. Often a trellis is used to support vines or other climbing plants.

they are to provide effective shading. The typical pergola shown in the left side of Fig. 9.17h provides little shade when it is needed most—around the noon hours. Pergolas should have the beams (louvers) tilted toward the north in order to create meaningful shade in the summer (Fig. 9.17h, right). Interesting nontraditional shading structures are shown in Figs. 9.17i and j.

When the outdoor shading system is fixed and permanent, it should be designed to let the winter sun enter while rejecting the summer sun (Fig. 9.17k). The author has seen many shading structures that created more shade in the winter than in the summer. Designing a successful shading structure is not as simple as it might seem. The best way to design a shading system for an outdoor space as well as for a building is to use physical models on a heliodon. This technique will now be explained.

Figure 9.17f This pergola was designed so that most of the shade comes from the vine that it supports.

Figure 9.17g This arbor is located in the garden of the Governor's Palace, Colonial Williamsburg, Virginia. (Courtesy of Richard Kenworthy.)

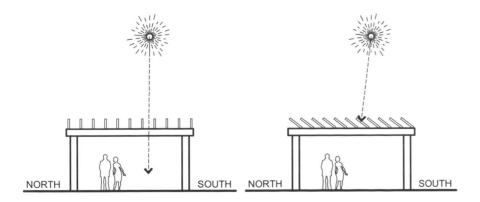

Figure 9.17h The typical pergola has shading elements that are on edge like joists. Such a design will provide little shade at 12 noon. Instead, the louvers should be tilted toward the north.

Figure 9.17i Perforated screen shading structure. (Courtesy of *ARAMCO World* magazine.)

Figure 9.17k Fixed, outdoor shading systems should allow hot air to escape and winter sun to enter, as in this structure in San Jose, California.

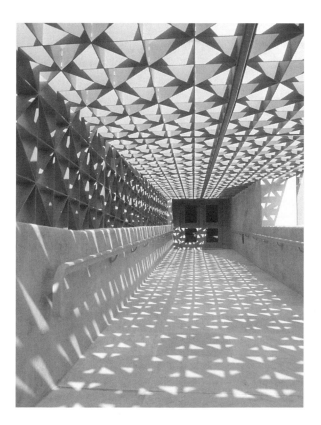

Figure 9.17j Antione Predock used a trellis of steel bars to shade outdoor walkways and sculpture gardens at the Fine Arts Center at Arizona State University in Tempe.

9.18 USING PHYSICAL MODELS FOR SHADING DESIGN

Heliodons were introduced earlier, and the author suggested that building or buying a heliodon is an excellent investment for an architectural office or school. Appendix I gives detailed instructions for making and using a heliodon. One of its main applications is the design of shading devices. Testing a model of a shading device not only gives feedback on the performance of the device but also teaches the designer much about the whole question of sun shading. Since this method of design is conceptually simple, it is easy to learn and remember. The step-by-step procedure for designing shading devices by means of physical models is followed by an illustrative example.

Basic Procedure for Shading Design by Means of Physical Models

1. Build a scale model of the building, a typical portion of the building facade, or a typical window.

2. Set up the heliodon and adjust it for the correct latitude (see Appendix I).

3. Place the model on the center of the heliodon tilt table. Be sure to orient the model properly (e.g., a south window should face south, as shown in Fig. 9.18a).

4. Determine the end of the over- and underheated periods from Tables 9.5B and 9.5C for internally and envelope-dominated buildings, respectively.

5. Move the heliodon light vertically to match the date of the end of the overheated period, check the shading on the model, and adjust the overhang as necessary.

6. Rotate the model stand to simulate the changing shadows at different hours on that date.

7. Make more adjustments, if necessary, on the model to achieve the desired shading.

8. Move the heliodon light vertically to match the date of the end of the underheated period (winter), and check the sun penetration.

9. Make changes on the model if the sun penetration is not sufficient.

10. Rotate the model stand to simulate the changing shadows for various hours on this date.

11. Repeat steps 5 to 10 until an acceptable design has been developed.

Illustrative Example

Problem

A horizontal overhang is required for a small office building (envelope-dominated) in Indianapolis, Indiana. Daylighting will not be considered in this example. The overhang is for a 5-ft-wide (1.5 m) and 4-ft-high (1.2m) window on a wall facing south.

Solution

1. Build a model of the window with some of the surrounding wall. For convenience, the model should be about 6 in. (15 cm) on a side (Fig. 9.18a). Use a clear plastic film, such as acetate, for the glazing.

2. Appendix I explains how to set up and use the heliodon. Adjust the tilt table for the latitude of Indianapolis, which is 40°N latitude.

3. With pushpins or double-stick tape, tack the model to the center of the tilt table and orient it south (Fig. 9.18a).

4. From Fig. 5.5, determine that Indianapolis is in climate region 3. Since it is given that the building is envelope-dominated, use Table 9.5C to determine that the overheated period ends about September 15 and the underheated period ends about May 7.

5. Move the heliodon light vertically to correspond with September 15. Cut and attach an overhang of such length that the shadow just reaches the windowsill (Fig. 9.18a).

6. When one rotates the model stand, the shadows for different times of the day can be investigated. Note how the sun outflanks the window before and after noon because the overhang was not wide enough (Fig. 9.18b).

7. The overhang is extended on each side of the window (Fig. 9.18c).

8. Move the lamp to the position corresponding to the end of the underheated period, which we determined above to be about

Figure 9.18a A model of a south window is placed facing south on the tilt table of the heliodon. Note that the overhang fully shades the window at 12 noon at the end of the overheated period (September 15) for this design.

Figure 9.18b The heliodon now simulates 4 P.M. on September 15. Note how the sun is outflanking the overhang.

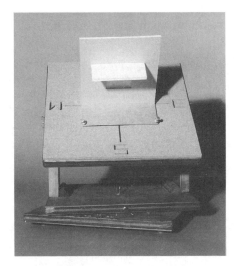

Figure 9.18c The overhang is redesigned by making it wider.

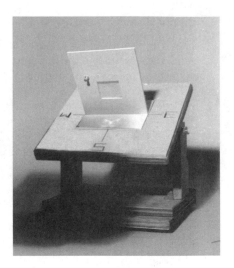

Figure 9.18d The heliodon light is readjusted to simulate the shading just before the end of the underheated period (May 7 in this case), at which time sun is still desired. Instead, the window is in shade.

Figure 9.18e The overhang is rotated up until the window is fully exposed to the winter sun. This determines the position for the overhang during the whole underheated period.

Figure 9.18f The model shows that at very large angles of incidence the sun is mostly reflected off the glazing. Note the long shadow of the pushpin and the reflections onto the ground below the window.

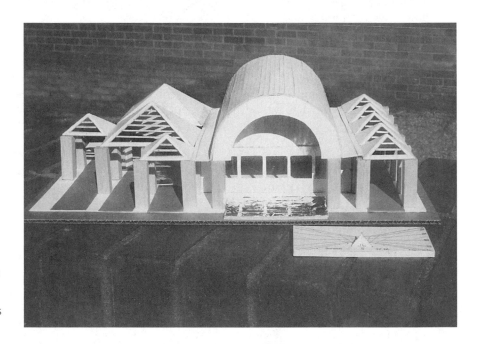

Figure 9.18g No matter how complicated the shading problem is, physical modeling can help the designer. Also note the sundial, which can be used as an alternative method to test models (see Appendix I).

May 7. At this time, the window should still be in sun and not shaded (Fig. 9.18d). Since a shorter overhang would decrease the summer shading, use a movable overhang instead.

9. Swing the overhang up until the window is fully exposed to the winter sun (Fig. 9.18e).
10. Rotate the model stand to see how shade changes during different hours of the day.

11. The solution in this case is for an overhang that is moved twice a year. During the summer, the overhang is as shown in Fig. 9.18d, and during the winter it is up, as in Fig. 9.18e.

Model testing can reveal many surprises. For example, little sun penetrates the glazing at acute sun angles. The glazing acts almost like a mirror at these angles (Fig. 9.18f). This phenomenon is explained later in this chapter.

Even complicated shading problems are easy to solve by physical modeling. For example, the analysis of a shading system for a complex building with odd angles and round features (Fig. 9.18g) is no more difficult than the analysis for a conventional building. Figure 9.18g also shows how a sundial can be used with a heliodon to test models. See Appendix I, Section I.4, for an explanation of this alternate method of testing models.

Since heliodons can also easily simulate the shading from trees, neighboring buildings, and landforms, their use is also very appropriate for site planning and landscape architecture (Chapter 11).

9.19 GLAZING AS THE SHADING ELEMENT

Even the clearest and thinnest glass does not transmit 100 percent of the incident solar radiation. The radiation that is not transmitted is either absorbed or reflected off the surface (Fig. 9.19a). The amount that is absorbed depends on the type of, additives to, and thickness of the glazing. The amount that is reflected depends on the nature of the surface and the angle of incidence of the radiation. Each of these factors will be explained below, starting with absorption.

Most types of **clear** glass and plastic vary only slightly in the amount of radiation they absorb. The thickness is not critical either. Absorption is mainly a function of additives that give the glazing a tint or shade of gray. Although tinted glazing reduces the light transmission, it usually does not decrease the heat gain by much because the absorbed radiation is then reradiated indoors (Fig. 9.19b). One type of tinted glazing is called

heat absorbing because it absorbs the short-wave infrared part of solar radiation much more than the visible part. But even this type of glazing reduces the solar heat gain by only a small amount.

Tinted glass was very popular in the 1960s because it reduced, even if only slightly, the solar load through glass-curtain walls. It also provided color to what was otherwise often stark architecture. It was originally available only in greens, grays, and browns, but recently it has also become available in blue and its popularity is again on the rise.

Glazing also blocks solar radiation by reflection. The graph in Fig. 9.19d shows how transmittance is a function of the angle of incidence. It also shows how the angle of incidence is always measured from the normal to the surface. Notice that the transmittance is almost constant for an angle of incidence from 0° to about 45°. Above 70°, however, there is a pronounced reduction in the transmittance of solar radiation through glazing. Several architects have used this phenomenon as a shading strategy. One of the most dramatic examples is the Tempe, Arizona, City Hall (Fig. 9.19e).

The amount of solar radiation that is reflected from glazing can be increased significantly by adding a reflective coating. One surface of the glazing is covered with a metallic

coating thin enough that some solar radiation still penetrates. The percentage reflectance depends on the thickness of this coating, and a mirror is nothing more than a coating that is thick enough so that no light is transmitted. **Reflective glazing** can be extremely effective in blocking solar radiation while still allowing a view (Fig. 9.19c). It is most appropriate on the east- and west-facing windows and south windows where winter heat is not required.

When reflective glazing became available in the 1970s, it quickly became popular for several reasons. It blocked solar radiation better than heat-absorbing glass, and did it without any color distortion. Compare the total solar transmittance in Figs. 9.19a–c. Reflective glazing also mirrored dramatic images of other buildings, trees, clouds, etc.

Although tinted and reflective glazing systems can be effective shading devices, they are very undiscerning. They do not differentiate between light from the sun and light from the view. They filter out light whether daylighting is desired or not. They shade equally on cloudy days and sunny days. And they block the desirable winter sun as much as the undesirable summer sun. Thus, tinted or reflective glazing is not appropriate where either daylighting or solar heating is desired.

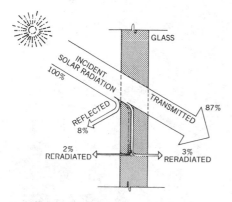

Figure 9.19a The total heat gain from the incident solar radiation consists of both the transmitted and reradiated components. For clear glazing, about 90 percent of the incident solar radiation ends up as heat gain.

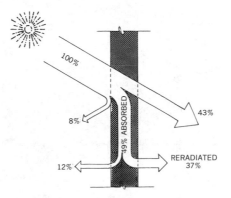

Figure 9.19b Since with tinted or heat-absorbing glass a large proportion of the absorbed solar radiation is reradiated indoors, the total heat gain is quite high (80 percent in this example).

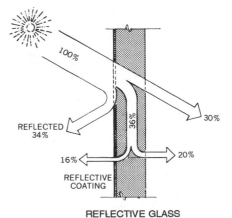

Figure 9.19c Reflective glazing effectively blocks solar radiation without color distortion. Reflective glass is available in a variety of reflectances (50 percent in this example).

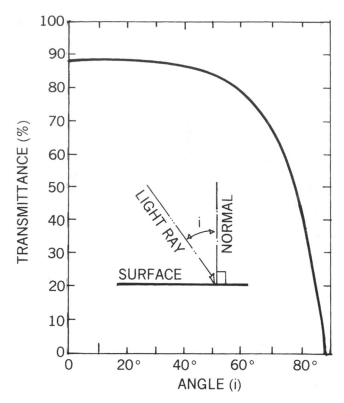

Figure 9.19d The transmittance of solar radiation through glazing is a function of the angle of incidence, which is always measured from the normal to the surface. Maximum transmission occurs when the light is perpendicular to the glass (angle i = 0), and transmission is zero when the light is almost parallel to the glass (angle i > 87°).

When the glazing is expected to do all the shading, it has to be of a very-low-transmittance type. The view through this kind of glazing makes even the sunniest day look dark and gloomy. Thus, external overhangs, fins, etc., which are more discerning, are usually still the best shading devices. Tinted or reflective glazing is appropriate, however, for blocking diffuse sky radiation, the low sun where no other shading would allow a view, and for glare control, which will be discussed in Chapter 13.

The directionally selective control possible with external shading can also be achieved by the glazing itself in certain special circumstances. The opaque mortar joints in glass-block construction can act as an eggcrate shading system. A new type of glass incorporates photoetched slats that can be ordered at any preset angle. The resultant effect will be similar to the horizontal louvers illustrated in Fig. 9.3d.

When daylighting is desired and solar heating is not, having the visible component of solar radiation pass through while heat radiation is blocked would be advantageous.

Figure 9.19e The City Hall of Tempe, Arizona, is an inverted pyramid as a consequence of a shading concept. When the sun is high in the sky, the building shades itself. At low sun angles, much of the solar radiation is reflected off the glazing because of the very large angle of incidence.

Certain "spectrally selective" glazing systems can do that to a limited extent. In Chapter 13, curve 3 of Fig. 13.12c illustrates spectrally selective low-e glazing which transmits cooler daylight than other glazing materials, because it transmits a much higher ratio of visible-to-infrared radiation.

Much research and development work is being done on dynamic glazing systems. These are known as **responsive glazing** systems because they change in response to light, heat, or electricity. The sunglasses that darken when exposed to sunlight are an example of this type of glass.

Responsive glazing can be either passive or active. Passive glazing responds directly to environmental conditions, such as light level or temperature (photochromics or thermochromics, respectively). The active system can be controlled as needed and can include such devices as liquid crystal, dispersed particle, and electrochromics.

Photochromics: These materials change their transparency in response to light intensity. They are ideal for automatically controlling the quantity of daylight allowed into a building. The goal is to let in just enough light to eliminate the need for electric lighting, but not so much that the cooling load would increase.

Thermochromics: These materials change transparency in response to temperature. They are transparent when cold and reflective white when hot. They can be used in skylights, where the loss of transparency on a hot day is not a problem, as it would be in a view window. These materials could also be used to prevent passive solar heating systems from overheating in the summer.

Liquid-Crystal Glazing: When electric power is applied, the transparent liquid crystals align and become translucent. Thus, liquid-crystal glazing has little application for shading, but its real potential is in privacy control.

Dispersed-Particle Glazing: Although similar to liquid-crystal glazing, this material is more promising for solar control because the applied power can change the transmittance of the material in a range between clear and dark states, thereby preserving the view.

Electrochromic Glazing: This is the most promising material for shading because it can change transparency—not translucency—continuously over a wide range (about 10 to 70 percent) and can be easily controlled. Consequently, either a computer, a photocell, a thermostat, or the occupant can adjust the transparency as the local conditions require.

Rules for Glazing Selection

1. Shading with glazing should be an auxiliary system to the main outdoor shading of overhangs and fins.
2. Use clear glazing when winter solar heating is a major concern (especially on a south facade).
3. Use reflective glazing when solar heat gain must be minimized and the use of external shading devices is not possible (especially on east and west facades).
4. Use the new selective low-e glazing when solar heat gain must be minimized but daylighting is still desired and the use of external shading devices is not an option.
5. Blue-green heat-absorbing glazing or other tinted glazing materials are a less efficient alternative to reflective glazing.

9.20 INTERIOR SHADING DEVICES

From an energy-rejection point of view, external shading devices are by far the most effective. But for a number of practical reasons, interior devices, such as curtains, roller shades, venetian blinds, and shutters, are also very important (Fig. 9.20a). Interior devices are often less expensive than external shading devices, since they do not have to resist the elements. They are also very adjustable and movable, which enables them to respond easily to changing requirements. Besides shading, these devices provide numerous other benefits, such as privacy, glare control, insulation, and interior aesthetics. At night, they also prevent the "black hole" effect created by exposed windows.

Since internal devices are usually included whether or not external devices are supplied, we should use them to our advantage. They should be used to stop the sun when it outflanks the exterior shading devices. They are also useful for those exceptionally hot days during the transition or underheated periods of the year when exterior shading is not designed to work. In the form of venetian blinds or light shelves (Fig. 9.20b), they can also produce fine daylighting.

One of the main drawbacks of interior devices is that they are not always discerning. They cannot block the sun while admitting the view, something that can be effectively done with an external overhang. Since they block the solar radiation on the inside of the glazing, much of the heat remains indoors. The side of the shade facing the glass should be as light as possible (white) in order to reflect solar radiation back out through the glass before it is converted to heat.

When indoor roller shades are used in conjunction with overhangs, the shades should move up from the windowsill instead of down from the window head (Fig. 9.20c). The lower portion of a window always needs more shade than the upper. Thus, some view, privacy, and daylighting can be maintained while still shading the sun.

There are, however, a few very sophisticated interior shading systems. The Occidental (Hooker) Chemical Corporate Office Building in Niagara Falls, New York, is a good example. The window wall consists of horizontal louvers between two layers of glass that are about 4 ft (1.2 m) apart (see Fig. 13.11k). The heat that builds up in this space during the summer is allowed to vent out through the roof. Shading is only one of the functions

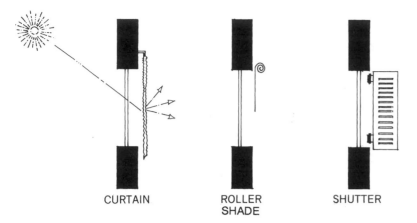

Figure 9.20a Interior shading devices for solar control.

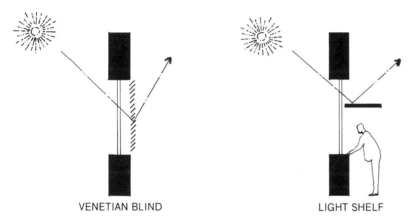

Figure 9.20b Interior shading devices that contribute to quality daylighting.

Figure 9.20c When roller shades roll up, they not only shade better but also offer better privacy.

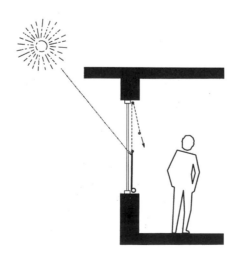

of the louvers. They also reflect daylight into the interior, and they can close up to further insulate the building at night.

As stated before, one of the best inventions of all time is the venetian blind. It is extremely flexible and can be used in a very directionally selective way (i.e., it can block the sun but not the view or can send the light to the ceiling for quality daylighting). Recently, venetian blinds have become even better. A new type, with tiny perforations, allows some light and view to enter even when the shades are completely closed. Although venetian blinds come in many colors, the ones with white or mirrored finishes are most functional for heating, cooling, and daylighting.

9.21 SHADING COEFFICIENT AND SOLAR HEAT-GAIN COEFFICIENT

Some of the shading devices mentioned in this chapter can be compared in a quantitative way by the concept of the **shading coefficient** (SC). Although this coefficient was developed for use in analytical work, we will use it here as a rough way to compare various shading devices. The author uses the word "rough" because the SC does not account for the fact that often we want to block the high summer sun and not the low winter sun, or that we want to block the sun but not the view, as is possible with directionally selective shading systems, such as a horizontal overhang. Because the effectiveness of external shading devices depends on the specific design and sun angles, it is not possible to assign a precise number to most exterior devices such as overhangs and trees. Nevertheless, Table 9.21 gives us some idea of the relative effectiveness of the various shading devices.

The traditional SC is counterintuitive because a value of 1 equals no shading, while a value of 0 indicates that no sunlight can enter. For this

Table 9.21 Shading Coefficients (SC) and Solar Heat Gain Coefficients (SHGC) for Various Shading Devices

Device	SC	SHGC
Single glazing		
Clear glass, 1/8 in (3 mm) thick	1.0	0.86
Clear glass, 1/4 in. (6 mm) thick	0.94	0.81
Heat absorbing or tinted	0.6–0.8	0.5–0.7
Reflective	0.2–0.5	0.2–0.4
Double glazing		
Clear	0.84	0.73
Bronze	0.5–0.7	0.4–0.6
Low-e clear	0.6–0.8	0.5–0.7
Spectrally selective	0.4–0.5	0.3–0.4
Triple-clear	0.7–0.8	0.6–0.7
Glass block	0.1–0.7	
Interior shading		
Venetian blinds	0.4–0.7	
Roller shades	0.2–0.6	
Curtains	0.4–0.8	
External shading		
Eggcrate	0.1–0.3	
Horizontal overhang	0.1–0.6	
Vertical fins	0.1–0.6	
Trees	0.2–0.6	

Notes:
The smaller the number, the less solar radiation enters through a window. A value of zero indicates that the window allows no solar radiation to enter, either directly or reradiated after being absorbed.
Ranges are given either because of the large variety of glazing types available (e.g., slightly or heavily tinted) or because of the varying geometry due to differences in orientation, sun angle, size and type of shading device, and variations in window size.
Source: ASHRAE Fundamentals Handbook (1997) and Egan (1975).

and other reasons, the SC is being replaced by the much more logical solar heat-gain coefficient (SHGC), where a value of 1 equals no blockage of sunlight and 0 equals no sunlight entering the window. Table 9.21 also gives the SHGC for various glazing systems.

Table 9.21 indicates that the best shading systems, such as horizontal overhangs, are very hard to quantify. The table shows that the SC of a horizontal overhang can vary from 0.1 (excellent) to 0.6 (poor). This is further evidence that most exterior shading devices need to be analyzed with a heliodon or a very sophisticated computer program in order to understand their effectiveness.

9.22 REFLECTION FROM ROOFS AND WALLS

The U.S. Environmental Protection Agency (EPA) says that for low-rise commercial buildings, the heat gain through the roof is about 50 percent of the heat gain for the entire building. This heat gain can be reduced not only by using more insulation but also by reflecting the sun's radiation. The American Society of Heating, Refrigeration, and Air-conditioning Engineers (ASHRAE) states that the heat gain through a white roof is half of that of a black roof, and the heat gain through a white wall is two-thirds of that of a black wall. Thus, in hot climates, the walls should have a light color and the roof should be white.

Walls

Since there is no law that requires every exterior wall to have the same color, a building could have a white east and west wall to reflect the summer sun, a dark but shaded south wall to increase winter solar gain, and a north wall of any color desired. However, in very hot climates, the south and north walls should also be light in color. For those wall systems that must be painted for protection in any case, the designer simply needs to specify a light color. For exposed concrete, a white cement can be specified; for brick, the choice is paint, a white cement coating, or a white glaze.

In dark urban canyons, white walls also increase the light level on the ground both during the day and at night. White exterior walls also increase the daylighting for the lower floors.

Roofs

There is little opposition to using white membranes on flat roofs. However, there is great opposition to using white for sloped roofs. In the hot American South, black roofs are very common. When the author recommends white roofs, he is almost always told that white roofs are ugly. However, when he presents the photo of a very attractive building with a white roof (Fig. 9.22a), that argument is abandoned and the excuse that white roofs get dirty is raised instead. The reason for the popularity of black roofs in the South is a mystery, but there is one intriguing explanation.

When General William Tecumseh Sherman marched through the South toward the end of the Civil War, he ordered most buildings to be burned. In order to cause ongoing discomfort, he ordered that all rebuilt houses have black roofs. That inappropriate color has now become the desired traditional color.

Because dark-colored sloped roofs are popular in all parts of the world, the roofing industry has produced dark-colored cool roofs, which even at first glance appear to be an oxymoron.

Cool Roofs

Cool roofs are most likely when the roof surface is white. A dark roof can be 90°F (50°C) hotter than the ambient air temperature, while a white roof will be only about 18°F (10°C) hotter. However, there are misleading claims that dark roofs can be made "cool" by means of high-tech coatings. Figure 9.22b shows that although a high-tech "cool" dark bronze coating is three times more reflective than an ordinary dark bronze coating, it is still three times less reflective than an ordinary white roof. Thus, a dark bronze "cool" roof is not cool but only less hot than a regular dark bronze roof. For a truly cool roof, the roof surface must be as light as possible. See Table 9.22 for the solar reflectance (albedo) of various surface finishes.

Usually we can predict how much the sun will heat a surface by how it appears to us (e.g., black will get much hotter than white). However, there are two exceptions to this rule. The first exception results from the technology known as "cool coatings". In normal colors, just as much solar infrared radiation as reflected as visible radiation, but the high-tech "cool coatings" reflect much more solar infrared than visible solar radiation.

(Fig. 9.22c). This behavior is most significant with dark colors (Fig. 9.22b).

Appearances also mislead us when the surface is polished metal. Although such surfaces reflect solar radiation much like white colors, they are poor emitters and, therefore, get much warmer than light colors. See Section 3.11 for an explanation of this phenomenon. The **solar reflectance index** was developed to describe the behavior of a surface in regard not

Figure 9.22a White sloped roofs are not only very sustainable but also beautiful. White metal is the coolest roofing material and, because of its smoothness, does not collect much dirt.

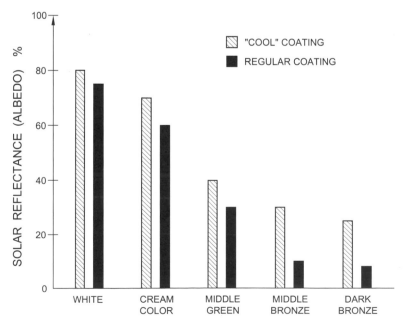

Figure 9.22b This chart shows that "cool coatings" are not cool—only less hot. For example, although the dark bronze "cool coating" reflects three times as much solar radiation as a normal dark bronze coating, it is only one-third as good as a regular white roof. Thus, a sustainable roof is a white or very light-colored roof.

Table 9.22 Solar Reflectance (Albedo)

Surface	Solar Reflectance	
	Normal Finish	"Cool"*
White—high reflectance	85	—
White—typical	75	80
Cream-color coating	60	67
Galvanized steel	50	—
Aluminum	50	—
Weathered concrete	35	—
Light gray coating	30	50
Middle green coating	30	40
Brick red coating	25	30
Dark green coating	25	30
White asphalt shingles	20	—
Dark bronze coating	10	25
Dark asphalt shingles	10	—
Black membrane	5	—

*Available only as a special coating.

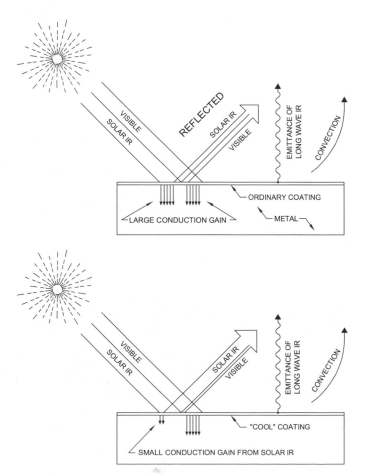

Figure 9.22c Ordinary finishes (top) reflect the short-wave (solar) infrared much like the visible part of the spectrum. However, "cool coatings" (bottom) reflect more of the solar infrared than the visible radiation.

only to the solar reflectance (albedo) but also the emittance of the surface. Materials with low emittance (polished metals) will always be hotter than materials with high emittance even when their solar reflectance is the same.

9.23 CONCLUSION

The ideal building from a shading point of view will have windows only on the north and south facades, with some type of horizontal overhang protecting the south-facing windows. The size and kind of overhang will depend on the type of building, climate, and latitude of the building site.

Even if there are windows on all sides, as there often will be, a building should not look the same from each direction. Each orientation faces a very different environment. James M. Fitch, in his *American Building; 2. The Environmental Forces That Shape It* (1999), pointed out that moving from the south side of a building to the north side is similar in climate change to traveling from Florida to Maine. A building can still have unity without the various facades being identical. Even the east and west facades, which are symmetrical from a solar point of view, should rarely be identical. They differ because afternoon temperatures are much higher than morning temperatures and because site conditions are rarely the same (e.g., trees toward the east but not the west). One of the buildings at the University of California at Davis exemplifies very well this unity with diversity (Figs. 9.23a and b).

If Le Corbusier had his way with the United Nations Building in New York City, our cities might have a very different appearance today. Le Corbusier wanted to use a brise-soleil to shield the exposed glazing. Not only were there no shading devices, but the building is so oriented that the glass facades face mostly east and west, while the solid stone facades face mostly north and south. Just rotating the plan could have greatly improved the performance

Figure 9.23a The south and east facades of the Biological Sciences Building at the University of California at Davis illustrate how unity can be maintained while each orientation responds to its unique conditions.

of the building. Instead of a symbol of energy-conscious design, the building became the prototype for the glass-slab office tower that could be made habitable only by use of energy-guzzling mechanical equipment (Fig. 9.23c).

Frank Lloyd Wright also had a different image of the high-rise building. His Price Tower makes full use of shading devices (Fig. 9.23d). He, like many other great architects, realized that shading devices were central to the practice of architecture, because they not only solve an important functional problem but also make a very strong aesthetic statement. This powerful potential for aesthetic expression has been largely ignored in recent years. The energy crisis of 1973 renewed our interest in this very important and visible part of architecture. And global warming makes it imperative to create sustainable low-energy buildings. Such buildings must shade the sun during the overheated part of the year.

Figure 9.23b The north and west facades of the same building shown in Fig. 9.23a. Shading requires a different response on each orientation.

Figure 9.23c The office slab of the United Nations headquarters in New York City, 1950, became the prototype for many office buildings. Le Corbusier was very upset when he discovered that the blank walls faced mostly north and south, while the glass facades faced mostly east and west and were in no way protected by sunshades. (Courtesy of New York Convention and Visitors' Bureau, Inc.)

Figure 9.23d The Price Tower, Bartlesville, Oklahoma, designed by Frank Lloyd Wright, uses sunshading as a major design concept. (Photograph by James Bradley.)

KEY IDEAS OF CHAPTER 9

1. Shading is an integral part of architecture that has traditionally offered great opportunity for aesthetic expression (e.g., the Greek portico).
2. Every orientation should have a different shading strategy.
3. **Maximize south glazing** because it is the only orientation that not only can be effectively shaded in the summer while preserving the view but also can harvest a maximum of solar radiation in the winter.
4. **Maximize north glazing** in very hot climates that have no or mild winters.
5. **Minimize east and west glazing** because it is impossible to fully shade those orientations while maintaining the view.
6. Glazing on the east and west facades should face north or south.
7. Movable shading devices are much better than fixed devices because the thermal year and the solar year are out of phase and because of the variability of the weather.
8. Plants can be excellent shading devices. Deciduous plants can act as movable shading devices.
9. On the east and west facades, the horizontal overhang is usually preferred over vertical fins because the overhang preserves the view better while the solar energy blocked is about the same.
10. **Exterior shading is superior** to both interior shading and the shading from the glazing itself.
11. Use indoor shading devices to back up the outdoor shading
12. Light transmission through glazing is a function of the angle of incidence.
13. Outdoor spaces should be carefully shaded to make them attractive in the summer.
14. Since walls and especially roofs are hard to shade, use very light colors to reflect the solar radiation. In hot climates, white roofs are best. "Cool coatings" are not as cool as white coatings.

References

ASHRAE. *ASHRAE Fundamentals Handbook*. Atlanta: ASHRAE.

Egan, M. D. *Concepts in Thermal Comfort*. Englewood Cliffs, NJ: Prentice Hall, rev. ed. 1999.

Fitch, J. M., with W. Bobenkausen. *American Building: 2. The Environmental Forces That Shape It*. New York: Schocken, 1999.

Resources

FURTHER READING

(See the Bibliography in the back of the book for full citations.)

ASHRAE. *ASHRAE Fundamentals Handbook*.

Baird, G. *The Architectural Expressions of Environmental Control Systems*.

Brown, G. Z., and M. DeKay. *Sun, Wind, and Light*, 2nd ed.

Carmody, J. et al. *Residential Windows: A Guide to New Technologies and Energy Performance*, 3rd ed.

Carmody, J. et al. *Window Systems for High-Performance Buildings*.

Egan, M. D. *Concepts in Thermal Comfort*.

Fitch, J. M., with W. Bobenhausen. *American Building: 2. The Environmental Forces That Shape It*.

Franta, G., K. Anstead, and G. D. Ander. *Glazing Design Handbook for Energy Efficiency*.

Kwok, Alison G., and Walter T. Grondzik. *The Green Studio Handbook: Environmental Strategies for Schematic Design*.

Olgyay, A., and V. Olgyay. *Solar Control and Shading Devices*.

Ramsey Sleeper Architectural Graphic Standards, 11th ed. CD-ROM version is also available.

Stein, B., J. S. Reynolds, W. T. Grondzik, and A. G. Kwok. *Mechanical and Electrical Equipment for Buildings*, 10th ed.

PASSIVE COOLING

True regional character cannot be found through a sentimental or imitative
approach by incorporating either old emblems or the newest local fashions
which disappear as fast as they appear. But if you take, for instance, the basic
difference imposed on architectural design by the climatic conditions of
California, say, as against Massachusetts, you will realize what diversity
of expression can result from this fact alone. . . .

Walter Gropius
Scope of Total Architecture, 1955

10.1 INTRODUCTION TO COOLING

To achieve thermal comfort in the summer in a more sustainable way, one should use the three-tier design approach. (Fig. 10.1). The first tier consists of **heat avoidance**. At this level, the designer does everything possible to minimize heat gain in the building. Strategies at this level include the appropriate use of shading, orientation, color, vegetation, insulation, daylight, and the control of internal heat sources. These and other heat-avoidance strategies are described throughout this book.

Since heat avoidance is usually not sufficient by itself to keep temperatures low enough all summer, the second tier of response, **passive cooling**, is used. With some passive cooling systems, temperatures are actually lowered and not just minimized, as is the case with heat avoidance. Passive cooling also includes the use of ventilation to shift the comfort zone to higher temperatures. The major passive cooling strategies will be discussed in this chapter.

In many climates, there will be times when the combined effort of heat avoidance and passive cooling is still not sufficient to maintain thermal comfort. For this reason, the third tier of **mechanical equipment** is usually required. In a rational design process, as described here, this equipment must cool only what heat avoidance and passive cooling could not accomplish. Consequently, the mechanical equipment will be quite small and will use only modest amounts of energy.

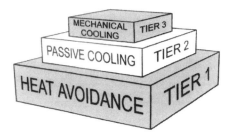

Figure 10.1 Cooling needs of buildings are best and most sustainably achieved by the three-tier design approach. This chapter covers tier two.

10.2 HISTORICAL AND INDIGENOUS USE OF PASSIVE COOLING

Examples are sometime better than definitions in explaining concepts. The following examples of historical and indigenous buildings will illustrate what is meant by passive cooling.

Passive cooling is much more dependent on climate than passive heating. Thus, the passive cooling strategies for hot and dry climates are very different from those for hot and humid climates.

In hot and dry climates, one usually finds buildings with few and small windows, light surface colors, and massive construction, such as adobe, brick, or stone (Fig. 10.2a). The massive materials not only retard and delay the progress of heat through the walls, but also act as a heat sink during the day. Since hot and dry climates have high diurnal temperature ranges, the nights tend to be cool. Thus, the mass cools at night and then acts as a heat sink the next day. To prevent the heat sink from being overwhelmed, small windows and light colors are used to minimize the heat gain. Closed shutters further reduce the daytime heat gain, while still allowing good night ventilation when they are open.

In urban settings and other places with little wind, wind scoops are sometimes used to maximize ventilation. Wind scoops were already used several thousand years ago in Egypt (Fig. 10.2b), and they are still found in the Middle East today. When there is a strong prevailing wind direction, as in Hyderabad, Pakistan, the scoops are all aimed in the same direction (Fig. 10.2c). In other areas, where there is no prevailing wind direction, such as Dubai on the Persian Gulf, wind towers with many openings are used. These rectangular towers are divided by diagonal walls, which create four separate airwells facing four different directions (Fig. 10.2d).

Wind towers have shutters to keep out unwanted ventilation. In dry climates, they also have a means of evaporating water to cool the incoming air. Some wind towers have porous jugs of water at their base, while others use fountains or trickling water (Fig. 10.2e).

The mashrabiya is another popular wind-catching feature in the Arabic Middle East (Fig. 10.2f). These bay windows were comfortable places to sit and sleep, since the delicate wood screens kept most of the sun out yet allowed the breezes to blow through. Evaporation from porous jugs of water placed in the mashrabiya cooled not

Figure 10.2a Hot and dry climates typically have buildings with small windows, light colors, and massive construction. Thera, Santorini, Greece. (From *Proceedings of the International Passive and Hybrid Cooling Conference*, Miami Beach, Florida, Nov. 6–16, © American Solar Energy Society, 1981.)

Figure 10.2b Ancient Egyptian houses used wind scoops to maximize ventilation. (Replica of a wall painting in the Tomb of Nebamun, circa 1300 B.C., courtesy of the Metropolitan Museum of Art, New York City, #30.4.57.)

Figure 10.2c The wind towers in Hyderabad, Pakistan, all face the prevailing wind.

Figure 10.2d The wind towers in Dubai, United Arab Emirates, are designed to catch the wind from any direction. (Photograph by Mostafa Howeedy.)

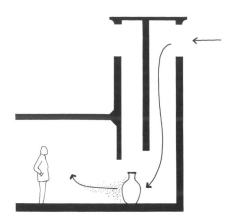

Figure 10.2e Some wind towers in hot and dry areas cool the incoming air by evaporation.

Figure 10.2f A mashrabiya is a screened bay window popular in the Arabic Middle East. It shades, ventilates, and provides evaporative cooling. Cairo, Egypt. (Photograph by Mostafa Howeedy.)

Figure 10.2g In the evening, the orchestra platform provided entertainment while the water cooled the air at the Panch Mahal Palace at Fathepur, India. (Photograph by Lena Choudhary.)

only drinking water but the houses as well. The mashrabiya also satisfied the cultural need to give women an inconspicious place to view the activity of the outside world.

Wherever the humidity is low, evaporative cooling is very effective. Fountains, pools, water trickling down walls, and transpiration from plants can all be used for evaporative cooling (Fig. 10.2g). The results are best if the evaporation occurs indoors or in the incoming air stream. In India, it was quite common to hang wetted mats at openings to cool the incoming air. Indian palaces had pools, streams, and waterfalls brought indoors to make the cooling more effective.

Evaporative cooling of courtyards is especially effective when the courtyard

is the main source of air for the building (Fig. 10.2h). Small and deep courtyards or atriums are beneficial in hot and dry climates, not only because they are self-shading most of the day, but also because they block the hot wind that would blow away the cool air. This benefit is a liability in hot and humid climates, where cross-ventilation is desirable.

Massive domed structures are an appropriate strategy in hot and dry regions. Besides the thermal benefit of their mass, their form yields two different benefits. During the day, the sun sees little more than the horizontal footprint of the dome, while at night almost a full hemisphere sees the night sky. Thus, radiant heating is minimized while radiant cooling

is maximized. Domes also have high spaces where stratification will enable the occupants to inhabit the cooler lower levels (Fig. 10.2i). Sometimes vents are located at the top to allow the hottest air to escape (Fig. 10.2j). The most dramatic example of this kind of dome is the Pantheon, in Rome. Its "oculus" allows light to enter while the hot air escapes. The same concept was used in the U.S. Pavilion, Expo '67, in Montreal. The upper panels of the geodesic dome had round openings to vent the hot air (Fig. 9.16a).

A large quantity of earth or rock is an effective barrier to the extreme temperatures in hot and dry climates. The deep earth is usually near the mean annual temperature of a region, which in many cases is cool enough

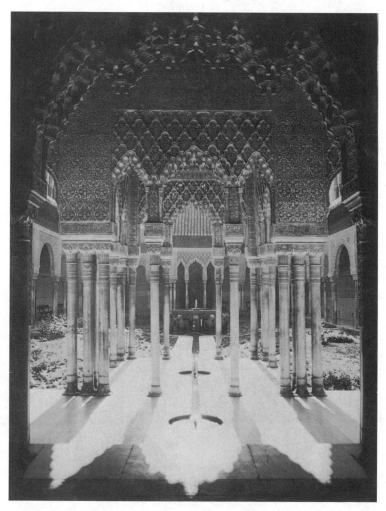

Figure 10.2h A small shaded courtyard was cooled by a series of fountains. Court of the Lions, Alhambra, Spain. (Courtesy of *ARAMCO World* magazine.)

Figure 10.2i The trulli are conical stone houses in Apulia, Italy. Their large mass and high ceilings, with the resultant stratification of air, make these houses fairly comfortable. (From *Proceedings of the International Passive and Hybrid Cooling Conference*, Miami Beach, Florida, Nov. 6–16, © American Solar Energy Society, 1981.)

Figure 10.2j Small domes made of sun-dried mud bricks work well in very hot and dry climates, such as those found in Egypt. Small vents allow the hot air to escape and a small amount of light to enter. Narrow alleys enable buildings to shade each other. Small courtyards provide outdoor sleeping areas at night. (Courtesy of the Egyptian Tourist Authority.)

Figure 10.2k Dwellings and churches are carved from the volcanic tuffa cones in Cappadocia, Turkey. (Photograph by Tarik Orgen.)

for the soil to act as a heat sink during summer days. Earth sheltering is discussed in more detail in Chapter 15.

In Cappadocia, Turkey, thousands of dwellings and churches have been excavated from the volcanic tuffa cones over the last 2000 years (Fig. 10.2k). Many of these spaces are still inhabited today, in part because they provide effective protection from extreme heat and cold.

A structure need not be completely earth-sheltered to benefit from earth contact cooling. The dwellings leaning against the cliffs at Mesa Verde, Colorado, make use of the heat-sink capacity of both the rock cliff and the massive stone walls. The overhanging, south-facing cliffs also offer much shade during summer days (Fig. 10.2l). In areas where rock was not available, thick earthen walls were used. The Navajo of the dry Southwest built **hogans** for the insulating effect of their thick earthen walls and roofs (Fig. 10.2m). The Spanish settlers used adobe for the same purpose (Fig. 10.2n).

In hot and humid climates, we find a different kind of building, one in which the emphasis is on natural ventilation. In very humid climates, mass is a liability and very lightweight structures are best. Although the sun is not as strong as in dry climates, the humidity is so uncomfortable that any additional heating from the sun is very objectionable. Thus, in very humid regions, we find buildings

with large windows, large overhangs, and low mass (Fig. 10.2o). These buildings are often set on stilts to catch more wind and to rise above the humidity near the ground. High ceilings allow the air to stratify, and vents at the gable or ridge allow the hottest air to escape (Fig. 1.2c).

Much of Japan has very hot and humid summers. To maximize natural ventilation, the traditional Japanese house uses post-and-beam construction, which allows the lightweight paper wall panels to be moved out of the way in the summer (Fig. 10.2p).

Large overhanging roofs protect these panels and also create an outdoor space called an **engawa**. Large gable vents further increase the ventilation through the building (Fig. 10.2q).

Gulf Coast houses and their elaborate version, the French Louisiana plantation houses, were well adapted to the very humid climate (Fig. 10.2r). In that region, a typical house had its main living space, built of a light wood frame, raised off the damp and muggy ground on a brick structure. Higher up, there was more wind and less humidity. The main living spaces

Figure 10.2l The cliff dwellings at Mesa Verde, Colorado, benefit from the heat-sink capacity of the stone walls and rock cliff.

Figure 10.2m The Navajo hogan, with its thick earthen walls, provides comfort in the hot and dry Southwest.

Figure 10.2n Spanish missionaries and settlers used thick adobe walls for thermal comfort.

Figure 10.2o These "chickees," built by the Indians of southern Florida, respond to the hot and humid climate by maximizing ventilation and shade while minimizing thermal mass. The diagonal poles successfully resist hurricane winds.

Figure 10.2p Ventilation is maximized by movable wall panels in traditional Japanese houses. (Courtesy of Japan National Tourist Organization.)

Figure 10.2q The movable wall panels open onto the engawa (veranda), which is protected by a large overhang. Also note the large gable vent. Japanese Garden, Portland, Oregon.

Figure 10.2r This Gulf Coast house incorporated many cooling concepts appropriate for hot and humid climates. Note the large shaded porch, ventilating dormers, large windows, and ventilation under the house.

Figure 10.2s The breezy passage of the dog trot house was a favorite for both man and beast during the hot and humid summers.

had many tall openings to maximize ventilation. The ceiling was very high (sometimes as high as 14 ft) (4.2 m) to permit the air to stratify and the people to occupy the lower, cooler layers. Vents in the ceiling and high attic allowed the stack effect to exhaust the hottest air from the building. Deep verandas shaded the walls and created cool outdoor areas.

The common open central hallway was derived from the **dog trot** houses of the early pioneers of that region, who built one roof over two log cabins spaced about 10 ft (3 m) apart (Fig. 10.2s). In the summer, this shady, breezy outdoor space became a desirable hangout for dogs and people alike.

Many of these same concepts were incorporated in the Classical Revival

architecture that was so popular in the South during the nineteenth century. As was mentioned in Chapter 9, the classical portico was a very suitable way to build the large overhangs needed to shade the high doors and windows. These openings were often as high as 12 ft (3.6 m), and the windows were frequently triple hung so that two-thirds of the window could be opened. Louvered shutters allowed ventilation when sun shading and privacy were desired (Fig. 10.2t). The classical image of white buildings was also very appropriate for the hot climate.

The Waverly plantation is a good example of the classical idiom adapted to the climate (Fig. 10.2u). It has a large, many-windowed belvedere, which offers a panoramic view, light, and a strong stack effect through the two-story stair hall. Since every door has operable transoms, all rooms have cross-ventilation from three sides (Fig 10.2v). The author visited this non-air-conditioned building on a hot, humid summer day and found it to be comfortably cool inside.

Often the temperate climate is the hardest to design for. This is partly true because many so-called temperate climates actually have very hot summers and very cold winters. Buildings in such climates cannot be designed to respond to either hot or cold conditions alone. Rather, they must be designed for both summer and winter, which often make opposing demands on the architect. The Governor's Mansion in Williamsburg, Virginia, is located in such a climate. The building is compact, and the windows are medium-sized (Fig. 10.2w). The brick construction allows passive cooling during much of the summer when the humidity is low enough. The massive fireplaces act as additional heat sinks in the summer, as well as heat storage mediums in the winter. Every room has openings on all four walls for maximum cross-ventilation. The little tower on the roof has several different names, depending on its main function. It is a "belvedere" if the panoramic view is most important, it

Figure 10.2u The Waverly plantation near Columbus, Mississippi, has a large belvedere for view, light, and ventilation. (Photograph by Paul B. Watkins. Courtesy of the Mississippi Department of Economic Development. Division of Tourism.)

Figure 10.2t Shutters with adjustable louvers were almost universally used in the old South.

Figure 10.2v A strong stack effect is created by the octagonal belvedere over the open stair hall of the Waverly plantation. All interior doors have transoms. [From *Mississippi Houses: Yesterday Toward Tomorrow*, by Robert Ford (copyright).]

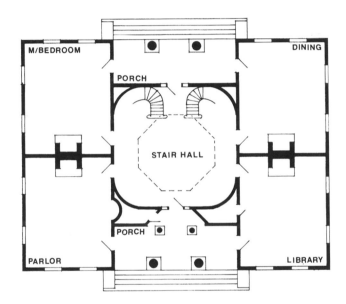

Figure 10.2w The Governor's Mansion in Colonial Williamsburg, Virginia, is well suited for a "temperate" climate. (Courtesy of the Colonial Williamsburg Foundation.)

is a "lantern" if it acts as a skylight, it is a "cupola" if it has a small dome on it and is mainly for decoration or image, and it is a "monitor" if ventilation is most important. In the Governor's Mansion, the tower's main purpose was to create the image of a governmental building. It usually had several of the above functions and sometimes all.

10.3 PASSIVE COOLING SYSTEMS

The passive cooling systems described here include not only the well-known traditional techniques mentioned above, but also more sophisticated modern techniques. As much as possible, passive cooling uses natural forces, energies, and heat sinks. When some fans and pumps are used, the systems are sometimes called **hybrid**. Because the systems described here use only small, low-energy pumps and fans, if any, these systems are also included under the passive category.

Since the goal is to create thermal comfort during the summer (the over-heated period), we can either cool the building or raise the comfort zone sufficiently to include the high indoor temperature. In the first case, we have to remove heat from the building by finding a heat sink for it. In the second case, we modify one of the other factors of the thermal environment (i.e., humidity, MRT, or air speed) so that the comfort zone shifts to higher temperatures. In this second case,

people will feel more comfortable even though the building is not actually being cooled.

There are five methods of passive cooling:

Types of Passive Cooling Systems

I. Cooling with Ventilation
   A. *Comfort ventilation*: Ventilation during the day and night to increase evaporation from the skin and thereby increasing thermal comfort.
   B. *Night flush cooling*: Ventilation to precool the building for the next day.
II. Radiant Cooling
   A. *Direct radiant cooling*: A building's roof structure cools by radiation to the night sky.
   B. *Indirect radiant cooling*: Radiation to the night sky cools a heat-transfer fluid, which then cools the building.
III. Evaporative Cooling
   A. *Direct evaporation*: Water is sprayed into the air entering a building. This lowers the air's temperature but raises its humidity.
   B. *Indirect evaporative cooling*: Evaporation cools the incoming air of the building without raising the indoor humidity.
IV. Earth Cooling
   A. *Direct coupling*: An earth-sheltered building loses heat directly to the earth.
   B. *Indirect coupling*: Air enters the building by way of earth tubes.

V. Dehumidification with a Desiccant: Removal of latent heat.

A combination of these techniques is sometimes necessary. Each of these techniques will now be discussed in more detail.

10.4 COMFORT VENTILATION VERSUS NIGHT-FLUSH COOLING

Until recently, ventilation was the major cooling technique throughout the world. It is important to note that not only are there two very different ventilation techniques, but also that they are mutually exclusive. **Comfort ventilation** brings in outdoor air, especially during the daytime, when temperatures are at their highest. The air is then passed directly over people to increase evaporative cooling on the skin. Although thermal comfort might be achieved, the warm air is actually heating the building.

Night-flush cooling is quite different. With this technique, cool night air is introduced to flush out the heat of the building, while during the day, very little outside air is brought indoors so that heat gain to the building can be minimized. Meanwhile, the mass of the relatively cool structure acts as a heat sink for the people inside. Before these techniques can be explained in more detail, some basic principles of air flow and their applications in buildings must be discussed.

10.5 BASIC PRINCIPLES OF AIR FLOW

To design successfully for ventilation in the summer or for wind protection in the winter, the following principles of air flow should be understood.

1. *Reason for the flow of air*: Air flows either because of natural convection currents, caused by differences in temperature, or because of differences in pressure (Fig. 10.5a).

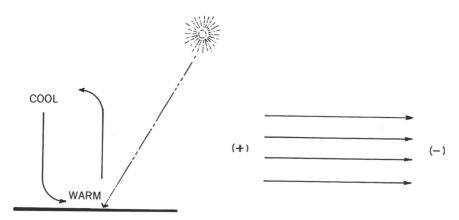

Figure 10.5a Air flows either because of natural convection or pressure differentials.

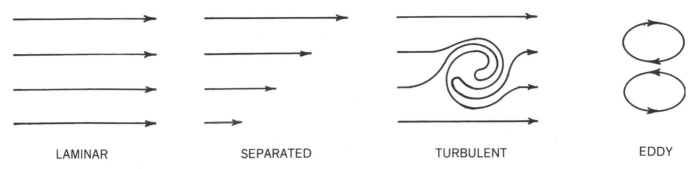

LAMINAR   SEPARATED   TURBULENT   EDDY

Figure 10.5b The four different kinds of air flow. (After Art Bowen, 1981.)

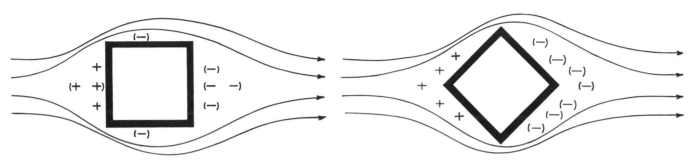

Figure 10.5c Air flowing around a building will cause uneven positive and negative pressure areas to develop. (After Art Bowen, 1981.)

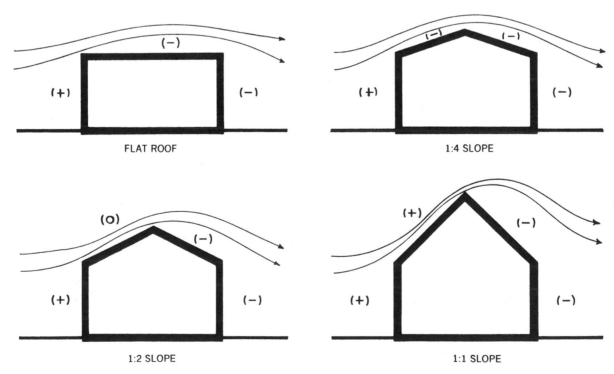

FLAT ROOF   1:4 SLOPE

1:2 SLOPE   1:1 SLOPE

Figure 10.5d The pressure on the leeward side of a roof is always negative (−), but on the windward side it depends on the slope of the roof. (After Art Bowen, 1981).

2. *Types of air flow:* There are four basic types of air flow: laminar, separated, turbulent, and eddy currents. Figure 10.5b illustrates the four types by means of lines representing air streams. These diagrams are similar to what one would see in a wind-tunnel test using smoke streams. Air flow changes from laminar to turbulent when it encounters sharp obstructions, such as buildings. Eddy currents are circular air flows induced by laminar air flows (Fig. 10.5e).

3. *Inertia:* Since air has some mass, moving air tends to go in a straight line. When forced to change direction, air streams will follow curves but never right angles.

4. *Conservation of air:* Since air is neither created nor destroyed at the building site, the air approaching a building must equal the air leaving the building. Thus, lines representing air streams should be drawn as continuous.

5. *High- and low-pressure areas:* As air hits the windward side of a building, it compresses and creates positive pressure (+). At the same time, air is sucked away from the leeward side, creating negative pressure (−).

   Air deflected around the sides will generally also create negative pressure. Note that these pressures are not uniformly distributed (Fig. 10.5c). The type of pressure created over the roof depends on the slope of the roof (Fig. 10.5d). These pressure areas around the building determine how air flows through the building.

   It should also be noted that these high- and low-pressure areas are not necessarily places of calm but also of air flow in the form of turbulence and eddy currents (Fig. 10.5e). Note how these currents reverse the air flow in certain locations. For simplicity's sake, turbulence and eddy currents, although usually present, are not shown on all diagrams.

6. *Bernoulli effect:* In the Bernoulli effect, an increase in the velocity of a fluid decreases its static pressure. Because of this phenomenon, there is negative pressure at the constriction of a venturi tube (Fig. 10.5f). A cross section of an airplane wing is like half a venturi tube (Fig. 10.5g).

   A gabled roof is also like half a venturi tube. Thus, air will be sucked out of any opening near the ridge (Fig. 10.5h). The effect can be made even stronger by designing the roof to be like a full venturi tube (Fig. 10.5i).

   There is another phenomenon at work here. The velocity of air

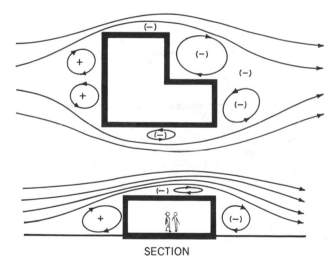

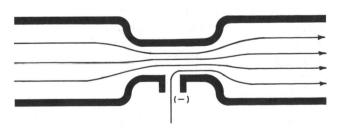

SECTION

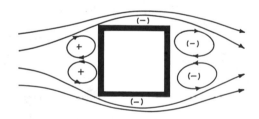

Figure 10.5e Turbulence and eddy currents occur in the high- and low-pressure areas around a building. (After Art Bowen, 1981.)

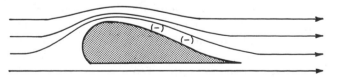

Figure 10.5f The venturi tube illustrates the Bernoulli effect: As the velocity of air increases, its static pressure decreases. Thus, an opening at the constriction would suck in air.

Figure 10.5g An airplane wing is like half of a venturi tube. In this case, the negative pressure is also called "lift".

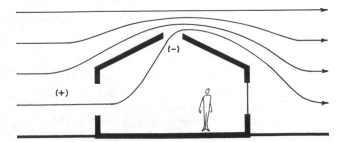

Figure 10.5h The venturi effect causes air to be exhausted through roof openings at or near the ridge.

Figure 10.5i Venturi passive ventilators with adjustable louvers are used at the Strasbourg, France, air freight terminal. Architects: Jockers Architekten, 2001.

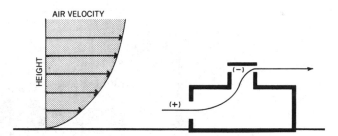

Figure 10.5j Because the air velocity increases rapidly with height above grade, the air has less static pressure at the roof than on the ground (the Bernoulli effect).

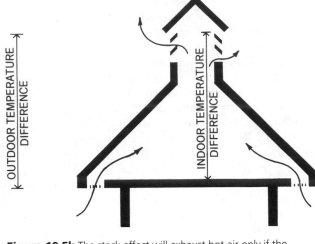

Figure 10.5k The stack effect will exhaust hot air only if the indoor-temperature difference is greater than the outdoor-temperature difference between the vertical openings.

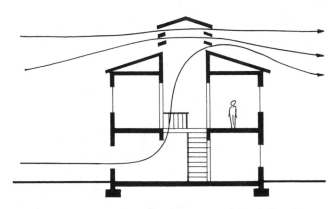

Figure 10.5l The central stair and geometry of this design allow effective vertical ventilation by the combined action of stratification, the stack effect, and both the Bernoulli and venturi effects.

increases rapidly with height above ground. Thus, the pressure at the ridge of a roof will be lower than that of windows at ground level. Consequently, even without the help of the geometry of a venturi tube, the Bernoulli effect will exhaust air through roof openings (Fig. 10.5j).

7. *Stack effect:* The stack effect can exhaust air from a building by the action of natural convection. The stack effect will exhaust air only if the indoor-temperature difference between two vertical openings is greater than the outdoor-temperature difference

between the same two openings (Fig. 10.5k). To maximize this basically weak effect, the openings should be as large and as far apart vertically as possible. The air should be able to flow freely from the lower to the higher opening (i.e., minimize obstructions).

The advantage of the stack effect over the Bernoulli effect is that it does not depend on wind. The disadvantage is that it is a very weak force and cannot move air quickly. It will, however, combine with the Bernoulli and venturi effects mentioned above to create particularly good vertical

ventilation on many hot summer days. Figure 10.5l illustrates how stratification, the stack effect, the shape of the roof (the venturi effect), and the increased wind velocity at the roof (the Bernoulli effect) can all combine to ventilate a building naturally. Roof monitors and ventilators high on the roof are especially helpful: because of stratification, the hottest indoor air is exhausted first.

The stack effect causes the lower part of a building with an atrium to have a negative pressure and the upper part to have a positive pressure. Somewhere in between will

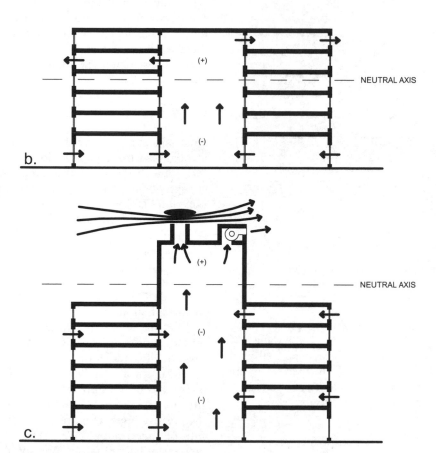

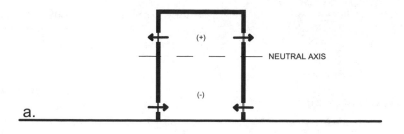

Figure 10.5m The stack effect causes negative pressure in the lower part of a space, positive pressure in the upper part, and zero pressure in between (top drawing). If this space were the atrium of a multistory building, the hot air would enter the upper floors (middle). To avoid this problem, the neutral axis must be raised by increasing the height of the atrium and using wind and/or exhaust fans (bottom).

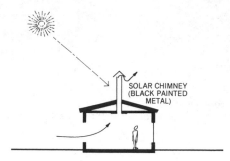

Figure 10.5n A solar chimney increases the stack effect without heating the indoors.

Figure 10.5o This outhouse is ventilated with a solar chimney. The author can verify that even on windless days, no odor was present when the sun was shining.

be the neutral axis (Fig. 10.5m, top). Consequently, hot air from the lower stories enters the upper floors (Fig. 10.5m, middle). To avoid this problem, the neutral axis must be raised above the top floor (Fig. 10.5m, bottom).

An interesting variation on the stack effect is the **solar chimney**. Since the stack effect is a function of temperature differences, heating the indoor air increases the air flow. But, of course, that would conflict with our goal of cooling the indoor air. Therefore, the solar chimney heats the air after it leaves the building (Figs. 10.5n and o). Thus, the stack effect is increased but without additional heating of the building.

10.6 AIR FLOW THROUGH BUILDINGS

The following factors determine the pattern of air flow through a building: pressure distribution around the building; direction of air entering windows; size, location, and details of windows; and interior partitioning details. Each of these factors will be considered in more detail.

Site Conditions

Adjacent buildings, walls, and vegetation on the site will greatly affect the air flow through a building. These site conditions will be discussed in Chapter 11.

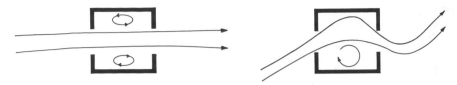

Figure 10.6a Usually indoor ventilation is better from oblique winds than from head-on winds because the oblique airstream covers more of the room.

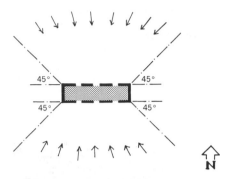

Figure 10.6b Acceptable wind directions for the orientation that is best for summer shade and winter sun.

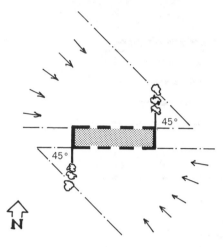

Figure 10.6c Deflecting walls and vegetation can be used to change air-flow direction so that the optimum solar orientation can be maintained.

Window Orientation and Wind Direction

Winds exert maximum pressure when they are perpendicular to a surface, and the pressure is reduced about 50 percent when the wind is at an oblique angle of about 45°. However, the indoor ventilation is often better with the oblique winds because they generate greater turbulence indoors (Fig 10.6a). Consequently, a fairly large range of wind directions will work for most designs. This is fortunate because it is a rare site that has winds blowing mainly from one direction. Even where there are strong prevailing directions, it might not be possible to face the building into the wind.

In most climates, the need for summer shade and winter sun calls for a building, orientation with the long axis in the east-west direction, and Fig. 10.6b shows the range of wind directions that works well with that orientation. Even when winds are east–west, the solar orientation usually has priority because winds can be rerouted more easily than the sun (Fig. 10.6c).

Window Locations

Cross-ventilation is so effective because air is both pushed and pulled through the building by a positive pressure on the windward side and by a negative pressure on the leeward side (Fig. 10.6d). Ventilation from windows on adjacent walls can be either good or bad, depending on the pressure distribution, which varies with wind direction (Fig. 10.6e).

Ventilation from windows on one side of a building can vary from fair to poor, depending on the location of windows. Since the pressure is greater at the center of the windward wall than at the edges, there is some pressure difference in the asymmetric placement of windows, while there is no pressure difference in the symmetric scheme (Fig. 10.6f).

Fin Walls

Fin walls can greatly increase the ventilation through windows on the same side of a building by changing the pressure distribution (Fig. 10.6g). Note, however, that each window must have only a single fin. Furthermore, fin walls will not work if they are placed on the same side of each window (Fig. 10.6h). Fin walls work best for winds at 45° to the window wall. Casement windows can act as fin walls at no extra cost.

The placement of windows on a wall determines not only the quantity but also the initial direction of the incoming air. The off-center placement of the window gives the airstream an initial deflection because the positive pressure is greater on one side of the window (Fig. 10.6i). To better ventilate the room, one should deflect the airstream in the opposite direction. A fin wall can be used to change the pressure balance and thus, the direction of the airstream (Fig. 10.6j).

Horizontal Overhangs and Air Flow

A horizontal overhang just above the window will cause the airstream to deflect up to the ceiling because the solid overhang prevents the positive pressure above it from balancing the positive pressure below the window (Fig. 10.6k). However, a louvered

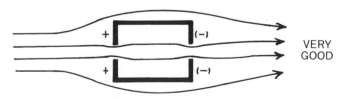

Figure 10.6d Cross-ventilation between windows on opposite walls is the ideal condition.

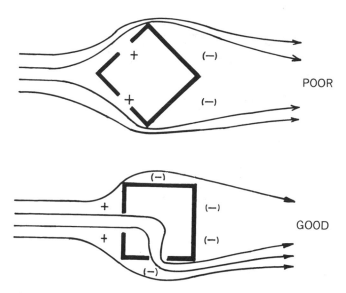

POOR

GOOD

Figure 10.6e Ventilation from windows on adjacent sides can be poor or good, depending on wind direction.

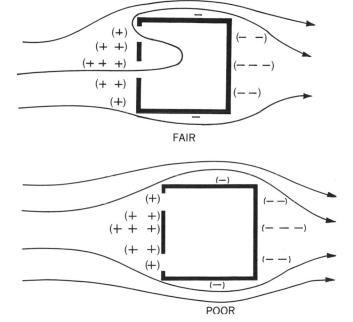

FAIR

POOR

Figure 10.6f Some ventilation is possible in the asymmetric placement of windows because the relative pressure is greater at the center than at the sides of the windward wall. (After Art Bowen, 1981.)

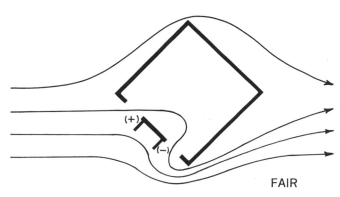

FAIR

Figure 10.6g Fin walls can significantly increase ventilation through windows on the same wall. (After Art Bowen, 1981.)

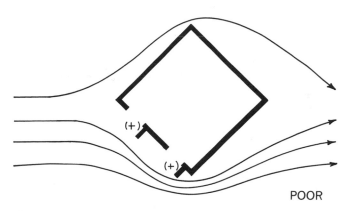

POOR

Figure 10.6h Poor ventilation results from fin walls placed on the same side of each window or when two fins are used on each window.

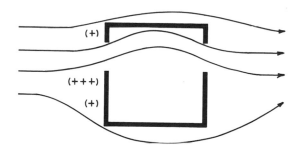

Figure 10.6i The greater positive pressure on one side of the window deflects the airstream in the wrong direction. Much of the room remains unventilated.

overhang or gap of 6 in. (15 cm) or more in the overhang will allow the positive pressure above it to affect the direction of the air flow (Fig. 10.6l). Placement of the overhang higher on the wall can also direct the airstream down to the occupants (Fig. 10.6m).

Window Types

The type and design of windows have a great effect on both the quantity and direction of air flow. Although double-hung, single-hung, and sliding windows do not change the direction

of the airstream, they do block at least 50 percent of the air flow. On the other hand, casement windows allow almost full air flow, but they can deflect the airstream (Fig. 10.6n). They also act as fin walls, as described above.

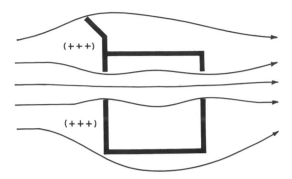

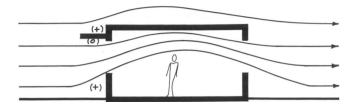

Figure 10.6k The solid horizontal overhang causes the air to deflect upward. (After Art Bowen, 1981.)

Figure 10.6j A fin wall can be used to direct the airstream through the center of the room.

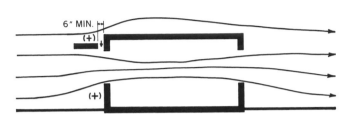

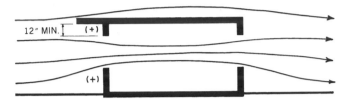

Figure 10.6m A solid horizontal overhang placed high above the window will also straighten out the airstream. (After Art Bowen, 1981.)

Figure 10.6l A louvered overhang or at least a gap in the overhang will permit the airstream to straighten out.

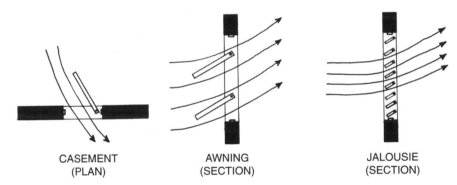

CASEMENT (PLAN)   AWNING (SECTION)   JALOUSIE (SECTION)

Figure 10.6n All but double-hung and sliding windows have a strong effect on the direction of the airstream.

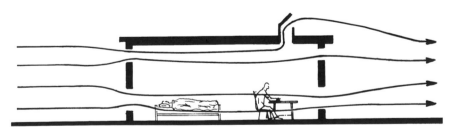

Figure 10.6o For comfort ventilation, openings should be at the level of the occupants. High openings vent the hot air collecting near the ceiling and are most useful for night-flush cooling. (After Art Bowen, 1981.)

For the vertical deflection of the airstream, use hopper, awning, or jalousie windows (Fig. 10.6n). These types also deflect the rain while still admitting air, which is very important in hot and humid climates. Unfortunately, with this kind of inclination, they deflect the wind upward over people's heads, which is undesirable for comfort ventilation.

Movable opaque louvers, frequently used on shutters, are like jalousie windows except that they also block the sun and view. The large amount of crack and resultant infiltration makes these types of windows and louvers inappropriate in climates with cold winters.

Horizontal strip or ribbon windows are often the best choice when good ventilation is required over large areas of a room.

Vertical Placement of Windows

The purpose of the air flow will determine the vertical placement and height of windows. For comfort ventilation, the windows should be low, at the level of the people in the room. That places the windowsill between 1 and 2 ft (30–60cm) above the floor for people seated or reclining. A low windowsill is especially important when hopper or jalousie windows are used because of their tendency to deflect air upward. Additional high windows or ceiling vents should be considered for exhausting the hot air that collects near the ceiling (Fig. 10.6o). High openings are also important for night-flush cooling where air must pass over the structure of the building.

Traditional buildings in the South had windows that were almost the full height of the room. Thomas Jefferson's home, Monticello, in Virginia, had triple-hung windows that went from the floor to the ceiling. By being triple-hung, the windows' upper and lower sashes could be opened for maximum ventilation. Jefferson could also open the lower two sashes to create a door to the porch.

It is often advantageous to place windows high on a wall where they are too high to reach for direct manual operation. Mechanical devices are readily available for both manual and automatic operation. Some work with mechanical linkage (Fig. 10.6p) and others with electric motors (Figs. 10.6q and r).

Inlet and Outlet Sizes and Locations

Generally, the inlet and outlet size should be about the same, since the amount of ventilation is mainly a function of the smaller opening. However, if one opening is smaller, it should usually be the inlet, because that maximizes the velocity of the indoor airstream, and it is the velocity that has the greatest effect on comfort. Although velocities higher than the wind can be achieved indoors by concentrating the air flow, the area served is, of course, decreased (Fig. 10.6s). The inlet opening not only determines the velocity, but also determines the air-flow pattern in the room. The location of the outlet, on the other hand, has little effect on the air velocity and flow pattern.

However, because many locations have no prevailing wind, most naturally ventilated buildings must be designed to function under many different wind directions. Thus, it is usually best to have inlets and outlets the same size.

Insect Screens

Air flow is decreased about 50 percent by an insect screen. The actual resistance is a function of the angle

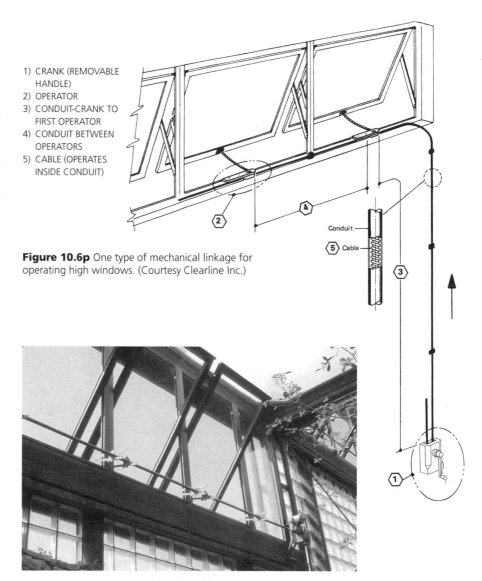

1) CRANK (REMOVABLE HANDLE)
2) OPERATOR
3) CONDUIT-CRANK TO FIRST OPERATOR
4) CONDUIT BETWEEN OPERATORS
5) CABLE (OPERATES INSIDE CONDUIT)

Figure 10.6p One type of mechanical linkage for operating high windows. (Courtesy Clearline Inc.)

Figure 10.6q Each motor opens a bank of pivoting windows high above the floor in a greenhouse at Callaway Gardens, Georgia.

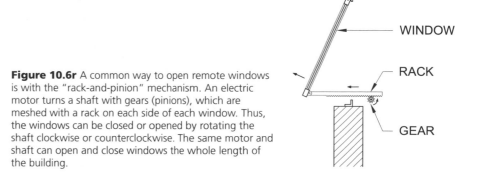

Figure 10.6r A common way to open remote windows is with the "rack-and-pinion" mechanism. An electric motor turns a shaft with gears (pinions), which are meshed with a rack on each side of each window. Thus, the windows can be closed or opened by rotating the shaft clockwise or counterclockwise. The same motor and shaft can open and close windows the whole length of the building.

at which the wind strikes the screen, with the lowest resistance for a head-on wind. To compensate for the effect of the screen, larger window openings are required. A screened-in porch is especially effective because of the very large screen area that it provides (Fig. 10.6t).

Roof Vents

Passive roof ventilators are typically used to lower attic temperatures. If, however, local winds are high enough, and the ventilator is large enough or high enough on the roof, these devices can also be used to ventilate habitable spaces. The common wind turbine enhances ventilation about 30 percent over an open stack. Research has shown that other designs can enhance the air flow as much as 120 percent (Fig. 10.6u).

The BedZED housing project uses rotating vents with wind vanes so that the opening is always on the leeward side to maximize the negative pressure (Fig. 10.6v). Also see Fig. 7.12d and e. Although the BRE office building uses the simpler open-stack ventilators, significant ventilation is achieved by the height of the opening (Fig. 10.6w).

Although cupolas, monitors, and roof vents are often a part of traditional architecture (see Figs. 10.2u and w), they can also be integrated very successfully into modern architecture (Figs. 10.6x and y). Some kind of shutter or trapdoor is required to prevent unwanted ventilation, especially in the winter.

Fans

In most climates, wind is not always present in sufficient quantity when needed, and usually there is less wind at night than during the day. Thus, fans are often required to augment the wind.

There are three quite different purposes for fans. The first is to exhaust hot, humid, and polluted air. This is part of the heat-avoidance strategy and is discussed in Chapter 15. The second is to bring in outdoor air to either cool people (comfort

Figure 10.6s Inlets and outlets should be the same size. If they cannot be the same size, the inlet should be smaller to maximize the velocity. (After Art Bowen, 1981.)

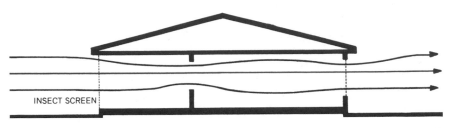

Figure 10.6t The resistance to air flow by insect screens can be largely overcome by means of larger openings or screened-in porches.

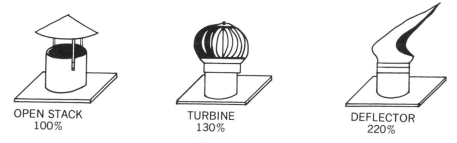

Figure 10.6u The design of a roof ventilator has a great effect on its performance. Percentages show relative effectiveness. (After Shubert and Hahn, 1983.)

Figure 10.6v The Bedford Zero Energy Development (BedZED) in London, England uses rotating ventilators to maximize the air exhausted from the building by the wind. Architects: Bill Dunster Architects. Engineers: ARUP. (Photo courtesy ARUP.)

Figure 10.6w The Building Research Establishment (BRE) office building uses open stacks with great height to maximize both the *stack effect* and *wind effect* to ventilate the building naturally. Architect: Fielden Clegg. Location: Garston, England, 1991–1997. (Photo: Bruce Haglund.)

Figure 10.6x The Animal Foundation Dog Adoption Park uses monitors placed high and oriented to the local winds to maximize the natural ventilation. Location: Las Vegas, Nevada, 2005. Architect: Tate Snyder Kimsey.

ventilation) or cool the building at night (night-flush cooling). The third purpose is to circulate indoor air at those times when the indoor air is cooler than the outdoor air.

Separate fans are required for each purpose. Window or **whole-house fans** are used for comfort ventilation or night-flush cooling (Fig. 10.6z). Ceiling or table fans are used whenever the indoor air is cooler and/or less humid than the outdoor air.

Partitions and Interior Planning

Open plans are preferable because partitions increase the resistance to air flow, thereby decreasing total ventilation.

When partitions are used but are in one apartment or one tenant area, cross-ventilation is often possible by leaving doors open between rooms. Cross-ventilation is almost never possible, however, when a public double-loaded corridor plan is used. Before air conditioning became available **transoms** (windows above doors) allowed for some cross-ventilation.

Figure 10.6y Monitors on the roof of the bathing pavilions at Callaway Gardens, Georgia.

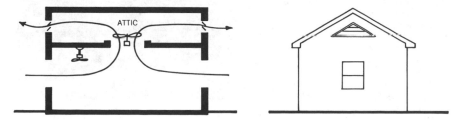

Figure 10.6z Whole-house or window fans are used to bring in outdoor air for either comfort ventilation or night-flush cooling. Ceiling or table fans are mainly used when the air temperature and humidity are lower indoors than outdoors.

277

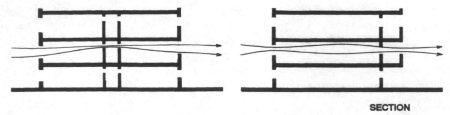

Figure 10.6aa In regard to natural ventilation, single-loaded corridor plans *(right)* are far superior to double-loaded plans *(left)*.

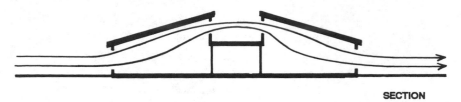

Figure 10.6bb In single-story buildings, a double-loaded corridor plan can use clerestory windows instead of transoms.

Figure 10.6cc The Unite d'Habitation at Marseilles, France, was designed by Le Corbusier to provide cross-ventilation for each apartment. (Photograph by Alan Cook.)

An alternative to the double-loaded corridor is the open single-loaded corridor since it permits full cross-ventilation (Fig. 10.6aa). Single-story buildings can improve on the double-loaded corridor by using clerestory windows instead of transoms (Fig. 10.6bb).

Le Corbusier came up with an ingenious solution for cross-ventilation in his Unite d'Habitation at Marseilles (Fig. 10.6cc). The building has a corridor on only every third floor, and each apartment is a duplex with an opening to the corridor as well as the opposite sides of the building (Fig. 10.6dd). The balconies have perforated parapets to further encourage ventilation, and they form a giant brise-soleil for sun shading.

Le Corbusier opened the area under the building to the wind by resting the building on columns that he called **pilotis**. In a hot climate, such an area becomes a cool, breezy place in summer, but in a cold climate the same area becomes very unpleasant in the winter. The wind patterns around buildings will be discussed further in Chapter 11.

10.7 EXAMPLE OF VENTILATION DESIGN

Ventilation design is greatly aided by the use of **air-flow diagrams**. These diagrams are based on the general principles and rules mentioned above and not on precise calculations. They are largely the product of a trial-and-error process. The following steps are a guide to making these air-flow diagrams.

Air-Flow Diagrams

1. Determine a common summer-wind direction from local weather data or from the wind roses given in Fig. 5.6f.
2. On an overlay of the plan and site, draw a series of arrows parallel to the chosen wind direction on the upwind side of the building and their continuation on the downwind side. (Fig. 10.7a).

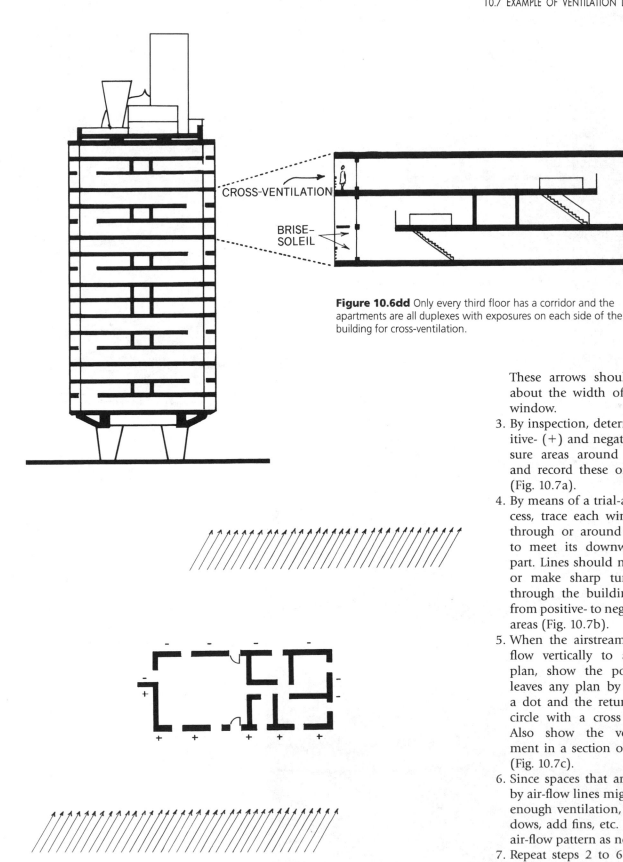

CROSS-VENTILATION

BRISE–SOLEIL

Figure 10.6dd Only every third floor has a corridor and the apartments are all duplexes with exposures on each side of the building for cross-ventilation.

Figure 10.7a The initial steps for drawing an air-flow diagram.

These arrows should be spaced about the width of the smallest window.

3. By inspection, determine the positive- (+) and negative- (−) pressure areas around the building and record these on the overlay (Fig. 10.7a).

4. By means of a trial-and-error process, trace each windward arrow through or around the building to meet its downwind counterpart. Lines should not cross, end, or make sharp turns. Air flow through the building should go from positive- to negative-pressure areas (Fig. 10.7b).

5. When the airstream is forced to flow vertically to another floor plan, show the point where it leaves any plan by a circle with a dot and the return point by a circle with a cross (Fig. 10.7b). Also show the vertical movement in a section of the building (Fig. 10.7c).

6. Since spaces that are not crossed by air-flow lines might not receive enough ventilation, relocate windows, add fins, etc. to change the air-flow pattern as necessary.

7. Repeat steps 2 to 6 until a good air-flow pattern has been achieved.

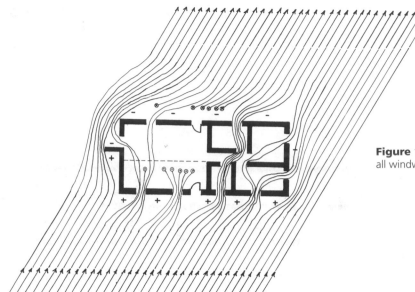

Figure 10.7b The completed air-flow diagram has connected all windward and leeward arrows.

Figure 10.7c Air flow should also be checked in section. (This technique is based on work by Prof. Murray Milne, UCLA.)

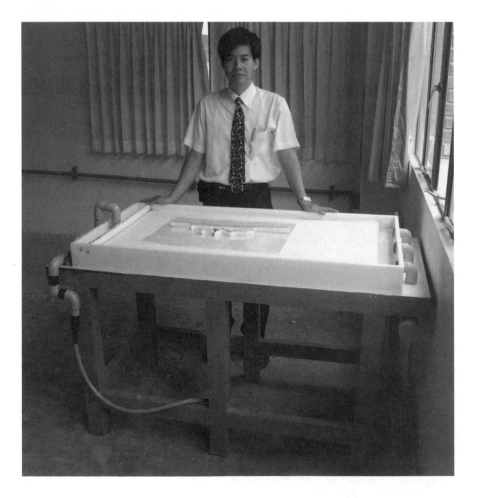

Fig. 10.7d This water table at Chiang Mai University in Thailand allows effective ventilation studies by using streams of colored water to simulate air flow through a building. See Appendix N for more information about the water table.

This technique is based on work by Prof. Murray Milne, UCLA.

Ventilation can also be designed and tested with a water table apparatus, as shown in Fig. 10.7d. Water flow is used as an analogy for wind. A section of the building is modeled in slight three dimensions about 3/4 in. (2 cm) thick. Water is thus allowed to flow through the model. When dye is added to the water supply, it quickly becomes apparent to what extent water flows through the model, thereby predicting how the wind will flow through the building. See Appendix N for a full description of the water table and for detailed construction drawings.

10.8 COMFORT VENTILATION

Air passing over the skin creates a physiological cooling effect by evaporating moisture from the surface of the skin. The term **comfort ventilation** is used for this technique of using air motion across the skin to promote thermal comfort. This passive cooling technique is useful for certain periods of the day and year in most climates, but it is especially appropriate in hot and humid climates, where it is typical for air temperatures to be only moderately hot and ventilation is required to control indoor humidity. See Fig. 4.11 for the conditions under which comfort ventilation is appropriate.

Comfort ventilation can rarely be completely passive because in most climates winds are not always sufficient to create the necessary indoor air velocities. Window or whole-house attic fans are usually needed to supplement the wind. See Table 10.8 for the effect on comfort due to various air velocities. For comfort ventilation, the air-flow techniques mentioned above should be used to maximize the air flow **across the occupants** of the building.

If the climate is extremely humid, if little or no heating is required, and if air conditioning will not be used, lightweight construction is appropriate. In such climates, any thermal mass

Table 10.8 Air Velocities and Thermal Comfort

Air Velocity				Equivalent Temperature Reduction*		
I-P		SI				
fpm	mph	[m/s]	[kph]	°F	[°C]	Effect on Comfort
10	0.1	0.05	0.2	0	0	Stagnant air, slightly uncomfortable
40	0.5	0.2	0.8	2	1.1	Barely noticeable but comfortable
50	0.6	0.25	1.0	2.4	1.3	Design velocity for air outlets that are near occupants
80	1	0.4	1.6	3.5	1.9	Noticeable and comfortable
160	2	0.8	3.2	5	2.8	Very noticeable but acceptable in certain high-activity areas if air is warm
200	2.3	1.0	3.7	6	3.3	Upper limit for air-conditioned spaces Good air velocity for natural ventilation in hot and dry climates
400	4.5	2.0	7.2	7	3.9	Good air velocity for ventilation in hot and humid climates
900	10	4.5	16	9	5.0	Considered a gentle breeze when felt outdoors

*The values in this column are the number of degrees that the temperature would have to drop to create the same cooling effect as the given air velocity.

Figure 10.8a The Mayan Indians of the hot and humid Yucatan Peninsula build lightweight, porous buildings for maximum comfort. Note that although mud and rocks are available, experience has led the Mayans to the most comfortable construction method.

will only store up the heat of the day to make the nights less comfortable (Fig 10.8a). In the United States, only southern Florida and Hawaii (climate region 16) fit in this category. In these climates, a moderate amount of insulation is still required to keep the indoor surfaces from getting too hot due to the action of the sun on the roof and walls. The insulation keeps the mean radiant temperature (MRT) from rising far above the indoor air temperature, since that would decrease thermal comfort. Insulation is also required when the building is air conditioned. Thermal mass is also helpful

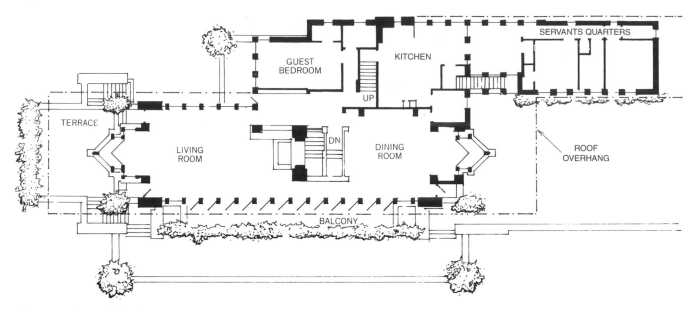

Figure 10.8b Frank Lloyd Wright's Robie House (1909) in Chicago has whole walls of doors and windows that open for cross-ventilation. It also has large roof overhangs to keep out the sun and rain.

for buildings that are mostly air conditioned even in humid climates. It allows the air conditioning to be turned off during times of peak electrical demand, because the mass will prevent quick temperature changes.

Some control is also possible over the temperature of the incoming air. For example, tests have shown that when the air temperature above unshaded asphalt was 110°F (43°C), it was only 90°F (32°C) over an adjacent shaded lawn. The lower the incoming air temperature, the more effective will be comfort ventilation.

For comfort ventilation, the operable window area should be about 20 percent of the floor area, with the openings split about equally between windward and leeward walls. The windows should also be well shaded on the exterior, as explained in Chapter 9. One of the examples presented there was Frank Lloyd Wright's Robie House (Fig. 9.1i). It has very large roof overhangs to shade walls made entirely of glass doors and windows that can be opened for ventilation (Fig. 10.8b). Since Chicago has very hot and humid summers, plentiful ventilation and full shade were the major cooling strategies before air conditioning became available.

Large overhangs are also needed to keep the rain out. Besides the difficulty of closing windows just before a rain, the relative humidity increases with rain, consequently, windows need to remain open during the rain.

Comfort ventilation is most effective when the indoor temperature and humidity are above the outdoor level. This is often the case because of internal heat sources and the heating effect of the sun. Thus, comfort ventilation not only brings in cooler air whenever possible but also produces thermal comfort from the resultant air motion. However, when it is much hotter outdoors than indoors, the windows should be closed to avoid excessive heating of the building with hot outdoor air. Ceiling fans can be used to circulate the cooler indoor air.

Rules for Comfort Ventilation in Hot and Very Humid Climates

1. See Fig. 4.11 for the climatic conditions for which comfort ventilation is appropriate.
2. Use fans to supplement the wind.
3. Maximize the air flow across the occupants.
4. Lightweight construction is appropriate only in climates that are

very humid, do not require passive solar heating, and use little if any air conditioning.
5. Use at least a moderate amount of insulation to keep the MRT near the air temperature.
6. Operable window area should be about 20 percent of the floor area, split about equally between windward and leeward walls. Larger window areas can be used in tropical climates.
7. Windows should be open both during the day and during the night.

10.9 NIGHT-FLUSH COOLING

In all but the most humid climates, the night air is significantly cooler than the daytime air. This cool night air can be used to flush out the heat from a building's mass. The precooled mass can then act as a heat sink during the following day by absorbing heat. Since the ventilation removes the heat from the mass of the building at night, this time-tested passive technique is called **night-flush cooling**.

This cooling strategy works best in hot and dry climates because of

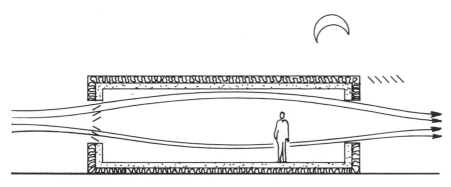

Figure 10.9a With night-flush cooling, night ventilation cools the mass of the building.

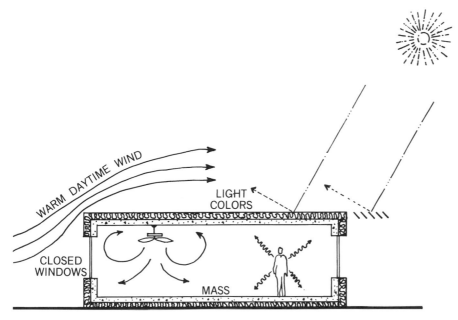

Figure 10.9b During the day, the night-flush cooled mass acts as a heat sink. Light colors, insulation, shading, and closed windows keep the heat gain to a minimum. Interior circulating fans can be used for additional comfort.

the large diurnal (daily) temperature ranges found there—above 30°F (17°C). A large range implies cool nighttime temperatures of about 70°F (21°C) even though daytime temperatures are quite high—about 100°F (38°C). However, good results are also possible in somewhat humid climates, which have only modest diurnal temperature ranges—about 20°F (11°C). The map of the United States in Fig. 5.6c illustrates that most of the country, including the humid East, has diurnal temperature ranges of more than 20°F (11°C). The daily ranges are smaller only very close to the coast.

Night-flush cooling works in two stages. At night, natural ventilation or fans bring cool outdoor air in contact with the indoor mass, thereby cooling it (Fig. 10.9a). The next morning, the windows are closed to prevent heating the building with outdoor air (Fig. 10.9b). The mass now acts as a heat sink and thus keeps the indoor air temperature from rising as fast as it would otherwise. However, when the indoor air temperature has risen above the comfort zone, internal circulating fans are required to maintain comfort for additional hours. As with passive heating, a significant

temperature range indoors will result. Although more thermal mass will reduce the swing, it is advantageous to allow night flushing to cool the building below the comfort zone in preparation for the hot day to follow.

The thermal mass is critical, because without it there is no heat sink to cool the building during the day. The requirements for the mass are similar to those for passive solar heating, and, of course, the mass can serve both purposes. Ideally, the mass should equal 80 lb per square foot (390 kg/m²) of floor area (concrete weighs about 150 lb/ft³ (2400 kg/m³). The surface area of the mass should be more than two times the floor area.

Minimize the heat gain to minimize the amount of mass required. Use heat-avoidance techniques, such as well-shaded windows, a heavily insulated envelope, and light colors. These and many other heat-avoidance techniques are mentioned throughout this book.

To flush out the heat at night, the operable window area should be about 10 to 15 percent of the floor area. When natural ventilation is not sufficient, exhaust fans should be used. With night-flush cooling, the air flow should be directed **over the mass**, not over the occupants.

In normal buildings, it is difficult to completely flush the mass of its heat at night. A more sophisticated version of convective cooling passes the night air through channels in the structural mass. The Emerald PUD Building in Eugene, Oregon, uses night-flush cooling as a major design strategy. Cool night air is passed through a hollow-core concrete floor and roof planks. This excellent design also incorporates many other energy-conscious design concepts, and it is more fully explained as a case study in Section 17.4.

The Bateson State Office Building in Sacramento, California, uses two different night-flush cooling techniques. Night air cools both the exposed interior concrete structure for direct cooling and a rock bed for indirect cooling. This building is also discussed as a case study in Section 17.6.

Rules for Night-Flush Cooling

1. Night-flush cooling works best in hot and dry climates with a daily temperature range that exceeds 30°F (17°C) but is still effective in somewhat humid regions as long as the daily range is above 20°F (11°C).
2. Except for areas with consistent night winds, window or whole-house fans should be used. Ceiling or other circulating indoor fans should be used during the day when the windows are closed.
3. Ideally, there should be about 80 lb of mass for each square foot (390 kg/m²) of floor area, and the surface area of this mass should be more than two times the floor area. The mass has to be on the indoor side of the insulation.
4. The air flow at night must be directed over the mass to ensure good heat transfer.
5. The window area should be between 10 and 15 percent of the floor area.
6. Windows should be open at night and closed during the day.

Before we look at other passive-cooling strategies, it is worthwhile to note that natural ventilation is by far the most common passive-cooling technique. It can save much energy, provide better indoor air quality, and increase occupant satisfaction. Since people desire to control their immediate environment, operable windows are very popular. To prevent conflict with the air-conditioning system, the architect and engineer need to cooperate at all stages of the design process.

10.10 SMART FACADES AND ROOFS

Also known as "double-skin facades" and "climate walls," smart facades have many functions and they are dynamic, unlike most curtain walls. The smartest facades save energy and increase comfort by integrating all of the following: passive solar collection, shading, daylighting, increased thermal resistance, mechanical systems, and natural ventilation. Smart facades

usually have a double-glazed unit, an air space between 6 and 30 in. (15–75 cm) deep, and a layer of safety or laminated glass on the outside (Fig. 10.10a). The air space in smart facades is usually divided into vertical and horizontal compartments to control the spread of fire and noise and to prevent the stack effect from transferring hot, stale air from lower floors to upper floors.

Most smart facades are dynamic by means of venetian blinds and operable windows. The shading and daylighting benefits of the blinds are described in Chapters 9 and 13. The operable windows provide ventilation for both quality indoor air (Chapter 16) and passive cooling, which is discussed here. Smart facades can support both comfort ventilation and night-flush cooling

in a more controlled manner than windows, because they prevent the entry of rain, control noise, and prevent excessively high airspeeds even on the fiftieth floor on a windy day. One of the most famous smart facades is found on the Commerzbank, described as a case study in Section 17.7.

Certain building types can use smart roofs that retract when not needed. Baseball stadiums are the best examples, but enclosed swimming pools are the most common application. Movable roofs are also used for playgrounds, zoos, greenhouses, atriums, and pedestrian streets. Preengineered systems make movable roofs an economical solution for reducing cooling loads where glass roofs are desired. Of course, they also create delight. (Fig. 10.10b).

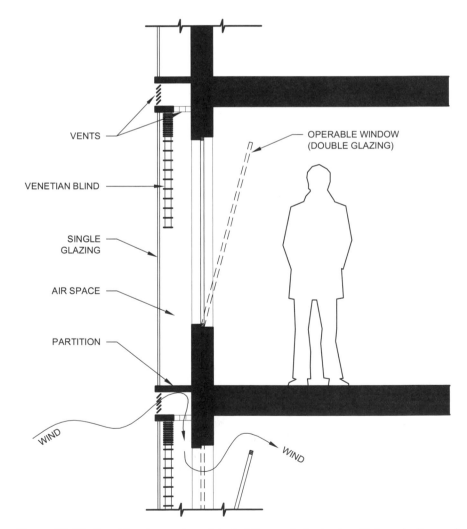

Figure 10.10a Smart facades are dynamic in that they control natural ventilation, shading, and daylighting all of which change with time.

Figure 10.10b Many spaces, such as this Best Western Lamplighter Inn, London, Ontario, benefit from having the roof open up on hot days. (Project by Open Aire Inc., www.openaire.com)

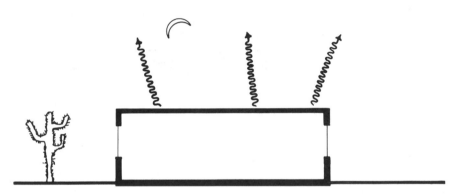

Figure 10.11a On clear nights with little humidity, there is strong radiant cooling to the cold night sky (outer space).

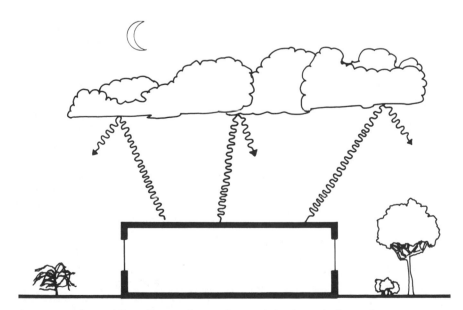

Figure 10.11b Humidity reduces radiant cooling, and clouds practically stop it.

10.11 RADIANT COOLING

As was explained in Chapter 3, all objects emit and absorb radiant energy, and an object will cool by radiation if the net flow is outward. At night the long-wave infrared radiation from a clear sky (outer space) is much less than the long-wave infrared radiation emitted from a building, and thus there is a net flow to the sky (Fig. 10.11a).

In hot and dry climates, traditional buildings used deep courtyards and narrow alleys to expose the massive walls to only a few hours of direct sunlight. However, all of the walls radiated to the cold night sky all night long. Thus, the walls were quite cool by morning. As mentioned in Chapter 9, shading the courtyards and narrow streets during the day provided even more comfort.

Since the roof has the greatest exposure to the sky, it is the best location for a long-wave radiator. Since only shiny metal surfaces are poor emitters, any other surface will be a good choice for a long-wave radiator. Painted metal (any color) is especially good because the metal conducts heat quickly to the painted surface, which then readily emits the energy. Such a radiator on a clear night will cool as much as 12°F (7°C) below the cool night air. On humid nights, radiant cooling is less efficient but a temperature depression of about 7°F (4°C) is still possible. Clouds, on the other hand, almost completely block the radiant cooling effect (Fig. 10.11b).

Direct Radiant Cooling

Potentially the most efficient approach to radiant cooling is to make the roof itself the radiator. For example, an exposed-concrete roof will rapidly lose heat by radiating to the night sky. The next day, the cool mass of concrete can effectively cool a building by acting as a heat sink. The roof, however, must then be protected from the heat of the sun and hot air. Consequently, insulation must be added to the roof every morning and removed every evening.

Harold Hay has designed and built several buildings using this concept, except that he used plastic bags filled

285

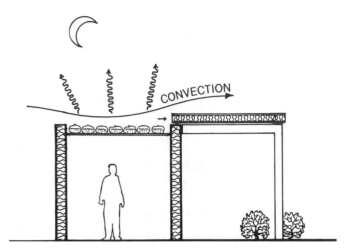

Figure 10.11c During a summer night, the insulation is removed and the bags of water are allowed to give up their heat by radiant cooling.

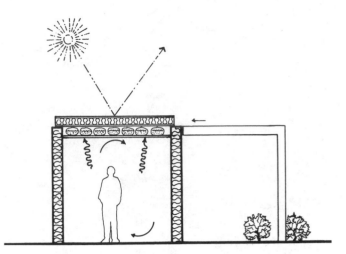

Figure 10.11d During a summer day, the water bags are insulated from the sun and hot outdoor air, while they act as a heat sink for the space below.

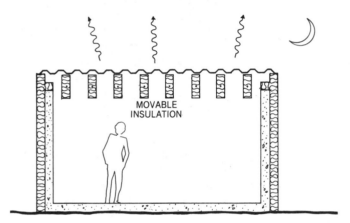

Figure 10.11e At night, the movable insulation is in the open position so that the building's heat can be radiated away. This is an example of direct radiant cooling.

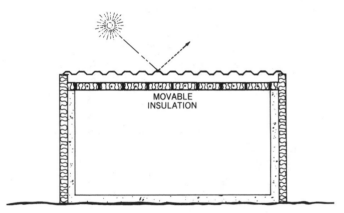

Figure 10.11f During the day, the insulation is in the closed position to keep the heat out. The cool interior mass now acts as a heat sink.

with water rather than concrete for the heat-sink material. At night, the water bags are exposed to the night sky by removing the insulation that covered them during the day (Fig. 10.11c). When the sun rises the next day, the water bags are covered by the movable insulation. During the day, the water bags, which are supported by a metal deck, cool the indoors by acting as a heat sink (Fig. 10.11d). Although this "roof pond" concept has been tested and shown to be very effective, an inexpensive, reliable, and convenient movable insulation system has still not been achieved.

Another direct-cooling strategy uses a lightweight radiator with movable insulation on the inside. This eliminates two of the problems associated with the above concept: a heavy roof structure and a movable insulation system exposed to the weather. With this system, a painted sheet-metal radiator, which is also the roof, covers movable insulation (Fig. 10.11e). At night, this insulation is in the open position so that heat from the building can migrate up and be emitted from the radiator. For the cooling effect to be useful during the day, sufficient mass must be present in the building to act as a heat sink. Also, during the day, the insulation is moved into the closed position to block the heat gain from the roof (Fig. 10.11f).

Indirect Radiant Cooling

The difficulty with movable insulation suggests the use of specialized radiators that use a heat-transfer fluid. This approach is much like active solar heating in reverse. In Fig. 10.11g the painted metal radiator cools air at night, which is then blown into the building to cool the indoor mass. The next morning the fan is turned off, and the building is sealed. The cooled indoor mass now acts as a heat sink. The radiator is vented during the day to reduce the heat load to the building (Fig. 10.11h). Unless the radiator is also used for passive heating, it should be painted white, since

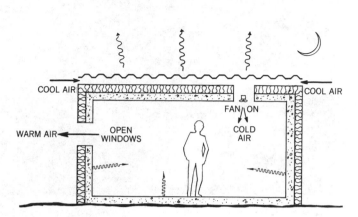

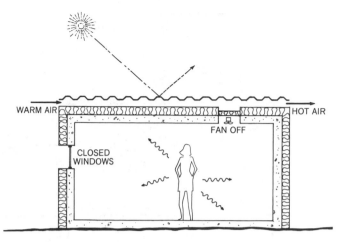

Figure 10.11g The specialized radiator cools air, which is then blown into the building to cool the thermal mass. This is an example of indirect radiant cooling.

Figure 10.11h During the day, the radiator is vented outdoors, while the building is sealed and the cooled mass acts as a heat sink.

that color is a good emitter of long-wave radiation and a poor absorber of short-wave (solar) radiation.

If there is not enough exposed mass in the building, a rock bed can be used. At night, the cooled air is blown through the rock bed to flush out the heat. During the day, indoor air blown across the rock bed is cooled by giving up its heat to the rocks. This is one of the passive cooling techniques used by the Bateson State office building (see Section 17.6).

Rules for Radiant Cooling

1. Radiant cooling will not work well in very cloudy regions. It performs best under clear skies and low humidity, but will still work at lower efficiency in temperate regions.
2. This cooling concept applies mainly to one-story buildings.
3. Unless the radiator is also used for passive heating, the radiator should be painted white.
4. Since the cooling effect is small, the whole roof area should be used.
5. Thermal mass is needed to act as a heat sink during the day.

10.12 EVAPORATIVE COOLING

When water evaporates, it draws a large amount of sensible heat from its surroundings and converts this heat into latent heat in the form of water vapor. As sensible heat is converted to latent heat, the temperature drops. This phenomenon is used to cool buildings in two very different ways. If the water evaporates in the building or in the fresh-air intake, the air will be not only cooled, but also humidified. This method is called "direct evaporative cooling." If, however, the building or indoor air is cooled by evaporation without humidifying the indoor air, the method is called "indirect evaporative cooling."

Evaporative cooling is much less energy intensive than conventional cooling, with energy savings of 30 to 90 percent. The required equipment is also much less expensive. Another environmental benefit is that no CFCs are used. The water usage of 3 to 11 gal (11 to 42 liters) per day for a house is not a serious problem in most areas. Since modern water closets use 1.6 gpf (6 lpf), the coolers use the equivalent of two to seven flushes per day. The main drawback to evaporative cooling is that its use is limited to dry climates.

Direct Evaporative Cooling

When water evaporates in the indoor air, the temperature drops but the humidity goes up. In hot and dry climates, the increase in humidity actually improves comfort. However, **direct evaporative cooling** is not appropriate in humid climates because the cooling effect is low and the humidity is already too high. See Fig. 4.11 for the kind of climate that supports direct evaporative cooling. On the map of the United States in Fig. 5.6c, direct evaporative cooling is effective for all regions with a daily temperature range above 30°F (17°C) and partially effective in regions with a daily temperature range of 25° to 29°F (14–16°C). Horticultural greenhouses are an exception because most plants thrive on high humidity but not high temperature.

The most popular form of direct evaporative cooling is accomplished with commercially available **evaporative coolers** (swamp coolers). Although they look like active mechanical devices from the outside, they are actually quite simple and use little energy (Figs. 10.12a and b). A fan is used to bring outdoor air into the building by way of a wet screen. A modest amount of water is required to keep the screen wet. To maintain comfort, a high rate of ventilation is required during the day (about twenty air changes per hour).

Misting the air has become a popular direct evaporative-cooling strategy. Water under high pressure is atomized into tiny droplets, which then readily evaporate to cool the air.

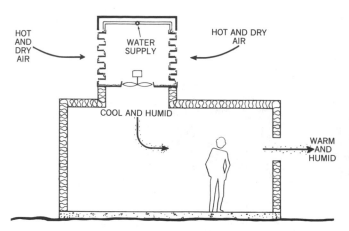

Figure 10.12a Evaporative coolers (swamp coolers) look a great deal like central air conditioning units, but their cooling mechanism is very simple and inexpensive. They are appropriate only in dry climates.

Figure 10.12b Evaporative coolers are widely used in hot and dry regions. This is an example of a direct evaporative cooler on the roof of a house.

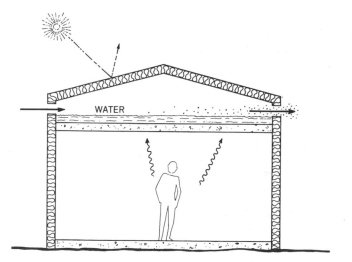

Figure 10.12c This indirect evaporative-cooling system uses a roof pond. Note that no humidity is added to the indoors.

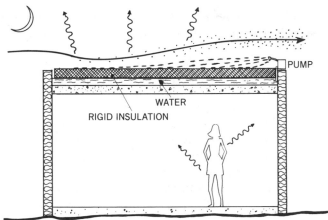

Figure 10.12d This indirect evaporative-cooling system uses floating insulation instead of a second roof to protect the water from the sun and heat of the day.

Misting is mainly used to cool outdoor spaces. Unfortunately, if the area is too sunny or too windy, the benefit of misting will be minimal. However, the cooling effect can be significant in sheltered outdoor spaces and greenhouses. Misting is often used more for the atmosphere it creates than for its cooling benefits.

Indirect Evaporative Cooling

The cooling effect from evaporation can also be used to cool the roof of a building, which then becomes a heat sink to cool the interior. This technique is an example of **indirect evaporative cooling**, and its main advantage is that the indoor air is cooled without increasing its humidity.

A critical aspect of evaporative cooling is that the heat of vaporization must come from what is to be cooled. Thus, spraying a sunlit roof is not especially good because most of the water will be evaporated by the heat of the sun. On the other hand, the heat to evaporate water at night or from a shaded roof pond comes mainly from the building itself.

Figure 10.12c illustrates the basic features of roof-pond cooling. An insulated roof shades the pond from the sun. Openings in the roof enable air currents to pass over the pond during the summer. As water evaporates, the pond will become cooler and, together with the ceiling structure, will act as a heat sink for the interior of the building. During the winter, the pond is drained and the roof openings are closed. The main disadvantage of this system is the cost of the double-roof structure and waterproofing.

A clever alternative to the above roof pond is the roof pond with floating insulation. A double-roof structure is no longer needed because the insulation floats on the roof pond (Fig. 10.12d). At night, a pump sprays the water over the top of the insulation,

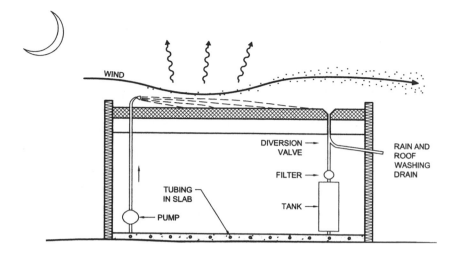

Figure 10.12e Water that is cooled by both evaporation and radiation to the night sky is used to cool the floor slab to create a heat sink for the next day. Additional water can be cooled and stored in tanks for use in fan-coil units the next day.

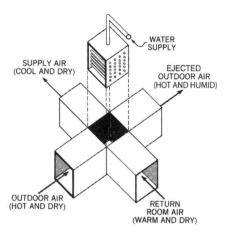

Figure 10.12f Indirect evaporative coolers reduce the indoor air temperature without increasing its humidity.

and it cools by both evaporation and radiation. When the sun rises, the pump stops and the water remains under the insulation, where it is protected from the heat of the day. Meanwhile, the water together with the roof structure acts as a heat sink for the interior. Although the cooling occurs only at night, it is very effective because of the combined action of evaporation and radiation.

A more conventional version of the water spray design is to store the cooled water in a tank and to precool the floor slab at night (Fig. 10.12e). At night the water is sprayed on a conventional roof, where it is cooled by both evaporation and radiation to the night sky. The cooled water is then pumped through tubing embedded in the floor slab and then stored in a tank for the next day. Of course, the tubing in the floor slab can also be used for radiant heating in the winter. The cooled water stored in the tank can be used with fan-coil units the next day (see Fig. 16.14q–s).

Indirect evaporative coolers are now commercially available as packaged units. They are similar to the evaporative coolers mentioned above except that they do not humidify the indoor air (Fig. 10.12f). Outdoor air is used to evaporate water off the surface of tubes. The necessary heat of vaporization is drawn in part from these tubes, through which indoor air is flowing. Thus, indoor air is cooled but not humidified. These units are sometimes used in series with evaporative coolers for extra cooling with less humidification.

Indirect evaporative cooling has two advantages over direct evaporative cooling: the indoor air is not humidified, and it can be used in climates too humid for direct evaporative cooling. Thus, the climates that have a daily range of 25° to 29°F (14°–16°C), which is marginal for direct evaporative cooling, can be effectively cooled by indirect evaporative coolers. Fig. 5.6c shows these climates to be a significant part of the United States.

Rules for Evaporative Cooling

1. Direct evaporative cooling is appropriate only in dry climates.

2. Indirect evaporative cooling works best in dry climates but can also be used in somewhat humid climates because it does not add to the indoor humidity.
3. A combination of direct and indirect is sometimes the best choice.

10.13 COOL TOWERS

Cool towers are passive evaporative coolers that act like reverse chimneys (Fig. 10.13a). At the top of the tower, water is sprayed on absorbent pads. As air enters the top of the tower, it is cooled, becomes denser, and sinks. The cool air then enters the building through openings that look like fireplaces. Thus, instead of hot air flowing up, cool air flows down the passive downdraft **cool towers**. Consequently, cool air is supplied to the buildings without the need for fans.

Cool towers have been working successfully at the Zion National Park Visitors Center in Utah since the year 2000 (Fig. 10.13b). The buildings also use natural ventilation as much as possible, with the cool towers reserved for the hottest weather. In addition, the buildings use many other energy-responsive strategies to achieve 70 percent annual energy savings compared to similar conventional buildings. For the passive heating strategies used, see Fig. 7.9e.

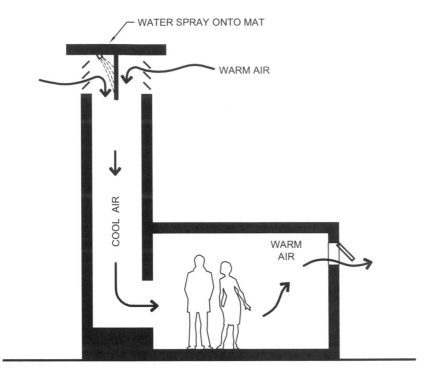

Figure 10.13a In cool towers, air is cooled by evaporation, which then sinks to fill the building with cool air.

Figure 10.13b The Zion National Park Visitors Center in Utah is kept comfortable in the hot and dry summer by means of cool towers.

10.14 EARTH COOLING

Before earth-cooling techniques can be discussed, the thermal properties of soil must be considered. Earth, especially wet earth, is both a good conductor and storer of heat (i.e., it has high heat capacity). The temperature at the surface is the result of solar gain, radiant loss, and heat conduction to or from lower layers of the ground. Since air is heated mainly by its contact with the earth, the surface soil temperature is about the same as the air temperature with its large annual fluctuations. However, due to the large time lag of earth, the soil temperature fluctuates less and less as the soil depth increases. At about 20 ft (6 m) in depth, the summer/winter fluctuations have almost disappeared and a year-round steady-state temperature exists, which is equal to the average annual air temperature.

The graph of Fig. 10.14a shows the earth temperatures as a function of depth. One curve represents the maximum summer temperatures, and the other represents the minimum winter temperatures of the soil. The ground temperatures at any depth fluctuate left and right between these curves.

Since the ground temperature is always below the maximum air temperature, the deep earth can always be used as a heat sink in the summer. However, unless the temperature difference is great enough, earth cooling might not be practical. The map of Fig. 10.14b shows that the deep soil temperatures are low enough for earth cooling (approx. 60°F (15°C) or less) in much of the country. Even if the soil is too warm for actual cooling, it will, nevertheless, be much cooler than the outdoor air. Earth sheltering, which is described in Section (15.12) can be very advantageous in some climates.

Cooling the Earth

Since the sun heats the soil, shading the surface significantly reduces the maximum earth temperature. Water evaporating directly from the surface will also cool the soil. Both techniques together can reduce soil surface temperatures as much as 18°F (10°C). It must be noted, however, that transpiration from plants (especially trees and bushes) is not very helpful because the evaporation occurs in the air high above the soil.

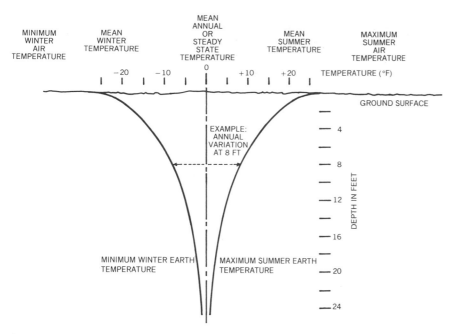

Figure 10.14a Soil temperature varies with time of year and depth below grade. To find the maximum or minimum soil temperature at any depth, first find the mean annual steady-state temperature from Fig. 10.14b and then, according to depth, add (summer) or subtract (winter) the deviation from the centerline.

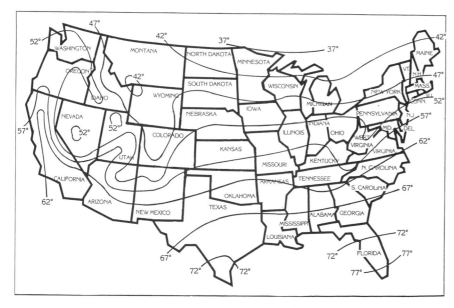

Figure 10.14b Deep-earth temperatures are approximately equal to these well-water temperatures. (Reprinted with permission of National Water Well Association.)

A canopy of trees, an elevated patio deck, and even a building over a crawl space are all possibilities for shading soil while letting air motion cause evaporation from the surface (Fig. 10.14c). When rain is not sufficient, a sprinkler should keep the soil moist. However, when sprinklers are used, they should operate only at night; otherwise, sun-warmed water will percolate into the soil. In dry climates, a light-colored gravel

bed about 4 in. (10 cm) deep can effectively shade the soil while still allowing evaporation from the earth's surface below the gravel (Fig. 10.14d).

Direct Earth Coupling

When earth-sheltered buildings have their walls in direct contact with the ground (i.e., there is little or no insulation in the walls), we say that there is **direct earth coupling**. In regions where the mean annual temperature is below 60°F, (15°C) direct coupling will be a significant source of cooling. This asset becomes a liability, however, in the winter, when excess heat will be lost to the cold ground. One solution is to insulate the earth around the building from the cold winter air but not from the building (Fig. 10.14e). This horizontal insulation buried in the ground will bring the steady-state temperature closer to the surface and closer to the building. In much of the United States, it would be an advantage to have a building surrounded by the local steady-state (i.e., deep-earth) temperature.

Indirect Earth Coupling

A building can be indirectly coupled to the earth by means of earth tubes. When cooling is desired, air is drawn through the tubes into the building (Fig. 10.14f). The earth acts as a heat sink to cool the air.

To get the maximum cooling effect, the tubes should be buried as deeply as possible to take advantage of that constant, deep-earth temperature, which is the coolest available in the summer. Deep below the surface, the soil is also more likely to be moist during the summer. Since wet soil has much higher conductivity than dry soil, there is more heat transfer per foot of tubing. Nevertheless, very long pipes are needed to cool a building.

Use an open-loop system if large amounts of fresh air are required. On the other hand, a closed-loop system offers greater efficiency and reduced condensation.

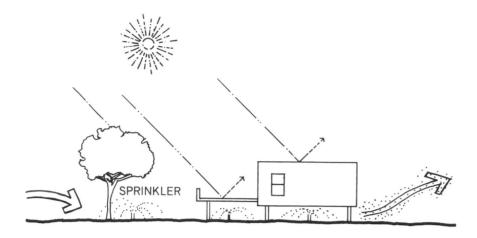

Figure 10.14c Soil can be cooled significantly below its natural temperature by shading it and by keeping it wet for evaporative cooling. However, it is best to wet the soil at night.

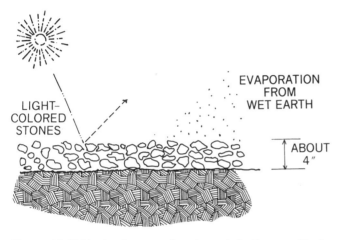

Figure 10.14d In dry climates, soil can be cooled with a gravel bed, which shades the soil while it allows evaporation to occur.

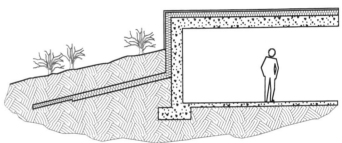

Figure 10.14e In earth-sheltered buildings in cold climates, the earth should be insulated from the cold winter air.

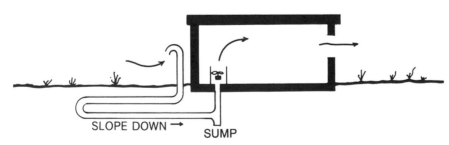

Figure 10.14f Indirect earth cooling is possible by means of tubes buried in the ground. Sloped tubes and a sump are required to catch condensation. An open-loop system is shown, while a closed-loop system would return the air from indoors.

The greatest problem with earth tubes is condensation, which occurs mainly in humid climates where the earth temperature is frequently below the dew point, or saturation temperature, of the air. The tubes, therefore, must be sloped to drain into a sump. The consequences of biological activity (e.g., mold growth) in the moist tubes are unknown at this time, and caution is advised. Condensation is not a big problem in dry climates. Tubes must be absolutely tight to prevent radon gas or water from entering. (Radon is discussed further in Section 16.17.)

Earth tubes have not become popular because of the health risks and high cost.

Factors for Earth Cooling Design

1. The steady-state deep-earth temperature is similar to the mean annual temperature at any location (Fig. 10.14b).
2. Directly coupled earth cooling works well when the steady-state earth temperature is a little below 60°F (15°C). If the earth is much colder, the building must be insulated from the ground.
3. Earth tubes are best in dry climates.
4. In humid climates, the condensation on walls or in earth tubes might cause biological activity, which is a health risk.

10.15 DEHUMIDIFICATION WITH A DESICCANT

In humid regions, dehumidifying the air in summer is very desirable for thermal comfort and control of mildew. Two fundamental ways to remove moisture from the air exist. With the first method, the air is cooled below the dew point temperature. Water will then condense out of the air. Conventional air conditioning and dehumidification use this principle. Some of the passive cooling techniques mentioned above will also dehumidify in the same way. For example, in humid climates, water will often condense in earth tubes.

The second method involves the use of a **desiccant** (drying agent). A number of chemicals, such as silica gel, natural zeolite, activated alumina, and calcium chloride, will absorb large amounts of water vapor from the air. However, there are two serious difficulties with the use of these materials. First, when water vapor is absorbed and turned into liquid water, heat is given off. This is the same heat that was required to vaporize the water in the first place (heat of vaporization). Thus, if a desiccant is placed in a room, it will heat the air as it de-humidifies it (i.e., the desiccant converts latent heat into sensible heat). Thermal comfort will, therefore, require another cooling stage to lower the temperature of the air.

The second problem with the use of a desiccant is that the material soon becomes saturated with water and stops dehumidifying. The desiccant must then be **regenerated** by boiling off the water. Although desiccant dehumidification works in theory, no one has been able to build an inexpensive system due to its inherent complexity.

10.16 CONCLUSION

Passive cooling strategies have the greatest potential in hot and dry climates. Just about every cooling technique will work there. On the other hand, in *very* humid regions only comfort ventilation will be very helpful. However, many regions that are considered hot and humid are humid for only part of the overheated period. There are often many months that are hot but not humid. In such regions, night-flush cooling and night-radiation cooling can be beneficial. Most of the eastern United States has this moderately humid climate, where passive cooling can replace or reduce the need for air conditioning much of the summer. However, in every climate, the first and best strategy for summer comfort is heat avoidance.

KEY IDEAS OF CHAPTER 10

1. Make full use of **heat avoidance** before applying any passive cooling strategies.
2. **Comfort ventilation** is used day and night to cool people and to keep the indoor temperature close to the outdoor temperature. This type of ventilation is used mainly in very humid climates and in temperate climates when the humidity is high.
3. **Night-flush cooling** uses night ventilation to cool the mass of the building. During the day, the windows are closed, and the mass acts as a heat sink. This passive cooling strategy is used in both dry climates and temperate climates whenever the humidity is low.
4. Air flows from positive- to negative-pressure areas.
5. There is a positive pressure on the windward side, and a negative pressure on both the leeward side and the sides of the building parallel to the wind.
6. Hot air can be exhausted from the top of a building by stratification, the stack effect, the shape of the roof (the venturi effect), and the increased wind velocity found at higher elevations (the Bernoulli effect).
7. Use cross-ventilation whenever possible.
8. Have air flow across people for comfort ventilation and across the building mass for night-flush cooling.
9. **Radiant cooling** from the roof works well in climates in which the humidity is low and clouds are few.
10. Use **direct evaporative cooling** in dry climates.
11. Use **indirect evaporative cooling** in slightly humid climates.
12. Use **earth cooling** mainly in the North and West. Condensation can be a problem in the humid Southeast.

Resources

FURTHER READING

(See Bibliography in back of book for full citations.)

Abrams, D. W. *Low-Energy Cooling.*
Akbari, H., et al. *Cooling Our Communities: A Guidebook on Tree Planting and Light-Colored Surfacing.*
Allard, F., ed. *Natural Ventilation in Buildings.*
Baird, G. *The Architectural Expression of Environmental Control Systems.*
Boutet, T.S. *Controlling Air Movement: A Manual for Architects and Builders.*
Brown, G. Z., and M. DeKay. *Sun, Wind, and Light: Architectural Design Strategies,* 2nd ed.
Cook, J. "Cooling as the Absence of Heat."
Cook, J., ed. *Passive Cooling.*
Daniels, K. *The Technology of Ecological Building: Basic Principles and Measures, Examples and Ideas.*
Environmental Protection Agency. "Cooling Our Communities."
Givoni, B. *Climate Considerations in Building and Urban Design.*
Givoni, B. *Man, Climate and Architecture.*
Givoni, B. *Passive and Low Energy Cooling of Buildings.*
Golany, G. *Housing in Arid Lands— Design and Planning.*

Konya, A. *Design Primer for Hot Climates.*

Kwok, Alison G., and Walter T. Grondzik. *The Green Studio Handbook: Environmental Strategies for Schematic Design.*

Olgyay, V. *Design with Climate.*

Santamouris, M., and D. Asimakopoulos, eds. *Passive Cooling of Buildings.*

Solar Energy Research Inst. *Cooling with Ventilation.*

Stein, B., J. S. Reynolds, W. T. Grondzik, and A. G. Kwok. *Mechanical and Electrical Equipment for Buildings,* 10th ed.

Underground Space Ctr. Unv. Minn. *Earth Sheltered Housing Design: Guidelines, Examples, and References.*

Watson, D., and K. Labs. *Climatic Design: Energy Efficient Building Principles and Practices.*

REFERENCE

Schubert, R. P., and P. Hahn. From *Progress in Passive Solar Energy* by American Solar Energy Society, Boulder, CO, 1983.

11

SITE DESIGN, COMMUNITY PLANNING, AND LANDSCAPING

Study nature, love nature, stay close to nature, it will never fail you.

Frank Lloyd Wright,

The sun is fundamental to all life. It is the source of our vision, our warmth, our energy, and the rhythm of our lives. Its movements inform our perceptions of time and space and our scale in the universe. . . . Assured access to the sun is thus important to the quality of our lives.

Ralph L. Knowles,
Sun Rhythm Form

295

11.1 INTRODUCTION

The heating, cooling, and lighting of a building are very much affected by the site and community in which the building is located. Although many aspects of a site have an impact on a building, only those that affect solar access and wind penetration will be discussed here. All of the strategies discussed fall under tiers one and two of the three-tier design approach (Fig. 11.1a).

The ancient Greeks realized the importance of site and community planning for the heating and cooling of buildings. Since they wanted their buildings to face the winter sun and reject the summer sun, their new towns were built on southern slopes and the streets ran east–west whenever possible. The ancient Greek city of Olynthus was planned so that most buildings could front on east–west streets (Fig. 11.1b). See Fig. 2.16 to understand how the buildings were designed to take advantage of this street layout. The ancient Greeks considered their solar design of buildings and cities to be modern and civilized.

The Romans were also convinced of the value of solar heating, so much so that they protected solar access by law. The great Justinian Code of the sixth century states that sunshine may not be blocked from reaching a helio-caminus (sunroom).

While winter heating was critical to the ancient Greeks and Romans, summer shade was also very desirable.

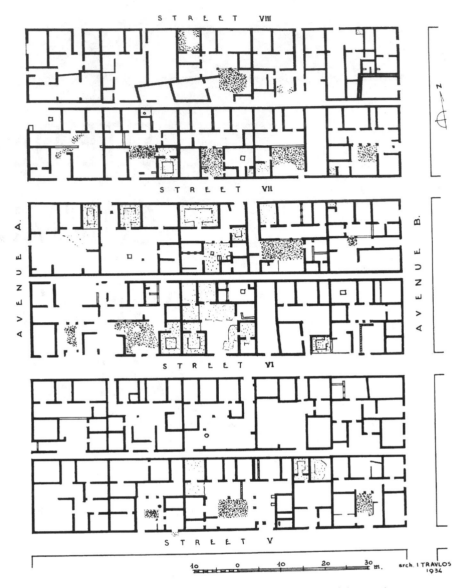

Figure 11.1b The ancient Greek city of Olynthus was oriented toward the sun. (From *Excavations at Olynthus. Part 8, The Hellenic House* © Johns Hopkins University Press, 1938.)

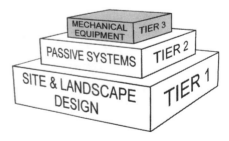

Figure 11.1a The heating, cooling, and lighting needs of a building are best and most sustainably achieved by the three-tier design approach, and this chapter covers tiers one and two.

By building continuous rows of homes along east–west streets, only the end units would be exposed to the low morning and afternoon summer sun.

In climates with very hot summers and mild winters, shade is more desirable than solar access. Often multistory buildings are built on narrow streets to create shade both for the street and for the buildings (Fig. 11.1c). When buildings are not tall enough to cast much shade, pedestrian streets can have their own shading system (Fig. 11.1d). And when protection from rain as well as sun is desirable, arcades and colonnades are frequently used (Fig. 11.1e).

Wind is also an important factor in vernacular design. When there is too much wind and the temperature is cool, windbreaks are common, and windbreaks of dense vegetation are most common (Fig. 11.1f). On the other hand, when the climate is warm and humid, cross-ventilation is very desirable. Many native communities maximize the benefit of natural ventilation by building far apart and by eliminating low vegetation that would block the cooling breezes (Fig. 11.1g).

Figure 11.1c Multistory buildings facing narrow streets create desirable shade in very hot climates, as here in Jidda, Saudi Arabia. (Photograph by Richard Millman.)

Figure 11.1d The shading structure over this Moroccan street blocks much of the sun but still allows air and daylight to filter through. (Courtesy of Moroccan National Tourist Office.)

Figure 11.1e This colonnade in Santa Fe, New Mexico, protects pedestrians from rain as well as sun, and it shades the windows and walls.

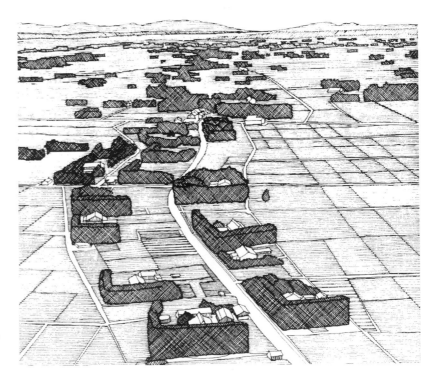

Figure 11.1f Farms in the Shimane Prefecture of Japan use L-shaped windbreaks for protection from the cold wind. (From *Sun, Wind, and Light: Architectural Design Strategies* by G. Z. Brown, © John Wiley, 1985.)

Figure 11.1g In hot and humid climates, such as that of Tocamacho, Honduras, buildings are set far apart to maximize the cooling breezes. (From *Sun, Wind, and Light: Architectural Design Strategies* by G. Z. Brown, © John Wiley, 1985.)

11.2 SITE SELECTION

When the United States was first settled and land was still plentiful, farms were built almost exclusively on south slopes. It was well known that a south slope is warmer and has the longest growing season. When a choice of sites is available, a south slope is still the best for most building types.

In the winter, the south slope is warmest for two reasons. It receives the most solar energy on each square foot of land because it most directly faces the winter sun (Fig. 11.2a). This phenomenon, called the "cosine law," was discussed in depth in Chapter 6. The south slope also experiences the least shading because objects cast their shortest shadows on south slopes (Fig. 11.2b).

Figure 11.2c illustrates the variation in microclimate with different slope orientations. The south slope gets the most sun and is the warmest in the winter, while the west slope is the hottest in the summer. The north slope is the shadiest and coldest, while the hilltop is the windiest

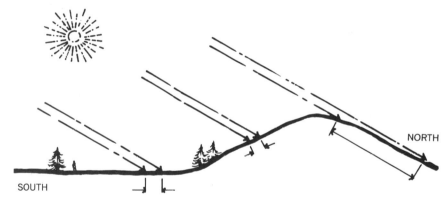

Figure 11.2a In winter, south-sloping land receives the most sunshine because of the cosine law. For the same reason, north-facing slopes receive very little solar heating because a given sunbeam is spread over much more land.

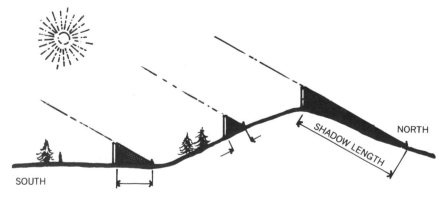

Figure 11.2b South-sloping land also experiences the least shade.

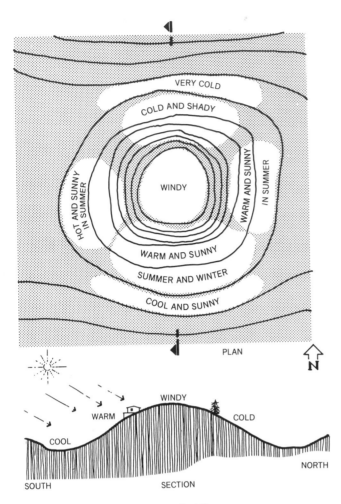

Figure 11.2c Microclimates around a hill.

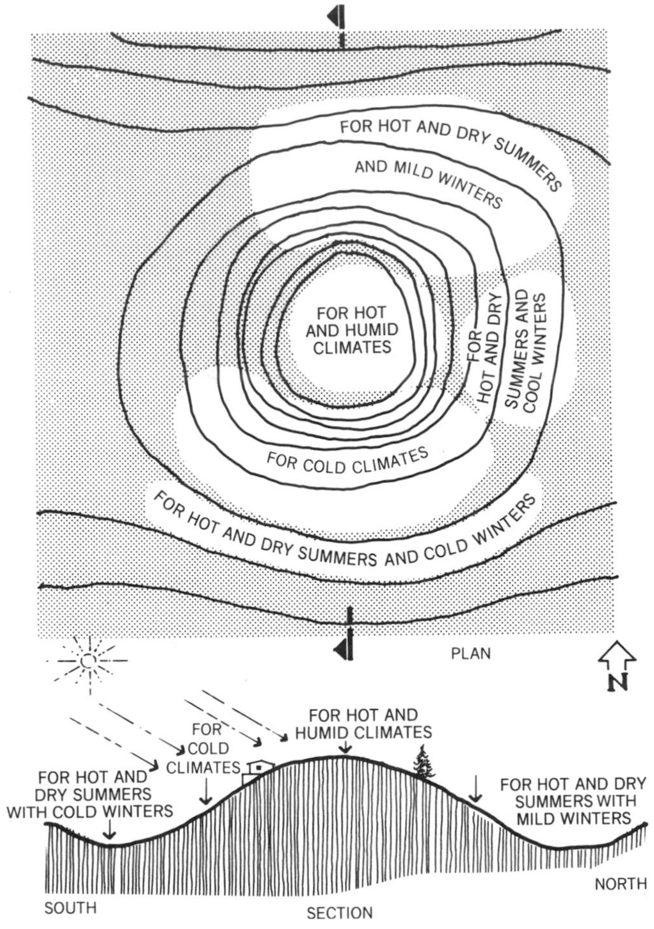

Figure 11.2d Preferred building sites around a hill in response to climate for envelope-dominated buildings.

location. Low areas tend to be cooler than slopes because cold air drains into them and collects there.

The best site for a building on hilly land depends on both climate and building type. For envelope-dominated buildings, such as residences and small office buildings, the climate would suggest the sites shown in Fig. 11.2d.

For example, in

Cold climates: South slopes maximize solar collection and are shielded from cold northern winds. Avoid the windy hilltops and low-lying areas that collect pools of cold air.

Hot and dry climates: Build in low-lying areas that collect cool air. If winters are very cold, build on the bottom of the south slope. If winters are mild, build on the

north or east slope, but in all cases avoid the west slope.

Hot and humid climates: Maximize natural ventilation by building on hilltops but avoid the west side of hilltops because of the hot afternoon sun.

For internally dominated buildings, such as large office buildings that require little if any solar heating, the north and northeast slopes are best. Also appropriate are the cool, low-lying areas especially to the north of hills.

11.3 SOLAR ACCESS

Nothing is as certain and consistent as the sun's motion across the sky. It is, therefore, possible to design for solar access with great accuracy, barring the possibility that future construction on neighboring property will block the

sun. If neighbors are sufficiently far-away or if restrictions exist on what can be built next door, solar access can be assured.

Although laws protecting solar access are rare, they do exist in the United States and they have existed for centuries in England. These legal aspects of solar access will be considered later. A discussion of the physical principles of solar access must come first.

In Chapter 6, the sun's motion was explained by means of a sky dome.

That part of the sky dome through which *useful* solar energy passes was called the **solar window** (Fig. 6.8b). The bottom of this solar window is defined by the sun path of the winter solstice (December 21). The sides of the window are usually set at 9 A.M. and 3 P.M. The window thus includes the time period during which more than 80 percent of the winter solar

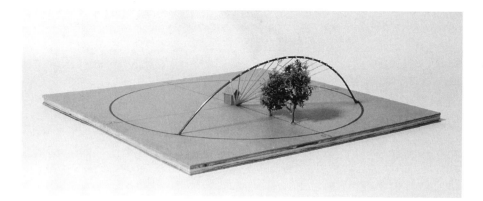

Figure 11.3a The solar-access boundary is a conical surface generated by sunrays on December 21 from 9 A.M. to 3 P.M. Any trees or buildings projecting through this surface will obstruct solar access to the site.

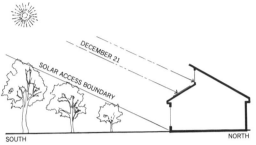

Figure 11.3b The solar-access boundary determines how high objects can be before they obstruct the sun.

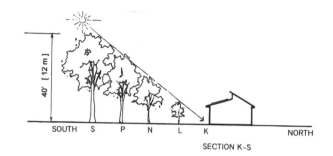

SECTION K–S

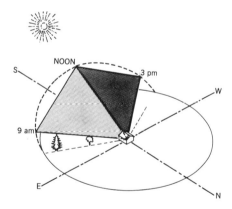

Figure 11.3c To simplify construction of the solar-access boundary, two inclined planes replace the conical surface.

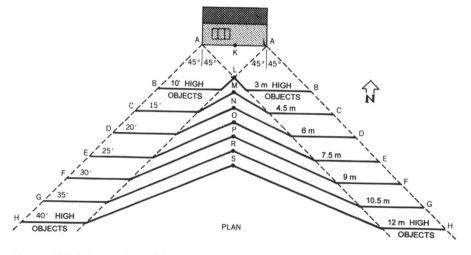

PLAN

Figure 11.3d Contour lines of the solar-access boundary. The lines define the maximum height objects can reach without blocking the sun. The horizontal distances are a function of latitude.

radiation is available. Of course, if sunlight is available before 9 A.M. or after 3 P.M., it should be used.

The conical surface generated by the sun's rays on the winter solstice from 9 A.M. to 3 P.M. is called the **solar-access boundary**. Any object that projects through this surface will obstruct the winter sun (Fig. 11.3a). A north–south section through this solar-access boundary is shown in Fig. 11.3b.

Because the conical surface of the solar-access boundary is difficult to deal with, a simplified surface is often used instead (Fig. 11.3c). In plan, this simplified surface can be defined by contour lines, which not only define the elevation of the solar-access boundary but at the same time define the maximum height an object can have without penetrating the boundary and obstructing the sun. The solar

contour lines for a simple rectangular building are given in Fig. 11.3d. Since the slope of the boundary is a function of latitude, use Tables 11.3A and B to determine the location of the contour lines for the latitude in question. Use Table 11.3A for due south, and use Table 11.3B for 45° from due south.

To draw a section of the solar-access boundary, use Tables 11.3A and B,

Table 11.3A Distances to the Solar-access Boundary due South of a Building in Feet (meters)

Lat.	Alt. at Noon	Distances in Feet (Meters)*						
		KL	KM	KN	KO	KP	KR	KS
0	67		6 (1.8)	8 (2.4)	11 (3.3)	13 (3.9)	15 (4.5)	17 (5.1)
4	63	5 (1.5)	8 (2.4)	10 (3)	13 (3.9)	15 (4.5)	18 (5.4)	20 (6)
8	59	6 (1.8)	9 (2.7)	12 (3.6)	15 (4.5)	18 (5.4)	21 (6.3)	24 (7.2)
12	55	7 (2.1)	11 (3.3)	14 (4.2)	18 (5.4)	21 (6.3)	25 (7.5)	28 (8.4)
16	51	8 (2.4)	12 (3.6)	16 (4.8)	20 (6)	24 (7.2)	28 (8.4)	32 (9.6)
20	47	9 (2.7)	14 (4.2)	19 (5.7)	23 (6.9)	28 (8.4)	33 (9.9)	37 (11)
24	43	11 (3.3)	16 (4.8)	21 (6.3)	27 (8.1)	32 (9.6)	38 (11)	43 (13)
28	39	12 (3.6)	19 (5.7)	25 (7.5)	31 (9.3)	37 (11)	43 (13)	49 (15)
32	35	14 (4.2)	21 (6.3)	29 (8.7)	36 (11)	43 (13)	50 (15)	57 (17.)
36	31	17 (5.1)	25 (7.5)	33 (9.9)	42 (13)	50 (15)	58 (17)	67 (20)
40	27	20 (6)	29 (8.7)	39 (12)	49 (15)	59 (18)	69 (21)	79 (24)
44	23	24 (7.2)	35 (11)	47 (14)	59 (18)	71 (21)	82 (25)	94 (28)
48	19	29 (8.7)	44 (13)	58 (17)	73 (22)	87 (26)	102 (31)	116 (35)
52	15	37 (11)	56 (17)	75 (23)	93 (28)	112 (34)	131 (39)	149 (45)
56	11	51 (15)	77 (23)	103 (31)	129 (39)	154 (46)	180 (54)	206 (62)

*See Fig 11.3d for a definition of KL, KM, etc.

Table 11.3B Distances to the Solar Access Boundary at 45° Azimuth from South in Feet (meters)

Lat.	Alt. at 45° Azimuth	Distances in Feet (Meters)*						
		AB	AC	AD	AE	AF	AG	AH
0	56	7 (2.1)	10 (3)	13 (3.9)	17 (5.1)	20 (6)	24 (7.2)	27 (8)
4	50	8 (2.4)	13 (3.9)	17 (5.1)	21 (6.3)	25 (7.5)	29 (8.7)	34 (10)
8	45	10 (3)	15 (4.5)	20 (6)	25 (7.5)	30 (9)	35 (11)	40 (12)
12	40	12 (3.6)	18 (5.4)	24 (7.2)	30 (9)	36 (11)	42 (13)	48 (14)
16	35	14 (4.2)	21 (6.3)	29 (8.7)	36 (11)	43 (13)	50 (15)	57 (17)
20	30	17 (5.1)	26 (7.8)	35 (10.5)	43 (12.9)	52 (15.6)	61 (18.3)	69 (20.7)
24	26	21 (6.3)	31 (9.3)	41 (12)	51 (15)	62 (19)	72 (22)	82 (25)
28	23	24 (7.2)	35 (11)	47 (14)	59 (18)	71 (21)	82 (25)	94 (28)
32	18	31 (9.3)	46 (14)	62 (19)	77 (23)	92 (28)	108 (32)	123 (37)
36	15	37 (11)	56 (17)	75 (23)	93 (28)	112 (34)	131 (39)	149 (45)
40	12	47 (14)	71 (21)	94 (28)	118 (35)	141 (42)	165 (50)	188 (56)
44	8	71 (21)	107 (32)	142 (43)	178 (53)	213 (64)	249 (75)	285 (86)
48	6	95 (29)	143 (43)	190 (57)	238 (71)	285 (86)	333 (100)	381 (114)
52	3	191 (57)	286 (86)	382 (115)	477 (143)	572 (172)	668 (200)	763 (229)
56	0							

*See Fig 11.3d for a definition of AB, AC, etc.

which also present the solar altitude angles. Use Table 11.3A when the sun is due south (12 noon), and use Table 11.3B to draw a section at 45° to south (approximately 9 A.M. and 3 P.M.).

The contour lines shown in Fig. 11.3d are for a building on level ground. Any rise or fall of the land will have a positive or negative effect on how high objects can be before they block the winter sun. To account for the effect of sloping land, superimpose the contour lines for the solar-access boundary and the contour lines for the slope of the land as

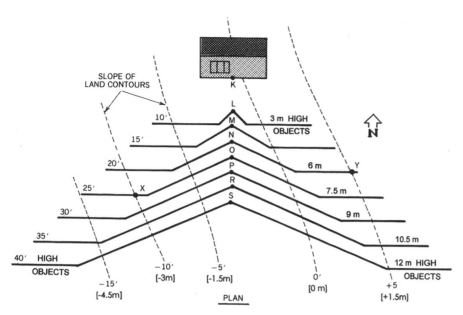

Figure 11.3e Sloping land will affect how high objects can be before they block the winter sun.

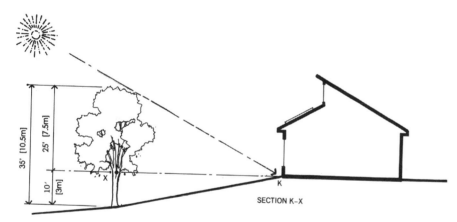

Figure 11.3f Down-sloping land increases the height objects can reach before they block the sun.

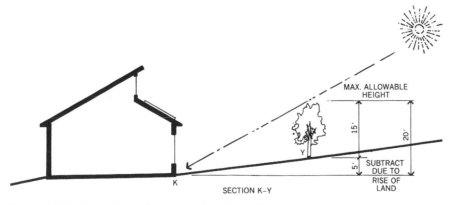

Figure 11.3g Up-sloping land decreases the height objects can reach before they block the sun.

in Fig. 11.3e. Where the land is lower than the building, add the drop in elevation to the height of the solar-access boundary. For example, at point X, an object can be 35 ft (10.5 m) high without blocking the sun because the total height from grade level to the solar-access boundary has increased (Fig. 11.3f). However, at point Y, an object can be only 15 ft (4.5 m) high because the rise of the land has decreased the distance from grade level to the solar-access boundary (Fig. 11.3g).

For passive solar heating through south-facing windows, the solar-access boundary should start from the base of the building, as was discussed above. However, if solar access is required only for the roof or clerestory windows, the solar-access boundary should be raised as shown in Fig. 11.3h.

The solar-access boundary reaches 45° east and west of south even if a building is not facing due south. The distances from Table 11.3A can still be used as before, However, the contour lines will look a little different, as can be seen in Fig. 11.3i.

Some books suggest using deciduous trees on the south side, as shown in Fig. 11.3j, to produce summer shade while still permitting access to the winter sun. Unfortunately, deciduous trees without their leaves still block a significant amount of sunlight. Most deciduous trees block 30 to 60 percent of sunlight (Figs. 11.3k and 11.9c). Also, if the roof has collectors for domestic hot water, pool heating, or PV, it should *not* be shaded in the summer. Thus, on the south side of buildings, trees should usually be kept below the solar-access boundary (Fig. 11.3b).

If large trees already exist on the south side of a building in very hot climates with mild winters, it may not be appropriate to cut them down to improve the solar access. The summer shade from mature trees might be more valuable than the winter sun (Fig. 11.3l). However, in most climates, the energy from the sun is too valuable to not use. Every square

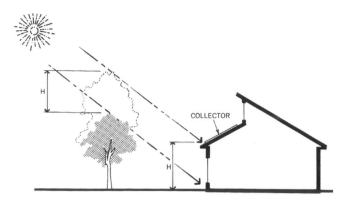

Figure 11.3h If solar access is required only for the roof, raise the solar-access boundary by the height of the roof.

foot (meter) of the south facade and south-facing roof should be used to collect daylight, PV electricity, and hot water all year long and passive solar in the winter.

For additional information about solar-access boundaries, see Chapter 7 of *Energy Conserving Site Design* by McPherson. Since the above-mentioned graphic method can become very complicated except in the simplest situations, the author highly recommends the use of physical models in conjunction with a heliodon, which will be described in Section 11.7.

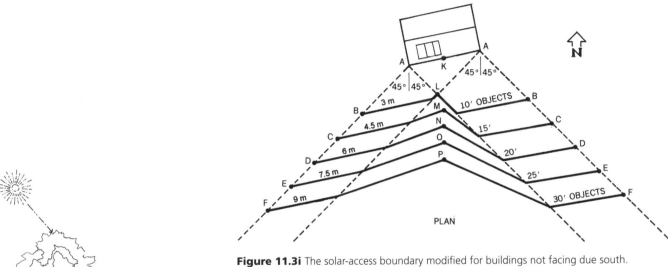

Figure 11.3i The solar-access boundary modified for buildings not facing due south.

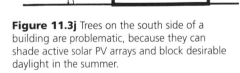

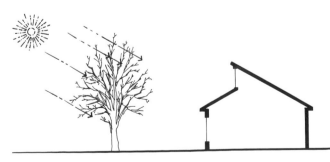

Figure 11.3j Trees on the south side of a building are problematic, because they can shade active solar PV arrays and block desirable daylight in the summer.

Figure 11.3k Even without leaves, deciduous trees still block 30 to 60 percent of sunshine.

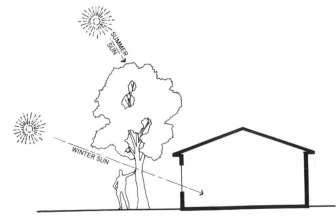

Figure 11.3l If large trees exist on the south side in hot climates, trim the lower branches to form a high canopy.

11.4 SHADOW PATTERNS

When designing only one building on a site, solar access is best achieved by working with the solar-access boundary. When designing a complex of buildings or a whole development, **shadow patterns** are more useful for achieving solar access to all of the buildings. By drawing the shadow pattern for each building and tree, it is possible to quickly determine conflicts in solar access (Fig. 11.4a). The main difficulty with this technique is the generation of accurate shadow patterns.

A shadow pattern is a composite of all shadows cast during winter hours when access to the sun is most valuable. It is generally agreed that solar access should be maintained, if possible, from about 9 A.M. to 3 P.M. during the winter months. During those six hours, more than 80 percent of a winter's total daily solar radiation will fall on a building.

The easiest way to understand shadow patterns is by examining the shadows cast by a vertical pole. Figure 11.4b illustrates the shadows cast by a pole on December 21. The same pole is shown in plan in Fig. 11.4c with the shadows cast at each hour between 9 A.M. and 3 P.M. at 36° N latitude. The shaded area represents the land where solar access is blocked by the pole at some time during these hours and is called the "shadow pattern" of the pole. Of course, the taller the pole, the longer the shadow pattern. In addition, the shadow pattern will be longer at higher latitudes and shorter at lower latitudes.

To make the construction of shadow patterns easier, we can determine the shadow lengths only for the hours of 9 A.M., 12 noon, and 3 P.M. and then connect them with straight lines (Fig. 11.4d). The construction of a shadow pattern is further simplified by drawing the ends of the shadow pattern at 45°, which corresponds closely with 9 A.M. and 3 P.M. (actual azimuth at these times varies with latitude). The length of the shadow is determined by drawing a section through the pole at

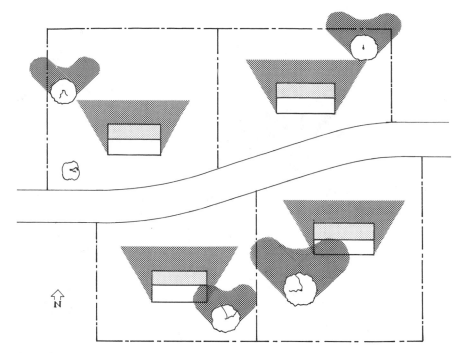

Figure 11.4a Shadow patterns demonstrate conflicts in solar access. Notice that the trees shade the lower two buildings during the winter.

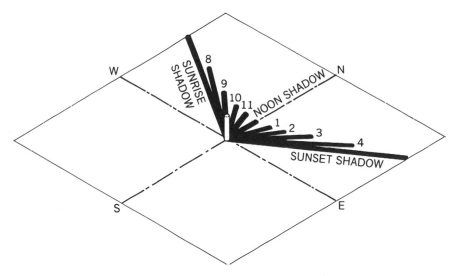

Figure 11.4b Shadows cast by a vertical pole from sunrise to sunset on December 21 (shadows vary with latitude).

12 noon and 9 A.M./3 P.M. (45° azimuth) (Fig. 11.4e). Use Tables 11.3A and B for the altitude angles of the sun at those times.

To construct the shadow pattern for a building, we assume that the building consists of a series of poles (Fig. 11.4f). The morning, noon, and

afternoon shadows are then constructed from these poles (Fig. 11.4g). The composite of these shadows creates the shadow pattern (Fig. 11.4h). Additional poles would be required for more complex buildings.

The shading pattern, like the solar-access boundary, is affected

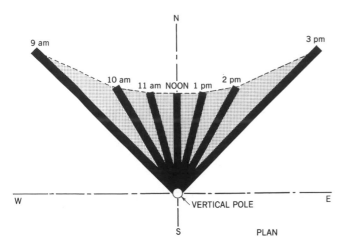

Figure 11.4c Plan view of shadows cast by a pole at 36° N latitude on December 21.

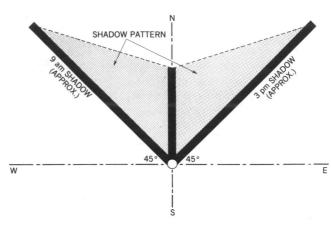

Figure 11.4d Simplified shadow pattern of a pole on December 21.

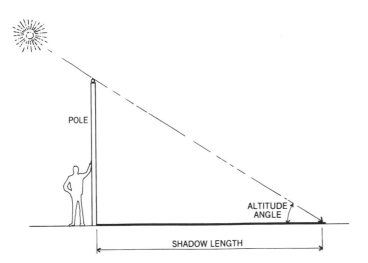

Figure 11.4e Determination of shadow length.

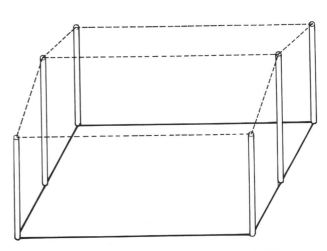

Figure 11.4f To generate the shadow pattern of a building, assume that the building consists of a series of poles.

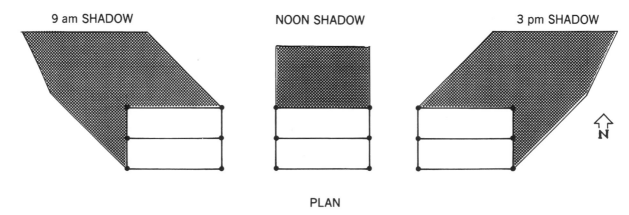

PLAN

Figure 11.4g The morning, noon, and afternoon shadows on December 21 are constructed by assuming six poles. (After *Solar Energy Planning* by P. Tabb, 1984.)

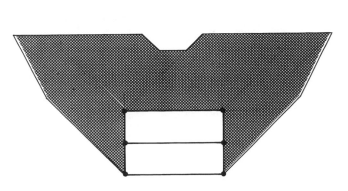

Figure 11.4h The shadow pattern is the composite of the morning, noon, and afternoon shadows. (After *Solar Energy Planning* by P. Tabb, 1984.)

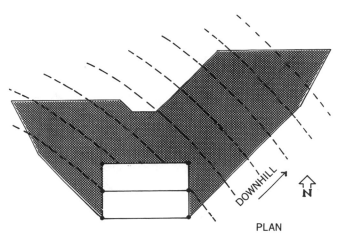

Figure 11.4i Sloping land changes the length of the shadow pattern. (After *Solar Energy Planning* by P. Tabb, 1984.)

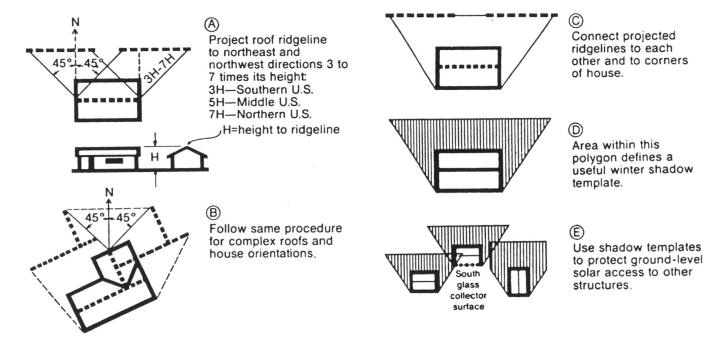

Ⓐ Project roof ridgeline to northeast and northwest directions 3 to 7 times its height
3H—Southern U.S.
5H—Middle U.S.
7H—Northern U.S.
H=height to ridgeline

Ⓑ Follow same procedure for complex roofs and house orientations.

Ⓒ Connect projected ridgelines to each other and to corners of house.

Ⓓ Area within this polygon defines a useful winter shadow template.

Ⓔ Use shadow templates to protect ground-level solar access to other structures.

Figure 11.4j Quick method for constructing shadow patterns (templates). (Reprinted with permission from *Energy Conserving Site Design* by E. Gregory McPherson, © 1984, The American Society of Landscape Architects.)

by the slope of the land (Fig. 11.4i). Also, just because the footprint of a building is shaded, it cannot be assumed that the roof is also shaded. Because of the limitations and complexity of this graphic method, it is often easier to use physical models for generating accurate shadow patterns and for determining how a building is actually shaded. The use of physical models for this purpose will be explained below.

However, there is a quick graphic method for creating approximate shadow patterns for simple buildings on flat land. Figure 11.4j illustrates this quick method for a gabled house, while Fig. 11.4k illustrates the quick method for creating shadow patterns for trees.

It is important to remember that some solar access is better than none. Even if solar access cannot be provided from 9 A.M. to 3 P.M., assured access from 10 A.M. to 2 P.M. would still make available over 60 percent of the total daily solar radiation in the winter.

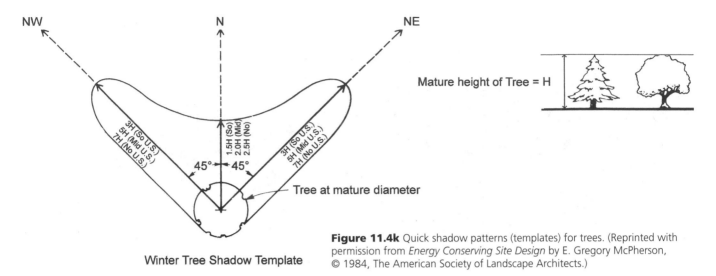

Winter Tree Shadow Template

Figure 11.4k Quick shadow patterns (templates) for trees. (Reprinted with permission from *Energy Conserving Site Design* by E. Gregory McPherson, © 1984, The American Society of Landscape Architects.)

11.5 SITE PLANNING

Access to winter sun and avoidance of summer sun are greatly affected by building orientation. Because it is common in suburban areas for buildings, and especially homes, to present their long facade to the street, building orientation is determined largely by road design.

Fortunately, there is a road orientation that is ideal for both winter-heating and summer-cooling needs. Streets that run east–west not only maximize winter solar access from the south but also maximize shade from the low morning and afternoon summer sun (Fig. 11.5a). On the other hand, with north–south streets there is little if any winter solar access, and the large east and west facades are exposed to the summer sun (Fig. 11.5b).

It is usually possible to design new developments to maximize the lots fronting on east–west streets. A good example of this, the Village Homes subdivisions in Davis, California, is described at the end of the chapter (Figs. 11.13b and c). The performance of buildings on north–south streets can be improved significantly by a number of different methods. Orienting the short facade to the street is the most obvious technique (Fig. 11.5c). The use of **flag lots**, interior lots with only driveway access to the street, is less common but is a

very effective technique for achieving a good orientation for each building, as well as a quiet off-the-street location for some buildings (Fig. 11.5d). The increasing popularity of duplexes makes the technique shown in Fig. 11.5e very promising.

Good orientation can also be achieved on diagonal streets if the buildings are rotated to face south. Although the practice of orienting facades parallel to streets is a widely held convention, it is almost never required by codes. There are a number of benefits in the alternate arrangement shown in Fig. 11.5f. Besides the better solar orientations, this arrangement yields much greater privacy since windows do not face each other. There are also aesthetic possibilities in this nonconventional design (Fig. 11.5g).

Although lots facing east–west streets have the greatest potential for good solar access and shading, these benefits are not guaranteed.

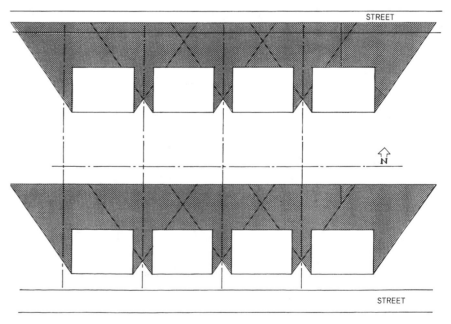

Figure 11.5a East–west streets are ideal for both winter solar access from the south and summer shading from the low east and west sun.

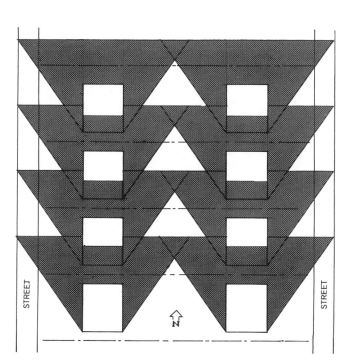

Figure 11.5b With conventional development, north–south streets promote neither solar access in winter nor shading on east or west facades in summer. Note how the buildings shade each other in the winter.

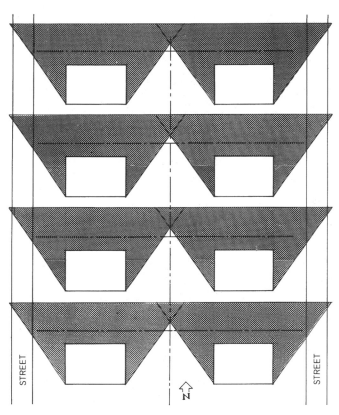

Figure 11.5c Buildings on north–south streets should have their narrow facade face the street.

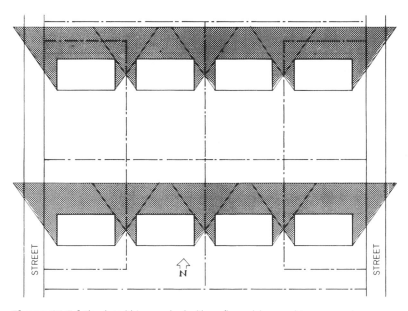

Figure 11.5d Flag lots (driveway looks like a flagpole) can achieve a good orientation for each building on a north–south street.

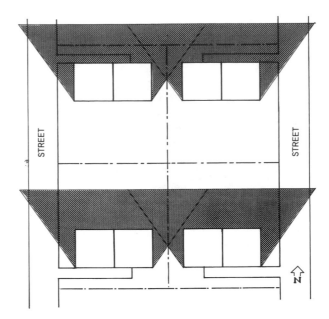

Figure 11.5e Duplexes can achieve good solar access even on a north–south street with this arrangement.

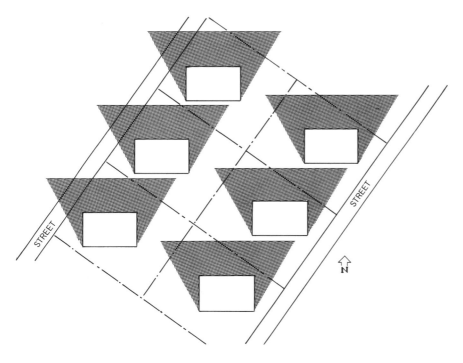

Figure 11.5f Even on diagonal streets, buildings can be oriented toward the south.

For example, uneven setbacks can significantly reduce both winter sun and summer shading (Figs. 11.5h and i). Also, for buildings two or more stories high, the north–south separation between buildings becomes critical. Deep lots are better than shallow lots on east–west streets (Fig. 11.5j). However, when depth of lots is not sufficient, the designer must adjust setback requirements to benefit solar access.

Adjust the size, shape, and location of buildings to maximize solar access. Since streets are in most cases fairly wide, it is usually best to have the higher buildings and trees on the south side of east–west streets (Fig. 11.5k). If sufficient spacing is not possible, collect the sun at the roof level with south-facing clerestory windows and rooftop collectors (Fig. 11.5l).

The foregoing discussion on solar access focused on the most challenging

demand: passive solar space heating in winter. Solar access for domestic hot water and PV can be easier to achieve because much of the solar collection occurs during the higher sun angles of spring and summer. Access for daylighting is also less demanding because of the year-round use of the sun and because both diffuse-sky radiation and reflected sunlight are useful. Thus, daylighting can be achieved with considerably less solar access than was

Figure 11.5g This site design shows a prototypical subdivision for solar access. It illustrates that although east–west streets are best, other street orientations and cul-de-sacs are still workable. (Courtesy Prof. Michael Underhill, Arizona State University.)

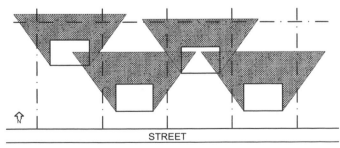

Figure 11.5h Uneven setbacks cause both winter and summer problems.

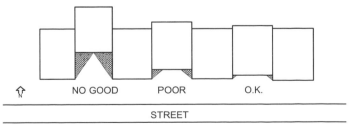

Figure 11.5i Very small setbacks, like those sometimes used in row housing, can be acceptable.

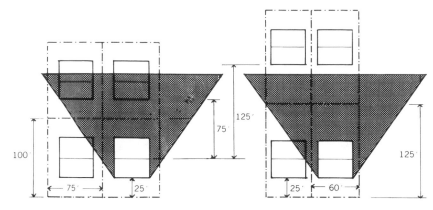

Figure 11.5j On east–west streets, deep lots are better than wide lots for solar access.

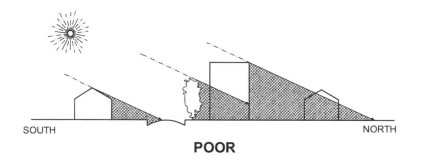

POOR

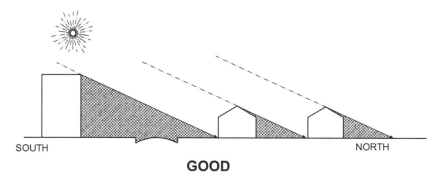

GOOD

Figure 11.5k Place taller buildings and trees on the south side of east–west streets to take advantage of the wide right of way of the streets.

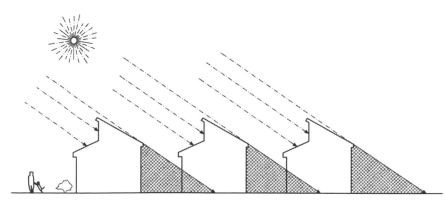

Figure 11.5l When solar access is not possible for the whole building, clerestories and active roof collectors should be used.

described here for space heating. See Chapter 13 for guidelines on daylighting design.

11.6 SOLAR ZONING

As the above discussion shows, solar access is very much dependent on what occurs on neighboring properties in all but the largest sites. Thus, solar-access laws are very important. However, since the United States does not have a doctrine of "ancient light" like that of England and since there is no constitutional right to solar access, state and local laws must be passed to ensure solar access. Although a few states, such as California and New Mexico, have passed solar-rights acts, most protection comes from zoning codes. Because of the many variables involved, this type of zoning must be very local in nature. Climate, latitude, terrain, population density, and local tradition all play an important part.

The amount of solar access to be achieved is another variable in the creation of zoning laws. If only the roofs of buildings require solar access, zoning will be least restrictive and easiest to achieve (Fig. 11.6a). Although south-wall access for passive solar is more difficult to achieve, it should be provided if possible. Providing south-lot access is less critical than it might seem because the sun is normally required there only in the spring and fall when the sun is higher in the sky. At least in northern climates, outdoor spaces are usually too cold in winter even if sunlight were available.

"Solar zoning" controls the shadows cast by a building on neighboring properties by defining the buildable volume on a site. Conventional zoning usually defines a rectangular solid (Fig. 11.6b), while solar zoning defines a sloped volume. Zoning can define this sloped buildable volume in several ways. In the **bulk-plane method,** a plane slopes up from the north property line (Fig. 11.6c). The **solar-envelope method** is more sophisticated but also more complicated (Fig. 11.6d). Professor Ralph Knowles

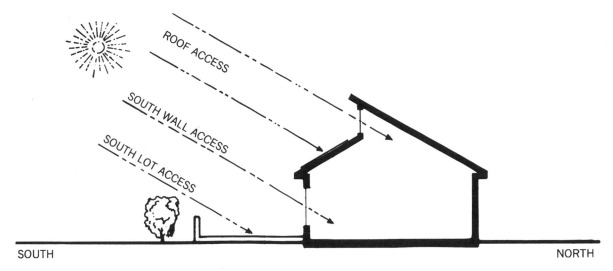

Figure 11.6a The three levels of solar access.

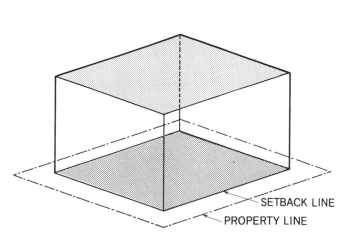

Figure 11.6b Conventional zoning.

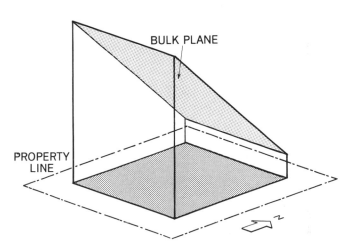

Figure 11.6c Bulk-plane zoning.

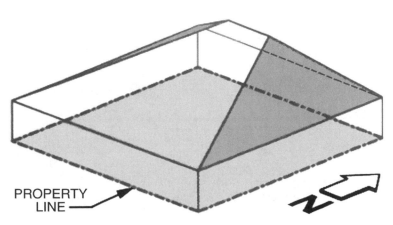

Figure 11.6d Solar-envelope zoning.

at the University of Southern California has developed this method in great detail. It has the potential for not only ensuring high-quality solar access, but also generating attractive architecture (Figs. 11.6e and f). The **solar-fence method** is the third solar zoning strategy, and it utilizes an imaginary wall of prescribed height over which no shadow can be cast (Fig. 11.6g).

In addition to zoning, several other possible ways exist to ensure solar access. Legal agreements or contracts can be set up between neighbors. For example, solar easements can be placed on neighboring

Figure 11.6e Example of architectural form encouraged by solar-envelope zoning. The model was created in Ralph Knowles's studio at the University of Southern California. (Photo courtesy Ralph Knowles ©.)

Figure 11.6f This development in downtown Denver, Colorado, demonstrates the kind of architecture that solar-envelope zoning would encourage.

properties. This is most effective in new developments where solar covenants and restrictions can guarantee solar access for all. For further discussion on the legal ways of ensuring solar access, see *Solar Energy Planning* by Phillip Tabb and *Protecting Solar Access for Residential Development*, U.S. Department of Housing and Urban Development.

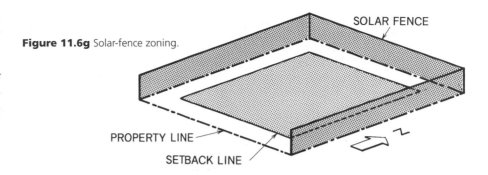

Figure 11.6g Solar-fence zoning.

11.7 PHYSICAL MODELS

As was mentioned several times before, the use of a physical model in conjunction with a heliodon is a very powerful design tool. With a physical model of the site, solar access can be accurately determined no matter how complex the situation is. The shading due to any number of buildings, trees, and the lay of the land is, therefore, easy to analyze for any latitude, time of year, and time of day (Fig. 11.7a).

Physical models can also be used to easily generate shadow patterns no matter how complex the building or site is. The following procedure is illustrated with a building on the side of a hill sloping down to the northeast at 32°N latitude.

Procedure for Creating Shadow Patterns

1. Place the model of the building with the site on the heliodon (see Appendix I for details on how to use the heliodon).
2. Illuminate the model to simulate shadows on December 21 at 9 A.M. (Fig. 11.7b).
3. Outline the shadows. (If drawing the shadow pattern directly on the model is not desirable, then first tape down a sheet of paper.)
4. Repeat steps 2 and 3 for 12 noon (Fig. 11.7c).
5. Repeat steps 2 and 3 again for 3 P.M. (Fig. 11.7d).
6. The composite of the above three shadows is a rough shadow pattern (Fig. 11.7e). A more refined shadow pattern can be obtained by also drawing the shadows for 10 A.M., 11 A.M., 1 A.M., and 2 P.M.

Figure 11.7a Physical modeling is an excellent design tool for providing each site with access to the sun. Note how an east–west street (left to right in the model) promotes solar access, while the north–south street inhibits it.

Figure 11.7b The shadow for December 21 at 9 A.M. is shown.

Figure 11.7c The shadow for December 21 at noon is shown. Note the dashed outline for the 9 A.M. shadow.

Figure 11.7d The shadow for December 21 at 3 P.M. is shown. Note the outlines for both the 9 A.M. and noon shadows.

Figure 11.7e The composite of the three shadows forms the shadow pattern.

11.8 WIND AND SITE DESIGN

Since in most climates the wind is an asset in the summer and a liability in winter, a different wind strategy is required for summer and winter. Fortunately, this is made easier by a significant change in wind direction from summer to winter in many parts of the United States (see the wind roses in Figs. 5.6d–g).

Even if a particular region does not have a strong prevailing wind direction in winter, it is safe to say that the northerly winds will be the colder ones, and it is from these that the primary protection is required. Thus, it seems possible to design a site that diminishes the cooling effect of the northerly winds in the winter while still encouraging the more southerly summer winds. Much easier to design for are those few climates that are either so cold or so hot that only winter or summer winds need to be considered.

The design implications of wind on the building itself are discussed in Chapter 10 (passive cooling) and Chapter 15 (infiltration). In this chapter, the impact of the wind on site design will be investigated.

In winter, the main purpose of blocking the wind is to reduce the heat loss that infiltration causes. Although infiltration is normally responsible for about one-third of the total heat loss in homes, on a windy day on an open site, infiltration can account for more than 50 percent of the total heat loss. Since infiltration is approximately proportional to the square of the wind velocity, a small reduction in wind speed will have a large effect on heat loss. For example, if the wind speed is cut in half, the infiltration heat loss will be only one-fourth as large (Fig. 11.8a).

It is worthwhile to block the winter wind for several other reasons. Heat transmission through the building envelope is also affected by wind speed. The heat loss from door operations is greatly reduced if the entrance is protected from the wind. Finally

outdoor spaces are usable in winter only if they are protected from the cold winds.

Windscreens can effectively reduce the wind velocity by three methods: deflection of air to higher elevations, creation of turbulence, and absorption of energy by frictional drag. Solid windbreaks, such as buildings, tend to use the first two methods the most, while porous windbreaks, such as trees, rely mainly on the third method. Figure 11.8b illustrates the effect of porosity and height on the performance of a windbreak. Since the depth of wind protection is proportional to the height of the windbreak, the horizontal axis of the graph depicts multiples of the height of the windbreak. Notice that the densest windbreak results in the greatest reduction of air velocity but also has the smallest downwind coverage. Thus, dense windbreaks should be used on small lots or whenever the building is close to the windbreak, while medium-dense windbreaks would be better for protection at distances greater than four times the height of the windbreak.

Since windbreaks are never continuous, the end condition must be considered. At gaps or ends of windbreaks, the air velocity is actually

greater than the free wind (Fig. 11.8c). This phenomenon can be an asset in the summer but certainly is not in the winter. The same undesirable situation arises in cities where buildings channel the wind along streets. A similar situation also occurs at passages through buildings, such as dogtrots (Fig. 10.2s). Buildings raised on columns (e.g., Le Corbusier's pilotis) create very windy conditions at grade level and are recommended only for climates without cold winters (Fig. 11.8d). Even without underpasses, high-rise buildings often create such high winds at grade level that entrance doors are prevented from closing. This occurs because much of the wind hitting the facade of the building is deflected downward, as shown in Fig. 11.8e. By the simple addition of a lower extension or large canopy, this downward wind can be deflected before reaching pedestrians at grade level (Fig. 11.8f).

To design a community or even a small development, it would be advantageous to place the higher buildings on the northern end. Not only will this arrangement block some of the cold northern wind, it also will provide better access to the winter sun (Fig. 11.8g).

Windbreaks can also be used to control snow, dust, or sand, which are

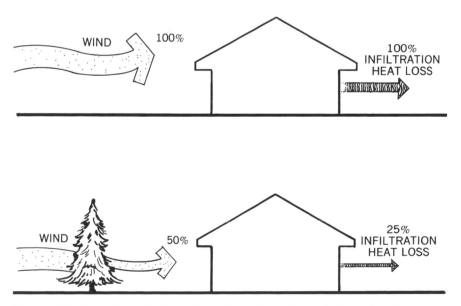

Figure 11.8a A small reduction in wind velocity results in a high reduction in heat loss.

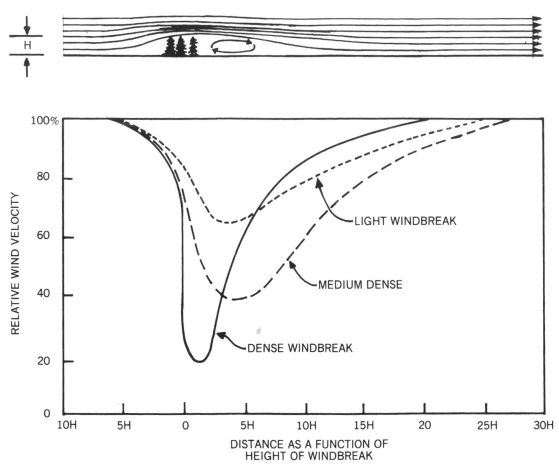

Figure 11.8b Wind protection is a function of both the height of a windbreak and its porosity. [After Naegeli (1946), cited in J. M. Caborn (1957). *Shelterbelts and Microclimate*, Edinburgh, Scotland: H. M. Stationery Office.]

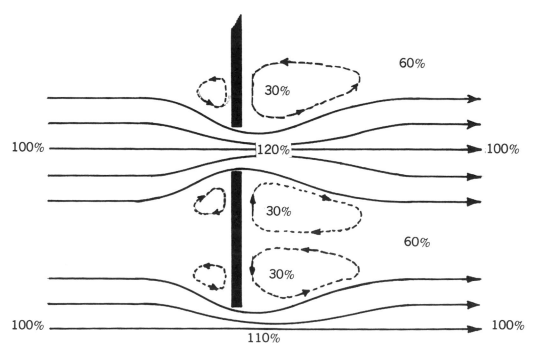

Figure 11.8c In gaps or at ends of windbreaks, the air velocity is actually higher than the free-wind speed.

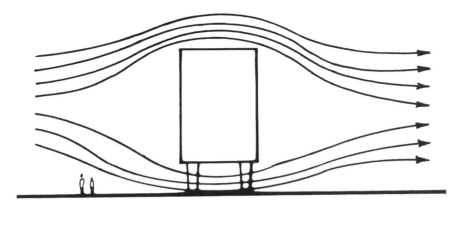

Figure 11.8d Buildings on columns (pilotis) experience very high wind speeds at ground level.

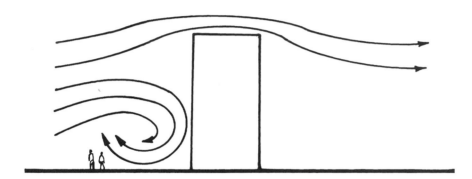

Figure 11.8e Tall buildings often generate severely windy conditions at ground level.

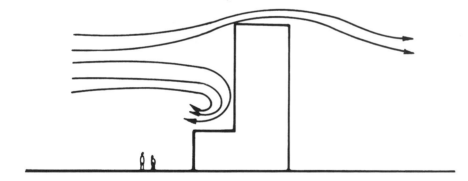

Figure 11.8f A building extension deflects winds away from ground-level areas.

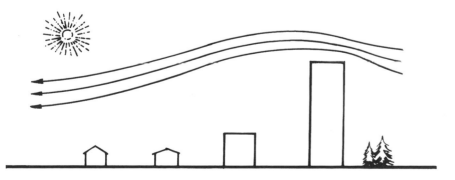

Figure 11.8g Tall buildings placed toward the north not only protect from the cold winter winds but also permit good solar access.

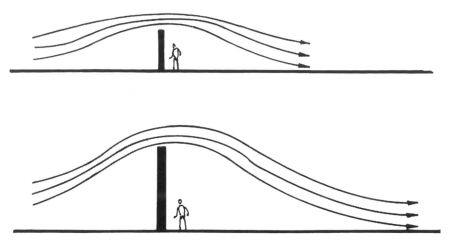

Figure 11.8h The higher the windbreak, the larger the wind shadow.

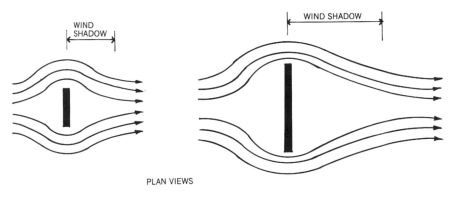

PLAN VIEWS

Figure 11.8i Up to a point, the width of a windbreak also affects the length of a wind shadow. In this plan view, both windbreaks are of the same height.

carried by the wind and will settle out in the "windstill" area behind a windbreak. Thus, snowfences are used in snow country, and garden walls surround buildings in areas prone to dust storms or sandstorms. For lightweight dust, the protective walls need to be as high as the building, but for relatively heavy sand even 6-ft (2 m) walls will reduce the wind velocity enough for the sand particles to settle out.

Guidelines for Windbreak Design

1. The higher the windbreak, the longer will be the wind shadow (Fig. 11.8h).
2. To get full benefit of height, the width of the windbreak should be at least ten times the height (Fig. 11.8i).
3. The porosity of the windbreak determines both the length of the wind shadow and the reduction of wind velocity (Fig. 11.8b).

In summer or in climates with mild winters, breezes are welcome. Instead of being used for windbreaks, trees can be used to funnel more of the wind into the building (Fig. 11.8j). Even if the trees do not create a funnel, they can still increase ventilation by preventing the wind from easily spilling around the sides of the building (Fig. 11.8k). This concept works best

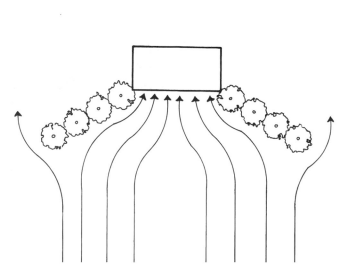

Figure 11.8j Trees and bushes can funnel breezes through buildings.

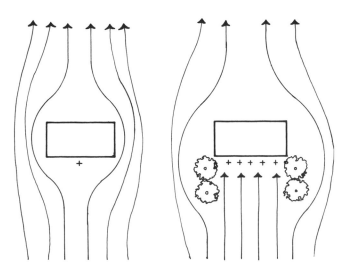

Figure 11.8k By preventing the wind from spilling around the sides of a building, a few trees or bushes can significantly increase natural ventilation.

Figure 11.8l To maximize summer winds, use trees with high canopies.

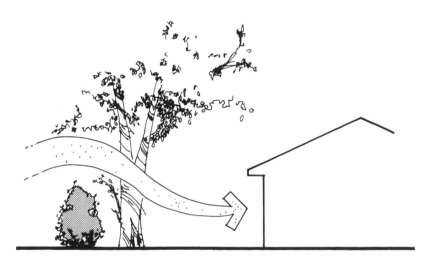

Figure 11.8m To maximize summer ventilation, place bushes away from the building and trees, as shown.

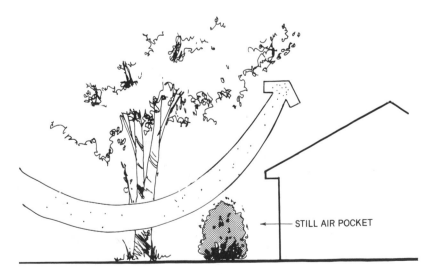

STILL AIR POCKET

Figure 11.8n Placing bushes between the building and trees is good for winter wind protection but not good for summer ventilation.

when the wind comes predominantly from the south because it is then easier to maintain winter solar access and winter wind protection. When there is no dominant summer wind direction, shade trees with a high canopy are desirable (Fig. 11.8l). If bushes are used, they should be placed away from the building, as shown in Fig. 11.8m. If, instead, they are placed between the trees and buildings, the wind will be deflected over the building (Fig. 11.8n). This is the appropriate way to place bushes on the north side for winter wind protection.

By staggering the location of buildings, cooling breezes can be maximized (Fig. 11.8o). Since buildings cannot be moved for the winter, this strategy is appropriate only for hot and humid climates with mild winters. In cold climates where the priority is protection from the cold winter winds, row or cluster housing is most appropriate (Fig. 11.8p).

By placing a pool of water upwind or by building downwind from an existing lake, the air can be cooled by evaporation before entering a building. This strategy works best is hot and dry climates but can also be used in moderately humid areas. However, it is definitely counterproductive in very humid areas, where additional humidity is to be avoided. Pools and fountains were popular among the Romans in part for their cooling benefits (Figs. 11.8q and r). Frank Lloyd

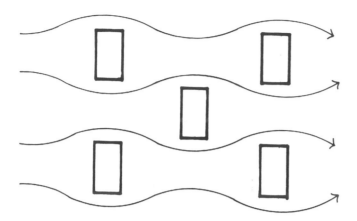

Figure 11.8o In hot and humid climates, buildings should be staggered to promote natural ventilation.

Figure 11.8p Use row or cluster housing for protection against wind in cold climates.

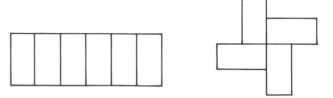

Figure 11.8q Large pools of water frequently helped cool Roman villas. The Getty Museum in California is a careful replica of a Roman villa. (Courtesy of the John Paul Getty Museum, Malibu, California. Julius Schulman, photographer.)

Figure 11.8r This dining terrace in the House of Loreio Tiburtino in Pompeii, Italy, is cooled by an indoor canal. A grapevine-covered pergola provides shade. The terrace is oriented to the south for winter heating. (Courtesy Richard Kenworthy, photographer.)

Wright also recognized the advantages of fountains in hot and dry climates. At Taliesin West, he used several pools and fountains, at least in part, to cool the desert air (Fig. 11.8s).

11.9 PLANTS AND VEGETATION

Plants are immensely useful in the heating, cooling, and lighting of buildings. Although plants are very popular, they are usually used for their aesthetic and psychological benefits. The famous biologist E. O. Wilson holds the theory that people experience **biophilia**, an innate need for contact with a wide variety of species of animals and plants (Kellert and Wilson, 1993).

Plants have been shown to enhance human health and performance. People recoving in hospitals healed faster when they had views of greenery rather than views of another building (Ulrich, 1984). Larger views, especially of greenery, improved the scores of students in classrooms and the performance of office workers (Heschong, 2003). There is much

Figure 11.8s In Taliesin West, near Phoeniz, Arizona, Frank Lloyd Wright used pools and fountains to help cool the desert air.

evidence that people want and need views of green plants. Ideally, along with their aesthetic and psychological function, plants can act as windbreaks in the winter, as shading devices and evaporative coolers in the summer, and as light filters all year long (Fig. 11.9a and b). Vegetation can reduce erosion and attract wildlife. It can also reduce noise, dust, and other air pollution. It is sometimes most useful in blocking visual pollution or in creating privacy. Of course, just as in the design elements of the building itself, the more functions vegetation has, the better.

Before we discuss specific design techniques, some general comments about plants are in order. Perennial plants are usually better than annuals because they do not have to start from the beginning each year. Deciduous plants can be very useful for solar access, but some cautions are in order. It must be understood that even without leaves, the branches create significant shade (30 to 60 percent). A few trees shade even more of the winter sun. For example, some oaks hold onto their dead leaves and, thus, shade

up to 80 percent of the winter sun (Fig. 11.9c). The best trees are those that have a dense summer canopy and an almost branchless, open winter canopy. Certain species will be deciduous only if the temperature gets cold enough.

Thus, the same plant might be deciduous in the north and evergreen in the south. The times of defoliation in fall and foliation in spring vary with species. Some deciduous plants respond to length of daylight rather than

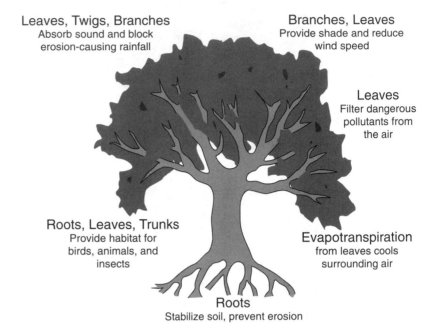

Leaves, Twigs, Branches
Absorb sound and block
erosion-causing rainfall

Branches, Leaves
Provide shade and reduce
wind speed

Leaves
Filter dangerous
pollutants from
the air

Roots, Leaves, Trunks
Provide habitat for
birds, animals, and
insects

Evapotranspiration
from leaves cools
surrounding air

Roots
Stabilize soil, prevent erosion

Figure 11.9a Besides the many benefits of trees described in this diagram, there are also psychological and aesthetic benefits.

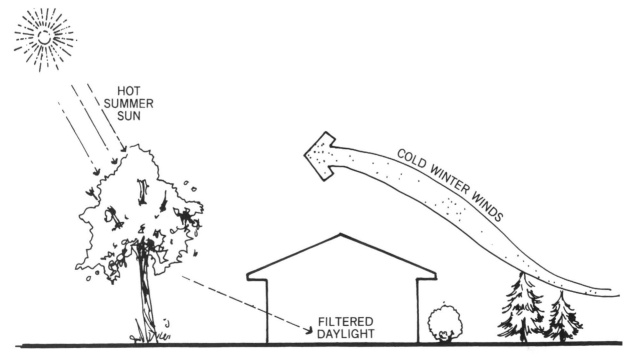

HOT
SUMMER
SUN

COLD WINTER WINDS

FILTERED
DAYLIGHT

Figure 11.9b Plants can reduce winter heating and summer cooling as much as 50 percent. Plants can also improve the quality of daylight by filtering and diffusing the light.

Figure 11.9c Deciduous trees vary greatly in the amount of sunlight they block in the winter (30 to 60 percent). A few deciduous trees, like this particular oak, do not even lose their dead leaves until spring.

temperature and, thus, might defoliate at the wrong time. This is especially true when bright outdoor lighting at night confuses the biological timing of the plants.

The size and shape of a fully grown tree or shrub vary not only with species, but also with local growing conditions. See Table 11.9 for a sample of tree sizes, growth rates, percentage of winter and summer sun blockage, and time of fall defoliation and spring foliation. The location of the hardiness zones listed in the table are shown on the map of Fig. 11.9d. Since a design is often based on the more mature size of a tree or bush, the growth rate is very important. Choosing a fast-growing tree or bush (2 ft or more per year) is not always a

good choice because most fast-growing trees are weak-wooded (have poor strength). However, a vine can be the ideal fast-growing plant. Since some vines grow as much as 40 ft (12 m) per year, a vine can create as much shade in three years as it can take a tree ten years to achieve. Physical strength is not required since a vine can be supported by a man-made structure such as a wall, a trellis, or a cable network. Unlike a tree, the growth of a vine can be directed exactly where it is needed (Fig. 11.12g).

The growth rate of any tree, shrub, or vine can be accelerated by supplying ample nutrients and a steady source of water. A drip-irrigation system is excellent for this purpose. And, of course, starting with a large plant will further

shorten the time required to reach maturity.

Sometimes it is desirable to stop the growth of a plant when it has reached the desired size. That this is possible is proven by the existence of bonsai plants. The usual methods for creating bonsai include limiting the supply of nutrients, limiting the space for root growth, pruning, and using wire chokes to constrict the flow of nutrients. However, for the health of the plant, sufficient water must always be supplied.

Plants promote heating primarily by reducing infiltration and partly by creating still-air spaces next to buildings, which act as extra insulation. Use dense evergreen trees and shrubs for breaking the wind.

Table 11.9 Useful Trees

Name	Shape	Mature Size FT (M) HT × Spread	Growth Rate	Shade Provided Winter	Shade Provided Summer	Time in Leaf Fall Defoliates	Time in Leaf Spring in Leaf	USDA Hardiness Zone	Site Features
Acacia greggii (catclaw acacia)	spreading	15(5) × 10(3)	moderate	light	light	late	early	7–11	sun/dry soils
Acer platanoides (Norway maple)	round	50(15) × 40(12)	moderate	light	dense	late	early	3–8	sun/well-drained soils
Acer rubrum (red maple)	oval/round	60(18) × 40(12)	fast	light	moderate	average	average	3–9	sun-partial shade/moist soils
Acer saccharinum (silver maple)	oval/round	75(23) × 40(12)	fast	moderate	dense	average	average	3–9	sun/wide variety of soils
Acer saccharum (sugar maple)	oval/spreading	75(23) × 40(12)	moderate/fast	moderate	dense	average	average	3–8	sun/moist well-drained, acid soils
Betula nigra (river birch)	oval	30(9) × 20(6)	fast	light	moderate	early	early	4–9	sun/moist, sandy, acid soil
Cercidium floridum (blue Palo Verde)	spreading	30(9) × 30(9)	moderate	light	light	late	late	8–11	sun/dry soils
Cercis canadensis (eastern redbud)	spreading	30(9) × 35(11)	moderate	light	light	late	average	4–9	sun-shade/moist-dry soils
Chilopsis linearis (desert willow)	vase	20(6) × 15(5)	fast	light	light	average	average	8–10	sun/dry, alkalinesoils
Cornus florida (flowering dogwood) select disease-resistant hybrids	round	35(11) × 35(11)	slow	light	medium	early	late	6–9	partial shade/moist, well-drained soils
Cornus kousa (Kousa dogwood)	round	25(8) × 20(6)	moderate	moderate	moderate	early	late	4–8	sun-part shade
Fagus sylvatica (European beech)	oval/round	100(30) × 70(21)	slow	moderate	dense	late	late	4–8	sun/moist, well-drained soils
Fraxinus pennsylvanica (green ash)	oval/round	50(15) × 30(9)	moderate	light	moderate	average	average	3–9	sun/wide variety of soils
Fraxinun veluntina (Arizona ash)	pyramid	35(11) × 25(8)	fast	light	moderate	average	average	7–9	sun/tolerates dry alkaline soil
Ginkgo biloba (ginkgo)	pyramid	70(21) × 40(12)	moderate/slow	light	dense	average	late	4–9	sun/wide variety of soils
Gleditsia triacanthos var. inermis (honey locust)	oval/spreading	60(18) × 20(6)	fast	light	moderate	early	late	4–9	sun-part shade/dry-wet soils
Gymnocladus dioica (Kentucky coffeetree)	oval	60(18) × 40(12)	slow	light	light	average	average	4–8	sun/wide variety of soils
Lagerstroemia indica (crepe myrtle)	vase	20(6) × 15(4)	moderate	light	moderate	late	late	7–10	sun/moist soil
Liquidambar styraciflua (sweet gum) select fruitless cultivar	pyramid	80(24) × 40(12)	moderate/fast	moderate	moderate	late	average	5–10	sun/rich, wet, acid soils
Liriodendron tulipifera (tulip poplar)	columnar/oval	80(24) × 40(12)	moderate	moderate	dense	average	average	4–9	sun/moist, fertile soil
Magnolia acuminata (cucumber magnolia)	pyramid/spreading	80(24) × 70(21)	moderate	light	medium	average	average	4–8	sun/moist, slightly acid soils
Pistacia chinensis (Chinese pistache)	oval/round	40(12) × 40(12)	slow	medium	dense	average	average	8–10	sun/well-drained soil
Platanus x acerifolia (London planetree)	pyramid/spreading	90(27) × 70(21)	moderate/fast	light	moderate	late	late	4–8	sun/wide variety of soils
Platanus occidentalis (American sycamore)	round	90(27) × 90(27)	moderate/fast	light	moderate	late	late	4–9	sun/moist soils
Populus deltoides (eastern cottonwood), select seedless cultivars	vase	75(23) × 50(15)	fast	light	light	early	early	2–9	sun/moist soil/invasive roots
Prosopis glandulosa (honey mesquite)	spreading	25(8) × 15(4)	fast	light	light	early	late	8–9	sun/dry, alkaline soils
Quercus palustris (pin oak)	pyramid/columnar	75(23) × 40(12)	moderate	moderate	moderate	early	early	5–10	sun/acid soils
Quercus phellos (willow oak)	round	60(18) × 40(12)	moderate	medium	dense	late	late	6–9	sun/moist, well-drained soils
Robinia pseudoacacia (black locust)	columnar	50(15) × 30(9)	moderate/fast	moderate	moderate	early	late	3–8	sun/wide variety of soils
Tilia cordata (littleleaf linden)	pyramid	50(15) × 40(12)	moderate/slow	moderate	dense	early	late	3–7	sun/wide variety of soils
Zelkova serrata (Japanese zelkova)	vase	70(21) × 20(6)	moderate	light	moderate	average	late	5–8	sun/moist soils

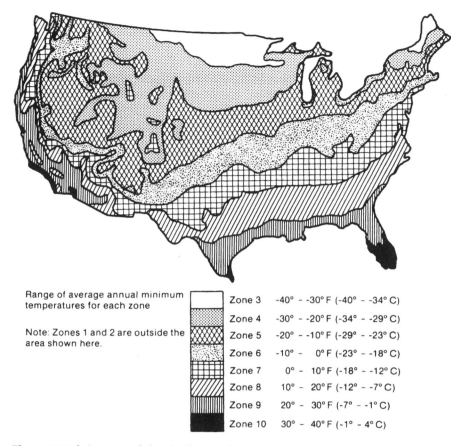

Range of average annual minimum temperatures for each zone	Zone 3	-40° – -30° F (-40° – -34° C)
	Zone 4	-30° – -20° F (-34° – -29° C)
	Zone 5	-20° – -10° F (-29° – -23° C)
Note: Zones 1 and 2 are outside the area shown here.	Zone 6	-10° – 0° F (-23° – -18° C)
	Zone 7	0° – 10° F (-18° – -12° C)
	Zone 8	10° – 20° F (-12° – -7° C)
	Zone 9	20° – 30° F (-7° – -1° C)
	Zone 10	30° – 40° F (-1° – 4° C)

Figure 11.9d The zones of plant hardiness as listed in Table 11.9. (From Richard Montgomery, *Passive Solar Journal*, Vol. 4 (1), p. 91. Courtesy of the American Solar Energy Society.)

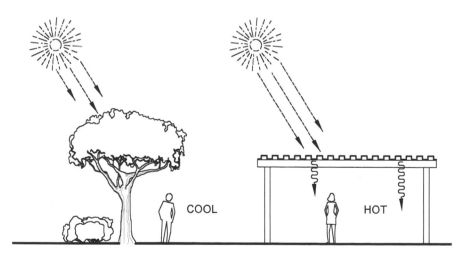

Figure 11.9e Shade from trees is so effective because trees do not get hot and reradiate heat (long-wave infrared), as do most man-made shade structures. Trees cool themselves by transpiration.

Summer cooling is more complicated, with most of the benefit derived from the shade that the plants provide. The shade from a tree is better than the shade from a man-made canopy because the tree does not heat up and reradiate down (Fig. 11.9e). This is the case because of the multiple layers that are ventilated and because the leaves stay cool by the transpiration (evaporation) of water from the leaves. Since only a small amount of the sun's energy is used in photosynthesis, the chemical energy created has little effect on reducing the temperature.

Transpiration cools not only the plant, but also the air in contact with the vegetation (Fig. 11.9f). Thus, the cooling load on a building surrounded by lawns will be smaller than on a building surrounded by asphalt or concrete. Trees are even more effective than grass in providing comfort. They provide shade, and unlike grass, their evaporative cooling occurs high above the ground and, therefore, does not raise the humidity level at the ground.

During the summer, grassy areas are superior to paved areas not only during the day but also at night. Because of the high surface temperatures and good conductivity of pavement, large amounts of heat are stored during the day. Consequently, in the evening and all night long, the paved areas will be warmer than grassy areas. Using large amounts of water, however, to achieve cooling is not the answer in the dry Southwest, nor even in the Southeast, which is also experiencing water shortages. For example, Georgia, Alabama, and Florida are in the courts fighting over the water in the Chattahoochee River. It is becoming increasingly important to use a **xeriscape** design, which is landscaping that saves water and energy. Incidentally, the word "xeriscape" has the same Greek root as "Xerox," which refers to a "dry" process.

Usually the best plants to use are native varieties that have adapted to the local climate, soil, and pathogens. Thus, less water, fertilizer, and chemicals are needed for healthy plant growth. It is not unrealistic to expect a reduction of up to 50 percent in the cooling load when an envelope-dominated building is effectively shaded by plants. A 60 percent reduction in the use of electricity was realized in a Florida school when plants shaded the walls and windows. In another experiment, the temperature

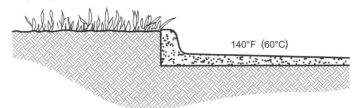

Figure 11.9f Since air is heated by contact with the ground, the air over asphalt is much hotter than the air over grass. On some days, the temperature of asphalt can reach 160°F (71°C). The asphalt will also store more heat to make nighttimes less comfortable in summer.

Figure 11.9g At night, it is warmer under trees than in an open field because the trees block the outgoing heat radiation.

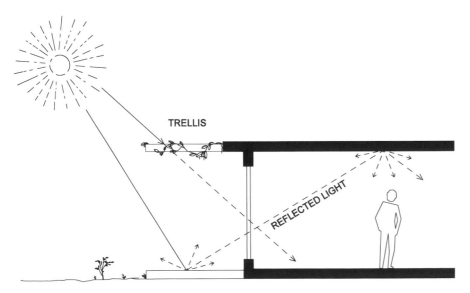

Figure 11.9h Quality daylight can sometimes be achieved by blocking direct sunlight while encouraging reflected sunlight.

inside a mobile home was reduced 20°F (11°F) when it was well shaded by plants.

At night, trees work against natural cooling by blocking long-wave radiation. There will be more radiant cooling in an open field than under a canopy of trees (Fig. 11.9g). Consequently, the diurnal temperature range is much smaller under trees than in an open field, and radiant cooling at night is not feasible under trees.

Plants can also improve the quality of daylight entering through windows. Direct sunlight can be scattered and reduced in intensity, while the glare from the bright sky can be moderated by plants (Fig. 11.9i). Vines across the windows or trees farther away can have the same beneficial effect. Since light reflected off the ground penetrates deeper into a building than direct light, it is sometimes desirable not to have vegetation right outside a window on the ground (Fig. 11.9h). See Chapter 13 for a detailed discussion on daylighting.

There is no doubt that the proper choice and positioning of plants can greatly improve the microclimate of a site. However, choosing a specific plant can be difficult not only because of the tremendous variety that exists, but also because of the specific needs of plants, such as minimum safe temperatures, rainfall, exposure to sun, and soil type. For these reasons, advice should be obtained from such sources as local nurseries, agricultural extension agents, state foresters, and landscape architects. **Rule of thumb: Choose plants suited for the local environment.**

11.10 GREEN ROOFS

Greek soldiers returning from Babylon in 500 B.C. reported that the city was overflowing with green plants and flowers. They said that plants were hanging everywhere from the roofs of houses and temples. If the "Hanging Gardens" could be created in Babylon in 600 B.C., then surely we could do the same today. Our cities would be

Figure 11.9i Plants can soften and diffuse daylight and reduce the glare from the bright sky and light-colored surfaces. Apartment complex in Vienna designed by F. Hundertwasser.

Figure 11.10a Greenery will make cities move livable, healthier, and cooler. A city covered with plants would convince many suburbanites that the long commute to get away from the inhumane urban core was unnecessary. LDS Assembly Hall, Salt Lake City, Utah. Architects: Zimmer Gunsel Fraca Partnership. Area of green roof: 70,000 ft²(6300 m²) in 2000. (Courtesy American Hydrotech Inc.)

Figure 11.10b Although the thermal benefits of green roofs are greatest in hot climates, their many other benefits also make them popular in cold climates. Vancouver City Library, British Columbia, Canada. Architects: Moshe Safdie & Associates. Area of green roof: 8000 ft² (720 m²) in 2002. (Courtesy American Hydrotech Inc.)

more pleasant to live in if the roofs were mostly covered with plants (Fig. 11.10a). Fortunately, green roofs are becoming very popular because they reduce the cooling load on buildings, reduce the heat island effect in cities, reduce storm water runoff, reduce noise transmission, reduce air pollutants that normally collect on roofs and are then flushed into streams, extend the life of roof membranes, create wildlife habitat, and make buildings and cities more humane (Fig. 11.10b).

If the green roof is designed to grow only grass and small flowers, the soil can be as little as 2 in. (5 cm) thick. Such a green roof is called **extensive**, while an **intensive** roof will have about 6 in. (15 cm) of soil to grow larger flowers and small shrubs. If large shrubs or small trees are desired, then deeper pockets of soil must be provided, but such pockets would be a significant load and should be placed over or near columns. Extensive green roofs add a dead weight as low as 13 lb/ft² (63 kg/m²), while intensive roofs weigh about 40 lb/ft² (200 kg/m²). These dead weights are much less than normal soil weights would suggest, because the planting medium that is typically used consists of 80 percent lightweight aggregates such as perlite, vermiculite, and expanded shale. The

remaining 20 percent consists of high water-absorbing material which could be organic.

Besides the soil, there are several other important parts to a green roof system (Fig. 11.10c). To thrive, plants need just the right amount of water—both too much and too little are bad. Thus, a drainage/retention layer regulates the moisture content by draining excess water. Below that layer are the root barrier and waterproof membranes that protect the roof insulation. It must be emphasized that green roofs need just as much insulation as regular roofs for reducing heat loss in the winter. For backup, there may be another waterproof membrane under the insulation. Although other systems vary somewhat, they all need to address the same problems. One alternative system consists of modular trays that come ready from the nursery to place on the roof membrane (Figs. 11.10d and e).

One of the great advantages of green roofs is the reduction of storm water runoff, which has both economic and environmental benefits. In nature, rainwater gets absorbed by the soil, and whatever does not evaporate or is not used by plants makes its way slowly to streams. Meanwhile, the nonporous surfaces of cities cause storm water to surge into

Figure 11.10c An extensive green roof system for growing grass and small flowers is shown. Many layers are required to perform all the functions of a successful green roof. An intensive system would have more growing medium (soil) to allow larger plants to grow. (Courtesy American Hydrotech Inc.)

streams, causing erosion and poor water quality. Green roofs, however, absorb much of the rainfall, which is then used by the plants, while the rest is discharged into the storm-water system but with a delay. Thus, the building's discharge rate is greatly diminished in size, protecting both the local ecology and requiring a smaller and cheaper municipal storm-water drainage system.

The other important benefit of green roofs is the reduced summer

Figure 11.10d Some green roofs are made of modular trays that come with plants from the nursery and are placed on conventional roof membranes. (Courtesy GreenGrid.)

Figure 11.10e This roof garden, or intensive green roof, is made from modular trays. Taller plants that need more soil have deeper trays. (Courtesy GreenGrid.)

cooling load. Although wet soil is a poor insulator, the **transpiration** from the plants and **evaporation** from the soil (**evapotranspiration** for the combination) cool the plants, soil, and contiguous air. Thus, the cooling load on the building is greatly reduced. In a single-story building, the cooling load can be reduced as much as 30 percent. Green roofs also reduce the urban heat island effect.

Because the wet soil does not reduce heat loss, the insulation required in the winter will be the same as for a building with no green roof. Thus, the thermal benefits of green roofs are greatest for buildings in hot climates and cities in most climates. However, green roofs are also popular in colder climates because of the many other benefits mentioned before. They are especially desirable in special situations such as proximity to airports or noisy highways for the acoustical benefit. A properly designed green roof can also be economical for several reasons, including the 100–500 percent extension on the life of the roof membrane. And if

all of these benefits are not convincing enough, one LEED point can be earned by having at least 50 percent of a commercial roof green.

Rules for Green Roofs

1. Use only quality green roof systems to prevent water damage.
2. Account for the higher dead load. Deep soil pockets for trees should be placed near vertical supports and not near the middle of long spans.
3. Use the same amount of insulation as if the roof were not green.
4. Consider making the green roof an accessible roof garden.

11.11 LAWNS

Lawns became popular in eighteenth-century England, where rich landowners wanted vistas and improved-upon nature. Their lawns were "mowed" mainly by sheep, cattle, and horses because cutting short grass with a scythe was expensive. To eliminate the need for grazing animals, the first

mechanical lawn mower was patented in 1830. In the United States, lawns did not become popular until after the Civil War because they were a luxury. Although lawns are very practical for sports, for children to play, and for picnicking, most lawns are purely for show (aesthetic and status reasons). Presently, the area of lawns in the United States is about equal to the area of Pennsylvania.

Unfortunately, lawns have a high economic and environmental cost. Mowing lawns accounts for 5 percent of U.S. air pollution and much of the noise pollution, especially on days of rest. Lawns consume about 30 percent of drinking water in the eastern United States and about 60 percent in the West. Because of the desire to have a lawn look as perfect as Astroturf, the resultant use of fertilizer, herbicide, and insecticide pollutes the environment. Any deviant like the beautiful and beneficial dandelion is considered an evil pest to be exterminated at any cost.

Fortunately, there are good alternatives. Maintaining or restoring the native natural environment is the best option. It will require little, if any, watering, fertilizer, pesticide, or herbicide. If views and vistas are desired, then native grasses and flowers can be planted. Of course, lawns for sports, play, and picnicking should be kept. In addition, when a decorative lawn is desired, only small patches should be used. The resulting landscaping will be less expensive, healthier for both wildlife and humans, and more beautiful than the present monoculture lawns.

11.12 LANDSCAPING

The concepts discussed above can now be combined into landscaping techniques that promote the heating, cooling, and lighting of buildings. Figure 11.12a illustrates the general tree-planting logic for most of the country, while Figs. 11.12b–e present landscaping techniques appropriate for four different climates (temperate, very cold, hot and dry, and hot and humid).

When trees are not available to shade the east, west, and north windows, high bushes or a vine-covered trellis can be used. Bushes can shade windows just like vertical fins, which were discussed in Chapter 9. And, like fins, shrubs should extend above the windows and be fairly deep (Fig. 11.12f). A vertical vine-covered trellis is very effective on east and west facades, while a horizontal trellis can be used on any orientation (Fig. 11.12g).

Outdoor shading structures, such as trellises, pergolas, and arbors, are described in Fig. 9.17e, f, and g. Other functional landscaping elements include allees, pleached allees, and hedgerows (Fig. 11.12h). **Allees** are garden walks bordered with shrubs and trees; they primarily control sight lines but can also be used for providing shade and/or to control air movement. In **pleached allees**, closely spaced trees or tall shrubs are intertwined and pruned to form a tunnel-like structure. Not only do these features effectively frame views, they also create cool, shady walkways.

The term **hedgerow** refers to a row of bushes, shrubs, or trees forming a hedge. Depending on the orientation, such hedges can be used for shading, wind protection, or wind funneling.

As mentioned before, pools of water and especially fountains can be used to cool the air. However, if these features are used in hot and humid climates, they should be placed downwind to avoid adding more humidity to the air. On the other hand, in very dry climates, the water should be placed in a sheltered courtyard. Unless the water is chlorinated, a healthy ecosystem should be created. As waterfalls or fountains cool the air, they also oxygenate the water for fish and snails, which are required to control mosquitoes and algae growth. In very hot climates, the water should be shaded to prevent overheating and excessive algae growth (Fig. 11.12i). A natural black dye added to the water will also prevent algae growth. The water should also circulate and not become stagnant.

A private sunny garden is considered a basic amenity in much of the world. It is, therefore, surprising how little use is made of roof gardens in the cities of the world. Use light-colored paving materials to prevent heat buildup that could make its way through the roof. A vine-covered trellis can be a lightweight element for creating shade.

Of course, the design of roof gardens will vary with climate. A design of a roof garden for a northern climate might include high parapet walls on the north, east, and west facades to deflect the cold winds. An open or glass railing on the south side would allow the winter sun to enter (Fig. 11.12j). A roof garden in a hot and humid climate, on the other hand, would be open to cooling breezes and be well shaded by trees, trellises, etc. (Fig. 11.12k). In hot and dry climates, gardens are typically surrounded by walls to keep out the hot wind. Thus, such gardens would be more like the design shown in Fig. 11.12j.

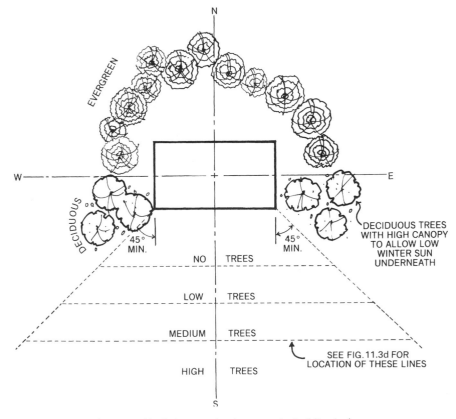

Figure 11.12a The general logic for tree planting around a building is shown.

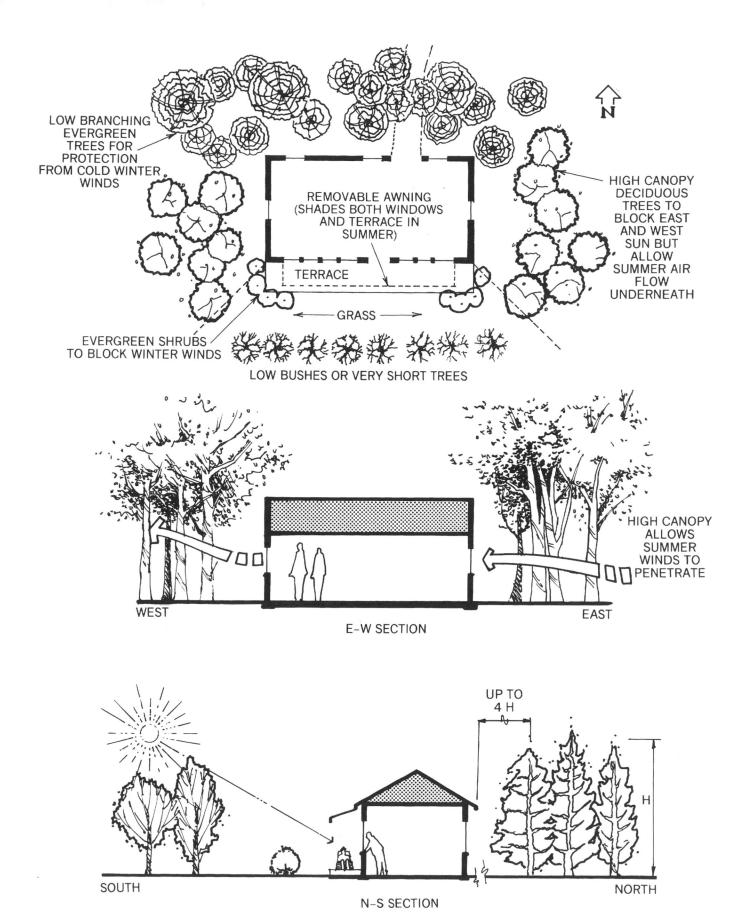

LOW BRANCHING EVERGREEN TREES FOR PROTECTION FROM COLD WINTER WINDS

HIGH CANOPY DECIDUOUS TREES TO BLOCK EAST AND WEST SUN BUT ALLOW SUMMER AIR FLOW UNDERNEATH

REMOVABLE AWNING (SHADES BOTH WINDOWS AND TERRACE IN SUMMER)

TERRACE

GRASS

EVERGREEN SHRUBS TO BLOCK WINTER WINDS

LOW BUSHES OR VERY SHORT TREES

WEST

EAST

HIGH CANOPY ALLOWS SUMMER WINDS TO PENETRATE

E-W SECTION

UP TO 4 H

SOUTH

NORTH

H

N-S SECTION

Figure 11.12b Landscaping techniques for a temperate climate. The windbreak on the north side of the building should be no farther away than four times its height. Contrary to their name, temperate climates are hot in the summer and cold in the winter.

333

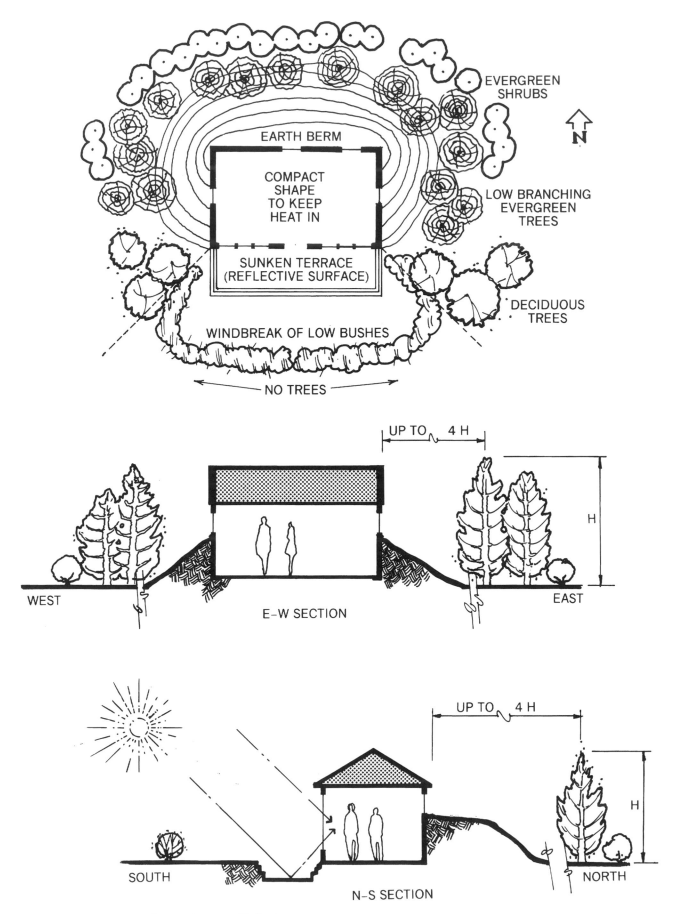

EVERGREEN SHRUBS

EARTH BERM

COMPACT SHAPE TO KEEP HEAT IN

LOW BRANCHING EVERGREEN TREES

SUNKEN TERRACE (REFLECTIVE SURFACE)

DECIDUOUS TREES

WINDBREAK OF LOW BUSHES

← NO TREES →

N

UP TO 4 H

H

WEST

EAST

E–W SECTION

UP TO 4 H

H

SOUTH

NORTH

N–S SECTION

Figure 11.12c Landscaping techniques for very cold climates.

334

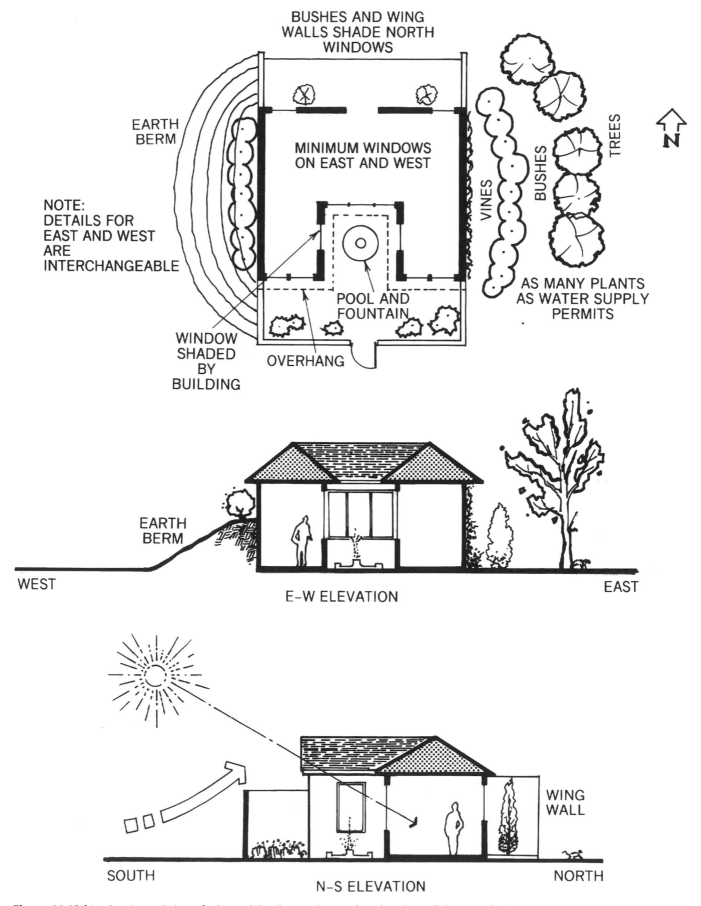

BUSHES AND WING WALLS SHADE NORTH WINDOWS

EARTH BERM

NOTE: DETAILS FOR EAST AND WEST ARE INTERCHANGEABLE

MINIMUM WINDOWS ON EAST AND WEST

VINES

BUSHES

TREES

N

AS MANY PLANTS AS WATER SUPPLY PERMITS

POOL AND FOUNTAIN

WINDOW SHADED BY BUILDING

OVERHANG

EARTH BERM

WEST

E–W ELEVATION

EAST

WING WALL

SOUTH

N–S ELEVATION

NORTH

Figure 11.12d Landscaping techniques for hot and dry climates. Courtyards and garden walls keep out the hot winds and conserve cool, moist air.

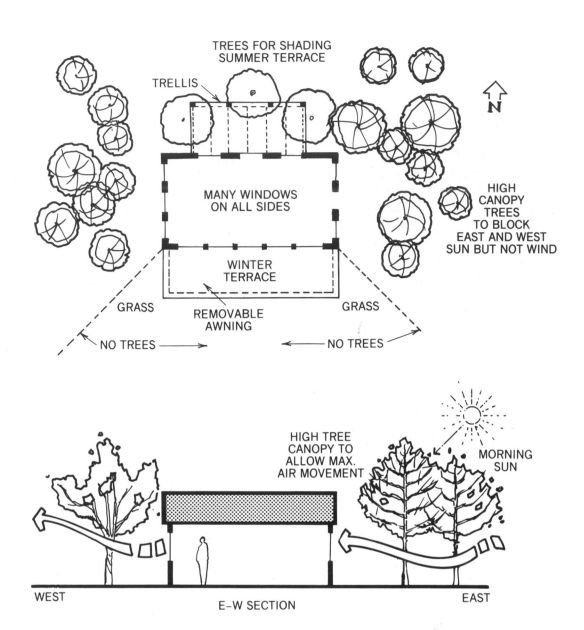

TREES FOR SHADING
SUMMER TERRACE

TRELLIS

N

MANY WINDOWS
ON ALL SIDES

HIGH
CANOPY
TREES
TO BLOCK
EAST AND WEST
SUN BUT NOT WIND

WINTER
TERRACE

GRASS

GRASS

REMOVABLE
AWNING

NO TREES →   ← NO TREES

HIGH TREE
CANOPY TO
ALLOW MAX.
AIR MOVEMENT

MORNING
SUN

WEST   EAST
E–W SECTION

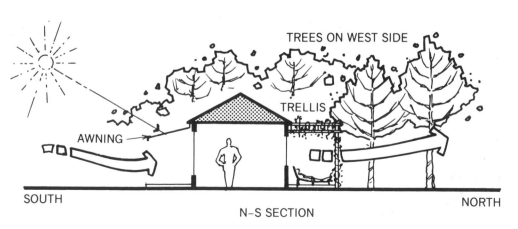

TREES ON WEST SIDE

TRELLIS

AWNING

SOUTH   NORTH
N–S SECTION

Figure 11.12e Landscaping techniques for hot and humid climates.

336

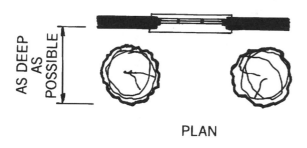

PLAN

Figure 11.12f Bushes can act as vertical fins to block the low sun on north facades. On east and west windows, only the bush on the north side should be used if winters are cold.

Figure 11.12g Vine-covered trellises are effective devices for creating shade. A newly planted vine will provide shade much sooner than a newly planted tree.

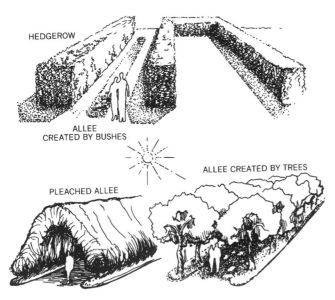

Figure 11.12h Landscaping elements for creating shade and/or controlling air movement.

Figure 11.12i Waterfalls, fountains, and pools can cool the air in all but very humid climates. If the climate is very hot, the water should be shaded by trees, bushes, lily pads, etc.

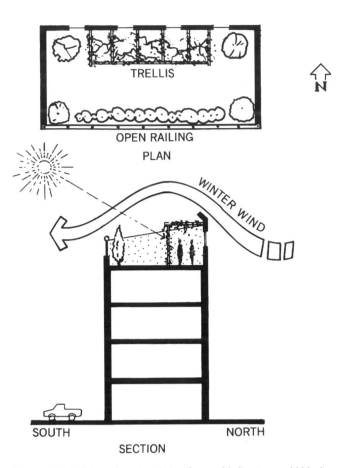

Figure 11.12j A roof-garden design for a cold climate would block the cold northern winds while allowing the winter sun to enter. In hot and dry climates, the garden needs to be protected from winds in all directions.

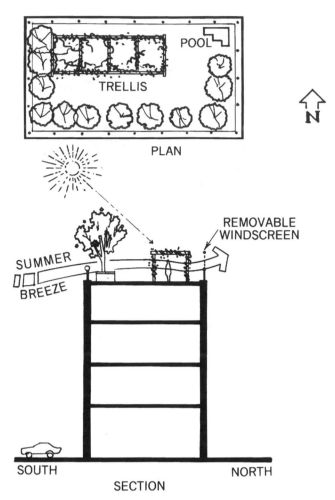

Figure 11.12k A roof-garden design for a hot and humid climate would maximize natural ventilation.

11.13 COMMUNITY DESIGN

Community planning can either promote or hinder the design of each lot. Outside of Phoenix, Arizona, is a place called Sun City. Although the name might suggest a place in harmony with the sun, the street layout shows a total disregard for sun angles (Fig. 11.13a). On circular streets, every building has a different orientation. Only two buildings on each street have the ideal east–west orientation, where the small facades face east and west and where shading from neighbors is at a maximum.

A quite different approach is illustrated in the street plan of Village Homes in Davis, California

(Fig. 11.13b). Although the site runs north–south, the streets run mostly east–west. Cluster housing is used to save both land and energy (Fig. 11.13c). Bicycle and pedestrian paths are included in part to reduce the use of automobiles. Studies have shown that houses in Village Homes use on average about half of the energy required by comparable nonsolar buildings in the same area. In addition, these houses tend to be more comfortable, desirable, and economical. Their success and popularity are indicated by their high resale value.

As much as possible, Village Homes encourages employment opportunities within the community. Tremendous amounts of energy and

time could be saved if people did not have to commute so much. Although the heavy use of automobiles is a major part of America's national energy drain, that aspect of sustainability is unfortunately beyond the scope of this book.

The existence of communities such as Village Homes is in part due to the zoning technique called **planned unit development** (PUD). PUD provisions allow for modification of lot size, shape, and placement for increasing siting flexibility. Thus, solar access and community open land can be maximized.

Besides creating more sustainable suburban designs, cities could be built as attractive alternatives to suburban

Figure 11.13a With a circular street layout, every building has a different orientation, and only a small number have the ideal east–west orientation.

Figure 11.13b In the community of Village Homes in Davis, California, most streets run east–west for winter solar access and summer shading. (From *Village Homes' Solar House Design* by David Bainbridge, Judy Corbett, John Hofacre. Rodale Press, 1979. © Michael N. Corbett.)

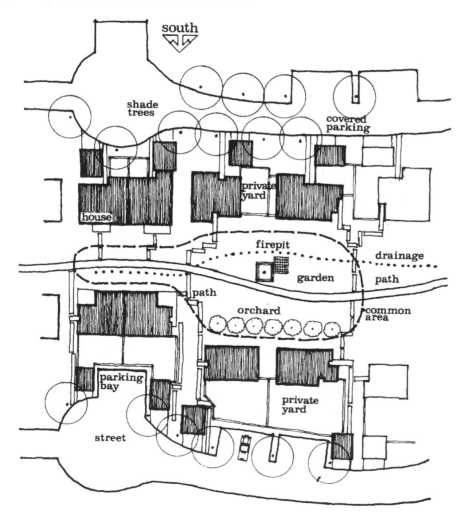

Figure 11.13c Cluster housing saves land and energy. The saved land is used for pedestrian/bicycle paths, recreation, vegetable gardens, and orchards. (From *Village Homes' Solar House Design* by David Bainbridge, Judy Corbett, John Hofacre. Rodale Press, 1979 © John C. Hofacre.)

living. Although there are many reasons to live in the suburbs, the presence of a great amount of greenery is a major attraction. Roof gardens, green balconies, small private gardens, large public gardens, and trees and flowers along all streets could make a city not only cooler and healthier but also an attractive alternative to suburban living.

Although everyone seems to agree that **sprawl** is undesirable, the solutions presented suggest otherwise. What is presented as **smart growth** is often **greenwash**. The basic causes of sprawl are usually not addressed. At least 50 percent of sprawl is the result of population growth. The rest of it is caused by various factors such as a desire to live in nature, which present cities don't provide, and a desire to buy larger houses (i.e., growing affluence). Thus, we come back to Paul Ehrlich's equation, which was described in Section 2.5:

$$I = P \cdot A \cdot T$$

To reduce the impact on the environment (I), we need to reduce population growth (P), have a higher quality of life rather than growing affluence (A), and make technology (T) work for the environment rather than against it. Thus, if we need to stop or reduce the growth of population and affluence, the term "smart growth" is an oxymoron.

Instead of sprawl and ugly cities, we should have "sustainable communities"; fortunately, several such communities are being built around the world:

1. Solar City, Linz, Austria, Architects: READ (Renewable Energy in Architecture and Design); Thomas Herzog + Partner; Sir Norman Foster and Partners; Richard Rogers Partnership
2. Beddington Zero Energy Development (BedZED) Bill Dunster Architects (see Fig. 7.12d and e, and Fig. 10.6v)

3. Dongton near Shanghai, China, by ARUP
4. Hyungbaiyu Cradle to Cradle, Village Master Plan, Benxi, China, by William McDonough & Partners

11.14 COOLING OUR COMMUNITIES

Urban areas are much hotter than the rural areas around them. Figure 5.3e and Color Plate 12 show the **heat-island effect** caused mainly by the excessive absorption of solar energy. The darker the surfaces, the more heat is absorbed, with black roofs reaching a temperature of 160°F (71°C). For every 1°F (0.6°C) increase in urban temperature, electricity use increases 2 percent and the production of smog increases 3 percent. Significantly cooler communities are possible by using light-colored materials for roofs, walls, and especially paved surfaces. Materials should have a very high albedo (a factor that measures the reflectivity of solar radiation). A surface with an albedo of 1 reflects all radiation, while a surface with an albedo of 0 absorbs all radiation. Black roofs are especially bad because they heat both the buildings and the urban area.

Certain paved areas, such as driveways and parking areas, not only can be made of light-colored materials, such as concrete, but also can be made of special blocks that allow grass to grow in the openings. All plants cool by transpiration. Trees have the double benefit of creating shade, while the transpiration occurs high above the ground where the increase in humidity will blow away faster. Significant comfort and energy savings are possible from ordinances requiring the use of light colors, the planting of trees, green roofs, and other plant covers.

Much excellent information is available on how to cool our communities, and many organizations have been set up to promote this goal. See especially:

1. www.coolcommunities.org
2. www.nationaltreetrust.org
3. *Cooling Our Communities: A Guidebook on Tree Planting and Light Colored Surfacing*, U.S. Environmental Protection Agency (1992).

11.15 CONCLUSION

Site and community planning can have a tremendous effect on energy consumption. For example, the annual per capita energy use in New York City is about one-half of the U.S. average.

In Davis, California, good planning and building design has resulted in some houses that have achieved 100 percent natural cooling and 80 percent solar heating.

Planning decisions made today will be with us for decades, if not centuries. It *will* be very unfortunate if future interest in solar energy is frustrated by the poor planning decisions made today. It is almost certain that PV electricity, the almost ideal energy source, will become economical in the near future (see Section 8.2). When that day arrives, some buildings will be able to make much better use of it than others. For architects and others with great aesthetic sensibilities, a world with jury-rigged solar collectors on a multitude of misoriented buildings will be a constant irritation. Thus, providing proper orientation and solar access is critical.

The proper layout of streets, the proper design of building lots, the proper orientation of buildings, and an abundance of nature will not only reward us now but also create a decent legacy for our children and our children's children.

KEY IDEAS OF CHAPTER 11

1. East-west streets offer the best access to the winter sun and the best shading from the summer sun.
2. The solar-access boundary can be used on plans and sections to ensure winter solar access.
3. Shadow patterns can be used on site plans to ensure winter solar access to all buildings.
4. Solar zoning ensures solar access through ordinances.

5. Use physical models as a design tool for ensuring winter solar access and summer shading.
6. Use site features to block the cold winter wind and to funnel in the summer wind.
7. Use plants to block the winter wind and the summer sun.
8. Landscaping that supports the heating, cooling, and lighting of buildings varies with the climate.

9. Because of their many advantages, green roofs are highly recommended.
10. Lawns, which are an environmental liability, should be used only when necessary.
11. Design communities for sustainability. Emphasize east–west streets, and de-emphasize the need for automobiles.

References

Heschong, Lisa. "Classrooms and Windows" and "Offices with Windows," 2003. www.h_m_g.com.

Kellert, Stephen R., and Edward O. Wilson. *The Biophilia Hypothesis*. Washington, DC: Island Press, 1993.

McPherson, E. Gregory. *Energy Conserving Site Design*. Waldorf, MD: American Society of Landscape Architects, 1984.

Ulrich, R. S. "View Through Windows May Influence Recovery from Surgery." *Science*, Vol. 24, 920–921 (1984).

Resources

FURTHER READING

(See Bibliography in back of book for full citations.

Akbari, H., et al. *Cooling Our Communities: A Guidebook on Tree Planting and Light-Colored Surfacing.*

Boutet, T. S. *Controlling Air Movement: A Manual for Architects and Builders.*

Brown, G. Z., and M. DeKay. *Sun, Wind, and Light: Architectural Design Strategies*, 2nd ed.

Brown, R., and T. Gillespie. *Microclimatic Climate Design: Creating Thermal Comfort and Energy Efficiency.*

Druse, K., and M. Roach. *The Natural Habitat Garden.*

Dunnett, N. and N. Kingsbury. *Planting Green Roofs and Living Walls.*

Earth Pledge. *Green Roofs: Ecological Design and Construction.*

Foster R. S. *Homeowner's Guide to Landscaping That Saves Energy Dollars.**

Francis, M. *Village Homes: A Community by Design: Case Studies in Land and Community Design.*

Givoni, B. *Climate Considerations in Building and Urban Design.*

Groesbeck, W., and J. Stiefel. *The Resource Guide to Sustainable Landscapes and Gardens*, 2nd ed.

Hightshoe, G. L. *Native Trees, Shrubs, and Vines for Urban and Rural America: A Planting Design Manual for Environmental Designers.*

Hottes, A. C. *Climbers and Ground Covers, Including a Vast Array of Hardy and Subtropical Vines Which Climb or Creep.**

Jaffe M. S., and E. Duncan. *Protecting Solar Access for Residential Development: A Guidebook for Planning Officials.*

Knowles, R. L. *Energy and Form: An Ecological Approach to Urban Growth*

Kwok, Alison G., and Walter T. Grondzik. *The Green Studio Handbook: Environmental Strategies for Schematic Design*

Knowles, R. L. *Sun Rhythm Form.*

Lyle, J. T. *Design for Human Ecosystems: Landscape, Land Use, and Natural Resources.*

McHarg, I. L. *Design with Nature.*

McPherson, E. G., ed. *Energy Conserving Site Design.*

Moffat, A., and M. Schiler. *Energy-Efficient and Environmental Landscaping.*

Moffat, A., and M. Schiler. *Landscape Design that Saves Energy.**

Norwood, K., and K. Smith. *Rebuilding Community in America: Housing for Ecological Living, Personal Empowerment, and the New Extended Family.*

Ottsen, C. *The Native Plant Primer: Trees, Shrubs, and Wildflowers for Natural Gardens.*

Petit, J., D. Bassert, and C. Kollin. *Building Greener Neighborhoods: Trees as Part of the Plan*, 2nd ed.

Robinette, G. O. *Energy Efficient Site Design.*

Robinette, G. O. and C. McClenon. *Landscape Planning for Energy Conservation.*

Rocky Mountain Institute Staff. *Green Development: Integrating Ecology and Real Estate.*

Tabb, P. *Solar Energy Planning: A Guide to Residential Development.*

U.S. Department of Energy, Office of Project and Facilities Management. *Site Development Planning for Energy Management. Cooling Our Communities: A Guidebook on Tree Planting and Light Colored Surfacing.* U.S. EPA.

U.S. Department of Housing and Urban Development. *Protecting Solar Access for Residential Development.*

Van der Ryn, S., and P. Calthorpe. *Sustainable Communities: A New Design Synthesis for Cities, Suburbs, and Towns.*

Vickery, R. L. *Sharing Architecture.*

Watson, D., and K. Labs. *Climatic Design: Energy Efficient Building Principles and Practices.*

PAPERS

Knowles, R. L. "The Solar Envelope." At www-rcf.usc.edu/ ~ rknowles

---

* These books have extensive lists of plants that are useful for energy-conscious landscape design.

LIGHTING | 12

More and more, it seems to me, light is the beautifier of the building.
Frank Lloyd Wright, **The Natural House,**
©*Frank Lloyd Wright Foundation, 1958*

The design of human environments is, in effect, the design of human
sensory experience; all visual design is de facto also lighting design. . . .
William M. C. Lam, **Perception and Lighting as**
Formgivers for Architecture

12.1 INTRODUCTION

The form of a building is known to us primarily by the way it reflects light. Sensitive designers have always understood that what we see is a consequence of both the quality of the physical design and the quality of light falling on it. The ancient Egyptians found that shallow, negative relief created powerful patterns under the very clear, bright, and direct sunlight of Egypt (Fig. 12.1a). The Greeks found that relief sculpture and moldings were well modeled under the somewhat less bright sun of Greece (Fig. 12.1b). The designers of the Gothic cathedrals had to create powerful statements in the cloudy and diffused light of northern Europe. Here, sculpture in the round could be placed in niches and portals and still be seen because of the softness of the shadows (Fig. 12.1c). Most of the sculpture of a Gothic cathedral would disappear in the dark shadows of an Egyptian sun. The quality of light and the quality of architecture are inextricably intertwined.

Sometimes the architect must accept the light as it is and design the form in response to it. At other times, both the form and the light source are under the architect's control. This is true not only for the interior, but also for the exterior at night. Thus, the architect creates the visual environment by both molding the material and controlling the lighting.

The following three chapters on lighting present the information required by the designer to create a quality and creative lighting environment.

Such an environment includes the lighting necessary for satisfying aesthetic and biological needs, as well as the lighting required to perform certain tasks. Since a quality lighting environment is not achieved by supplying large quantities of light, the emphasis in this book is not on the quantification of light. This chapter explains the basic concepts required for a creative and quality lighting environment, which is achieved primarily through the geometric manipulation of light and the color of finishes. This aspect of lighting is tier one of the three-tier design approach (Fig. 12.1d). Tier two consists of the natural energy of daylighting, and tier three consists of electric lighting. To design quality lighting, we must start with an understanding of light, vision, and perception.

Figure 12.1a Low sunken relief is ideal for the very bright and direct sun of Egypt. (Courtesy of the Egyptian Tourist Authority.)

Figure 12.1b High relief is modeled well by the direct sun of Greece.

Figure 12.1c The cloudy and subdued lighting of northern Europe allows highly sculptured forms. Even when the sun does come out, as in this photograph, it is not so intense that details are lost in dark shadows. (Photograph by Nicholas Davis.)

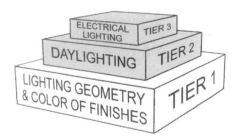

Figure 12.1d High-quality and more sustainable lighting is best achieved via the three-tier design approach. This chapter covers tier one.

12.2 LIGHT

Light is defined as that portion of the electromagnetic spectrum to which our eyes are visually sensitive (Fig. 12.2a). In Fig. 6.2b, we see the intensity of the solar radiation reaching the earth as a function of wavelength. It is no accident that our eyes have evolved to make use of that portion of the solar radiation that is most intense.

Not all animals are limited to the visible spectrum. Rattlesnakes can see the infrared radiation emitted by a warm-blooded animal. Many insects can see ultraviolet radiation, and to them, flowers look quite different. We can get a notion of how the world looks to them when we see certain materials illuminated by **black light**, which is ultraviolet light just beyond violet. Certain materials **fluoresce** (glow) when exposed to radiation at this wavelength. Ultraviolet radiation of a somewhat shorter wavelength causes our skin to tan or burn. Even shorter ultraviolet radiation is so destructive that it is germicidal and can be used in sterilization (Fig. 12.2a). Although we cannot see beyond the visible spectrum, we can feel infrared radiation on our skin as heat.

Lumen

The rate at which a light source emits light energy is analogous to the rate at which water sprays out of a garden hose (Fig. 12.2b). The power with which light is emitted from a lamp is called **luminous flux** and is measured in **lumens**. We can say that the quantity of light a lamp emits in all directions is indicated by its lumen value (Fig. 12.2c). The same unit is used in the SI system (Table 12.2).

Efficacy

Using efficient lamps saves not only money but energy and, therefore, the environment. The ratio of light output to energy input is called **efficacy**.

$$\frac{\text{light out}}{\text{energy in}} = \frac{\text{lumens}}{\text{watts}} = \text{efficacy}$$

Thus, the efficacy of the lamps in Fig. 12.2c is:

Incandescent: $\dfrac{1740 \text{ lm}}{100 \text{ W}} = 17.4$

Fluorescent: $\dfrac{7800 \text{ lm}}{100 \text{ W}} = 78$

High pressure sodium: $\dfrac{9500 \text{ lm}}{100 \text{ W}} = 95$

Note that fluorescent lamps emit about four times as much light as incandescent lamps with the same amount of electricity.

Candlepower

Lumens, however, do not reveal how the emitted light is distributed. In Fig. 12.2d, we see two reflector lamps that give off equal amounts of light (lumens) but with very different distribution patterns. The spot lamp has an intense, narrow beam, while the flood lamp has a much wider beam with less intensity. **Candlepower**, measured in **candelas**, describes the intensity of the beam in any direction. Manufacturers supply candlepower distribution graphs for each of their lighting fixtures (Fig. 12.2e). The SI system uses the term **candela**, and both units have the same magnitude (Table 12.2).

Table 12.2 Comparison of the Inch-Pound (I-P) and Systeme International (SI) Lighting Units			
	(I-P)	**(SI)**	**Conversion Factor**
Supply of light	Lumen (lm)	Lumen (lm)	1
Luminous intensity	Candlepower (cp) or candela (cd)	Candela (cd)	1
Illuminance	Footcandle (fc)	Lux (lx)	1 fc ≈ 10 lx*
Luminance	cd/ft²	cd/m²	1 cd/ft² ≈ 0.1 cd/m²*

*Approximations are appropriate because both the eye and most light meters have a high tolerance.

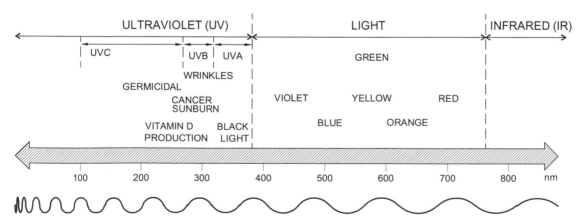

Figure 12.2a Light is only a small part of the electromagnetic spectrum. Light is the radiation to which our eyes are visually sensitive.

Figure 12.2b The supply of light and its water analogy.

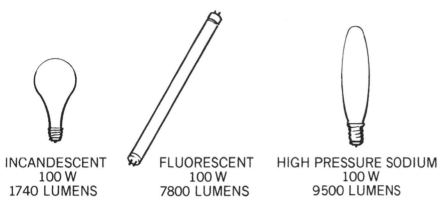

INCANDESCENT	FLUORESCENT	HIGH PRESSURE SODIUM
100 W	100 W	100 W
1740 LUMENS	7800 LUMENS	9500 LUMENS

Figure 12.2c The power or rate at which lamps emit light is measured in lumens. Because of large differences in efficiency, lamps of equal wattage can emit very different amounts of light.

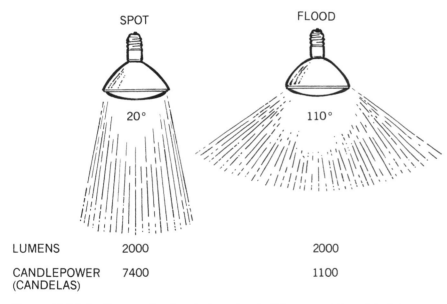

	SPOT	FLOOD
	20°	110°
LUMENS	2000	2000
CANDLEPOWER (CANDELAS)	7400	1100

Figure 12.2d Candlepower describes the intensity of a light source. Although both lamps emit the same amount of light (lumens), the intensity and width of the beams are very different. *Average value of the central 10° cone.

Illuminance

The lumens from a light source will illuminate a surface. A meaningful comparison of various illumination schemes is possible only when we compare the light falling on equal areas. **Illuminance** is, therefore, equal to the number of lumens falling on each square foot (meter) of a surface. The unit of illumination is the **footcandle (lux)**. For example, when the light of 80 lumens falls uniformly on a 4 ft² table, the illumination of that table is 20 lumens per square foot, or 20 footcandles (see Fig. 12.2f and Sidebox 12.2a for the SI example). Illumination is measured with footcandle (lux) meters, which are also known as **illuminance meters** or **photometers**. Such instruments are available in a wide range of prices.

Brightness/Luminance

The words **brightness** and **luminance** are closely related. The brightness of an object refers to the perception of a human observer, while the object's luminance refers to the objective measurement of a light meter. The perception of brightness is a function of the object's actual luminance, the adaptation of the eye, and the brightness of adjacent objects. Although the words are interchangeable much of the time, under certain conditions a significant discrepancy exists between what we see (brightness) and what a light meter reads (luminance).

Luminance is the amount of light that is reflected off an object's surface and reaches the eye. The luminance of an object is a function of the illumination; the geometry of the viewer in relation to the light source; the **specularity**, or mirror-like reflection, of the object; and the color, or reflectance, of the object (Fig. 12.2g). Light emitted from glowing or translucent objects is also called **luminance**. Thus, we can talk of the luminance of a table, an electric lamp, or a translucent window.

It is usually more important to consider the perceived brightness than the objective luminance. Lights will generally appear much brighter at night than during the day, but they will register the same luminance on a light meter at any time. Since we design lighting for people and not light meters, it is usually more important to focus on brightness than luminance.

Conversions Between System International and American System

In lighting, the switch to the Systeme International (SI) from the inch-pound (I-P) will be rather painless.

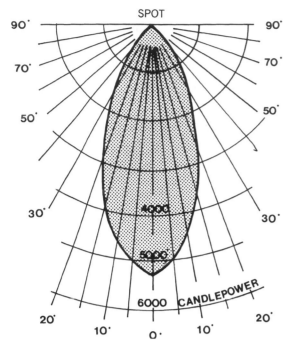
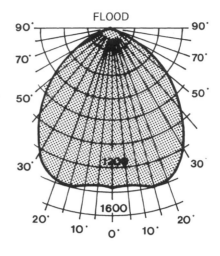

SPOT

FLOOD

Figure 12.2e Candlepower distribution curves illustrate how light is emitted from lamps and lighting fixtures. In this vertical section, the distance from the center determines the intensity of the light in that direction.

SIDEBOX 12.2A

Illuminance (inch-pound system)

$$\text{footcandles} = \frac{\text{lumens}}{\text{square feet of area}}$$

or

$$\text{fc} = \frac{\text{lm}}{\text{ft}^2}$$

Thus, the illumination of the table in Figure 12.2f is:

$$\text{Illuminance} = \frac{80\ \text{lm}}{4\ \text{ft}^2} = 20\ \text{fc}$$

Illuminance (SI system)

$$\text{lux} = \frac{\text{lumens}}{\text{square meter}}$$

or

$$\text{lx} = \frac{\text{lm}}{\text{m}^2}$$

Thus, the illumination of the table in Figure 12.2f is:

$$\text{illuminance} = \frac{80\ \text{lm}}{4\ \text{ft}^2\ (0.09\ \text{m}^2/\text{ft}^2)}$$

$$= 222\ \text{lux}$$

Note that this answer is approximately ten times larger than the 20 footcandles answer above, as is expected from the approximate conversion factor given in Table 12.2.

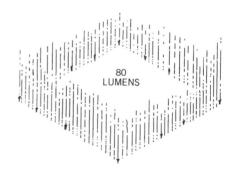

80 LUMENS

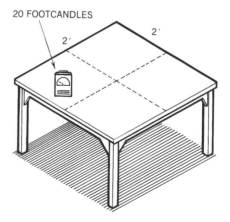

20 FOOTCANDLES

Figure 12.2f Illumination (footcandles) is the amount of light (lumens) falling on 1 square foot. Illumination can be measured with a photometer (light meter). In the SI system, illumination is measured in lux.

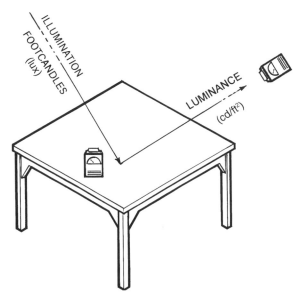

Figure 12.2g The luminance of the table is a function of the illumination, the color (reflectance), and the smoothness (specularity) of the table. Except for a perfectly flat (matte) surface, the luminance is also a function of the direction of the illumination and the direction of the luminance measurement.

Both systems use the unit of the lumen, and the unit of candlepower is equal to the SI candela. Lux is the SI unit for illumination and is approximately equal to one-tenth of a foot-candle or

1 footcandle = approximately 10 lux

(see Table 12.2).

12.3 REFLECTANCE/ TRANSMITTANCE

Light falling on an object can be transmitted, absorbed, or reflected. The **reflectance factor (RF)** indicates how much of the light falling on a surface is reflected. To determine the RF of a surface, divide the reflected light by the incident light. Since the reflected light (brightness) is always less than the incident light (illumination), the RF is always less than 1, and since a little light is always reflected, the RF is never 0. A white surface has an RF of about 0.85, while a black surface has an RF of only 0.05. The RF does not predict how the light will be reflected, only how much. Very smooth polished surfaces, such as mirrors, produce specular reflections where the angle of incidence is equal to the angle of reflection. Very flat or matte surfaces scatter the light to produce diffuse reflections. Most materials reflect light in both a specular and a diffuse manner (Fig. 12.3a).

Similarly, the **transmittance factor** describes the amount of light that is transmitted compared to the incident light. To determine the transmittance factor of a surface, divide the transmitted light by the incident light. A clear, **transparent** material transmits the image of the light sources, while a diffusing **translucent** material like frosted glass scatters the light, thereby obscuring the image of the light sources (Fig. 12.3b). In general, diffusion does not affect the quantity of light transmitted (both clear and frosted glass transmit about 85 percent of the incident light).

There are three aspects to the reflection of light: the quantity (the RF), its manner (specular versus diffuse), and spectral selection (color). We have discussed the first two and will now discuss the third.

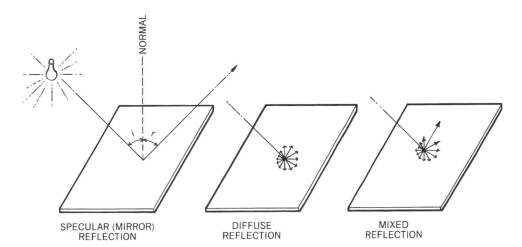

SPECULAR (MIRROR) REFLECTION   DIFFUSE REFLECTION   MIXED REFLECTION

Figure 12.3a The characteristics of a surface determine not only how much but also in what way light is reflected. Most real materials tend to give mixed reflections.

Figure 12.3b Transparent materials do not distort the transmitted image, while translucent (frosted or milky) materials diffuse the light and destroy any image.

12.4 COLOR

White light is a mixture of various wavelengths of visible light. Figure 12.4a illustrates the composition of daylight on a clear day in June at noon. The horizontal axis describes the colors (wavelengths in millionths of a meter) and the vertical axis the amount of light (relative energy) at the various wavelengths. This kind of graph is the best way to describe the color composition of any light, and it is known as a **Spectral Energy distribution (SED)** or **Spectral Power distribution (SPD)** diagram. The mostly horizontal curve reflects the even mixture of the various colors that make up daylight. Only violet light is present in less quantity. North light, which is often considered the ideal white light for painters, is a less even mixture. It has more light in the blue end than the red end of the spectrum, as can be seen in the SED diagram of north light (Fig. 12.4b). Also compare color plates 6 and 7.

Artists' studios used to face north not because north light was considered to have the best color balance but because, until recently, it was the most consistent source of white light. The main advantage of north glazing is the constancy of the light. Light from windows with other orientations varies greatly throughout the day and year. Late-afternoon daylight has much more energy in the red end of the spectrum and less in the blue end. Although all of the above varieties of daylight and many artificial light sources supply "white" light, there is a great difference in the composition of these sources.

The color of a surface is due not only to its spectrally selective reflectance characteristics but also to the spectral composition of the illumination. A completely saturated (pure) red paint that is illuminated by monochromatic (pure) red light will appear bright red because most of the light is reflected (Fig. 12.4c). However, if this same red paint is illuminated

with monochromatic blue light, it will appear black because the color red absorbs all colors except red (Fig. 12.4d). Unless the red paint is illuminated with light that contains red, it will not appear red.

In the real world, where the colors are not completely saturated (pure), the situation is more complicated.

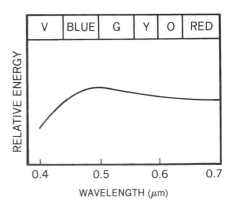

Figure 12.4a The spectral-energy distribution (SED) of average daylight at noon on a clear day in June. Notice the almost even distribution of the various colors. (See also Color Plate 6).

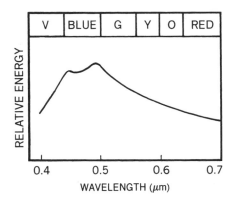

Figure 12.4b The spectral-energy distribution of daylight from a north-facing window. Note that there is more energy in the blue end than the red end of the spectrum. (See also Color Plate 7).

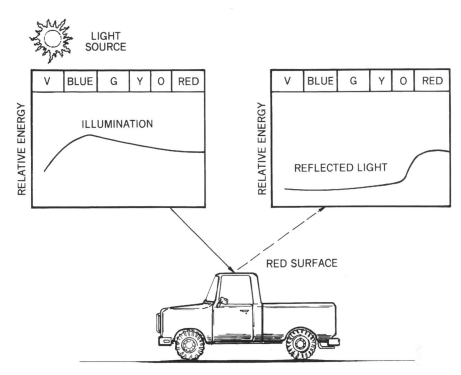

Figure 12.4e A red car will appear red if it is illuminated by a full-spectrum white light source, such as the sun.

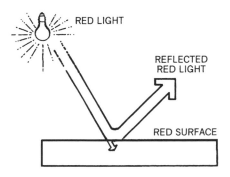

Figure 12.4c A red-colored surface reflects most red light and absorbs most of the light of the other colors.

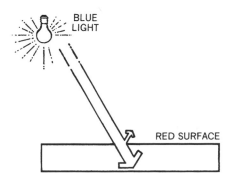

Figure 12.4d Under pure blue light, a pure red color will appear black since almost no light is reflected.

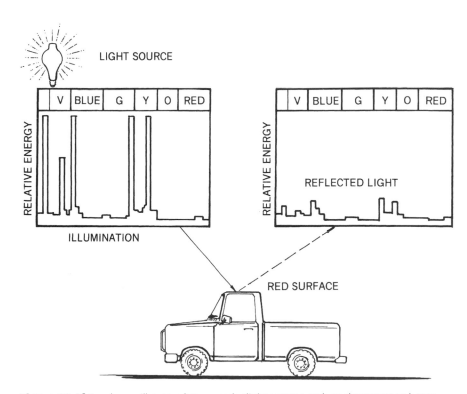

Figure 12.4f A red car will appear brown under light sources such as clear mercury lamps because these lamps emit only small amounts of red light. Thus, only a very small amount of red light is reflected from the car.

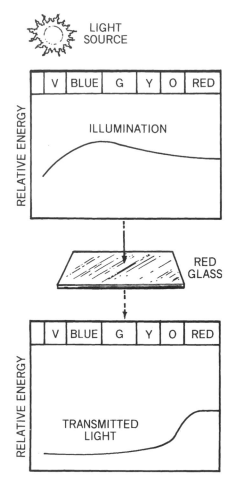

Figure 12.4g Red glass transmits most of the red light but only very little of the other colors.

Figure 12.4i This device is used for comparing the color-rendering effect of two different light sources on the same color samples.

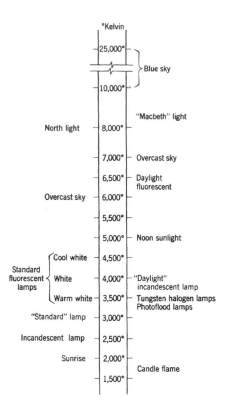

Figure 12.4h The color-temperature scale gives a rough indication of the color balance (spectral-energy distribution) of various sources of "white" light. (From *Mechanical and Electrical Equipment for Buildings*, by B. Stein et al., 10th ed., © John Wiley & Sons, Inc., 2006.)

Ordinary colors, such as red, reflect not only most of the red light, but also small amounts of the other colors. This can create problems when the illumination does not have a good mixture of the various colors. A bright red car reflects plenty of red light when it is illuminated by daylight (Fig. 12.4e). However, when this same bright red car is parked at night under a clear mercury street light, it will appear to be brown (Fig. 12.4f). Since clear mercury lamps emit mostly blue, green, and yellow light, there is little red light that the car can reflect. Although much of the light of the other colors is absorbed, enough blue and green is reflected to overwhelm the red light.

When an object's color is very important, as, for example, in the displaying of meat or tomatoes, the selection of the light source is critical. A full-spectrum white light source will accurately render the red colors of these items. To make them look even fresher and more appetizing, a light source rich in red could be used.

The transmission of light through colored glass or plastic is a selective process similar to reflection. A white light viewed through red glass will appear red because red light is mostly transmitted, and the light of the other colors is mostly absorbed (Fig. 12.4g).

Color Temperature

To completely describe the color content of a light source, the amount of light at each wavelength must be defined as in the SED diagrams of Color Plates 6 to 14. Because this method is quite cumbersome, the concept of **color temperature (CT)** is often used. Many materials, when heated, first glow red, then white, and finally blue. Thus, there is a relation between temperature and color. A CT scale was developed that describes the color of a light source in Kelvin (Fig. 12.4h and Color Plate 17).

CT is mostly used to describe the warmness or coolness of a light source. Low-CT or warm light sources tend to render red colors well, while high-CT or cool light sources tend to render blue colors well. It must be noted, however, that this scale can give only a very crude description of the color-rendering ability of light sources. Another attempt to simplify the description of light sources was the development of the **color-rendering index (CRI)**, but it, too, has limitations and must be used with care. The CRI compares light sources to a standard source of white light. A perfect match would yield a CRI of 100, which is the value of daylight. A CRI of 90 is considered quite good, and a CRI of 70 is sometimes still acceptable (Color Plate 18).

Because of the simplicity of the CRI, it is tempting to rely on it too much. The CRI can be used only to compare light sources of the same color temperatures. Even then there is no guarantee that any specific color will appear natural.

Color selection or matching is best accomplished by actual tests. If colors are to be matched or selected, they must be examined with the type of light source by which they will be illuminated. Many designers have been shocked when they saw their carefully chosen colors under a different light source. The effect of light sources on color appearance is called **color rendition** and will be discussed in Chapter 14.

To see how two different light sources will render a specific color sample, a side-by-side comparison can be made with the setup shown in Fig. 12.4i. A divider prevents light from either source from crossing over to the other color sample. Both samples must be seen at the same time because of a phenomenon of perception called "color constancy," explained in Section 12.6.

Rules for Choosing White Light Sources

1. Full-spectrum white light is required for the accurate judgment of color.
2. People prefer white light sources between 3000°K (warm white) and 4100°K (cool white).
3. Warmer colors are preferred when illumination levels are low and to complement skin tones.
4. Cooler colors are preferred at high light levels and in hot climates.
5. Use 5000°K (cold white) light where very accurate color judgments must be made, as in studios.
6. Use a source with a CRI above 90 where color is important, and above 80 whenever possible. A CRI below 60 is unacceptable in most situations.

12.5 VISION

Vision is the ability to gain information through light entering the eyes. Rather than compare the eye to a photographic camera, which is the usual analogy, let's compare it to the video camera of a robot (Fig. 12.5a). The light rays that enter the video camera are transformed into electrical signals, and the robot's computer then processes these signals for their information content. The meaning of the signals is determined by both the hardware and software of the robot. Similarly, our eyes convert light into electrical signals that the brain then processes (Fig. 12.5b). Here also, the meaning of the visual information is a consequence of the hardware (eye and brain) and the software (associations, memory, and intelligence). The brain's interpretation of what the eyes see is called "perception." Although a lighting design must ultimately be based on an understanding of perception, we must start by understanding vision.

Light enters the eye through an opening called the **pupil** and is focused on the light-sensitive lining at the back of the eye called the **retina**. The retina consists of **cone** cells that are sensitive to colors and **rod** cells that respond to motion and dim lighting conditions.

To accommodate the large range of brightness levels in our environment, the eye adapts by varying the size of the pupil with the muscle called the **iris**, as well as by a change in the sensitivity of the retina. The eye is able to see effectively in a range of brightness of 1000 to 1 and to partially see in a range of over 100,000,000 to 1. However, it takes about an hour for the eye to make a full adaptation; in the meantime, vision is not at its best.

Table 12.5 lists commonly experienced brightness levels and shows how these relate to vision. Although

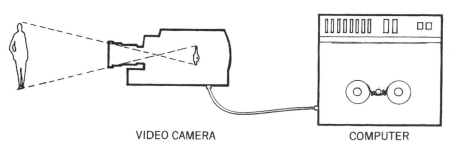

Figure 12.5a In robots that can "see," the computer brain interprets the electrical signals that come from the video camera.

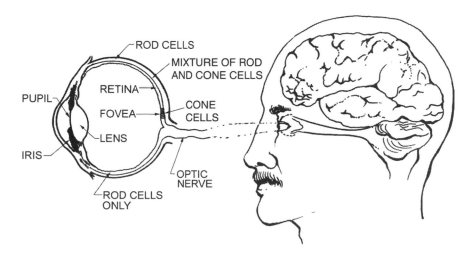

Figure 12.5b Light falling on the retina causes electrical signals to flow to the brain, which then interprets these signals for meaning.

Table 12.5 Commonly Experienced Brightness Levels

	Brightness		
	cd/ft²	cd/m²	
Sidewalk on a dark night	0.0003	0.00003	
Sidewalk in moonlight	0.003	0.0003	Poor vision
Sidewalk under a dim streetlight	0.03	0.003	
Book illuminated by a candle	0.3	0.03	
Wall in an office	3	0.3	Normal indoor brightness
Well-illuminated drafting table	30	3	
Sidewalk on a cloudy day	300	30	Normal outdoor brightness
Fresh snow on a sunny day	3,000	300	
500-W incandescent lamp	30,000	3,000	Blinding glare

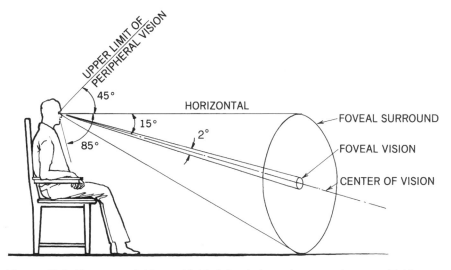

Figure 12.5c The center of vision and field of view is shown for a seated person with his head and eyes in the normal relaxed position. The foveal surround is a 30° cone within which brightness ratios must be carefully controlled.

each item listed is ten times brighter than the previous item, we don't see it as ten times brighter. This illustrates the nonlinear sensitivity of the eyes and the consequence that it takes large increases in light for the eyes to notice a small increase in brightness.

Although rapid and extreme changes in brightness cause stress and fatigue, the eye is very well adapted to the gradual changes in brightness that are associated with daylighting. Because of the eye's adaptation, we perceive only small changes in light levels when clouds move across the sky. A gradual change in brightness is not a liability and might even be an asset because changes are more stimulating than static conditions.

A very small area of the retina surrounding the center of vision called the **fovea** consists mainly of cone cells. Here, the eye receives most of the information on detail and color (Fig. 12.5b). The foveal (sharp) vision occurs in a 2° cone around the center of vision, which moves as the eye scans. Focus, color, and awareness in the field of view decrease with distance from the central 2° cone of vision, because the density of cone cells decreases while that of rod cells increases. Rod cells respond to low light levels and movement but not to color or detail. Awareness is still quite high in the **foveal surround** which is within a 30° cone around the center of vision. The nose, cheeks, and eyebrows are the limiting factors for peripheral vision, and the total field is, therefore, about 130° in the vertical direction and about 180° in the horizontal direction.

For a seated person whose head and eyes are at rest, the center of vision is about 15° below horizontal (Fig. 12.5c). The location and brightness of objects in the field of view will have a major impact on the quality of the lighting environment, as discussed in more detail later.

12.6 PERCEPTION

The ancient Greeks realized that we do not perceive the world as it actually is. They found that when they built their early temples with straight lines, right angles, and uniform spacing of columns, the results were perceived not as they built them (Fig. 12.6a) but distorted, as shown in Fig. 12.6b. Consequently, the Greeks built later temples, like the Parthenon, in a very cleverly distorted manner (Fig. 12.6c) so that they would be perceived as correct (Fig. 12.6a).

In the Parthenon, the columns are all inclined inward to prevent the illusion that they are falling outward. The columns have a slight bulge (entasis) to counteract the illusion of concavity that characterizes columns with straight sides. The column spacing and thickness vary because of the effect of high brightness ratios. Figure 12.6d illustrates how bright columns on a dark background look sturdier than dark columns on a bright background. This is important because the Parthenon's central columns are seen against the dark, shaded building wall, while the end columns are seen against the bright sky. Therefore, the ancient Greeks made the end columns thicker than the central columns.

This example of temple design was not included to suggest that we should proportion our buildings as

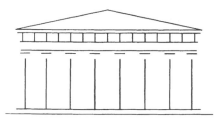

Figure 12.6a Greek temples appear to be built with straight lines, square corners, and uniform spacing of the repeating elements.

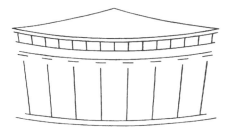

Figure 12.6b When a temple was actually built as shown in Fig. 12.6a, it was perceived as distorted in this manner (optical illusions).

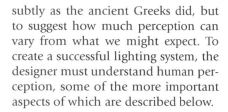

Figure 12.6c The Parthenon was actually built in this distorted way so that it would be perceived as shown in Fig. 12.6a.

COLUMNS

Figure 12.6d Some columns appear bright because of the shaded wall behind them. Corner columns seen against the bright sky seem dark in comparison. Because the darker corner columns appear smaller and weaker than the brighter columns, the Greeks made the end columns stouter than the central columns. (Figures 12.6a–d are from Banister Fletcher's *A History of Architecture, 19th ed., edited by John Musgrove*, © Royal Institute of British Architects, 1987.)

subtly as the ancient Greeks did, but to suggest how much perception can vary from what we might expect. To create a successful lighting system, the designer must understand human perception, some of the more important aspects of which are described below.

Relativity of Brightness

The absolute value of brightness, as measured by a **photometer (light meter)** is called **luminance.** A human being, however, judges the brightness of an object relative to the brightness of the surroundings. Since the Renaissance, painters have used this principle to create the illusion of bright sunshine. The puddle of light on the table in the painting in Fig. 12.6e will appear as bright sunshine no matter how little light illuminates the painting. The painter was able to

"highlight" objects by creating a dark setting rather than by high illumination levels. Figure 12.6f shows this same principle in an abstract diagram. The middle gray triangles are identical in every way, including their reflectance factor. Their luminance, as measured by a photometer, will be the same but their perceived brightness will depend on the brightness of the surrounding area.

Because of the importance of this aspect of perception, one more example is in order. Car headlamps seem very bright at night but are just noticeable during the day. Although a meter would show the luminance to be the same, the brightness we perceive depends on the brightness of the headlamps relative to the overall lighting condition. This is partly due to the fact that at night, our wide-open pupils allow much of the light of the

Figure 12.6e This Italian painter of the nineteenth century fully understood the concept of relativity of brightness. He could simulate bright sunshine by creating dark surroundings. The mind visualizes bright sunshine no matter how little light is falling on this painting. *The 26th of April 1859*, painted by Odoardo Borrani in 1861. (Courtesy of the Guiliano Matteucci-Studio d'Arte Matteucci, Rome, Italy.)

headlights to enter, while during the day, our small pupils shield us from the excess light of the headlights.

Brightness Constancy

To make sense of the visual environment, the brain has to make adjustments to what the eyes see. For example, in a room with windows on one end, the ceiling plane will appear of constant brightness, although a photometer would clearly show greater luminance near the windows. The brain knows that the reflectance factor is constant and that it is the illumination level that is varying. Consequently, the brain interprets the ceiling as having uniform brightness. This ability of the brain to ignore differences in luminance under certain conditions is called **brightness constancy**.

Color Constancy

It is common to have the experience of photographing a white building at sunset and then being surprised when the photograph comes back showing a pink building. The photograph tells the truth. Our perception fooled us into seeing a white building when we took the picture. Our brain "filtered" out much of the red light from the setting sun, something a camera can do also — but only when the lens is covered with a color filter or the "white balance" is adjusted in a digital camera. This ability of the brain to eliminate some of the differences in color due to differences in illumination is called **color constancy**. This ability has very important survival implications because, without it, we would never recognize our own home if we returned at a different time of day.

Color constancy is not possible, however, if more than one type of light source is used simultaneously. Figure 12.6g illustrates what happens if an object is illuminated by north light from one side and an incandescent lamp from the other. One shadow will appear bluish and the other reddish because the brain

cannot adjust to the color balance of each source simultaneously. A lighting design with different light sources must take this into account. Often, the best solution is not to mix light sources that are very different. The placement of clear window glazing adjacent to tinted glazing should also be avoided.

Although the brain makes some adjustment to perceived colors, cold north light will never look the same as warm, sunny sunlight. The adjustment due to color constancy is limited.

Other Color Perception Phenomena

The warm colors (red, orange, and yellow) appear to advance toward the eye, while the cool colors (blue, green and dark gray) appear to recede. The choice of wall colors can make a space seem larger or smaller than it actually is.

Prolonged concentration on any color will result in an afterimage of the complementary color. A surgeon staring at a bright red organ will see a green organ as an afterimage when

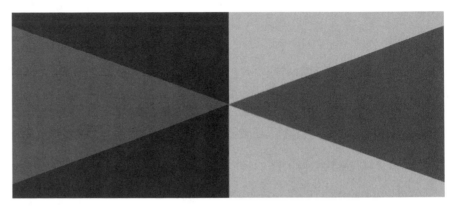

Figure 12.6f The two isosceles triangles are exactly the same, yet they appear to have different reflectance factors because of the phenomenon of the relativity of brightness. To see the triangles as equal, cover the dark areas around the left triangle with two pieces of white paper.

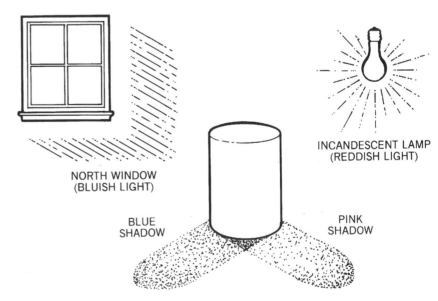

Figure 12.6g When more than one type of white light is used, color constancy cannot operate. One consequence is that shadows appear colored. However, if either source is eliminated, the remaining shadow will appear normal because color constancy can then be activated by the brain.

Figure 12.6h Venetian blinds are often disturbing because of the figure/background confusion.

Figure 12.6i The brain perceives only a bar and a circle.

Figure 12.6j The brain perceives an exclamation mark rather than a bar and a circle. This perception of greater meaning is explained by Gestalt Theory.

Figure 12.6k Since the brain is not sure if there is greater meaning, this pattern is disturbing.

she moves her eyes to look elsewhere. To minimize this upsetting phenomenon, hospitals now use green sheets and wall surfaces in their operating rooms. A green afterimage superimposed on a green sheet is much less noticeable than when it is superimposed on a white sheet.

Figure/Background Effect

The brain is always trying to sort out the visual signal from the visual noise. When this becomes difficult or impossible, the image becomes disturbing. Figure 12.6h illustrates a view interrupted by venetian blinds. In many cases, a properly designed overhang could achieve the same shading without any obstruction of the view.

Gestalt Theory

The purpose of seeing is to gather information. The brain is always looking for meaningful patterns. In Fig. 12.6i, we see only a small circle and a long rectangle. But in Fig. 12.6j, the first thing we see is the exclamation mark. In Fig. 12.6k, we see a disturbing arrangement because it reminds us of something, but it is not quite right. The brain's search for greater meaning than the separate parts would suggest is called **Gestalt Theory.** A particular lighting scheme will, therefore, be successful not only because all the parts are well designed but also because the

whole composition is meaningful and not disturbing or distracting.

Other Perception Phenomena

Bright ceilings and upper walls make a room look larger and friendly, while dark ceilings and upper walls make a room seem smaller and less inviting.

Dramatic lighting is achieved by utilizing large brightness ratios in the field of view.

Romantic light, as from a candle on a dining table in a dark room, has several benefits. It creates an intimate space, it emits a very warm light whose reds complement skin complexion, and the nearly horizontal light tends to make facial wrinkles disappear.

12.7 PERFORMANCE OF A VISUAL TASK

Many factors affect the performance of a visual task (i.e., a task like reading, where visibility is important). Some of these factors are inherent in the task, some describe the lighting conditions, and the remainder reflect the condition of the observer. Most of the important factors can be easily understood by examining the common but critical seeing task of reading an interstate-highway sign (Fig. 12.7). Since the time of exposure is very limited, the signs are made large, bright, of high contrast, and of a consistent design. They are either well illuminated at night, or the lettering uses reflective materials. Sometimes, however, they are obscured by the glare of oncoming cars. The health and alertness of the driver are also factors. Thus, we can see that the basic

Figure 12.7 Since exposure time is limited, the other factors of visual performance are used to their maximum effect: size/proximity, brightness (night illumination), contrast, and familiarity (always white on green for exit signs.)

factors that affect the performance of a visual task can be categorized as:

A. The task
   1. Size/proximity
   2. Exposure time
   3. Brightness
   4. Contrast
   5. Familiarity
B. The Lighting Condition
   1. Illumination level
   2. Brightness ratios
   3. Glare
C. The Observer
   1. Condition of eyes
   2. Adaptation
   3. Fatigue level
   4. Health
   5. Effect of drugs and alcohol.

Most of these factors will now be discussed in more detail.

12.8 CHARACTERISTICS OF THE VISUAL TASK

Size/Proximity

The most important characteristic of a visual task is the **exposure angle**, which is a function of the viewed object's size and proximity. The exposure angle will increase when the object is either enlarged or brought closer (Fig. 12.8a). In most cases, the brain then determines the cause by its familiarity with the real world and by means of binocular vision.

Whenever possible, the designer should increase the size of the task because a small increase in size is equivalent to a very large increase in illumination level. For example, a 25 percent increase in lettering size on a blackboard increases the visual performance as much as a change in illumination from 10 to 1000 footcandles (100 to 10,000 lux).

Exposure Time

Other factors of visual performance can offset a short exposure time, but, as with size, very high increases of illumination are required to offset small decreases in the exposure time. Thus, exposure time should not be cut short if at all possible.

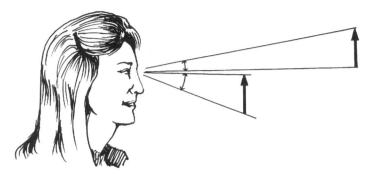

Figure 12.8a Size and proximity together determine the exposure angle.

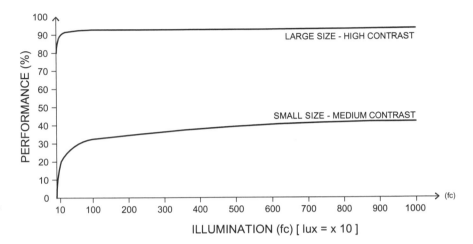

Figure 12.8b At first, visual performance improves rapidly with increase in illumination (brightness), but soon the law of diminishing returns governs. Above about 100 fc (1000 lux) there is little benefit with even large increases of illumination. For tasks of large size and high contrast, even 10 footcandles (100 lux) are enough. This graph also shows that no amount of light can make the performance of tasks of small size and medium contrast be the same as the performance of tasks of large size and high contrast. Thus, whenever possible, both the task and lighting should be adjusted. (After Boyce et al., 2000.)

Brightness

Figure 12.8b illustrates how an increase in task brightness, caused by increased illumination, at first results in significant improvements in visual performance, but additional increases yield smaller and smaller benefits. The "law of diminishing returns" is in effect because of the nonlinear relationship between brightness and visual performance. For example, in raising the illumination from 0 to 50 footcandles (0 to 500 lux), the brightness also increases, and the visual performance improves to about 85 percent of the maximum performance, while another increase of 50 footcandles (500 lux) improves the visual performance only by 5 percent. Since large increases in brightness are made possible only by large increases in illumination, high brightness is a very expensive route to visual performance.

The discussion so far has been about absolute brightness (luminance), but, as we saw earlier, we perceive brightness in relative terms. Therefore, it is often possible to increase performance by reducing the background brightness, thereby increasing the relative brightness of the task. The reduction of the background brightness increases the eye's sensitivity to light, making the task easier to see.

Figure 12.8c Fragile artifacts from ancient Egypt are brightly illuminated by only 4 footcandles [40 lux] of illumination because of the very dark background. The designer used the phenomenon of perception called "relativity of brightness". (Courtesy of Memphis State Photo Services, Memphis State University, TN.)

HIGH CONTRAST ILLUMINATION OF ONE FOOTCANDLE IS SUFFICIENT	LOW CONTRAST ILLUMINATION OF OVER 100 FOOTCANDLES IS REQUIRED

Figure 12.8d Contrast is an extremely important factor for the performance of many visual tasks. High levels of illumination are required to compensate for poor contrast.

This concept is used to its fullest by museums exhibiting artifacts that light can damage. Wood, paper, cloth, and natural pigments all fade significantly when exposed to light. Such damage can be minimized by keeping the light level as low as possible. The museum shown in Fig. 12.8c manages to highlight its fragile objects with fewer than 4 footcandles (40 lux) of illumination simply by having an even darker background illumination.

Although ultraviolet radiation causes the most damage to delicate objects, visible light also causes some fading. Short-wavelength radiation, such as that of violet and blue, is worse than the long-wavelength radiation of red.

Contrast

The difference in brightness between a detail and its immediate background is called **contrast**. Most critical visual tasks will benefit when the contrast between the task and its immediate surroundings is maximized. Writing,

for example, is most easily seen when the contrast between ink and paper is at a maximum. When contrast decreases, the other factors of visual performance can be adjusted to compensate. Again, however, very large increases of illumination are required to offset poor contrast (Fig. 12.8d).

It is important to note that the concept of contrast refers to detailed visual tasks (foveal vision), such as the print on a piece of paper. It does not refer to the brightness relationship of the paper to the desk or the desk to surrounding area. The brightness differences in these peripheral areas will have different effects on vision and will be discussed later.

12.9 ILLUMINATION LEVEL

Since brightness is directly proportional to illumination, the previous discussion on brightness is directly relevant to illumination. The graph in Fig. 12.8b describes either the relationship between visual performance and illumination or brightness. As the light level increases to about 50 footcandles (500 lux), there is a significant improvement in visual performance. Above 100 footcandles (1000 lux), however, the law of diminishing returns begins to govern, and large increases in illumination result in only minor improvements in visual performance. The main reason for this is that the pupil gets smaller as the illumination increases. Thus, the amount of light reaching the retina increases only slightly.

It is, therefore, usually appropriate to keep the general area illumination below 30 footcandles (300 lux) and to supply higher light levels only if specific tasks require it. The additional light should be localized to the tasks that require it. This nonuniform approach to lighting is called **task lighting**.

The Illuminating Engineering Society of North America (IESNA) publishes recommended illumination levels for various activities. These recommendations are based on such factors as task activity, required speed,

Table 12.9 Guidelines for Illumination Levels*

Approximate Type of Activity	Examples	fc	lux
1. General lighting throughout space			
a. Public spaces with dark surroundings	Corridors at night	3	30
b. Simple orientation for short, temporary visits	Residential (nonwork), restaurants	8	80
c. Working spaces where visual tasks are only occasionally performed	Corridors, lobbies, churches	15	150
2. Illumination on task			
a. Performance of visual tasks of high contrast or large size	Residential (kitchens and other work areas), hotels	30	300
b. Performance of visual tasks of medium contrast or small size	Offices, classrooms, banks	75	750
c. Performance of visual tasks of low contrast and very small size over a prolonged period	Studios, critical work areas	150	1500

*Based on IESNA recommendations. Precise values are not appropriate because of the large tolerance of human vision. However, the following adjustments should be made:

1. Increase illumination about 50 percent for any of the following reasons: room surfaces are dark, many people are over age fifty, or the tasks are difficult and/or critical.
2. Decrease the illumination about 50 percent for any of the following reasons: the quality of the lighting is very high, the room surfaces are very light, most people are below age forty, or the tasks are neither difficult nor critical.

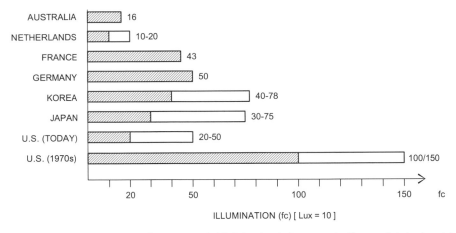

Figure 12.9 A comparison of recommended lighting levels for general office work in horizontal footcandles. Note that some countries recommend ranges instead of a specific value. Also note how the recommended illumination levels have dropped in the United States since the 1970. (After Mills and Borg. "Rethinking Light Levels." IAEEL Newsletter, 7 (20), 4–7 (1998).)

required accuracy, room-surface reflection factors (dark finishes require more light) and occupantage. For example, people in their twenties have a visual performance that is four times better than, that of people in their fifties and eight times better than that of people in their sixties. Higher illumination levels can help to offset the handicap of older eyes.

At the schematic design stage, however, only a very rough approximation of illumination levels is required for determining lighting strategies and for model studies. Table 12.9 gives guidelines for illumination levels appropriate for various activities. Unless otherwise specified, illumination levels are always given for horizontal work surfaces, and

most tasks are performed on tables or desks that are about 2½ ft (75 cm) high.

The ASHRAE Standard 90-75, which has been widely accepted as an energy code, makes the following recommendations about lighting:

1. Task lighting should be consistent with the IESNA recommendations.
2. General area lighting should be one-third of task lighting.
3. Noncritical circulation lighting should be one-third of general area lighting.

For example, in an office the task lighting might be 75 footcandles (750 lux), the general area lighting 25 footcandles (250 lux), and the corridor 8 footcandles (80 lux).

There is nothing absolute about these recommended light levels, as can be seen by the dramatic decrease in recommended light levels in the United States in the last thirty years (Fig. 12.9). Also, consider the very large discrepancy in what is recommended in various industrialized countries. Much more important than quantity is the quality of the light. The following discussion will explain the critical aspects of quality light.

To further demonstrate that the quantity of light is not the primary goal in lighting design, it is worth while to discuss the **Hawthorne effect**. A series of studies around 1930 on the effect of light levels on productivity showed that both an increase and a decrease in illumination levels could cause an increase in productivity. This apparently absurd result indicated that other factors were much more important than illumination levels in affecting productivity in a visual task. Further research showed that motivation and attitudes toward the job had a far greater impact. A good way for a lighting designer to incorporate the Hawthorne effect would be to give each worker control over his or her own lighting. Both physiological and psychological needs are addressed by a task light that has both flexible arms and a brightness adjustment.

12.10 BRIGHTNESS RATIOS

Although the eye can adapt to large variations in brightness, it cannot adapt to two very different brightness levels simultaneously. This problem can be easily visualized by looking at photographs of a building entrance. In Fig. 12.10a, the camera was set to correctly expose the exterior; consequently, the view of the interior is too dark to see. On the other hand, in Fig. 12.10b, we see the same entrance where the camera was set to correctly expose the interior, and the result is that the outdoors are too bright to see. There is no way that the camera itself can overcome the problem of the excessive brightness ratio between indoors and outdoors. Professional photographers usually wait until early evening, when the indoor and outdoor brightnesses are equal. Another option is to greatly increase the indoor illumination.

Although the eye can minimize this problem by concentrating on one brightness area at a time, all brightness areas in the field of view have some impact. The result of too high a **brightness ratio** is visual stress. If the eye keeps switching back and forth between areas of very different brightness, the additional stress of constant readaptation will also be present.

Lighting designers can avoid these sources of visual stress by controlling the brightness ratios in the field of view. They can accomplish this by adjusting reflectance factors as well as the illumination of surfaces, since brightness is a function of both. The eye is most sensitive to brightness ratios near the center of vision and least sensitive at the edge of peripheral vision. Consequently, the acceptable brightness ratios depend on the part of the field of view that is affected. For good visual performance such as that required in an office, the brightness ratios should be kept within the limits shown in Table 12.10.

The first step in designing brightness ratios is to choose the reflectance factors of all large surfaces. In work areas, such as offices, the following *minimum* reflectances are recommended: ceiling, 80 percent; vertical surfaces, such as walls, 60 percent; and floors, 40 percent (Fig. 12.11k). Dark walls, especially, should be avoided. A small sample of dark wood paneling can be quite attractive, but a whole wall of it is likely to be oppressive. Additional control of brightness ratios is then achieved by selective illumination. Although the illumination on the work surface is more

Figure 12.10a In this photograph, the camera was adjusted to correctly expose the high brightness of the exterior. We cannot see indoors because the brightness there is too low compared to the outdoors. This is a problem of excessive brightness ratios.

Figure 12.10b In this photograph, the camera was adjusted to correctly expose the interior. Consequently, we cannot clearly see the outdoor view because it is too bright compared to the interior. This is a problem of excessive brightness ratios.

Table 12.10 Maximum Recommended Brightness Ratios for Indoor Lighting*

Ratio	Areas	Example
3:1	Task to immediate surroundings	Book to desk top
5:1	Task to general surroundings	Book to nearby partitions
10:1	Task to remote surroundings	Book to remote wall
20:1	Light source to large adjacent area	Window to adjacent wall

*For high visual performance in a normal work area, these brightness ratios should not be greatly exceeded. However, uniform brightness is not desirable either. The task should be slightly brighter than the immediate surroundings to avoid distraction. This table does not apply in situations in which dramatic highlighting, mood lighting, or aesthetic concerns should be dominant.

Figure 12.10c Although this room has more than enough illumination on the horizontal work surface, it appears dark because of the low brightness of the vertical surfaces. (Photograph by James Benya.)

Figure 12.10d Additional illumination on the vertical surfaces makes this room appear less dark. (Photograph by James Benya.)

than adequate, the walls in Fig. 12.10c are not bright enough. Figure 12.10d shows the same room with additional illumination on the vertical surfaces.

12.11 GLARE

Glare is "visual noise" that interferes with visual performance. Two kinds of glare exist, direct and reflected, and each can have very detrimental effects on the ability to see.

Direct Glare

Direct glare is caused by a light source sufficiently bright to cause annoyance, discomfort, or loss in visual performance. It is called **discomfort glare** when it produces physical discomfort and **disability glare** when it reduces visual performance and visibility. The severity of the glare that a light source causes is due largely to its brightness. Both absolute brightness and apparent brightness produce glare. High-beam headlights can cause blinding glare at night, but hardly any glare during the day. Similarly, a bare lamp against a black ceiling causes much more glare than the same lamp seen against a white ceiling. This is one of several reasons why ceilings should usually be white.

Direct glare is also a consequence of geometry. The closer an offending light source is to the center of vision, the worse the glare. For this reason, windows are often a serious source of glare (Fig. 12.11a). Of all the lights in Fig. 12.11a, lamp C is closest to the center of vision and, therefore, a serious source of glare, while lamp A is not a source of glare at all because it is completely outside the field of view for the observer at the location shown. Geometry also affects the exposure angle, which is a function of both size and proximity. Large exposure angles from large or close light sources also result in more glare than small exposure angles from small or more distant light sources. Thus, glare changes greatly from point to point in a room.

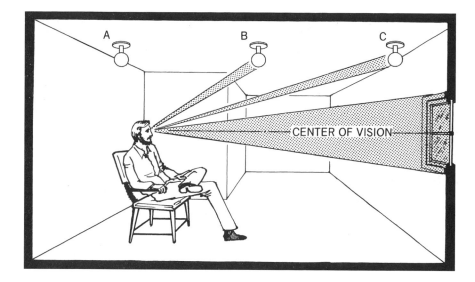

Figure 12.11a Light sources near the center of vision cause more direct glare than those at the edge of the field of view. For the person seated as shown, light A causes no glare at all.

Since ceiling-mounted lighting fixtures are a likely source of direct glare, much research has been conducted to quantify and reduce the glare these fixtures cause. **Eggcrates**, parabolic louvers, lenses, and diffusers are commonly used to minimize glare from lighting fixtures (Fig. 12.11b). These optical controllers eliminate or reduce the light emitted in the direct-glare zone (Fig. 12.11c). Note how the direct-glare zone of the light source (45° below the horizontal) corresponds to the direct-glare zone of the viewer (45° above the horizontal). Because indirect lighting uses the ceiling as a large-area, low-brightness reflector, it creates almost no glare at all. The impact of lighting-fixture design and the benefits of indirect lighting are explained in more detail in Chapter 14.

Since lighting fixtures vary greatly in the amount of direct glare that they produce, the concept of **visual comfort probability (VCP)** was developed. The VCP factor predicts the percentage of people who will find a specific lighting system acceptable with regard to glare. Indirect lighting fixtures, because of their low brightness, come close to the maximum of 100 percent.

We must not forget that lighting design is a problem not just in physics, but also in human perception.

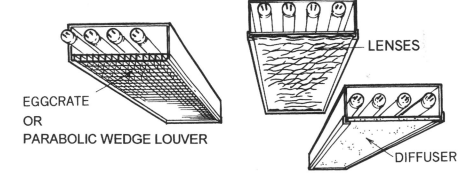

Figure 12.11b Eggcrates, parabolic louvers, baffles, and lenses limit direct glare by controlling the direction of the emitted light. Diffusers limit glare by reducing the brightness of the light source.

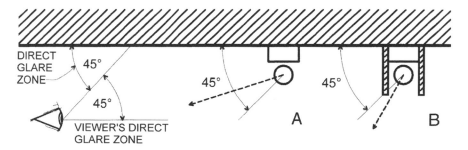

Figure 12.11c Lighting fixture A causes glare because light is emitted within the direct-glare zone, while the shielded fixture B does not cause direct glare. Note how the fixture's and viewer's direct-glare zones correspond.

The same light source that creates glare in an office might create sparkle in a nightclub. What is noise in one situation can be an information signal in another.

Indirect Glare

Reflections of light sources on glossy tabletops or polished floors cause a problem similar to direct glare. Note the reflected glare from the polished floor and glossy metal lockers in the photo of Fig. 12.10b. **Indirect glare** is often best avoided by specifying flat or matte finishes. However, when the task has a glossy surface, the lighting system has to be designed to avoid producing this reflected glare. If shiny surfaces cannot be avoided, then indirect glare can be minimized by using a diffused light source or by working with geometry, as will be explained in the following section on veiling reflections.

Veiling Reflections

The reflections of bright light sources on such tasks as glossy printed pages are known as **veiling reflections** because they reduce the contrast necessary for good visual performance (Fig. 12.11d). The sheen of the reflected light hides

Figure 12.11d Veiling reflections impair the visual performance of a task by reducing contrast.

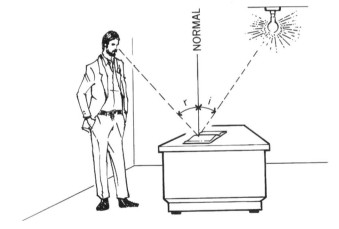

Figure 12.11e Veiling reflections are at a maximum when the angle of incidence (i) equals the angle of reflection (r).

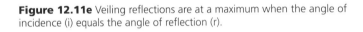
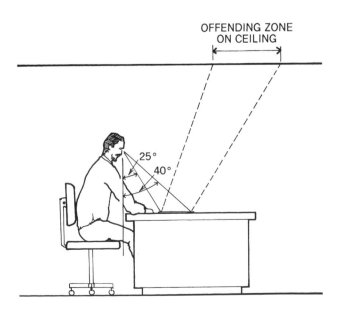

Figure 12.11f Any light source in the offending zone can create severe veiling reflections for a person working at a table or desk. The offending zone will shift if the task or table is tilted (e.g., a drafting table).

or veils the image of a picture or text. Veiling reflections are specular, or mirror-like, reflections that are most severe on very smooth materials, but exist to a lesser degree also on semigloss surfaces. Pencil marks and some inks quickly disappear under veiling reflections because of their glossy finish.

Their sheen will be just as bright as the white background and all contrast is lost (Fig. 12.11d).

Veiling reflections are at a maximum when the angle of incidence, established by the light source, equals the angle of reflection, established by the location of the eye (Fig. 12.11e).

Most people seated at a desk will do their reading and writing in a zone ranging from 25° to 40° measured from the vertical. Any glossy material in this zone will reflect light from a corresponding zone in the ceiling (Fig. 12.11f). Any light source in this **offending zone** of the ceiling will be a cause of veiling reflections. In an existing lighting design, this offending zone is easy to spot simply by substituting a mirror for the visual task (Fig. 12.11g). Similarly, an imagined mirror can help visualize the offending zone in a proposed design. Thus, it is easy to understand how the offending zone shifts if the task is tilted (Fig. 12.11h). It is also easy to understand that light sources behind or to the right or left of the viewer cannot be seen in a mirror on the table and, thus, are not in the offending zone (Fig. 12.11i). However, if the task is nearly vertical, as with a computer monitor, the offending zone will be behind the viewer (Fig. 12.11j).

Veiling reflections are the most serious problem that the lighting designer faces. It is a problem not only for people working behind a desk but also for others, such as workers handling smooth parts, people viewing artwork through glass, etc.

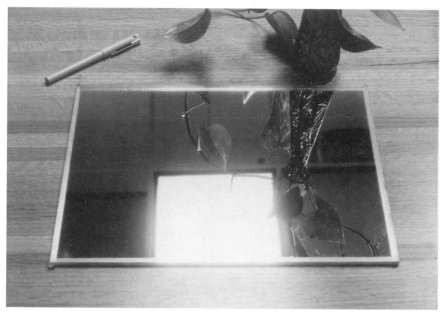

Figure 12.11g By replacing the task with a mirror, any bright light source in the offending zone will be visible. Hold the mirror vertically if the task is in a vertical plane (e.g., a painting or computer monitor).

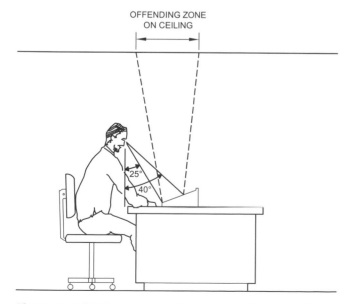

Figure 12.11h When the task is tilted, the offending zone shifts.

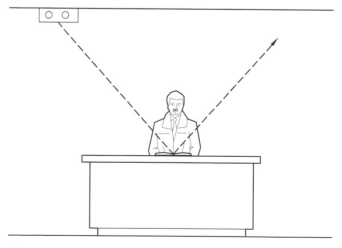

Figure 12.11i To prevent both veiling reflections from front lighting and the casting of shadows from back lighting, the light should come from the sides.

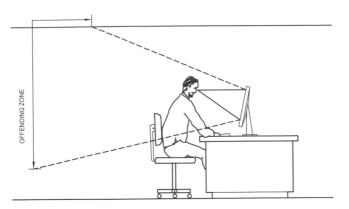

Figure 12.11j The rear wall and ceiling become the offending zone when the task is vertical or nearly vertical.

Figure 12.11k Sources of direct glare and veiling reflections are shown. Recommended reflectance factors are also shown. (Courtesy of General Electric Lighting.)

The problem is getting even more serious with the growing use of computers. The avoidance of glare and veiling reflections is the top priority in most lighting designs. Figure 12.11k illustrates the sources of veiling reflections and direct glare. The diagram also shows common reflectances that will produce acceptable brightness ratios in the field of view. Much of the remainder of this chapter and the following chapters on daylighting and electric lighting discuss how to control glare and veiling reflections.

12.12 EQUIVALENT SPHERICAL ILLUMINATION

Veiling reflections are so detrimental to visual performance that increased lighting at the wrong angle can actually reduce our ability to see. Above a certain minimum, the quality of the light is more important than the quantity. Ordinary "raw" footcandles of illumination, as measured by a photometer, can be meaningless if the geometry of the lighting is not included. To correct this serious deficiency, the concept of **equivalent spherical illumination (ESI)** was developed.

Sphere illumination is a standard reference condition with which the actual illumination can be compared. In sphere illumination, the task receives light from a uniformly illuminated hemisphere (Fig. 12.12a). Since the task is illuminated from all directions, only a small amount of the total light will cause veiling reflections. Although spherical illumination is of high quality, it could be improved by eliminating that small portion of light causing veiling reflections. Sphere illumination is a valuable concept not because it represents the best possible lighting, but because it is a very good reproducible standard with which any actual lighting system can be compared.

An actual lighting system that supplied an illumination of 250 footcandles (2500 lux) might be no better than an equivalent spherical illumination of 50 ESI footcandles (500 lux). This means that the quality of the actual system is so poor that 200 out 250 footcandles (2000 out of 2500 lux) are noneffective. Therefore, the ESI footcandles can tell us how effective the raw footcandles are. ESI enables us to describe the quality as well as the quantity of the illumination.

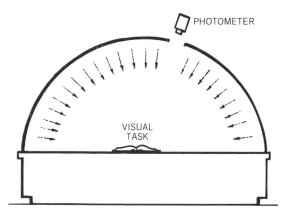

Figure 12.12a Test chamber for measuring equivalent spherical illumination (ESI).

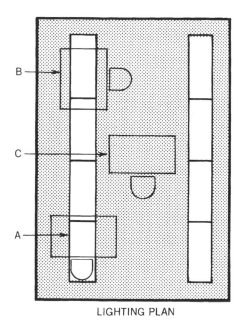

LIGHTING PLAN

	DESK		
	A	B	C
RAW FOOTCANDLES	100	120	90
ESI FOOTCANDLES	17	30	90

Figure 12.12b This reflected ceiling plan also shows the location of the desks. A comparison of raw and ESI footcandles for three different locations clearly shows that desk C has the best lighting. Although desk B has the highest illumination level, the veiling reflections neutralize most of the footcandles. Desk A has the worst lighting of all.

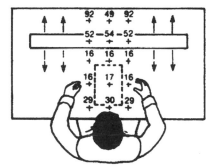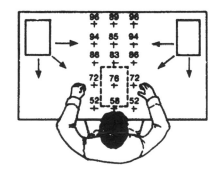

Figure 12.13a The ESI footcandles are quite low for the lighting fixture in front of the task because of the veiling reflections. With fixtures on both sides, there will be almost no veiling reflections, and consequently the ESI footcandles are much higher, although the total wattage is lower. Left: one 40 W lamp; right: two 14 W lamps. Two fixtures are used to prevent shadows from hands. (Courtesy of Cooper Lighting.)

In the lighting layout plan shown in Fig. 12.12b, we can see that the quality of the lighting varies greatly with location and that raw footcandles are not a good indication of visual performance. Notice that if only raw footcandles were considered, location C would be the worst choice for the desk because it has the lowest illumination level. In fact, location C is by far the best, as the very high ESI footcandle level indicates. Locations A and B will both experience serious veiling reflections from the overhead lighting fixtures. This situation can be visualized via the mirror test (Fig. 12.11g). Imagine a mirror placed on each desk in place of the task. The person occupying desk A will see the most lighting fixture in the offending zone, while the person at desk C will see only the ceiling in the offending zone.

Since quality compensates for quantity, the lighting levels that the IESNA recommends can be reduced by 25 percent if veiling reflections are largely avoided. Recommended light levels are still given in raw footcandles because it is very difficult and expensive to measure ESI footcandles.

12.13 ACTIVITY NEEDS

The requirements for good visual performance, mentioned so far, apply to most visual tasks. However, additional requirements vary with the specific visual task.

1. *Reading and writing:* The avoidance of veiling reflections has the highest priority for the activities of reading and writing. Light should, therefore, come from the sides or from behind but never from in front of the observer. Notice in Fig. 12.13a how much higher the ESI footcandles are on a desk when the light comes from the sides rather than from in front. The light should come from at least two sources to prevent workers from casting shadows on their own task.

2. *Drafting and drawing:* Because of the somewhat glossy finish of drafting films, pencil lines, and ink, veiling reflections are a major problem. Shadows from drafting instruments also obscure the work. Very diffuse general lighting with task lighting from either side is appropriate on both accounts.

3. *Observing sculpture:* Shades and shadows are necessary in understanding the three-dimensional form of an object. The appropriate lighting should, therefore, have a strong directional component (Fig. 12.13b). Unless there is some diffused light, however, the shadows will be so dark that many details will be obscured (Fig. 12.13c), but completely diffused lighting is not appropriate either because it makes objects appear flat and some three-dimensional details will tend to disappear (Fig. 12.13d). Usually, the directional light should come from above and slightly to one side because that is the way the sun generally illuminates objects, and we are used to that kind of modeling. Seeing familiar objects like the human face lit from below can be a very eerie experience.

4. *Seeing texture:* The appearance of texture depends on the pattern created by shades and shadows.

Figure 12.13b The best modeling occurs with strong directional light along with some diffused light to soften the shades and shadows.

Figure 12.13c If all the light comes from one direction, strong shadows and shade will obscure much of the object.

Figure 12.13d Some parts of an object will appear flat under completely diffused light.

Figure 12.13e Texture is most visible under glancing light. Note the long shadow of the pushpin in the upper right corner.

Figure 12.13f The same texture seen under straight-on or diffused light. Note the lack of a shadow from the pushpin.

Figure 12.13g It is impossible to appreciate this glass-covered work of art in a famous museum because of the reflected glare caused by a circular downlight (top center of picture) and because of the veiling reflections caused by bright surfaces behind the viewer.

A texture is, therefore, made most visible by glancing light that maximizes the shades and shadows (Fig. 12.13e). The same material seen under diffused or straight-on lighting will appear to have almost no texture (Fig. 12.13f). Glancing light can also be used to investigate surface imperfections; conversely, glancing light should be avoided if surface imperfections are to be hidden.

5. *Looking at paintings:* When one highlights paintings, glossy artwork, or art behind glass, the challenge is to prevent specular reflections of the light sources into the viewers' eyes. Many a fine print protected by glass has become invisible because of veiling reflections (Fig. 12.13g). The accent light must be placed in front of the offending zone so that people of various heights and at different locations will not see the specular reflection of the light source (Fig. 12.13h). However, if the light is too close to the wall above the painting, the top of the picture frame will cast a shadow

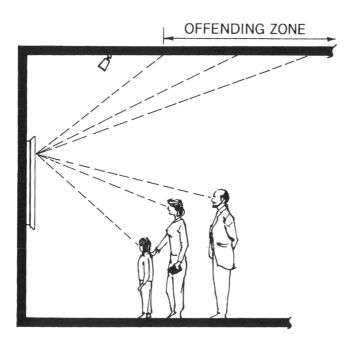

Figure 12.13h Accent lighting must be placed in front of the offending zone.

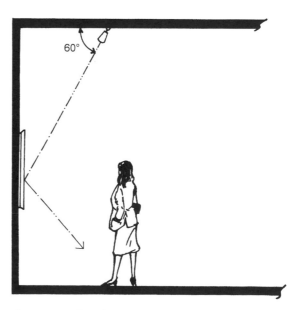

Figure 12.13i Under normal conditions, a 60° fixture aiming angle is quite satisfactory.

Figure 12.13j These two photos are taken from outdoors looking through the storefront of a sporting goods store. With normal glass (right) the reflections of the bright outdoors overwhelm the transmitted image. However, when the storefront is replaced with special antireflective coating glass (left), the reflected image almost disappears. (Courtesy Schott Co.)

and the texture of the painting will be overemphasized. In most cases, a 60° aiming angle will be a good compromise (Fig. 12.13i).

When the artwork is covered with glass, special antireflectivity glass, which makes the lighting much less critical, can be specified (Fig. 12.13j).

6. *Windows:* Because glass transmits about 90 percent and reflects about 10 percent of the light, we always see both the transmitted and reflected images simultaneously. The relative strength of each image depends on the brightness of each scene. When we look out of a window during the day, the outdoor image overwhelms the indoor image to the point where the reflected indoor image is rarely seen. However, at night, the windows act as a dark mirror. Many people find this "black hole effect" unpleasant. Also, since about 90 percent of the light striking the windows is lost, large window areas create

an inefficient lighting system. The best solution is to have movable window coverings such as curtains, shades, or venetian blinds that can be used as sunshades during the day and light reflectors at night.

7. *Computer Monitors:* The tasks of looking at computer monitors is now almost universal. The glossy surface and vertical screen make veiling reflections a problem. Avoid bright light sources or bright surfaces behind the operator (Fig. 12.11j). If it is not possible to eliminate these offending light sources, place a partition behind the operator. Indirect lighting from large areas of ceiling and walls works quite well, as does direct, almost vertical lighting from the ceiling. Unlike most tasks, more light makes it harder to see the screen. The best approach is to have low-level ambient illumination of about 10 footcandles (100 lux) and task lights for any printed material that needs to be referred to.

Computer monitors can be purchased with low-reflectance glass or retrofitted with a low-reflectance screen. Either approach makes the lighting less critical.

12.14 BIOLOGICAL NEEDS

A good lighting design must address not only the previously mentioned requirements for visual performance, but also the biological needs shared by all human beings, independent of culture and style. These needs relate to the biological requirements of orientation, stimulation, sustenance, defense, and survival. The following list of biological needs is largely based on the book *Perception and Lighting as Formgivers for Architecture*, by William Lam (1992):

1. *The Need for Spatial Orientation:* The lighting system must help define slopes and changes of level. It must also help people know where they are and where

Figure 12.14a An elevator lobby or reception area can become the focus for direction by making it brighter than the corridor leading to it. (Photograph courtesy of Hubbell/Lighting Division.)

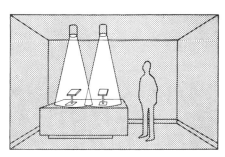

Figure 12.14b Important areas can be highlighted, while less important areas can receive subdued illumination. (From *Architectural Graphic Standards,* Ramsey/Sleeper, 8th ed. John R. Hoke, editor, © John Wiley & Sons. Inc., 1988.)

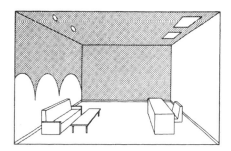

Figure 12.14c Changing light levels can help define personal space. (From Architectural Graphic Standards, Ramsey/Sleeper, 8th ed. John R. Hoke, editor, © John Wiley & Sons, Inc., 1988.)

to go. For example, an elevator lobby or reception area might be brighter than the corridor leading to it because people's attention is drawn to bright lights (Fig. 12.14a). Windows are very helpful in relating one's position inside a building to the outside world.

2. *The Need for Time Orientation:* Jet lag is a result of internal clocks being out of synchronization with what the eyes see. The internal clock might expect darkness and the time for sleep, while the eyes experience bright sunshine. Melatonin might be produced or suppressed at the wrong times during a person's circadian rhythm. The least stress occurs when the eyes see what the internal clocks expect. For example, views of the exterior through clear glazing give people the feedback on the progress of time that their internal clocks seem to need.

3. *The Need to Understand Structural Form:* The need to understand the physical world is frustrated by lighting that contradicts the physical reality, by excessive darkness or by excessively diffuse lighting. Directional light gives form to objects, while diffuse light tends to flatten their appearance. The sculpture in Fig. 12.13b is well modeled by the mostly directional light, while it loses its three-dimensional quality when illuminated by completely diffuse lighting (Fig. 12.13d). Fog and luminous ceilings both create this excessively diffuse type of lighting.

4. *The Need to Focus on Activities:* To prevent information overload, the brain has to focus its attention on the most important aspects of its environment and largely ignore the rest. The lighting can help by creating order and by highlighting the areas and activities that are most relevant. Low illumination for the less important areas is just as important as highlighting (Fig. 12.14b).

5. *The Need for Personal Space:* Light and dark areas in a large room can help define the personal space of each individual (Fig. 12.14c). Uniform lighting tends to reduce individuality, while local or furniture-integrated lighting emphasizes personal territory. People appreciate the ability to control their own environment. A study by Steelcase, the office furniture company, showed that about 75 percent of office workers would like to control their own lighting. Personal lighting fixtures that can be adjusted are an easy way to satisfy this need for control.

6. *The Need for Cheerful Spaces:* Dark walls and ceilings create a cave-like atmosphere (see Fig. 12.10c). This gloom can be caused by specifying dark surfaces, low illumination levels, or excessively vertical light. However, a dark restaurant with candlelight is not gloomy because we expect it to be dark. A space is, therefore, gloomy only if we expect it to be bright and it is not. Small patches of sunlight can be especially welcome in the winter. Direct sunlight, however, must be kept off the task to prevent excessive brightness ratios at the center of vision. Gloom can also be created without dark surfaces. Most people find the lighting from an overcast rainy day to be quite gloomy. An all-indirect-lighting scheme, as shown in Fig. 12.14d, can create this same dull, dreary appearance. Instead, a combination of direct, indirect, and accent lights creates a most interesting and cheerful design (Fig. 12.14e).

7. *The Need for Interesting Visual Input:* Dull spaces are not made interesting just by increasing the light levels. A very barren space might be interesting for a short period, when it is first perceived, but it will not remain interesting for long. Furthermore, there is a need to look up occasionally from one's work and to scan the environment. Interesting objects, such as

Figure 12.14d An all-indirect-lighting scheme creates a feeling of gloom. (Photograph by James Benya.)

Figure 12.14e A cheerful and interesting lighting design is achieved by the combination of direct, indirect, and accent lights. (Photograph by James Benya.)

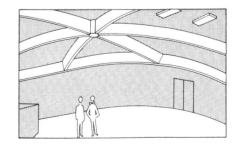

Figure 12.14f When the lighting fixture pattern is not in harmony with the structure, the need for order is frustrated. (From *Architectural Graphic Standards*, Ramsey/Sleeper, 8th ed. John R. Hoke, editor, © John Wiley & Sons, Inc., 1988.)

Figure 12.14g Light-colored buildings can be a source of gentle, diffused area lighting at night. (Courtesy Spaulding Lighting, Inc.)

windows, people, paintings, sculpture, and plants, can act as visual rest centers. Viewing distant objects allows the eye muscles to relax.

8. *The Need for Order in the Visual Environment:* When order is expected but not present, we perceive chaos. For example, when the lighting fixtures in the ceiling have no relationship with the structure, we find the design disturbing (Fig. 12.14f).

9. *The Need for Security:* Darkness is a lack of visual information. In a situation in which we expect danger, this lack of information causes fear. Dark alleys, dark corners, and shadows from trees are best eliminated by numerous closely spaced street lights and not by a few very bright lights. Just as bright areas appear brighter if they are adjacent to dark areas, dark areas are darker if they are adjacent to bright areas. Low brightness ratios are best. Light-colored buildings help greatly by reflecting diffuse light into dark corners (Fig. 12.14g).

Most lighting systems that satisfy these biological needs automatically also satisfy the needs of the visual tasks mentioned before.

12.15 LIGHT AND HEALTH

In northern latitudes, where winter days are short, depression is more common in the winter than in the summer. Dr. Alfred J. Lewy discovered that light therapy could help some patients who become depressed during the short winter days. This illness is now called **seasonal affective disorder (SAD)**.

Research has shown that bright light (more than 150 footcandles or 1500 lux) through the eyes will cause the pineal gland in the brain to stop making melatonin, which is produced whenever people are in the dark. High melatonin levels cause drowsiness, while low levels produce alertness; thus, melatonin plays a critical part in our circadian cycles.

Recent research has discovered new light-sensitive cells in the retina that have no function in seeing. It is believed that these special ganglion cells directly affect the endocrine cycle, which in turn controls the circadian cycle.

Many industrial accidents occur during the night shift. It is now believed that many of these accidents, as well as jet lag, result from drowsiness caused by activity at a time when our internal clocks tell us to be sleeping. Research in light therapy shows promising developments in several areas: fighting SAD depression, making people more alert at night, regulating sleep cycles for older people, and alleviating the problem of jet lag. Research also suggests that periods of high light levels are needed in the morning to suppress the previous night's melatonin production. The easiest way for architects to supply this light is with views of the bright outdoors and with the introduction of high levels of daylight (about 250 footcandles or 2500 lux).

Other photobiological effects of light exist besides melatonin suppression. Excessive ultraviolet (UV) radiation can cause serious burns to skin and eyes, blindness, and, in some cases, skin cancer. For this reason, most lamps sold in the United States have glass covers that absorb most of the damaging UV radiation. However, excessive visible light, especially blue and violet light, can also cause serious eye and skin burns. Light also plays a role in a variety of body functions, and it is used in the treatment of such diseases as hyperbilirubinemia, psoriasis, and vitamin D deficiency (rickets).

A few people seem to get headaches from the 120 flashes per second that fluorescent lights operating with magnetic ballasts create (see Chapter 14). This problem is easily solved by switching to electronic ballasts, which have the additional benefit of increased efficiency.

12.16 THE POETRY OF LIGHT

The previous objective discussion of lighting principles was both necessary and useful. A full understanding of lighting also requires a poetic perspective. Richard Kelly, who was one of the foremost lighting designers, fully understood the role of poetry in design conceptualization. His own words say it best:

> In dealing with our visual environment, the psychological sensations can be broken down into three elements of visual design. They are focal glow, ambient luminescence and the play of brilliants.
>
> **Focal glow** is the campfire of all time . . . the welcoming gleam of the open door . . . the sunburst through the clouds. . . . The attraction of the focal glow commands attention and creates interest. It fixes gaze, concentrates the mind, and tells people what to look at. It separates the important from the unimportant. . . .
>
> **Ambient luminescence** is a snowy morning in open country. It is twilight haze on a mountaintop . . . a cloudy day on the ocean . . . a white tent at high noon. . . . It fills people with a sense of freedom of space and can suggest infinity. . . .
>
> The background of ambient luminescence is created at night by fixtures that throw light to walls, curtains, screens, ceilings and over floors for indirect reflection from these surfaces.
>
> **Play of brilliants** is aurora borealis. . . . Play of brilliants is Times Square at night. . . . It is sunlight on a tumbling brook. . . . It is a birch tree interlaced by a motor car's headlights. Play of brilliants is the magic of the Christmas tree . . . the fantasy excitement of carnival lights and restrained gaiety of Japanese lanterns. . . . A play of brilliants excites the optic nerves, stimulates the body and spirit, and charms the senses . . .

12.17 RULES FOR LIGHTING DESIGN

The following rules are for general lighting principles. Specific rules for electric lighting and daylighting will be given in the next two chapters.

1. First, establish the lighting program by fully determining what the seeing task is in each space. For example, is the illumination mainly for vertical or horizontal surfaces? Are colors very important? Does the task consist of very fine print? Will daylighting be used to reduce the need for electric lighting?

2. Illuminate those things that we want or need to see. Since this usually includes the walls and some furnishings, the light reflected from these surfaces can supply much of the required illumination. Except for decorative light fixtures, such as chandeliers, we usually want to see objects, not light sources.

3. Quality lighting is largely a problem of geometry. Direct glare and veiling reflections are avoided mainly by manipulating the geometry between the viewer and the light source. The main light source should never be in front of the viewer. Glare can also be prevented by baffling the light sources from normal viewing angles. Baffles can be louvers, eggcrates, or parts of a building. With indirect lighting, the ceiling becomes a large-area, low-brightness source with minimal glare and veiling reflections (Fig. 12.17a).

4. In most situations, the best lighting consists of a combination of direct and diffuse light. The resulting soft shadows and shading enable us to fully understand the three-dimensional quality of our world.

5. "Darkness is as important as light: it is the counterpoint of light—each complements the other" (Hopkinson). Avoid, however, very large brightness ratios that force the eye to readapt continually.

6. An object or area can be highlighted by either increasing its brightness or reducing the brightness of the immediate surroundings. The absolute brightness matters little. What does matter is that the brightness ratio should be about 10 to 1 (Fig. 12.17b) for the purpose of highlighting.

Figure 12.17a Direct glare from bright lighting fixtures is not a problem with an indirect lighting system. The whole ceiling becomes a low brightness source. The uplights are part of the office furniture. (Courtesy, © Peerless Lighting Corporation.)

Figure 12.17b This artwork is highlighted by reducing the background brightness. MIT Chapel by Eero Saarinen.

7. Paint is one of the most powerful lighting tools. In most cases, light colors are desirable, and with indirect lighting, the most reflective white is almost mandatory. This is one of the most economical lighting tools; usually it costs nothing because paint or some finish is specified anyway. Dark colors should be considered only when drama rather than performance of visual tasks is the goal for the lighting design. Important examples of places where drama is the goal are certain museums and theaters; here the highlighting of objects or the stage, respectively, draws the viewer's attention. Dark paint is often used to hide the clutter of pipes, ducts, and beams where a suspended ceiling is not possible or desirable. In such a case, direct lighting that does not depend on reflections off the ceiling should be used. Remember, you cannot make a room with dark finishes look light.

8. Use daylighting wherever possible. Most people prefer the quality and variety of daylight. They especially desire and need the views that often accompany daylighting. Eye muscles are released only when we look at a distant object. There is evidence that both health and productivity benefit from the use of daylight in buildings. Recent research has shown that children perform better in daylit than in electrically lit classrooms.

9. Flexibility and quality are more important than the quantity of light, and these goals are most easily achieved with task/ambient lighting. Flexible task lights provide many benefits: they are energy efficient, they provide very high quality light, they work well with computers, they respond well to individual users' needs, and they provide user satisfaction because they allow occupants to control their own lighting environment. The task/ambient lighting system also provides a low level of background lighting for the whole space.

12.18 CAREER POSSIBILITIES

Because lighting is so important and complex, a new profession of lighting designers has emerged. Since the emphasis is on both functional design and aesthetics, architects have a good appreciation and background for this field. With some additional education and experience, an architect can become a lighting consultant, working on a wide variety of projects with some of the world's most prominent architects and interior designers. For more information, contact the International Association of Lighting Designers (IALD) (www.iald.org). For a master's degree in lighting, consider the Lighting Research Center at Rensselaer Polytechnic Institute (www.lrc.rpi.edu).

Since 1998, the National Council for the Qualifications for the Lighting Professions (NCQLP) has administered a national certification test for lighting designers. Architects qualify for taking the test that leads to the title "Lighting Certified" (LC). See www.ncqlp.org for information about the test.

12.19 CONCLUSION

The importance of quality over quantity cannot be overemphasized because for too long the general opinion has been "more is better." It is a bit strange that this attitude was so widely held, because we do not hold it in regard to the other senses. We do not appreciate sound according to its loudness. The difference between noise and music is certainly not its volume. We do not appreciate touch by its hardness. And we do not appreciate smell or taste by its strength. In each case, a minimum level is required, but above that, it is quality and not quantity that counts. Our sense of sight is no different in this regard.

Ignoring quality has always impaired visual performance. Often, the detrimental effects are not even recognized. There is, however, a very dramatic example in which the impairment of visual performance could not be ignored. The Houston Astrodome was built with translucent plastic bubbles over a very interesting steel structure, as seen in Fig. 12.18a. The illumination level was high enough indoors to allow grass to grow on the playing field. However, high-flying balls could not be seen against the visual "noise" of the structure. The problem was solved by painting over the skylights and using electric lights even during the day. Since the grass then died, it was replaced by Astroturf. This disaster occurred because lighting was considered only as a problem of quantity and not as a problem of quality that must be integrated with the architecture. A pneumatic structure, on the other hand, solves the lighting problem in a well-integrated manner (Fig. 12.18b). It creates a neutral background for the ball, it allows soft daylight to enter, and at night it reflects low-brightness light from electric light sources.

Figure 12.18a The structure and skylights of the Houston Astrodome had created an interesting visual pattern, which, unfortunately, became very strong visual noise when people tried to see a high-flying ball.

Figure 12.18b Pneumatic structures with translucent membranes are an example of well-integrated designs. These structures provide daylight without visual noise, and at night they work well with indirect lighting. (Courtesy of Tensar Structures, Inc.)

To best satisfy all the biological and activities needs, one must usually integrate daylighting and electric lighting. With the basic concepts of this chapter and the more specific information of the next two chapters on daylighting and electric lighting, designers should be able to design a high-quality-lighting environment that will satisfy the environmental, biological, psychological, aesthetic, and activity needs of the occupants.

KEY IDEAS OF CHAPTER 12

1. The rate at which light is emitted from a source is measured in **lumens**, while the intensity in any direction is called **candlepower** and is measured in **candelas**.
2. Illumination (illuminance) is measured in **footcandles** (lux).
3. **Luminance** is measured brightness, and its units are candelas per square foot (candelas per square meter).
4. The reflectance factor (reflectance) describes how much of the light falling on an object is reflected.
5. Light can be reflected in a specular, diffuse, or mixed fashion.
6. The color of an opaque object is the result of both the spectrally selective reflections of the object and the spectral composition of the light source.

7. The consistency of white light can be described by color temperature K, by the color-rendering index (CRI), or by a spectral-energy distribution diagram (SED), which is also known as a spectral power distribution diagram (SPD).

8. The iris controls the size of the pupil to adjust the amount of light falling on the retina.

9. Lighting should be designed for what people perceive, not for what meters measure.

10. The performance of a visual task is a nonlinear function of brightness (i.e., a little light is very helpful but a lot of light is only slightly better).

11. Use IESNA (Illuminating Engineering Society of North America) recommendations for task lighting, one-third of those levels for general illumination, and only one-third of those levels for circulation areas (i.e., one-ninth of task levels). Use somewhat higher levels for daylighting in summer, and use much higher levels for daylighting in winter.

12. Rules for quality lighting
    a. Control brightness ratios
    b. Avoid glare
    c. Avoid veiling reflections.

13. Don't forget the poetry of light
    a. Focal glow
    b. Ambient luminescence
    c. Play of brilliants.

14. Rules for lighting design
    a. Determine the visual task.
    b. Illuminate the things that we want or need to see.
    c. Quality lighting is largely a problem of geometry.
    d. Darkness is as important as light.
    e. Use light-color finishes whenever possible.
    f. Use efficient electric lighting.
    g. Use daylighting wherever possible.
    h. Flexibility and quality are much more important than the quantity of light above the minimum task-illumination level. Use task/ambient lighting.

References

Boyce, Peter, R. *Human Factors in Lighting*, 2nd edition
Hopkinson, R. G., *Architectural Physics: Lighting*, 1963
Lam, William M. C. *Perception and Lighting as Formgivers for Architecture*, Christopher Hugh Ripman, ed. New York: Van Nostrand Reinhold, 1992.

Resources

FURTHER READING

(See the Bibliography in the back of the book for full citations.

Boyce, P. R. *Human Factors in Lighting*, 2nd ed.
Brown, G. Z., and M. DeKay. *Sun, Wind, and Light: Architectural Design Strategies*, 2nd ed.
Cuttle, *Lighting by Design*.
DiLaura, D. *A History of Light and Lighting*.
Egah, M. D. and V. Olgyay. *Architectural Lighting*, 2nd ed.

Flynn, J. E., et al. *Architectural Interior Systems: Lighting, Acoustics, and Air-Conditioning*.
Futagawa, Y., ed. *Light and Space: Modern Architecture*.
Gordon, G., and J. L. Nuckolls. *Interior Lighting for Designers*, 4th ed.
Grosslight, J. *Light, Light, Light: Effective Use of Daylight and Electric Lighting in Residential and Commercial Spaces*, 3rd ed.
IESNA. *Lighting Handbook*. 2000
Karlen, M. and J. Benya. *Lighting Design Basics*.
Kwok, Alison G., and Walter T. Grondzik. *The Green Studio Handbook: Environmental Strategies for Schematic Design*.
Lam, W. M. C. *Perception and Lighting as Formgivers for Architecture*.
Millet, M. S. *Light Revealing Architecture*.
Moore, F. *Environmental Control Systems*.
Schiler, M. *Simplified Design of Building Lighting*.
Steffy, G. R. *Architectural Lighting Design*, 2nd ed.
Steffy, G. R. *Time-Saver Standards for Architectural Lighting*.

Stein, B., J. S. Reynolds, W. T. Grondzik, and A. G. Kwok. *Mechanical and Electrical Equipment for Buildings*, 10th ed. A basic resource.

ORGANIZATIONS

(See Appendix K for full citations.)

IESNA (Illuminating Engineering Society of North America)
www.iesna.org
International Association of Lighting Designers (IALD).
www.iald.org
LBNL (Lawrence Berkeley National Laboratory)
www.eande.lbl.gov
Lighting Design Lab
www.northwestlighting.com
Lighting Research Center-Rensselaer Polytechnic Institute
www.erc.rpi.edu

DAYLIGHTING

We were born of light. The seasons are felt through light.
We only know the world as it is evoked by light . . . .
To me natural light is the only light, because it has mood—it provides
a ground of common agreement for man—it puts us in touch with the
eternal. Natural light is the only light that makes architecture architecture.

Louis I. Kahn

13.1 HISTORY OF DAYLIGHTING

Until the second half of the twentieth century, when fluorescent lighting and cheap electricity became available, the history of daylighting and the history of architecture were one. From the Roman groin vault (Fig. 1.3c), to the Crystal Palace of the nineteenth century, the major structural changes in buildings reflected the goal of increasing the amount of light that was collected. Because artificial lighting had been both poor and expensive until then, buildings had to make full use of daylight.

Gothic architecture was primarily a result of the quest for maximum window area. Only small windows were possible when a barrel vault rested on

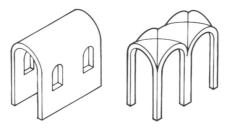

Figure 13.1a Because few windows were possible in the massive bearing walls required to support the Romanesque barrel vault, the Gothic builders turned to the Roman groin vault. (From *Architectural Lighting*, 1987. © Architectural Lighting. Reprinted Courtesy of Cassandra Publishing Corporation, Eugene, OR.)

a bearing wall. The Roman groin vault supplanted the barrel vault partly because it allowed large windows in the vaulted spaces (Fig. 13.1a). Gothic groin vaulting with flying buttresses provided a skeleton construction that permitted the use of very large windows (Fig. 13.1b).

Large and numerous windows were a dominant characteristic of Renaissance architecture. Windows dominated the facade, especially in regions with cloudy climates such as England. The increase in window size was so striking that one English manor was immortalized in rhyme: "Hardwick Hall, more window than wall" (Fig. 13.1c). Bay windows, too, became very popular (see Figs. 16.2d). Although the facades of such Renaissance palaces were designed to give the impression of great massive structures, their E- and H-shaped floor plans provided for their ventilation and daylight requirements. As a matter of fact, such shapes were typical of floor plans for most large buildings until the twentieth century (Fig. 13.1d). These buildings or their wings were rarely more than 60 ft (18 m) deep so that no point would be more than 30 ft (9 m) from a window. High ceilings with high windows allowed daylight to reach about 30 ft (9 m) in from the exterior walls, while today's lower ceiling allow daylight to reach only about 15 ft (4.5 m).

During the nineteenth century, all-glass buildings became possible because of the increased availability of glass combined with the new ways of using iron for structures. The Crystal Palace by Paxton is the most famous example (Fig. 4.2d). Also see the galleria in Fig. 4.2c.

More modest amounts of glass and iron could be found in many buildings of the day. The Bradbury Building, designed around a glass-covered atrium, is a precursor for many of today's office buildings (Fig. 13.1e).

In older neighborhoods of many cities, such as New York City, it is still possible to find sidewalks paved with glass blocks that allow daylight to enter basements. New York City enacted zoning codes to ensure minimum levels of daylighting. In England, laws that tried to ensure access to daylight date back as far as the year 1189.

Figure 13.1b Groin vaulting and flying buttresses allowed Gothic cathedrals to have windows where there had been walls.

Figure 13.1c Hardwick Hall, Derbyshire, England, 1597 more window than wall. (From *Mansions of England in Olden Times*, by Joseph Nash, Henry Sotheran & Co., 1871.)

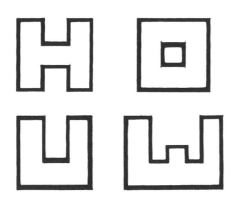

Figure 13.1d These were the common floor plans for large buildings prior to the twentieth century because of the need for light and ventilation.

Figure 13.1e The Bradbury Building, Los Angeles, 1893, has a glass-covered atrium as the circulation core. Delicate ironwork allows light to filter down to the ground level. The building was cooled by natural ventilation. Air entered exterior windows, passed through transoms and interior windows facing the atrium, and then left through mechanically operated hopper windows just below the skylight.

Figure 13.1f The Guggenheim Museum, New York City, 1959, by Frank Lloyd Wright uses a glass-domed atrium for diffused daylighting.

The masters of twentieth-century architecture continued to use daylight for both functional and dramatic purposes. In New York's Guggenheim Museum, Frank Lloyd Wright used daylight to illuminate the artwork both with indirect light from ribbon windows and with light from an atrium covered by a glass dome (Figs. 13.1f and 13.1g). In the Johnson Wax Administration Building in Racine, Wisconsin, he created a space with no apparent upper boundaries by letting daylight enter continuously along the upper walls and the edge of the roof. Daylight also enters through skylights around the mushroom columns (Figs. 13.1h and 13.2i).

Le Corbusier created very dramatic effects with the splayed windows and light towers of the chapel at Ronchamp (Figs. 13.1j, 13.1k and 13.1l). Eero Saarinen used a fascinating form of daylight in the MIT chapel. A skylight over the altar was fitted with a black eggcrate so that only vertical light could enter the chapel. This vertical light was then reflected into the room by a sculpture consisting of small brass reflectors like leaves on a tree (see Fig. 12.17b).

This short history demonstrates what an important role daylight has had in architecture. We will look at more examples after we discuss some of the basic daylighting concepts.

Figure 13.1g Continuous strip windows bring additional daylight to the gallery space. (Courtesy of New York City Convention and Visitors Bureau, Inc.)

Figure 13.1h The Johnson Wax Administration Building, Racine, Wisconsin, 1939, by Frank Lloyd Wright. Note the skylights between the mushroom columns, as well as the glazing at the junction of roof and walls. The two circular shafts (center left) are fresh-air intakes ("nostrils" as Wright called them). (Courtesy of SC Johnson Wax.)

Figure 13.1i Glazing dematerialized the upper walls and ceiling of the Johnson Wax Administration Building. (Courtesy of SC Johnson Wax.)

Figure 13.1j In Notre Dame du Haut at Ronchamp, France, 1955, Le Corbusier used thick walls with splayed windows, colored glass, and light scoops to bring carefully controlled light into the interior. (Photograph by William Gwin.)

Figure 13.1k Interior of Notre Dame du Haut. (Photograph-by William Gwin.)

Figure 13.1l Slit openings in the light scoops are seen in this rear view of a model of Notre Dame du Haut built by Simon Piltzer at the University of Southern California in Los Angeles.

13.2 WHY DAYLIGHTING?

Daylighting became a minor architectural issue as we entered the second half of the twentieth century because of the availability of efficient electric light sources; cheap, abundant electricity; and the perceived superiority of electric lighting. Perhaps the most important advantage of electric lighting was—and still is—the ease and flexibility it permitted in floor-plan design by enabling designers to ignore window locations.

Supplying adequate daylight to work areas can be quite a challenge because of the great variability in available daylight. Electric lighting is so much simpler. It offers consistent lighting that can be easily quantified. But it also has some drawbacks.

The energy crisis of the mid-1970s led to a reexamination of the potential for daylighting. At first, only the energy implications were emphasized, but now daylighting is also valued for its aesthetic possibilities and its ability to satisfy biological and human needs.

About half of all the lighting energy used by buildings could be saved through daylighting. For some building types, such as offices, schools, libraries, and museums, daylighting can save even more energy. For example, in buildings such as schools and offices about 70 percent of the lighting energy can be saved through daylighting. Since in these kinds of buildings lighting is the main energy user (Fig. 13.2a), daylighting will significantly reduce the total energy consumption. It gets even better. Daylighting can also reduce the heating and cooling energy consumption because it can be cooler than electric lighting in the summer, and it can passively heat a building in the winter.

Even today, much of the nation's work is still done during daylight hours.

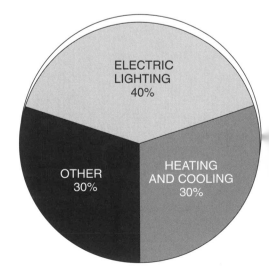

Figure 13.2a Typical distribution of energy use for buildings such as offices, schools, and many industrial facilities.

Most people work about 2000 hours each year (40 hours/week × 50 weeks), and over 80 percent of those hours occur when useful daylight is available.

There is another energy-related factor in using daylight, and it is usually the more important factor in terms of money. Figure 13.2b shows the rate at which energy is used in a typical office building during a sunny summer day. The horizontal axis represents time and the vertical axis describes the rate at which electricity is used. The greatest annual **electrical demand** usually occurs during sunny summer afternoons, when the air conditioning is working at full capacity. Since the sun creates this maximum cooling load, it simultaneously also supplies the maximum amount of daylight. Consequently, some or most of the electric lights, which consume about 40 percent of the total energy, are then not needed. The maximum demand for electrical power can, therefore, be reduced up to 40 percent by the proper utilization of daylighting.

Electric power plants are, and must be, built and sized not for the total energy used but for the maximum demand. Heavy consumers of electricity are, therefore, charged not only for the total energy they use, but also for the maximum demand they make. For such users (e.g., large office buildings, schools, and factories), daylighting can significantly reduce the cost of electricity because of both the reduced energy use and the reduced "demand charge." Much of the extra cost for the daylighting design can be offset by savings in demand charges. Society also benefits if the demand for electricity can be reduced because fewer electric power plants will have to be built in the future. The energy and electrical demand savings of daylight are greatly underutilized, in part, because most designers and building owners underestimate its potential (Fig. 13.2c).

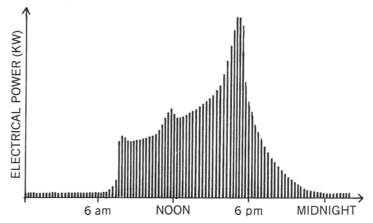

Figure 13.2b In most parts of the country, the maximum demand for electricity in an office building occurs on a hot summer afternoon, when daylighting is plentiful.

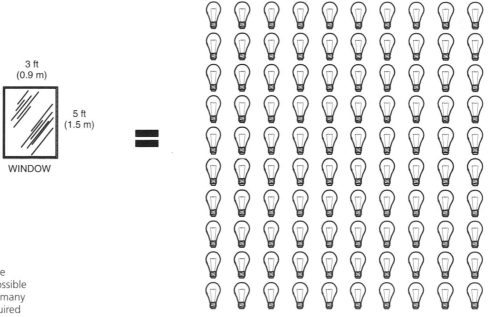

Figure 13.2c To get an indication of the energy and electrical demand savings possible with daylighting, this figure shows how many 60 W incandescent lamps would be required to produce the same amount of light as a 3 × 5 ft (0.9 × 1.5 m) window. (After Rocky Mountain Institute.)

100 - 60 W LAMPS

The dynamic nature of daylight is now seen as a virtue rather than a liability. It satisfies the biological need to respond to the natural rhythms of the day. The generally slow but occasionally dramatic changes in the quality and intensity of natural light can be stimulating.

Recent research by the Heschong-Mahone Group (www.h_m_g.com) showed an improvement of about 20 percent in the performance of students in daylit schools over standard schools. The same researchers also discovered that daylighting can increase retail sales by about 3 percent. Although 3 percent seems very small, the amount of money involved is tremendous and can easily pay for any extra expense of the daylighting design.

Some other countries have long understood the benefits and importance of daylighting. In Europe, building codes require workers to have access to both views and daylighting.

Daylighting is also a strategy for getting a building LEED (Leadership and Energy and Environmental Design) accredited. Table 13.2 shows how points can be earned for daylighting and views.

Even when daylighting was completely ignored, architects continued to use plenty of windows for the enjoyment of views, for visual relief, and for satisfying biological needs. The irony is that the all-glass-curtain walls were most popular in the 1960s, when daylighting was not utilized. Consequently, daylighting design does not require adding windows to otherwise windowless buildings. In most cases, it does not even

require increasing the window area. Daylighting design does, however, require the careful design of the fenestration for the proper distribution and quality of daylighting.

13.3 THE NATURE OF DAYLIGHT

The daylight that enters a window can have several sources: direct sunlight, clear sky, clouds, or reflections from the ground and nearby buildings (Fig. 13.3a). The light from each source varies not only in quantity and heat content, but also in such qualities as color, diffuseness, and efficacy.

Although sky conditions can be infinitely variable, it is useful to understand the daylight from the two extreme conditions: overcast sky and clear sky with sunlight. A daylighting design that works under both of these conditions will also work under most other sky conditions.

The brightness distribution of an overcast sky is typically three times greater at the zenith than at the horizon (Fig. 13.3b). Although the illumination from an overcast day is relatively low (500–2000 footcandles) (5000–20,000 lux), it is still ten to fifty times greater than what is needed indoors.

On a clear day, the brightest part of the sky, which is in the direction of the sun, is about ten times brighter than the darkest part of the

sky, which is found at about 90° to the sun (Fig. 13.3c). Under a clear sky, the illumination is quite high (6,000–10,000 footcandles [60,000–100,000 lux]) or 100 to 200 times greater than the requirements for good indoor illumination. Furthermore, the illumination remains high much of each day. Figure 13.3d shows that as the sun's altitude drops from its highest point at noon, the illumination changes very little at first. Thus, for much of each day around the noon hours, daylighting remains very high and fairly constant. Under such conditions, a 1 ft² (0.6 m²) window could illuminate over 250 ft² (23 m²) of floor area. Even on overcast days, that same window could still illuminate about 50 ft² (4.5 m²) of floor area. Thus, well-designed windows and skylights can be quite small (Fig. 13.3e).

The main difficulty with the clear sky is the challenge of direct sunlight, which is not only extremely bright but is continually changing direction. Consequently, to understand clear-day illumination, it is necessary to also understand solar geometry, as explained in Chapter 6.

In most climates, there are enough days of each sky condition to make it necessary to design for both conditions. The main exceptions are parts of the Pacific Northwest, where overcast skies predominate, and the Southwest, where clear skies predominate. Under overcast skies, the main challenge for

Table 13.2 Leed Points for Daylighting	
Strategy	Points
75% of building is daylit	1
90% of building is daylit	2
Views for 90% of occupants	1
Daylighting contributes to total energy efficiency of building	Up to 10

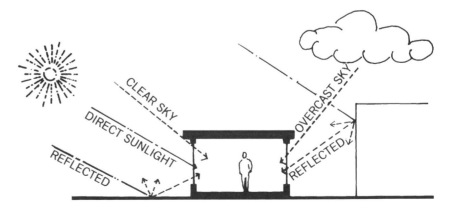

Figure 13.3a The various sources of daylight are shown. Reflected light from light-colored pavement and buildings can be significant. Light reflected from reflective glazing can almost equal direct sunshine.

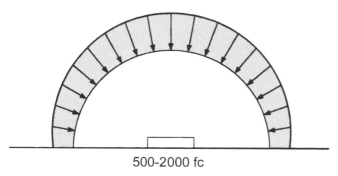

500-2000 fc

Figure 13.3b The brightness distribution on an overcast day is typically about three times greater at the zenith than at the horizon. (After *Architectural Lighting*, 1987. © *Architectural Lighting*. Reprinted courtesy of Cassandra Publishing Corporation, Eugene, OR.)

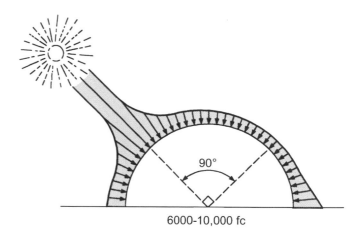

6000-10,000 fc

Figure 13.3c The brightness distribution on a clear day is typically about ten times greater near the sun than at the darkest part of the sky. (After *Architectural Lighting*, 1987. © *Architectural Lighting*. Reprinted courtesy of Cassandra Publishing Corporation, Eugene, OR.)

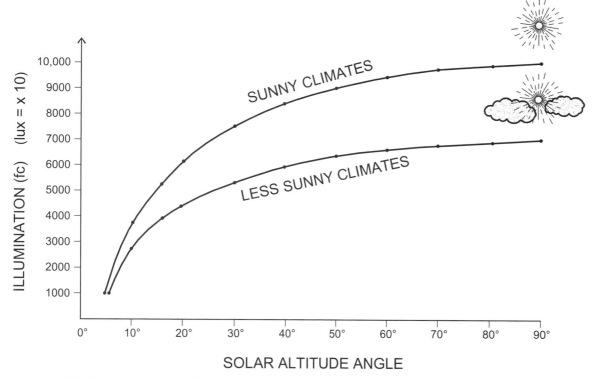

Figure 13.3d This graph shows how the illumination of sunlight (on a surface perpendicular to the sunrays) varies with the altitude angle of the sun. Notice that the illumination rises very quickly as the sun rises and then levels off. Thus, the illumination is quite constant for several hours before and after noon. (After Hopkinson Petherbridge, and Longmore, *Daylighting*, 1966.)

the designer is one of quantity, while for clear-sky conditions the challenge is one of quality.

The daylight from clear skies consists primarily of the two components of skylight and direct sunlight. The light from the blue sky is diffuse and of low brightness, while the direct sunlight is very directional and extremely bright. Because of the potential for glare, excessive brightness ratios, and overheating, it is sometimes assumed that direct sunlight should be excluded from a building. It is

sometimes erroneously believed that direct sunshine is appropriate only for solar heating. Figure 13.6a illustrates the efficacy (lumens/watt) of various light sources. Although direct-beam sunlight has a lower efficacy than skylight, its efficacy is comparable to the

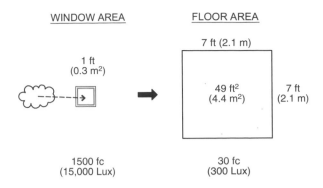

WINDOW AREA

1 ft
(0.3 m²)

1500 fc
(15,000 Lux)

FLOOR AREA

7 ft (2.1 m)

49 ft²
(4.4 m²)

7 ft
(2.1 m)

30 fc
(300 Lux)

OVERCAST CONDITION

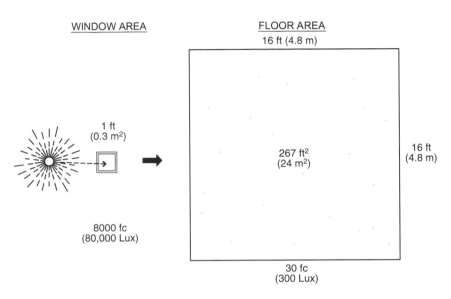

WINDOW AREA

1 ft
(0.3 m²)

8000 fc
(80,000 Lux)

FLOOR AREA

16 ft (4.8 m)

267 ft²
(24 m²)

16 ft
(4.8 m)

30 fc
(300 Lux)

CLEAR SKY WITH SUN CONDITION

Figure 13.3e Sunlight is such an abundant source of light that a window can illuminate a floor area about 250 times the size of the window if the light is distributed evenly. Even on overcast days, a window can illuminate a floor area about 50 times the size of the window.

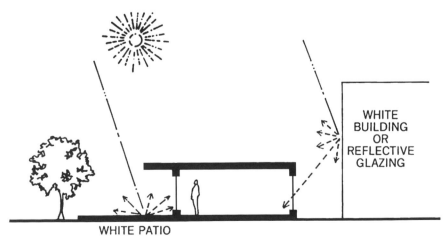

WHITE
BUILDING
OR
REFLECTIVE
GLAZING

WHITE PATIO

Figure 13.3f Sometimes reflected light is the major source of daylight. Under certain circumstances, a north window can receive as much light as a south window.

best electric sources, while its color-rendering ability is superior. Since direct sunlight is an extremely abundant and free source of light, it should be utilized in any daylight design. With the proper design it can supply high quality as well as high quantity daylight.

The light from clear skies, especially the light from the northern sky, is rich in the blue end of the spectrum. While the color-rendering quality of such light is excellent, it is on the cool side (Color Plate 15).

Reflected light from the ground and neighboring structures is often a significant source of daylight (Fig. 13.3f). The reflectance factor of the reflecting surface is critical in this regard. A white-painted building will frequently reflect about 80 percent of the incident light, while lush green grass will reflect about 10 percent and mostly green light. Table 13.3 gives the reflectance factors in percent for some common surfaces.

Table 13.3 Typical Reflectance Factors	
Material	**Reflectance (Percent)**
Aluminum, reflectors	90–98
Aluminum, polished	70–85
Asphalt	10
Brick, red	25–45
Concrete	30–50
Glass	
Clear or tinted	7
Reflective	20–40
Grass	
Dark green	10
Dry	35
Mirror (glass)	80–90
Paint	
Black	4
White	70–90
Porcelain enamel (white)	60–90
Snow	60–75
Stone	5–50
Vegetation, average	25
Wood	5–40

13.4 CONCEPTUAL MODEL*

Direct-beam light can be nicely modeled with arrows, but a diffused source cannot. To understand and to predict the effect of a diffused light source, a different kind of visual model is required. The illumination due to a diffused light source is similar to the concept of mean radiant temperature (MRT) described in Section 3.12. The illuminating effect of a diffused source on a point is a function of both the brightness of the source and the apparent size of the source, which is defined by the exposure angle. Figure 13.4a illustrates the fact that illumination increases with the brightness of the source.

Figures 13.4b–d illustrate how the exposure angle is a function of source size, distance, and tilt. In Fig. 13.4b, we see a plan of two desks in a room. The desks are equally far from two windows of equal brightness but different sizes. Obviously, desk B has worse illumination because it has a smaller exposure angle due to the smaller window.

In Fig. 13.4c, we see two desks that are both illuminated by the same window. Desk B has again worse illumination because of its smaller exposure angle, which is due to the greater distance to the window.

Finally, in Fig. 13.4d, both desks are equally far from the window. Desk B is again more poorly illuminated, but this time the smaller exposure angle is due to the tilt of the source relative to desk B.

In Fig. 13.4e, we see a section of the same room. The two main sources of daylight for a point on the table are the sky and the ceiling. Some of the daylight entering the window is reflected off the ceiling, which, in turn, becomes a low-brightness source for the table. The illumination from the ceiling is significant, even though the brightness is low, because of the large apparent size of this source. The sky, despite its smaller apparent size,

---

*This section is based on material from *Concepts and Practice of Architectural Daylighting* by Fuller Moore (1985).

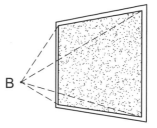
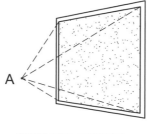

Figure 13.4a The illumination of a point by a diffuse source like a window is a function of both the brightness of the source and the exposure angle. In this example, the exposure angle (solid angle) has been held constant and only the brightness varied. (After Moore, 1985)

BRIGHTER SOURCE   LESS BRIGHT SOURCE

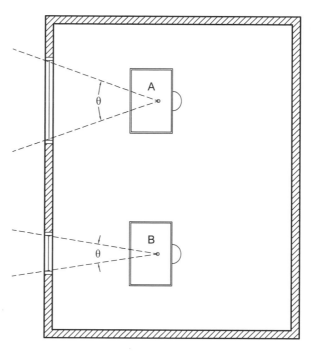

Figure 13.4b SOURCE SIZE: This Figure shows a floor plan with two desks equally far from two windows of equal brightness. Desk B will receive less illumination because the smaller window produces a smaller exposure angle.

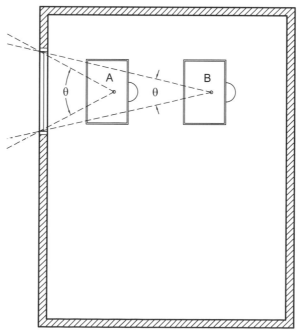

Figure 13.4c DISTANCE TO SOURCE: In this figure, both desks receive light from the same window. This time, desk B has a smaller exposure angle and gets less light because it is farther from the window.

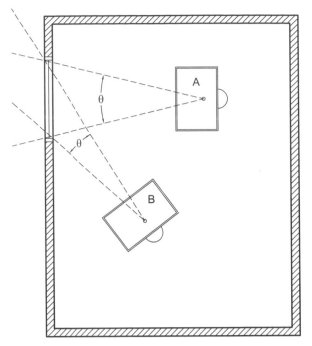

Figure 13.4d TILT OF SOURCE: In this figure, both desks are illuminated by the same window and they are equally far from the window. However, desk B now has a smaller exposure angle because the window is tilted relative to the desk.

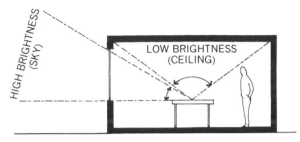

Figure 13.4e To determine the total illumination on the table, one must consider the brightness and exposure angle of each source. (After Moore, 1985.)

is the major source of light because it is much brighter than the ceiling. If the walls are of a light color, they will also reflect some light on the table. For simplicity, the contribution of the walls is not shown in Fig. 13.4e.

13.5 ILLUMINATION AND THE DAYLIGHT FACTOR

One of the best ways for the architect to determine both the quantity and the quality of a daylighting design is through the use of physical models. Although most daylighting model tests are conducted under the real sky, the actual measured illumination is of limited usefulness. Unless the model can be tested under the worst daylight conditions, the illumination inside the model will not indicate the lowest illumination level to be expected. Fortunately, it is not necessary to test the model under the worst conditions because of a concept called the **daylight factor**. The daylight factor is the ratio of the illumination indoors to outdoors on an overcast day

(Fig. 13.5), which is an indication of the effectiveness of a design in bringing daylight indoors. For example:

A daylight factor of 5 percent means that on an overcast day when the illumination is 2000 footcandles outdoors, the illumination indoors will be 100 footcandles 2000 fc × 0.05 = 100 fc) (20,000 × 0.05 = 1000 lux). Note that the daylighting factor is independent of the units used.

Although winter overcast skies are usually the worst design condition, the model can be tested under an overcast sky at any time of year or day.

Table 13.5A presents typical daylight factors for different kinds of spaces. If the measured daylight factor is greater than that of Table 13.5A, there will be more than enough daylight for most of the year. By multiplying the daylight factor by the average minimum daylight of Table 13.5B, one can also determine the average minimum indoor illumination.

Remember, however, that absolute illumination is not a good indicator of visibility because of the eye's great power of adaptation. The relative brightness between the interior and the window is, however, a critical consideration in daylight design, and the daylight factor is a good indicator of this relationship. The higher the factor, the less extreme are the brightness differences.

If a design excludes direct sunlight, clear days will behave similarly to the overcast conditions described above. If direct sunlight is included, as it generally should be, then the model will have to be tested with a heliodon to simulate the various sun angles

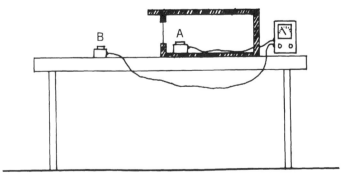

Figure 13.5 The daylight factor (D.F.) is determined by the ratio of indoor to outdoor illumination on an overcast day. D.F. = A/B.

Table 13.5A Typical Minimum Daylight Factors

Type of Space	Daylight Factor (%)
Art studios, galleries	4–6
Factories, laboratories	3–5
Offices, classrooms, gymnasiums, kitchens	2
Lobbies, lounges, living rooms, churches	1
Corridors, bedrooms	0.5

Table 13.5B Average Illumination From Overcast Skies*

North Latitude (degrees)†	Illumination	
	footcandles	lux
46	700	7000
42	750	7500
38	800	8000
34	850	8500
30	900	9000

*The illumination values are typical for overcast-sky conditions, available about 85 percent of the day 8 A.M. to 4 P.M. For more detailed information, see *IESNA Lighting Handbook* (2000).
†See map of Fig. 5.6d.

throughout the year. Model testing will be explained later in this chapter.

Often, models are used to compare alternative designs. Since actual outdoor lighting varies greatly from hour to hour and day to day, footcandle measurements made at different times cannot be compared, but the daylight factor can. As the outdoor illumination changes, the indoor illumination changes proportionally and the daylight factor remains constant for any particular design for overcast skies.

13.6 LIGHT WITHOUT HEAT?

All light, whether electric or natural, is radiant energy that is eventually absorbed and turned into heat. In the winter this heat is an asset and in the summer a liability. Thus, we want to collect as much daylight as possible in the winter and as little as possible in the summer. As long as the collected light is *quality light*, there is no maximum in the underheated period because our pupils can shut out any excess. On the other hand, we want to collect just enough daylight in the summer so that the electric lights can be turned off.

At the same illumination level, daylight is cooler than electric lighting.

Figure 13.6a shows the efficacy of various light sources. Note that light from the sky has the highest light-to-heat ratio. Although sunlight intro- duces more heat per unit of light than light from the sky, it is still better than any white, electric light source. For the same light level, incandescent lamps introduce about six times more heat than daylighting, and fluorescent lamps introduce about two times more heat than daylighting (60 lumens/watt for fluorescent lamps versus 120 lumens/watt for daylighting).

In the winter, there is no limit to the amount of sunlight that might be introduced as long as glare and excessive-brightness ratios are controlled. After all, the daylighting indoors can never be brighter than the daylighting outdoors, for which the eyes evolved.

The seasonal problem of daylighting is most acute with skylights since horizontal openings receive much more sunlight in the summer than in the winter. South-facing vertical glazing is much better in this regard because it captures more sunlight in the winter than in the summer (Fig. 13.6b).

Rules

1. During the summer, introduce just enough daylight so that the electric lights can be turned off. The

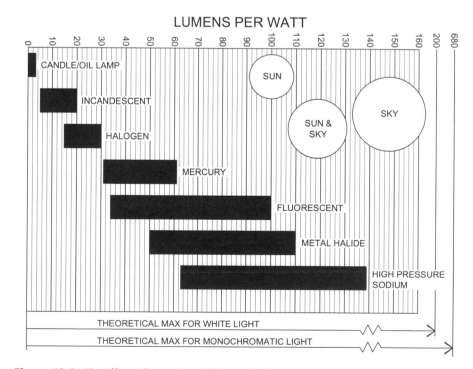

Figure 13.6a The efficacy (lumens/watt) of various light sources is compared.

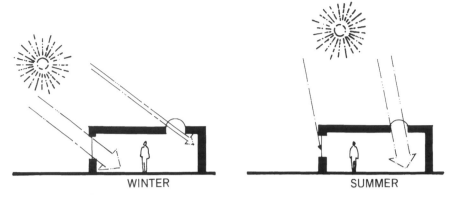

Figure 13.6b South-facing vertical glazing is more in phase with sunshine demand than is horizontal (skylight) glazing. Although the amount of daylight collected should be just adequate in the summer, there is almost no limit to the amount that is desirable in the winter.

a building through glazing just as visible light does, but it contributes nothing to lighting. Light reflected off clouds or from the blue sky has a smaller proportion to this infrared radiation and, therefore, has a higher efficacy (lumens/watt) (Fig. 13.6a).

Most materials have the same reflectance for short-wave infrared as for visible light. For example, the light reflected into a clerestory from a white roof has the same ratio of visible to short-wave infrared as the original sunlight did.

Glazing, however, can be made to exclude some of the short-wave

sunlight must be well distributed, and it must not raise the illumination levels much above what is required.

2. During the winter, introduce as much sunlight as possible in those buildings that need heating. There is no upper limit as long as it does not create glare or excessive brightness ratios.

3. Any building that does not need heating, such as an internally dominated buildings in a mild climate, should obey rule 1 in winter as well as in summer.

13.7 COOL DAYLIGHT

Because internally dominated buildings in warm climates need no heating, we would like to collect the coolest daylight possible. In addition to the fact that the amount of heat entering a building is a function of the amount of daylight, the amount of heat is also a function of the source of that daylight. Figure 13.7 (lower graph) illustrates the fact that about 50 percent of solar radiation is in the infrared part of the electromagnetic spectrum. This radiation enters

Figure 13.7 An ideal spectrally selective coating allows the visible but not the infrared part of the solar radiation to pass through the glazing. Compare this behavior to that of regular glass. Two actual cool glazing products are shown to illustrate what is possible today.

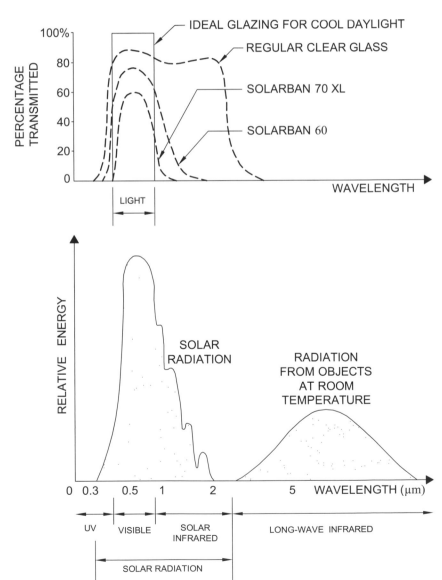

infrared. Tinted glazing is not a good choice for daylight because it blocks light as well as infrared radiation, it distorts the color of the daylight (and view), and it gets very hot and thereby still heats the building unnecessarily. Reflective glazing is only a little better. Although it does not distort the color or heat the glass, it reflects light as much as the infrared, radiation.

Heat-absorbing glass was developed to block more of this unwanted infrared radiation than light. Although it absorbs a slightly larger proportion of infrared than visible light, much of the absorbed radiation is reradiated inside and makes the glass uncomfortably hot. Its green tint also affects the color of the view. What is really needed for cool daylight is a **selective glass** that reflects the infrared but not the visible portion of daylight (see the upper graph of Fig. 13.7). There are now some new glazing materials commercially available that do this, and they are generally known as **spectrally selective low-e glazing.**

The ideal glazing type shown in Fig. 13.7 (top) not only filters out the solar infrared but also the ultraviolet (UV) radiation that fades colored materials, such as carpets, fabrics, artwork, paints, and wood. Special coatings or films on glass can filter out 100 percent of UV radiation. It is important to note, however, that visible light (blue especially) fades colors at one-third the rate of UV radiation. Valuable and delicate artifacts need to be shielded from both UV radiation and high-level light (i.e., above 15 footcandles [150 lux]).

Visible transmittance (VT) is the factor that quantifies the amount of visible light that passes through glazing. It varies from 0.9 for very clear glass to less than 0.1 for highly reflective or tinted glass. For cool daylight, the VT should be high while the transmission of the solar infrared should be low.

As mentioned in Section 9.21, the **solar heat-gain coefficient (SHGC)** is a factor that quantifies the total solar radiation (visible and solar infrared) that passes through glazing. When

one compares the VT to the SHGC, one can predict the coolness of the transmitted light. The ratio of the VT to the SHGC is called the **light-to-solar-gain (LSG) ratio** (see Sidebox 13.7). The higher the ratio, the cooler the light. See Table 13.7 for the LSG ratio for various types of glazing. Note that tinted glazing has a low LSG ratio because it blocks visible light more than solar heat which is certainly not desirable for daylighting purposes. On the other hand, spectrally selective glazing has a high LSG ratio because solar infrared is blocked much more than light.

The same logic applies if you replace the SHGC with the still used but older shading coefficient (SC). Thus, the following recommendation:

Rule of thumb: The VT factor should be much larger than the SHGC or the SC when one is choosing glazing for cool daylighting purposes.

13.8 GOALS OF DAYLIGHTING

As stated above, the *quantity* goals of daylighting are to collect just enough light in the summer so that the electric lights can be turned off and to collect as much sunshine as possible in the winter to help meet the heating demand. The quality goals are the same as for electric lighting, and the main ones are: minimize

glare, minimize veiling reflections, avoid excessive brightness ratios, and supply fairly even ambient illumination throughout a space.

Ordinary windows have trouble meeting these goals. The diagram in Fig. 13.8a shows that typically there is too little light at the back of the room and more than enough right inside the window. Thus, the first goal is to get more light deeper into the building both to raise the illumination level there and to reduce the illumination gradient across the room (Fig. 13.8b).

Table 13.7 Light-to-Solar-Gain (LSG) Ratios for Various Glazing Systems

Glass Type (All Double-Glazed)	Visible Transmittance (VT)	Solar Heat-Gain Coefficient (SHGC)	Light-to-Solar-Gain Ratio (LSG)
Clear	0.82	0.75	1.20
Bronze	0.62	0.60	1.03
Reflective	0.20	0.16	1.25
Spectrally selective	0.70	0.46	1.52

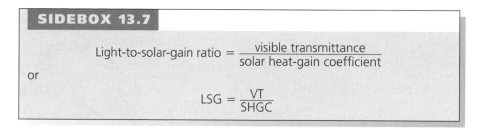

SIDEBOX 13.7

$$\text{Light-to-solar-gain ratio} = \frac{\text{visible transmittance}}{\text{solar heat-gain coefficient}}$$

or

$$\text{LSG} = \frac{\text{VT}}{\text{SHGC}}$$

Figure 13.8a The light from windows creates an excessive illumination gradient across the room (too dark near the back wall compared to the area near the window).

Figure 13.8b One goal of daylighting design is to create a more acceptable illumination gradient.

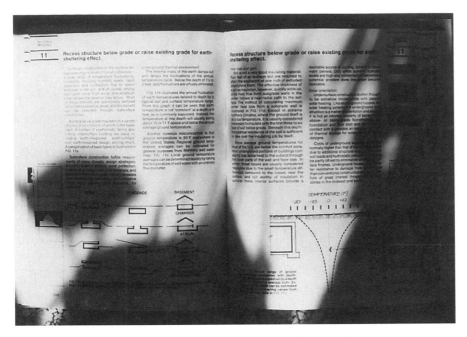

Figure 13.8c Excessive brightness ratios can result from puddles of sunlight.

Figure 13.8d Veiling reflections are a common problem from any overhead lighting.

The second goal is to reduce or prevent the severe direct glare of unprotected windows and skylights. This glare is aggravated if the walls adjacent to the windows are not illuminated and, therefore, appear quite dark (see Fig. 13.10f).

If a beam of sunlight creates a puddle of light over part of the work area, severe and unacceptable brightness ratios will exist. Thus, the third goal is to prevent excessive brightness ratios, especially those caused by direct sunlight on or near the task (Fig. 13.8c).

Although the low-angle light from windows is usually not a source of veiling reflections, the light from overhead openings can be (Fig. 13.8d). Thus, the fourth goal is to prevent or minimize veiling reflections,

especially from skylights and clerestory windows.

In most situations, lighting should not be too directional because of the glare and dark shadows that result. The fifth goal, therefore, is to diffuse the light by means of multiple reflections off the ceiling and walls.

In areas where there are no critical visual tasks, the drama and excitement of direct sunlight can be a positive design element. Therefore, the sixth goal, which is limited to those spaces in which there are few if any critical visual tasks, is to use the full aesthetic potential of daylighting and sunlight. In all spaces, however, the dynamic nature of daylight should be seen as an asset rather than a liability. The ever-changing nature of daylight needs only to be limited—not eliminated.

Unlike electric lighting, daylighting cannot just be added to the building. Daylighting design is part of the fundamental building design from the first line drawn. Form and orientation are the most critical aspects of daylighting. Next come window size and location. Even indoor partitions are critical because they stop the spread of light unless they are made of glass.

The remainder of this chapter discusses techniques and strategies for achieving the above-mentioned goals.

13.9 BASIC DAYLIGHTING STRATEGIES

Although advanced daylighting is primarily a second-tier strategy (Fig. 13.9a), it is important to utilize as many of the tier one strategies listed below as possible to enhance and prepare for the daylighting design.

Guidelines

1. *Orientation*: Because of the usefulness of direct sunlight, the south orientation is usually best for daylighting. The south side of a building gets sunlight most consistently throughout the day and the year. This extra sunlight is especially welcome in the winter, when its heating effect is usually desirable. Sun-control devices are also most effective on this orientation.

   The second best orientation for daylighting is north because of the constancy of the light. Although the quantity of north light is rather low, the quality is high if a cool white light is acceptable (see Color Plate 15). There is also little problem with glare from the direct sun. In very hot climates, the north orientation might even be preferable to the south orientation.

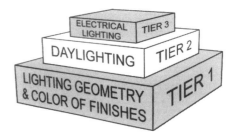

Figure 13.9a The best and most sustainable lighting is achieved by the three-tier design approach, and this chapter covers primarily tier two (daylighting).

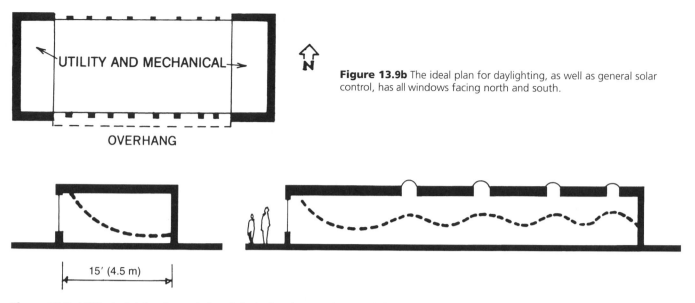

Figure 13.9b The ideal plan for daylighting, as well as general solar control, has all windows facing north and south.

Figure 13.9c While daylighting from windows is limited to the area about 15 ft from the outside walls, roof openings can yield fairly uniform lighting over unlimited areas.

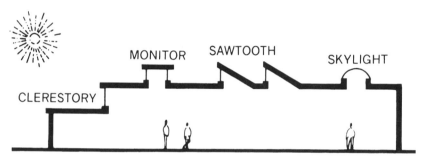

Figure 13.9d The various possibilities for overhead openings for daylighting.

The worst orientations are east and west. Not only do these orientations receive sunlight for only half of each day, but the sunlight is at a maximum during summer instead of winter. The worst problem, however, is that the east or west sun is low in the sky and, therefore, creates very difficult glare and shading problems. Figure 13.9b illustrates an ideal floor plan in regard to building orientation.

Rules for Orientation

1. (a) For daylighting when winter heat is desirable, use south-facing glazing.
   (b) For daylighting when winter heat is not desirable, use north-facing glazing.

   (c) For daylighting without summer overheating or severe glare, *avoid* east and west glazing.

2. *Lighting Through the Roof:* Except for the use of light wells, only one story or the top floor of multistory buildings can use overhead openings. When applicable, horizontal openings (skylights) offer two important advantages. First, they allow fairly uniform illumination over very large interior areas, while daylighting from windows is limited to about a 15-ft (4.5 m) depth (Fig. 13.9c). Second, horizontal openings also receive much more light than vertical openings. Unfortunately, there are also two important problems associated with skylights. The intensity of light is greater in the summer than in the winter—just the opposite of what we want. It is also difficult to shade horizontal glazing. For these two reasons, it is usually more appropriate to use vertical glazing on the roof in the form of clerestory windows, monitors, or sawtooth arrangements (Fig. 13.9d).

3. *Form:* The form of the building not only determines the mix of vertical and horizontal openings that is possible, but also how much of the floor area will have access to daylighting. Generally, in multistory buildings a 15-ft (4.5 m) perimeter zone can be fully daylit and another 15 ft (4.5 m) beyond that can be partially daylit. All three floor plans in Fig. 13.9e have the same area (10,000 ft) (900 m²). In the square plan, 16 percent is not daylit at all, and another 33 percent can be only partially daylit. The rectangular plan can eliminate the core area that receives no daylight, but it still has a large area that is only partially daylit, while the atrium scheme is able to have all of its area daylit. Of course, the actual percentage of core versus perimeter zones depends on the actual area. Larger buildings will have larger cores and less surface area.

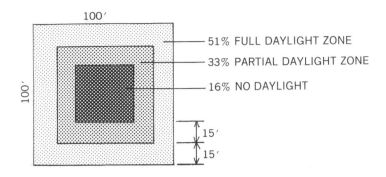

51% FULL DAYLIGHT ZONE

33% PARTIAL DAYLIGHT ZONE

16% NO DAYLIGHT

100'

100'

15'

15'

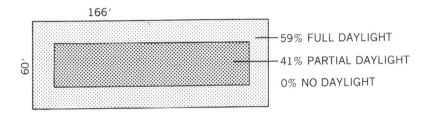

166'

60'

59% FULL DAYLIGHT

41% PARTIAL DAYLIGHT

0% NO DAYLIGHT

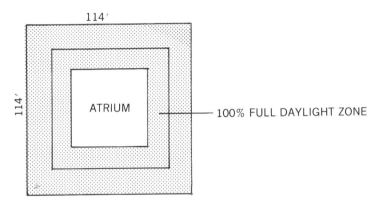

114'

114'

ATRIUM

100% FULL DAYLIGHT ZONE

Figure 13.9e These alternative plans of a multistory office building illustrate the effect of massing on the availability of daylight.

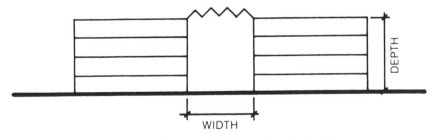

DEPTH

WIDTH

Figure 13.9f It is not the actual depth or width but their ratio that determines how much daylight will be available at the base of an atrium.

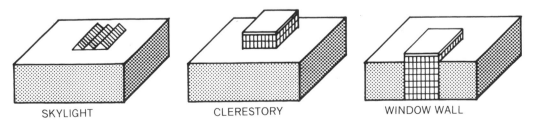

SKYLIGHT

CLERESTORY

WINDOW WALL

The modern atrium is typically an enclosed space whose temperature is maintained close to the indoor conditions. Buildings with atriums are, therefore, compact from a thermal point of view and yet have a large exposure to daylight. The amount of light available at the base of the atrium depends on a number of factors: the translucency of the atrium roof, the reflectance of atrium walls, and the geometry of the space (depth versus width), as shown in Fig. 13.9f. Physical models are the best way to determine the amount of daylight that can be expected at the bottom of an atrium. When atriums get too small to be useful spaces, they are known instead as "light wells." Atriums can be illuminated by skylights, clerestories, or window walls (Fig. 13.9g). The advantage of each approach will be explained below in the discussion of windows, skylights, and clerestories.

One of the most sophisticated modern atrium buildings, the Bateson State Office Building in Sacramento, California, is discussed further as a case study in Section 17.6.

4. *Space Planning:* Open space planning is very advantageous for bringing light to the interior. Glass partitions can furnish acoustical privacy without blocking the light. When visual privacy is also needed, venetian blinds or translucent materials could be used. Alternatively, the partitions could have glass above eye level only (Fig. 13.9h). Sometimes the partitions must be fire rated, and any partition facing an egress corridor

Figure 13.9g Generic types of daylit atriums.

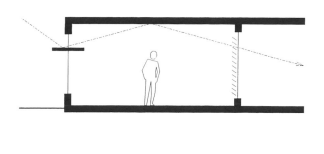

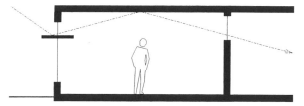

Figure 13.9h Full- or partial-height glass partitions can enable borrowed light to enter interior spaces.

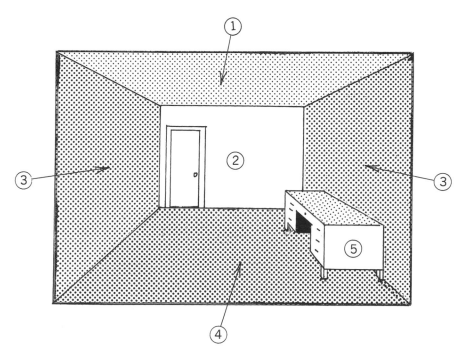

Figure 13.9i For good distribution and penetration of light, the order of importance for high reflectance finishes is shown (e.g., 1 should have the highest reflectance factor).

reduce dark shadows, glare, and excessive-brightness ratios. The ceiling should have the highest reflectance factor possible. The floor and small pieces of furniture are the least critical reflectors and, therefore, *might* have fairly low reflectance factors (dark finishes). The descending order of importance for reflecting surfaces is: ceiling, back wall, side walls, floor, and small pieces of furniture (Fig. 13.9i).

6. *View and Daylighting:* Use separate openings for view and daylighting. Use high windows, clerestories, or skylights for excellent daylighting, and use low windows at eye level for view. High glazing should be clear or spectrally selective to maximize the daylight collected. The view glazing is more flexible in that it can be tinted or reflective to control heat gain and/or glare.

13.10 BASIC WINDOW STRATEGIES

To understand window daylighting strategies, it is worthwhile to first examine the lighting from an ordinary window. As mentioned earlier, the illumination is greatest just inside the window and rapidly drops off to inadequate levels for most visual tasks (Fig. 13.10a left). The view of the sky is often a source of direct glare, and direct sunlight entering the window creates excessive-brightness ratios (puddles of sunlight as well as overheating during the summer. To overcome these negative characteristics of ordinary windows, designers should keep in mind the following strategies:

Guidelines

1. *Windows should be high on the wall, widely distributed, and of optimum area.* Daylight penetration into a space will increase with the mounting height of the window (Fig. 13.10a right). The useful depth of a daylit space is limited to about 1½ times the height of the top of the window. Whenever

must be fire rated. Fortunately, new fire-resistant glazing systems allow a two-hour rating even with unlimited glazing areas.

5. *Color:* Use *light* colors both indoors and outdoors to reflect more light into the building and farther into the interior. Light-colored roofs can greatly increase the light that clerestories collect. Windows adjacent

or opposite to light-colored rather than dark exterior walls will receive more daylight. Light-colored facades are especially important in urban areas to increase the availability of daylighting at the lower floors and sidewalks.

Light-colored interiors will not only reflect light farther into the building, but also diffuse it to

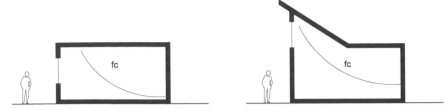

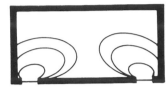

Figure 13.10a Daylight penetration increases with window height.

Figure 13.10b These plans, with contours of equal illumination, illustrate how light distribution is improved by admitting daylight from more than one point.

Figure 13.10c Strip or ribbon windows, as seen here in the Maison LaRoche by Le Corbusier, admit uniform light, which is further improved by placing the windows high on the wall. Note that photographic film exaggerates brightness ratios. (Photograph by William Gwin.)

possible, ceiling heights should be increased so that windows can be mounted higher.

Daylight will be more uniformly distributed in a space if windows are horizontal rather than vertical and if they are spread out rather than concentrated (Fig. 13.10b). Architects, such as Le Corbusier, often used high ribbon windows for these reasons (Fig. 13.10c).

Window area as a percentage of floor area should generally not exceed 20 percent because of summer overheating and winter heat losses. By means of reflectors, small-window areas can collect large amounts of daylight. However, in very cloudy or cold climates, movable shading systems and high-performance windows can increase the optimum window area.

2. *If possible, place windows on more than one wall.* Whenever possible, avoid **unilateral lighting** (windows on one wall only), and use **bilateral lighting** (windows on two walls) for much better light distribution and reduced glare (Fig. 13.10d). Windows on adjacent walls are especially effective in reducing glare. The windows on each wall illuminate the adjacent walls and, therefore, reduce the contrast between each window and its surrounding wall.

3. *Place windows adjacent to interior walls.* Here, the interior walls adjacent to windows act as low-brightness reflectors to reduce the overly strong directionality of daylight (Fig. 13.10e). The glare of the window is also reduced because of the reduced brightness ratio between the window and its surrounding wall due to reflections back from the side wall (Fig. 13.10f).

4. *Splay walls to reduce the contrast between windows and walls.* Windows create less glare when the adjacent

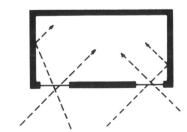

Figure 13.10d Bilateral lighting is usually preferable to unilateral lighting (plan view).

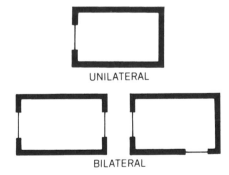

Figure 13.10e Light distribution and quality are improved by the reflection off sidewalls.

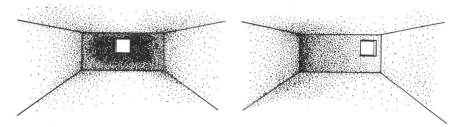

Figure 13.10f The glare from a window next to a sidewall is less severe than that from a window in the middle of a room.

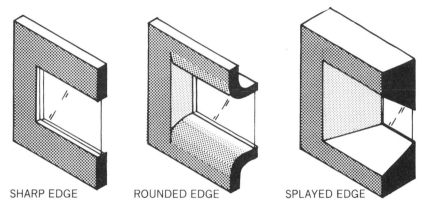

SHARP EDGE   ROUNDED EDGE   SPLAYED EDGE

Figure 13.10g The excessive contrast between a window and a wall can be reduced by splaying or rounding the inside edges. (After M. D. Egan, *Concepts in Architectural Lighting.*)

walls are not dark in comparison to the window. Splayed or rounded edges create a transition of brightness that is more comfortable to the eye (Fig. 13.10g).

5. *Filter daylight.* Sunlight can be filtered and softened by trees or by such devices as trellises and screens (Fig. 13.10h). Translucent glazing or very light drapes, however, can make the direct-glare problem much worse. Although they diffuse direct sunlight, they often become excessively bright sources of light in the process (Fig 13.10i).

6. *Shade windows from excess sunlight in summer.* Ideally, only a small amount of sunlight should be admitted through the windows in the summer and a maximum amount in the winter. At all times, however, the light should be diffused by reflecting it off the ceiling. Overhangs on south windows can provide this ideal seasonal control. They can also eliminate puddles of sunlight, reduce glare, and even out the light gradient across the room. If

Figure 13.10h Trees, supported on a grid of wires, filter the light before it enters the Kimbell Art Museum, Fort Worth, Texas. Louis I. Kahn, architect.

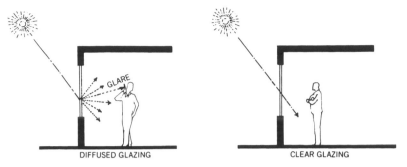

Figure 13.10i Translucent glazing can be a major source of glare because some of the sunlight is directed into the eyes of the observer.

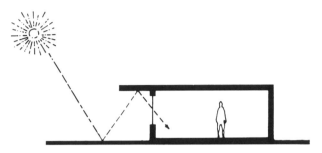

Figure 13.10j Large, horizontal overhangs block too much light unless both the ground and the underside of the overhang have high reflectance values.

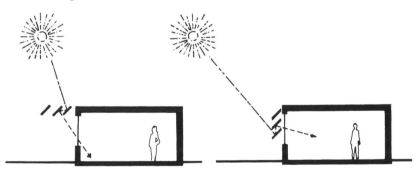

Figure 13.10k Light-colored louvers block direct sunlight but allow some diffused light to enter the windows.

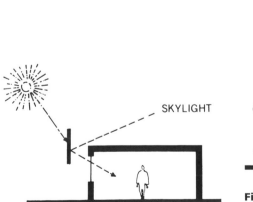

Figure 13.10m A vertical panel can block direct sunlight while it reflects diffuse skylight.

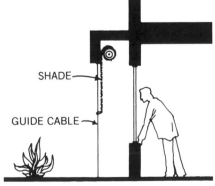

Figure 13.10n On the east and west facades, the Bateson Building in Sacramento, California, uses exterior translucent roller shades that automatically respond to sun and wind conditions. See also Section 17.6.

a large, solid horizontal overhang is used, its underside should be painted white to reflect ground light (Fig. 13.10j). A light-colored overhang, especially with louvers, will also reduce the brightness ratio between itself and the sky.

Louvers in a vertical or horizontal plane painted a light color are beneficial because they block direct sunlight, yet reflect diffused sunlight (Fig. 13.10k). A vertical panel in front of a window can block direct sunlight while reflecting diffused skylight into the window (Fig. 13.10m).

Chapter 9 contains an extensive description of shading devices. Physical models can be used to determine how well these and other devices can admit quality daylight while shading direct sunlight. Of course, in certain spaces, such as lobbies, lounges, and living rooms, where visual tasks are not critical, some direct sunlight can be welcome for its visual and psychological benefits, especially in winter.

7. *Use movable shades.* A dynamic environment calls for a dynamic response. Variations in daylighting are especially pronounced on the east and west exposures, which receive diffused light for half a day and direct sunshine for the other half. Movable shades, venetian blinds, or curtains can respond to these extreme conditions. To reduce heat gain, the interior shading devices must be highly reflective.

Although indoor shading is simpler, outdoor shading is more effective. Movable outdoor venetian blinds are very popular in Germany and Austria. They are sturdy enough to resist wind, snow, and ice, and they are usually made of reflective aluminum to either reflect the sun away or to the ceiling indoors (Fig. 9.4l).

The Bateson Building uses exterior roller shades for the same purpose (Fig. 13.10n). The fabric is translucent so that some light still enters even when most of the sun is blocked.

13.11 ADVANCED WINDOW STRATEGIES

The challenges of getting daylight from windows farther into the building while still maintaining the quality of the lighting can best be met by reflecting daylight off the ceiling. In one-story buildings, walkways, roads, and light-colored patios can reflect a significant amount of light to the ceiling (Fig. 13.11a). In multistory buildings,

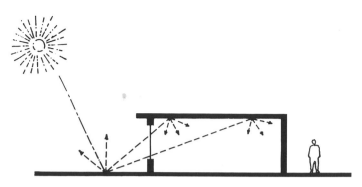

Figure 13.11a Light-colored pavement or gravel can reflect light deep into the interior.

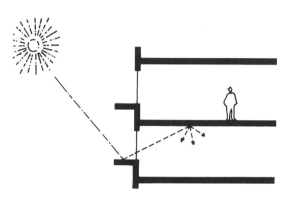

Figure 13.11b Wide windowsills can be used as light reflectors to send light deep into the interior.

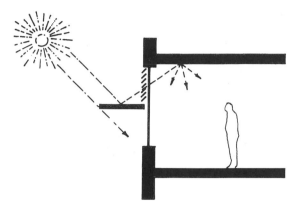

Figure 13.11c Light shelves are usually placed above eye level to prevent glare from the top of the shelf. In this position, they also act as overhangs for the view windows underneath. Louvers can be used to prevent glare from the clear glazing above the light shelf.

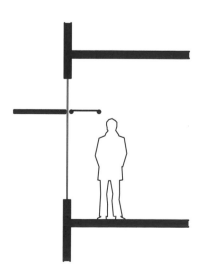

Figure 13.11d A second light shelf on the interior is more effective in collecting daylight than using louvers to control the sunlight entering through the upper (daylight) glazing (see Fig. 13.11c). Unlike the outdoor light shelf, the indoor light shelf can be very delicate (e.g., a white film or fabric stretched on a light metal frame.

parts of the structure can be used to reflect light indoors. Deep windowsills can be quite effective but are a potential source of glare (Fig. 13.11b). Light shelves prevent glare when placed just above eye level (Fig. 13.11c). If glazing is used below the light shelf, it will be mainly for view. The light shelf acts as an overhang for this lower glazing to prevent direct sunlight from entering and creating puddles of sunlight. The overhang also reduces glare by blocking the view of the bright sky in the lower window. Glare from the upper window can be controlled by louvers (Fig. 13.11c) or by an additional light shelf on the inside (Fig. 13.11d). Light shelves will not only improve the quality of the daylighting, but also increase the depth of the daylighting zone (Fig. 13.11e).

Light shelves must be much longer on east and west windows than

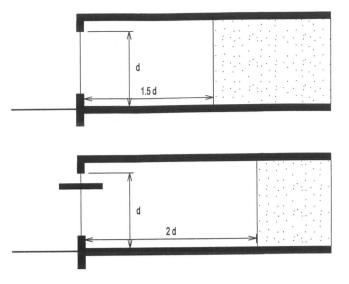

Figure 13.11e A rule of thumb for daylight penetration is 1½ times the height of a standard window and 2 times the height of a window with a light shelf for south-facing windows under direct sunlight. (After *Tips for Daylighting* by Jennifer O'Connor, © Regents of the University of California, 1997.)

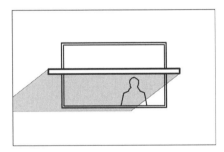

SOUTH-FACING WINDOWS

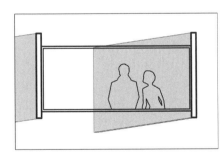

NORTH-FACING WINDOWS

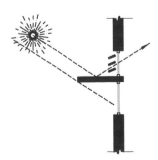

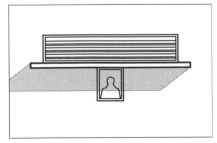

EAST-OR WEST-FACING WINDOWS

on south windows, and they are not needed at all on north windows. Thus, every orientation needs a different window design (Fig. 13.11f). Since east and west windows are exposed to the low summer sun, they need extra-deep light shelves, louvers, ribbon windows, and an occasional view window.

The Ventura Coastal Corporation's Administration Building is an excellent example of a building using light shelves (Fig. 13.11g). A sloped ceiling allows the windows to be large and high for extensive daylight penetration and the necessary mechanical equipment to be concentrated near the center of the building where more room exists above the ceiling (Fig. 13.11h). North windows are also very large and high because of the sloping ceiling. In this very mild climate, the north-facing clerestory brings light into the center of the building so that the illumination from daylighting is more evenly distributed.

Figure 13.11f Each orientation should have a different window design. Light shelves work very well on south windows, but not on north windows, where they block more daylight than they collect. North windows, however, need fins to shade the early morning and late afternoon sun. Ribbon windows with deep light shelves and louvers work best on the east and west, and view windows should be few and small.

Figure 13.11g The Ventura Coastal Corporation's Administration Building in Ventura, California, uses light shelves to daylight the building. Architect: Scott Ellinwood. (Courtesy of and © Mike Urbanek, 1211 Maricopa Highway, Ojai, CA 93023.)

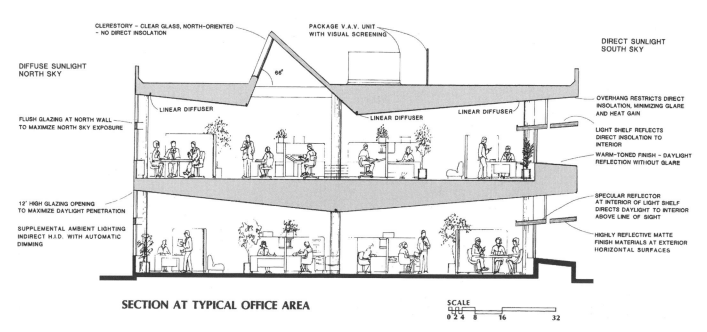

Figure 13.11h Light shelves, sloped ceilings, clerestories, north-facing windows, and open planning all help to illuminate the Ventura Coastal Corporation's Administration Building during the day. (Courtesy of and © Mike Urbanek, 1211 Maricopa Highway, Ojai, CA 93023.)

Figure 13.11i Thin metal light shelves are supported by cables. The top of the shelf is a high-reflectance white, while the rest is painted a bright yellow. The photo was taken before the indoor light shelves were installed.

The very thin metal light shelves of the Florida Solar Energy Center are made hurricane-safe via cable stays (Fig. 13.11i). One of the most effective strategies for reflecting light onto the ceiling is the use of venetian blinds. Outdoor venetian blinds are more effective in stopping heat gain than interior blinds, and they add a rich texture to the facade (see again Fig. 9.4l). The venetian blind's main drawback, dirt accumulation, can largely be avoided by sandwiching the blind between two layers of glass (Fig. 13.11j). Miniature slats reduce the annoying figure/background effect described in Fig. 12.6h. Dynamic systems such as venetian blinds are much more effective than static systems because they can better respond to the varying conditions of daylight and sunlight.

The Hooker office building in Niagara Falls, New York (1981), is covered by two glass skins that create a 4 ft (1.2 m) air space in which horizontal louvers have been placed (Fig. 13.11k). These white louvers are automatically rotated to control daylight entering the building. Direct sunlight is always intercepted and reflected to the ceiling. For insulating purposes, the louvers rotate to form an additional barrier at night.

These **double skin** or **climate facades** are very popular in Europe because of their energy efficiency (see Section 10.10). Double skin facades are especially appropriate for naturally ventilated buildings because they can control wind and rain much better than a single-skin facade.

In all cases, the ceiling should be a diffuse reflector, but the devices reflecting light onto the ceiling *could* have a specular finish in order to maximize the depth of sunlight penetration. Figures like 13.11b were drawn for clarity as if the reflectors had a specular finish. Unless they are specifically labeled, do not assume that the reflectors shown in the diagrams must be specular in nature. A disadvantage of specular reflectors is that they often cast excessively bright patches of sunlight on the ceiling. Curved specular reflectors minimize this problem by spreading the sunlight over a large part of the ceiling (Fig. 13.11l). Matte reflectors, on the other hand, create a very even distribution of light and are much less sensitive to sun angles. Model studies are a good way to determine whether specular or diffuse reflectors should be used.

When venetian blinds are rotated to block the summer sun or to maximize the winter sun, they often block the view. To correct this problem and eliminate the need for seasonal adjustments, a new type of venetian blind has been developed. The special shape of the louvers automatically blocks the summer sun and collects the winter sun with minimum obstruction of the view (Fig. 13.11m).

Rules for Advanced Daylighting from Windows

1. Use light shelves on the south facade.
2. Use small fins on north windows.
3. Use a dynamic system like outdoor venetian blinds on the east and west facades.
4. Use a backup system like venetian blinds on all interior facades for blocking low sun angles, glare control, and room darkening.

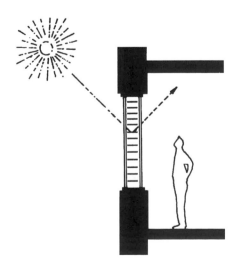

Figure 13.11j Venetian blinds are very effective in redirecting light up to the ceiling, controlling glare, and limiting the collection of light. They are especially appropriate on east and west facade because of their adjustability. They are most effective when placed outdoors.

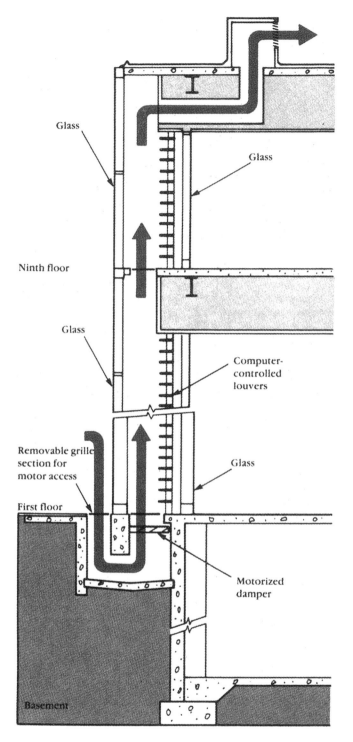

Glass

Ninth floor

Glass

Computer-controlled louvers

Removable grille section for motor access

First floor

Basement

Glass

Glass

Motorized damper

Figure 13.11k The Occidental Hooker Chemical Corporate Office Building, Niagara Falls, New York, uses computer-controlled louvers to regulate the light and heat entering the building. In summer, the hot air generated between the inner and outer glazing is vented outdoors. In winter, this hot air is sent to the north side of the building to provide heat. (From *Architectural Lighting*, 1987. © *Architectural Lighting*. Reprinted courtesy of Cassandra Publishing Corporation, Eugene, OR.)

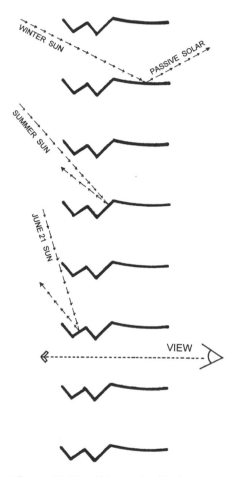

WINTER SUN

PASSIVE SOLAR

SUMMER SUN

JUNE 21 SUN

VIEW

Figure 13.11m This venetian blind was designed to reject the summer sun and collect the winter sun while remaining essentially horizontal in order to maximize the view.

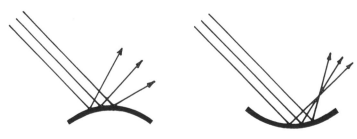

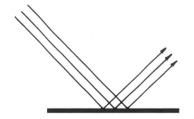

Figure 13.11l Both concave and convex specular reflectors can be used to distribute daylight over a wide area of the ceiling.

13.12 WINDOW GLAZING MATERIALS

Choosing the right glazing material is critical to a successful daylighting design. Transparent glazing comes in a variety of types: clear, tinted, heat-absorbing, reflective, and spectrally selective.

The tinted, heat-absorbing, and reflective types are rarely appropriate for the collection of daylight because they reduce light transmittance. They are sometimes used to control the glare caused by the excessive-brightness ratios between windows and walls. These three types of glazing do not, however, solve the problem automatically because they reduce the interior brightnesses as much as they reduce the brightness of the view. Thus, the brightness ratios remain the same—as does the glare. Tinted or reflective glazing can reduce glare from view windows only if the interior is also illuminated by other sources, such as skylights, clerestories, or the daylighting glazing above Light shelves, and not by the view windows alone. When there are other light sources, reducing the transmission of the view glazing reduces the glare because the reduced brightness of the view window is closer to the interior brightness (Fig. 13.12a). Of course, electric lights can also increase interior brightness, but using them to reduce the glare from sunlight defeats the whole idea of daylighting.

As mentioned earlier in this chapter in the section on cool daylight, one should use spectrally selective glazing when mainly light—and little or no heat—is required as illustrated in Fig. 13.12b and curve 3 in Fig. 13.12c. On the other hand, in buildings where winter heat is desired, a traditional low-e glazing should be used, since it transmits both the visible and solar infrared (curve 2 in Fig. 13.12c). When neither heat nor much light is required, as in view windows on the east and west facades, then a low-transmission, spectrally selective low-e coating should be used that blocks some light and most solar infrared (curve 4 in Fig. 13.12c). However, avoid dark-tinted glazing, because it can create a gloomy atmosphere and unnecessary heat gain.

Thus, it is no longer appropriate to use the same glazing for all orientations. Instead, an efficient, sustainable design will "tune" the glazing for each orientation as a function of building type and climate.

Most glass blocks are not especially useful for daylighting because they afford little control over the direction or quality of the light (Fig. 13.12d top). They also do not provide access to views, and they have poor thermal performance. However, one type of glass block is made especially for

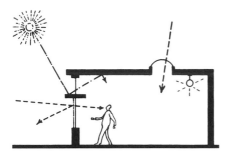

Figure 13.12a Tinted or reflective glazing in the view windows will reduce glare only if the space is lighted by other sources such as skylights, clerestories, or daylight glazing above the light shelves.

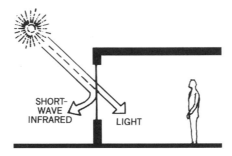

Figure 13.12b A selectively reflecting glazing blocks the sun's infrared radiation while it transmits the visible radiation.

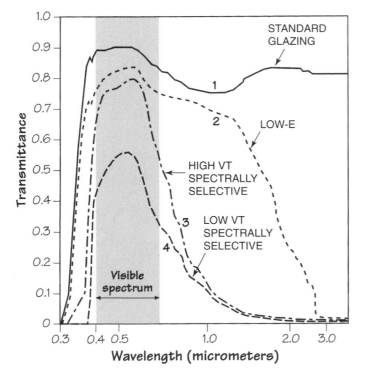

Figure 13.12c Curve 1 represents ordinary clear glazing. Use high-transmission, low-e glazing (curve 2) when winter heat is a priority. Use high-transmission, spectrally selective glazing (curve 3) when much cool daylight is desired, and use spectrally selective glazing (curve 4) for an east- or west-view window that has inadequate outdoor shading. (From *Residential Windows: A Guide to New Technologies and Energy Performance* by John Carmody, Stephen Selkowitz, and Lisa Heschong. © 1996 by John Carmody, Stephen Selkowitz, and Lisa Heschong. Reprinted by permission of W. W. Norton & Company, Inc.)

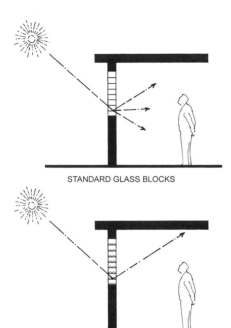

STANDARD GLASS BLOCKS

LIGHT-DIRECTING GLASS BLOCKS

Figure 13.12d Light-directing glass blocks refract the light up to the ceiling. Keep blocks high on the wall to avoid glare.

daylighting design. It is called **light-directing** because of built-in prisms that refract the light up toward the ceiling for even and deep penetration of daylight into a space (Fig. 13.12d bottom). These light-directing blocks were once very common but are now quite hard to obtain. At least one Japanese firm (Nippon Electric Glass Co.), however, still exports them to the United States.

Translucent glazing material with very high light transmittance and a small area is not usually appropriate for window glazing for several reasons. A translucent material becomes an excessively bright source when sunlight falls on it (see Fig. 13.10i). Because it diffuses light in all directions equally, it is not very helpful in improving the illumination gradient across the room. And, of course, translucent glazing does not allow for a view.

On the other hand, translucent glazing materials of relatively low light transmittance can be used successfully for daylighting when the glazing area is quite big. A large area of low-transmittance glazing, especially overhead, creates a large, low-brightness source that will contribute a significant amount of light without glare (see Fig. 13.17a). A discussion of translucent walls and roofs will follow later.

Section 9.18 describes various glazing types with an emphasis on shading rather than daylighting. Because shading and daylighting are so intertwined, it may be worthwhile to read Section 9.19 again.

Rules for Glazing Selection

1. For south glazing:
   a. use high solar heat gain low-e clear glazing if winter heat is desired.
   b. use high light-to-solar-gain (LSG) low-e glazing if winter heat is not desired.
2. For east and west glazing:
   a. minimize glazing area.
   b. use high LSG low-e glazing in cold climates.
   c. use low visible transmittance selective low-e glazing for hot climates.
3. For north glazing, use high visible transmittance low-e clear glazing.

4. For horizontal glazing or skylights:
   a. minimize skylights and maximize clerestories.
   b. use translucent high solar gain low-e glazing in cold climates.
   c. use translucent high LSG low-e glazing in hot climates.
5. Clerestory (vertical) glazing:
   a. same as windows.
   b. can be translucent.

13.13 TOP LIGHTING

Skylights, monitors, and clerestories are all methods of **top lighting**. The advantages of top lighting are the potential for high-quality and high-quantity illumination over a large area. Unfortunately, top lighting also has some serious drawbacks. It is not a workable strategy for multistory buildings, and since it does not satisfy the need for view and orientation, it should supplement, not replace, windows.

Top lighting, like all lighting from above, can cause glare and veiling reflections. These reflections are best avoided by keeping light sources out of the offending zones. This is possible, of course, only when the location of the visual task is fixed and the roof openings can be appropriately placed (Fig. 13.13a). Usually, the best solution is to carefully diffuse the light so that there are no bright sources to cause veiling reflections. Either reflect the light off the ceiling (Fig. 13.14f) or use baffles or banners to shield, and diffuse the light sources (Fig. 13.13b and Color Plates 15 and 16). Both of

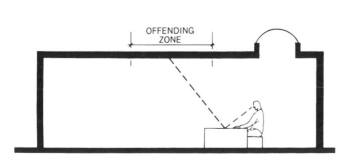

Figure 13.13a Veiling reflections are avoided when skylights are placed outside the offending zone.

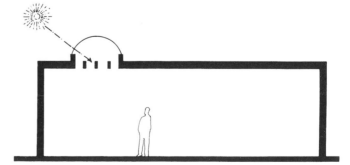

Figure 13.13b A system of baffles can control direct glare and to some extent veiling reflections.

these strategies also solve the problem, of direct glare and puddles of sunlight falling on the work surfaces. Because skylights behave differently from monitors and clerestories, they are discussed separately.

13.14 SKYLIGHT STRATEGIES

Skylights are horizontal or slightly sloped, glazed openings in the roof. As such, they see a large part of the unobstructed sky and, consequently, transmit very high levels of illumination. Because beams of direct sunlight are not desirable for difficult visual tasks, the entering sunlight must be diffused in some manner. For skylights, unlike windows, translucent glazing can be appropriate since there is no view to block and direct glare can be largely avoided.

A fundamental problem with all skylights is that they face the summer sun more than the winter sun. Thus, they collect much more light and heat in the summer than the winter, which is exactly the opposite of what is needed. As a result, clerestories should be used instead of skylights whenever possible. Nevertheless, because skylights are inexpensive and popular, they will be discussed here.

Guidelines

1. *Skylight spacing for uniform lighting.* If there are no windows, the skylights should be spaced, as shown in Fig. 13.14a. With windows, the skylights can be farther from the perimeter, as shown in Fig. 13.14b.
2. *Use splayed openings to increase the apparent size of skylights.* Better light distribution and less glare result when the walls of the light well are sloped (Fig. 13.14c).
3. *Place the skylight high in a space.* A skylight mounted high above a space will enable the light to diffuse before it reaches the floor (Fig. 13.14d). Direct glare is largely prevented, because the bright skylight is at the edge of or beyond the observer's field of view.

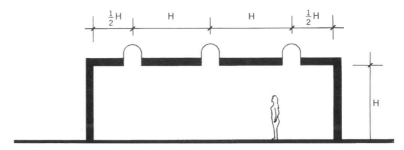

Figure 13.14a Recommended spacing for skylights without windows as a function of ceiling height.

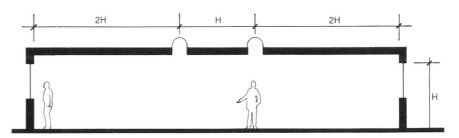

Figure 13.14b Recommended spacing for skylights with high windows as a function of ceiling height.

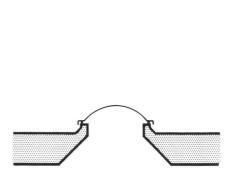

Figure 13.14c Splayed openings distribute light better and cause less glare than square openings.

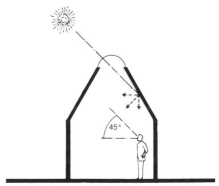

Figure 13.14d In high, narrow rooms, glare is minimal because the high light source is outside the field of view.

4. *Place skylights near walls.* Any wall, and especially the north wall, can be used as a diffuse reflector for a skylight (Fig 13.14e). The bright wall will make the space appear larger and more cheerful. The north wall will balance the illumination from the south window. Avoid puddles of sunlight on the lower parts of the walls.
5. *Use interior reflectors to diffuse the sunlight.* A skylight can deliver very uniform and diffused light when a reflector is suspended under

the opening to bounce light up to the ceiling (Fig. 13.14f). Louis I. Kahn used this strategy very successfully in the Kimbell Art Museum (Fig. 13.14g). The light entering a continuous skylight is reflected by a daylight fixture onto the underside of the concrete barrel vault. The result is extremely high-quality lighting. No direct glare results because the daylight fixture shields the skylight from view. Small perforations in the daylight fixture allow some light

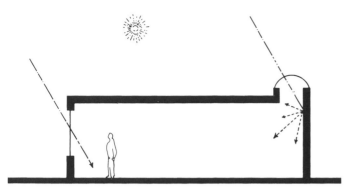

Figure 13.14e Place a skylight in front of a north wall for more uniform lighting and less glare.

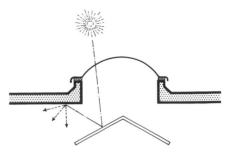

Figure 13.14f Use interior reflectors (daylight fixtures) to diffuse sunlight and reduce glare.

Figure 13.14g In the Kimbell Art Museum, Fort Worth, Texas, Louis I. Kahn successfully used daylight fixtures to diffuse light and to eliminate direct glare.

to filter through, so the fixture does not appear dark against the bright ceiling.

The author believes that if Louis I. Kahn were alive today and were designing this museum, he would use clerestories rather than skylights in order to avoid the large summer heat gain and to collect more winter sun.

The Menil Collection in Houston, Texas, designed by architect Renzo Piano, in 1982, uses skylights with diffusing baffles in all parts of the building except the two-story section (Fig. 13.14h). The skylight glazing is slightly sloped for drainage (Fig. 13.14i). The ferro-cement baffles were carefully designed to keep all direct sunlight out of the building. Baffles can also be made of light-colored and/or translucent cloth panels (Fig. 13.15i). A weakness of this design is the use of skylights, which cause overheating in the summer. In his latest design, the addition to the High Museum in Atlanta, Georgia (2005), Renzo Piano avoided this problem by using clerestories instead of skylights (see Fig. 13.15r).

6. *Use exterior shades and reflectors to improve the summer/winter balance.* Shade the skylight from the summer sun, and use reflectors to increase the collection of the winter sun (Fig. 13.14j). Movable devices can be more effective (see Figs. 7.6f, 7.6g, and 17.5f.

7. *Quantity controls:* Some spaces, such as classrooms when using audiovisuals, need to control the amount of daylight any time of the year. Figure 13.14k shows a skylight with operable louvers that can be controlled manually or automatically by photo sensors to maintain the daylight illumination at a constant level.

Figure 13.14h All gallery spaces in the Menil Collection, designed by Renzo Piano, are daylit except for those under the second story. However, the color of the daylight varies for those areas in direct sunlight and those areas in shade that are receiving only skylight. (See Color Plate 15).

Figure 13.14i The glazing in the Menil Collection is above the baffles, which allow only soft, diffused daylight to enter.

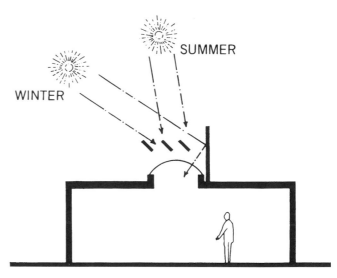

Figure 13.14j Shade the skylight from some of the summer sun, and use a reflector to increase the winter collection.

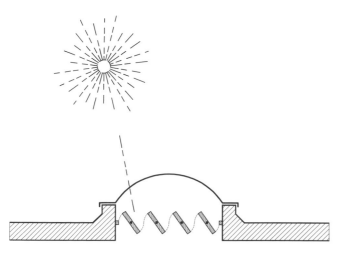

Figure 13.14k Some spaces, such as offices, need to modulate the light level, while other spaces, such as classrooms, need to block all light when viewing audiovisuals. Operable louvers, to adjust the light levels, can be controlled manually or automatically as needed.

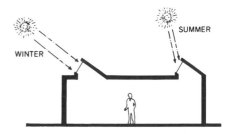

Figure 13.14l Steeply sloped skylights perform better than horizontal ones because they collect more winter light and less summer light.

8. *Use steeply sloped skylights to improve the summer/winter balance.* Since horizontal skylights collect more light and heat in summer than winter, skylights *steeply sloped toward the north or south* will supply light more uniformly throughout the year (Fig. 13.14l). As the slope is increased, the skylights eventually turn into monitors or clerestories, as described in the next section.

9. *Use sunlight for dramatic effect.* In lobbies, lounges, and other spaces without critical visual tasks, use sunlight and sun puddles to create delight. Splashes of sunlight moving slowly across surfaces can create dramatic effects and display the passage of time. To minimize summer overheating, use either small skylights or large skylights with reflective glazing, **frets** (Fig. 13.14o) painted on the glass, or covered with PV cells (Fig. 8.11b) to block a significant amount of the sun.

Perhaps no modern building uses daylighting as exuberantly as the Crystal Cathedral, Garden

Figure 13.14m Highly reflective glazing and a gossamer space frame filter the light entering the Crystal Cathedral, Garden Grove, California, by Johnson and Burgee.

Figure 13.14n Overheating problems in the Crystal Cathedral, Garden Grove, California, are minimized by the highly reflective glazing and large sections of window wall that can be opened. Only one of many operable panels is open (see left center).

Figure 13.14o For a dramatic effect, I. M. Pei allowed direct sunlight to enter the central circulation space of the East Wing, National Gallery of Art, Washington, D.C. However, to reduce overheating from the large skylight, a fret of white parallel bars was attached to the glazing (see upper left corner of photo).

Grove, California (Fig. 13.14m). The walls and roof are all glass, supported by a gossamer space frame. The light is filtered first by the highly reflective glazing (8 percent transmittance) and then again by the white space frame. From the outside, the building is a large mirror mainly reflecting the blue sky (Fig. 13.14n). Overheating is minimized by the low-transmission glass, by large wall and roof panels that can open for natural ventilation, by stratification, and by the fact that the building is primarily used either in the morning or in the evening in the rather mild climate found just south of Los Angeles.

In the East Wing of the National Gallery, Washington, D.C., I. M. Pei used skylights in the form of tetrahedrons to create dramatic daylighting in the atrium lobby (Fig. 13.14o). To limit the solar gain through the very large skylight, a fret of parallel white lines was applied to the glass.

13.15 CLERESTORIES, MONITORS, AND LIGHT SCOOPS

Clerestories, monitors, and light scoops are all raised above the main roof in order to bring light to the center of the space (Fig. 13.15a). The word "monitor" is ordinarily used when the windows face more than one direction and are operable (Fig. 13.15b), while the term "light scoops" is ordinarily used when the clerestory windows face one direction only and the opposite side is curved to reflect the light down (Fig. 13.15c). These devices have been used in architecture for at least 4000 years to bring daylight into the central area of a large space. Egyptian hypostyle halls had taller columns in the center to raise the roof, thereby creating a clerestory for light and ventilation.

The vertical or near-vertical glazing of clerestories has the characteristics of windows rather than skylights. When they face south, clerestories have the desirable effect of collecting more sunlight in the winter than in the summer. Vertical south-facing

openings can also be shaded easily from unwanted direct sunlight. North-facing openings deliver a low but constant light with little or no glare. East and west openings are usually avoided because of the difficulty in shading the low sun, and they receive more summer sun than winter sun.

Another advantage of clerestory lighting is the diffused nature of the light, which results because much of the entering light is reflected off the ceiling (Fig. 13.15d). Since the light can be easily diffused once inside, the glazing can be transparent.

The main disadvantage of any vertical opening is that it sees less of the sky than a horizontal opening and, consequently, collects less light. As with skylights, direct glare and veiling reflections can be serious problems. The following are some of the more common strategies for clerestories, monitors, and light scoops.

Guidelines For Clerestories

1. *Orientation.* Face openings south to get the most winter solar heating and good lighting all year. Design openings carefully to prevent problems associated with direct sunlight. In extremely hot climates with no winters, north clerestories are preferred, while in hot climates with short winters, a combination of north and south glazing might be best. Avoid east and west glazing as much as possible.

2. *Spacing:* Figure 13.15e illustrates spacing for typical clerestories.

3. *Reflective roof:* Use a high-reflectance white roof to reflect more light through the clerestory glazing. To maximize winter collection, a specular reflector can be mounted on the roof just outside the glazing. Once indoors, the light needs to be reflected off a high-reflectance white ceiling (Fig. 13.15d).

4. *Suncatcher Baffles:* Use suncatcher baffles outside of north clerestories to increase light collection on clear, sunny days (Fig. 13.15f).

Figure 13.15a These south-facing clerestories illuminate classrooms at the Durant Middle School, Raleigh, North Carolina. The sawtooth arrangement keeps one clerestory from shading the next, and the sloped ceiling more efficiently directs the light down. (Innovative Design, Architect.)

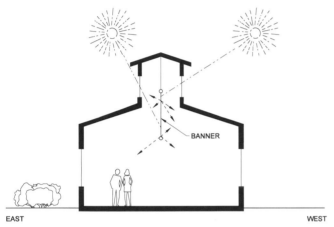

EAST   WEST

Figure 13.15b Monitors usually ventilate and light the center of large spaces. A banner is an effective technique for diffusing the sunlight. Also see color plate 8.

Figure 13.15c These light scoops on the roof of the Florida Solar Energy Center in the town to Cocoa face north because passive solar heating is not required for this building in that climate.

Although east and west clerestories are not usually recommended, their performance can be greatly improved via suncatcher baffles. Ordinarily, east clerestories receive too much morning sun and not enough afternoon light. A suncatcher can produce a more balanced light level by shading some of the morning sunlight while increasing the afternoon reflected light (Fig. 13.15g). Of course, the same is true for west clerestories.

5. *Reflecting Light Off Interior Walls.* Walls can act as large, low-brightness diffusers. A well-lit wall will appear to recede, thereby making the room seem larger and more cheerful than it actually is. Furthermore, glare from a direct view of the sky or the sun can be completely avoided (Fig. 13.15h). Le Corbusier used this technique in Notre Dame du Haut, where the towers act as clerestories. As a result, the interior walls of the towers glow with a soft light (Fig. 13.15m).

6. *Diffusing baffles:* Use diffusing baffles to prevent puddles of sunlight on work surfaces, to spread the light more evenly over the work areas, and to eliminate glare from the clerestory (Fig. 13.1l). The baffle spacing must be designed both to prevent

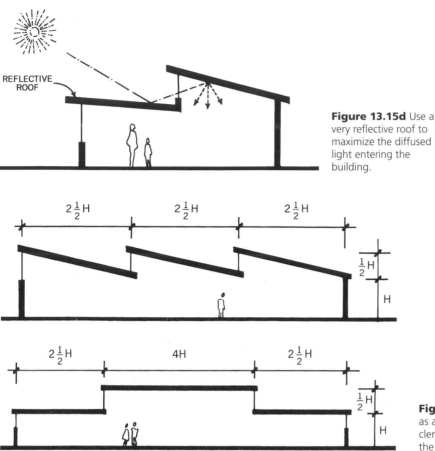

Figure 13.15d Use a very reflective roof to maximize the diffused light entering the building.

Figure 13.15e Typical spacing of clerestories is shown as a function of ceiling height. It is usually best to have clerestories face either north or south, depending on the climate.

direct sunlight from entering the space and to prevent direct glare in the field of view below 45° (Fig. 13.15j). The baffles should have a matte, high-reflectance finish or be highly translucent.

The Mt. Airy Public Library in North Carolina is an excellent example of a building largely daylit by clerestory windows. The axonometric view in Fig. 13.15k shows the location of the south-facing clerestories, and Fig. 13.15m illustrates how the direct sunlight is captured and diffused. Also, note how the electric lights and mechanical equipment

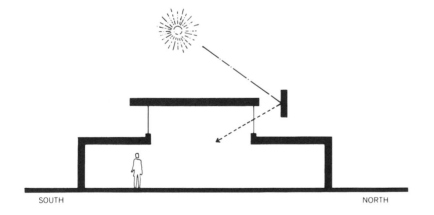

SOUTH NORTH

Figure 13.15f A suncatcher baffle outside a north window can significantly increase daylighting on a sunny day. (After Lam, *Sunlighting as Formgiver for Architecture*, 1986.)

AFTERNOON SUN

MORNING SUN

WEST EAST

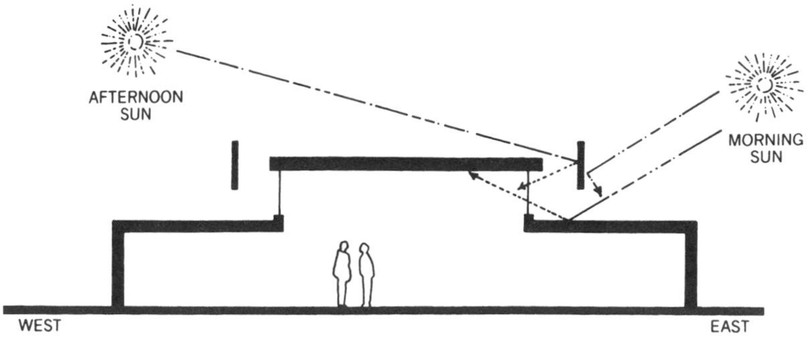

Figure 13.15g Suncatcher baffles can greatly improve the performance of east and west clerestories. (After Lam, *Sunlighting as Formgiver for Architecture*, 1986).

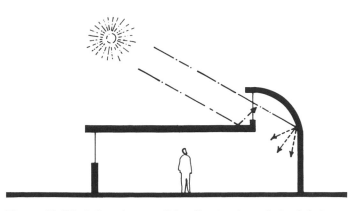

Figure 13.15h Reflect clerestory light off an interior wall. South-facing clerestories work best in this regard.

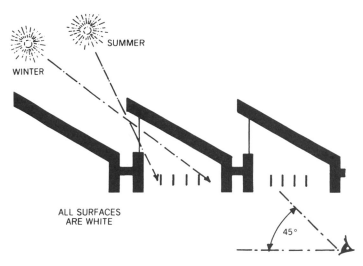

Figure 13.15j The baffles for the public library in Mt. Airy, North Carolina, not only prevent direct sunlight from entering, but also prevent glare within the normal field of view.

Figure 13.15i These cloth baffles prevent glare and diffuse the light entering from a south-facing clerestory at the Durant Middle School, Raleigh, North Carolina. (Innovative Design, Architect.)

are integrated into the daylighting system (Fig 13.15m). This building also uses light shelves on the windows (Fig. 13.15n).

Alvar Aalto, the master of daylighting, made extensive use of clerestories and light baffles in the Parochial Church of Riola, Italy (Fig. 13.15o). He used the concrete structure to create both the light scoops and the baffles (Fig. 13.15p). Although his light scoops face north for cool, constant light, a good case could have been made for them facing south or especially east (Fig. 13.15q). East-facing light scoops might seem contradictory, given everything said before, but not if one considers the building type, a church that is used primarily on Sunday mornings and rarely in the afternoon.

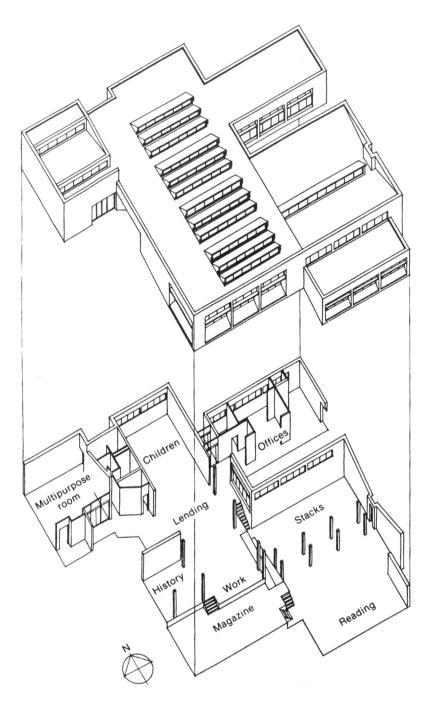

As was mentioned before, clerestories are superior to skylights because skylights collect the most sun in the summer and least in the winter—just the opposite of what we want. One architect who has come to recognize this situation is Renzo Piano. Unlike his earlier Menil gallery, which uses skylights, his addition to the High Museum in Atlanta, Georgia, uses a clerestory-like design (Fig. 13.15r). Although the actual glazing is horizontal, the light scoops prevent any direct sun from entering the building (Fig. 13.15s).

7. *Quantity controls:* Many toplit spaces, such as classrooms when using audiovisuals, need the ability to reduce or eliminate daylighting. Since clerestories have most of the properties of windows, venetian blinds, vertical blinds, roll-up shades, or curtains can be effectively used. All of the devices are easily operated remotely through electrical or mechanical means.

Figure 13.15k Axonometric view of the Mt. Airy Public Library in North Carolina. Architects: Edward Mazria Assoc. and J. N. Pease Assoc. [From *Passive Solar Journal,* Vol 3(4). © American Solar Energy Society.]

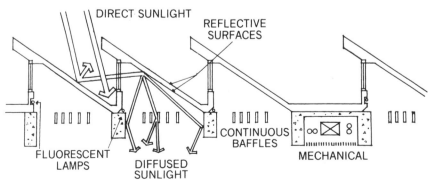

Figure 13.15m Section through the clerestory of the Mt. Airy Public Library, in North Carolina. [From *Passive Solar Journal,* Vol. 3(4). © American Solar Energy Society.]

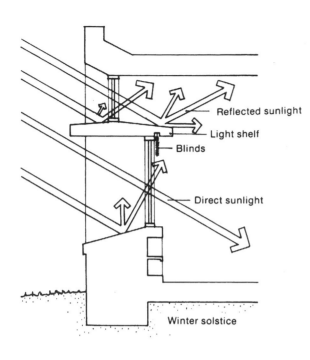
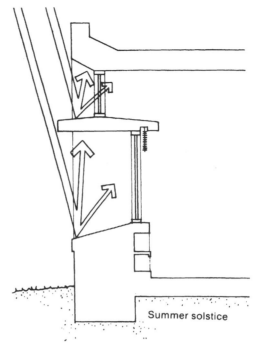

Reflected sunlight

Light shelf

Blinds

Direct sunlight

Winter solstice

Summer solstice

Figure 13.15n Sections through south windows of the Mt. Airy Public Library in North Carolina. More reflected sunlight can enter in the winter than the summer. [From *Passive Solar Journal*, Vol. 3(4). © American Solar Energy Society.]

Figure 13.15o Clerestories can also be used in the form of light scoops. The Parochial Church of Riola, Italy (1978), designed by Alvar Aalto, uses bent concrete frames to support the roof and to block the glare from the light scoops. (Photograph by William Gwin.)

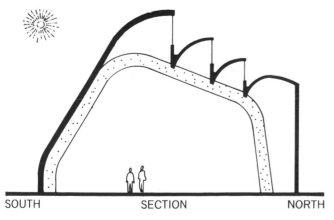

SOUTH   SECTION   NORTH

Figure 13.15p A section of the Parochial Church of Riola, Italy.

Figure 13.15q The light scoops of the Parochial Church of Riola, Italy, collect constant and cool north light. (Photograph by Clark Lundell.)

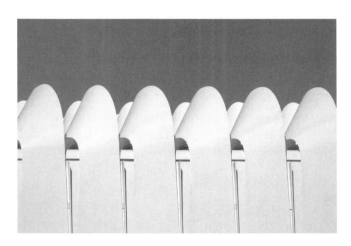

Figure 13.15r In the design of the addition to the High Museum in Atlanta, Georgia, Renzo Piano uses light scoops to control the collection of sunlight. The opening at the base of each light scoop is for reducing wind loads.

Figure 13.15s No direct sunray can ever enter the High Museum in Alanta, Georgia. The evenness of the diffused daylighting is most obvious where the partition meets the ceiling—almost no scallops.

13. 16 SPECIAL DAYLIGHTING TECHNIQUES

The following daylighting strategies may be useful for special lighting problems:

1. *Light Wells or Shafts:* Light wells become more efficient as the width-to-depth ratio increases because less light is absorbed by the reduced number of reflections (Fig. 13.9f). If the well walls were very reflective, more light would be transmitted or the well could be made narrower for the same light transmission. With modern, very reflective, specular (mirrored) surfaces, which absorb as little as 2 percent at each reflectance, it is possible to successfully transmit light one story with fairly small light wells. Moshe Safdie and associates used such light shafts in the National Gallery of Canada (Fig. 13.16a). Physical models were used to prove the viability of this strategy.

2. *Tubular Skylights:* Duct-like tubes are commercially available with highly reflective, specular inner surfaces that transmit about 50 percent of the outdoor light through the attic (Fig. 13.16b). The amount of light depends largely on the diameter and length. Circular tubes are available in a range of sizes from 8 to 24 in. (20–60 cm) in diameter, and square tubes are as large as 4 ft^2 (1.2 m^2). Although they are an economic way to add light shafts to one-story, gabled, or flat-roofed buildings, the quality of the light is not much better than that of a ceiling-mounted, circular, fluorescent lamp. Both the quantity and quality of the lighting are improved by splaying the ceiling around the light tube (Fig. 13.16b).

3. *Beamed Daylighting.* A mirror mounted on a heliostat can track the sun and reflect a vertical beam of light through the roof regardless of the sun angle. Because the sunlight enters a building at a constant angle, it can be easily and effectively controlled.

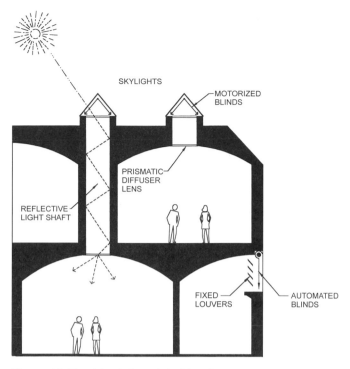

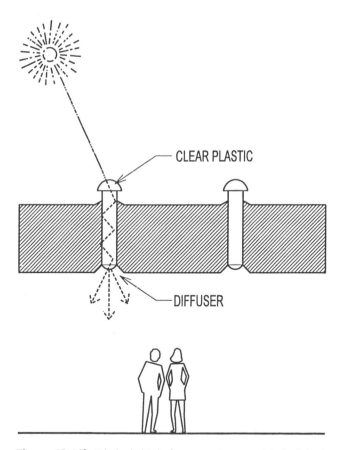

Figure 13.16a Light shafts with highly reflective specular surfaces bring daylight through the second floor to the ground floor galleries at the National Gallery of Canada in Ottawa, Ontario, Canada, designed by Moshe Safdie and Associates.

Figure 13.16b Tubular light shafts are most appropriate for bringing daylight into the interior areas of existing buildings. When used in new construction, the lower opening should be splayed as much as possible.

When large mirrors mounted on heliostats are used to light whole sections of a building, the technique is known as **beamed daylighting**. The Civil/Mineral Engineering Building at the University of Minnesota in St. Paul exemplifies this concept. Mirrors and lenses are used to beam sunlight throughout the building (Fig. 13.16c). Where

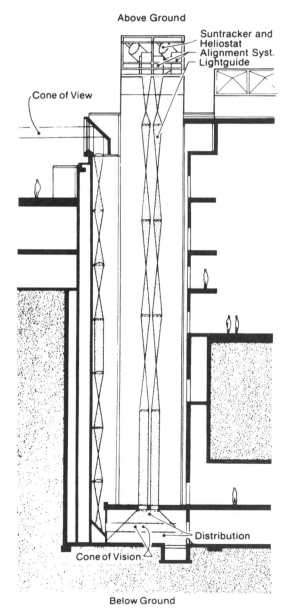

Figure 13.16c The Civil/Mineral Engineering Building at the University of Minnesota in St. Paul uses beamed daylighting to light underground areas of the building. Images of the outdoors can also be beamed to the far interior or underground. (From *Building Control Systems* by V Bradshaw, © John Wiley & Sons, Inc. 1985.)

Figure 13.16d A giant one-axis heliostat reflects sunlight into the lobby of the Hong-Kong Bank. (Courtesy Foster Associates. © Ian Lambot, photographer.)

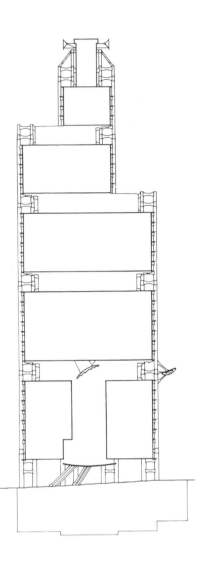

Figure 13.16e This section of the Hong Kong Bank shows how the heliostat reflects sunlight onto a mirror hanging at an angle from the ceiling of the ten-story-high lobby. The sunlight is thus reflected down to the otherwise dark lobby floor. (Courtesy Foster Associates.)

light is required, a diffusing element intercepts the beam and scatters the light.

Figure 13.16c also shows how a similar type of optical system can be used to transmit views of the outdoors deep into the building or underground. The Hong Kong Bank, designed by Foster Associates, uses a one-axis heliodon to reflect a beam of sunlight horizontally into the building (Fig. 13.16d). When the beam hits the 45° tilted mirrors at the top of the atrium, sunlight is reflected down to the floor of the atrium deep inside the building (Fig. 13.16e).

4. *Fiber optics and light pipes:* Unlike the above-mentioned systems, which use surface reflections to conduct light, fiber optics and light pipes use the much more efficient phenomenon of total internal reflection. These light guides are illuminated on one end with daylight or an electric light that is almost parallel to the light guide. Since diffused skylight cannot be focused, these light guides only work with sunlight. A heliostat (Fig. 13.16f) is used to track the sun and reflect the sunrays as a narrow beam into the ends of the light guides, which can be made either of fiber optics or light pipes.

Fiber optics uses thin glass or plastic fibers or plastic rods to conduct light very efficiently by total internal reflection. Because

Figure 13.16f This commercially available heliostat feeds sunlight into a fiber-optic bundle to illuminate a series of small displays indoors.

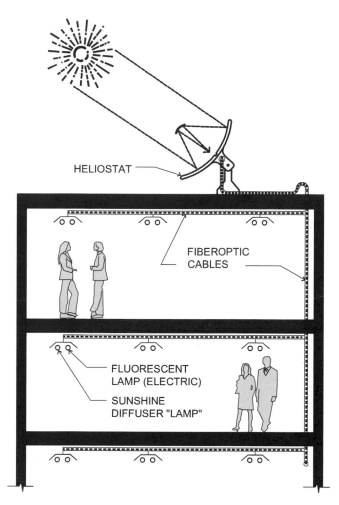

HELIOSTAT

FIBEROPTIC CABLES

FLUORESCENT LAMP (ELECTRIC)

SUNSHINE DIFFUSER "LAMP"

Figure 13.16g In the Hybrid Solar Lighting system, the large heliostat mirror focuses the full solar spectrum on a cap that not only converts the solar infrared to electricity with PV cells, but also reflects the visible radiation (light) into the ends of the fiber-optic system. The indoor hybrid lighting fixtures have both electric lamps powered by the PV and diffuser "lamps" powered by the optical fibers.

Light pipes are hollow, duct-like light guides made of prismatic, plastic film that transmit light by total internal reflection, unlike the tubular skylights mentioned above, which use surface reflection. Since light pipes are essentially straight elements, mirrors are used to change direction. Figure 14.12a and 14.12b show how light pipes and fiber optics work with electric light sources.

5. *Prismatic Systems:* Popular daylighting techniques in the early twentieth century, prismatic systems are being rediscovered. One of the main challenges for daylighting has always been the need to get quality light deep into the interior of a building from the window wall. Glass or plastic prisms can be placed at the top of windows to refract light up to the ceiling, much like light shelves (Fig. 13.16h). This system is similar to the prismatic light–directing glass blocks seen in Fig. 13.12d. See the references Baker et al. (1993) and Willmert (1999) at the end of this chapter for more information on prismatic systems.

6. *Glass Floors:* In the nineteenth century, glass paving blocks were commonly used to enable light to

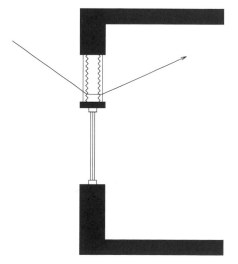

Figure 13.16h Prisms can refract light farther into the building, much like the way light shelves reflect the light.

the fibers or rods are thin, they can make fairly sharp turns. Thus, light is conducted almost as easily as electricity is conducted in wires. When the light gets to the end of the fiber, a fiber-optic lighting fixture will create the desired illumination pattern. Like electric lighting fixtures, fiber-optic fixtures can be made in the whole range from spot lighting to linear diffusers.

The Oak Ridge National Laboratory has developed a complete fiber-optic system that is now commercially available. They call this system "Hybrid Solar Lighting" because it uses not only the visible part of the solar spectrum (45 percent) but also the short-wave (solar) infrared part of the spectrum (50 percent). The heliostat divides the solar radiation, with light directed into the optical fibers or rods and the infrared radiation directed to PV cells (Fig. 13.16g). Thus, the indoor hybrid fixtures have both electric lamps powered by PV and optical diffusing "lamps" powered by light. In this system, a 4 ft (1.2 m) diameter heliostat can illuminate about 1000 ft^2 (90 m^2) of floor area.

Figure 13.16i Glass block pavers can transmit light deep into buildings. (Courtesy Innovative Building Products, Inc.)

Figure 13.16j Laminated glass floors and stair treads allow daylight to reach lower levels. The glass is usually textured or diffusing for reasons of modesty. (Courtesy Innovative Building Products, Inc.)

reach basements. In some of the older commercial areas of New York City, one can still walk on glass-block-embedded sidewalks that have withstood a century of trucks parked on them. Although glass blocks are making a comeback mostly for stylish reasons, they are still a wonderful way to bring light from one floor to the next (Fig. 13.16i).

Because of the brittle nature of glass, the blocks had to be small so that the failure of one unit would not result in a serious overall failure. Today, laminated glass can accomplish the same thing. As in automobile windshields and bulletproof glass, the failure of one or more glass laminations does not result in a catastrophic failure of the whole unit. Since glass has become a predictable material, engineers can calculate the thickness and number of laminations based on the size of the glass floor panel and its loading. Glass floors in block or panel form can be a powerful tool for transmitting daylight to the lower floors (Fig. 13.16j).

13.17 TRANSLUCENT WALLS AND ROOFS

Most translucent walls and roofs are made of either fabric membranes or composite panels. Membrane tension structures are most appropriate for large spaces with long spans. The translucent membranes provide a very diffused, low-brightness, low-glare light source. Unfortunately, none of the available translucent-membrane materials has a very good insulating value; consequently, membrane roofs are appropriate only for special building types.

Many stadiums, tennis courts, and other similar facilities are now covered with these translucent membranes. They are usually made of a Teflon- or silicon-coated fiberglass fabric. Even though the light transmittance of those fabrics is often less than 10 percent, abundant high-quality light is available inside because of the very large area of the translucent material. The Denver Airport is an excellent example of the high-quality daylight that filters through such membranes (Fig. 13.17a). Overheating is avoided because the white membrane reflects about 90 percent of the solar radiation (Fig. 13.17b).

Sometimes double membranes are used to increase the insulating value of the skin to a point at which heating becomes feasible, but a double membrane with an R-value of about 2 is still a poor thermal envelope.

For good thermal resistance with translucency, a composite sandwich panel system is appropriate (Fig. 13.17c). Panels with only air

Figure 13.17a Although the roof membrane of the Denver Airport Terminal Building has very low transmittance, there is ample quality daylight because of the large-area, low-brightness translucent roof. (Courtesy of and © Greg Stueber, photographer.)

Figure 13.17b Overheating is minimized because about 90 percent of sunlight is reflected off the white membrane. Furthermore, the high ceiling enables the heat to rise, which is an advantage in the summer but a disadvantage in the winter.

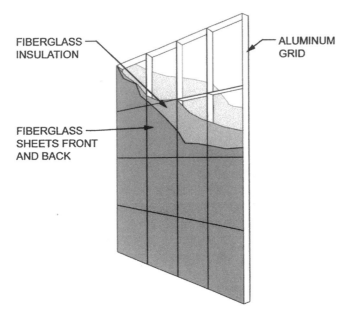

FIBERGLASS INSULATION

ALUMINUM GRID

FIBERGLASS SHEETS FRONT AND BACK

Figure 13.17c As the thermal resistance of translucent, composite sandwich panels is increased by the addition of fiberglass, the light transmittance is decreased. The panels can be used for walls and roofs of various shapes (e.g., barrel vaults)

Table 13.17 Properties of Translucent Panels and Membranes

System	Thickness I-P (in.)	Thickness SI (mm)	R-Value I-P	R-Value SI	Solar Transmission %
Fiberglass membrane	1/16	2	1–2	0.18–0.35	5–10
Composite sandwich panel with fiberglass insulation*	2¾	70	2	0.35	50
	2¾		3	0.53	25
	2¾		5	0.88	15
	2¾		10	1.75	10
Composite sandwich panel with aerogel insulation	1/2	13	4	0.7	73
	1	25	8	1.4	53
	1¼	31	10	1.75	45
	2½	63	20	3.5	21

*Although the panel thickness is fixed, the amount of insulation in the cavity can be varied.

spaces have an R_{I-P} value of about 2, ($R_{SI} = 0.35$), but if translucent fiberglass is added, the R_{I-P} value can be raised as high as 10 ($R_{SI} = 1.75$). Unfortunately, as fiberglass is added to increase the thermal resistance, the transmittance of light decreases significantly. However, if silica aerogel is used instead of fiberglass, the panel can have both high thermal resistance and high solar transmittance (see Table 13.17). Even so, solar transmission always decreases with increasing thermal resistance, as shown in Fig. 13.17d.

A delightful by-product of the translucency is the nighttime glow of the building walls and/or roof (Fig. 13.17e).

13. 18 ELECTRIC LIGHTING AS A SUPPLEMENT TO DAYLIGHTING

Even if a building is designed to be fully daylit, an electric lighting system is still required for stormy weather and nighttime use. A daylit building can save a significant amount of energy and electrical demand only if the electric lights are turned off when sufficient daylight is available. Although people can be relied upon to turn the lights on, few will turn the lights off when they are no longer necessary. This is understandable, because having both daylight and the electric lights on, thereby doubling the required illumination, is not visually objectionable and barely noticeable. The eye easily adapts to the higher illumination.

Consequently, automatic controls are necessary if daylighting is to save electricity. These controls consist of a photocell placed in the ceiling of the work area and a control panel of either the on/off or the dimming type. The on/off type is less expensive, while the dimming type saves more energy and is less disturbing to the users. To take advantage of these automatic controls, the lighting fixtures must be arranged to complement the available daylight. Figure 13.18a illustrates how the lighting gradient from part of the electric lighting can supplement the lighting gradient from daylighting. Figure 13.18b illustrates how the fixtures are arranged in rows parallel to the windows so that any number of rows can be on or off as needed.

Fluorescent lighting is the best choice for dimming and switching. The lamps can be dimmed to about 15 percent of their light output without changes in color, and they can be turned on and off almost instantaneously. Since most high-intensity discharge sources (metal halide and high-pressure sodium) have a long restrike time (five to ten minutes), they are not as suitable for switching strategies but they can be dimmed to about 50 percent of the normal light output.

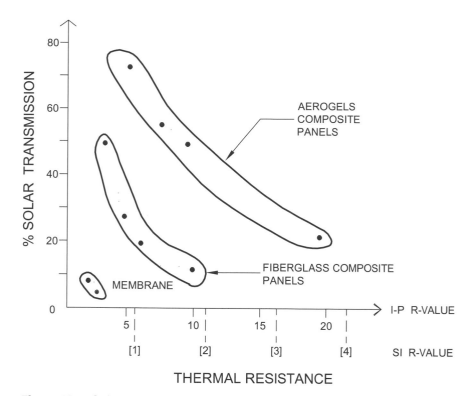

Figure 13.17d Like windows, translucent panels lose solar transmittance as their thermal resistance is increased. The points represent specific commercially available panels and membranes.

The controls described above use sensors to control all the lighting fixtures in a zone simultaneously. A promising alternative is to have each fixture control itself. One system, called "Day Switch," uses an inexpensive electronic device in conjunction with the ballast of a fluorescent lighting fixture. With its own built-in sensor, it dims the fluorescent fixture as needed.

Not only do people leave electric lights on when there is more than enough daylight, they also leave them on when no one is in the room. **Occupancy sensors** are a very cost-effective solution to this problem. These sensors use either infrared radiation or ultrasonic vibrations to detect the presence of people. Combination occupancy and light-sensing devices are also available for daylit spaces.

Daylighting should usually serve as the ambient part of a task/ambient lighting system. As described in the previous chapter, the ambient illumination is usually about one-third of the recommended task illumination. The user-controllable, electric task lighting then gives people the control they need to get abundant high-quality light for their tasks.

Figure 13.17e Translucent and insulated composite walls provide increased lighting by day and a spectacular luminescent architecture by night. (PA Technology, Princeton, NJ, by Richard Rogers, Kelbaugh & Lee Architects, photographs courtesy Kalwall Corporation.)

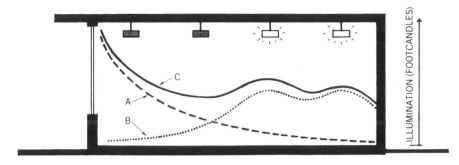

Figure 13.18a Daylighting (curve A) is supplemented by part of the electric lighting (curve B) to create a rather uniform light level (curve C).

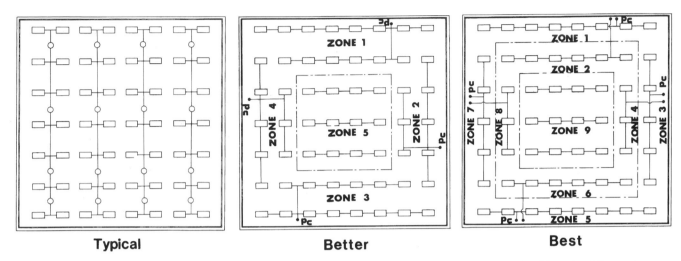

Typical   Better   Best

Figure 13.18b These reflected ceiling plans are for a building with windows on all four sides. Lighting zones should consist of fixtures in rows parallel to the windows on each orientation. "Pc" stands for photocell light sensor. (From *Daylighting: Performance and Design*, by Gregg D. Ander. © Gregg D. Ander, AIA., Southern California Edison.)

13.19 PHYSICAL MODELING

Simulation with physical models is by far the best tool for designing daylighting for a number of reasons:

1. Because of the physics of light, no error due to scale is introduced. Consequently, the model can reproduce exactly the conditions of the actual building. Photographs made of a real space and of an accurate model show identical lighting patterns (Fig. 13.19a).
2. No matter how complicated the design, a model can accurately predict the result.
3. Physical models illustrate both the qualitative and quantitative aspects of a lighting system (Figs. 13.19b and c). This is especially significant since glare, veiling reflections, and brightness ratios are often more important than illumination levels (Fig. 13.19d).

4. Simple hand calculations or software can produce erroneous conclusions because of the very complex nature of daylighting, while sophisticated computer programs require significant time and experience to run. On the other hand, physical modeling requires little learning time and provides very reliable feedback and insight for both present and future projects.
5. Physical modeling is a familiar, popular, and appropriate medium for architectural design.
6. Physical models are very effective in communicating with the client as well as with the design team.
7. Although physical models are expensive to build and test, the resultant quality of design and improved skills of the designer make the investment worthwhile. Excellent results are obtainable from even crude study models as

long as a few basic requirements are met.

Important Considerations for Physical Modeling

1. Architectural elements that affect the light entering a space must be carefully modeled (e.g., the size, depth, and location of windows, overhangs, mullions, and baffles). Use plastic film to simulate glazing, especially if tinted, reflective, or translucent glazing is being modeled.
2. Reflectance factors should be reasonably close to the desired finishes. The best solution is to use actual finishes whenever possible.
3. External objects that reflect or block light entering the windows should be included in the model test. Include adjacent walls, trees, ground finishes, and anything

Figure 13.19a The photo on the left is of an actual room, while the photo on the right is of a model of the same room. Both pictures were taken at the same time so that the available daylighting was identical. This side-by-side comparison shows that there is no inherent scaling error with light. (University of California, Davis Daylight Design Class—Design 198. Taught by Professor Konstantines Papamichael, Ph. D., Spring 2006.)

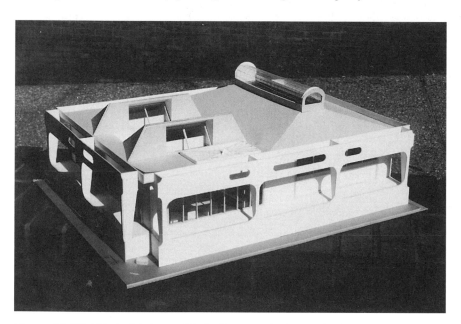

Figure 13.19b This daylighting model of a library was built as a school project at Auburn University, School of Architecture in Auburn, Alabama, by S. Etemadi, T. Peters, and C. Scaglione.

2. Use modular construction so that alternative schemes can be easily tested. For example, the model might be constructed with interchangeable window walls.

3. Add view-ports on the sides and back for observing or photographing the model. Make the ports large enough for a camera lens to get an unobstructed view and for the photometer probe to pass through. A 2 in.² (5 cm²) hole is usually sufficient. To see what a person inside the modeled space would see, place the view-port at eye level (i.e., 5.5 ft. [1.7 m] to scale). Windows on the model cannot be used as view-ports because the observer's head would block a significant amount of light.

4. The quality of the model and the effort expended in its construction depend on the purpose of the model. If the model is not going to be used for presentations to clients, even a crude model is sufficient for determining illumination levels and gross glare problems.

5. Since furniture can have an important effect on the lighting, especially if it is dark, large, and extensive, it should be included. Simple blocks painted with colors of the appropriate reflectance

else that will reflect light into or prevent light from entering the model.

4. Opaque walls must be modeled with opaque materials. Note that foam core boards are translucent unless covered with opaque paper. All joints must be sealed with opaque material, such as black-cloth tape, black duct tape, or aluminum tape. Vinyl (electrical) tape is not useful because it does not stick well to cardboard.

5. Test the model under the appropriate sky conditions as described below.

Helpful Hints for Constructing Models

1. Use a scale of at least 1/2 in. = 1 ft (1:25) if possible, but for larger spaces or buildings this scale can result in difficult models to build and transport. A scale of 3/8 in. = 1 ft (1:33) can still work quite well for large models.

Figure 13.19c A part of the library's roof is lifted off to show the interior.

Figure 13.19d This photograph taken through a view-port shows the quality of the daylighting. Glare, excessive brightness ratios (puddles of sunlight), and the general lighting atmosphere are all easily and accurately determined.

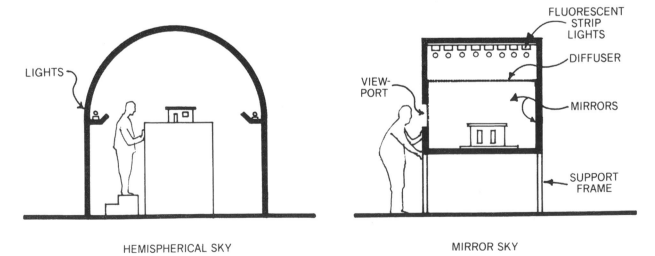

HEMISPHERICAL SKY

MIRROR SKY

Figure 13.19e Artificial skies for testing models usually consist of either a white dome or a mirror-lined box.

428

Figure 13.19f This view of the inside of a mirror sky shows how a standard overcast sky is created, but it also shows the confusing images that multiple mirrors create.

factors can act as furniture in crude models (Fig. 13.19d).

6. A photometer (light meter) is a very valuable instrument for measuring the illumination (footcandles or lux) inside the model. The less expensive meters are usually quite adequate, but be sure to get a meter with a remote sensor.

Testing the Model

The climate of the site will determine which of the two critical sky conditions must be utilized in testing the model. In most parts of the United States, a model must be tested under both an overcast sky and a clear sky with sun. The overcast sky determines whether minimum illumination levels will be met, and the clear sky with sun indicates possible problems with glare and excessive-brightness ratios.

For consistent results, artificial skies are sometimes used for the model tests (Fig. 13.19e). Unfortunately, artificial skies are not available to most designers. The hemispherical artificial skies are more accurate but are very expensive and bulky to build.* The rectilinear mirror skies are smaller and less expensive but still quite rare (Fig. 13.19e). See Fig. 13.19f for the confusing effect that opposing mirrors create. Also, most artificial skies simulate only standard overcast conditions, yet the consequences of direct sunlight are most critical. Thus, for a number of reasons, the real sky and sun are usually used to test daylighting models.

Avoid testing a model under partly cloudy conditions because the lighting will change too quickly to

---

* An artificial sky can be purchased from Beijing J-T Science Technology Co. Ltd. www.bjsjjt.com.

allow reliable observations. Although overcast and clear skies are quite consistent from minute to minute, they vary greatly from day to day. For this reason, all quantitative comparisons between alternative schemes should be based on the daylight factor and not footcandles or lux. The daylight factor is a relative factor determined by measuring the horizontal indoor and outdoor illumination levels more or less at the same time. Under overcast skies, the daylight factor remains constant even when the outdoor illumination changes. See Section 13.5 for a discussion of the daylight factor. **Rule of thumb: The design alternative with the highest daylight factor yields the highest indoor illumination.**

The human eye is the ideal tool for checking qualitative aspects of the design. The eye is also quite good at determining the adequacy of illumination levels. To get accurate results, look into the view-ports for several minutes to allow your eyes to adapt to the lower light levels inside the model.

Outdoor Model-Testing Procedure for Overcast Skies

1. Place the model in the correct orientation on a table at the actual site or at a site with similar sky access and ground reflectances. If neither of the above is possible, include the major site characteristics in the model to simulate the horizon profile (e.g., high buildings or trees) and test it on a roof or other clear site.
2. Place the photometer sensor at the various critical points inside the model to be tested. Usually, the critical points to check are the center of a room and 3 ft (1 m) from each corner. The top of the sensor should be about 30 in. (75 cm) to scale above the floor in the model.
3. Measure the horizontal outdoor illumination level by moving the sensor to point B (Fig. 13.19g), then calculate the daylight factor (D.F. = A/B)

4. Use the view-ports on the sides and back of the model to check visually for glare, excessive-brightness ratios, and the general quality of the lighting. Use hands or a black cloth to prevent stray light from entering the view-port during observations. Take photographs for a permanent record.

Outdoor Model-Testing Procedure for Clear Skies

The procedure is basically the same as that for overcast skies except that the model must be tilted to simulate the range of sun angles throughout the day and year (Fig. 13.19h). At a minimum, the model should be tested for the conditions of June 21 at 8 A.M., noon, and 4 P.M., and for the conditions at December 21 at 9 A.M.,

noon, and 3 P.M. It is very important to test the model under varying sun angles to prevent potentially serious glare and sun puddle problems. One can best accomplish this procedure by means of a heliodon and sundial, as described in Appendix I. Use the directions given under "Alternative Mode of Use of the Heliodon."

Photographing the Model

Photographs greatly enhance the usefulness of physical models as design tools. Photographs of model interiors facilitate the careful analysis and comparison of various lighting schemes. Photographs of well-constructed models also make for effective presentations to clients. Remember, though, that the camera does not see the way the human eye does. Brightness ratios

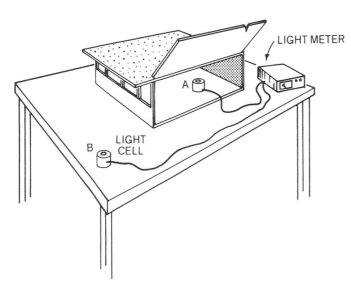

Figure 13.19g The daylight factor is determined by dividing the indoor illumination by the outdoor illumination. When the same cell is used for both measurements, the time between readings must be minimized.

Figure 13.19h A tabletop heliodon is used to hold the daylighting model at various orientations and tilt angles as determined by the sundial mounted on the model. View-ports allow observation of the lighting without affecting the light collected by the windows.

always appear worse in photos than they are in reality. The eye can also change focus as required, while the camera freezes one view. Either the near or the far image might be out of focus. Nevertheless, photography is a valuable adjunct to physical modeling. The following suggestions are for photographing the interiors of physical models.

1. Use wide-angle lenses for their large field of view as well the increased depth-of-field.
2. Depth-of-field can also be maximized by using a tripod, which will allow for slow shutter speeds and therefore small apertures.
3. **Bracket** each photograph by taking shots at least one-half exposure setting higher and one-half setting lower than what the camera meter says.
4. Keep the center of the lens at eye level of a standing scale figure in the model.
5. Do not allow light to leak into the model through the view port around the camera lens. Use a black cloth if necessary.

More Information on Physical Modeling

For more information on model building and testing, see *Simulating Daylight with Architectural Models*, edited by Marc Schiler (see the Bibliography book for the full citation).

13.20 GUIDELINES FOR DAYLIGHTING

1. General principles.
   a. Integrate daylighting design with the architecture.
   b. Integrate daylighting design with the other building systems.
   c. Design the building as a lighting fixture (luminaire).
2. Use top lighting whenever possible.
   a. Use clerestories and avoid skylights.
   b. Face clerestories south if there is a significant heating load.
   c. Face clerestories north if the building has no or minor heating load.
   d. Use east and/or west clerestories only if south or north clerestories are impossible.
   e. Use louvers or baffles to diffuse light, to avoid glare, and to prevent puddles of sunlight
3. For daylighting from windows:
   a. Design the form of the building to maximize the daylit areas. Use a long rectangle or an atrium.
   b. Maximize south windows if winter heating is required.
   c. Maximize north windows if winter heating is *not* required.
   d. Avoid east and west windows.
   e. Use light shelves except on the north facade.
   f. Use separate view and daylight windows. Have daylight windows high on the wall.
   g. Use venetian blinds or shades for backup and flexibility.
   h. Use open floor plans (avoid partitions) for maximum light penetration and views.
   i. Use glass partitions for borrowed daylight.
   j. Use light colors on the exterior to reflect light into the windows and clerestories.
   k. Use light colors on the interior to maximize light penetration, to diffuse the light, and to minimize glare.

13.21 CONCLUSION

As Louis I. Kahn suggests at the beginning of this chapter, daylighting brings meaning and richness to architecture. People want and need natural light for psychological, spiritual, and physiological reasons. Although more complicated to design than electric lighting, daylighting has profound aesthetic consequences for both the interior and exterior of buildings. The various daylighting strategies, such as light shelves and clerestories, change the appearance of buildings. Daylighting allows architects to economically justify additional visual elements that enrich the design.

The environment is also enriched. With daylighting, fewer fossil energy sources need to be extracted from the earth and less pollution is dumped into the environment. Daylighting is an important strategy in the effort to reduce global warming. Thus, daylighting enriches life as well as architecture.

KEY IDEAS OF CHAPTER 13

1. Until the mid-twentieth century, all buildings were daylit.
2. Daylighting is still appropriate because:
   a. People need and enjoy the qualities of daylight.
   b. It saves energy for a sustainable future, and it can reduce electrical demand. It helps fight global warming.
3. Daylight is a very plentiful resource. On an overcast day, the illumination on the roof is about 30 times what is required indoors, and on a sunny day it is about 160 times greater (varies with latitude).
4. Daylighting designs should distribute light evenly throughout the space throughout the day.
5. South lighting is best because it is warm, plentiful, easy to control, and in tune with the seasons (maximum in winter and minimum in the summer).
6. North lighting is second best because it is constant and cool. However, it is not as plentiful or warm as south lighting.

7. Avoid east and west lighting if possible because of the glare from low sun angles and summer overheating.

8. Although all light turns into heat, electric light sources heat a building more than daylight.

9. In the summer, introduce only enough daylight to supply the required illumination levels; in winter, collect all the daylight possible (except in internally dominated buildings in mild climates).

10. Use spectrally selective glazing for cool daylighting on east and west facades.

11. When winter heating is not desired, use spectrally selective glazing for cool daylight even on the south facade.

12. Use top lighting whenever possible.

13. Use clerestories rather than skylights.

14. Use light shelves.

15. Use electric lighting as a supplement to daylighting.

16. Use physical models to help design high-quality daylighting.

17. Use photocell controls to automatically dim or turn off lights when sufficient daylight is present.

References

Baker, N., A. Fanchiotti, and K. Steemers, eds. *Daylighting in Architecture*. London: James & *IESNA LIGHTING HANDBOOK*, 9th ed., 2000 James, 1993.

Loftness, Vivian. "Improving Energy Efficiency in the U.S.: Technologies and Policies for 2010 to 2050," prepared for the PEW Center on Global Climate Change, 2004.

Moore, Fuller. *Concepts and Practice of Architectural Daylighting*. New York: Van Nostrand Reinhold, 1985.

Wilmert, Todd. "Prismatic daylighting systems, once commonly used, reemerge as a promising technology for the future." *Architectural Record*, August 1999, pp. 177–179.

Resources

FURTHER READING

(See the Bibliography in the back of the book for full citations.

Ander, G. D. *Daylighting Performance and Design*, 2nd ed.

Baird, G. *The Architectural Expression of Environmental Control Systems*.

Brown, G. Z., and M. DeKay. *Sun, Wind, and Light: Architectural Design Strategies*, 2nd ed.

Carmody, J., S. Selkowitz, and L. Heschong. *Residential Windows: A Guide to New Technologies and Energy Performance*, 3rd ed.

Carmody, J., S. Selkowitz, E. S. Lee, D. Arastem, and T. Willmert. *Windows Systems for High-Performance Buildings*.

Commission of the European Communities Directorate-General XII for Science Research and Development. *Daylighting in Architecture: A European Reference Book*.

Daniels, K. *The Technology of Ecological Building: Basic Principles and Measures, Examples, and Ideas*.

Egan, M. D. *Architectural Lighting*, 2nd ed., 2002

Energy Design Resources. *Skylighting Guidelines*

Evans B. E. *Daylight in Architecture*.

Fitch, J. M., with W. Bobenhausen. *American Building:2. The Environmental Forces That Shape It*.

Flynn, J. E., J. A. Kremers, A. W. Segil, G. Steffy. *Architectural Interior Systems: Lighting, Acoustics, Air-Conditioning*, 3rd ed.

Franta, G., K. Anstead, and G. D. Ander. *Glazing Design Handbook for Engergy Efficiency*.

Futagawa, Y., ed. *Light and Space: Modern Architecture*.

Guzowski, M. *Daylighting for Sustainable Design*.

Hopkinson, R. G., P. Petherbridge, and J. Longmore. *Daylighting*.

Kwok, Alison G., and Walter T. Grondzik. *The Green Studio Handook: Environmental Strategies for Schematic Design*.

Lam, W.M.C. *Sunlighting as Formgiver for Architecture*.

Millet, M. S. *Light Revealing Architecture*.

Moore, F. *Concepts and Practice of Architectural Daylighting*.

Phillips, D. *Daylighting: Natural Light in Architecture*.

Phillips, D. *Lighting Modern Buildings*.

Robbins, C. *Daylighting: Design and Analysis*.

Schiler, M. *Simplified Design of Building Lighting*.

Schiler, M. *Simulating Daylighting with Architectural Models*.

Steffy, G. R. *Architectural Lighting Design*, 2nd ed.

Steffy, G. R. *Time-Saver Standards for Architectural Lighting*.

Stein, B., J. S. Reynolds, W. T. Grondzik, and A. G. Kwok. *Mechanical and Electrical Equipment for Buildings*, 10th ed.

ORGANIZATIONS

(See Appendix K for full citations.)

California Collaborative for High Performance School (CHPS) www.chps.net

Heschong-Mahone Group www.h-m-g.com

IESNA Illuminating Engineering Society of North America www.iesna.org

International Association of Lighting Designer (IALD) www.iald.org

Lawrence Berkeley National Laboratory (LBNL) www.eande.lbl.gov

Lighting Design Lab www.northwest-lighting.com

Lighting Research Center, Rensselaer Polytechnic Institute www.lrc.rpi.edu

ELECTRIC LIGHTING

Light has always been recognized as one of the most powerful formgivers available to the designer. . . . Theoretically, the possibilities for imaginative lighting are limitless. And, theoretically, our ability to create great architecture should have increased in proportion to the availability of more, and more versatile, artificial [light] sources. Yet we have scarcely begun to scratch the surface of these "limitless" possibilities.

William M. C. Lam,

Perception and Lighting as Formgivers for Architecture, 1977

14.1 HISTORY OF LIGHT SOURCES

Throughout most of human history, activities requiring good light were reserved for daylight hours. This was true not only because of the poor quality of the available light sources, but more so because of the expense. Oil lamps (Fig. 14.1a) and candles, the main sources of light, were so expensive that even the rich did not use more than a few at a time. For the poor, the choice was often light or food since lamps burned cooking oil and most candles were made from animal fat (tallow). During the eighteenth and early nineteenth centuries, the whaling industry existed mainly for supplying oil and wax for lighting needs. An energy crisis

Figure 14.1a The history of the oil lamp is about as old as the history of humanity.

Figure 14.1b The kerosene lamp launched the petroleum age in the mid-nineteenth century.

was developing due to the overhunting of sperm whales. Fortunately for both whales and lighting, kerosene, which is extracted from petroleum, replaced the whale oil, and the petroleum age was born (Fig. 14.1b).

Coal gas was another important light source in the nineteenth century. At first, it was considered safe only for street lighting (Fig. 14.1c), but eventually it was accepted indoors as well. The light, however, was not much better than that from oil lamps until the invention of the mineral-impregnated mantle in the 1880s (Fig. 14.1d), which greatly improved both the quality and quantity of gas light. Since gas lighting, even with the mantle, still caused many fires and generated much heat, and since the products of combustion were a serious health hazard, it was quickly replaced by electric lighting at the beginning of the twentieth century.

Thomas Edison did not invent the idea of the electric incandescent lamp, but he was the first to make

Figure 14.1c The mantles can be seen in this two-burner streetlight in old Mobile, Alabama. Lamplighters used to turn the gas on and off. Today, gaslights are wasteful because there is no economical way to turn them on and off every day.

it practical, around 1880. He also developed efficient electric generators and distribution systems without which the electric lamp was worthless. Although the incandescent lamp was an excellent light source for general illumination compared to what was available before, the development of discharge and LED lamps has made the incandescent lamp obsolete. The first major new lamp was the fluorescent lamp, which was introduced in the late 1930s.

Until the invention of gas and electric lighting, streets and public buildings were largely abandoned after dark. Now more and more facilities, such as offices, factories, stores, and even outdoor sporting areas, are available twenty four hours a day. It has been suggested that the today's frontier is not space but nighttime.

Neither during the day nor during the night is quality and more sustainable lighting achieved merely by supplying electric lights. As mentioned in the previous two chapters, electric

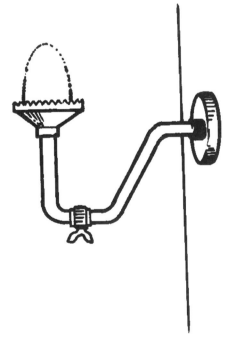

Figure 14.1d Not until the invention of the mantle did gas lamps significantly improve the quality of artificial lighting.

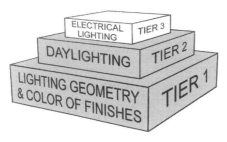

Figure 14.1e The best and most sustainable lighting design results when the three-tier design approach is applied, and this chapter covers tier three (electric lighting).

lighting is part of the third tier of the three-tier design approach for lighting. The architect should make full use of geometry, color of finishes, and day-lighting before the electric lighting system is designed (Fig. 14.1e).

14.2 LIGHT SOURCES

Figure 14.2a shows the primary sources of electric light for buildings. Figure 14.2b shows the relative efficiency of various light sources by giving the number of lumens emitted for each watt of electricity used. This specific ratio of **lumens per watt** is called **efficacy**. The figure clearly shows that although the modern incandescent lamp was once considered a good light source, it is inefficient when compared to the modern discharge lamps such as fluorescent, metal halide, and high pressure sodium lamps. The efficacy of each lamp type is shown as a range because efficacy is a function of several factors including wattage. High-wattage lamps have greater efficacy than low-wattage

lamps. For example, a 100-watt lamp gives off much more light than the combined effect of two 50-watt lamps. The spectral distribution also influences the efficacy of lamps. Unfortunately, the lamps with the best-quality white light do not have the highest efficacy.

The theoretical maximum efficacy is where 100 percent of the electrical energy is converted into light. For monochromatic yellow-green light, this would be about 680 lumens/watt, while for white light it is only about 200 lumens/watt. This difference exists because the human eye is not equally sensitive to all colors. Since the eye is most sensitive to yellow-green light, a lamp of that color will have the highest efficacy. The eye is not very sensitive to such colors as red and blue, and any light containing these colors, such as

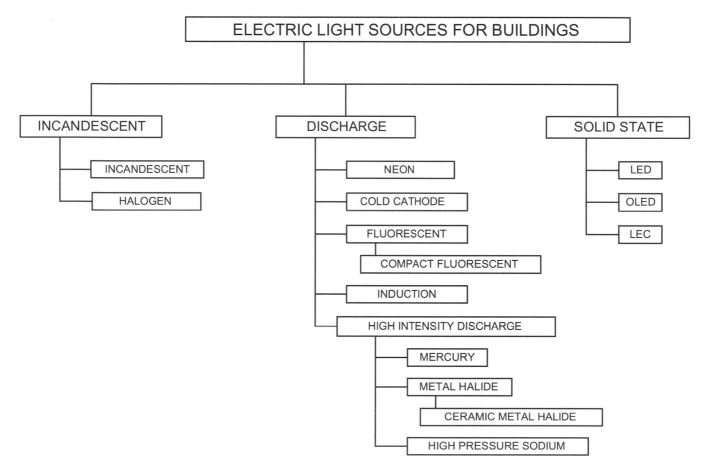

Figure. 14.2a This chart shows the primary sources of electric lighting for buildings. At present, discharge lamps are the primary source, but in the future, they may be replaced by the solid state LED (light-emitting diode), OLED (organic light-emitting diodes), and LEC (light-emitting capacitor) sources.

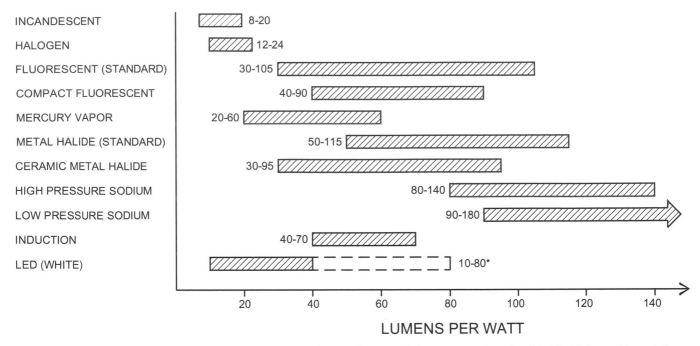

Figure. 14.2b The efficacy of lamps is always a range because of several factors, including wattage, the color of "white" light, and lamp design (e.g., reflector lamps). The efficacy of LED lamps is improving rapidly, while most of the other lamps are approaching their limit.

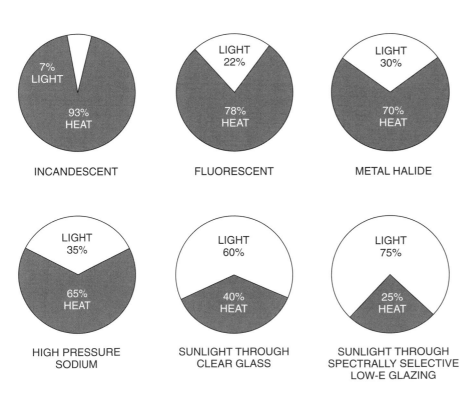

Figure 14.2c These pie charts show how much of the electrical energy is converted into light and how much is converted directly into heat. Clearly, the incandescent lamp is a very hot and inefficient light source since only 7 percent of the electricity is converted into light. It is important to note that daylight is the coolest light source only if the *quantity* that is brought into the building is carefully controlled.

white, will have a lower efficacy than yellow-green monochromatic light. Therefore, whenever color rendition is important, we must accept the lower efficacy of white light.

The modern incandescent lamp turns only about 7 percent of the electricity into light; the other 93 percent is immediately turned into heat (Fig.14.2c). Although the fluorescent lamp is a great improvement, it still converts only about 22 percent of the electricity into light. Consequently, lighting, and especially incandescent lighting, not only uses large amounts of valuable electrical energy but also contributes greatly to the air-conditioning load of a building.

Building codes regulate energy efficiency by specifying the maximum number of watts per square foot (watts per square meter) of floor area that is permitted. See Table 14.2 for the efficiency requirements of various codes.

As discussed in the previous chapter, daylighting has a higher efficacy than any white electric light source, and it is free. Thus, electric lighting should be supplemental to daylight whenever possible. Electric light sources will now be discussed in ascending order of efficacy.

Table 14.2 Lighting Efficiency		
w/ft²	**w/m²**	**Code**
5	54	Typical before energy codes
1.5	16	ASHRAE 90.1-1999
1.2	13	ASHRAE 90.1-2004
1.1	11.8	Oregon State Code
1.0	10.8	Washington State Code
0.9	9.7	LEED
0.45	4.8	Possible during the day if daylighting is used

14.3 INCANDESCENT AND HALOGEN LAMPS

Although incandescent lamps are obsolete for general illumination, they are still used for a number of special applications. Since they are good at creating sparkle, they remain popular in decorative lighting fixtures such as chandeliers. Although their first cost is low, their operating cost is very high in terms of both money and the environment. Several countries, including Korea, already prohibit the sale of most incandescent lamps, and many others, such as Canada and Australia, are phasing them out.

In an incandescent lamp, light is emitted by electrically heating a tungsten filament until it is reddish-white-hot (Fig. 14.3a). By increasing the current, the filament gets hotter and the light gets whiter (higher color temperature). Unfortunately, a hotter filament also burns out faster. Thus, the manufacturers build their incandescent lamps with an optimum design, balancing the life of the lamp and the amount of light emitted. The life of a typical incandescent lamp is about 1000 hours. Since long-life incandescent lamps last for only about 3000 hours and are even less efficient than regular lamps, and since other types of lamps have a life as long as 100,000 hours with high efficacy, long-life incandescent lamps should *never* be used.

Incandescent lamps wear out as the tungsten filament evaporates and condenses on the inside of the bulb, which causes the darkening of the glass. Eventually, as the filaments get thinner, it breaks. However, this evaporation of the filament can be reduced by adding halogen elements to the inert gases inside the lamp. These types of incandescent lamps can, therefore, be operated at higher temperatures without shortening lamp life excessively. This variation of the incandescent lamp is known as the **tungsten halogen** or **quartz iodine lamp** (Fig. 14.3b). Because of their intense light and small size, they are very popular as automobile headlamps, projector lamps, and spotlights for accent lighting.

One of the main advantages of halogen lamps is the optical control that is possible. A point source of light at the focal point of a parabolic reflector will produce a beam of parallel light (Fig. 14.3c). Although there is no point source of light available, halogen lamps come closer than most other types of lamps. A tightly wound coil of a coil, as shown in Fig. 14.3a,

Figure 14.3a The tungsten filaments of incandescent lamps are frequently coils of coils to concentrate the light source. (Courtesy of Osram-Sylvania.)

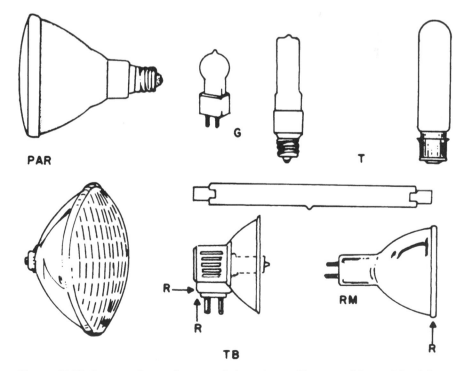

PAR

G

T

TB

RM

Figure 14.3b Common shapes of tungsten halogen lamps. (Courtesy of Osram-Sylvania.)

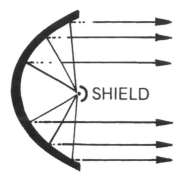

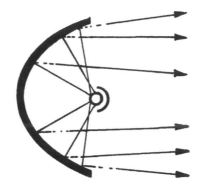

Figure 14.3c Parabolic reflectors will reflect light as a parallel beam if a point source is located at the focal point. Since all real sources are larger than a point, lamps cannot generate completely parallel beams of light.

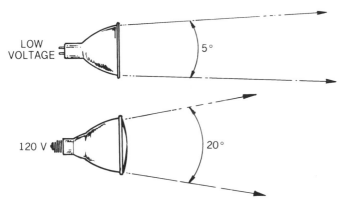

Figure 14.3d Low-voltage lamps can generate beams of light narrower than is possible with regular line voltage (120, 210, etc. volts) lamps.

when placed at the focal point of a parabolic reflector, will create a narrow but not parallel beam of light.

Low-voltage (usually 12-volt) lamps have smaller filaments than 120-volt lamps and are, therefore, more of a point light source than regular lamps. They can yield beams as narrow as 5°, while regular 120-volt or higher lamps produce light beams 20° or wider (Fig. 14.3d). This makes low-voltage lamps very appropriate for accent lighting. They can save energy as well because, with the narrow beam, more light is on target and less is spilled on adjacent areas.

The color-rendering quality of incandescent lamps is generally considered to be very good. Like daylight, the incandescent lamp emits a continuous spectrum, but unlike daylight, the color spectrum is dominated by the reds and oranges

(Color Plate 8). The warm colors, including skin tones, are, therefore, complemented.

Because of the above-mentioned reasons of sparkle, beam control, and very good color rendition, a few incandescent and especially halogen lamps will continue to find specialty applications. Halogen lamps can be appropriate for accent lighting of small areas or objects, such as retail displays, sculpture, and paintings. Halogen lamps are especially appropriate when sparkle and specular reflectances are desired in the display of glassware, silverware, or jewelry.

Incandescent lighting is *not* appropriate in situations where moderate or high levels of illumination are required over large areas. The low efficacy of these lamps makes such applications extremely energy wasteful and very expensive. Since their use

also increases the cooling load on a building, it is appropriate to include part of the cost of the large air-conditioning equipment and the additional cost of operating the cooling equipment as part of the cost of inefficient lighting. It is, therefore, clear that incandescent lamps should be used as little as possible and halogen lamps should be used sparingly.

14.4 DISCHARGE LAMPS

A major improvement in electric lighting came first with the development of the fluorescent lamp and then again with the development of high-intensity discharge lamps (mercury, metal-halide, high-pressure sodium). All of these lamps are based on a phenomenon known as **discharge**, in which an ionized gas rather than a glowing hot solid tungsten filament emits light.

All discharge lamps require an extra device known as a **ballast** (Fig. 14.4), which first ignites the lamp with a high voltage and then limits the electric current to the proper operating level. Traditional ballasts that were made of copper coils are being replaced by electronic ballasts, which are more efficient and less noisy. The electronic ballasts also eliminate the problem caused by magnetic ballasts that which produce 120 flashes per second that disturb some sensitive people.

The long life and high efficacy of the discharge lamps are more than enough to offset the extra cost of the ballast and the higher cost of each lamp when compared to incandescent lamps.

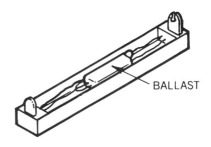

Figure 14.4 All discharge lamps require a ballast first to start the lamp and then to maintain the proper operating current.

Although discharge lamps are much better for sustainability than incandescent lamps, they have one important liability. They all use mercury, which is a very toxic element. The lamp manufacturers are redesigning their discharge lamps to use less mercury, but when the lamps are thrown away, the mercury enters the environment. One of the potential benefits of LEDs is that they use no mercury.

Since the various groups of discharge lamps have significant differences, each group will be discussed separately.

14.5 FLUORESCENT LAMPS

Although the fluorescent lamp was first introduced in the 1930s, it is still very popular. It is available in a wide variety of sizes, colors, wattages, and shapes (Fig. 14.5a). Because of the concern with energy, **compact fluorescent lamps** have been developed that can directly replace the much less efficient incandescent lamp (Fig. 14.5b). Because of global warming, it is imperative to minimize the use of incandescent lamps, and compact fluorescents make that easy and even cost effective.

In the fluorescent lamp, the radiation is emitted from a low-pressure mercury vapor that is ionized. Since much of the radiation is in the ultraviolet part of the spectrum, the inside surface of the glass tube is coated with phosphors to convert that invisible radiation into light (Fig. 14.5c). By using different kinds of phosphors, fluorescent lamps can be designed to emit various types of white light. For example, warm white lamps emit more energy in the red end of the spectrum, while cool white lamps emit more energy in the blue end of the spectrum (Color Plates 9 and 10). Specially formulated fluorescent lamps are available that give excellent color rendition.

Because of its traditionally large physical size, the fluorescent lamp had been suitable only as a large area source of light. This made it an excellent source for diffused lighting but an inappropriate source when beam control was required.

The large physical size was also a disadvantage when a small fixture size was desired. The availability of compact fluorescent lamps now allows manufacturers to make incandescent-like luminaires for them. Also, much more slender linear fluorescent lamps are now available (Fig. 14.5d). These new lamps are not only more efficient than standard lamps, but they also allow the creation of slender luminaires with a good amount of beam control.

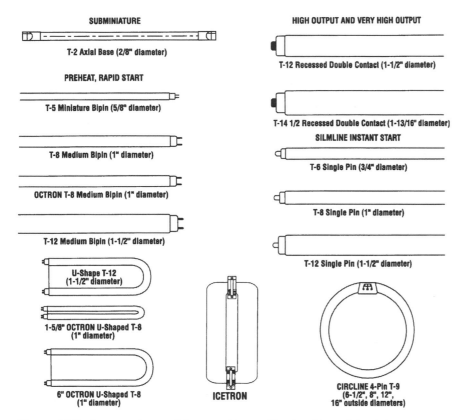

Figure 14.5a Common shapes of fluorescent lamps. (Courtesy Osram Sylvania.)

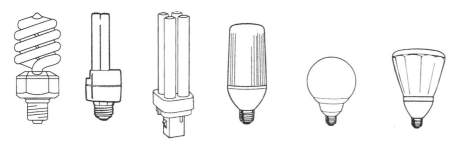

Figure 14.5b Compact fluorescent lamps are widely used around the world as replacements for incandescent lamps because of their high efficacy, warm color, and small size. The spiral shape is a result of the goal to get the most light out of the smallest-size fluorescent lamp. (Courtesy Osram Sylvania and Duro-Test Lighting for the spiral lamp.)

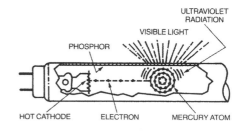

Figure 14.5c The basic features of a fluorescent lamp are shown. The ultraviolet radiation is converted into visible light by the phosphor coating on the inside of the glass tube. (Courtesy of GTE Products Corporation, Sylvania Lighting Center.)

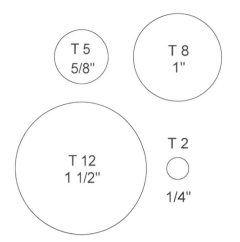

Figure 14.5d In standard fluorescent lamp designation, the T stands for "tubular" and the number after the T stands for the diameter in one-eighths of an inch. Although the T12 was the traditional size for decades, it is now obsolete in new fixtures. The T8 and T5 are now considered the standard sizes. The T5 is available in up to 5 ft (1.5 m) lengths, while the longest T2 is only 20 in. (0.5 m) long.

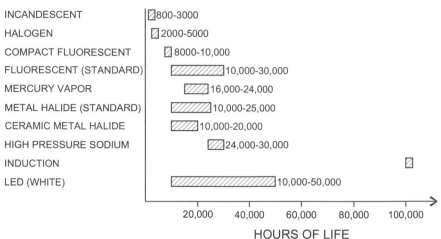

Figure. 14.5e The operating life of lamps varies tremendously. By modern standards, the life of incandescent and halogen lamps is very poor.

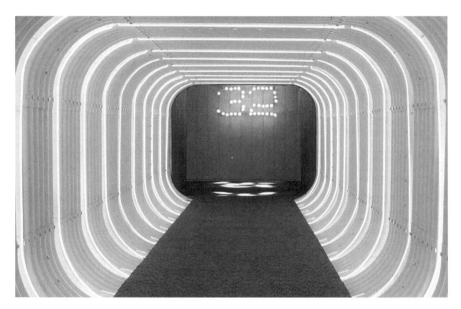

Figure 14.5f Neon lights help define the entranceway into this office building on John Street in New York City.

Long lamp life is another great virtue of the fluorescent lamp, but frequent starting cycles decrease the life of the lamp slightly. It was once considered prudent to leave lamps on to maximize their life, but the high cost of energy and the need to protect the environment make it proper to turn lights off when they are not required. The life of fluorescent lamps varies greatly by type. Some of the best lamps can now last for 30,000 hours. See Figure 14.5e for the expected life of various types of lamps.

Most fluorescent lamp ballasts are of the **instant start** kind, but **rapid start** ballasts are also used. However, a new ballast called **programmed start** has many advantages and is likely to become the dominant ballast in the future.

Neon Lamps

Neon lamps are close relatives of fluorescent lamps. These lamps use such gases as neon, which gives off red light, and argon, which gives off blue light. Through the use of different combinations of gases, colored glass, and phosphors, a large variety of rich, colored light sources is possible.

The main advantage of these lamps is that they can be custom made to almost any desired shape. Neon, which uses about 0.5 in. (13 mm) diameter glass tubes, can be bent into very complex shapes. Neon lamps are hard-wired into place, and have long lives of about 25,000 hours. Neon is not suitable for area lighting because the light output is only one-sixth of that of an equally long fluorescent lamp. Rather, it is appropriate for applications that require special colors and shapes. These lamps are most suitable when the shape of the lamp is closely integrated with the form of the architecture (Fig. 14.5f) or when the shape of the lamp is itself the design element. However, LEDs, discussed below, are replacing neon in many applications.

Cold-Cathode Lamps

Cold-cathode lighting fits somewhere between fluorescent and neon lighting. Like fluorescent lighting, cold-cathode lighting uses phosphors to

Figure 14.5g Cold-cathode tubes used for both form generation and illumination in the Town Center, Boca Raton, FL. (Courtesy of National Cathode Corporation.)

produce mainly white light, but it has a much lower efficacy than fluorescent lighting. Like neon, it is custom made for a particular project, and like neon, it is for decorative rather than functional purposes (Fig. 14.5g).

14.6 HIGH INTENSITY DISCHARGE LAMPS (MERCURY, METAL HALIDE, AND HIGH PRESSURE SODIUM)

High intensity discharge lamps are very efficient light sources that in size and shape are more like incandescent than fluorescent lamps (Fig. 14.6a), but like all discharge lamps they need a ballast to work. In all of the high intensity discharge lamps, the light is emitted from a small arc tube located inside a protective outer bulb (Fig. 14.6b). The relatively small size of this arc tube permits some optical control similar to that possible with a point source (see Fig. 14.3c). When increased color rendition is desired, metal halides are added to the mercury in the arc tube or phosphors are added to the inside of the outer bulb. However, the addition of phosphors greatly increases the size of the source, and some optical control is lost.

High intensity discharge lamps have two other important characteristics in common. They all require a few minutes to reach maximum light output, and they will not restrike immediately when there is a temporary voltage interruption. The lamps must cool for about five minutes before the arc can restrike. Recently, a few instant-restrike lamps have come on the market. In public areas, a supplementary emergency light source such as a fluorescent lamp should be part of the design.

Mercury Lamps

Besides having lower efficacy than other discharge lamps, mercury lamps have poor color rendition. They produce a very cool light, rich in blue and green and deficient in the red and orange parts of the spectrum. Because of their blue-green light, mercury lamps are still appropriate in landscape lighting, but otherwise they are largely obsolete.

Metal Halide Lamps

The white light that metal halide lamps emit is moderately cool, but there is enough energy in each part of the spectrum to give very good color rendition (Color Plate 11). Metal halide lamps are appropriate for stores, offices, schools, industrial plants, and outdoors where color rendition is important. These lamps are some of the best sources of light today because they combine in one lamp many desirable characteristics: high efficacy (50–115 lumens/watt), long life (10,000–25,000 hours), very good color rendition, and small size for optical control.

Ceramic Metal Halide

Ceramic metal halide (CMH) lamps are different enough from other metal halide lamps to require a separate discussion. Because of their very good color properties and small size, they can replace halogen lamps. Since CMH lamps last about four times longer and have about four times the efficacy of halogen lamps, they are superior to halogen lamps except

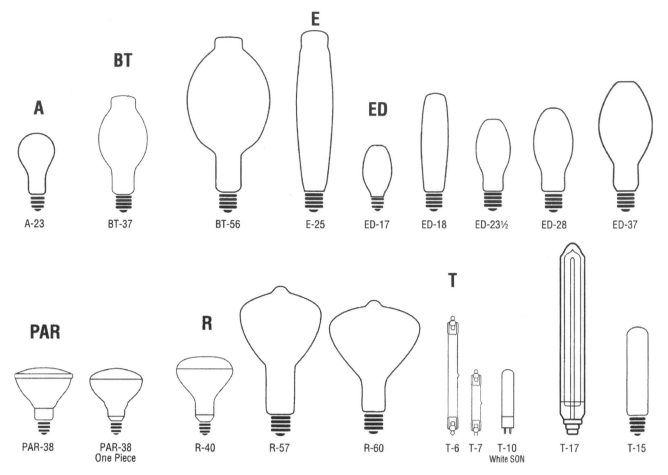

Figure 14.6a The common shapes of high intensity discharge lamps. (Courtesy of Philips Lighting.)

when color rendition is the top priority (85 CRI vs. 100 CRI for halogen lamps) (see Color Plate 12).

High Pressure Sodium Lamps

When high efficacy (60–140 lumens/watt) and long life are of prime importance, the high pressure sodium (HPS) lamp group is usually the design choice. Although the color rendition of HPS lamps is not very good, some people find the warm golden-white light acceptable when color is not important. Most of the emitted energy is in the yellow and orange parts of the spectrum (Color Plate 13).

HPS lighting is most appropriate for outdoor applications, such as lighting for streets, parking areas, sports areas, and building floodlighting. Research has shown, however, that for low-light-level peripheral vision (e.g.,

to see a deer at the side of the road or a mugger at the edge of a parking lot), white sources, such as metal halide lamps, far outperform poor color sources such as HPS lamps. Indoor spaces where color rendition is not important can also make use of the lamps' high efficacy. HPS lighting is quite appropriate for many industrial and warehouse spaces.

Because of improvements in metal halide lamps, it is now possible to get both high efficacy and good color rendition. Thus, many designers now specify metal halide where previously they would have specified HPS lamps.

A low pressure sodium lamp group also exists. Although it has the highest efficacy of any lamp group (130–180 lumens/watt), its monochromatic yellow light is unacceptable in most applications (see Color Plate 14).

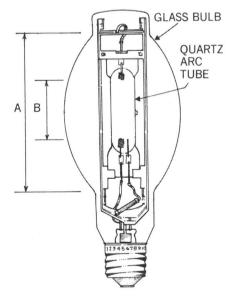

Figure 14.6b High intensity discharge lamps generate the light in the arc tube. This relatively small source (dimension B) allows a fair amount of optical control. When a phosphor coating on the bulb is used, however, the light source is much larger (dimension A) and beam control becomes difficult. (Courtesy of Osram-Sylvania.)

Induction Lamp

The induction lamp is also known as the "electrodeless fluorescent lamp," and its main virtue is its extremely long life of 100,000 hours. Although it has very good color rendition and efficacy, its high cost makes it appropriate only where lamp replacement is extremely difficult.

Sulfur Lamp

For both technical and practical reasons, the sulfur lamp is not being sold currently. Unlike all the other light sources discussed above, the sulfur lamp only comes in the super-large

size. Although its physical size is only that of a golf ball, the light output is equal to that of about seventy-five 100-watt incandescent lamps. It is hard to find applications for lamps emitting 130,000 lumens.

14.7 COMPARISON OF THE MAJOR LIGHTING SOURCES

To help designers choose the best light source for their needs, Table 14.7 compares the major lamp groups by providing the advantages, disadvantages, and major applications for each group.

Some of the most important considerations in choosing a lighting system

are the lighting effect desired, color rendition, energy consumption, illumination level, maintenance costs, and initial costs. When we consider energy consumption and illumination level, lamp efficacy (lumens/watt) is the prime factor. Typical ranges of efficacy, as well as lamp life, are also found in Table 14.7.

14.8 SOLID STATE LIGHTING

Solid state lighting (SSL) uses the same technology as the computer industry. SSL is extremely resistant to physical abuse and also very long-lasting. It is developing very rapidly, and it has the potential to become the

Table 14.7 Comparison of The Major Lamp Groups

Lamp Group	Advantages	Disadvantages	Applications	Efficacy (Lumens/Watt)	Life (Hours)
Incandescent	Obsolete except for a few specialty applications such as sparkle in decorative fixtures	Extremely low efficacy (a major burden on the environment); very low lamp life	As decorative light sources in chandeliers and similar fixtures.	8–20	800–3,000
Halogen	Excellent optical control (e.g., very narrow beams of light are possible) Excellent color rendition (especially warm colors and skin tones) Very low initial cost (especially useful when many low-wattage lamps are used) Flexible (easily dimmed or replaced with another lamp of a different wattage) Very small fixtures are possible No mercury	Very low efficacy (high energy costs) and burden on the environment Very low lamp life (high maintenance costs) Adds high heat load to buildings, thereby increasing cooling load	For spotlighting, accent, highlighting and sparkle (residential, restaurants, lounges, museums)	12–24	2,000–5,000
Fluorescent	Very good for diffused, wide-area, low-brightness lighting Very good color rendition Very good efficacy Long lamp life	Limited optical control (no narrow beams possible) Sensitive to temperature and, therefore, not used outdoors in cold climates Contains mercury	For diffused even lighting of a large area (offices, schools, residential, industrial)	30–105	10,000–30,000
Compact fluorescent	Relatively small size that allows for small fixtures.	Color rendition not as good as that of incandescent or halogen lamps that it replaces	Replaces most incandescent and many halogen lamps	40–90	8,000–10,000

(Continued)

Table 14.7 (*Continued*)

Lamp Group	Advantages	Disadvantages	Applications	Efficacy (Lumens/Watt)	Life (Hours)
	Can directly replace incandescent lamps in most existing fixtures Good optical control allows some beam control High efficacy Long life Low cost Very good color rendition	Beam control limited Contains mercury	Good for small fixtures such as table lamps, canned downlights, and wall sconces		
Metal Halide	Good to very good optical control Very good color rendition High efficacy Long lamp life Small fixtures possible	5 to 10 minute delay in start or restart Contains mercury	For diffused lighting or wide beams (offices, stores, schools, industrial, outdoor) Good for high-bay spaces	50–115	10,000–25,000
Ceramic metal halide	Small size allows for small fixtures Very good beam control Very good color rendition Very good replacement for halogen lighting, with four times its life and efficacy	Lower efficacy and life than standard metal halide Color rendition is not as good as that of the halogen lamps it replaces Contains mercury	Very good replacement for halogen lamps Spot and highlighting	30–95	10,000–20,000
High Pressure Sodium	Good optical control Very high efficacy Very long lamp life	Color rendition is poor (mostly orange and yellow) About 5-minute delay in start or restart Contains mercury	For diffused lighting or wide beams where color is not important (outdoor, industrial, warehouses, interior and exterior floodlighting)	80–140	24,000–30,000
LED (light-Emitting diode)	Very small source Very durable Long life Excellent source of pure colors such as red, green, blue, etc. No mercury Potential to become a major light source Good source for small amount of white light, as in task lights	Not yet a source of white area lighting Few fixtures available at present	Decorative lighting, especially in pure colors Accent lighting Task lighting Exit and emergency directional lighting Wayfinding	10–60	10,000–50,000

ideal light source, with 200 lumens per watt for white light. The most fully developed type of SSL lamp, the **light emitting diodes (LED)**, is described below. Only time will tell what role organic light emitting diodes (OLEDs) and light emitting capacitors (LECs) will have in building lighting.

An LED is like a PV (solar) cell operating backward. Instead of light generating electricity, electricity generates light. However, the light is generated at a specific wavelength (color). Thus, LEDs are great for producing pure colored light

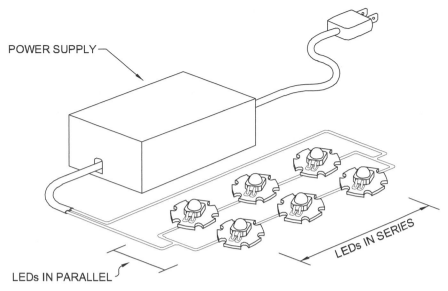

POWER SUPPLY

LEDs IN SERIES

LEDs IN PARALLEL

Figure 14.8a Because LEDs are small, most applications use many of them in one lamp/fixture. They are connected to a power supply either in series or parallel. Because the light is produced by many small units, LEDs are ideal for creative, decorative, and task lighting. As their efficacy increases, they are also being used for general area lighting.

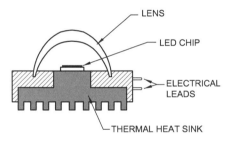

LENS

LED CHIP

ELECTRICAL LEADS

THERMAL HEAT SINK

Figure. 14.8b An LED used for lighting is the size of a large coin, while the actual light emitting diode (chip) is the size of a tiny coin. The lens directs the light, and the heat sink is necessary to prevent the chip from overheating. Although their efficacy is high, most of the electricity is still converted to heat.

for decorative or communication purposes. To generate white light, the light from different colored LEDs must be mixed or phosphors (as in fluorescent lamps) must be used to convert colored light to white light. Either way, the process of creating white light gets more complicated and expensive.

At present, LEDs are most practical where colored light or small amounts of white light are needed. Thus, LEDs

are most appropriate for decorative, task, and accent lighting. LEDs are also appropriate for wayfinding and as exit signs, directional lights, and low-level path lighting. LEDs are available in a large variety of sizes and wattages. Continuing rapid progress indicates that white LEDs are becoming available for area lighting as well (Fig. 14.8a). And since they contain no mercury, they will be great for the environment.

Although LEDs do not need a ballast, they do need a power supply, which adds both cost and additional energy loss. Unlike all of the other light sources, LEDs produce very little heat in the form of infrared radiation. Thus, they are very good for illuminating chocolate and refrigerated foods. However, they do produce large amounts of sensible heat for which a heat sink is needed. LEDs are usually mounted on metal blocks that conduct the heat away from the diodes into the air behind the lamp (Fig. 14.8b).

It is likely that LEDs and other SSL lighting systems will be the primary

sources of light for buildings in the future.

14.9 LUMINAIRES

Lighting fixtures, also called **luminaires**, should not be confused with luminaries which refer either to Mexican Christmas lanterns or to persons of brilliant achievement who have shed light on the unknown. Luminaires have three major functions: supporting the lamp with some kind of socket, supplying power to the lamp, and modifying the light from the lamp to achieve a desired light pattern and to reduce glare. Typical luminaires are divided into six generic categories by the way they distribute light up or down (Table 14.9).

Luminaires with a sizable direct component are most appropriate when high illumination levels are required over a large area or when the ceiling and walls have a low reflectance factor. Although their energy efficiency is high, the quality of light is usually not. Direct glare, veiling reflections, and unwanted shadows are all reduced or eliminated by the fixtures with a large indirect component. Task/ambient lighting provides the best of both approaches and is discussed further below.

The quality of the lighting from direct fixtures can be improved by the design of the fixtures. The following section describes the various techniques used to improve these types of luminaires.

14.10 LENSES, DIFFUSERS, AND BAFFLES

The distribution of light from a luminaire (in a vertical plane) is often defined by a curve on a polar-coordinate graph, where the distance from the center represents the candle-power (candelas) in that direction. The candlepower distribution curve of

Table 14.9 Lighting Fixtures (Luminaires)

Illustration*	Type	
	0%–10% 90%–100%	*Direct:* Direct lighting fixtures send most of the light down to the workplane. Since little light is absorbed by the ceiling or walls, this is an efficient way to achieve high illumination on the workplane. Direct glare and veiling reflections are often a problem, however. Also, shadows on the task are a problem when the fixture-to-fixture spacing is too large.
	10%–40% 60%–90%	*Semidirect:* Semidirect fixtures are very similar to direct luminaires except that a small amount of light is sent up to reflect off the ceiling. Since this creates some diffused light as well as a brighter ceiling, both shadows and the apparent brightness of the fixtures are reduced. Veiling reflections can still be a problem, however.
	40%–60% 40%–60%	*General diffuse:* This type of fixture distributes the light more or less equally in all directions. The horizontal component can cause severe direct glare unless the diffusing element is large and a low-wattage lamp is used.
	40%–60% 40%–60%	*Direct–indirect:* This luminaire distributes the light about equally up and down. Since there is little light in the horizontal direction, direct glare is not a severe problem. The large indirect component also minimizes shadows and veiling reflections.
	60%–90% 10%–40%	*Semi-indirect:* This fixture type reflects much of the light off the ceiling and, thus, yields high-quality lighting. The efficiency is reduced, however, especially when the ceiling and walls are not of a high-reflectance white.
	90%–100% 0%–10%	*Indirect:* Almost all of the light is directed up to the ceiling in this fixture type. Therefore, ceiling and wall reflectance factors must be as high as possible. The very diffused lighting eliminates almost all direct glare, veiling reflections, and shadows. The resultant condition is often used for ambient lighting.

a semidirect lighting fixture is shown in Fig. 14.10a. The up-directed light will reflect off the ceiling to reduce both direct glare and veiling reflections. For the same goal, some direct-lighting fixtures are designed to distribute light in a **batwing light pattern** (Fig. 14.10b). The high-angle light that causes the direct glare and the low-angle light that causes the veiling reflections are thereby avoided as much as possible.

Because the brightness of a room is judged largely by the brightness of the walls, wallwasher luminaires are sometimes used. Often asymmetric luminaires are used to illuminate the wall evenly (Fig. 14.10c).

Lenses, prisms, diffusers, baffles, and reflectors are all used in fixtures to control the manner in which light is distributed from the lamps.

Baffles, Louvers, and Eggcrate Devices

These devices limit direct glare by restricting the angle at which light leaves the fixture (Fig. 14.10d). If these devices are painted white, they, in turn, can become a source of glare. If, on the other hand, they are painted black, much of the light is absorbed and the efficiency of the fixture is very low. These devices can be small and part of the luminaire or they can be large and part of the architecture (e.g., waffle slab or joists). One-way baffles, such as louvers, joists, and beams, are useful only if viewed perpendicular to their direction (Fig. 14.10e).

Parabolic Louvers

This type of louver is made of parabolic wedges (Fig. 14.10f) with a specular finish. These devices are extremely effective in preventing direct glare because the light distribution is almost straight down. Thus, these fixtures have a high visual comfort probability (VCP). They are also very good in preventing veiling reflections in computer monitors (Fig. 14.10g). The penalty for having mostly vertical light is that vertical surfaces such as walls are not well illuminated. This type of louver also does not solve the problem of veiling reflections on horizontal surfaces.

Diffusing Glass or Plastic

Translucent or surface "frosted" sheets diffuse the emitted light more or less equally in all directions. The horizontal component of this distributed light is a cause of significant direct glare. Consequently, these devices have limited usefulness.

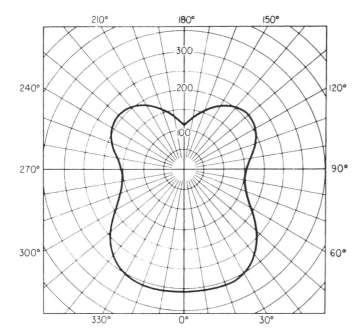

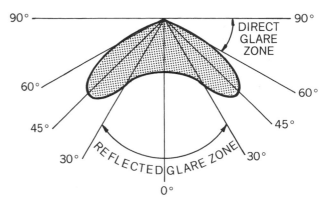

Figure 14.10b For luminaires that have no uplight, only the bottom half of the polar coordinate graph is shown. Light that leaves the luminaire from 0 to 30° zone tends to cause veiling reflections, while light in the 60 to 90° zone tends to cause direct glare. Fixtures with batwing light-distribution patterns yield a better-quality light because they minimize the light output in these problematic zones. However, they are not ideal when computers are used.

Figure 14.10a Manufacturers generally supply candlepower (candela) distribution curves for their lighting fixtures. In this vertical section, the distance from the center determines the intensity of the light in that direction. This curve is for a semidirect lighting fixture. (Courtesy of Osram-Sylvania.)

Figure. 14.10c Wallwashers are often used to illuminate walls. These luminaires are sometimes asymmetric versions of regular ceiling lighting fixtures.

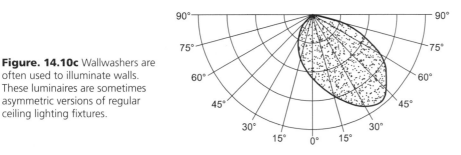

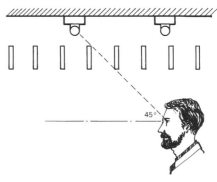

Figure 14.10d Baffles, louvers, and eggcrates are used to shield against direct glare. The direct view of the light sources should be shielded up to at least 45°.

Figure 14.10e One-way baffles are effective only when people are limited to viewing the ceiling from one direction. For example, in a corridor, the baffles should be oriented perpendicular to the length of the corridor. Use eggcrates when shielding is required in two directions.

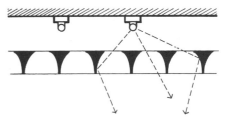

Figure 14.10f Parabolic louvers are very effective in reducing direct glare.

Figure 14.10g The left photo shows the room after the luminaire lenses were replaced with parabolic louvers. The reduction in direct glare and veiling reflections in the computer monitor at the left and center is very significant. However, notice that while horizontal surfaces are brighter, vertical surfaces are darker (note books on the left). To counter the negative effect of dark walls that results from parapolic louvers, a wallwasher was added (see the right rear walls). (Courtesy of American Louver Company.)

Lenses and Prisms on Clear Sheets

When the surface of clear sheets of glass or plastic is formed into small lenses or prisms, good optical control is possible. The light is refracted so that more of the distribution is down and direct glare is reduced. Round fixtures can use fresnel lenses that can either concentrate the light like a convex lens or disperse the light like a concave lens. Fresnel lenses are much less expensive than regular lenses because they consist of flat sheets with beveled grooves (Fig. 14.10h).

14.11 LIGHTING SYSTEMS

Lighting systems can be divided into six generic types. In many applications, a combination of these basic systems is used.

General Lighting

General lighting usually consists of more or less uniformly spaced, ceiling-mounted direct lighting fixtures (Fig. 14.11a). It is a very popular system because of the flexibility in arranging and rearranging work areas. Since the illumination is roughly equal everywhere, furniture placement is relatively easy. The energy

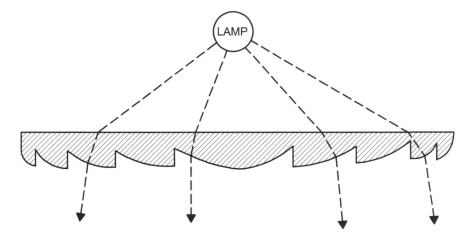

Figure 14.10h Lenses and prisms refract the light down to reduce direct glare. Fresnel lenses are made of thin plates but act as if they were thick convex or concave lenses. The light bends twice: on entering glass and on leaving glass.

efficiency is usually low because non-critical work areas receive as much light as task areas. Light quality, especially veiling reflections, is also a problem, since it is hard to find a work area that does not have a lighting fixture in the offending zone (see Fig. 12.11k).

Localized Lighting

Localized lighting is a nonuniform arrangement in which the lighting fixtures are concentrated over the

work areas (Fig. 14.11b). Fairly high efficiency is possible since nonwork areas are not illuminated to the same degree as work areas. Veiling reflections and direct glare can be reduced because this system affords some freedom in fixture placement. Flexibility in rearranging the furniture is reduced, however, even if track lighting or other adjustable systems are used.

Ambient Lighting

Ambient lighting is indirect lighting reflected off the ceiling and walls. It

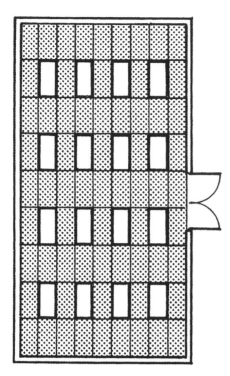

Figure 14.11a This reflected-ceiling plan shows the regular layout of direct luminaires, which is typical of general lighting systems. This approach is very flexible but not very efficient or interesting.

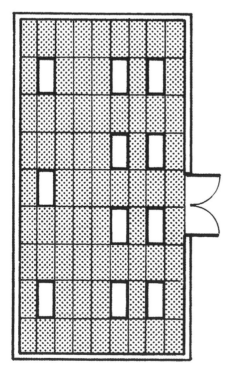

Figure 14.11b This reflected-ceiling plan illustrates localized lighting. In this system, direct fixtures are placed only where they are needed. It is efficient but not very flexible.

is a diffused, low-illumination, level lighting that is sufficient for easy visual tasks and circulation. It is usually used in conjunction with task lighting and is then known as **task/ambient lighting.** Direct glare and veiling reflections can be almost completely avoided with this approach. The luminaires creating the ambient lighting can be suspended from the ceiling, mounted on walls, supported by pedestals, or integrated into the furniture (Figs. 14.11c–f). To prevent hot spots, the indirect fixtures should be at least 12 in. (30 cm) below the ceiling, and to prevent direct glare, they should be above eye level (Fig. 14.11d). The ambient illumination level should be about one-third of the task light level.

Task Lighting

The greatest flexibility, quality, and energy efficiency are possible with **task lighting** attached to or resting on the furniture (Figs. 14.11e and f). Direct

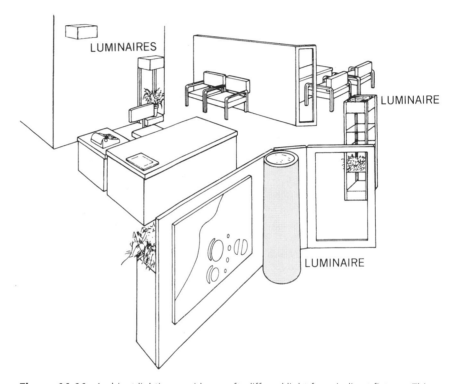

Figure 14.11c Ambient lighting provides a soft, diffused light from indirect fixtures. This diagram shows the luminaires mounted either on pedestals (torchieres) or on the wall (sconces). (Courtesy of Cooper Lighting.)

Figure 14.11d Ambient lighting from furniture-integrated lighting fixtures. (Courtesy of Cooper Lighting.)

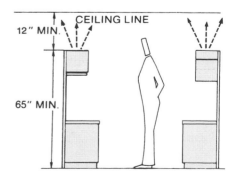

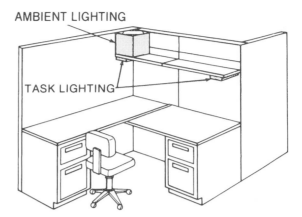

Figure 14.11f Note how the task lights are mounted on each side and not in front of the work area because of the problem of veiling reflections. Since an indirect luminaire is included in the office furniture, this system is known as task/ambient lighting. (Courtesy of Cooper Lighting.)

Figure 14.11e Ambient lighting from pendent indirect luminaires together with task lighting on desks creates high-quality task/ambient lighting. (Courtesy of Peerless Lighting Corporation.)

glare and veiling reflections can be completely prevented when the fixtures are placed properly (see Fig. 12.13a). Since only the task and its immediate area are illuminated, the energy efficiency is also very high. The individual control possible with this personal lighting system can also have significant psychological benefits for workers, who traditionally have little influence over their environment. To avoid dark surrounding areas and excessive-brightness ratios, some background illumination is required. Since indirect luminaires are often used to complement the task lighting, this combination is known as **task/ambient lighting**. Not only is

task/ambient lighting the most sustainable, it also uses about 35 percent less energy than standard lighting and is the highest-quality lighting.

Rule: Use task/ambient lighting whenever possible.

Accent Lighting

Accent lighting is used whenever an object or a part of the building is to be highlighted (Fig. 14.11g). **Accent** illumination should be about ten times higher than the surrounding light level. Since this type of lighting is very variable and is a very powerful generator of

the visual experience, designers should give it careful attention.

Decorative Lighting

With a **decorative-lighting** system, unlike all of the others, the lamps and fixtures themselves are the object to be viewed (e.g., chandeliers). Although glare is in this case called "sparkle," it can still be annoying if it is too bright or if a difficult visual task has to be performed. In most cases, the decorative lighting also supplies some of the functional lighting.

14.12 REMOTE-SOURCE LIGHTING SYSTEMS

In remote-source lighting systems, light is efficiently transmitted inside a light guide by the phenomenon of **total internal reflection**. When the light enters the light guide as a sufficiently narrow beam, the walls of the light guide behave like perfect mirrors. Light guides can be made of hollow plastic pipes, solid plastic rods, or fibers of glass or plastic. Because of the need for narrow beams, sunlight and small, compact light sources are best. The light guides can be designed to be end-emitting or side-emitting to form a linear light source. Remote-source lighting has many benefits: filtering out

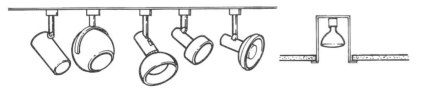

Figure 14.11g Accent lighting is usually achieved with track lighting or canned downlights. To highlight only small areas or objects, low-voltage fixtures with narrow beams of light are especially appropriate. Instead of a centrally located step-down transformer, each luminaire can have its own small transformer.

ultraviolet and infrared energy, separating the light from almost all of the heat generated by the lamp, removing the light source from a hazardous area, simplifying maintenance, and reducing energy consumption.

Light pipes are made of a prismatic, plastic film with a narrow-beam light source at one end (Fig 14.12a). For use as a linear diffuser, a mirror is placed at the opposite end, and a special diffusing film is placed where the light is to be extracted. Mirrors are used to make turns in the otherwise straight pipes. Light pipes can deliver large amounts of light to areas difficult or dangerous to reach for relamping. Applications include outlining the tops of skyscrapers and illuminating large and high spaces, such as airplane hangars.

Fiber-optic lighting uses special flexible, plastic rods or fibers of plastic or glass to guide the light. A very narrow-beam light source is needed, because the light must enter the fibers almost parallel to their length in order for total internal reflections to occur (Fig. 14.12b). The main applications are for the display of ultraviolet sensitive objects (museums), small objects (crystal and jewelry), and objects that need to remain cool (chocolate).

Fiber-optic lighting is also appropriate for decorative or functional lighting where numerous small-light sources and the convenience of one centralized lamp are desired. Troublesome electric wires connected to lamps can be replaced by water-resistant, safe optical fibers. Flexible plastic rods that look a little like neon lighting are used to show direction, create patterns and signs, and safely illuminate pools.

Light can also be transmitted by the use of mirrors and lenses. This kind of beamed lighting was described in Section 13.16.

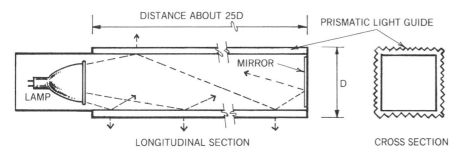

Figure 14.12a Light guides, or light pipes, convey light a distance of about 25 diameters. The light can be conveyed to the end with small losses, or a linear light source can be created by modifying the light guide to increase the losses along its length.

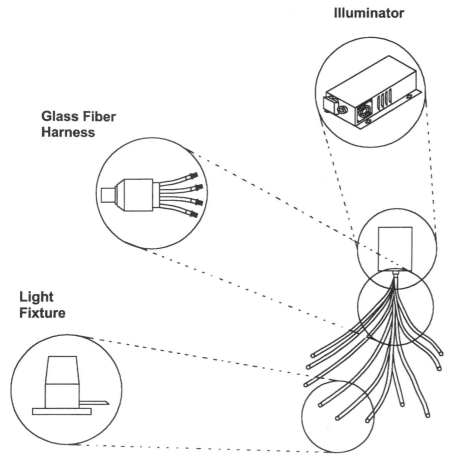

Figure 14.12b A fiber-optic lighting system consists of a light source (can contain a rotating color wheel), a fiber harness, and lighting fixtures that can deliver the light in any pattern desired from beam to diffused source. (Courtesy Lucifer Lighting Co.)

14.13 VISUALIZING LIGHT DISTRIBUTION

For both electric lighting and daylighting, it is very valuable to develop an intuitive understanding of the light distribution from various sources.

Let us first consider how illumination changes with distance from various light sources. For a point light source, the illumination (footcandles) (Lux) is inversely proportional to the square of the distance. Notice that in Fig. 14.13a when the distance doubles (1 to 2), the illumination is reduced to one-fourth (100 to 25). In most applications, incandescent and high intensity discharge lamps can be treated as point sources. The main implication of this principle is that point sources should usually be as close as possible to the visual task.

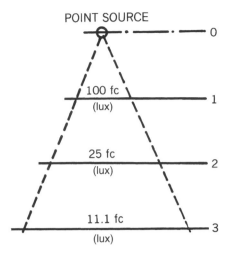

POINT SOURCE
0
100 fc
(lux)
1
25 fc
(lux)
2
11.1 fc
(lux)
3

Figure 14.13a The illumination from a point source is inversely proportional to the square of the distance (feet, meters, or any other unit).

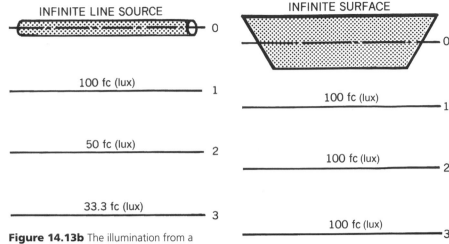

INFINITE LINE SOURCE
0
100 fc (lux)
1
50 fc (lux)
2
33.3 fc (lux)
3

Figure 14.13b The illumination from a line source of infinite length is inversely proportional to the distance.

INFINITE SURFACE
0
100 fc (lux)
1
100 fc (lux)
2
100 fc (lux)
3

Figure 14.13c The illumination from a surface of infinite area is constant with distance.

FIXTURE
MOUNTING DISTANCE
A
A
DISTANCE
DISTANCE
5
10
20
30
14'
12'
10'
8'
6'
4'
2'
0'
2'
4'
6'

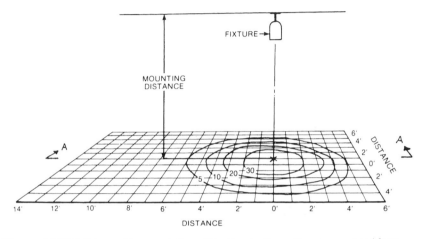

Figure 14.13d This graphic presentation of the illumination pattern is generated from isofootcandle (isolux) lines connecting points of equal illumination. (Courtesy of Cooper Lighting.)

To calculate the illumination from a point light source, see Sidebox 14.13.

A line source of infinite length is shown in Fig. 14.13b. In this case, the illumination is inversely proportional to the distance. When the distance is doubled (1 to 2), the illumination is halved (100 to 50). A long string of fluorescent lamps would create such a situation.

A surface source of infinite area is shown in Fig. 14.13c. In this case, the illumination does *not* vary with distance. A typical example of this kind of light source would be well-distributed indirect lighting in a large room. See Section 13.4 for visualizing the illumination from a finite area source.

The illumination also does not change with distance in a parallel beam of light. It is extremely difficult, however, to create a parallel beam, as was explained in Fig. 14.3c. Of the common light sources used in buildings, only direct sunlight acts as a beam of parallel light. However, luminaires with optics can come close.

The above discussion demonstrated how illumination varies with distance from the source. The following discussion will describe how the light source at a fixed location is

SIDEBOX 14.13

Illumination from a point light source is proportional to the candlepower and inversely proportional to the square of the distance.

$$\text{Footcandles} = \frac{\text{candlepower}}{(\text{feet})^2}$$

$$\text{fc} = \frac{\text{cd}}{(\text{ft})^2}$$

Example: What is the illumination on the ground directly under a streetlight that is 20 ft high and has a light intensity of 10,000 cp straight down?

$$\text{fc} = \frac{\text{cp}}{(\text{ft})^2} = \frac{10{,}000}{(20)^2} = 25 \text{ fc}$$

or in SI

$$\text{Lux} = \frac{\text{candela}}{(\text{meter})^2}$$

$$= \frac{\text{cd}}{\text{m}^2}$$

Example: What is the illumination on the ground directly under a streetlight that is 7 m high and has a light intensity of 15,000 cd straight down?

$$\text{Lux} = \frac{\text{cd}}{\text{m}^2} = \frac{15{,}000}{(7)^2} = 306 \text{ lux}$$

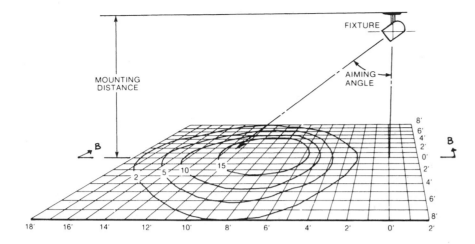

Figure 14.13e When light is not aimed straight at a surface, the isofootcandle (isolux) lines are elongated. The lines are now of reduced intensity and cover a larger area. (Courtesy of Cooper Lighting.)

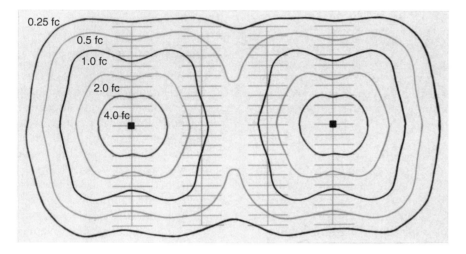

Figure 14.13f Isofootcandle (isolux) lines used to define the lighting pattern from parking-lot lighting. (Courtesy of Spaulding Lighting, Inc.)

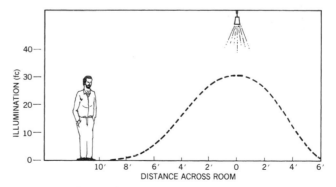

Figure 14.13g In this alternate graphic method of defining the lighting pattern, a curve of the illumination across a room is plotted on top of a section of the space. This diagram, in fact, is section A–A of the room in Fig. 14.13d.

distributed over the workplane. Two major ways exist to graphically display the illumination at the workplane. The first uses points of equal illumination to plot the contour lines of the light pattern in plan. Figure 14.13d illustrates this method for a common light source aimed straight down. Note the concentric pattern of **isofootcandle (isolux)** rings. In Fig. 14.13e, we see the pattern created when the same source is *not* aimed straight down. Note that the intensities are less but the area of illumination is greater. This is another example of the consequence of the cosine law, which was explained in Fig. 6.5c. Figure 14.13f illustrates this method as applied to outdoor lighting.

The second graphic method shows a graph of the light distribution superimposed on a section of the room. Figure 14.13g uses this method to show the same lighting situation shown in Fig. 14.13d, but only at section A–A. Similarly, Fig. 14.13h shows section B–B of the pattern shown in Fig. 14.13e. When more than one fixture is used, the effect of each is combined for the total because illumination is additive (Fig. 14.13i).

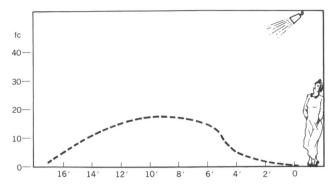

Figure 14.13h This diagram plots the illumination across the room at section B–B of Fig. 14.13e. Again, we can see that when the light source is not aimed normal (perpendicular) to the workplane, the maximum illumination is reduced and the light is spread over a larger area.

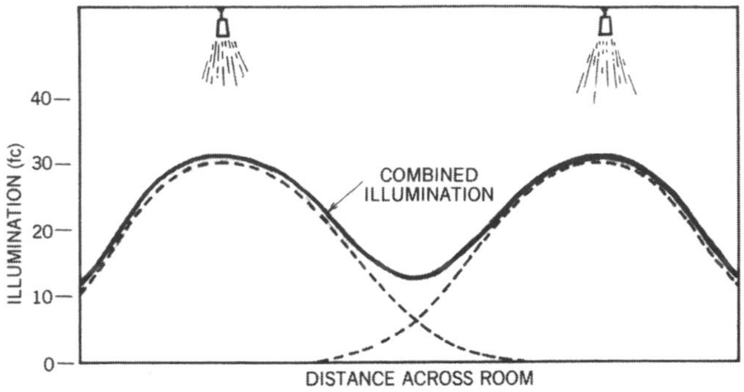

Figure 14.13i When more than one light source is present, the curve defining the combined effect is the sum of the individual curves.

14.14 ARCHITECTURAL LIGHTING

The lighting equipment can either consist of prefabricated luminaires or be an integral part of the building fabric. In the latter case, it is often known as **architectural lighting**. Ceiling-based systems will be discussed first.

Cove Lighting

Indirect lighting of the ceiling from continuous wall-mounted fixtures is called **cove lighting** (Fig. 14.14a). Besides creating a soft, diffused ambient light, coves create a feeling of spaciousness because bright surfaces (in this case the ceiling) seem to recede. The cove must be placed high enough so that a direct view of the light source is not possible, and at the same time it must be far enough

from the ceiling to prevent excessive brightness (hot spots) right above the lamps. The inside of the cove, the upper walls, and the ceiling must all be covered with a high-reflectance white paint. Larger rooms require cove lighting on two, three, or four sides.

Coffer Lighting

Coffers (pockets) in the ceiling can be illuminated in a variety of ways. Large coffers often have cove lighting around their bottom edges (Fig. 14.14b), which makes them appear similar to skylights. This technique is sometimes used inappropriately on real skylights as nighttime illumination. In such a design, most of the light is lost through the skylight. Furthermore, simulating daylight at night is not only aesthetically inappropriate but also confusing

to our circadian rhythms. Small coffers can be illuminated by recessed luminaires (Fig. 14.14c).

Luminous-Ceiling Lighting

The **luminous ceiling** provides a large area source of uniform illumination by means of diffuser elements suspended below uniformly spaced fluorescent lamps (Fig. 14.14d). The mind often associates this uniform high-brightness ceiling with a gloomy overcast sky. In the worst case, it is similar to being in a fog, where the lighting is so diffused that the three-dimensional world appears rather flat. Another problem is that if a lamp burns out, a disturbing dark spot appears. For these and several other practical reasons, luminous ceilings are not used much anymore.

Wall Illumination

Although most visual tasks take place on the horizontal plane, the vertical surfaces have the greatest visual

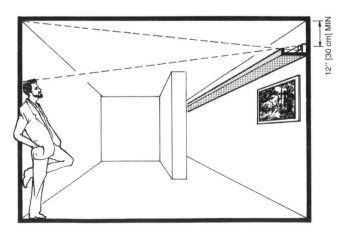

Figure 14.14a Ceilings appear to recede with cove lighting. Lamps must be shielded from view.

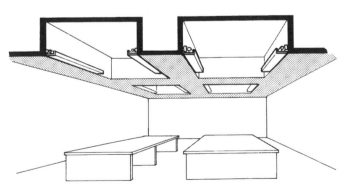

Figure 14.14b Large coffers are often illuminated with cove lighting.

Figure 14.14c Small coffers are best illuminated by direct luminaires in each coffer.

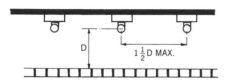

Figure 14.14d The very even brightness of luminous ceilings can create difficulties. Not only is it technically difficult to achieve, but it also tends to simulate a gloomy overcast sky.

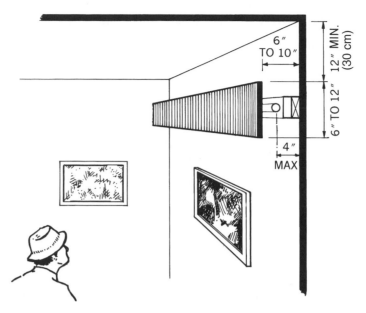

Figure 14.14e Valance lighting can increase the wall brightness, which is so very important in the overall visual appearance of a space. The specific design of a valance depends greatly on the expected viewing angles in a particular room. Note that the given dimensions were for T-12 fluorescent lamps. Smaller dimensions can be used with T-8 lamps and even smaller dimensions if T-5 lamps are used. However, do not reduce the minimum dimensions.

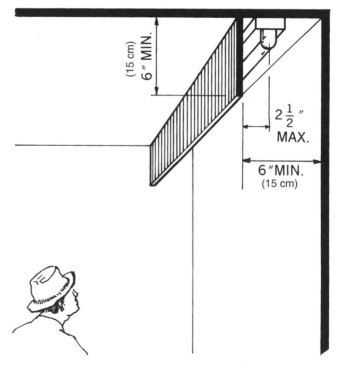

Figure 14.14f Because cornice lighting illuminates only the walls and not the ceiling, excessive brightness ratios can occur.

impact (see Figs. 12.10c and d). When we experience architecture, we are usually viewing vertical surfaces. Functional lighting systems for horizontal workplanes sometimes do not sufficiently illuminate the walls. Supplementary lighting fixtures mounted on the ceiling or walls can increase the brightness of the walls, emphasize texture, or accent certain features on the walls. Architectural lighting in the form of valances, cornices, and luminous panels is often used to illuminate the walls.

Valance (Bracket) Lighting

Valance (bracket) lighting illuminates the wall both above and below the shielding board (Fig. 14.14e). The placement and proportion of valance boards must result in complete shielding of the light sources as seen from common viewing angles. Valances should be placed at least 12 in. (30 cm) below the ceiling to prevent excessive ceiling brightness. If the valance must be close to the ceiling, a cornice, as described below, might be more appropriate.

Cornice (Soffit) Lighting

When a valance board is moved up to the ceiling, it is called a **cornice** (Fig. 14.14f). The wall is then illuminated only from above, and the ceiling, which receives no light from the cornice, might appear quite dark.

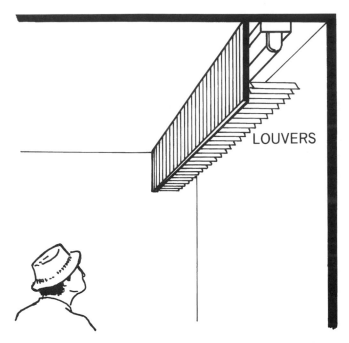

Figure 14.14g In many cases, the viewing angles are such that direct glare will result unless louvers or some other shielding devices are used in the cornice.

This is called **cornice lighting** or **soffit lighting**. If people are permitted to approach the wall, the light source will be visible unless additional shielding is provided. Cross louvers are quite effective in preventing this direct glare situation (Fig. 14.14g).

Luminous Wall Panels

Luminous wall panels must have very low surface brightness to prevent direct glare or excessive brightness ratios. Nevertheless, the viewer might feel frustrated because the luminous panel implies a window where the view to the outside is denied. The same sense of frustration often exists with the use of translucent glazing in real windows.

14.15 OUTDOOR LIGHTING

Like indoor lighting, outdoor lighting has both functional and aesthetic consideration, and as with indoor lighting, energy conservation is now a major consideration. In addition, it has become apparent that there are such things as light pollution and light trespass.

All animals, including humans, need darkness. Out circadian rhythms are interrupted when we are not exposed to enough darkness. Light trespass from our neighbors' lights can interfere with our production of melatonin, which in turn has an adverse effect on our health. There is also much scientific evidence that other animals are also greatly affected by light pollution. Sea turtles can't reproduce, birds fly into buildings, and trees grow and lose their leaves at the wrong time of year. These are just a few examples. Because much of humanity cannot see the Milky Way anymore and because astronomers are inhibited in their work by light pollution, the International Dark Sky Association was formed (www.darksky.org). This organization has increased an awareness of light pollution and light trespass. As a consequence, many communities are passing ordinances to control both of these problems.

Outdoor Area Lighting

The major steps in reducing light pollution are to reduce the illumination level used outdoors, to not use luminaries that allow light to go up into the sky, and to turn lights off when not needed (e.g., do not illuminate a parking lot when it is not used). Outdoor lighting should be controlled not only by a photocell switch to prevent lights from being on during daylight hours, but also a timer so that lights go off when they are no longer needed, because many outdoor lights do not need to be on all night. Also, **full cutoff** luminaries should be used to minimize the light going up into the sky.

Light trespass is avoided by the careful location and selection of luminaires. **Photometric** data in the form of candlepower (candela) curves describes the angles at which light is emitted from a fixture. Near property lines, asymmetric luminaires should be used (see Fig. 14.10c).

Outdoor Building Illumination

Buildings should be illuminated from the top rather than from below, which is the common practice (Fig. 14.15). There are many benefits to reversing this situation: instead of being spilled into the sky, light is spilled around the building; light reflected off the building illuminates the ground around the building, and fixtures facing down collect less dirt. Also, fixtures mounted on the ground aiming up at the building often cause serious glare problems (Fig. 14.15). Lighting fixtures around the top of the building can be an aesthetic asset rather than a liability. Throughout most of history, buildings ended with a "cap" of some kind. Architects are again seeking to make the tops of their buildings more interesting. A common device is to have a large ring around the top of building to support the window-washing equipment. Such a cap could easily support lighting fixtures aimed at the building.

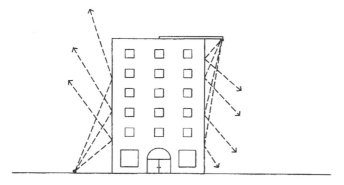

Figure. 14.15 When buildings are illuminated from below, which is the common situation, much of the light spills into the night sky (left side of the building). Instead, by illuminating buildings from above, this spilled light illuminates the landscape around the building (right side of the building).

Landscape Lighting

Landscape lighting should not try to simulate daylighting, but rather create a magical world where trees are illuminated from below and seen against a black sky. Special low-voltage (12-volt) fixtures are generally used because of their safety and economy. Because there is no shock hazard with low voltage, the electrical installation becomes simpler and less expensive. However, a step-down transformer is required, and the electrical conductors need to be much larger than those required for line voltage. To prevent light pollution, use uplighting sparingly and make sure it is mostly intercepted by the leaves of the trees.

14.16 EMERGENCY LIGHTING

Emergency lighting is required by code to allow people to safely exit a building. Exits must be clearly marked, and a lighted path must be provided even if there is a power failure for the normal lighting. Special lighting fixtures and exit signs are provided that will receive power either from a battery or an emergency generator when normal power is lost.

Exit signs are an ideal application for LED lamps, since they are low-power, require a very long life, and are monochromatic. The typical exit sign in the United States is red, while in most of the world it is green. Another problem with the existing system is that in case of fire, smoke rises and obscures high exit signs. For this reason, airlines have lighted strips on the floor to guide people to the exits. These lighted strips on the floor or low wall need not be electrified because photoluminescent materials can be used. Such materials absorb light and continue to glow even when no longer illuminated (Fig. 14.16). Although the brightness of the glow decreases with time, the human eye adapts to the lower light level. Consequently, the photoluminescent material can successfully guide people out of buildings in an emergency when the normal lighting is not functioning.

14.17 CONTROLS

Properly designed switching can yield functional, aesthetic, psychological, economic, and environmental benefits. Switching allows for the flexible use of spaces, as well as the creation of interesting and varying lighting environments. As mentioned before, the definition of personal space and the control over one's environment are important psychological needs that are partially satisfied by individual work area switching. Switching is also one of the best ways to conserve large amounts of energy (money and environment) simply by allowing unneeded lights to be turned off.

Although people can usually be relied on to turn lights on when it is too dark, they almost never turn lights off when they are not necessary. Consequently, to save energy, it is usually necessary to use automatic devices, such as occupancy sensors, photo sensors, timers, and remote switching equipment.

Occupancy sensors respond to people entering and leaving a room. They are based on either infrared or ultrasonic technology, each of which has advantages and disadvantages. Consequently, hybrid sensors that use both technologies have been developed.

Photo sensors respond to the availability of daylight. Most commonly, there is one sensor per room or zone, but lighting fixtures are now available with individual photo sensors.

Most **timers** are centrally located to turn lights on and off at a preset cycle. For example, they can turn the lights on just before people arrive at work and then turn them off when everybody has gone home. Centrally located timers are excellent whenever there is a regular schedule of activities. Timers can also be used for local control of lights. For example, many apartment houses and hotels in Europe have corridor timer-switches that turn lights on for about ten minutes, which is enough time to get to one's room or apartment. Thus, the corridor lights are on only when people use them. **Remote-control** switching enables people or a computer at a central location to control the lights. This central control of lights is part of what is now often called an **energy management system**. A computer using remote sensors and switches can be programmed to make efficient use of all energy used in a building.

Dimming is another powerful tool for the designer. Although incandescent lamps can be dimmed very easily, dimming them makes them even more inefficient and, therefore, should not be used. Halogen lamps are also easily dimmed, but again lose efficiency and, therefore, dimming should be used sparingly. Fortunately,

Figure. 14.16 Besides illuminated exit signs and directional lighting for emergencies, photoluminescent signs and strips can be used. These phosphorescent materials glow in the dark even with the loss of all electrical power. (Photos Courtesy of 3M.)

most discharge lamps can be dimmed, and fluorescent lamps can be dimmed at a reasonable cost. Most types of high intensity discharge lamps can now also be dimmed, but the special equipment required makes it somewhat more expensive. When daylighting is used, switching and dimming are especially important, and were discussed in the previous chapter.

14.18 MAINTENANCE

The two main considerations in maintaining a lighting system are the aging of the lamps and the accumulation of dirt on the lamp and fixture.

Figure 14.18 shows light output as a function of time for a certain lamp. As the lamp ages, its lumen output depreciates until the lamp fails. The rate of decline and the length of life vary greatly with the specific lamp type,

but the general pattern is the same for all. If a large **lamp lumen depreciation** is expected, the initial illumination level is increased to allow for the decline. If lamp life is short, lamp replacement must be made an easy operation. If replacement is difficult, a long-life lamp type should be chosen.

Light loss due to dirt accumulation is a separate problem. It is a function of the cleanliness of the work area and the design of the luminaire. For example,

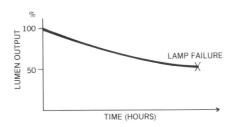

Figure 14.18 Lumen output typically declines over time until the lamp fails.

in dirty areas, such as a woodworking shop, indirect fixtures would not be appropriate because dirt accumulates mostly on the top side of lamps and fixtures. Manufacturers give information on how well their luminaires maintain light output under various levels of dirt accumulation. A **luminaire dirt depreciation factor** can be used to choose the right fixture for a specific environment. Nevertheless, periodic cleaning of lamps and luminaires is required even in clean areas. Thus, easy access for cleaning and relamping is an important design consideration.

14.19 RULES FOR ENERGY-EFFICIENT ELECTRIC LIGHTING DESIGN

With informed design and efficient equipment, high-quality lighting can be achieved with a power density below 1 watt per square foot (54 watts

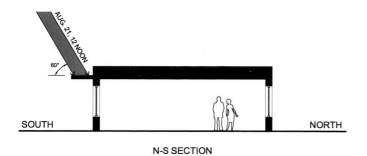

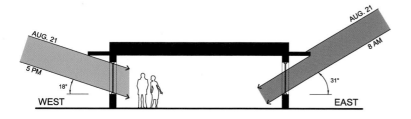

N-S SECTION

E-W SECTION

PLAN

N

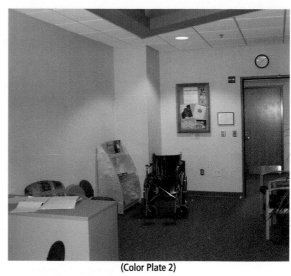

(Color Plate 2)

(Color Plate 3)

Color Plate 1 To learn, design, and present solar-responsive architecture, plans and sections should show sunbeams at critical times of the day and year. At least two sets of drawings are needed: one to show the summer sunbeams (shown) and another to show winter sunbeams (not shown).

Color Plates 2 and 3 Two images of the same room show how still air stratifies. Color Plate 2 is taken with light, and Color Plate 3 is a thermogram taken with a long-wave infrared radiation "camera." (Courtesy of Stockton Infrared)

(Color Plate 4)

(Color Plate 5)

Color Plates 4 and 5 These two thermograms show weak areas in the thermal envelope. Colors are used to represent temperatures. Blue is the lowest (coldest) and white is the highest (hottest) temperature. In the outdoor photo (Color Plate 4), the windows are hottest, because they lose the most heat. Orange indicates wall areas with little or no insulation. In the indoor photo (Color Plate 5), the windows are now blue, because they are the coldest surface. (Copyright Shell Infrared)

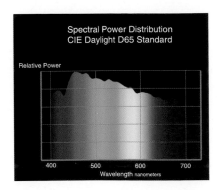

Spectral Power Distribution
CIE Daylight D65 Standard

Relative Power

400   500   600   700
Wavelength nanometers

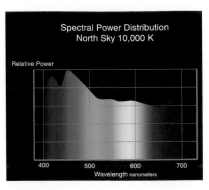

Spectral Power Distribution
North Sky 10,000 K

Relative Power

400   500   600   700
Wavelength nanometers

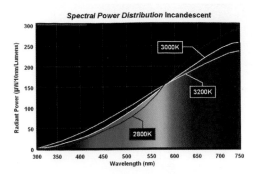

Spectral Power Distribution Incandescent

Color Plate 6 Standard daylight at noon, which includes sunlight, consists of almost equal amounts of all colors. It is an ideal light source. (Image courtesy of General Electric Company)

Color Plate 7 The light from the north sky is cool because of the large amount of blue light coming from the blue sky. (Image courtesy of General Electric Company)

Color Plate 8 Incandescent lamps (2800K) produce very warm light because of the preponderance of light at the red end of the spectrum. Color rendition is high, because all colors are present. Halogen lamps (3200K) have a whiter light, because there is less red and more blue light. Halogen lamps are often used where high color rendition is required. (Image courtesy of General Electric Company)

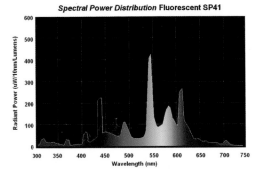

Spectral Power Distribution Fluorescent SP41

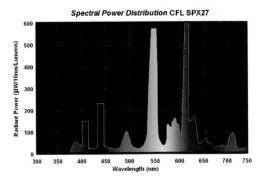

Spectral Power Distribution CFL SPX27

Color Plate 9 Because discharge lamps use ionization rather than incandescence, they produce much of their light at specific wavelengths. However, because of color addition (Color Plate 6), fluorescent lamps can be designed to create very good color rendition. (Image courtesy of General Electric Company)

Color Plate 10 This compact fluorescent was designed to create a warm white light (note the large amount of red light) to better replace the very inefficient incandescent lamp. (Image courtesy of General Electric Company)

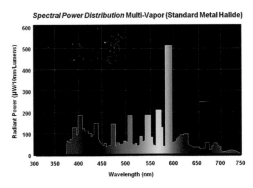

Spectral Power Distribution Multi-Vapor (Standard Metal Halide)

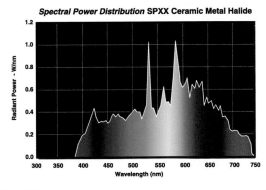

Spectral Power Distribution SPXX Ceramic Metal Halide

Color Plate 11 Metal halide lamps produce good color rendition at high efficacy in a compact light source. (Image courtesy of General Electric Company)

Color Plate 12 The ceramic metal halide lamp has very good color rendition, and it is more efficient than the halogen lamp it replaces. (Image courtesy of General Electric Company)

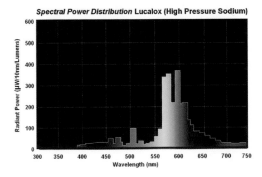

Spectral Power Distribution Lucalox (High Pressure Sodium)

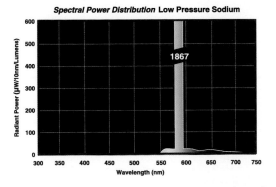

Spectral Power Distribution Low Pressure Sodium

1867

Color Plate 13 High-pressure sodium lamps have poor color rendition, because most of the light output is in the yellow/orange part of the spectrum. (Image courtesy of General Electric Company)

Color Plate 14 Low-pressure sodium lamps are appropriate only where color recognition is not important. They are monochromatic, because almost all light is emitted in the yellow part of the spectrum.

Color Plate 15 This photograph of the main lobby in the Menil Collection in Houston, Texas, clearly demonstrates how much cooler north lighting is than sunlight. The skylight over the lobby is partially shaded by the two-story portion of the museum on the left. The shaded section of the skylight is, therefore, only illuminated by the blue sky. The other portion at the far right is illuminated by both the blue sky and the warm sunlight. Also note the reddish white light produced by incandescent lamps in the side corridor.

Color Plate 16 Color can be used to create rich and humane architecture. The colorful banners in this library also act as baffles to diffuse daylight and to prevent glare from the skylights. (Photo courtesy Lisa Heschong, Heschong Mahone Group, Inc., 2002)

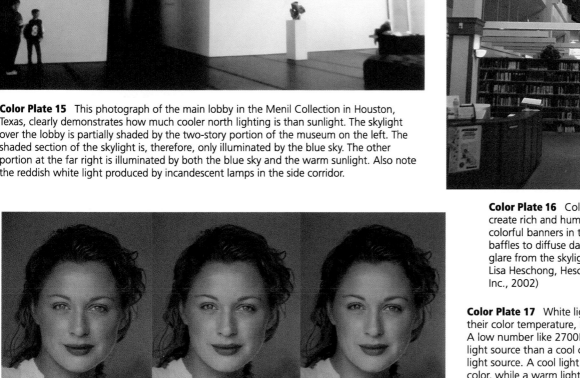

2700 K 3500 K 6500 K

Color temperature comparisons

Color Plate 17 White light sources vary in their color temperature, measured in Kelvin. A low number like 2700K is a much warmer light source than a cool color like a 6500K light source. A cool light source is bluish in color, while a warm light source is reddish in color. (Image courtesy of General Electric Company)

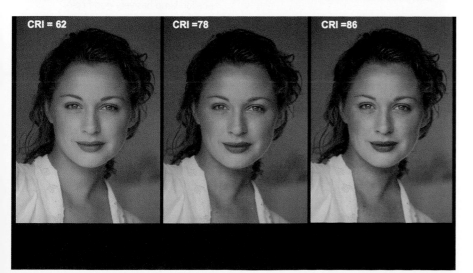

CRI = 62 CRI =78 CRI =86

Color Plate 18 The color-rendering quality of a white light source can also be described by the Color Rendering Index (CRI) from 1 (worst) to 100 (best). The higher the CRI, the truer the color. The illustration shows how poorly skin color appears with a CRI of 62 as compared to a CRI of 86. (Image courtesy of General Electric Company)

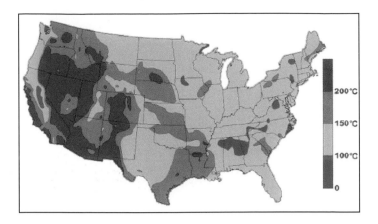

Color Plate 19 Most geothermal energy is found in the western part of the United States. (Source: U.S. Department of Energy)

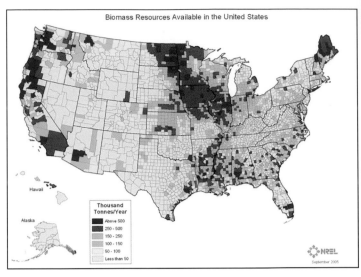

Biomass Resources Available in the United States

Color Plate 20 Biomass is most plentiful where good soil and water are both abundant.

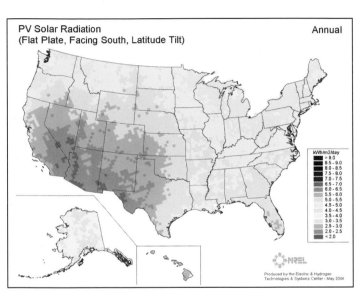

PV Solar Radiation
(Flat Plate, Facing South, Latitude Tilt)   Annual

Color Plate 21 Although solar energy is most available in the Southwest, there is more than enough available in the northern United States as well. It should be noted that the least sunny parts of the United States get more solar radiation than Germany, which is the world leader in using PV.

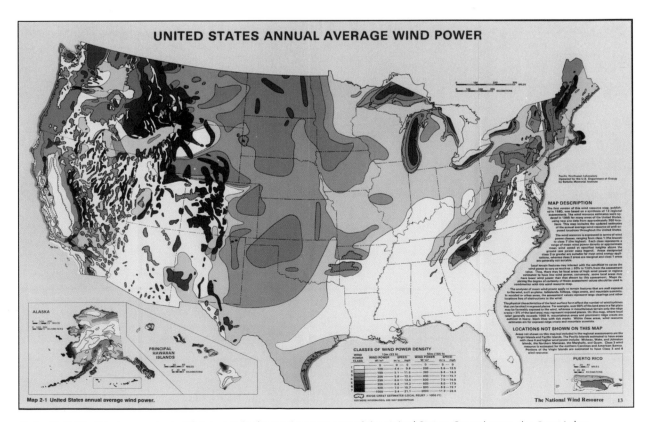

UNITED STATES ANNUAL AVERAGE WIND POWER

Map 2-1 United States annual average wind power.

The National Wind Resource   13

Color Plate 22 Wind energy is plentiful, except in the southeastern part of the United States. Coastal areas, the Great Lakes, mountains, and the Great Plains are all abundant sources of wind power.

per square meter). This is remarkable when you consider that the norm in the 1980s was more than five times higher (see Table 14.2). Use the following strategies to achieve a high-quality, energy efficient lighting system.

Rules for the Design of Efficient Electric Lighting

1. Use light-colored surfaces whenever possible for ceilings, walls, floors, and furniture.
2. Use local or task lighting to prevent the unnecessary high illumination of nonwork areas.
3. Use task/ambient lighting for most work areas.
4. Use electric lighting to complement daylighting (see the previous chapter for details).
5. Use the lowest recommended light level for electric lighting. For daylighting, however, the illumination can be set a little higher in the summer and can be much higher during the heating season.
6. Carefully control the direction of the light source to prevent glare and veiling reflections. A small amount of high-quality light can be more effective than a large amount of low-quality light.
7. Use high-efficiency lamps (e.g., metal halide and fluorescent).
8. Use efficient luminaires (e.g., avoid luminaires with black baffles and indirect fixtures in dirty areas).
9. Avoid light pollution and light trespass by using low levels of outdoor lighting, no uplighting, and special asymmetric luminaires to minimize projecting light where it is not wanted. Illuminate the exterior of buildings from the top down rather than from the bottom up, as is now standard practice.
10. Use the full potential of manual and automatic switching and dimming to save energy and the environment. Use occupancy sensors, photosensors, timers, and central energy-management systems whenever possible.

Many more specific suggestions for energy-conscious lighting are mentioned throughout the three chapters on lighting.

14.20 CONCLUSION

A good lighting design stresses flexibility and quality, not sheer quantity. It must satisfy biological as well as activity needs. In doing so, it must prevent direct glare, veiling reflections, and excessive-brightness ratios. In addition, in a world of limited resources, good lighting must be accomplished with a minimum of waste. Inefficient lighting systems not only guzzle huge amounts of electrical energy directly, but they also add greatly to the air-conditioning load, which then requires more equipment and still more electrical energy. Good lighting design is critical for a more sustainable world.

KEY IDEAS OF CHAPTER 14

1. One of the most important characteristics of a lamp is its efficacy (lumens per watt).
2. Another important characteristic of lamps is the color-rendering properties of the emitted light (i.e., whiteness of the light).
3. Incandescent lamps are obsolete for general illumination (even in homes). Use them only for special small-scale applications.
4. Compact fluorescent lamps are a good substitute for most incandescent-lamp applications.
5. Tungsten-halogen lamps should be used only where beam control is vital (e.g., highlighting small objects). Whenever possible, use the much more efficient ceramic metal halide lamps.
6. Use fluorescent or metal halide lamps for general illumination where color rendition is important.
7. Use HPS lamps where efficacy is more important than color rendition.
8. Task/ambient lighting offers both high-efficiency and high-quality lighting.
9. The illumination from a point light source is inversely proportional to the square of the distance.
10. The illumination from a linear light source is inversely proportional to the distance.
11. The illumination from an infinite-area light source does not vary with distance.
12. Avoid light pollution and light trespass for a healthier, more sustainable, and more beautiful world.
13. Use automatic controls, such as occupancy sensors and photocells, to eliminate waste.

Resources

FURTHER READING

(See the Bibliograpy in the back of the book for full citations.)

Brown, G. Z., and M. Dekay. Sun, Wind, and Light: *Architectural Design Strategies,* 2nd ed.

Cuttle, C. *Lighting by Design.*

Egan, M. D., and V. Olgyay. *Architectural Lighting,* 2nd ed.

Flynn, J. E., J. A. Kremers, A. W. Segil, G. Steffy. *Architectural Interior Systems: Lighting, Acoustics, Air Conditioning,* 3rd ed.

Futagawa, Y., ed. *Light and Space: Modern Architecture.*

Gordon, G., and J. L. Nuckolls. *Interior Lighting for Designers,* 4th ed.

Grosslight, J. *Light, Light, Light: Effective Use of Daylight and Electric Lighting in Residential and Commercial Spaces,* 3rd ed.

Grosslight, J. *Lighting Kitchens and Baths.*

IESNA. *Lighting Handbook.*

Ishii, M. *Lighting Horizons.*

Karlen, M. and J. Benya. *Lighting Design Basics.*

Kwok, A. G., and W. T. Grondzik. The *Green Studio Handbook: Environmental Strategies for Schematic Design.*

Lam, W. M. C. *Perception and Lighting as Formgivers for Architecture.*

Leslie, R. P., and K. M. Conway. *The Lighting Pattern Book for Homes.*

Leslie, R. P., and P. A. Rodgers. *The Outdoor Lighting Pattern Book.*

Millet, M. S. *Light Revealing Architecture.*

Neumann, D. *Architecture of the Night: The Illuminated Building.*

Schiler, M. *Simplified Design of Building Lighting.*

Steffy, G. R. *Architectural Lighting Design,* 2nd ed.

Steffy, G. R. *Time-Saver Standards for Architectural Lighting.*

Stein, B., J. S. Reynolds, W. T. Grondzik, and A. G. Kwok. *Mechanical and Electrical Equipment for Buildings,* 10th ed.

Trost, J. *Electrical and Lighting.*

ORGANIZATIONS

(See Appendix K for full citations.)

IESNA Illuminating Engineering Society of North America www.iesna.org

International Association of Lighting Designers (IALD) www.iald.org

Lawrence Berkeley National Laboratory (LBNL) www.eande.lbl.gov

Lighting Design Lab www.northwestlighting.com

Lighting Research Center at RPI www.lrc.rpi.edu

National Lighting Bureau www.nlb.org

OTHER RESOURCES

"Title 24—Residential Lighting Design Guide."

California Lighting Technology Center www.ucdavis.edu/title-24-residential-lighting-design-guide-files

CHAPTER 15

THE THERMAL ENVELOPE: KEEPING WARM AND STAYING COOL

Waste not, want not, is a maxim I would teach.
Let your watchword be dispatch, and practice what you preach.
Do not let your chances like sunbeams pass you by.
For you never miss the water till the well runs dry.

Rowland Howard, 1876

Reducing the size of the mechanical equipment is not just a free lunch,
but one they prepay you to eat.

Amory Lovins, Rocky Mountain Institute

461

15.1 BACKGROUND

This chapter discusses the creation of an efficient thermal envelope to minimize the heat loss in the winter and the heat gain in the summer. The

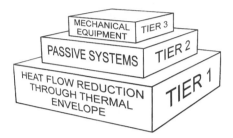

Figure 15.1a The best and most sustainable way to heat and cool a building is to use the three-tier design approach. This chapter covers strategies in tier one.

design of a tight thermal envelope is the first tier of the three-tier design approach to heating and cooling a building (Fig. 15.1a).

Suppose we wanted to keep a certain bucket full of water. Our common sense would have us repair the leaks, at least the major ones, rather than just refilling the bucket continuously. Yet with regard to energy, we usually keep a leaky building warm by pouring in more heat rather than patching the leaks (Fig. 15.1b). Perhaps if we could see the energy leaking out, we would have a different attitude. Fortunately, such **thermography** does exist now and is very effective in convincing people to upgrade their buildings. In a thermogram of the exterior of a building, hot and cold areas are shown

in different shades of gray or colors (Fig. 15.1c and Color Plate 4). A thermogram of the author (Fig. 15.1d) proves that he is not hot-headed.

President Jimmy Carter and President Ronald Reagan did not always agree, but they did agree that conservation implied a reduction of comfort. They were both wrong. From experience, we now know that comfort can be *increased* if the proper conservation techniques are used. For example, indoor comfort increases dramatically when insulation is added to the walls, the ceiling, and especially the windows. When the author moved into his present home, he was uncomfortably cold even when the thermostat was set at 80°F (27°C). The addition of ceiling insulation and insulating drapes over the windows now allows a thermostat setting of 70°F (21°C) to provide complete thermal comfort. Thus, insulation not only reduced energy consumption, but also increased thermal comfort by increasing the mean radiant temperature of the space.

Because conservation has such a negative connotation, it is better to talk of **energy efficiency**. It is not only possible but also more likely to have a higher standard of living through energy efficiency. After all, higher efficiency will

Figure 15.1b If we could see heat flowing out of a building as we see water leaking from a container, then our attitudes might be different.

MUCH HEAT
LOSS THROUGH
WINDOWS

MISSING
INSULATION

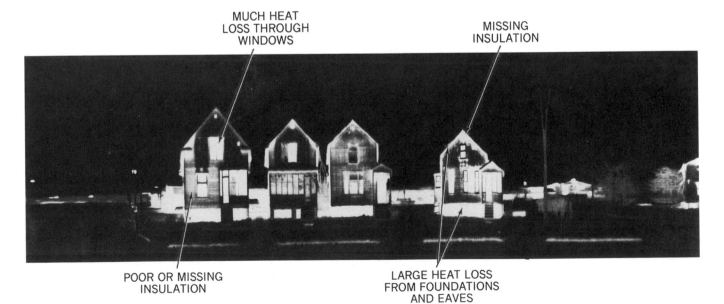

POOR OR MISSING
INSULATION

LARGE HEAT LOSS
FROM FOUNDATIONS
AND EAVES

Figure 15.1c Thermography can pinpoint the weakness in the thermal envelope. This winter thermogram indicates the warmest areas, which are a result of the greatest heat loss. [Vanscan (Thermogram) by Daedalus Enterprises, Inc.]

Figure 15.1d Thermogram of the author—a good likeness.

Figure 15.1e The traditional wattle-and-daub construction, so popular in old England, was unacceptable in the harsh climate of America. There was little insulation to counter heat flow, and infiltration was a major problem, as can be seen from the cracks in this demonstration wall.

enable us to meet the needs of heating, cooling, and lighting at less cost, leaving more money for other needs.

Making adjustments to new thermal realities has a long history in America. The early settlers in New England found that the wattle-and-daub construction method that they had brought from England was inappropriate in the harsh climate of the Northeast (Figure 15.1e). They quickly exhausted the local wood supply in trying to stay warm. Because bringing wood from great distances was expensive, they modified their building method and switched to clapboard siding for tighter construction and greater comfort. Although this was a great improvement in keeping the cold out, it was not as good as the log cabin technology that was brought to the United States later by the Swedish immigrants. Compared to the alternatives available in those days, the thick logs were good insulation, but the numerous joints were still a significant source of infiltration. It was the invention of that underappreciated material tar paper that really cut down on infiltration. By today's standards, wood is also a poor insulator. Today, controlling heat flow is not so much a technical problem as one of economics and concern for the planet.

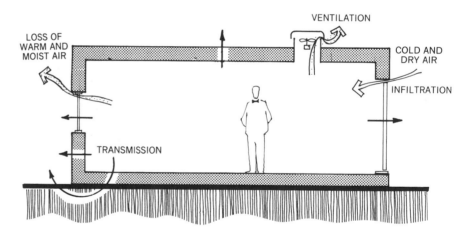

Figure 15.2a Heat is lost from a building by transmission, infiltration, and ventilation.

15.2 HEAT LOSS

Heat is lost from a building by transmission, infiltration, and ventilation (Fig. 15.2a). Heat is lost by **transmission** through the ceilings, walls, floors, windows, and doors. Heat flow by transmission occurs by a combination of conduction, convection, and radiation. The proportion of each depends mainly on the particular construction system (Fig. 15.2b).

The magnitude of heat loss rate through a building's skin is a function of the area, the temperature difference between the indoors and outdoors, and the thermal resistance of the skin (see Sidebox 15.2a). Thus, the heat loss can be minimized by the use of a compact design (minimum area), common walls (no temperature difference across walls), and plenty of insulation (large thermal resistance).

Heat is also lost by the **infiltration** of cold air through joints in the construction, as well as through

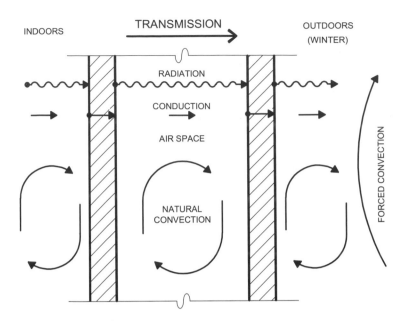

INDOORS

TRANSMISSION

OUTDOORS
(WINTER)

RADIATION

CONDUCTION

AIR SPACE

FORCED CONVECTION

NATURAL
CONVECTION

Figure 15.2b Heat flow by transmission consists of a combination of conduction, convection, and radiation. Winter heat loss is shown in this schematic wall detail consisting of two masonry wythes separated by an air space.

SIDEBOX 15.2a

Heat Loss Due to Transmission Through Walls, Windows, Doors, and Roofs

$$\text{Heat loss by transmission} = \frac{(\text{area}) \times (\text{temperature difference})}{(\text{thermal resistance})}$$

$$HL = \frac{A \times (T_i - T_o)}{R_T}$$

or the more conventional but not as conceptually clear format:

$$\text{since } U = \frac{1}{R_T} \quad \text{(see Section 3.17)}$$

$$HL = A \times U \times (T_i - T_o)$$

where U is the heat-flow coefficient and
where:

	I-P	SI
HL is the rate of heat loss	Btu/h	watts
A is the area	ft²	m²
T_i is the indoor design temperature	°F	°C
T_o is the outdoor design temperature	°F	°C
R_T is the total resistance	$\frac{(ft^2)(°F)}{Btu/h}$	$\frac{m^2(°C)}{W}$

I-P Example: What is the heat loss per hour through an 8-ft-high and 20-ft-long wall that has a total thermal resistance of 16 (R-value) if the indoor design temperature is 75°F and the outdoor design temperature is 20°F?

$$HL = \frac{(A) \times (T_i - T_o)}{R} = \frac{(20)(8)(75-20)}{16} = 550 \text{ BTU/h}$$

SI Example: What is the heat loss of a 3-m-high and 7-m-long wall that has a thermal resistance of $R[SI] = 4$ if the indoor design temperature is 20°C and the outdoor design temperature is −10°C?

$$HL = \frac{(A) \times (T_i - T_o)}{R_T} = \frac{(3)(7)(20-(-10))}{4} = 157.5 \text{ watts}$$

---

cracks around windows and doors. The heat loss due to infiltration is a function of how much cold air enters the building and the temperature difference between the indoor and outdoor air. The amount of cold air that infiltrates on the windward side of the building is equal to the amount of hot air that leaves on the leeward side. Thus, counting both the air entering and leaving is an error comparable to counting both heads and tails to determine the number of coins. Sidebox 15.2b shows how infiltration heat loss is calculated by the **air-change method.** A more complicated method uses the length of cracks at windows and doors. It is called the **crack method,** and although it is more accurate, the results are still rough approximations. However, the tightness of an existing building can be accurately determined by a **blower-door** test. If the indoor air is being humidified, latent as well as sensible heat will be lost by infiltration in the winter.

Heat loss due to **ventilation** is very much like infiltration except that it is a controlled and purposeful form of air exchange. Fortunately, heat-recovery devices, as described in Section 16.18, can save as much as 90 percent of the heat, both sensible and latent, that would otherwise be lost due to ventilation.

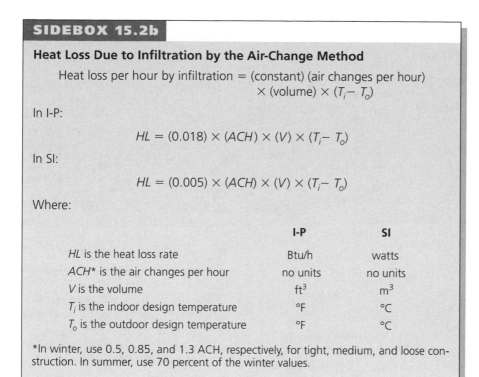

SIDEBOX 15.2b

Heat Loss Due to Infiltration by the Air-Change Method

Heat loss per hour by infiltration = (constant) (air changes per hour) × (volume) × ($T_i - T_o$)

In I-P:

$$HL = (0.018) \times (ACH) \times (V) \times (T_i - T_o)$$

In SI:

$$HL = (0.005) \times (ACH) \times (V) \times (T_i - T_o)$$

Where:

	I-P	SI
HL is the heat loss rate	Btu/h	watts
ACH^* is the air changes per hour	no units	no units
V is the volume	ft^3	m^3
T_i is the indoor design temperature	°F	°C
T_o is the outdoor design temperature	°F	°C

*In winter, use 0.5, 0.85, and 1.3 ACH, respectively, for tight, medium, and loose construction. In summer, use 70 percent of the winter values.

15.3 HEAT GAIN

Although heat gain in a building is similar to heat loss, some significant differences exist. Similar to winter, there is heat gain by transmission, infiltration, and ventilation. However, unlike winter, there is also heat gain due to internal heat sources, the effect of thermal mass, and, of course, the action of the sun (Fig. 15.3).

Depending on the building type, the internal heat sources can be either a major or a minor load. **Internally dominated buildings** are those that have a large amount of heat generated by people, lights, and appliances. The heat can be in both sensible and latent (water-vapor) form.

Thermal mass can reduce the heat gain when temperatures are fluctuating widely during a day. The insulating effect is most pronounced when the daily temperature range varies from above to below the comfort zone, a situation found in hot and dry climates. (This effect was explained in Section 3.19 and will be explained further in Section 15.11.

Infiltration is generally less of a problem in the summer than in the winter because of the lower wind velocities. Instead, ventilation is often a major source of heat gain. This is especially true in humid climates because of the large latent-heat component of the air. The same heat-recovery devices mentioned above for reducing heat loss can also be used to reduce both sensible and latent heat when ventilation brings in hot, humid summer air. Ventilation and heat-recovery devices are explained more fully in Section 16.18.

For windows, the part of the heat gain due to the temperature difference across the window is calculated the same way as in winter. Of course,

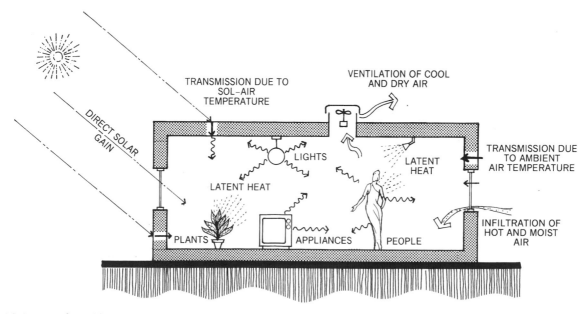

Figure 15.3 Sources of sensible and latent heat gain.

SIDEBOX 15.3a

Heat Gain Due to Solar Gain Through Glazing

The rate of solar heat gain through glazing = (area) × (solar heat gain factor) × (solar heat gain coefficient)

$$HG = (A) \times (SHGF) \times (SHGC)$$

Where

	I-P	SI
HG is the rate of solar heat gain through glazing	Btu/h	watts
A is the actual glazing area	ft^2	m^2
SHGF* is the unit solar heat gain	Btu/hft^2	Wm^2
SHGC† is the solar heat gain coefficient	no units	no units

*The Solar Heat Gain Factor SHGF is a function of latitude and orientation of glazing, time of year, and time of day. Values can be found in the *ASHRAE Handbook of Fundamentals.*
†The Solar Heat Gain Coefficient SHGC quantifies the amount of shading due to glazing type, trees, shading devices, etc. See Table 9.21 for values.

Example: What is the solar heat gain per hour through a clear 4- × 5-ft-double-glazed-window that is 80 percent glass and 20 percent frame? The window is at 40° N latitude and faces south. It is 11 A.M. on March 21. Where

$$HG = (A) \times (SHGF) \times (SHGC)$$

$$A \text{ (of glazing)} = (4 \times 5)(0.8) = 16 \text{ ft}^2$$

$$\text{SHGF from ASHRAE Handbook} = \frac{197 \text{ Btu/hr}}{\text{ft}^2}$$

SHGC (from Table 9.21) = 0.73

Therefore

$$HG = (16)(197)(0.73) = 2301 \text{ Btu/h}$$

SI Example: What is the solar heat gain rate through a clear 1-m × 2-m double-glazed window that is 80 percent glass and 20 percent frame? The window is at 40° N latitude and faces south. It is 11 A.M. on March 21. Where

$$HG = (A) \times (SHGF) \times (SHGC)$$

SHGF from *ASHRAE Handbook* = 622

$$= (1)(2)(0.8)(622)(0.73)$$

$$= 726 \text{ watts}$$

---

summer indoor and outdoor design temperatures are used. The part of the window heat gain due to solar radiation through the glazing is calculated as shown in Sidebox 15.3a. The second component of solar heat gain is a consequence of the surface heating of opaque surfaces. Dark colors absorb a large amount of solar radiation and get quite hot. This results in a higher temperature differential between indoors and outdoors than can be accounted for by the actual outdoor-air temperature.

This larger temperature differential is called the **sol-air temperature.** When the insulating effect of thermal mass is also included, the temperature differential used is called the "design-equivalent temperature difference."

Sidebox 15.3b illustrates how to calculate heat gain through the opaque parts of the building envelope.

Since sol-air temperatures are much lower with light-colored surfaces than with dark-colored surfaces, one of the most effective and certainly least expensive ways to reduce heat gain is to specify light-colored building finishes.

15.4 SOLAR REFLECTIVITY (ALBEDO)

The heat gain through a white roof will be about 50 percent of that of a black roof. The measure of a surface's reflectivity of solar radiation is called **albedo.** It varies from 0 percent to 100 percent, where a surface with an albedo of 0 percent would absorb all solar radiation and an albedo of 100 percent would reflect all solar radiation. See Table 15.4 for albedo values of typical building surfaces.

A textured, bumpy surface will absorb more radiation than a smooth surface of the same material and color. Studies done at the Oak Ridge National Laboratory in Tennessee have shown that the temperature of dark-colored roofs routinely exceeds 160°F (71°C) on sunny summer days, while flat white surfaces only reach about 135°F (57°C), and glossy white surfaces rarely exceed 120°F (48°C) (Akbati et al., *Cooling Our Communities*, 1992). Other studies have shown that the total air conditioning can be reduced by 20 percent just by changing the albedo of the roof and walls from a typical medium-dark value of 30 percent to a light-colored value of 90 percent. During initial design and construction there is usually no cost penalty for choosing light colors, but the savings go on for the life of the material.

Although polished metal surfaces have high reflectivity (albedo), they have low emissivity and, therefore, get much warmer than surfaces with light colors, which have a high emissivity (see Section 3.11). Clearly then, light colors should be used in hot

SIDEBOX 15.3b

Heat Gain Through Walls and Roofs

$$HG = \frac{(A) \times (DETD)}{R_T} \quad \text{or} \quad (A) \times (U) \times (DETD)*$$

where

	I-P	SI
HG is the rate of heat gain	Btu/h	watts
$DETD$ is the design-equivalent temperature difference[†]	°F	°C
R_T is the total resistance of the wall or roof structure	$\frac{(ft^2)(°F)}{Btu/h}$	$\frac{(m^2)(°C)}{W}$

*Because $U = \frac{1}{R_T}$.

[†]$DETD$ is a function not only of the temperature difference across the building envelope but also of the thermal mass and the color of the outdoor surface.

Table 15.4 Albedo of Typical Building Surfaces

Building Surface	% Albedo*
White paint	50–90
Highly reflective roof[†]	60–70
Colored paint	10–40
Brick and stone	10–40
Concrete	10–40
Red/brown tile roof	10–40
Grass	20–30
Trees	10–20
Corrugated roof	10–20
Tar and gravel roof	5–20
Asphalt paving	5–20

* Albedo describes the reflectivity of the total solar spectrum (ultraviolet, visible, and infrared), while the reflectance factor (RF) only describes the reflectivity of light. Values from Akbari et al., eds., *Cooling Our Communities* (1992).

[†]A white roof with some dirt accumulation

climates. In dense urban areas, the paving and other surfaces between buildings should also have a high albedo. Researchers have found that in a typical American city, the value of the albedo can be realistically raised by about 15 percent and this increase in reflectivity will result in a drop of a city's temperature of about 5°F (3°C). In such a city, a light-colored building will benefit both from less heat gain from direct solar radiation and because the outdoor-air temperature will be lower. It should be stressed that although grass and trees have a low albedo, they do not heat a building or city. Transpiration from plants more than offsets the absorption due to their dark color.

It should be relatively easy to convince people to use light colors in hot climates. Light colors not only save money, energy, and the environment, but also are traditional in hot climates (Fig. 15.4 and Fig. 9.22a). Yet for some unknown reason, many people are convinced that black roofs are beautiful and white roofs are ugly. After being shown the picture of the building in Fig. 15.4, most people admit that white roofs are not ugly. They then argue that white roofs can't be used because they get dirty. However, the author has found that smooth white metal roofs get no more stained than black shingle roofs.

15.5 COMPACTNESS, EXPOSED AREA, AND THERMAL PLANNING

Compactness

Until the advent of modern architecture, buildings generally consisted of simple volumes richly decorated. Modern architecture changed that situation and created buildings of complex volumes simply decorated. Unfortunately, complex volumes usually result in large surface-area-to-volume ratios. For example, the compact cube and the spread-out alternative in Fig. 15.5a have the same volume, yet the surface area of the dispersed volume is 60 percent greater than that of the cube. In most cases, a building with more surface area requires more resources of every kind for both construction and operation. Throughout history, compact buildings were built not just for the poor and frugal middle class, but also for the rich and powerful (Fig. 15.5b).

A note of caution is in order here because we can easily learn the wrong lessons from the past. For example, our image of a traditional home is one with many wings. This can be a misleading prototype because authentic old homes almost always started out as compact designs. It was only after many generations of additions that the quaint nostalgic image we have today emerged (Fig. 15.5c).

There are some exceptions to the rule that compact designs are more sustainable. When natural ventilation is the dominant cooling strategy and

Figure 15.4 White roofs are not ugly! Black or dark roofs are an unfortunate tradition in the hot American South.

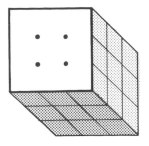

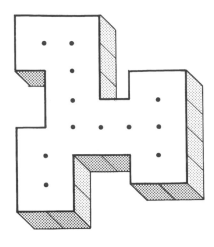

Figure 15.5a Although the volumes are equal, the less compact form (right) has 60 percent more surface area.

Figure 15.5b Like most palaces throughout time, the Andrew Carnegie mansion of Fifth Avenue in New York City is a spacious, ornate, but compact building.

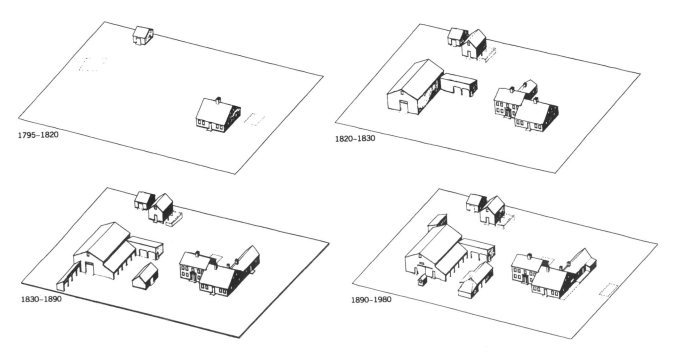

1795–1820

1820–1830

1830–1890

1890–1980

Figure 15.5c Evolution of the Nutting Farm. Note especially the changes in the residence. (Reproduced from *Big House, Little House Back House Barn* by Thomas C. Hubka, by permission of the University Press of New England. Copyright 1984, 1985, 1987 by Trustees of Dartmouth College.)

the climate has mild winters, an open, spread-out plan might be best. If daylighting in a large multistory building has a high priority, a more spread-out plan might also be in order. The glass-covered atrium is usually the result of a simultaneous desire for more surface area for daylighting and less

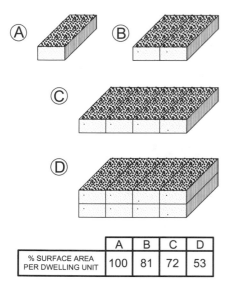

% SURFACE AREA PER DWELLING UNIT	A	B	C	D
	100	81	72	53

Figure 15.5d Through the sharing of walls, attached units can significantly reduce the amount of exposed surface area.

surface area for heating and cooling needs (See Fig. 13.9e).

Exposure

Ultimately, what counts is not total surface but exposed surface. Through the sharing of walls (partly walls), great savings in heating and cooling are possible For example, row housing of four attached units has about 30 percent less surface area than four detached units (Fig. 15.5d).

Exposure can also be reduced by the arrangement of the floor plan for thermal planning. Spaces that require or tolerate cooler temperatures should be placed on the north side of the building. Buffer spaces, such as garages, should be on the north to protect against the cold or on the west to protect against summer heat.

Thermal Planning

Solar thermal conditions around a building are shown for both summer and winter in Fig. 15.5e. A bubble diagram for a residence based on the solar/thermal conditions is shown in Fig. 15.5f. The kitchen would be on

the northeast because it needs little heat, while the breakfast area would be on the southeast to receive morning sun all year. The utility and garage areas would be on the northwest to buffer against the winter cold and summer heat. Bedrooms are on the north because they are used little during the day and a cool room is better for sleeping.

A plan based on this diagram would be in harmony with our circadian rhythms, thereby promoting both physical and mental well-being (Fig. 15.5g). Consider preparing and eating breakfast with bright, cheerful sunlight. You would spend the day in the family room with warm, south lighting, and at night you would sleep in the pleasantly cool bedrooms on the north.

Another example of solar/thermal planning is the bubble diagram for an elementary school (Fig. 15.5h). The classrooms face southeast for year-round warm south lighting from early morning until early afternoon, while the gymnasium is on the north because it needs to be the coolest space.

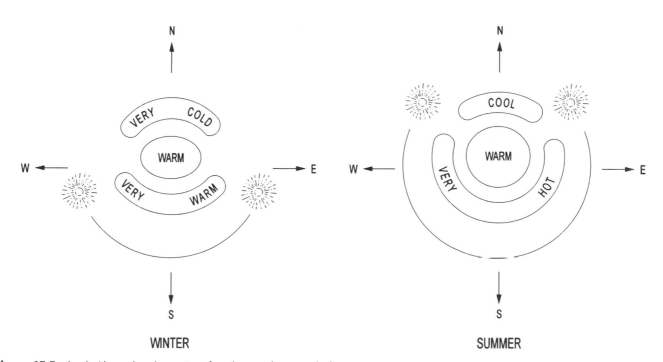

Figure 15.5e A solar/thermal zoning pattern for winter and summer is shown.

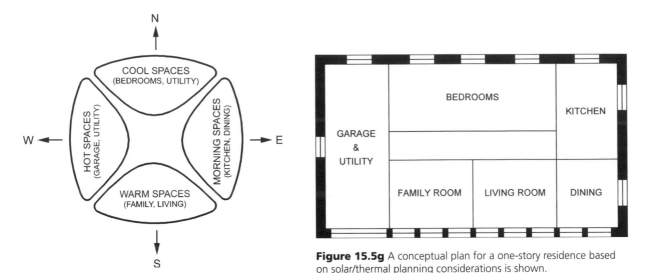

Figure 15.5f A solar/thermal bubble diagram for designing a one-story residence is shown.

Figure 15.5g A conceptual plan for a one-story residence based on solar/thermal planning considerations is shown.

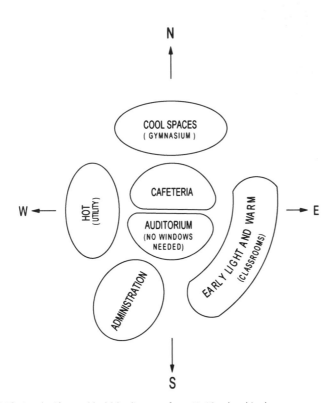

Figure 15.5h A solar/thermal bubble diagram for a K–12 school is shown.

15.6 INSULATION MATERIALS

Thirty-five years ago, many buildings were still built without insulation in the walls. As a consequence of the energy crisis of 1973, the question is no longer whether insulation should be used but rather which material and how much.

In general, "the more insulation the better" is a good principle to start with for a number of reasons: insulation not only saves money, but also increases thermal comfort; it helps create more sustainable buildings; it is relatively inexpensive; it is very durable; it functions in both summer and winter; and it is much easier to install during initial construction than to retrofit later. There is, of course, a limit to how much should be used. The "law of diminishing returns" says that every time you double the amount of insulation, you cut the heat loss in half. This is great the first few times as the heat loss goes from 1 to ½ to ¼, etc. Unfortunately, the cost keeps up with the thickness of insulation, while the heat loss decreases by ever smaller amounts (e.g., from 1/32 to 1/64 to 1/128, etc.). This simplistic approach to building economics has done much damage. A more realistic approach is to see how the cost of the whole building increases as more insulation is used. As Amory Lovins says, "You can tunnel through the cost barrier." As more insulation is used, the mechanical heating and cooling systems get smaller and less expensive. In many climates, superinsulation can eliminate the heating system altogether, and in some climates it also eliminates the cooling system. Thus, large amounts of insulation can be less expensive than small amounts even for the initial costs.

Large amounts of insulation also provide a passive security system.

When there is a power failure in the winter in superinsulated building, the temperature indoors will drop more slowly and less far than in a conventional building. It is surprising that in a world where people crave security, they don't make their homes more secure. Furthermore, since future energy supplies and cost are uncertain, it is wise to be conservative and to **use as much insulation as possible.**

Table 15.6A gives recommended insulation levels. These values and those required by codes should be considered *minimum* values. Consider

that **superinsulated buildings,** which are gaining in popularity, use about twice these levels. The main obstacle to using high levels of insulation is not so much the cost of the insulation but the need to change construction details to allow the use of thicker insulating materials.

The bar chart of Fig. 15.6a compares various insulating materials to each other and to common building materials by showing the thermal resistance of 1-in. (1m)-thick samples. Thus, it is easy to determine how many inches (meters) of insulation are required to achieve the R-value

desired. Obviously, the materials with a high R-value per inch will result in a thinner wall or roof system.

Other important characteristics of insulating materials are moisture resistance, fire resistance, potential for generating toxic smoke, physical strength, and stability over time. Table 15.6B summarizes the important characteristics of common insulation materials. Although all tables and figures in this book give both I-P and SI values, use Table 15.6C to convert R- and U- values for items not given.

Most insulation materials used in buildings fit into one of the following five categories: blankets, loose fill, foamed-in-place, boards, and radiant barriers. Most insulating materials work by creating miniature air spaces. The main exception is **reflective insulation,** which uses larger air spaces faced with foil on one or both sides. This material acts mainly as a **radiation barrier.** Another insulating system that does not use miniature air spaces is vacuum insulation. All of these insulation types will now be described.

Batts and Blankets

Although most blankets or batts are made of fiberglass or rock wool, cotton is also being used. Blankets come in continuous rolls, while batts are cut to length. The batts and blankets are made to fit between studs, joists, or rafters. Both fiberglass and rock wool are very resistant to fire, moisture, and organic attack. The main health hazard is present during installation and comes from inhaling the short fibers that become airborne.

Loose Fill

Loose-fill materials consist primarily of fiberglass, cellulose (ground-up newspapers), and expanded minerals, such as perlite and vermiculite. The fiberglass and cellulose types are blown into stud spaces and attics. Cellulose is a good, safe product if properly treated with borates to make it fire-retardant and resistant to organic attack. Care must be taken

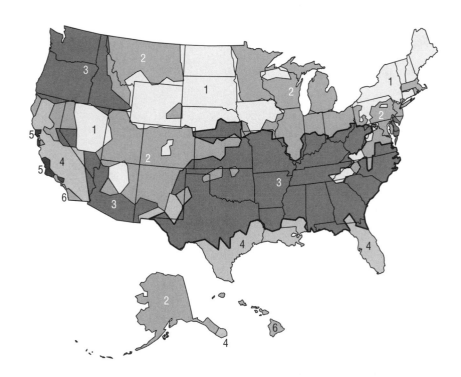

Table 15.6A	Recommend Minimum Insulation Levels									
	Ceiling		Walls		Floor		Slab Edge[†]		Basement[†]	
Zone*	I-P	SI	I-P	SI	I-P	SI	I-P	SI	I-P	SI
1	50	8.7	20	3.5	25	4.3	15	2.6	15	2.6
2	50	8.7	20	3.5	25	4.3	10	1.7	15	2.6
3	50	8.7	20	3.5	25	4.3	10	1./	10	1.7
4	40	6.9	14	2.4	14	2.4	5	0.9	10	1.7
5	40	6.9	14	2.4	14	2.4	5	0.9	5	0.9
6	40	6.9	14	2.4	12	2.1	5	0.9	5	0.9

*See map above for zones.
[†]Insulate whole height of foundation wall.
Source: Map from the Department of Energy; see www.eere.energy.gov.

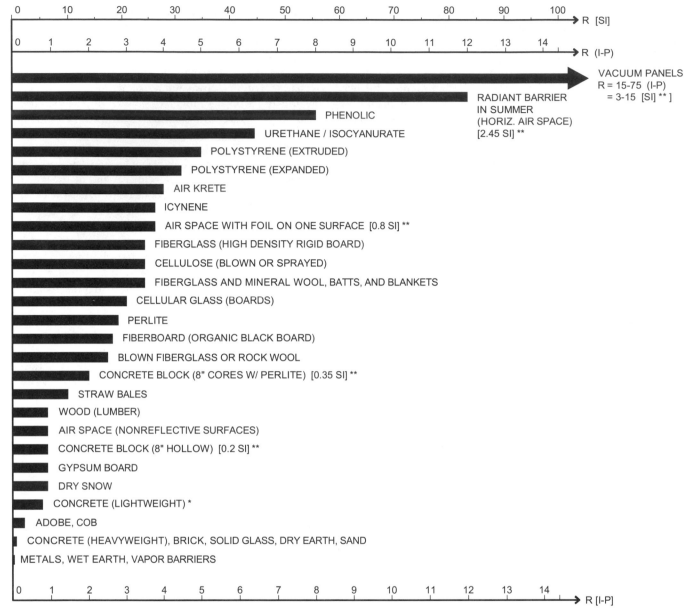

Figure 15.6a A comparison of the thermal resistance of various materials. All values are for 1-in. thick [1 m SI] samples, unless otherwise indicated. The actual resistance of a sample varies with density, temperature, material composition and, in some cases, moisture content.

* The resistance of lightweight concrete varies greatly with density and aggregate used (R-values vary from 0.2 to 2.0 (1.4 to 14 SI)).

** Not per inch (0 meter) but for actual thickness of block or air space.

to prevent inhalation of the fine particles both during installation and afterward. Perlite consists of lightweight granules that are usually poured into masonry wall cavities.

Foamed-in-Place

Most foamed-in-place insulation materials are made of plastics. The main exceptions are foamed glass and Air Krete ™, which are foamed minerals that have the advantages of acting as a fire stop and of not releasing toxic gases. The plastic foams vary tremendously because of both the base materials and the foaming agents. Foams can be sprayed into cavities or on surfaces (e.g., basement walls) both during construction and for retrofit.

In all cases, the cured material needs to be covered to protect the foam and or the occupants. Toxic smoke from burning plastic is a severe hazard, and off-gassing from aging plastic foams is a potential hazard, especially for chemically sensitive people. Because there are many differences among the plastic foams, see Table 15.6B for the specific characteristics of each type.

Table 15.6B Insulation Materials

Material	Physical format	Resistance R(I–P)*	Resistance R[SI]†	Comments
Fiberglass and rockwool	Batts	3–4	21–28	Good fire resistance
	Loose fill	2.2–3	15–21	Hard to completely fill air spaces
	Boards	3–4	21–28	Moisture reduces R-value
				Health danger to installers
				Use formaldehyde-free types
Perlite	Loose fill	2.5–3.3	17–23	Very inert volcanic rock
				Some dust
				Very fire resistant
Cellulose	Loose fill or sprayed	3.2–3.7	22–26	Made from recycled newspaper treated with borates
				Environmentally safe
				Easy to fully fill air spaces
				Must be kept dry
Cotton	Batts	3.0–3.7	21–26	Made from cotton and polyester mill scraps
				Very sustainable
Icynene™	Spray-in	3.6	25	Plastic foam using water as foaming agent
				No off-gassing
				Sustainable
				Provides air sealing
Air-Krete™	Spray-in	3.9	27	All-mineral content
				Inert
				Very fire resistant
				Sustainable
				Remains friable
Expanded polystyrene (EPS)	Boards	3.6–4.2	25–29	Plastic foam
				Water resistant
				Must be protected from fire
Extruded polystyrene (XPS)	Boards	4.5–5	31–35	Plastic foam
				Very water resistant
				Must be protected from fire
				Can be used below grade
Polyiso-cyanurate	Boards	5.6–6.3	39–44	Plastic foam
				Must be protected from water and fire
				Some off-gassing
				Very good sheathing material
Polyiso-cyanurate with foil facing	Boards	7	49	Like regular polyisocyanurate, but has a higher R-value because there is no off-gassing
Urethane	Spray-in	3.6–6.8	25–47	Plastic foam
	Spray-on			R-value is a function of density
				Must be protected from fire
				Provides air sealing
				Forms a skin that is water resistant
Phenolic foam	Boards	8.2	57	Plastic foam
				Fire and water resistant
				Very low off-gassing
				Good structural strength
Radiant barrier	Metal film	4–12	30–80	Radiant barrier must face an air space
				R-value is a function of air space orientation and direction of heat flow
				Best for preventing heat gain through the roof
Vacuum	Panel	15–50	100–350	Because most heat flow is through the edges, larger panels are better
				Quality is most important to prevent loss of vacuum

*Resistance is $\dfrac{(ft^2)(°F)}{Btu/h}$ per inch of thickness except for the radiant barrier.

†Resistance is $\dfrac{(m^2)(°C)}{W}$ per meter of thickness except for the radiant barrier.

Table 15.6C I-P to SI Conversion Factors		
Multiply	**By**	**To Get**
Resistance per inch (I-P)	6.933	Resistance per meter (SI)
Actual resistance (I-P)	0.1735	Actual resistance (SI)
U-coefficient (I-P)	5.73	U-coefficient (SI)

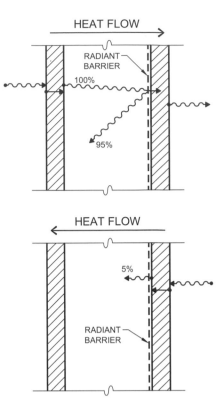

Figure 15.6c All radiant barriers act as either reflectors or nonemitters, depending on the direction of heat flow. A radiant barrier will reduce heat transfer either by reflecting 95 percent of the heat radiation or by emitting only 5 percent of that emitted by nonradiant barrier materials.

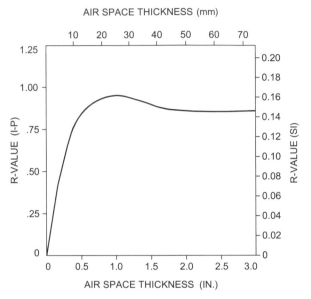

Figure 15.6b The optimum wall or window air space thickness is about ¾ in. (2 cm). Note that this is for air spaces not faced with reflective material. (After *Climatic Design* by D. Watson and K. Labs, 1983.)

Boards

Although most insulation boards are made of foamed plastics, some are made from recycled or waste organic material. For example, Homosote™ is made from recycled newspapers. Boards can also be made of fiberglass. Because boards made of polystyrene are very resistant to moisture, they are frequently used to insulate below grade. Extruded polystyrene is both more resistant to moisture migration and has a higher R-value than the less expensive, expanded polystyrene (bead board) material.

Boards made of isocyanurate have very high R-values but are damaged by moisture and off-gassing. For that reason, they are usually covered with a protective foil coating. All plastic insulation boards should be covered to prevent damage to themselves from such forces as ultraviolet radiation in sunlight, water, and physical attack. They also need to be covered to minimize off-gassing and to prevent toxic smoke from being generated during a fire.

Air Spaces and Radiant Barriers

Large plain air spaces are a poor way to insulate. As Fig. 15.6b shows, the R-value of an air space of any size is always less than 1 (0.16). The optimum size is about ¾ in. (2 cm). For smaller air spaces conduction increases, and for those larger than ¾ in. (2 cm), convection heat transfer increases. For more thermal resistance, air spaces should be filled with either insulation or a radiant barrier.

Although radiant barriers only affect the radiant transfer of heat, their effect can be quite significant. A radiant barrier consists of a highly polished metal foil that is both a poor emitter and a poor absorber (i.e., a good reflector) of heat radiation. Radiant barriers are usually made of aluminum, and they must face an air space at least ½ in. (12 mm) thick. They are usually applied to one or both of the materials facing the air spaces (Fig. 15.6c). The first surface of foil stops about 95 percent of the radiant heat flow and the second surface stops another 4.8 percent, for a total of 99.8 blockage of radiation. Additional layers of foil help little except to create additional air spaces, which reduce the convection heat flow. Although radiation is independent of orientation, heat flow by convection is very much dependent on both the orientation of the air space and the direction of heat flow. As a result, the resistance of air spaces and reflective insulation varies greatly with the location in the structure and the time of year. Table 15.6D gives the resistance of air spaces and reflective insulation for different orientations and heat-flow directions. Note the tremendous range of R-values for air spaces that are all about the same size but have radiant barriers.

The best application for a radiation barrier is in hot climates just under the roof. Experiments in Florida have shown that the summer heat gain through the roof can be reduced as much as 40 percent. In buildings with rafters, the foil should be attached to the underside of the rafter to create two air spaces, each facing a radiant barrier. Since radiant barriers are effective only when the foil faces an air space, a finished attic or vaulted ceiling will not achieve the double radiant-barrier benefit. Since working with the thin foil is difficult, most builders use foil preapplied to sheathing panels.

Vacuum-Insulated Panels (VIPs)

To keep drinks hot or cold, a vacuum bottle is unbeatable. The vacuum stops all conduction and convection heat transfer, while a silver coating on the bottle stops most radiant heat transfer (Fig. 15.6d). The bottle resists being crushed by the 1 ton/ft^2 (10,300 kg/m^2) atmospheric pressure only because of the sharp curvature of the glass, which acts as either a compression or a tension ring. Flat panels do not have that geometric advantage, and, therefore, need a spacer to keep from being crushed (Fig. 15.6e). Because the thermal resistance of the "vacuum" panel depends partly on the resistance of the spacer, the R-value of VIPs varies widely (15–75 I-P [2.5–13 SI]). The best spacer is aerogel, which will be described along with windows below.

Since the edges of the vacuum panels are heat bridges, larger panels have a higher total R-value. For example, a particular kind of VIP will have an R-value of 20 if it is 1 ft^2 in area and an R-value of 40 if its area is 8 ft^2 (or, in SI, a 0.1 m^2 panel has an R-value of 4, while a 0.8 m^2 panel has an R-value of 8).

Table 15.6D R-Values of Air Spaces and Radiant Barriers*

Position of Air Space	Air Space I-P	Air Space SI	Air Space with Radiant Barrier[†] I-P	Air Space with Radiant Barrier[†] SI
Wall	1	0.17	4	0.6
Ceiling in winter (heat flow up)	1	0.17	3	0.5
Ceiling in summer (heat flow down)	1	0.17	12	2.0

*Values vary somewhat with the size of the air space and with temperature.
[†]Values shown are for an air space with a radiant barrier on one surface facing the air space. Increase the value 5 percent for radiant barriers on both surfaces.

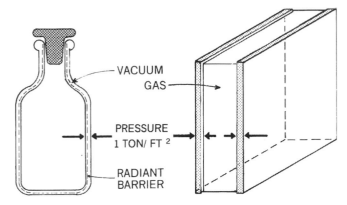

Figure 15.6d A vacuum bottle can stop most heat flow. It resists the 1-ton-per-square-foot [100,000 pascals] atmospheric pressure by its sharp curvature, something a flat panel cannot do without a spacer.

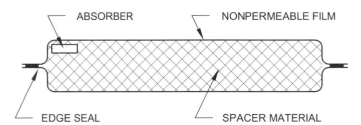

Figure 15.6e A vacuum-insulated panel VIP needs a spacer material to resist atmospheric pressure. It also requires an absorber, which consists of a desiccant to absorb water vapor and a "getter" to absorb other gases to help preserve the vacuum. Although VIPs have great potential to save energy, their main weakness, as with windows, is edge losses. Thus, use the largest panels possible.

15.7 THE THERMAL ENVELOPE

The total thermal resistance of a wall, roof, or floor construction is simply the sum of the resistances of all the component parts. Determining the total resistance of a wall or roof section is useful for comparing alternatives, for complying with codes, and for calculating heat loss. Many codes, company literature, and equations describe the thermal characteristic of a wall or roof by a quantity called the **U-coefficient** rather than the total R-value. The U-coefficient is the reciprocal of the total R-value. The author feels that the U-coefficient is a somewhat counterintuitive concept and that it is, therefore, usually better to think in terms of the total R-value. (See Sidebox 15.7 and the accompanying diagram.) After all, it is easy to understand that a large

Total Resistance and U-Coefficient

The total resistance of a wall, roof, window, or door equals the sum of all the resistances of the components:

$$R_T = \Sigma R = R_1 + R_2 + R_3 \ldots$$

where

R_T = the total thermal resistance of the construction detail in R-value

$$R_{I\text{-}P} = \frac{(ft^2) \times (°F)}{Btu/hour} \text{ or } R_{SI} = \frac{(m^2) \times (°C)}{W}$$

R_1, R_2, etc. = the thermal resistance of each component

Also, the heat-flow coefficient equals the reciprocal of the total resistance of a wall, roof, door, or window:

$$U = \frac{1}{R_T}$$

where

U = the heat flow coefficient of the construction detail in U-value,

$$U_{I\text{-}P} = \frac{Btu/hour}{(ft^2) \times (°F)} \quad \text{or} \quad U_{SI} = \frac{W}{(m^2) \times (°C)}$$

Example: Find the total resistance and U-value for the wood-framed wall detail below,

Component	R-Values*	
	R(I-P)	R(SI)
Indoor air film	0.7	0.12
½ in. (12 mm) gypsum board	0.45	0.08
3½ in (87 mm) air space	1.0	0.17
½ in (12 mm) extruded polystyrene board	2.5	0.43
½ in (12 mm) plywood siding	0.6	0.11
Outdoor air film	0.2	0.03
Total resistance (R_T)	5.45	0.94
Total U-coefficient=1/R_T	0.18	1.06

*See Appendix L for an abbreviated list of R-values and U-coefficients. See the *ASHRAE Handbook of Fundamentals* for a complete list of values.

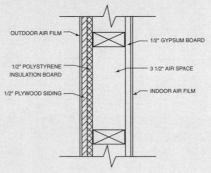

total R-value is desirable, while it is harder to remember that a small U-coefficient is equally desirable.

Just as a container holding water should have no holes, a building holding heat in or out should have no thermal holes or thermal bridges. The thermal envelope should be a continuous unbroken skin around the conditioned spaces.

Walls

Although wall details vary tremendously, a few typical details are shown in Fig. 15.7a. Note that most insulation materials should not be exposed either indoors or outdoors. Also note that in walls with steel studs, the insulation between the studs is outflanked by the stud heat bridges. Therefore, the R-value of the insulation sheathing is especially important and should be increased. Heat bridges will be discussed in more detail in the next section. The role of thermal mass will be discussed in Section 15.11.

Climate or Smart Facades

These types of facades have an additional glass skin, not to increase the thermal resistance but rather to allow for solar control and natural ventilation. Thus, they are not discussed here but in the chapters on shading and passive cooling.

Roofs

In flat-roofed buildings, the insulation should be on the top of the roof deck to avoid structural members, lighting fixtures, or air ducts penetrating the thermal envelope. In buildings with sloped roofs, the insulation should follow the rafters or the top chord of trusses. If the ridge is very high, the insulation can more efficiently follow the collar beams (Fig. 15.7b). These locations for the thermal envelope place the ductwork on the indoor side of the thermal envelope, which is a very high priority.

Crawl Spaces

Crawl spaces should never be insulated because they need to be vented to prevent possible health problems from radon, mold, and mildew,

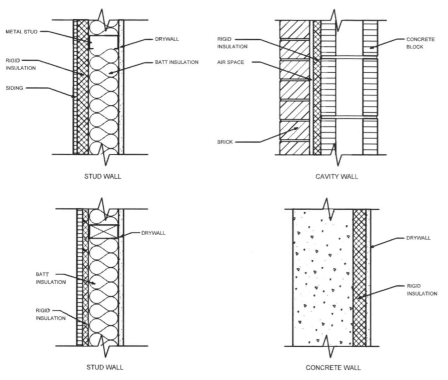

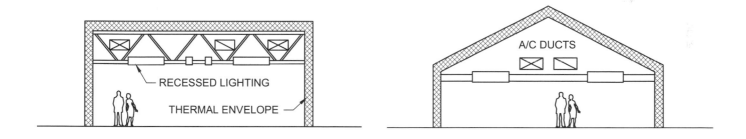

Figure 15.7a Various traditional wall details showing the type and location of insulation. Note the extra-thick insulating sheathing as the primary thermal envelope component when using steel studs, since they are good heat bridges.

whose future occurrence is hard to predict. Instead, the floor above the crawl space should be insulated (Fig. 15.7c). Furthermore, ducts should never be placed in crawl spaces, as will be explained in Section 16.16.

Slab-on-Grade

Insulation is usually not required under a slab-on-grade except around the outside edge. Rigid insulation should extend down to the frost line or an equal distance sideways. Thus, the heat flowing through the earth is forced to take a very long and, therefore, high-resistance path (Fig. 15.7d).

Basements

Basements should be insulated on the earth side of the foundation wall all the way down to the footing (Fig. 15.7e). Since thermal mass is beneficial indoors, it is best not to insulate the foundation wall on the inside, but instead to add plastic foam insulation on the outside. Care must be taken to

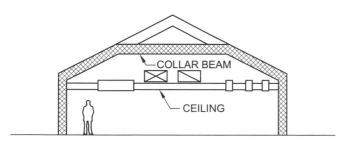

Figure 15.7b For flat-roofed buildings, the insulation should be on top of the roof deck so that all ducts, lights, and structural members are on the indoor side of the thermal envelope. On sloped roofs the insulation should follow the roof rafters and be placed between the rafters and/or on the roof deck. For steeply sloped roofs, the insulation can follow the collar beams, if they exist.

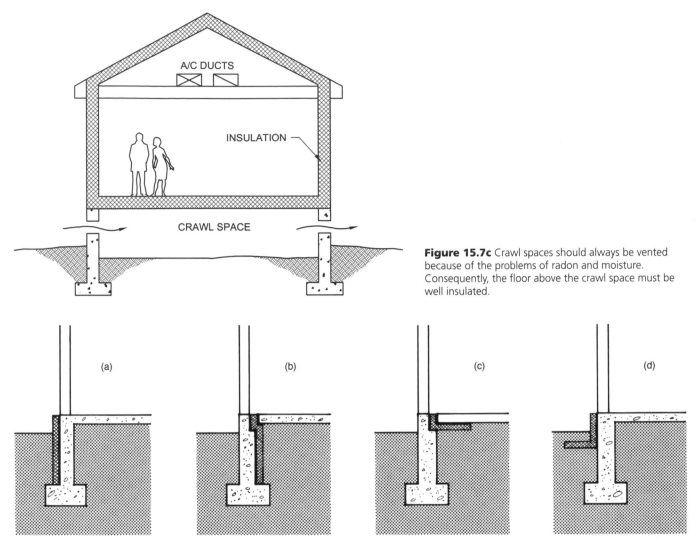

Figure 15.7c Crawl spaces should always be vented because of the problems of radon and moisture. Consequently, the floor above the crawl space must be well insulated.

Figure 15.7d Alternative methods for insulating the perimeter of a slab. In all cases, the insulation forces heat to take a long (high-resistance) path through the earth. Methods (a) and (d) are preferred.

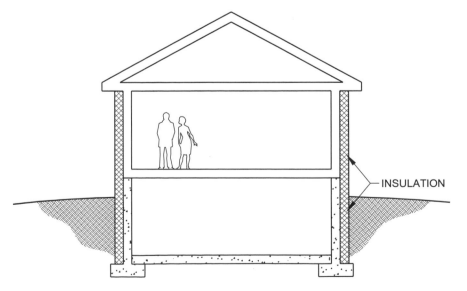

Figure 15.7e Insulate basement walls at least down to the frost line.

Figure 15.7f Insulating concrete forms (ICF) serve as both formwork and permanent insulation. Although mostly used for foundations, the forms are also used to build above grade walls.

protect the foam insulation where it is aboveground. Polystyrene insulation, the usual choice, must be protected from ultraviolet radiation and physical attack with a protective finish such as stucco, special paints, sheet metal, cement boards, or treated wood. Although termites don't eat plastic insulation, they have no trouble making tunnels in it to reach wood.

Instead of adding insulation to a concrete wall, many insulating concrete form (ICF) systems are available that initially act as formwork for the concrete and steel reinforcing rods and then remain in place as insulation (Fig. 15.7f). The ICFs are either preformed blocks or panels with plastic ties. Most ICFs are made of polystyrene because that plastic is unaffected by water and, therefore, is safe belowground. The ICF systems are also used to build strong, energy-efficient walls above grade. However, the present design of ICFs insulates the thermal mass from the indoors as well as from the outdoors. A better ICF system would consist of more insulation on the outdoor side and a noninsulating panel on the indoor side.

Structural Insulated Panels

Heat bridges are almost nonexistent with **structural insulated panels (SIPs)**, which are sandwich panels fabricated in a factory, shipped efficiently (no boxes full of air), and erected in as little as one day (Fig. 15.7g). The panels connect with splice plates so that there are no studs to act as heat bridges (Fig. 15.7h). Thus, a 4 in. (10 cm) nominal SIP wall has an R-value of 14, while a similar framed wall has an actual R-value of about 10 (in SI 2.4 rather than 1.7). Furthermore, there is much less infiltration with the SIP than with standard construction.

Structurally, SIP panels are also superior to conventional framing. The facing boards, which can be made of a variety of materials, carry most of the load in the efficient, stressed-skin mechanism. SIP systems also offer great design flexibility. The panels vary in thickness from 2 to 12 in. (5 to 30 cm) and can be as large as 8 × 24 ft (2.4 × 7.2 m).

Tilt-up

In **tilt-up** construction the concrete wall panels are cast directly on the floor slab to avoid the high cost of formwork. The panels are cast as a sandwich held together by special nonconducting connectors (Fig. 15.7i). Such tilt-up panels have many advantages: structural strength, insulating value, thermal mass, weather resistance, and fire resistance.

Figure 15.7g Structural insulated panels (SIP) create very high-quality thermal envelopes because of their high R-value and low infiltration. (Courtesy Winter Panel, Brattlebow, VT.)

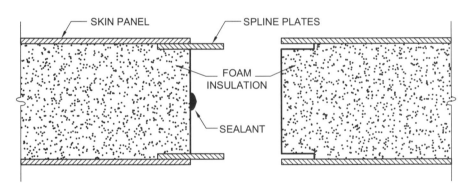

Figure 15.7h SIPs can eliminate studs by using splice plates that are glued and nailed into place. With sealant between panels, a very airtight building envelope is created. Skin panels can be made of OSB, drywall, or cement board.

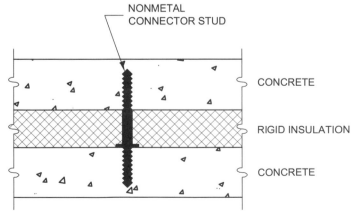

Figure 15.7i Tilt-up sandwich panels are held together by nonconducting connector studs.

Figure 15.7j The straw bales are generally used as in-fill panels, much as in half-timbered construction.

Straw Bales

Although straw bales are not as insulating as many advocates claim, the total R-value of a straw bale wall is excellent because the walls are so thick. Research at the Oak Ridge National Laboratory in Tennessee has shown straw bales to have an R-value of about 1.4 per inch (in SI 10 per meter). Their main virtue is that they are recycled natural materials. When covered with cement stucco, they become a safe and healthy building system. The bales should be used as an in-fill and not as structural material (Fig. 15.7j). Also see Fig. 17.2d of the Real Goods Solar Living Center.

Figure 15.7k Adobe or sun-dried mud bricks are being made in this Mayan village in Guatemala. The best adobe bricks are made of a clay-straw mixture. The straw gives the dried brick some strength in tension.

Adobe and Rammed Earth

Because traditional **adobe** or sun-dried mud brick construction uses no insulation, it is appropriate only for hot and dry climates with no winters (Fig. 15.7k). Insulation is a must whenever there is a need for heating or air conditioning. Unfortunately, there is no easy way to insulate adobe walls.

Instead of making bricks, the mud can be placed in forms much as concrete is placed in situ. The dry mud is then compacted, and the forms are removed. The result is similar to adobe but easier if power equipment is available. However, this **rammed earth** construction and adobe both have two serious weaknesses: (1) they have little resistance to earthquakes, and thus, they usually need a separate structural frame just like straw bales (Fig. 15.7j); and (2) it is difficult to insulate these systems.

15.8 HEAT BRIDGES

The actual heat gain and heat loss of a building are usually much greater than what the design of the thermal envelope would predict. Traditionally,

infiltration was the main cause of poor performance of the thermal envelope, but tighter construction and "house wraps" have reduced infiltration

significantly. Now the main problem is often a result of heat bridges and holes in the thermal envelope (Fig. 15.8a).

In framed construction, the wood studs, plates, and other framing members reduce the performance of the insulation by about 20 (i.e., de-rated to 80 percent). If steel studs are used, the insulation is de-rated to 50 percent (see Table 15.8). However, better detailing can greatly improve this situation. The basic strategy is to create a continuous unbroken thermal envelope over the whole building. Because insulating sheathing creates such a continuous thermal envelope, it should be given priority. Especially with steel studs, the sheathing is critical (Fig. 15.8b). Another approach to reducing heat bridges created by 2 × 4 wood framing is to use 2 × 6 members at a greater spacing (Fig. 15.8c).

Common heat bridges also result from the use of structural sheathing at corners to brace the building. Instead, use let-in diagonal bracing as shown

Figure 15.8a The saying "out of sight, out of mind" is usually appropriate for heat bridges, but not in this case. The significant heat bridges from the structure and roof fasteners are glaringly obvious in this photo of a snow-covered flat roof. (Courtesy: Thomas Kelly and the 2001 Company.)

Table 15.8 Thermal Bridging's Effect on Insulation	
Framing System*	**De-rating Factor(%)†**
2 × 4 wood	80
2 × 4 steel	50
SIP	93

*Normal conventional systems.
†A de-rating factor of 100 percent indicates that there are no heat bridges.

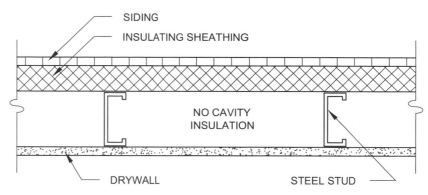

Figure 15.8b When steel studs are used, all of the insulation should be concentrated in the sheathing, because the cavity insulation is only 50 percent effective.

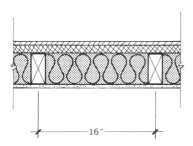 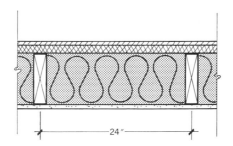

Figure 15.8c Heat bridges caused by studs are greatly reduced by using 2 × 6 studs every 24 in. instead of 2 × 4 studs every 16 in. on center.

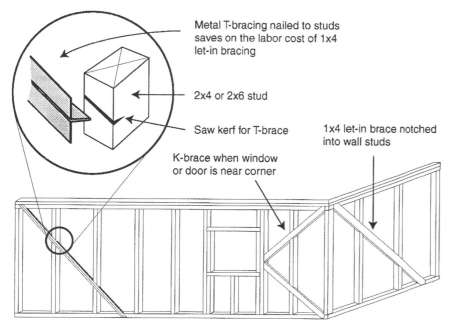

Metal T-bracing nailed to studs saves on the labor cost of 1x4 let-in bracing

2x4 or 2x6 stud

Saw kerf for T-brace

1x4 let-in brace notched into wall studs

K-brace when window or door is near corner

Figure 15.8d Let-in bracing using either wood or steel diagonal members allows for the uninterrupted use of insulating sheathing. (Courtesy Southface Energy Institute.)

in Fig. 15.8d. When trusses are used and the insulation is placed along the bottom chords, the web members all penetrate the insulation. When the trusses are made of steel, major heat bridges are created (Fig. 15.8e). Metal window frames and curtain wall systems without **thermal breaks** are heat bridges. Quality metal windows and curtain wall systems will have a plastic spacer to create a thermal break between the outdoor and indoor facing metal parts (Fig. 15.8f).

Poorly installed insulation is a significant problem because small air spaces act as thermal holes. For example, attic insulation with 5 percent voids can reduce the overall R-value by over 30 percent, and voids in insulation are quite common because of obstacles like electrical wires, pipes, framing members, and poor craftsmanship.

A major heat bridge problem exists in multistory apartment houses that have concrete balconies (Fig. 15.8g). A thermogram would show them for what they are: buildings with cooling fins in the winter and heating fins in the summer. Instead of cantilevers, balconies should be made of metal and hung from the building or supported by columns (Fig. 7.6 h).

A building with defects in its thermal envelope should be just as unacceptable as a building that lets the rain enter. Sustainability requires energy to be used efficiently and not wasted. Fortunately, awareness of thermal holes and thermal bridges

Figure 15.8e Serious heat bridges are created by the web members of steel trusses when the insulation is along the bottom chords. Not only is heat conducted efficiently through the insulation, but it is also transferred efficiently to or from the bottom chords of the truss, which are in contact with the interior of the building.

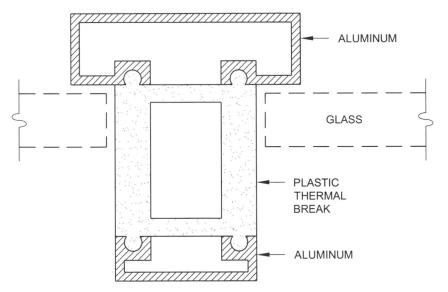

Figure 15.8f Metal windows and curtain wall systems should have thermal breaks to prevent heat bridges. A detail of a schematic mullion is shown.

can yield design details that largely eliminate these energy problems.

15.9 WINDOWS

The bar chart of Fig. 15.9a shows the comparative thermal resistance of different window systems. Note that although double glazing is about twice as good as single glazing in stopping heat flow, it is still only about one-ninth as effective as an ordinary insulated stud wall.

Even with a low-e coating, a double-glazed window has an R-value of 3, which is still only one sixth as good as a standard wall. However,

on south windows, that results in a heat gain during the whole winter, because the passive solar heating during the day exceeds the heat loss at night. Furthermore, windows with a rating of R-8 or higher are energy gainers even facing north. Thus, the old wisdom, to minimize windows in cold climates, has changed if high-performance windows are specified (Fig. 15.9b).

Consider the strange fact that switching from R-2 windows to R-4 windows will have the same benefit as switching the walls from R-19 to R-100. This unbelievable situation is correct because windows not only lose heat but also collect heat from sunlight. Thus, an opaque wall would have to have an R-value of 100 (17 SI) to have the same net heat loss as windows with an R-value of 4 (0.7 SI). Note that this average R-value is less for south windows and higher for north windows. Consequently, windows do not need to have the same R-value as walls in order to avoid being holes in the thermal envelope in the winter, and in the summer, shading is more important than thermal resistance.

The glazing itself, whether glass or plastic, has almost no thermal resistance. It is mainly the air spaces, the surface air films, and low-e coatings that resist the flow of heat (Fig. 15.9c). Single glazing has no air spaces, but it does have the slightly insulating stagnant air films that exist whenever air comes in contact with a building surface. The air spaces are normally filled with dry air, but the resistance of the "air" space can be significantly increased by replacing the air with argon, krypton, or xenon. The improvements are: argon +½, krypton +1; and xenon +1½ R-value.

The thermal resistance of a window consists of two parts: the glazing and the frame. In large windows, most of the heat is lost through the glazing, but in smaller windows, the frame becomes critical. Most frames are made of either wood, vinyl, fiberglass, or aluminum. Wood has good

Figure 15.8g Concrete balconies that cantilever from concrete floor slabs are major heat bridges. They turn a building into a giant radiator.

thermal properties, and when it is protected with vinyl or aluminum, it becomes a durable, low-maintenance product. Vinyl and fiberglass also have low conductance, while metal is acceptable only if it has thermal breaks.

In double or triple glazing, heat is also lost through the edge spacers (Fig 15.9d). High-performance windows use edge spacers with thermal breaks. The edge spacers not only maintain the size of the air space, but also keep moisture and dirt out in order to prevent condensation (fogging) inside the window.

The air films and air spaces only control the heat flow by conduction and convection. To reduce heat flow further, radiation must also be considered. Although clean glass is mostly transparent to solar radiation, it is opaque to heat radiation. Since most of this long-wave infrared (heat) radiation is absorbed, the glass gets warmer, and, consequently, more heat is given off from both indoor and outdoor surfaces (Fig. 15.9e). Thus, in effect, a significant amount of the heat radiation is lost through the glazing. Special coatings on the glass can dramatically reduce this radiant heat flow through the glazing.

Various types of reflective coatings are possible. A transparent silver coating (any polished metal) will not only reflect much of the long-wave heat radiation, but also much of the solar radiation (visible and short-wave infrared) (see Fig. 15.9f). Because it reflects heat radiation in the summer, it has a higher R-value than clear glazing. This kind of coating is appropriate for buildings that need year-round protection from the sun. However, if winter solar heating and/or daylighting is desirable, a different kind of coating will be required.

Special coatings are now available that transmit solar radiation but reflect long-wave infrared radiation. These **low-e** (low-emissivity) coatings are ideal for those buildings that need to reduce winter heat loss and at the same time allow the sun to shine in (i.e., passive solar) (Fig. 15.9g). Because the low-e windows reduce heat flow, they are given a higher R-value. The bar graph in Fig. 15.9a shows how each low-e coating is about equivalent to an additional pane of glass (and air space) in R-value but without the equivalent increase in the weight or cost of the glass. The cost of double-glazed low-e windows is low enough that it should be the minimum standard, except in the mildest climates. The benefits are many: significant energy savings, increased thermal comfort, reduced condensation (fogging), and reduced fading from ultraviolet radiation.

In chapter 13, Fig. 13.7, a slightly different low-e coating was described.

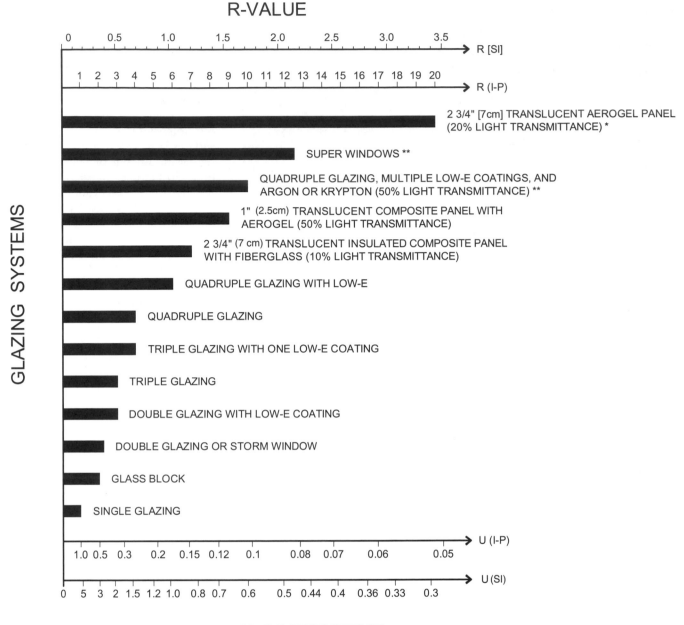

R-VALUE

U-COEFFICIENT

* MANUFACTURED BY KALWALL CO.
** MANUFACTURED BY SOUTH-WALL CO. AND OTHERS

Figure 15.9a The thermal resistance and U-coefficient of various window systems are shown. The values shown are for total resistance, which includes the resistance of the air films, air spaces, low-e coatings, and any special fill gases. Actual R-values vary somewhat with temperature, type of glazing, type of coating, thickness of air space, and the effect of the frame. Most plastics are similar to glass when used as glazing.

In those cases where the light but not the heat of the sun is desired, a **selective low-e** coating is used. This type of coating is transparent to visible radiation but reflective to both short- and long-wave infrared radiation. This kind of coating is appropriate for internally dominated buildings, such as large office buildings, in all but the coldest climates (Fig. 15.9h).

Because there are now many different kinds of low-e coatings available, glazing should be specified by both its R-value and its solar heat gain coefficient (SHGC). Thus, the

The way to insulate with a view.

One way to insulate.

Figure 15.9b Which building will require less heating energy? Until the 1980s, the building on the right would have had less heat loss, but with new, high-performance windows, the building on the left has the lower heating bills. (Courtesy Anderson Corp., Bayport, MN.)

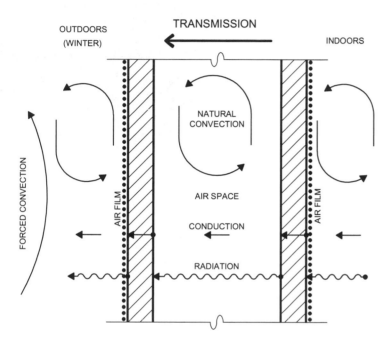

Figure 15.9c Since glass is a good conductor of heat, most of the resistance to heat flow comes from air films and air spaces (if any) and coatings (if any).

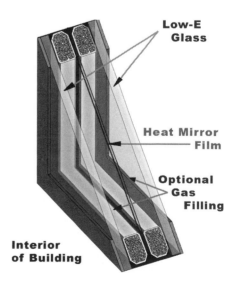

Figure 15.9d This cutaway drawing shows a special kind of triple-glazed window that uses a plastic film instead of the central glass pane to create a lighter and less expensive window. The center-of-glass thermal resistance varies with the fill gas used (argon krypton, or xenon) and the number of low-e coatings. R-values range from 4 to 9 (0.7 to 1.6 SI). Efforts are also being made to reduce the heat bridges of the edge spacers. (Heat Mirror is a registered trademark of Southwall Technologies, Inc.)

487

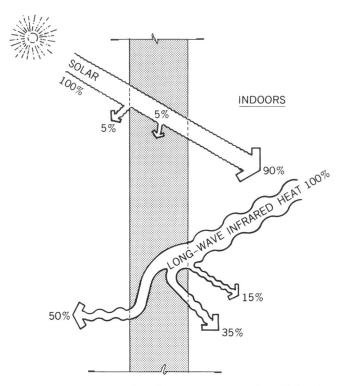

Figure 15.9e Although clear glass transmits most solar radiation, it absorbs most of the long-wave infrared (heat) radiation. Much of this absorbed heat is then lost outdoors. In the summer, the flow of heat radiation is from the outside in.

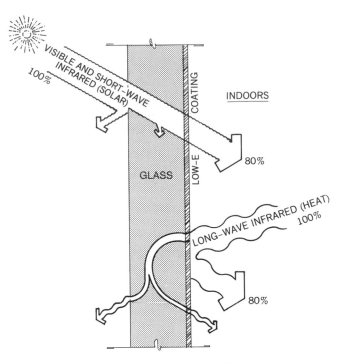

Figure 15.9g Low-e coatings are good for colder climates because they allow high transmission of solar radiation while they reflect heat radiation back inside.

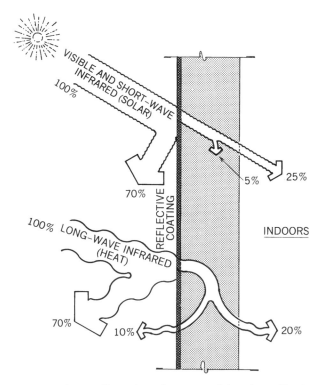

Figure 15.9f A metallic coating reflects most of the solar and heat radiation. Although good in summer, heat gain is also reduced in the winter, and daylighting is lost all year.

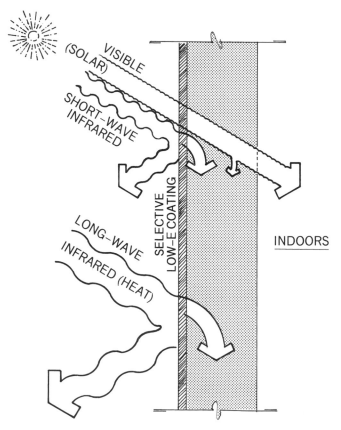

Figure 15.9h When light but not heat is desired, a spectrally selective low-e coating should be used.

low-e described above would be glazing with a high R-value and a high SHGC, while selective low-e would be specified by a high R-value and a low SHGC.

The National Fenestration Rating Council (NFRC), a nonprofit corporation, evaluates and labels windows of many companies. Such ratings promote quality, and NFRC ratings are increasingly being used by energy codes to maintain the minimum quality of construction.

As mentioned before, a dynamic environment requires a dynamic response. During the day, windows are an asset providing views, daylight, and solar heating, but at night, windows are a liability, because the lose light and, in the winter, they also lose heat. Movable insulation can respond to the dynamic needs of windows.

15.10 MOVABLE INSULATION

Movable insulation can greatly improve the performance of windows. The benefits of movable insulation are many: extra insulation on winter nights, higher mean radiant temperature at night, reflection of indoor light (elimination of the black hole effect of windows at night), extra insulation and shading during summer days when view and daylight are not needed (e.g., when no one is home), and aesthetic value.

Movable insulation for windows comes in many forms. Although outdoor shutters also provide extra security, they have limited thermal benefits because the wind tends to short-circuit the thermal performance of the shutters (Fig. 15.10a). Seals are less important indoors, but short-circuiting convection must still be prevented (Fig. 15.10b left).

Drapes with thermal liners are very appropriate since curtains of some kind are often specified anyway for aesthetic and lighting reasons. With an insulating foam or reflective films, drapes or shades can increase the R-value of a window as much as three R-units. Care must be taken, however,

to prevent the short-circuiting of the insulation by sealing the edges. (Fig. 15.10b right). Top and bottom seals are best accomplished by having the drapes extend from the ceiling to the window sill or floor, while magnetic strips or Velcro™ can be used to achieve good edge seals. The drapery should also contain a vapor barrier to reduce condensation on the windows.

Venetian blinds with a reflective coating or with insulated louvers can effectively control daylight, heat gain, and heat loss (Fig. 15.10c). The Hooker Chemical Corporate Office Building Headquarters in Niagara Falls, New York, is an excellent case study for this approach (see Fig. 13.11k).

15.11 INSULATING EFFECT FROM THERMAL MASS

Thermal mass has many benefits. It stores heat for passive solar, can be used as a heat sink for night-flush cooling, can eliminate peak demand due to air conditioning, and can reduce heat gain. Since thermal mass is usually expensive and since it has a high embodied energy content (especially if concrete), it should be used when it provides many benefits. In previous chapters, we have discussed the role of thermal mass for passive solar heating and passive cooling; in the next chapter, we will discuss how thermal mass can reduce peak loads

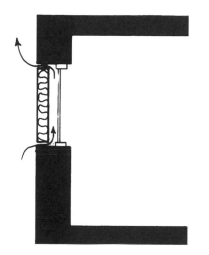

Figure 15.10a Without extra-good seals, the wind will short-circuit exterior insulating shutters.

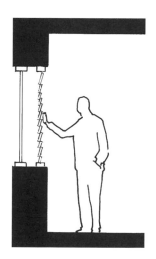

Figure 15.10c Venetian blinds with a reflective coating or insulated louvers can significantly improve the R-value of the windows when they are rotated into the closed position during nights and summer daytimes.

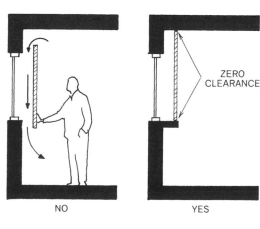

ZERO CLEARANCE

NO   YES

Figure 15.10b Prevent natural convection air currents from short-circuiting movable insulation, such as thermal drapery.

in an air-conditioning system. In this chapter on the thermal envelope, we will discuss how thermal mass can reduce heat gain in certain climates.

The time-lag property of materials can be used to reduce both the peak load and the total heat gain during the summer. Sections 3.18 and 3.19 explained the basic principles behind this phenomenon. The graph in Fig. 15.11a shows the time it takes for a heat wave to flow through a wall or roof. The length of time from when the outdoor temperature reaches its peak until the indoor temperature reaches its peak is called the **time lag.** The graph also shows how the indoor-temperature range is much smaller than the outdoor-temperature range in part because of the moderating effect of the mass. Traditional buildings in hot and dry climates were usually built of stone, soil, or adobe (Fig. 15.11b).

A structure can use thermal mass to reduce heat gain by delaying the entry of heat into the building until the sun has set. Since each orientation experiences its major heat gain at a different time, the amount of time lag required for each wall and roof is different (Fig. 15.11c). North, with its small heat gain, has little need for time lag. The morning load on the east wall must not be delayed to the afternoon because this would make matters only worse. Consequently, either a very long time lag (more than fourteen hours) or a very short time lag is required on the east. Since mass is expensive, mass with a fourteen-hour time lag is *not* recommended on the east. Instead, use either no mass or only a little mass in addition to a lot of insulation.

Although high sun angles reduce the summer heat gain on the south, the load is still significant. To delay the heat from midday until dark, about eight hours of time lag is recommended for the south wall. Although the west wall receives the maximum heat gain, the number of hours until sunset is fairly short. Thus, the west wall also suffices with about eight hours of time lag. Finally, since

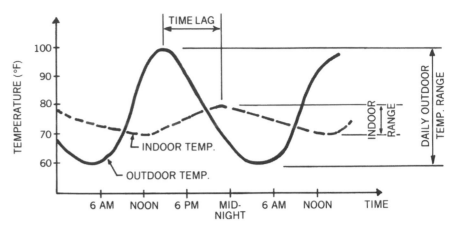

Figure 15.11a The difference between the times when the outdoor and indoor temperatures reach their peaks is called the time lag.

Figure. 15.11b Because adobe (sun-dried mud bricks) is a structurally weak material, the walls must be very thick, which increases adobe's thermal benefits in hot and dry climates. Since mud is an inexpensive material, adobe was popular when labor was also cheap, as seen in this historic New Mexico church.

the roof receives sunlight most of the day, it would require a very long time lag. Because it is very expensive to place mass on the roof, additional insulation rather than thermal mass is usually recommended there (Fig. 15.11c).

To help choose appropriate materials, Table 15.11c gives the time lag for 1-ft (30 cm)-thick walls for a variety of materials.

The time-lag property of materials should not be seen as a substitute for insulation but rather as an additional benefit of massive materials that are used for other purposes, such as heat storage and structural support.

If mass is used, should it be on the inside or on the outside of the insulation? For time-lag purposes, the location of the mass is not critical. On the outside of the insulation, the mass

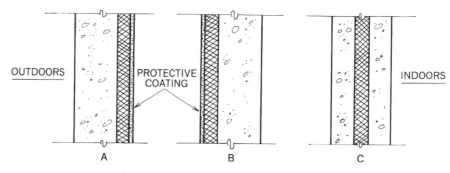

Figure 15.11d The placement of mass relative to the insulation is not critical in regard to time lag but it does have other implications. (A) Mass on outside: good for fire and weather resistance and good for appearance. (B) Mass on inside: good for night-flush cooling, passive solar heating, and peak air-conditioning load reduction. (C) Mass sandwich: for some of the benefits of both A and B.

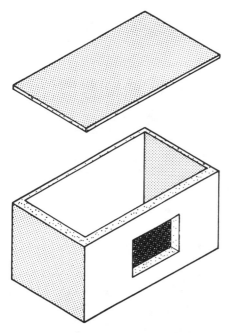

Figure 15.11c In most cases, the south and west walls should have enough mass to yield an eight-hour time lag, while north walls, east walls, and the roof should have little mass for time-lag purposes.

Table 15.11 Time Lag for 1-ft (30 cm)-Thick Walls of Common Building Materials	
Material	**Time Lag (hours)**
Adobe	10
Brick (common)	10
Brick (face)	6
Concrete (heavyweight)	8
Wood	20[a]

[a]Wood has such a long time lag because of its moisture content and high thermal resistance.

can also create an attractive as well as durable, weather-resistant skin. On the inside of the insulation, the mass can support night-flush cooling in the summer and passive solar heating in the winter. In order to achieve all of these benefits, one must often divide the mass by a layer of insulation (Fig. 15.11d).

The importance of light colors in reducing heat gain should not be forgotten. After all, time lag largely postpones heat gain, while light colors significantly reduce the heat gain.

Rules for Thermal Mass

1. Never use thermal mass without insulation.
2. Mass on the indoor side of the insulation is best.
3. Do not insulate the mass from the indoors.
4. Since concrete has a high embodied energy content, it should provide as many benefits as possible.

15.12 EARTH SHELTERING

A survey of indigenous underground dwellings around the world shows that most are found in hot and dry climates. In Matmata, Tunisia, chambers and a central courtyard are carved out of the local sandstone, and access to the 30-ft (9 m)-deep dwellings is by an inclined tunnel. Because of the dry climate, neither flooding nor condensation is a problem. More than 20 ft (6 m) of rock provides sufficient insulation, time lag, and heat-sink capability to create thermal comfort in the middle of a desert (Fig. 15.12a).

To understand the benefits of earth sheltering, one must understand the thermal properties of soil and rock. First, one must recognize that the insulating value of earth is very poor. It would take about 1 ft (30 cm) of soil to have the same R-value as 1 in. (2.5 cm) of wood, and it would take more than 10 ft (3 m) of earth to equal the R-value of an ordinary insulated

stud wall. Thus, earth is usually not a substitute for insulation. What, then, is the main benefit of earth in controlling the indoor environment?

Because of its massiveness, earth offers the benefits of time lag. In small amounts, the soil can delay and reduce the heat of the day just as massive construction, mentioned previously, does. In large quantities, the time lag of soil is about six months long. Thus, deep in the earth (about 20 ft (6 m) or more), the effect of summer heat and winter cold is averaged out to a constant steady-state temperature that is about equal to the mean annual temperature of that climate (see chapter 10, Fig. 10.14a). For example, at the Canadian border, the deep-earth temperature is about 45°F (8°C), while in southern Florida it is about 80°F (27°C) all year. See also the map in Fig. 10.14b for deep-ground temperature throughout the United States.

The ground is, therefore, cooler than the air in summer and warmer than the air in winter. This is a much milder environment than a building experiences aboveground. But the closer one comes to the surface, the more the ground temperature is like the outdoor air temperature. Consequently, the deeper the building is buried in the earth, the greater the thermal benefits. In much of the country, the earth can act as a heat sink to give free cooling, because the deep-earth temperature is sufficiently lower than the comfort zone. Also, the heating load is greatly reduced because the deep-earth temperature is much higher than the winter outdoor air temperature.

There are, however, a number of serious implications for underground construction. The biggest problems come from water. Thus, never build below the water table and avoid wet and humid locations. Have a fool-proof gravity-based way of draining storm water. Keep in mind that wet regions with soils that drain poorly require elaborate waterproofing efforts. Furthermore, in humid climates, condensation can form on the cool walls, causing mold and mildew.

Structural problems increase with the amount of earth cover. The main structural loads to be considered are of three types: weight of earth on roof, soil pressure on walls, and hydrostatic pressure on walls and floor.

Such problems as providing for exit requirements (code) and the psychological needs of people also exist. For example, most people want and need a view of the outdoors.

Where these problems can be solved, earth-sheltered buildings can offer substantial benefits, the greatest of which is security. By its very nature, an earth-sheltered building will be low to the ground and have a substantial structural system. Thus, it offers good protection against such forces as violent storms (tornadoes, hurricanes, lightning), earthquakes, vandalism, bombs (fallout shelter), temperature extremes, and noise (highway or airport) (Fig. 15.12b). In densely populated areas, the greatest benefit might be the retention of the natural landscape (Fig. 15.12c). Finally, from a heating and cooling point of view, these buildings are very comfortable and require substantially less energy than conventional buildings. For example, an underground factory in Kansas City required only one-third the heating and only one-twelfth the cooling equipment of a comparable aboveground building. Thus, earth sheltering also provides security from energy outages, shortages, and price increases.

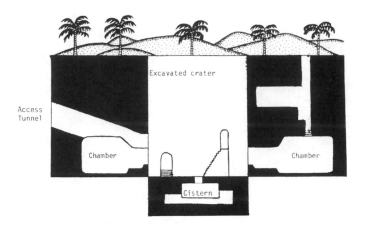

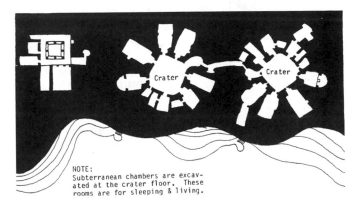

Figure 15.12a In Matmata, Tunisia, chambers and courtyards are cut from sandstone, which functions as both a heat sink and insulation. (From *Proceedings of the International Passive and Hybrid Cooling Conference*, Miami Beach, FL, Nov. 6–16, 1981. © American Solar Energy Society, 1981.)

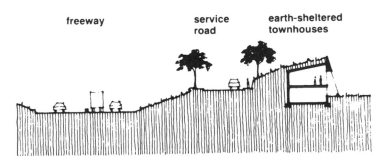

Figure 15.12b In densely populated areas, earth sheltering can help maintain the natural environment as well as protect from noise. (From *Earth Sheltered Housing Code: Zoning and Financial Issues*, by Underground Space Center, University of Minnesota. HUD, 1980.)

Four major schemes for the design of earth-sheltered buildings exist. The **below-grade scheme** offers the greatest benefits but also has the greatest liabilities (Fig. 15.12d). This type is usually built around sunken atriums or courtyards. The problem of flooding from storms can be partially solved by covering the atriums with domes. In the summer, the earth can act as a substantial heat sink and in the winter as an excellent buffer against the cold.

When an earth-sheltered structure is built on sloping land, the **at-grade scheme** is often the most advantageous,

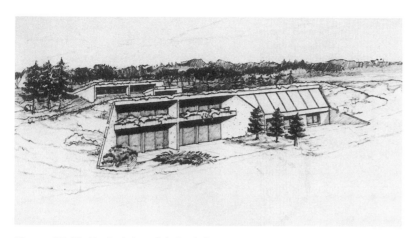

Figure 15.12c Earth-sheltered design helps preserve the natural landscape. ("Design for an Earth Sheltered House." Architect: Carmody and Ellison, St. Paul, MN. From *Earth Sheltered Housing Code: Zoning and Financial Issues,* by Underground Space Center, University of Minnesota. HUD, 1980.)

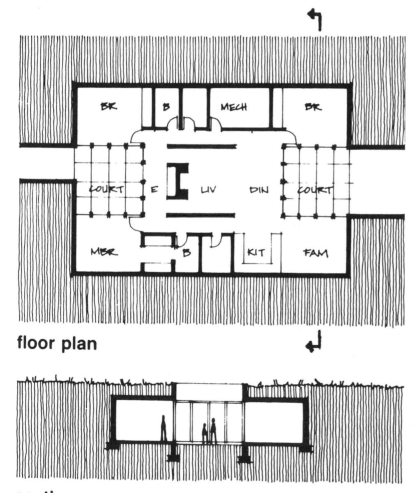

floor plan

section

Figure 15.12d Below-grade scheme: Rooms are arranged around one or more atriums. Drainage and fire exits are major considerations. (From *Earth Sheltered Housing Code: Zoning and Financial Issues,* by Underground Space Center, University of Minnesota. HUD, 1980.)

since water drains naturally, and there is easy access for people, light, and views (Fig. 15.12e). If built on a south slope, close to 100 percent passive solar heating is possible because of both the small heat loss and large thermal-storage mass of the earth.

On flat land, a mound of earth can be raised to protect a building that is built above grade (Fig. 15.12f). This scheme works well in hot and dry climates where time lag from day to night is very helpful.

Finally, one should consider the **berm-and-sod-roof scheme** when many openings are required for light and ventilation (Fig. 15.12g). However, the thermal benefits of earth berms are minimal except on west orientations in hot climates and north orientation to deflect the cold wind in cold climates (Fig. 15.12h). Likewise, sod roofs (green roofs) help only a little in cold climates but can significantly reduce the summer heat gain through the roof. Just 1 to 2 ft (30 to 60 cm) of earth will furnish sufficient daily time lag to reduce the overheating in hot and dry climates. Plants growing on the sod roof or berm will cool the earth by both shading and transpiration.

If berms are to have any benefit, they must be as continuous as possible. Each penetration of the berm is a major weakness, because of the way heat flows through soil. Heat tends to flow in a radial pattern, as shown in (Fig. 15.12i). A cut in the berm creates a thermal weakness not only at the exposed wall, but also in adjacent parts of the wall (Fig. 15.12j). Because of this heat short-circuiting, there should be as few penetrations as possible in any earth cover.

Although many factors determine the appropriateness of earth sheltering, one of the most important is climate. Earth sheltering is most advantageous in hot and dry climates and in regions that have both very hot summers and very cold winters. It is least advantageous in hot and humid regions, where water and mildew problems are common and where natural ventilation is a high priority.

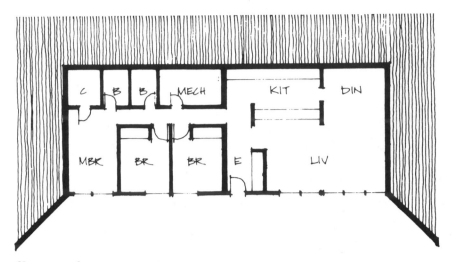

floor plan

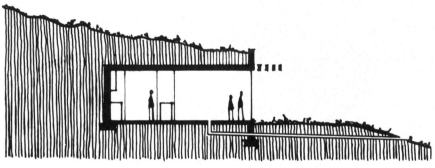

section

Figure 15.12e At-grade scheme:
Drainage, egress, and views are all very
good for an earth-sheltered structure built
at grade on a slope. (From *Earth Sheltered
Housing Code: Zoning and Financial Issues,*
by Underground Space Center, University of
Minnesota. HUD, 1980.)

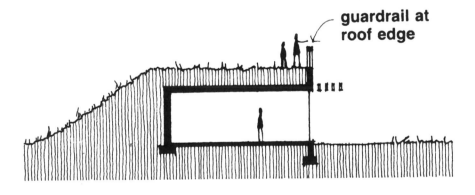

**guardrail at
roof edge**

Figure 15.12f Above-grade scheme:
On flat land with poor drainage, an artificial
mound might be the best strategy. (From
*Earth Sheltered Housing Code: Zoning and
Financial Issues,* by Underground Space
Center, University of Minnesota. HUD, 1980.)

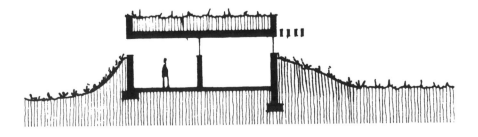

**Figure 15.12g Berm-and-sod-roof
scheme:** When natural ventilation, daylight,
and views are important, berms are appropriate.
Sod roofs (green roofs) are best for protection
from summer heat. (From *Earth Sheltered
Housing Code: Zoning and Financial Issues,*
by Underground Space Center, University of
Minnesota. HUD, 1980.)

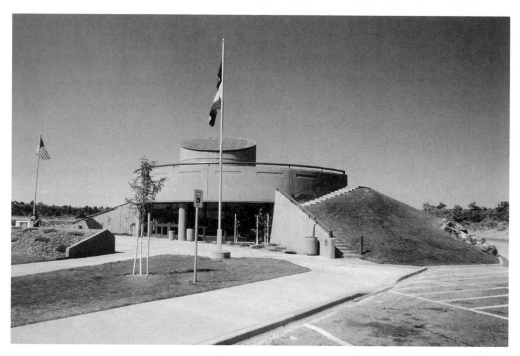

Figure 15.12h This highway rest area in Idaho uses earth berms both to deflect the northerly winter winds and to deflect the hot summer sun from the east and west facades. South glazing collects winter sun, while a south-facing overhang shades the south glazing from the summer sun.

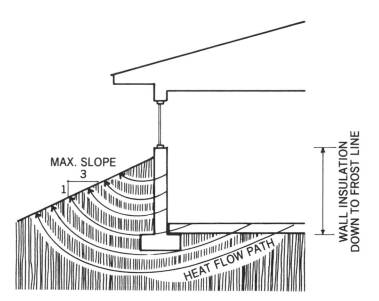

Figure 15.12i Since heat flows through earth in the radial pattern shown, the heat-flow path is quite long at the base of the wall and through the slab edge. Insulation (not shown for clarity) should, therefore, be thickest at the top of the earth-bermed wall.

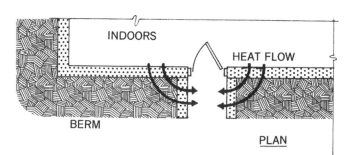

Figure 15.12j Minimize berm penetration because each opening is a major source of heat loss.

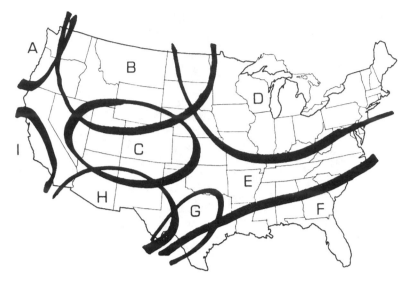

SYNOPSIS OF REGIONAL EARTH TEMPERING ISSUES

A. Cold, cloudy winters maximize value of earth tempering as a heat conservation measure. Cool soil and dry summers favor subgrade placement and earth cover, with little likelihood of condensation.

B. Severely cold winters demand major heat conservation measures, even though more sunshine is available here than on the coast. Dry summers and cool soil favor earth-covered roofs and ground coupling.

C. Good winter insulation offsets need for extraordinary winter heat conservation, but summer benefit is more important here than in zone B. Earth cover is advantageous, the ground offers some cooling, condensation is unlikely, and ventilation is not a major necessity.

D. Cold and often cloudy winters place a premium on heat conservation. Low summer ground temperatures offer a cooling source, but with possibility of condensation. High summer humidity makes ventilation the leading conventional summer climate control strategy. An aboveground super-insulated house designed to maximize ventilation is an important competing design approach.

E. Generally good winter sun and minor heating demand reduce the need for extreme heat conservation measures. The ground offers protection from overheated air, but not major cooling potential as a heat sink. The primacy of ventilation and the possibility of condensation compromise summer benefits. Quality of design will determine actual benefit realized here.

F. High ground temperatures. Persistent high humidity levels largely negate value of roof mass and establish ventilation as the only important summer cooling strategy. Any design that compromises ventilation effectiveness without contributing to cooling may be considered counterproductive.

G. This is a transition area between zones F and H, comments concerning which apply here in degree. The value of earth tempering increases moving westward through this zone and diminishes moving southward.

H. Summer ground temperatures are high but relatively much cooler than those of air. Aridity favors roof mass, reduces need for ventilation, eliminates concern about condensation. Potential for integrating earth tempering with other passive design alternatives is high.

I. Extraordinary means of climate control are not required due to relative moderateness of this zone. Earth tempering is compatible with other strategies, with no strong argument for or against it.

Figure 15.12k A summary of regional issues in regard to suitability of earth sheltering is shown. (From *Proceedings of the International Passive and Hybrid Cooling Conference,* Miami Beach, FL, Nov. 6–16, 1981. © American Solar Energy Society, 1981.)

The map and key in Fig. 15.12k give a more detailed breakdown of regional suitability of earth sheltering.

Rules for Earth Sheltering

1. Never build below or near the water table.
2. Use a gravity-based foolproof system for drainage.
3. It is most appropriate for climates with extreme temperatures.
4. It is least appropriate in wet, humid, and mild climates.
5. The ideal site is on a south-facing hillside where winter heating is needed and on a north-facing hillside where heating is not needed.

15.13 INFILTRATION AND VENTILATION

In a poorly constructed house with no weatherstripping on doors and windows, more than 50 percent of the heat loss can be due to infiltration. Good, tight construction techniques with quality weatherstripped windows and doors can reduce the loss from infiltration to about 30 percent of the total building heat loss, but that is still far too large for a sustainable world. Thus, a well designed air-barrier system is needed that can reduce the infiltration losses to less than 5 percent.

Infiltration is the unplanned introduction of outdoor air through windows, doors, or cracks in the construction due to wind and the stack effect, while the action of exhaust fans is called **ventilation**. In winter, as dry cold air enters, an equal amount of warm, moist air leaves the building (Fig. 15.13a). As a result, latent as well as sensible heat is lost. In summer, hot, moist air infiltrates and cool, dry air is lost. Consequently, the cooling load is also both latent and sensible.

Infiltration is controlled first by avoiding windy locations or by creating windbreaks. Minimizing doors and operable windows helps, but more important is the seal. A poorly fitted, unweatherstripped window has an infiltration rate five times as great as that of an average-fit weatherstripped

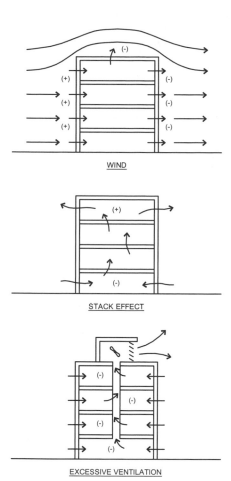

WIND

STACK EFFECT

EXCESSIVE VENTILATION

Figure 15.13a Infiltration is caused by the wind, stack effect, and improper ventilation. The taller the building, the greater the infiltration due to both the wind and the stack effect (see also Section 10.5). Proper ventilation, unlike what is shown, often causes the building to have a positive pressure, which prevents infiltration of outside air.

window. In buildings where doors are opened frequently, a vestibule can cut infiltration by 60 percent and revolving doors can cut infiltration by an amazing 98 percent (Fig. 15.13b).

Because ordinary construction systems have many cracks and porous components, a separate wind barrier is required. A 2005 study by the National Institute of Standards and Technology (NIST) shows that air-barrier systems can reduce air leakage by 85 percent. The most common kind of wind barrier is a woven fabric that comes in 9 or 10 ft (about 3 m) rolls in order to minimize the number of joints. Fabrics are often used because they are permeable to water vapor but resist water and wind. Because wind barriers also have to respond to water, they are discussed in more detail in the next section on moisture control.

When a building becomes very airtight, additional actions must be taken to prevent a new set of problems. Fireplaces and gas heating appliances could be starved for air, odors could build up, and eventually a shortage of oxygen for breathing could result. Often, there is also a problem of indoor air pollution caused by using toxic building materials, furniture, or cleaning materials. Thus, besides avoiding the use of toxic materials, provisions must be made to bring in sufficient fresh air in a controlled manner. This is called **ventilation** and

is described in more detail in the next chapter on mechanical equipment.

15.14 MOISTURE CONTROL

Excess moisture not only adds to the cooling load but also can cause serious problems in buildings. The structure can rust or rot, the insulation can become useless, and the paint can peel. Indoors, windows can fog up, and mold can grow, causing health problems. The moisture can come from the outside or be generated indoors. Although moisture in vapor form can cause mold to grow, it is mainly water in the liquid state inside the building fabric that causes most problems. Moisture can enter the building envelope as either water or water vapor that then condenses. Moisture can enter the building envelope in four ways: bulk moisture, capillary action, air leakage, and vapor diffusion.

1. **Bulk moisture** is liquid water that enters through holes, cracks, or gaps, and it is usually rainwater driven by gravity and wind. Proper design and quality construction will minimize the amount of bulk moisture penetrating the building skin. Every wall should have a **drainage plane** or **drainage cavity** right behind the **rain**

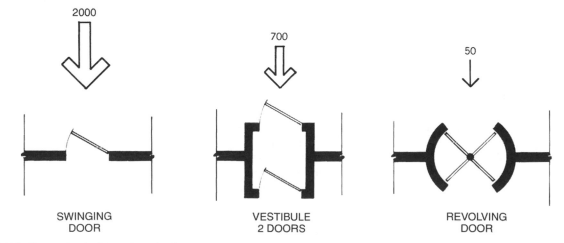

SWINGING DOOR

VESTIBULE 2 DOORS

REVOLVING DOOR

Figure 15.13b The number indicates the cubic feet of air infiltrating due to one-door operation.

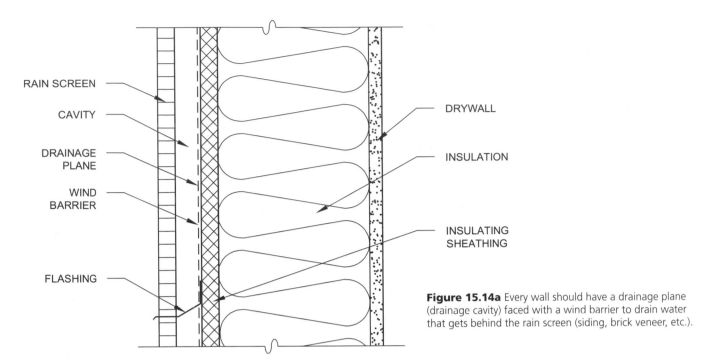

RAIN SCREEN

CAVITY

DRAINAGE PLANE

WIND BARRIER

FLASHING

DRYWALL

INSULATION

INSULATING SHEATHING

Figure 15.14a Every wall should have a drainage plane (drainage cavity) faced with a wind barrier to drain water that gets behind the rain screen (siding, brick veneer, etc.).

screen (siding, brick veneer, etc.) (Fig. 15.14a). On the indoor side of the cavity will be a wind barrier (also sometimes known as "house wrap") that also blocks liquid water. Thus, any water that gets behind the rain screen will flow down the cavity and be diverted back out by flashing. When the rain screen is not masonry, the cavity can be created by vertical furring (spacer) strips or by textured wind barriers that create vertical channels large enough to prevent capillary action (Fig. 15.14b).

2. **Capillary action** moves liquid water through porous materials and tiny holes by the surface tension on the water. The effect is strong enough to move water vertically against gravity. Capillary action is controlled primarily by fully sealing porous materials and tiny holes with some material, such as the asphaltic waterproofing on a concrete foundation wall.

3. **Air leakage** carries water vapor through holes and cracks in the building envelope by the action of the wind, fans, or the stack effect.

The wind barrier described above is designed to minimize air leakage in the building envelope.

4. Water vapor also enters the building fabric because of **vapor diffusion**, which is driven by a difference in vapor pressure. Water vapor moves from a higher concentration of moisture (high vapor pressure) to a lower concentration (low vapor pressure). Generally, that would be outward through the wall in the winter and inward in humid climates in the summer. Recent research has shown that vapor diffusion is much less of a problem than air leakage.

Water entering the building fabric through bulk-moisture flow is immediately ready to cause problems, but water vapor entering through air leakage or vapor diffusion will primarily cause problems if condensation occurs in the wall or roof. Condensation will occur if part of the construction is colder than the dew-point temperature of the moist air.

Condensation inside the building envelope can be prevented by not allowing the indoor air to be cooled to its dew point, also known as the "saturation point," "condensation point," or "100 percent relative humidity point." In regard to the building envelope, this phenomenon can be better understood with the concept of the **thermal gradient,** in which the temperatures across a wall (roof, etc.) are graphed on top of a drawing of the wall (roof, etc.), as shown in Fig. 15.14c. Thus, it is easy to determine the temperature in any part of the construction. For example, the temperature on the indoor side of the Fiberglas batts in Fig. 15.14c is 65°F (18°C), while on the outdoor side of the batts it is about 19°F (−7°C). As the indoor air slowly moves through the wall, its temperature drops, as the thermal gradient indicates. As the indoor air cools, its relative humidity (RH) will increase (see Section 4.5). Eventually, it will reach 100 percent RH, which is also known as the "saturation" or "dew point." At this point, water condenses out of the air and wets the insulation.

Rules to prevent condensation in the building envelope:

1. Use a wind barrier that reduces humid indoor air in the winter

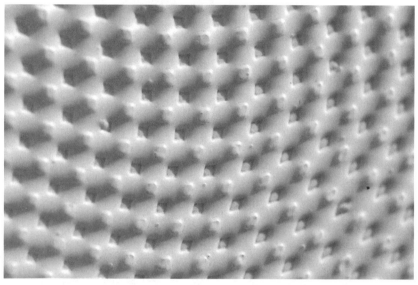

Figure 15.14b Water-resistant barriers in walls must not only stop water transmission but also allow water to drain down and out. Some water-resistant barriers create their own drainage channels (Vortec™ on the bottom and Delta-Dry™ on the top). (Valéron Vortec™ is a trademark of Valéron Strength Films®, an ITW company. Cosella – Dörlken 2006.)

and humid outdoor air in the summer from entering the thermal envelope. Keep in mind that air leakage is a problem 100 times greater than moisture diffusion.

2. Control indoor humidity with exhaust fans in moisture-producing areas such as bathrooms and kitchen stoves (Fig. 15.14d). If the indoor RH is still over 60 percent, use a dehumidifier.

3. Use tight construction to minimize water vapor from entering the building envelope.

4. Consider using insulation that is not porous. Water vapor will not condense in foam insulation because the water vapor can't penetrate the insulation. One of the advantages of SIP panels is that there is no condensation problem. In ordinary construction, an extra-thick layer of insulating sheathing can also prevent condensation in all but very cold climates.

5. In very cold climates, like that of Canada, use a vapor barrier in the location shown in Fig. 15.14c.

6. In cold climates, like that of the northern United States, consider using a "smart" vapor barrier (e.g., MemBrain™) whose permeability increases with the RH and therefore is less likely to trap moisture.

7. In most climates, do not use a vapor barrier because it is likely to trap moisture and prevent the building envelope from drying. A basic rule is never to have two vapor barriers, and since the insulating sheathing acts as a vapor barrier, there should be no other.

8. Design the building envelope so that it can dry out if and when it gets wet. If it dries quickly enough, no or little damage will occur.

9. Use **hygric buffer** materials that have a large moisture-storage capacity, because the stored water is then not available to cause rust, rot, or mold growth. Wood and masonry are excellent hygric buffers.

10. Attics, roofs, and sometimes walls should be vented to prevent water damage (Fig. 15.14e). These vents have the additional benefit of allowing hot air to escape in the summer. See Table 15.14 for recommended attic vent areas. For best results, half of the vent area should be in the soffit and half at the ridge. Continuous ridge vents, as shown in Fig. 15.14f, are very effective and highly recommended, as are aerodynamically designed roof vents (see Chapter 10, Fig. 10.6u). However, electrically powered roof vents are generally not economical.

11. In basements and earth-sheltered buildings, moisture is avoided by good drainage around the walls and carefully installed waterproofing. In buildings with crawl spaces, the soil should be covered with a polyethylene vapor barrier and the crawl space should be vented (see Table 15.14).

Rules for Moisture Control

1. Drain, drain, drain: Get rainwater off and away from the building.

2. Drainage plane: Always have a drainage plane or cavity in walls.

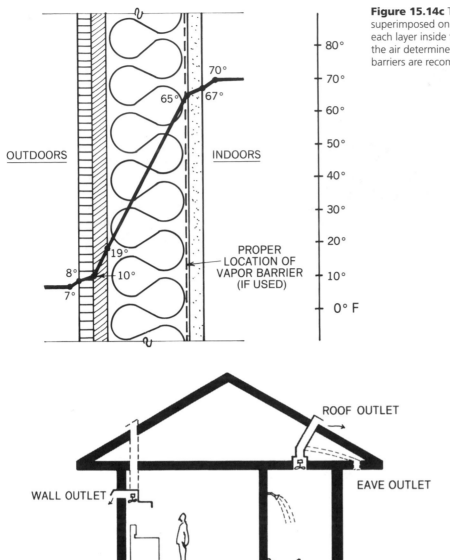

80°
70°
67°
70°
65°
60°
50°
40°
30°
20°
19°
10°
8°
10°
7°
0° F

OUTDOORS

INDOORS

PROPER
LOCATION OF
VAPOR BARRIER
(IF USED)

Figure 15.14c The graph of the thermal gradient, which is superimposed on a wall detail, clearly shows the temperature at each layer inside the construction. The dew-point temperature of the air determines where in the wall condensation will occur. Vapor barriers are recommended only in very cold climates.

ROOF OUTLET

WALL OUTLET

EAVE OUTLET

Figure 15.14d Moisture should be exhausted at the source. Vent it outside and never into the attic.

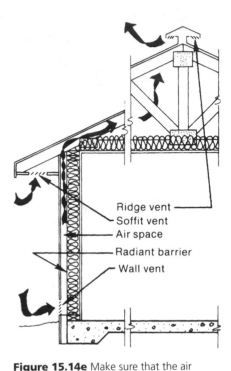

Ridge vent
Soffit vent
Air space
Radiant barrier
Wall vent

Figure 15.14e Make sure that the air flow from soffit to ridge or gable vents is not blocked by the ceiling insulation. When wall vents are used, it is as a passive cooling technique. (From *Cooling with Ventilation*. Golden, CO: Solar Energy Research Institute, 1986 (SERI/SP-273-2966; DE8601 701).)

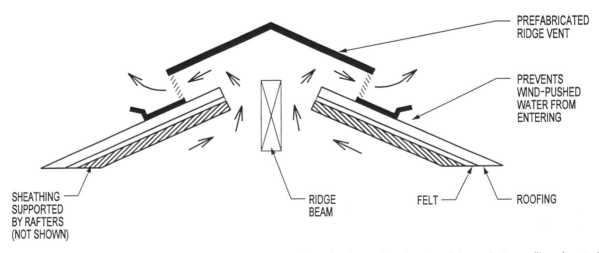

PREFABRICATED
RIDGE VENT

PREVENTS
WIND-PUSHED
WATER FROM
ENTERING

SHEATHING
SUPPORTED
BY RAFTERS
(NOT SHOWN)

RIDGE
BEAM

FELT

ROOFING

Figure 15.14f Continuous ridge vents efficiently evacuate hot and/or moist air by the combined action of the stack, Bernoulli, and venturi effects (See Fig. 10.5l). Ridge vents must be carefully designed to prevent wind-blown water from entering the building.

Table 15.14 Recommended Vent Areas	
Space Vented	**Vent Area/ Floor Area**
Crawl Space*	
No ground cover	1/150
With vapor barrier on ground	1/1500
Attic†	
No ceiling vapor barrier	1/150
With ceiling vapor barrier	1/300

*At least one vent near each corner of crawl space.

†Half at or near the ridge and half at the soffit.

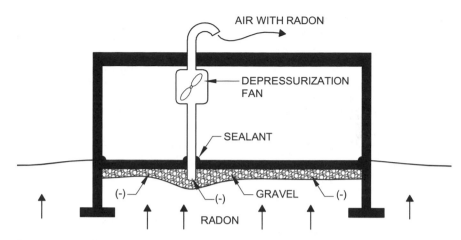

Figure 15.15 When radon is expected or found to be present, all slab penetrations should be sealed particularly well, the building's mechanical equipment should be run at a positive pressure, and the under-slab gravel should be depressurized.

3. Control indoor humidity: Use exhaust fans where humidity is produced.
4. Avoid condensation: Use insulation to prevent humid air from reaching its dew point.

15.15 RADON

The U.S. Surgeon General identified radon as the second leading cause of lung cancer after cigarettes. The element **radon** is a radioactive gas generated in the ground by the radioactive decay of uranium. Because it is a gas, it slowly moves up through the soil into the atmosphere or into a building. Because the stack effect or a faulty air-conditioning system can create negative pressure, radon can be sucked into a building. This problem is most severe with crawl spaces or slabs-on-grade that have many cracks, holes, or joints. Since there is no foolproof method for predicting the absence of radon, crawl spaces should always be vented and slabs well built and sealed. If radon is suspected because of information available before construction or is discovered by testing after the building is completed, then three additional techniques are available: (1) provide extra sealing of radon entry routes; (2) pressurize the building; and (3) depressurize the under-slab gravel (Fig. 15.15).

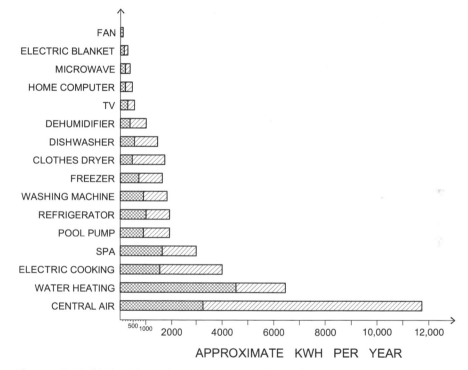

Figure 15.16 This chart shows the approximate annual use of electrical energy (KWH) by appliances in homes. After air conditioning, water heating is the next largest consumer of energy in the home. As mentioned before, active solar collectors should produce hot water. The rest of the appliances use less energy each, but together they are significant consumers of energy. Thus, always use the most efficient appliances possible. Because of the many variables, a range of energy use is given for each appliance.

15.16 APPLIANCES

Appliances vary greatly in the amount of energy they consume and, therefore, the amount of heat they give off. The cost of inefficient appliances is double, since first one must pay for using unnecessary energy and then pay again for extra cooling to have this unnecessary heat removed from the building in the summer.

By law, some appliances, like refrigerators, must state their efficiency with an Energy Efficiency Ratio (EER) label. To further help choose efficient appliances, the U.S. Environmental Protection Agency (EPA) introduced the **Energy Star** program in 1992. Appliances that exceed minimum efficiency standards are given the Energy Star stamp of approval. Thus, only lights and appliances that have the Energy Star label should be bought or specified.

Figure 15.16 is included to help focus attention on those appliances that use the most energy in the home. In residences, hotels, schools, restaurants, prisons, and similar buildings, a great deal of energy is used to heat domestic hot water. All such buildings should use active solar systems to generate most of the hot water needed. As mentioned earlier, the lighting system is often a major energy user and, therefore, also a major source of heat gain. Thus, in all buildings, but especially nonresidential buildings, the lighting system should use daylighting and have lamps of high efficacy and luminaires of high efficiency. By choosing the more efficient appliances, consumers will encourage manufactures to create even more efficient devices.

15.17 CONCLUSION

Every building should be energy-efficient. Such buildings can cost less initially because their heating and cooling equipment is smaller, and they certainly cost less to operate, since their energy bills will be much lower. Not only will owners save money and society save valuable energy, but it is the morally correct thing to do. The future of the planet depends on it.

This discussion on the techniques for keeping warm and staying cool finishes the discussion of that part of the heating, cooling, and lighting of buildings that is primarily in the domain of the architect. Although the mechanical heating and cooling systems discussed in the next chapter are mainly the responsibility of engineers, architects must still help to integrate these systems properly into the building. It is, therefore, vital for architects to have a general understanding of mechanical systems.

KEY IDEAS OF CHAPTER 15

1. Designing the thermal envelope is part of the first tier of the three-tier design approach. The better the thermal envelope, the less heating and cooling will be required.
2. Thermography can be used to find holes or weak areas in the thermal envelope.
3. Heat is lost by transmission through walls, roof, floors, windows, and doors; by infiltration through cracks; and by purposeful ventilation.
4. Heat is gained from transmission, ventilation, solar radiation, appliances, lighting, and people.
5. In most cases, a compact design will use fewer resources than a spread-out, extended design.
6. The extra heating effect of sunlight on a wall or roof is accounted for by the **sol-air temperature.**
7. The **design-equivalent temperature difference** is used when the insulating effect of mass is also considered.

8. In hot climates, use surfaces with high solar reflectivity (albedo).
9. **Thermal planning** arranges building spaces in accordance with their heat and temperature needs as related to solar orientation.
10. Insulation materials consist primarily of very small air spaces separated by a material of low thermal conductivity.
11. Shiny metal surfaces are good radiant barriers because they have both high reflectivity and low emissivity. Radiant barriers are most appropriate under roofs in hot climates.
12. Large air spaces should not be used because their R-value is about the same as that of small air spaces. Large air spaces should be subdivided into as many small air spaces as possible.
13. Log cabins should not be built because they waste wood and have mediocre thermal resistance.
14. Avoid creating heat bridges through the thermal envelope.

15. Structural insulated panels (SIPs) have both high thermal resistance and great structural strength.
16. Low-e, double-glazed (R-3) windows should be the minimum standard in all but the mildest climates.
17. Use high-performance (R-4 and higher) windows whenever possible.
18. Use **selective low-e** glazing when cool daylight is required.
19. Movable insulation over windows can reduce heat loss during winter nights and heat gain during summer days.
20. In hot climates with medium to large diurnal temperature ranges, massive walls will reduce the heat gain by the insulating effect of thermal mass.
21. Earth sheltering is most appropriate in climates with very hot summers and very cold winters. It is least appropriate in wet and humid regions.
22. Use earth sheltering only when positive-gravity drainage is assured.

23. Green roofs are mainly beneficial in reducing heat gain.
24. Moisture can enter a building in four ways: bulk moisture, capillary action, air leakage, and vapor diffusion.
25. Use vapor barriers to prevent condensation inside walls only in very cold climates.

26. Avoid creating excess moisture. Use exhaust fans where large quantities of water vapor are produced.
27. Use eave, ridge, and gable vents to prevent moisture problems in the roof.
28. Use a ground vapor barrier to prevent moisture problems in crawl spaces.

29. Vent crawl spaces to prevent both moisture and radon problems.
30. Infiltration barriers should stop the wind but not water vapor.

References

Akbari, Hashem, and others, eds. *Cooling Our Communities: A Guidebook on Tree Planting and Light-Colored Surfacing.* Washington, DC: EPA and DOE/Lawrence Berkeley Laboratory, 1992 [Lawrence Berkeley Laboratory LBL-31587].

Environmental Building News, October 1998.

Watson, Donald, and Kenneth Labs. *Climatic Design: Energy-Efficient Building Principles and Practices.* New York: McGraw-Hill, 1933.

Resources

FURTHER READING

(See the Bibliography in the back of the book for full citations.)

Boyer, L., and W. Grondzik. *Earth Shelter Technology.*

Brown, G. Z., and M. DeKay. *Sun, Wind and Light: Architecture Design Strategies,* 2nd ed.

Carmody, R. S. *Earth Sheltered Housing Design.*

Carmody, J., Selkowitz, S., Lee, E. S., Arasteh, D., and Willmert, T. *Window Systems for High-Performance Buildings.*

Carmody, J., Chistian, J., and Labs, K. *Builder's Foundation Handbook.*

Carmody R.S., S. Selkowitz, and L. Heschong. *Residential Windows: A Guide to New Technologies and Energy Performance,* 3rd ed.

Easton, D. *The Rammed Earth House.*

Franta, G., K. Anstead, and G. D. Ander. *Glazing Design Handbook for Energy Efficiency.*

Golany, G. *Design and Thermal Performance: Below Ground Dwellings in China.*

Hestnes, A. G., R. Hastings, and B. Saxhof, eds. *Solar Energy Houses: Strategies, Technologies, Examples.*

Houben, H., and H. Guillaud. *Earth Construction: A Comprehensive Guide.*

King, B. *Buildings of Earth and Straw: Structural Design for Rammed Earth and Straw-Bale Architecture.*

Krigger, J. T. *Residential Energy: Cost Savings and Comfort for Existing Buildings.*

Kwok, Alison G., and Walter T. Grondzik. *The Green Studio Handbook: Environmental Strategies for Schematic Design.*

Lstiburek, J. W. *Exemplary Home Builder's Field Guide.*

Lstiburek, J. W. *Builder's Guide to Cold Climates: Details for Design and Construction.*

Lstiburek, J. W. *Builder's Guide to Mixed Climates: Details for Design and Construction.*

Lstiburek, J. W., and J. Carmody. *Moisture Control Handbook: Principles and Practices for Residential and Small Commercial Buildings.*

Matus, V. *Design for Northern Climates: Cold-Climate Planning and Environmental Design.*

Norton, J. *Building with Earth: A Handbook.*

Stein, B., J. S. Reynolds, W. T. Grondzik, and A. G. Kwok. *Mechanical and Electrical Equipment for Buildings,* 10th ed.

Steven Winter Associates. *The Passive Solar Design and Construction Handbook.*

Underground Space Center. *Earth Sheltered Housing Design: Guidelines, Examples, and References.*

U.S. Department of Housing and Urban Development. *Moisture-Resistant Homes: A Best Practice Guide and Plan Review Tool for Builders and Designers with a Supplemental Guide for Homeowners.* www.huduser.org.

Watson, D., and W. M. C. Labs. *Climatic Design: Energy-Efficient Building Principles and Practices.*

ORGANIZATIONS

(See Appendix K for full citations.)

Energy Efficiency & Renewable Energy (U. S. DOE) www.eere.energy.gov

Energy Efficient Building Association www.eeba.org

Southface Energy Institute www.southface.org

MECHANICAL EQUIPMENT FOR HEATING AND COOLING

It is not a question of air conditioning versus sea breezes, or fluorescent tubes versus the sun. It is rather the necessity for integrating the two at the highest possible level.

James Marston Fitch
American Building: The Environmental Forces That Shape It, *1972*

16.1 INTRODUCTION

In most buildings, mechanical equipment (tier 3) is required to carry the thermal loads remaining after the techniques of heat retention or rejection (tier 1) and passive heating or cooling (tier 2) have been applied (Fig. 16.1). With the proper design of the building,

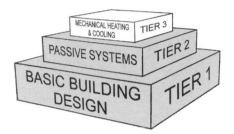

Figure 16.1 The heating and cooling needs of a building are best and most sustainably achieved by the three-tier design approach. This chapter discusses tier 3 (mechanical equipment).

as described in previous chapters, the size and energy demands of the heating and cooling equipment can be quite small. Since the heating and cooling equipment is bulky and must reach into every space, it is an important concern for the architectural designer.

Since the history of heating is much longer than the history of cooling, and since it is simpler to understand, it is discussed first.

16.2 HEATING

Conceptually, heating is very simple: a fuel is burned and heat is given off. The simplest heating system of all is a fire in the space to be warmed.

Until the twelfth century, it was almost universal practice—even in royal halls—to have a fire in the center of the room with the smoke exiting through the roof or a high window (Fig. 16.2a). The central

open fire was not only an efficient heater, it also provided light and a cooking fire. However, the smoke and flying cinders made the concept of cleanliness inconceivable. Around the Mediterranean Sea and in some other warm climates around the world, small portable heaters, such as **charcoal braziers**, were popular (Fig. 16.2b). The Japanese hibachi is a similar device. A real exception to these primitive heating systems was the Roman **hypocaust**, where warm air from a furnace passed under a floor and up through the walls (Fig. 16.2c). Traditional Korean buildings use a similar underfloor heating system. While the Roman hypocaust was only for the rich or the public baths, in Korea it was used by rich and poor alike. The rich had separate heating fires, while the poorer people directed the heat and smoke of their cooking fires under their bedrooms.

Figure 16.2a Some royal halls were still heated by an open fire as late as 1300 A.D. The hall of Penhurst Place. (From *The Mansions of England in Olden Time* by Joseph Nash, Henry Sotheran & Co., 1971.)

Figure 16.2b A portable charcoal brazier was used for heating and cooking.

In Europe the fireplace came about with the invention of the chimney in the twelfth century A.D. Although buildings were now relatively smoke-free, heating them became much harder because the efficiency of fireplaces is very low, about 10 percent. The fireplace remained popular in England because of the relatively mild climate (Fig. 16.2d), but in

Figure 16.2c Roman hypocaust heating. (Courtesy of Wirsbo Company.)

Figure 16.2d In England, fireplaces remained popular because of the relatively mild climate. In colder climates, the ceramic stove was preferred. (From *The Mansions of England in Olden Time* by Joseph Nash, Henry Sotheran & Co., 1971.)

colder parts of Europe, the ceramic stove with its much higher efficiency (between 30 and 40 percent) became popular (Fig. 16.2e).

The English settlers brought the fireplace to the New World, where the endless forests could feed the huge appetite of inefficient fireplaces in cold climates. Around big cities, like colonial Philadelphia, the forests were soon cut down, and an energy crisis developed. Benjamin Franklin responded by inventing a fuel-efficient cast-iron stove.

Franklin realized that the traditional fireplace has several serious deficiencies: it heats only by direct radiation, the hot gases carry most of the heat out through the chimney, and cold air is sucked into the building to replace the warmed room air pulled into the fire to support combustion. Franklin's design addressed all of these issues, and a good modern firepace must do the same. Today, metal fireplace inserts enable room air to circulate around the firebox (Fig. 16.2f). Sometimes a fan is used to increase the heat transfer from the firebox to the circulating room air. A special duct brings outdoor-combustion air to the fireplace. Thus, heated room air is not required to feed the fire. Doors are necessary to prevent any room air from being pulled into the fireplace. Otherwise, even when the fire has died out, the stack effect will continue to pull heated room air out through the chimney. But even with these features, modern fireplaces are still only about 30 percent efficient, while a modern metal stove can have an efficiency as high as 70 percent.

Central heating became quite popular in larger buildings in the nineteenth century. Gravity air and water systems worked especially well in multistory buildings with basements. The furnace or boiler, located in the basement next to the wood or coal bin, heated the air or water to create strong natural-convection currents (Fig. 16.2g). By adding pumps and fans, modern heating systems have become more flexible and respond faster.

Figure 16.2e In northern, central, and eastern Europe, masonry and ceramic stoves were used instead of the inefficient fireplace. Cast-iron and steel stoves are even more efficient because they conduct heat faster through the walls; however, the heavy masonry stoves stored heat for all-night warmth. In very cold climates like that of Russia, people lived and slept on top of very large masonry stoves.

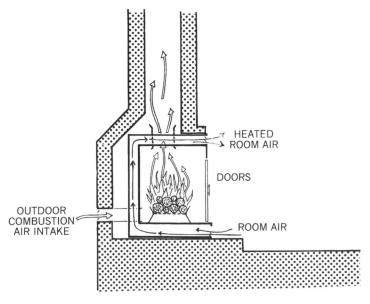

Figure 16.2f A modern, efficient fireplace must have doors, outdoor-combustion air intake, and a firebox around which room air can circulate.

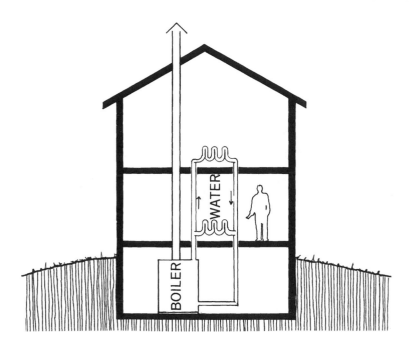

Figure 16.2g The first modern central heating system, which first appeared in the nineteenth century, used gravity hot-air or gravity hot-water systems. Large ducts or pipes allowed natural convection currents to transfer the heat from the basement to the rest of the house.

When choosing or designing a heating or cooling system for a building, one must first know how many different thermal zones are required.

16.3 THERMAL ZONES

Because not all parts of a building have the same heating or cooling demands, mechanical systems are designed to provide separate environmental control to building areas called **zones**. Each zone has a separate thermostat to control the temperature and sometimes a humidistat

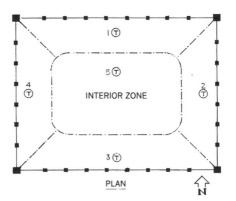

Figure 16.3 A large office building would require at least five zones based on differences in exposure. Each zone will have its own thermostat.

to control the moisture content of the air. One reason for separate zones is the difference in exposure. A north-facing space might require heating, while a south-facing space in the same building requires cooling. A west-facing room might require heating in the morning and cooling in the afternoon. Since interior spaces have only heat gains, they require heat removal all year. Thus, a large office building would be divided into at least five zones on the basis of exposure (Fig. 16.3).

Frequently, additional zones are required because of differences in scheduling and occupancy. For example, a large conference room requires separate thermal control; otherwise, it will be too cold when only a few people are present and too hot when the room is full. Buildings are often zoned on the basis of rental areas, too. The number of zones required is an important factor in choosing a particular mechanical system.

16.4 HEATING SYSTEMS

The two major considerations in choosing a heating system are the source of energy (fuel) used and the method of distribution within

the building. The choice of a fuel usually depends on both economic factors and what is available. The main choices are gas, oil, coal, electricity, solar energy, and the use of waste heat. Except in rural areas, wood is usually too polluting to be a practical fuel. In some areas, wood waste is shredded and compressed into pellets that can be automatically fed into high-efficiency, low-polluting burners.

Oil, coal, wood, bottled gas, and solar energy require building storage space (Fig. 16.4a). Electricity is popular because of its great convenience. Solar energy, the only renewable source in the list, was discussed in Chapters 7 and 8. Waste heat from a combined heat and power (CHP) systems was explained in Section 3.21.

Since the distribution system has a great effect on the architecture, one must select it with care. Heat can be distributed in a building by air, water, or electricity. Because of their large size, air ducts require the most forethought, while electric wires require the least (Fig. 16.4b). The space required for ducts and air-handling equipment varies between 1 and 5 percent of the total volume of a building. The advantages and disadvantages of air, water, and electric distribution systems are summarized in Table 16.4.

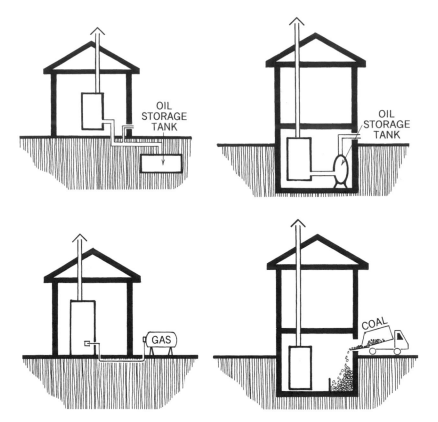

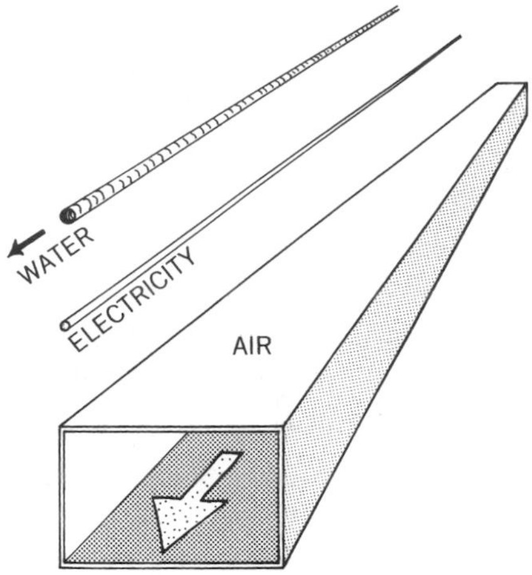

Figure 16.4b An air system requires a substantial amount of a building's volume for ducts and air-handling equipment (1–5 percent), while water and electrical systems require far less.

Figure 16.4a Oil, coal, wood, bottled gas, and solar energy require a significant amount of storage space.

Table 16.4	Heating Distribution Systems	
System	**Advantage**	**Disadvantage**
Air	Can also perform other functions such as ventilation, cooling, humidity control, and filtering. Prevents stratification and uneven temperatures by mixing air Very quick response to changes of temperature. No equipment required in rooms being heated.	Very bulky ducts require careful planning and space allocation. Can be noisy if not designed properly. Very difficult to use in renovations of old buildings. Zones are not easy to create in small buildings.
Water	Compact pipes are easily hidden within walls and floor. Can be combined with domestic hot water system. Good for radiant floor heating. Can be applied directly to cold walls and under windows. Easy zoning. Very quiet.	For the most part, can only heat and not cool (exceptions: fan-coil units and radiant ceiling panels) No ventilation. No humidity control. No filtering of air. Leaks can be a problem. Slightly bulky equipment in spaces being heated (baseboard and cabinet convectors). Radiant floors are slow to respond to temperature changes.
Electricity	Most compact. Quick response to temperature changes. Very easily zoned. Low initial cost. Good for spot heating. Very quiet if there is no fan.	Very expensive to operate (except heat pump). Not sustainable because of low source energy efficiency.

16.5 ELECTRIC HEATING

Although many different types of electric-heating devices exist, most use resistance-heating elements to convert electricity directly into heat. The exceptions are the heat pump and heat from the lighting system.

Figure 16.5a illustrates the general types of resistance-heating devices that are available for heating a room. A great advantage of all the devices shown is that they allow many heating zones to be easily established—each room or part thereof can be a separate zone. Electric boilers or furnaces to heat central hot-water or air systems do not have this advantage. Since electric resistance heating is expensive to operate and wasteful of source energy, one should use it only in mild climates or for spot-heating small areas.

The baseboard units heat by natural convection, while the unit heaters have fans for forced convection. Radiant heating is possible at three different intensities. Because of their large areas, radiant floors and ceilings can operate at rather low temperatures (80° and 110°F [25° and 45°C], respectively). Radiant panels on walls

or ceilings must be hotter (about 190°F [85°C]) to compensate for their smaller areas. They are used to increase the mean radiant temperature (MRT) near large areas of glazing or other cold spots. High intensity infrared lamps operate at over 1000°F (550°C) and, therefore, can be quite small. They look similar to fluorescent fixtures except that the linear quartz lamps glow red hot. These high intensity infrared heaters are designed to not heat air, but rather solid objects, such as walls, furniture, and people. Therefore, these heaters can be used outdoors for purposes such as keeping people warm in front of hotel or theater entrances and for melting snow. They are also often used for outdoor areas of restaurants to extend the hours of use. They are also appropriate in buildings, such as warehouses or aircraft hangars, where it is impractical to heat the air. High intensity infrared heaters can also be powered by gas instead of electricity.

With the above-mentioned resistance-heating devices, one unit of energy in the form of electricity is turned into one unit of heat—a poor choice because high-grade energy is thereby degraded into an equivalent

amount of low-grade energy. However, with a heat pump, about three units of heat energy can be created for every unit of electrical energy used. The secret of this apparent "free lunch" is that the electricity is not converted into heat, but is used instead to pump heat from outdoors to indoors. Heat is extracted from the cold outdoor air and added to the warm indoor air. Thus, in effect, the heat is pumped "uphill," which is what all refrigeration machines do. A heat pump is a special air conditioner running in reverse during the winter.

Heat pumps are appropriate where both summer cooling and winter heating are required. Since the efficiency of heat pumps drops with the outside temperature, they are not appropriate in very cold climates. The efficiency of heat pumps is described by the **coefficient of performance (COP)**, which is defined as

$$COP = \frac{energy\ out}{energy\ in}$$

In mild climates, a COP as high as 4 can be achieved, while in cold climates it will be under 2. Much better efficiencies are possible by coupling the heat pump with the ground rather than the outdoor air because the ground is much warmer in the winter and cooler in the summer. Ground-coupled heat-pump systems will be explained after heat pumps are discussed in Section 16.10.

Although lights are always a source of heat, they are no more efficient than resistance heating elements (COP = 1). There is a system, however, in which the lighting can be efficiently used for heating. In a large office building, a sizable interior zone requires cooling even in the winter (Fig. 16.3). If the warm return air from the core is further heated by being returned through the lighting fixtures, it will be warm enough to heat the perimeter area of the building (Fig. 16.5b). A side benefit of this system is that the lamps and fixtures last longer because they are cooled by the return air.

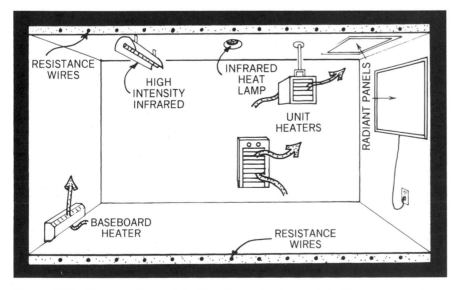

Figure 16.5a The various types of electric resistance heaters located within a room are shown.

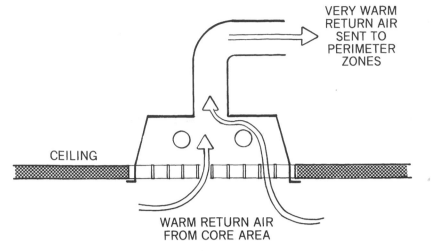

Figure 16.5b Air is heated by returning it through the lighting fixtures. The heated air can then be used to heat the perimeter areas of a building.

Radiant floor heating is a good match for active solar because solar collectors can efficiently produce the relatively low water temperatures needed (about 90°F) [32°C] (see Chapter 8).

Most hot-water systems use convectors to transfer the heat from the water to the air of each room (Fig. 16.6d). In the past, hot-water systems used cast-iron radiators, which, in fact, heated mostly by convection (Fig. 16.6e). Today, most convectors consist of fin-tubes or fin-coils to maximize the heat transfer by natural convection (Fig. 16.6f). Baseboard convectors are linear units placed parallel to exterior walls, while cabinet convectors concentrate the

16.6 HOT-WATER (HYDRONIC) HEATING

Any of the fuels mentioned before can be used to heat water in a **boiler** (Fig. 16.6a). The hot water can distribute the heat throughout the building in several ways.

One of the most comfortable hydronic heating systems is similar to the Roman hypocaust. Instead of fire, hot water is pumped through coils of plastic tubing embedded in the floor (Figs. 16.6b and 16.6c). When concrete slabs are used, the coils can be cast right into the slab. Although less common, radiant floor heating is also possible with wood floors.

A radiant floor will heat the space by both radiation and natural convection. Radiant floors are very comfortable because we enjoy having warm feet and cool heads. For the same reason, radiant ceilings are not very comfortable: they give us a warm head and cool feet. Because the coils are usually embedded in thermal mass, there is a long time lag in receiving heat after the system is turned on. This is an advantage in climates and buildings in which the heating demand is fairly constant, but this time lag is a disadvantage when the heating load is intermittent, and the system must respond quickly.

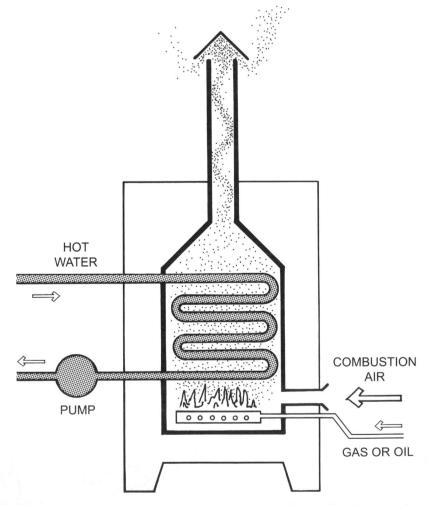

Figure 16.6a A conceptual section of a boiler for a hot-water (hydronic) heating system is shown. Wood pellets can also be used.

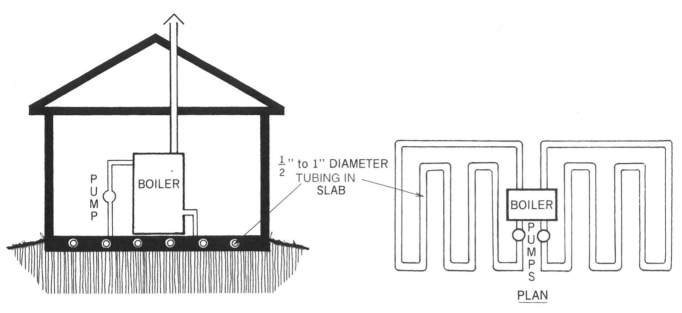

$\frac{1}{2}$'' to 1'' DIAMETER TUBING IN SLAB

PLAN

Figure 16.6b Radiant-floor hot-water heating systems use loops of continuous plastic tubing to minimize joints. A two-zone system is shown.

Figure 16.6c For slab-on-grade, radiant-floor heating, the concrete is poured over the plastic tubing. The various heating zones are made with continuous tubing, with all joints made above the slab to minimize leaks in the concrete.

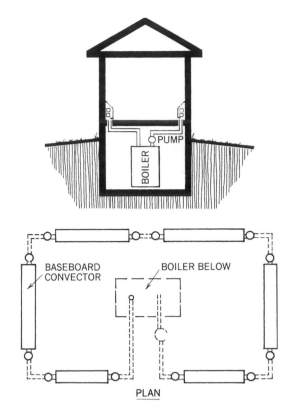

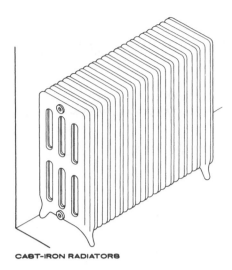

Figure 16.6e Cast-iron radiators heat primarily by convection. (From *Architectural Graphic Standards,* Ramsey/Sleeper 8th ed., John R. Hoke, editor, © John Wiley & Sons, Inc., 1988.)

Figure 16.6d A hot-water system with baseboard convectors, is shown.

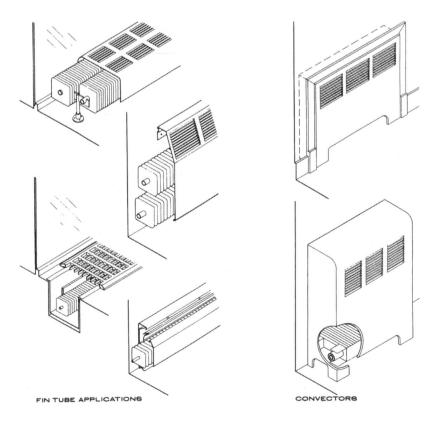

FIN TUBE APPLICATIONS

CONVECTORS

heating where it is most needed—under windows to counteract the cold downdraft and low MRT of the windows. When there is a large area of glazing from floor to ceiling, a below-floor convector can be used.

Most convectors are designed to be as unobtrusive as possible because it is assumed that mechanical equipment must be ugly. Some architects and manufacturers take a different approach, as can be seen in the elegant radiator/convectors in Fig. 16.6g.

Because convectors rely on natural convection, they must be placed low in a room. However, if a fan is used for forced convection, any mounting position is possible. Because such fan-coil units can also be used for cooling, they are discussed under cooling systems.

Figure 16.6f Baseboard convectors are unobtrusive but can be blocked by furniture. Cabinet convectors are usually placed under windows. Underfloor convectors are appropriate for areas with floor-to-ceiling glass. (From *Architectural Graphic Standards,* Ramsey/Sleeper, 8th ed., John R. Hoke, editor, © John Wiley & Sons, Inc., 1988.)

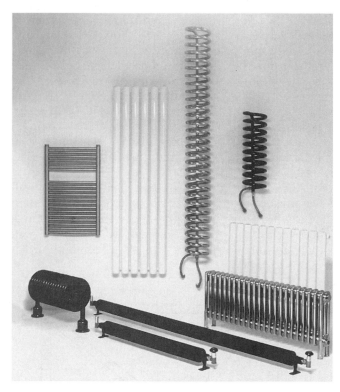

Figure 16.6g These sculptural, elegant convector/radiators are designed to be exposed to view. (Courtesy 3-D Laboratory, Inc.)

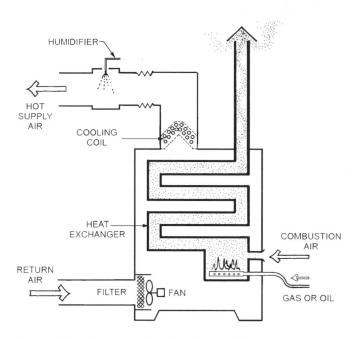

Figure 16.7a A conceptual section of a hot-air furnace with optional cooling coils and humidifier is shown.

16.7 HOT-AIR SYSTEMS

Air systems are popular because they can perform the whole range of air-conditioning functions: heating, cooling, humidification, dehumidification, filtering, ventilation, and air movement to eliminate stagnant and stratified air layers. Hot-air heating systems are especially popular where summer cooling is also required. Those hot-air systems that supply air at or near floor level around the perimeter of the building are most suitable for cold climates, where the heating season is the main consideration. These systems are discussed here, while those more suitable for hot climates will be discussed along with other cooling systems.

A hot-air furnace uses a heat exchanger to prevent combustion air from mixing with room air. A blower and filter are standard, while a humidifier and cooling coil are optional (Figs. 16.7a and b). Gas furnaces can be very efficient. Some pulse-type gas furnaces convert more

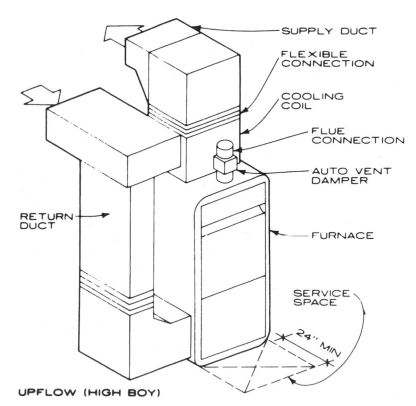

Figure 16.7b An isometric of a hot-air furnace with a cooling coil is shown. (From *Architectural Graphic Standards,* Ramsey/Sleeper, 8th ed., John R. Hoke, editor, © John Wiley & Sons, Inc., 1988.)

than 95 percent of the gas energy into useful heat.

For slab-on-grade construction in cold climates, the **loop-perimeter system** offers the greatest thermal comfort (Fig. 16.7c). The supply air heats the slab where it is coldest—at the edge. Thus, this system offers the benefits of both hot-air and radiant-slab heating. The main disadvantage is the high initial cost of the system.

The **radial-perimeter system** is a less expensive but also less comfortable way to heat slab-on-grade construction with hot air. This system is more suitable for crawl space construction (Fig. 16.7d). If the crawl space is high enough (about 4 ft), a special horizontal furnace can be used (Fig. 16.7e). The same horizontal furnaces are sometimes also used in attic spaces. The author has crawled through spaces so tight that it was a puzzle how the equipment and ducts were ever installed. Of course, the craftsmanship was very poor and the duct work was very leaky, which is not just inefficient but unhealthy, as will be explained later. Thus, the architect's design must also consider installation and servicing. By far the best solution, however, is to keep the ducts and equipment within the thermal envelope.

The **extended-plenum system** is appropriate for buildings with basements because it enables the supply ducts to run parallel and between the joists; consequently, much space and headroom are saved (Fig. 16.7f). With the emphasis on health and energy efficiency, it is increasingly common to use the extended-plenum system within the thermal envelope (Fig. 16.7g).

For heating single spaces, a **wall furnace** can be a practical solution because no duct work is required. When powered by gas, these wall furnaces can draw combustion air

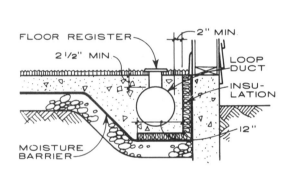
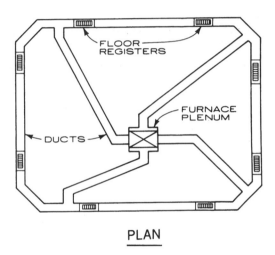

Figure 16.7c A loop-perimeter system for slab-on-grade construction is shown. (From *Architectural Graphic Standards,* Ramsey/Sleeper, 8th ed., John R. Hoke, editor, © John Wiley & Sons, Inc., 1988.)

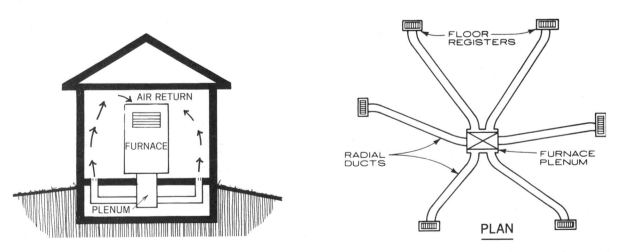

Figure 16.7d A radial-perimeter system for crawl space construction is shown. (From *Architectural Graphic Standards,* Ramsey/Sleeper, 8th ed., John R. Hoke, editor, © John Wiley & Sons, Inc., 1988.)

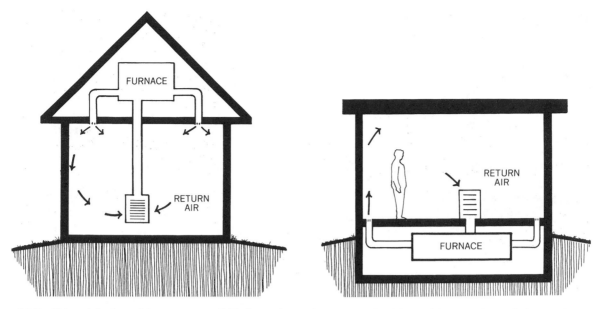

Figure 16.7e Although horizontal furnaces are available for use in crawl spaces or attics, it is much better to have all ducts and equipment within the thermal envelope for both health and efficiency reasons.

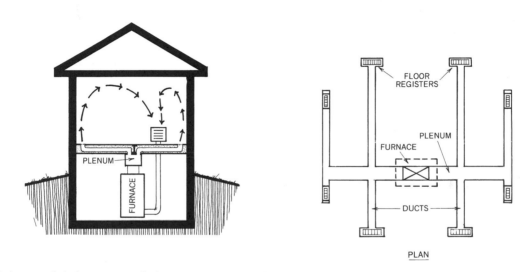

Figure 16.7f The extended-plenum system for basement construction has the supply ducts run parallel and between joists to save on headroom.

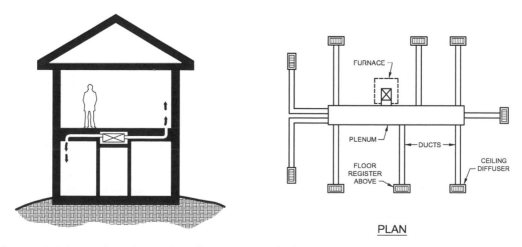

Figure 16.7g The extended plenum above the corridor ceiling system provides both health and energy efficiency benefits.

517

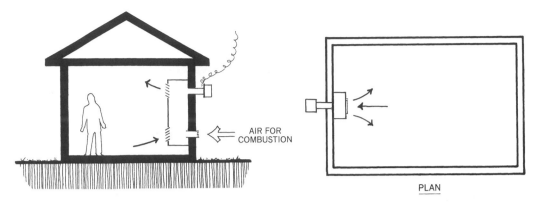

Figure 16.7h Wall furnaces can be appropriate for heating single spaces.

AIR FOR COMBUSTION

PLAN

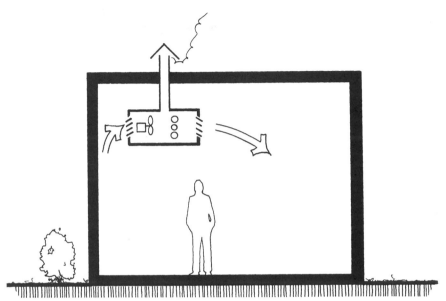

Figure 16.7i Unit heaters can be appropriate for spaces with high ceilings. A fan forces the hot air down. The heat source can be electricity, hot water, or gas. If gas is used, the heater must be vented.

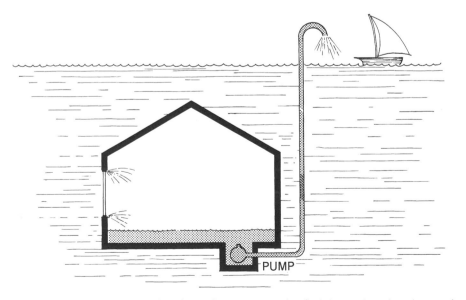

PUMP

Figure 16.8a In the water analogy for cooling, any water that finds its way into the submerged building must be pumped "uphill" to get it out.

and vent directly through the wall on which they are attached (Fig. 16.7h).

In utility spaces with high ceilings, **unit heaters** powered by gas, electricity, or hot water are often appropriate because they take up no floor area (Fig. 16.7i).

16.8 COOLING

Cooling is not as intuitively clear and simple as heating. Cooling, the removal of heat, can be better understood by means of a water analogy. A building in the summer is surrounded by heat trying to get in, just as water tries to get into a submerged building (Fig. 16.8a). The water in the analogy is gained both through the envelope and from internal sources. The natural tendency is for the water to flow into the building. Only by pumping it uphill can it be removed again.

In the same way, the natural tendency is for heat to flow inward when the outdoor temperature is higher than the indoor temperature. The only way to remove the heat is with a machine that pumps heat from a lower temperature to a higher temperature. Such a device is called a **refrigeration machine** (Fig. 16.8b). Before the invention of refrigeration machines about 150 years ago, there was no way to actively cool a building. Although blocks of ice harvested in winter could cool a building, the huge amount of ice required made that impractical on all but the smallest scales. One of the big trade items in the nineteenth century was

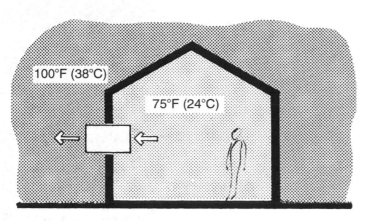

Figure 16.8b A refrigeration machine pumps heat from a lower to a higher temperature (e.g. 75° to 100° F) (24°–38°C).

ice, which was harvested from New England lakes in the winter and shipped to the South in the summer. Because of ice's high cost, it was primarily used for cooling drinks.

Until the late nineteenth century, the only way to achieve some summer comfort was to use the heat-rejection and passive-cooling techniques mentioned previously. Shading, natural ventilation, evaporative cooling, and thermal mass were the main techniques used.

In the 1840s, Dr. John Gorrie, a physician in Apalachicola, Florida, built the first refrigeration machine in an attempt to help his patients suffering from malaria. Although his machine worked, it was not used to cool buildings until the 1920s, when a new type of building had a special need for air conditioning. Because movie houses had to close their windows to keep the light out, they also kept the cooling breezes out. So, most people had their first experience with air conditioning at movie houses, where the marquees announced "air conditioned" in larger letters than the titles of the movies. Although air conditioning was still considered a luxury in the United States in the 1950s, it is now considered a necessity.

16.9 REFRIGERATION CYCLES

The refrigeration machine, which pumps heat, is the critical element of any cooling system. There are basically three refrigeration methods: vapor compression, absorption, and thermoelectric. The compression cycle is the most common, but the absorption cycle is often appropriate when a source of low-cost heat is available.

The thermoelectric cycle, which turns electricity directly into heating and cooling effects, is not used for buildings.

The Vapor Compression Refrigeration Cycle

The **vapor compression refrigeration cycle** depends on two physical properties of matter:

1. A large amount of **heat of vaporization** is required to change a liquid into a gas. Of course, this heat is released again when the gas condenses back into a liquid.
2. The boiling/condensation temperature of any material is a function of pressure. For example, 212°F (100°C) is the boiling point of water only at the pressure of sea level (14.7 lb/in.²) (101 KPa). When the pressure is reduced, the boiling point is also reduced.

The basic elements of a compression refrigeration machine are shown in Fig. 16.9a. Imagine that the valve is closed and the compressor has pumped most of the refrigerant into the condenser coil. When the valve is slightly opened, only a small stream of liquid refrigerant can enter the partial vacuum of the evaporator coil at point C (Fig. 16.9b). The refrigerant boils (evaporates) due to the very low pressure. To change state, the liquid will require the large amount of heat called "heat of vaporization." Thus, the evaporator coil will cool as it gives up its sensible heat to allow the liquid refrigerant to change into a gas (i.e., boil).

To keep the process going, the compressor continues to pump the refrigerant gas back into the condenser coil. A high pressure gas collects at point A. Since any gas under pressure heats up, the condenser coil gets hot. As the coil loses heat, the high pressure refrigerant gas will be able to condense and give up its heat of vaporization. Thus, a warm, high pressure liquid will collect at point B. The cycle now repeats as a small amount of liquid refrigerant enters the evaporation coil at point C and evaporates to collect as a low pressure gas at point D.

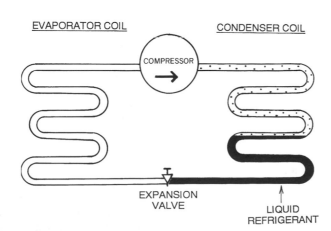

Figure 16.9a The basic components of a compressive refrigeration machine are shown.

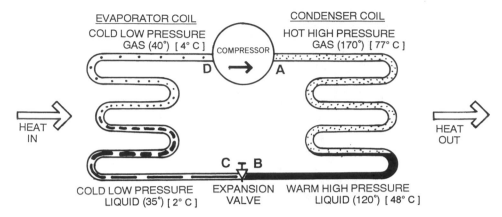

Figure 16.9b Where the refrigerant evaporates it absorbs heat (cools), and where it condenses it gives off heat.

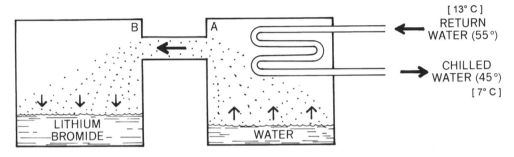

Figure 16.9c The first two chambers of an absorption refrigeration machine are shown.

Almost all refrigerants were made of **chlorofluorocarbons (CFCs)** until 1987, when the world agreed through the Montreal Protocol to phase out these ozone-damaging compounds.

New refrigerants made of **hydrofluorocarbons (HFCs)** are 90 percent less damaging to the ozone, but are still significant greenhouse gases when they escape from refrigeration machines. Other possible refrigerants include ammonia, propane, and isobutane, but these are all flammable, and ammonia is also toxic.

The Absorption Refrigeration Cycle

The **absorption refrigeration cycle** depends on the same two properties of matter described above for the compressive cycle, as well as a third property:

3. Some liquids have a strong tendency to absorb certain vapors. For example, water vapor is absorbed by liquid lithium bromide or ammonia.

The absorption refrigeration machine requires no pumps or other moving parts, but it does require a source of heat such as a gas flame or the waste heat from an industrial process. The machine consists of four interconnected chambers, of which the first two are shown in Fig. 16.9c.

In chamber A, water evaporates and in the process draws heat from the chilled water coil (output). The water vapor migrates to chamber B, where it is absorbed by the lithium bromide. Consequently, the vapor pressure is reduced, and more water can evaporate to continue the cooling process. Eventually, the lithium bromide will become too dilute to further absorb water. In chamber C (Fig. 16.9d), an external heat source boils the water off the lithium bromide. The concentrated lithium bromide is then returned to chamber B, while the water vapor is condensed back into water in chamber D. The last step is to return the liquid water back to chamber A so that the cycle can continue.

Because the absorption refrigeration-machine cycle is inherently inefficient, the cycle is economical only when an inexpensive source of heat is available. Solar-heated water may become such a source of heat when collectors are mass-produced and electricity becomes more expensive. Although the vapor compression cycle is more efficient, it requires a source of mechanical power, which is supplied by an electric motor running on valuable electricity.

In the vapor compression cycle, the power is required to drive refrigerant pumps that are of the reciprocating, scroll/screw, or centrifugal types. The reciprocating compressor is most appropriate for small to medium-sized buildings, while the centrifugal compressor is best for medium-sized to large buildings. When any of these refrigeration machines are used to chill water, they are known as **chillers.**

Sometimes **evaporative coolers** are included in a discussion of refrigeration machines. Although evaporative coolers often replace air conditioners in

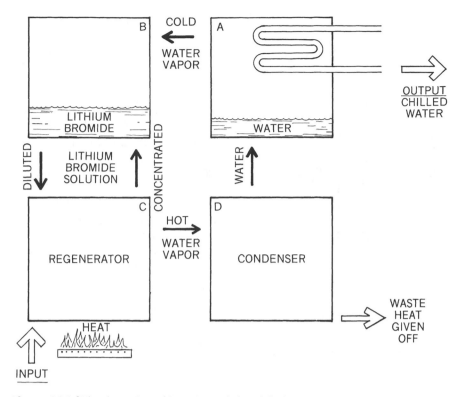

Figure 16.9d The absorption refrigeration cycle has chilled water as an output and a heat source as an input. Waste heat is given off in the process.

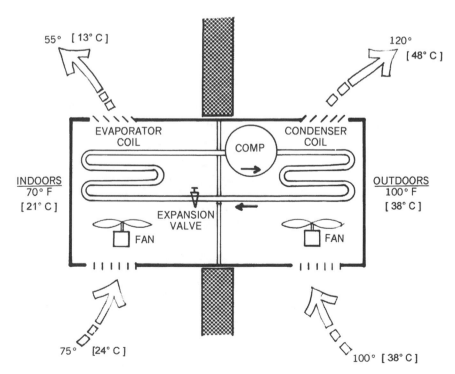

Figure 16.10a A simple through-the-wall air-conditioner unit essentially consists of a vapor compression refrigeration machine.

dry climates, most types do not remove total heat from a building. Instead, they convert sensible heat into latent heat, which in dry climates creates thermal comfort very economically. Because of their mechanical simplicity, they were discussed with other passive cooling systems in Chapter 10 (see Fig. 10.12a).

16.10 HEAT PUMPS

Every compressive refrigeration machine pumps heat from the evaporator coil to the condenser coil. Figure 16.10a illustrates a simple through-the-wall or window air-conditioner unit that is essentially a refrigeration machine. One fan cools indoor air by blowing it across the cold evaporator coil, while another fan heats outdoor air by blowing it across the condenser coil.

What would happen if the air-conditioning unit were turned around so that the evaporator coil were outdoors and the condenser coil were indoors? The outdoor air would then be cooled, and the indoor air would be heated—just what is needed in the winter.

Instead of turning the whole unit around, it is much easier to just reverse the flow of refrigerant. That also makes it unnecessary to go outside in the winter to reach the controls. A refrigeration machine in which the flow of refrigerant can be reversed is called a **heat pump.** The term is unfortunate because every refrigeration machine pumps heat, even if it is only in one direction. Heat pumps use reversing valves to change the direction of refrigerant flow (Fig. 16.10b).

Heat pumps are air conditioners that can switch to heating in the winter. Since, however, they extract heat from outdoor air, their efficiency drops as the outdoor air gets colder. Thus, heat pumps are most appropriate in those climates where summer cooling is required and where the winters are not too cold. Much of the United States fits into this category. When heat pumps are coupled with the ground instead of outdoor air, they are called "geo-exchange heat pumps."

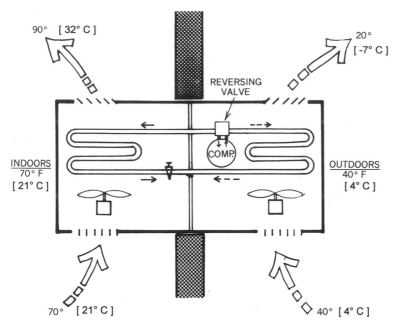

Figure 16.10b In a heat pump, the reversing valve allows the refrigerant to flow in either direction. In the winter condition shown, the outdoor coil becomes the evaporator and the indoor coil the condenser. An air-to-air heat pump is shown. In a ground-coupled heat pump, water would transfer the heat between the outdoor coil and the ground.

16.11 GEO-EXCHANGE

According to the Environmental Protection Agency (EPA), **geo-exchange** heat pumps are in many cases the most energy-efficient, environmentally clean, and cost-effective active space conditioning systems available.

Geo-exchange heat pumps are also known as **geothermal** or **ground-coupled** heat pumps. "Ground-coupled" is a good descriptive term, but "geothermal" is not because it is already in use to describe high-temperature heat obtained from deep within the earth (see the end of Section 2.18).

"Geo-exchange" is an excellent term, because in the summer, heat pumps move heat from indoors to the ground, which acts as a heat sink, and in the winter, the heat is moved back from the ground and pumped indoors again— a seasonal exchange with the earth (*geo*).

Water is used to transfer the heat from the heat pump to and from the upper layer of the earth (less than 100 ft (30 m). Four different methods are available, and the best choice depends on the local conditions. If a pond is available, it can be the most convenient heat source/heat sink (Fig.16.11a). Where groundwater is plentiful and well drilling is easy, an open-loop system can be used; here, the water is pumped out of the ground at one well and returned at another well (Fig. 16.11b). A closed vertical loop is usually preferred because much less pumping energy is required (Fig. 16.11c).

Vertical closed loops are preferred over horizontal closed loops because the deep ground is warmer in the winter and cooler in the summer than the shallow ground (see Section 10.14). Drilling deep holes can be expensive, however, especially if the ground is rocky. In such a case, if the site is large enough, horizontal loops in fairly deep trenches might be the most cost-effective alternative (Fig. 16.11d).

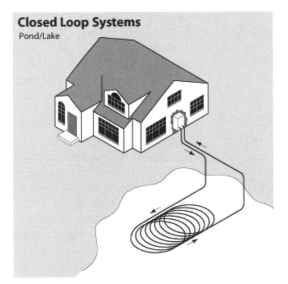

Figure 16.11a A geo-exchange heat-pump system can use a pond as the heat source/heat sink. (From U.S. Dept. of Energy, Office of Geothermal Technologies.)

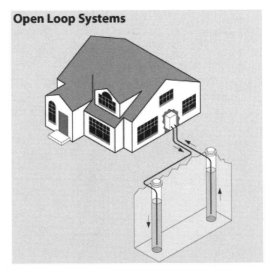

Figure 16.11b A geo-exchange heat-pump system can use groundwater as the heat source/heat sink. The water should be returned to the ground via a second well. (From U.S. Dept. of Energy, Office of Geothermal Technologies.)

Closed Loop Systems
Vertical

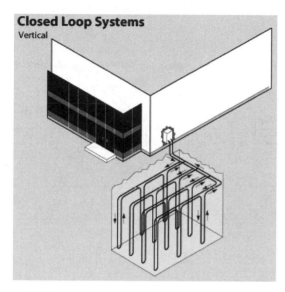

Figure 16.11c In most cases, vertical loops are the best option for geo-exchange heat pumps. (From U.S. Dept. of Energy, Office of Geothermal Technologies.)

Closed Loop Systems
Horizontal

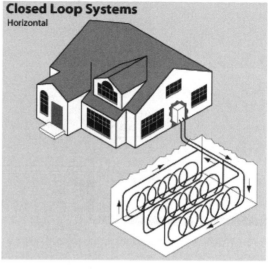

Figure 16.11d When soil conditions make vertical loops impractical, horizontal loops are acceptable. Trenches should be as deep as possible to obtain the best soil temperatures. (From U.S. Dept. of Energy, Office of Geothermal Technologies.)

Since ground-coupled heat pumps are indoors, protected from the elements, they last much longer and require much less maintenance than conventional air conditioners. These pumps also have the aesthetic advantages of being hidden indoors and of making almost no noise. During the summer, the heat removed from indoors is first used to heat hot water, in effect yielding free domestic hot water. A device called a **desuperheater** is added to a standard heat pump to heat the hot water. The rest of the year, the domestic hot water is heated efficiently from the ground like the rest of the building. The greatest benefit of geo-exchange heat pumps is their high efficiency. They use about 40 percent less energy than air-to-air heat pumps and about 70 percent less energy than standard air conditioning with electric resistance heating. Because ground temperatures are less extreme than air temperatures, geo-exchange heat pumps are appropriate in all but the coldest parts of the United States, and new types of heat pumps may even work there.

16.12 COOLING SYSTEMS

To cool a building, a refrigeration machine must pump heat from the various rooms into a heat sink. The heat sink is usually the outdoor air but can also be a body of water or the ground (Fig. 16.12a). Cooling

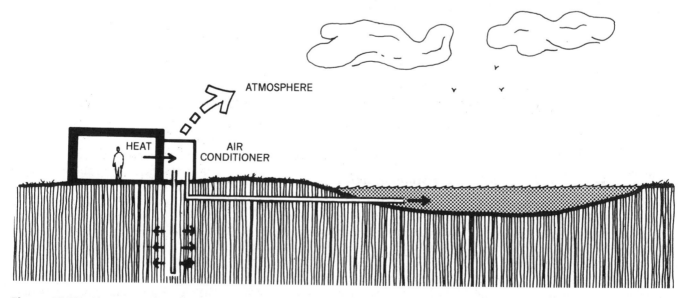

Figure 16.12a Air, water, or the ground can act as the heat sink for a building's cooling system.

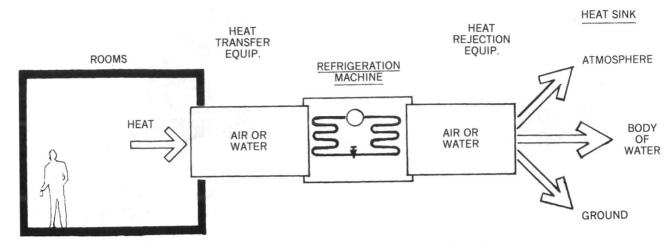

Figure 16.12b Cooling systems vary mainly in how heat is transferred to and from the refrigeration machine.

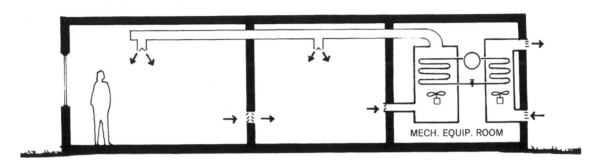

Figure 16.12c A schematic diagram of an all-air system is shown.

systems vary mostly by the way heat is transferred from the rooms to the refrigeration machine and from there to the heat sink (Fig. 16.12b). The choice of the heat-transfer methods depends on building type and size. Cooling systems are often classified by the fluids used to transfer the heat from the habitable spaces to the refrigeration machine. The four major categories are direct refrigerant, all-air, all-water, and combination air–water.

Direct Refrigerant Systems

The **direct refrigerant** or DX (direct expansion) **system** is the simplest, because it consists of little more than the basic refrigeration machine plus two fans. The indoor air is blown directly over the evaporator coil, and the outdoor air passes directly over the condenser coil (Fig. 16.13a and f). Direct refrigerant units are appropriate

for cooling small to medium-sized spaces or zones that require their own separate mechanical units.

All-Air Systems

In an all-air system, air is blown across the cold evaporator coil and then delivered by ducts to the rooms that require cooling (Fig. 16.12c). Air systems can effectively ventilate, filter, and dehumidify air. The main disadvantages are the bulky ductwork and large fan power required.

All-Water Systems

In an all-water system, the water is chilled by the evaporator coil and then delivered to fan-coil units in each space (Fig. 16.12d). Although the piping in the building takes up very little space, the fan-coil units in each room do require some space.

Another advantage of the all-water system is the small amount of energy required by the pumps as compared with fans. However, since ventilation must be supplied from windows, the all-water system is usually not suitable for interior rooms.

Combination Air–Water Systems

An air–water system is a combination of the above-mentioned air and water systems (Fig. 16.12e). The bulk of the cooling is handled by the water and fan-coil units, while a small air system completes the cooling and also ventilates, dehumidifies, and filters the air. Since most of the cooling is accomplished by the water system, the air ducts can be quite small.

The above systems describe how heat is transferred from building spaces to the refrigeration machine. The following discussion describes

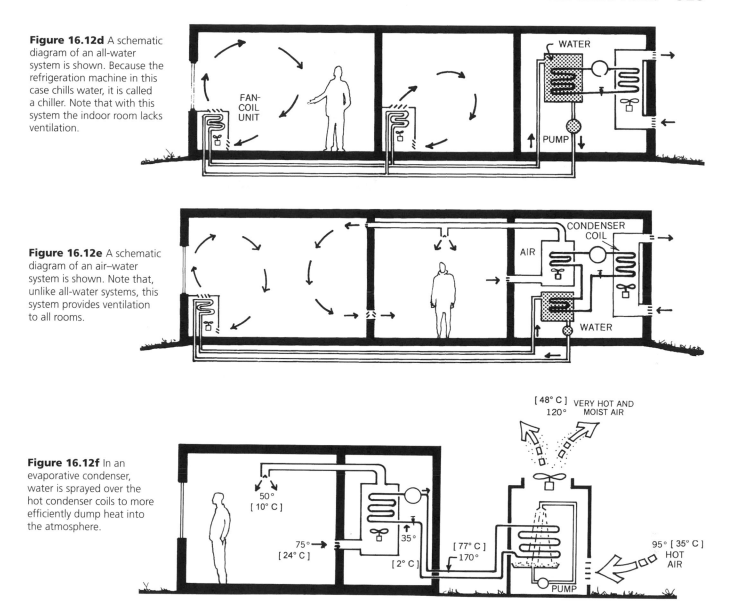

Figure 16.12d A schematic diagram of an all-water system is shown. Because the refrigeration machine in this case chills water, it is called a chiller. Note that with this system the indoor room lacks ventilation.

Figure 16.12e A schematic diagram of an air–water system is shown. Note that, unlike all-water systems, this system provides ventilation to all rooms.

Figure 16.12f In an evaporative condenser, water is sprayed over the hot condenser coils to more efficiently dump heat into the atmosphere.

how the heat from the refrigeration machine is dumped into the atmospheric heat sink.

Heat-Dumping Systems

In small buildings, the heat given off by a refrigeration machine is usually dumped into the atmosphere by blowing outdoor air over the condenser coil (Fig. 16.12e). To make this heat transfer more efficient, water can be sprayed over the condenser coil. Medium-sized buildings often use a specialized piece of equipment called an **evaporative condenser** to dump heat into the

atmosphere by evaporating water (Fig. 16.12f). A small amount of water must be continuously supplied to replace the water lost by evaporation. Since refrigerant lines are limited in length because of pressure loss due to friction, an evaporative condenser cannot be more than about 60 ft (18 m) from the compressor and evaporator coil. Thus, for large buildings, cooling towers are frequently a better choice.

A **cooling tower** also dumps heat into the atmosphere via the evaporation of water. However, the evaporating water is used to cool more water rather than refrigerant, as in

the evaporative condenser. This cooling water is then pumped to the refrigeration machine, where it cools the condenser coil (Fig. 16.12g). Although most of the water is recirculated, a small amount of makeup water is again required to replace the water lost by evaporation. Most cooling towers are placed on roofs (Fig. 16.12h), but when land is available, they can be equally well placed at grade (Fig. 16.12i). As a matter of fact, a cooling tower does not have to be a structure at all. A decorative fountain can be a very effective substitute for a cooling tower (Fig. 16.12j).

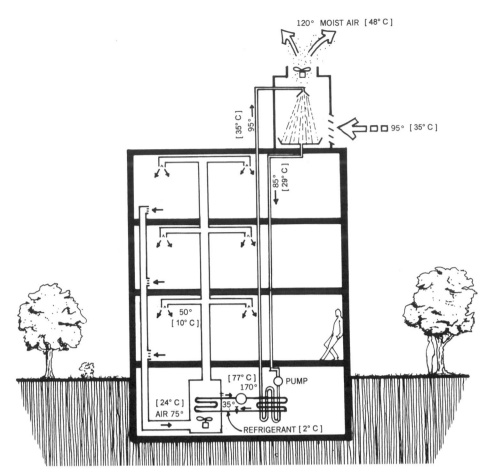

120° MOIST AIR [48° C]

[35° C] 95°

95° [35° C]

85° [29° C]

50° [10° C]

[77° C] 170°

PUMP

35°

[24° C] AIR 75°

REFRIGERANT [2° C]

Figure 16.12g A cooling tower cools water via evaporation. This cooling water is then used to cool the condenser coil located elsewhere.

Figure 16.12h In urban areas, cooling towers are typically located on rooftops. The cooling towers can be recognized by the circular fan housings.

Figure 16.12i The small raised cube at the left is a cooling tower for this office building, the Blue Cross and Blue Shield Building, in Maryland. Towson, Air is pulled in at the bottom and blown out the top.

526

Figure 16.12j These decorative fountains are used in place of a cooling tower at the West Point Pepperell factory, in Lanett, Alabama.

16.13 AIR CONDITIONING FOR SMALL BUILDINGS

Air conditioning is the year-round process that heats, cools, cleans, and circulates air. It also ventilates and controls the moisture content of the air. The various components of air-conditioning systems have been described above. Some of the most common air-conditioning systems will now be described first for small or one-story buildings and then for large, multistory buildings.

Through-the-Wall Unit

For air conditioning single spaces like motel rooms, a through-the-wall unit is often used. Each of these units essentially consists of a compressive refrigeration machine (Fig. 16.13a).

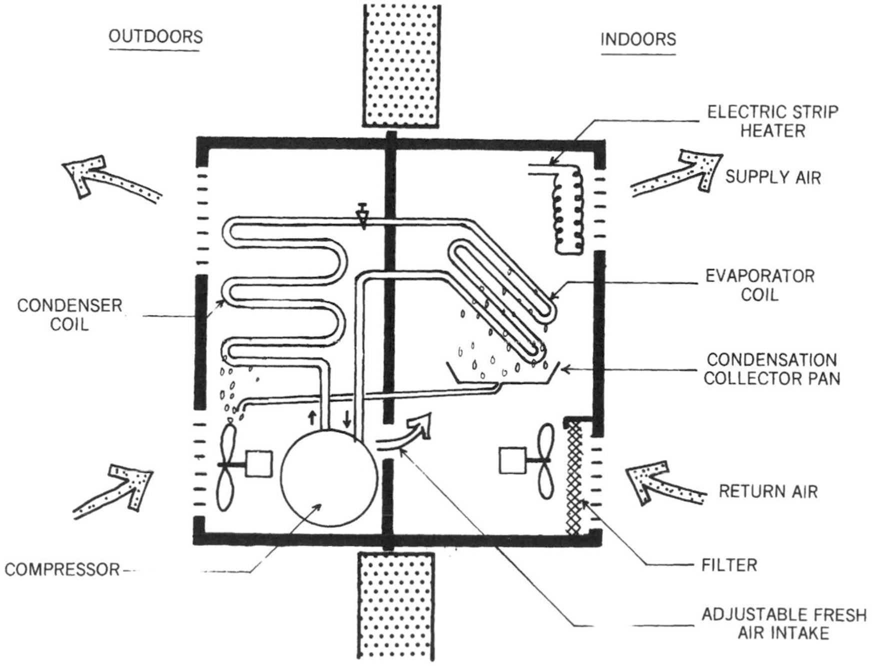

The condenser coil, compressor, and one fan are on the exterior side of an internal partition. The compressor is on the outside because it is the noisiest part of the equipment. On the interior side of the partition, there is the evaporator coil and a fan to blow air over it. As indoor air passes over the evaporator coil, its temperature is often lowered below its dew-point temperature in order to dehumidify the air. Consequently, condensation occurs, which must be collected and disposed of. Often, the condensation is used to help cool the condenser coil. An adjustable opening in the interior partition allows a controlled amount of fresh air to enter for ventilation purposes. Return air from the room first passes over a filter. An electric-strip heater is sometimes supplied for cold weather. Often, however, a heat pump is used instead of just a refrigeration machine for more efficient winter heating. The electric-strip heaters are then still included but are used for backup heating only when the outdoor temperatures are too low for the heat pump.

Packaged Systems

Like the previously described unit, **packaged systems** are preengineered, self-contained units where most of the mechanical equipment is assembled at the factory. Everything is in one unit except for the site-installed ducts.

OUTDOORS

INDOORS

ELECTRIC STRIP HEATER

SUPPLY AIR

EVAPORATOR COIL

CONDENSATION COLLECTOR PAN

CONDENSER COIL

RETURN AIR

FILTER

COMPRESSOR

ADJUSTABLE FRESH AIR INTAKE

Figure 16.13a A schematic diagram for a through-the-wall air-conditioning unit that can heat as well as cool is shown.

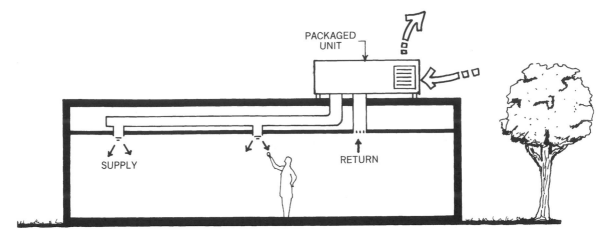

Figure 16.13b A packaged unit can contain both heating and cooling equipment.

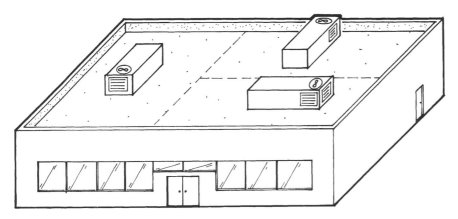

Figure 16.13c Rooftop packaged units are placed over the separate zones that they serve.

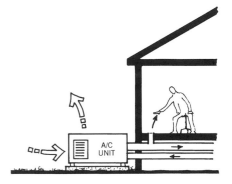

Figure 16.13d A packaged unit designed for crawl-space construction is shown.

Consequently, they offer low installation, operating, and maintenance costs. Usually, small buildings are served by one package, while larger buildings get several. Rooftop versions are the most common, with each unit serving a separate zone (Figs. 16.13b and c). Packaged units are sometimes also used on the ground for buildings with crawl spaces (Fig. 16.13d), above a suspended ceiling when there is enough space (Fig. 16.13e), or in an attic.

Packaged units can heat a building via electric strips, a heat pump, or a gas furnace. Electric-strip heaters are appropriate only in very mild climates. As mentioned before, heat pumps are an economical way to heat in much of the United States. In very cold climates, gas is the logical source of heat for the packaged units.

Split Systems

Most homes and many other small to medium-sized buildings find the **split system** to be most appropriate. In this system, the compressor and condenser coils are in an outdoor unit, while the air-handling unit with the evaporator coil is indoors (Fig. 16.13f). As in all cooling systems, condensation from the evaporator coil must be drained away. The **air-handling unit (AHU)** also contains the central heating system. As with packaged units, the heating is usually by electric strips, a heat pump, or a gas furnace.

Figures 16.13g and 16.13h illustrate the use of split systems for a small office building. The compressor/condenser units are shown on grade, although they could equally well be on the roof if free land were not

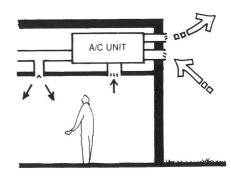

Figure 16.13e A packaged unit designed for placement above a suspended ceiling or in an attic is shown.

available. The air-handling units with their evaporator coils and heating systems are in a **mechanical-equipment room (MER)**. The supply ducts are above a suspended ceiling but on the indoor side of the roof insulation.

Thus, any heat loss from the ducts is into the air-conditioned space. The air is supplied to each room through a top register (high on the wall) or a ceiling diffuser. Return-air grilles and ducts bring the air back to the air-handling units. In homes, instead of grilles, smaller rooms often have undercut doors to allow air to enter the corridor, which can act as a return-air **plenum** (duct). Sections of both supply and return ducts are lined with sound-absorbing insulation to trap noise emitted by the air han-

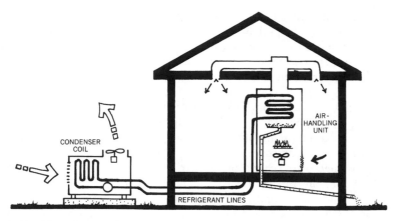

Figure 16.13f A schematic diagram of a split system is shown in this section.

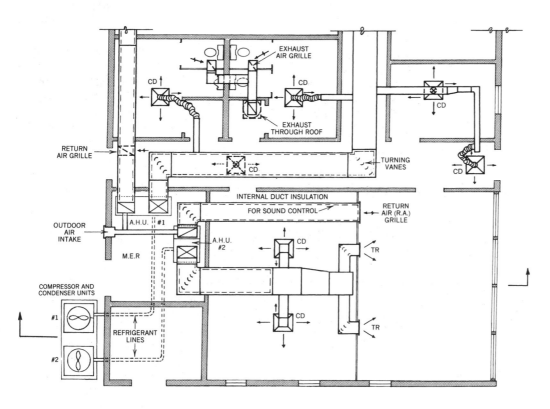

Figure 16.13g This plan shows a small two-zone office building served by two split systems. TR (top register), CD (ceiling diffuser), M.E.R. (mechanical-equipment room), A. H. U. (air-handling unit) Double diagonal lines define supply ducts in section, while a single diagonal line across a rectangle defines a return duct.

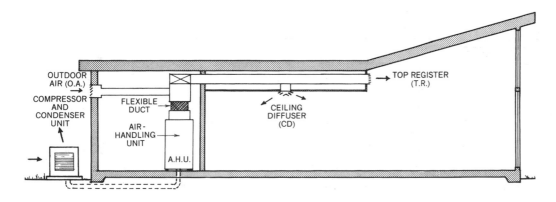

Figure 16.13h See the plan above for the location of this section.

dling units. A short piece of flexible duct (Fig. 16.13h) prevents vibrations from the air-handling unit from being transmitted throughout the building by the duct system. Ventilation is maintained by means of exhaust fans in the toilets and an outdoor-air intake into the return ducts in the MER.

The split system is very flexible because only two small copper tubes carrying refrigerant must connect the outdoor condenser/compressor with the indoor air-handling unit. However, these units cannot be much more than 60 ft (18 m) apart. Thus, the split system is appropriate for small to medium-sized buildings. Usually separate zones are served by having their own split units (Fig. 16.13i).

Ductless Split Systems

It is often difficult, if not impossible, to hide ducts when adding air conditioning to an existing building

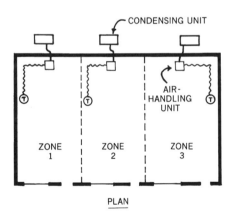

Figure 16.13i Each zone has its own split system controlled by a separate thermostat.

that has either inadequate or no air conditioning. Ducts are especially difficult to conceal in historic-preservation work. Ductless split systems require only two small copper refrigerant lines between the outdoor compressor/condenser unit and the mini-indoor air-handling units (Fig. 16.13j). The indoor units are compact, unobtrusive, and very quiet. The attractive indoor units are usually placed high on a wall, where they are out of the way and effective, and where condensation in the units can be easily drained away. One condenser/compressor unit can serve up to three mini-air-handling units as much as 160 ft (50 m) away. However, they are appropriate only for rooms with windows, since they do not introduce outside air.

16.14 AIR CONDITIONING FOR LARGE MULTISTORY BUILDINGS

Most large multistory buildings use highly centralized air-conditioning equipment. The roof and basement are the usual choice for these **central station systems** (Fig. 16.14a). The basement has the advantage of easy utility connections, noise isolation, not being valuable rental area, and the fact that structural loads are not a problem. The roof, on the other hand, is the ideal location for fresh-air intakes and heat rejection to the atmosphere. Since cooling towers are noisy, produce very hot and humid exhaust air, and can produce fog in cold weather, they are usually placed on the roof. In many buildings, the

equipment is divided, with some in the basement and some on the roof. To minimize the space lost to vertical air ducts, intermediate mechanical floors are used in very high buildings (Fig. 16.14a). If there is sufficient open land, the cooling tower and some of the other equipment might be placed on grade adjacent to the building (Fig. 16.12i).

In plan, most large multistory buildings have windows on all four sides and a core area for building services (Fig. 16.14b). Floor-to-floor heights of 13 or 14 ft (about 4 m) are often necessary to accommodate the horizontal ducts bringing conditioned air from the core to the perimeter. Lower floor-to-floor heights are possible with special compact mechanical systems or if the perimeter area is supplied with riser ducts at the perimeter (Fig. 16.14c).

When choosing a mechanical system for a building, one must consider the following: initial cost, life-cycle costs, energy consumption, space requirements, comfort level, and number of zones required. Both comfort and energy efficiency are greatly affected by the number of zones created. Since zones are expensive, however, their number is usually kept to a minimum. As was explained earlier in this chapter, the average large building has at least five zones because of orientation.

For the purpose of clarity, an example building with only three zones will be used to illustrate the major mechanical systems for large, multistory buildings (Fig. 16.14d). A section of this building is shown

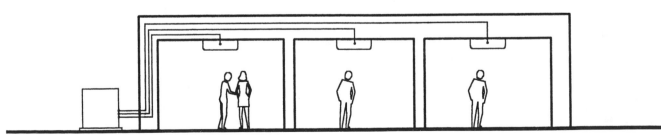

Figure 16.13j Ductless split systems are most advantageous in renovation work where ducts are hard to install or hide. One compressor/condenser unit can feed up to three mini–air-handling units.

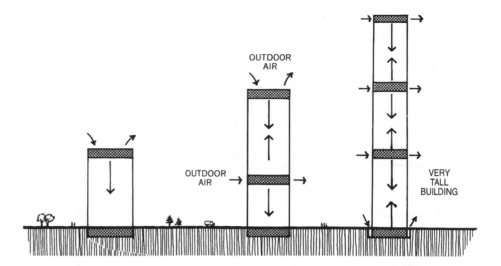

Figure 16.14a Common locations for centralized mechanical-equipment spaces in large multistory buildings are shown.

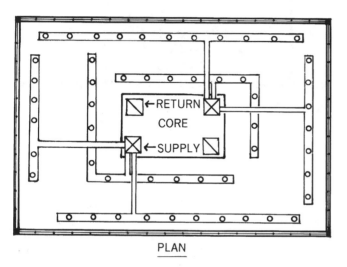

PLAN

Figure 16.14b A typical air-distribution plan with all risers in the core results in duct crossings and consequently a greater floor-to-floor height.

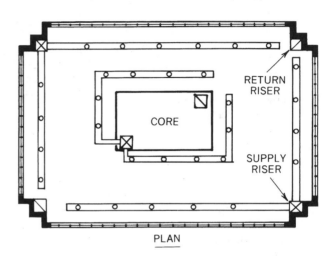

PLAN

Figure 16.14c One way to minimize floor-to-floor height is to supply the perimeter zones with separate perimeter risers. These ducts can be expressed on the facade.

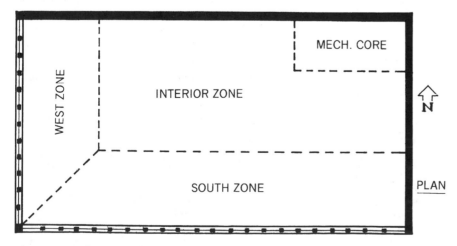

PLAN

Figure 16.14d A special three-zone floor plan is used to illustrate the major mechanical systems available for large buildings. This plan is actually the southwest quadrant of a typical large office building.

in Fig. 16.14e. As is typical in most tall office buildings, the mechanical equipment is shown to be on the roof. This section shows an all-air system served by a single central air-handling unit on the roof. To avoid the large vertical ducts, separate air-handling units could be placed on each floor with only hot and cold water circulating vertically (Fig. 16.14f). This alternative saves a great deal of energy because moving air great distances requires much more power than moving water.

The major mechanical systems available for large office buildings are illustrated by showing a typical floor plan and section of each. The

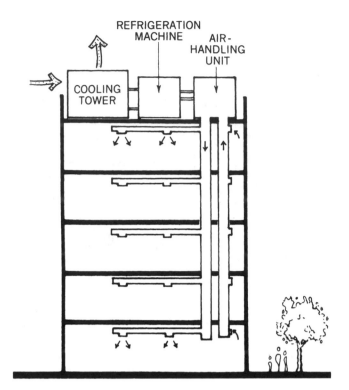

Figure 16.14e This section shows a typical multistory building with a rooftop central-station mechanical system. In this case, the air-handling unit on the roof serves all floors.

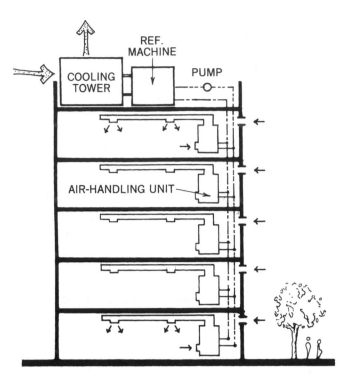

Figure 16.14f This section shows an alternate approach. Although much of the mechanical equipment is still on the roof, each floor has a separate air-handling unit. Because the refrigeration machine is now producing chilled water, it is called a "chiller."

equipment shown in each floor plan is above the ceiling unless otherwise noted. These systems are grouped by the heat-transfer medium used: all-air, air–water, and all-water.

Air systems are of two types: **constant-air-volume (CAV)** and **variable-air-volume (VAV)**. In CAV systems, the temperature control of a space is achieved by changing the temperature of a constant supply of air. In VAV systems, the temperature and humidity control of a space is achieved by varying the amount of supply air delivered to each space at a constant temperature. VAV systems are more widely used because they are more versatile and efficient than CAV systems.

All-Air Systems

The great advantage of all-air systems is that complete control over air quality is possible. The main disadvantages are that all-air systems are very bulky and a significant part of the building volume must be devoted to

the delivery of air. They are also less efficient because moving large quantities of air requires a great deal of power. It must be noted that for clarity, only the supply ducts are shown on each plan in the following examples. If an above ceiling plenum is not used, there will also be a sizable return-duct system on each floor.

1. *Single-Duct System with CAV*: The single-duct system is basically a one-zone system.

   Since a separate supply duct and air-handling unit is required for each zone, this system is most appropriate for small buildings or for medium-sized buildings with few zones (Fig. 16.14g).
2. *VAV System*: This is a single-duct system that can easily have many zones. A variable-volume control box is located wherever a duct enters a separate zone (Fig. 16.14h). A thermostat in each zone controls the air flow by operating a damper in the VAV

control box. Thus, if more cooling is required, more cool air is allowed to enter the zone. Since VAV systems cannot heat one zone while cooling another, they are basically cooling-only systems. Because heating is usually required only on the perimeter, a separate heating system can be supplied in conjunction with the VAV system. The low first cost and low energy usage make the VAV system very popular, and it is applicable to almost every building type.
3. *Terminal Reheat System (CAV)*: At first, the terminal reheat system looks just like the VAV system previously described, but, in fact, it is very different. Instead of VAV boxes, this system has terminal reheat boxes in which electric-strip heaters or hot-water coils reheat air previously cooled (Fig. 16.14i). For example, on a spring day, the zone with the greatest cooling load will

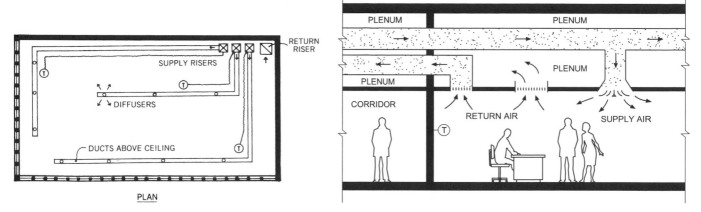

Figure 16.14g A single-duct system is shown. Return air can also travel through the above-ceiling plenum instead of the return air duct shown in the section.

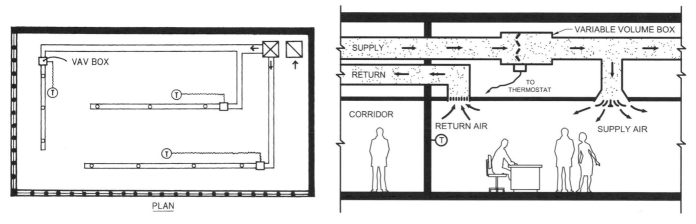

Figure 16.14h A variable-air volume (VAV) system is shown. Note the VAV control boxes for each zone.

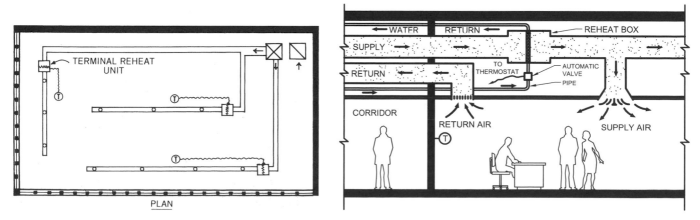

Figure 16.14i A terminal reheat system is shown. Note the terminal reheat boxes for each zone.

determine how much the air for the whole building is cooled. All other zones will then reheat the cold air to the desired temperature. Thus, most of the building is being heated and cooled simultaneously—a waste of energy. This system was popular in the past because it gave excellent control. It should not be used now except in special cases because of its high energy consumption. Terminal reheat systems can also be of the VAV type. In this case, the terminal reheat box also controls the volume of air. Thus, the control of space temperature is handled efficiently by varying the volume of the supply air, and the reheat function is called for only when some space needs heating while the others all need cooling.

4. *Multizone System:* In this mechanical system, every zone receives air at its required temperature through a separate duct (Fig. 16.14j). These ducts are supplied by a special multizone air-handling unit that custom-mixes hot and cold air for each zone. This is accomplished by means of motorized dampers located in the air-handling unit but controlled by thermostats in each zone. Depending on the temperature, the ratio of hot and cold air varies but the total amount of air is constant. The multizone unit is supplied with hot water, chilled water, and a small amount of fresh air.

Each multizone unit can handle up to about eight zones or about 30,000 ft². Because moderate air temperatures are created by mixing hot and cold air, this system is also somewhat wasteful of energy. First costs also are relatively high because of the duplication of ducts.

5. *Double-Duct System:* Like the multizone system, the double-duct system mixes hot and cold air to achieve the required air temperature. Instead of mixing the air at a central air-handling unit, mixing boxes are dispersed throughout the building (Fig. 16.14k). Thus, there is no limit to the number of

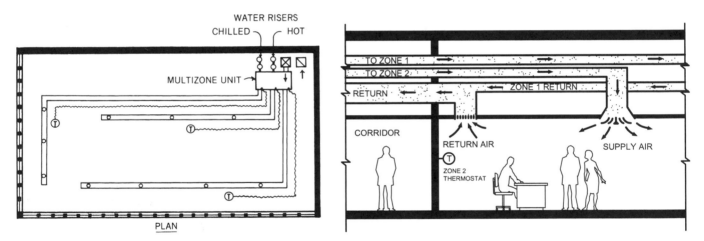

Figure 16.14j A multizone system is shown. Note that each zone has its own duct.

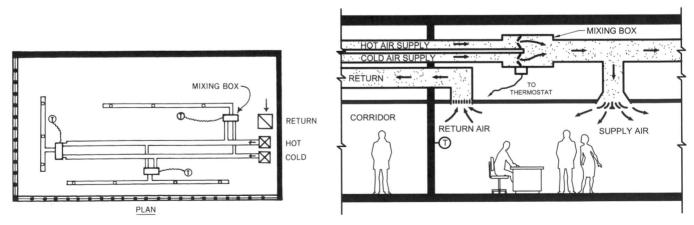

Figure 16.14k A double-duct system is shown. Note the mixing boxes for each zone.

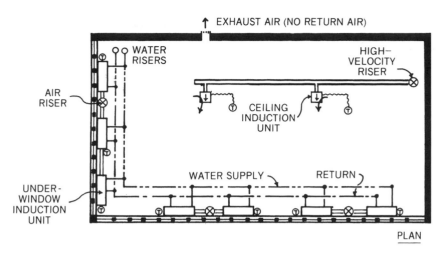

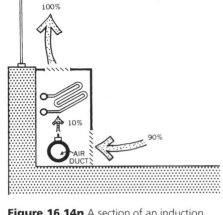

Figure 16.14n A section of an induction unit with cooling or heating coils is shown.

Figure 16.14m An induction system is shown. High-velocity air is also supplied at the perimeter to the induction units.

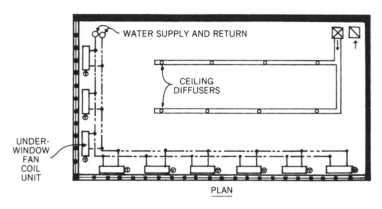

Figure 16.14o A fan-coil with supplementary air system is shown. The fan-coil units can be either above or below the windows.

zones possible. However, two sets of large supply ducts are necessary.

Although the double-duct system creates a high level of thermal comfort and allows for great zoning flexibility, it is very expensive, requires much building space, and is wasteful of energy.

Air–Water System

The following systems supply both air and water to each zone of a building. Although this increases the complexity of the mechanical systems, it greatly decreases the size of the equipment because of the immense heat-carrying capacity of water as opposed to air. Air is supplied mainly because of the need for ventilation.

6. *Induction System:* In an induction system, a small quantity of high velocity air is supplied to each zone to provide the required fresh air and to induce room air to circulate (Fig. 16.14m). Most induction units are found under windows, where they can effectively neutralize the heat gain or loss through the envelope (Fig. 16.14n). As the high velocity air shoots into the room, it induces a large amount of room air to circulate. This combination of room air (90 percent) and fresh air (10 percent) then passes over heating or cooling coils. Thus, most heating or cooling is accomplished with water, while ventilation and air motion are accomplished with a small amount of high-velocity

air. Local thermostats regulate the temperature by controlling the flow of either hot or cold water through the coils.

Unfortunately, high velocity (up to 6000 ft/min [30 m/s]) and, therefore, high pressure ducts are much more expensive than regular-velocity (up to 2000 ft/min [10 m/s]) ducts. High velocity air systems also consume much more fan power than normal-velocity systems. Because of these problems, induction systems are little used today.

7. *Fan-Coil with Supplementary Air:* This system also consists of two separate parts. For ventilation and cooling of the interior areas, there is an all-air system, and for neutralizing the heat gain or loss through the envelope, there are fan-coil units around the perimeter (Fig. 16.14o). The fan-coil units are described in more detail below under all-water systems.

8. *Radiant Panels with Supplementary Air:* Similar to radiant heating but in reverse, a cool surface can achieve thermal comfort by lowering the MRT. Moderately cool panels (about 65°F [18°c]) will suffice if their area is large. The ceiling is the best surface for radiant cooling because it is large, it is unobstructed by furniture, etc.,

and it can also cool by convection. Figure 16.14p shows three radiant cooling systems. Indoor rain from condensation on the ceiling can be prevented by controlling the humidity and panel temperature.

The supplementary air is dehumidified in order to control indoor humidity, and the large cooling panels are maintained above the dew-point temperature of the air.

All-Water Systems

Since these systems supply no air, they are appropriate when a large amount of ventilation either is not necessary or can be achieved locally by such means as opening windows.

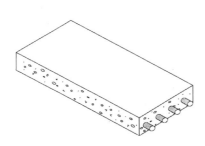

A **core-cooled** *ceiling is the cooling equivalent of a floor heating system. In this system, water is circulated through plastic tubes embedded in the core of a concrete ceiling. This layout allows the system to take advantage of the storage capacity of the concrete and provides the opportunity to shift the building peak load away from the utility grid peak.*

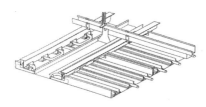

The most used system is the **panel system.** *It is usually built from aluminum panels, with metal tubes connected to the rear of the panel. An alternative is to build a "sandwich system," in which the water flow paths are included between two aluminum panels. The use of a highly conductive material in the panel construction provides the basis for a fast response of the system to changes in room loads.*

Cooling grids made of **capillary tubes** *placed close to each other can be embedded in plaster, gypsum board or mounted on ceiling panels. This system provides an even surface temperature distribution. Due to the flexibility of the plastic tubes, cooling grids might be the best choice for retrofit applications.*

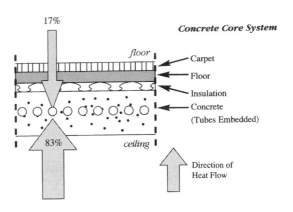

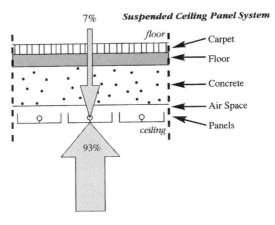

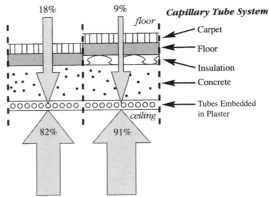

As shown by the arrows, most of the cooling effect occurs on the ceiling side of radiant panels.

Figure 16.14p Three different radiant cooling systems are shown. (From Lawrence Berkeley Laboratory, *Center for Building Science News,* Vol. 1, no. 4, Fall, 1994.)

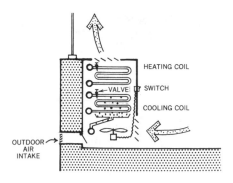

Figure 16.14q A schematic diagram of an under-window fan-coil unit (four-pipe system) with outdoor air intake and a condensation drain is shown.

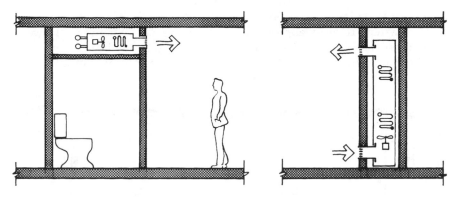

Figure 16.14r Fan-coil units can also be placed above a dropped ceiling or in a small closet.

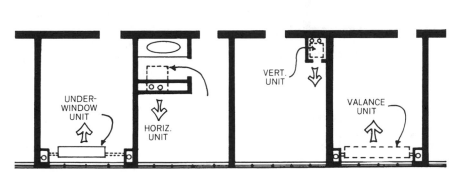

Figure 16.14s Four alternate fan-coil systems are shown in plan view: (1) under-window unit, (2) above-bathroom ceiling unit, (3) closet unit, and (4) valance (above-window) unit.

9. *Fan-Coil System:* The fan coil-unit, as the name implies, basically consists of a fan and a coil within which water circulates. The units are often in the form of cabinets for placement under windows (Fig. 16.14q). The fan blows room air across coils through which either hot or cold water circulates. Thermostatically controlled valves regulate the flow of water through the coils. A four-pipe system, which is shown, has two pipes for hot-water supply and return and another two pipes for cold-water supply and return (Fig. 16.14q). Thus, either heating or cooling is possible at any time of year. In the less expensive but also less comfortable two-pipe system, hot water circulates during the winter and cold water

in the summer. In such systems, it is not possible for an occupant to choose either heating or cooling. A three-pipe (hot, cold, and a common return) system also exists but wastes energy because hot and cold water return through the same pipe.

Condensation on the cooling coils must be collected in a pan and drained away. When the fan-coil unit is on an outside wall, it is possible to have an outdoor air intake connected to the unit. A three-speed fan switch or thermostat allows occupants to have control over the temperature.

Fan-coil units are most appropriate for air conditioning buildings with small zones (e.g., apartments, condominiums, motels, hotels, hospitals,

and schools). Besides the under-window location, fan-coil units are sometimes located above windows (valance units), in small closets, or in the dropped ceiling above a bathroom or hallway (Figs. 16.14r and s Fan-coil units come in many shapes and configurations to allow great flexibility in their use.

10. *Water-Loop Heat-Pump System:* With this system, each zone is heated or cooled by a separate water-to-air heat pump. A thermostat in each zone determines whether the local heat pump extracts heat from a water loop (heating mode) or injects heat into the water loop (cooling mode) (Fig. 16.14t). The water in the loop is circulated at between 60° and 90°F (15° and 32°C). In the summer, when most heat pumps are injecting heat into the loop, the excess heat is disposed of by a cooling tower. In winter, when most heat pumps are extracting heat, a solar collector or a central boiler keeps the water in the loop from dropping below 60°F (15°C).

The water-loop heat-pump system really shines in spring and fall or whenever about half the heat pumps are in the cooling mode and the other half are in the heating mode. In that case, the heat extracted from the water loop will roughly equal the heat injected, and neither cooling tower nor boiler needs to operate. This system is most appropriate in those buildings and climates where the simultaneous heating of some zones and cooling of others is common. However, the numerous heat pumps are a major maintenance problem.

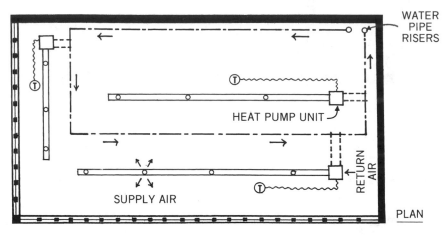

Figure 16.14t In a water-loop heat pump system, each zone has its own heat pump. All equipment is above the ceiling.

Table 16.15A Spatial Requirements for Mechanical Equipment

Equipment Type	Floor Area Required[a] (Percentage)	Required Ceiling Height[b] (Feet)
Room for refrigeration machine, heating unit, and pumps	1.5–4	9–18
Room for air-handling units		
All-air	2–4	9–18
Air–water	0.5–1.5	9–18
All-water	0–1[d]	N/A
Cooling tower	0.25	7–16[c]
Packaged (rooftop)	0–1	5–10[c]
Split units	1–3	8–9

[a]The required floor area is a percentage of the gross building area served (parking is excluded). Use the upper end of the range for small buildings and for large buildings with a great deal of mechanical equipment (e.g., laboratories and hospitals).
[b]Use the lower end of the range in ceiling height for smaller buildings.
[c]Since cooling towers and packaged units are usually not roofed over, the heights given are for the actual equipment, not ceiling height.
[d]The required area refers to fan-coil units.

Table 16.15B Cross-Sectional Area of Supply Ducts (Horizontal or Vertical)*

System	Cross-Sectional Duct Area of Conditioned Space per	
	1,000 ft²	100 m²
All-air	1–2 ft²	0.1–0.2 m²
Air–water	0.3–0.8 ft²	0.03–0.08 m²

*When used, return ducts are at least as large as these supply ducts. Use the large end of the range for spaces with large cooling loads or when ductwork has many turns. For the vertical-shaft space, use about twice the area of the duct risers.

16.15 DESIGN GUIDELINES FOR MECHANICAL SYSTEMS

Because the mechanical and electrical equipment requires 6 to 9 percent of the total floor area of most buildings, sufficient and properly located spaces should be allocated for it. By incorporating the following rules and design guidelines at the schematic design stage, one can prevent many serious design problems later on.

Sizing Guidelines

For the floor-area and ceiling-height requirements of the various parts of a mechanical system see Table 16.15A. Note that the spatial requirements for the air-handling units depend mostly on whether an all-air, air–water, or all-water system is used. Ducts for horizontal air distribution are usually above the ceiling and, therefore, do not use up any of the floor area. However, since floor-to-floor heights are very much dependent on the size of horizontal ducts, use Table 16.15B for a rough early estimate of duct sizes.

Location Guidelines

I. For medium-sized buildings:
   1. Place the equipment on the roof or
   2. Use a MER centrally located to minimize duct sizes, and place it along an outside wall for easy servicing (Fig. 16.15a).
II. For large multistory buildings:
   1. Place the centralized mechanical equipment in the basement, on the roof, or on intermediate floors (see Fig. 16.14a). However, basements are a problem in very tall buildings for chillers and boilers because of the pressures created by the water above and because of the long flue required for the boilers.
   2. The cooling tower should be placed on the roof or on out-of-the-way adjacent land (Fig. 16.15b).
   3. Any additional MER on each floor should be centrally located

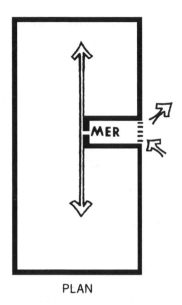

PLAN

Figure 16.15a Usually, MERs should be centrally located and have access to the outdoors.

to minimize duct sizes. If these MERs require large amounts of outdoor air, they should be located along an outside wall (Fig. 16.15a).

Noise Guidelines

1. Equipment placed outside can be a major source of noise to neighbors.
2. Surround the MER with massive material to stop sound and vibration transmission.
3. MERs and ducts should be lined with sound-absorbing insulation.
4. Do not locate a MER near quiet areas like libraries and conference rooms.

Residential Guidelines

1. Use one ton of cooling capacity for each 500 ft² (45 m²) of a standard house.
2. Use 1 ton of cooling capacity for each 1000 ft² (90 m²) of a modern, well-designed, and well-built house.

General Guidelines

1. The duct layout should be orderly and systematic, like the structural system.

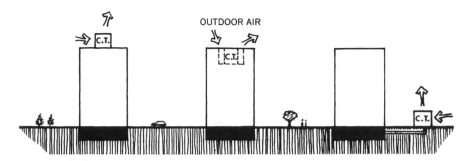

Figure 16.15b When the mechanical equipment is mainly in the basement, the cooling tower should still be on the roof or on an out-of-the-way location with good outdoor air circulation.

2. Avoid air ducts crossing each other.
3. Provide adequate access to large equipment that might have to be replaced.

16.16 AIR SUPPLY (DUCTS AND DIFFUSERS)

Air is usually supplied to rooms by means of round, rectangular, or oval ducts. However, building elements, such as hollow-core concrete planks and hollow beams, can also be used. Although round ducts are preferable for a number of reasons, they require clearances that are not always available. Consequently, rectangular ducts are very popular. However, the ratio of short to long sides, the aspect ratio, should not exceed 1:5 because the resulting high air-flow friction requires the ducts to have excessively large areas and perimeters (Fig. 16.16a).

At least another 2 in. (5 cm) must be added to the height and width when duct insulation is used. Insulation can be required for three reasons: to reduce heat gain or loss, to prevent condensation, and to control noise. To prevent condensation, a vapor barrier must be on the outside of the insulation, while for noise control, the insulation must be exposed to the airstream (Fig. 16.16b). Supply and return ducts transmit sound almost equally, because sound travels about 50 times faster than the velocity of air in ducts.

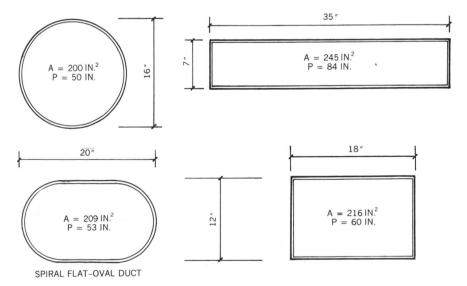

SPIRAL FLAT-OVAL DUCT

Figure 16.16a All these ducts have the same friction and, therefore, air-flow capacity. The circular duct requires the least volume and material but has the greatest depth. (A = area, p = perimeter). In this example, the actual sizes are not important—only the relative sizes.

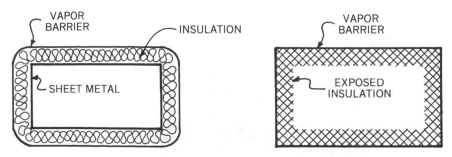

Figure 16.16b To prevent condensation on ducts, a vapor barrier must always be placed on the outside of the insulation. For noise control, porous fiberglass insulation must be exposed to the airstream.

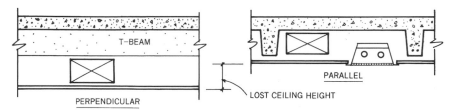

Figure 16.16c Coordinate ducts with beams and lighting fixtures to minimize the space required for the mechanical and electrical systems. Ducts should run parallel to beams.

Although the size of ducts can be decreased by increasing the air velocity, there are two important reasons for using large ducts and the resultant low velocity air flow. High velocity air flow requires significantly more fan power to generate, and it is much noisier than low velocity air flow.

A duct system is often described as a "tree system" in which the main trunk is the largest duct and the branches get progressively smaller (see Fig. 16.14e). As much as possible, ducts should run parallel to deep structural elements and lighting fixtures to prevent wasted space when various building elements cross each other (Fig. 16.16c).

Sometimes the return-air system has a duct "tree" as extensive as that of the supply-air system. Often, however, the corridor or plenum (space) above a hung ceiling is used instead of return-air ducts. To maintain acoustical privacy, short return-air ducts lined with sound-absorbing insulation should connect rooms with the plenum. Special return-air grilles with built-in sound traps are also available for doors or walls.

Supply ducts are also lined where necessary and permitted with sound-absorbing insulation to prevent the short-circuiting of sound from one room to the next. The insulation also reduces the noise transmitted through the air from the air-handling unit (see Fig. 16.13g). To prevent the ductwork itself from transmitting noise or vibration, a flexible fabric connection is used where the main ducts connect to the air-handling unit (see Fig. 16.13h).

The supply air enters a room through either a grille, register, or diffuser. A **supply grille** has adjustable vanes for controlling the direction of the air entering a room. A **register** is a grille that also has a **damper** behind it so that the amount as well as the direction of the air entering a room can be controlled.

In building types or climates where cooling predominates, the air is usually supplied high in each room. Although it is convenient to run ducts through an unheated attic or even on the roof, it is very undesirable from an energy point of view even if the ducts are well insulated. Thus, a dropped ceiling in the corridor is often appropriate not only for flat-roofed but also pitched-roof buildings (Fig. 16.16d).

When registers are mounted on upper walls, they are designed to throw the air about three-quarters of the distance across the room (Fig. 16.16d). When registers are mounted in the floor under windows or next to an outdoor wall, they are usually aimed up and, thus, are suitable only for small spaces (Fig. 16.16e).

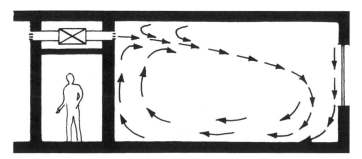

Figure 16.16d Air from an upper-wall register should be thrown about three-quarters of the distance across a room before it drops to the level of people's heads. This air supply method is common because it allows the ducts to be on the inside of the thermal envelope.

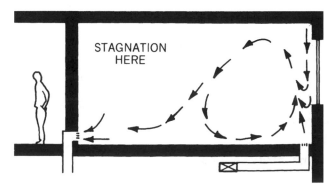

Figure 16.16e Floor registers cannot serve large spaces. They are good at countering the heating or cooling effect of windows.

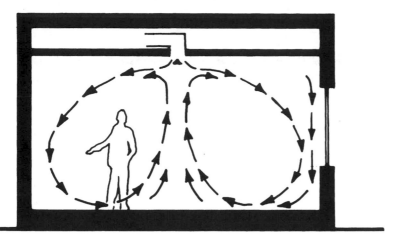

Figure 16.16f The proper air-flow pattern from a ceiling diffuser is shown.

When air is supplied from the ceiling, it has to be mixed rapidly with the room air to prevent the discomfort of cold air striking the occupants; consequently, a **diffuser** is used (Fig. 16.16f). Diffusers can be round, rectangular, or linear, and like registers, they have dampers for adjusting the volume of air being supplied. Supply air can also be diffused with large perforated ceiling panels (Fig. 16.16g).

The location of supply-air outlets is very important for the comfort of the occupants. The goal is to gently circulate all of the air in a room so that there are neither stagnant nor drafty areas. Make sure, too, that beams or other objects do not block the air supply from reaching all parts of a room (Fig. 16.16h). Where heating is the major problem, the supply outlets should be placed low.

Diffusers and registers are unnecessary when cloth ducts are used because they are fabricated with materials with different grades of porosity to allow for a range of draft-free air distribution. When nonporous fabric or plastic film is used, small holes are punched at frequent intervals for the supply air. The sections of lightweight, brightly colored fabric ducts are zippered together and hung from the ceiling (Fig. 16.16i).

In rooms with high ceilings, it is not necessary to cool the upper layers, which, because of stratification, are very warm. Air can be introduced through low wall or floor registers. Stratification, however, is a liability in cold climates. In the winter, the hot air collecting near the ceiling of

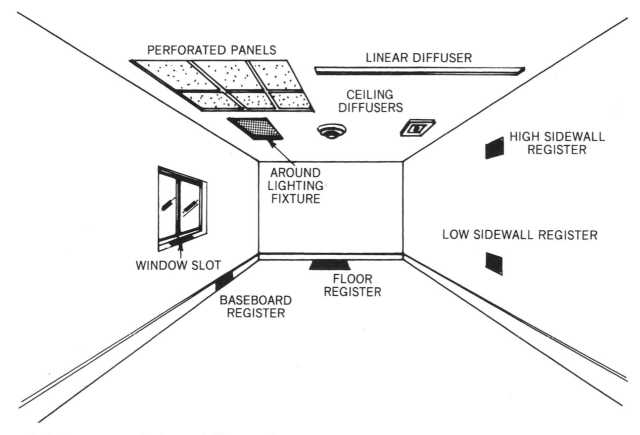

Figure 16.16g Common types of registers and diffusers are shown.

high spaces should be brought back down to the floor level by means of antistratification ducts or devices, as shown in Fig. 17.6d. In large theaters, good results are often achieved by supplying air all across the ceiling and returning it all across the floor under the seats (Fig. 16.16j). However, using displacement ventilation might be even better. Supplying air at the floor level and returning it at the ceiling has many advantages, as described in Section 16.18.

Return air generally leaves a room through a grille, but it can also leave through lighting fixtures, perforated ceiling panels, or undercut doors in homes. The location of the return-air grille has almost no effect on room air motion if supply outlets are properly located. However, to prevent the short-circuiting of the air, do not place return openings right next to supply

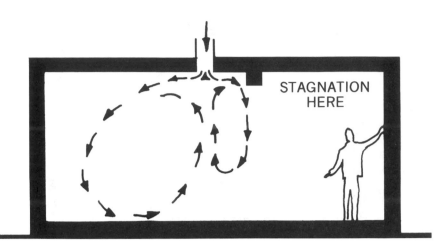

Figure 16.16h Locate air outlets carefully to avoid blocking the air flow with beams or other building elements.

outlets. Also avoid return grilles in the floor because dirt is sucked into them.

When ducts run through the basement, crawl space, or attic, tight-fitting ducts are important; otherwise, the

building will come under negative or positive pressure (Fig. 16.16k). If the return ducts leak, toxic material, such as radon or mildew, will be sucked into the return ducts. If the supply

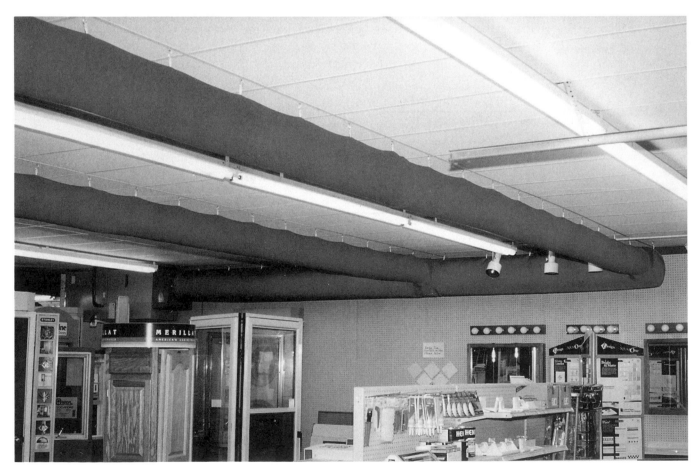

Figure 16.16i No drafts result when cloth ducts are used because the air is supplied along the entire length through the porous fabric. (Courtesy Air Sox, Inc.)

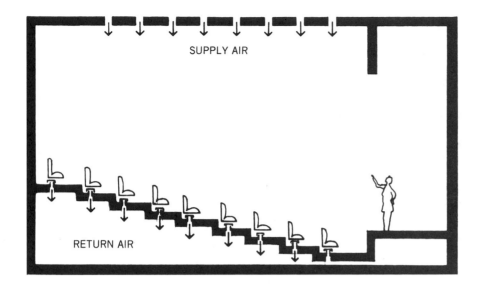

SUPPLY AIR

RETURN AIR

Figure 16.16j In large theaters, the air is often returned under the seating. However, reversing the flow might be even better, as is discussed under displacement ventilation.

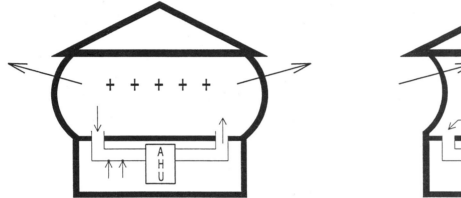

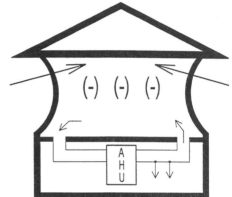

Figure 16.16k If the ducts are outside of the air-conditioned space, it is especially important to have no air leaks. Besides wasting energy, radon and toxic mildew can be sucked into the return duct or building. (After North Carolina Alternative Energy Corp. [AEC].)

ducts leak, the building comes under negative pressure, and outdoor, attic, and crawl space air will enter through all the cracks. Since duct leaks are hard to prevent, the ducts and equipment should be placed within the thermal envelope for health reasons as well as energy conservation.

kitchens, laboratories, and other such work areas). The air pressure in these areas should be kept slightly below that of the rest of the building to prevent the contaminated air from spreading. At the same time, the pressure

in the rest of the building should be slightly above the atmospheric pressure to prevent the infiltration of untreated air through cracks and joints in the building envelope (Fig. 16.17). These pressures can be maintained

16.17 VENTILATION

The excess carbon dioxide, water vapor, odors, and air pollutants that accumulate in a building must be exhausted. At the same time, an equal amount of fresh air must be introduced to replace the exhausted air. The air should be exhausted where the concentration of pollutants is greatest (e.g., toilets,

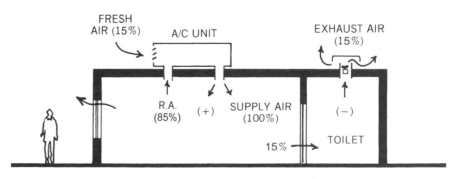

FRESH AIR (15%)   A/C UNIT   EXHAUST AIR (15%)

R.A. (85%)   (+)   SUPPLY AIR (100%)   (−)

15%   TOILET

Figure 16.17 A slight positive pressure in the building prevents infiltration, and a slight negative pressure in toilets prevent odors from spreading to adjacent spaces.

by the proper balance between the amount of air that is removed by exhaust fans and the amount brought in through the air-conditioning unit.

Normally, about 15 percent of the air circulated for heating or cooling will be outdoor air. Under certain circumstances, much larger amounts of outdoor air are introduced. For example, the American Society for Heating Refrigeration and Air Conditioning Engineers (ASHRAE) recommends five times as much outside air for smokers as for nonsmokers.

Outdoor air can also be used for cooling when its temperature is sufficiently below the indoor temperature. Mechanical systems designed to use cold outdoor air for cooling are said to have an **economizer cycle.**

Although mechanical ventilation is a standard part of air conditioning in larger buildings, it is usually left up to natural infiltration and operable windows to ventilate smaller buildings. As long as small buildings were not very airtight, this policy worked quite well. Now, however, many small, well-constructed, airtight buildings are suffering from indoor air pollution. Even some well-ventilated large buildings have problems with indoor-air quality, especially when they are new.

Indoor-air quality (IAQ) is affected by pollution from many sources. Besides the obvious sources from people and their activities, significant sources include unvented combustion, off-gassing of building materials and furnishings, cleaning materials, and the ground below the building. Eliminating the source of the pollutants is the best way to achieve IAQ. What can't be eliminated at the source should be extracted with exhaust fans. Dilution with fresh air should be the last method, although it is the most commonly used method for controlling IAQ.

Air pollution from combustion, which includes the odorless and deadly gas carbon monoxide, comes mainly from unvented kerosene and gas space heaters and attached garages. Carbon monoxide can also be generated by poorly maintained gas appliances, such as kitchen stoves. Tobacco smoke, fireplaces, and leaky wood stoves can also be a problem. Any indoor combustion should be directly vented outdoors.

Off-gassing of **volatile organic compounds (VOCs),** such as formaldehyde from plywood, particleboard, furniture, carpets, and drapes, can cause severe reactions in some people and is unhealthy for everyone. Use materials low in formaldehyde and VOCs and vent buildings well, especially when new. If loose asbestos is present, it should be immediately removed.

Radon gas, which is radioactive, odorless, and colorless, occurs naturally in the earth, from where it slowly makes its way to the surface. In those locations where there are high concentrations, radon gas must be blocked from entering the building (see Section 15.15).

Moisture in a crawl space or basement encourages mildew growth, which is highly allergenic and sometimes toxic. Certain types of microorganisms growing in moist buildings and air-conditioning equipment produce deadly toxins (e.g., like those that resulted in the fatal Legionnaire's disease). Keeping a building dry and properly maintaining air-conditioning equipment are the best ways to control these microorganisms.

Although indoor green plants can be a source of microorganisms if overwatered, they also scrub out the indoor air. Scientists from NASA have proven that properly maintained plants can clean the air of toxins. Scientist Bill Wolverton predicts that plants will be the technology of choice for improving IAQ in the twenty-first century.

IAQ Rules

1. Avoid using toxic cleaning materials.
2. Avoid storing toxic materials indoors.
3. Avoid specifying building materials that will off-gas.
4. Avoid specifying furniture that will off-gas.
5. Do not use unvented heaters.
6. Prevent water leaks (keep the building dry).
7. Dehumidify air if relative humidity is over 80 percent.
8. Minimize radon entry into the building.
9. Use exhaust fans where pollutants are generated.
10. Lastly, use ventilation to remove any remaining pollution.

16.18 ENERGY-EFFICIENT VENTILATION SYSTEMS

Although ventilation cannot be completely eliminated to save energy, there are several techniques available to greatly reduce the energy penalties of introducing outdoor air. If there is little or no off-gassing of toxic materials and if the buildup of carbon dioxide is the main reason for ventilation, it is possible to use **demand-controlled ventilation,** where the amount of outside air is adjusted by carbon dioxide sensors. Thus, ventilation can be reduced but not eliminated. However, the remaining ventilation can be made much more energy efficient by using a number of techniques. Zero energy ventilation is possible during a winter day by using a solar system to preheat the outdoor air (see Chapter 8, Section 8.24), and heat recovery equipment can save most of the energy lost to ventilation at any time of day or year.

Heat Recovery Ventilators

Heat recovery ventilators, also known as **heat exchangers** or **air-to-air heat exchangers,** can capture much of the heat that is ordinarily lost during ventilation. When air is exhausted from a building to make room for fresh outdoor air, a large amount of both sensible and latent heat is lost. In winter, cold, dry outdoor air must be heated and humidified, and in summer, the outdoor air must be cooled and

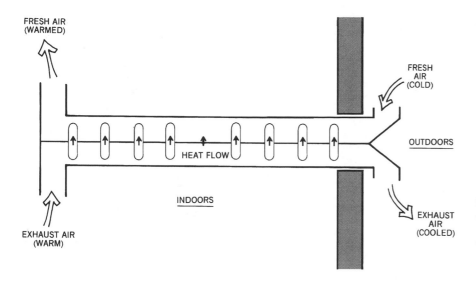

Figure 16.18a Heat-recovery ventilators allow part of the heat in exhaust air to be recovered without cross-contamination of the airstreams. Typically, the heat moves through metal partitions, but heat pipes can be used to improve the energy transfer.

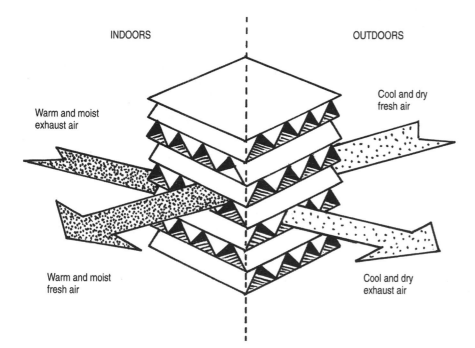

Figure 16.18b Some flat-plate heat exchangers transfer only sensible heat across metal partitions. The one shown uses composite-resin partitions to transfer latent as well as sensible heat (winter condition shown). (After Mitsubishi Electronics, HVAC Advanced Products Division.)

dehumidified. Some heat-recovery ventilators use fixed plates or heat pipes to capture only the sensible heat (Fig. 16.18a). Other ventilators are more sophisticated and recover both latent and sensible heat. The fixed plates in some heat exchangers are made of a special material that enables water vapor to move through the plates (Fig.16.18b). Another type recovers between 70 and 90 percent of

the heat by means of a heat-transfer wheel covered with lithium chloride, a chemical that absorbs water. As the wheel turns, both sensible and latent heat is transferred from one air stream to another (Fig. 16.18c).

Displacement Ventilation

The typical method of supplying cool and fresh air to spaces is shown in

the water analogy of Fig. 16.18d. The polluted, warm water in the pitcher (top) is being diluted by the addition of cool, clean water. A much more effective approach is the method used in the pitcher (bottom), where the cool, clean water is displacing the warmer polluted water. Similarly, a **displacement ventilation** system supplies fresh cool air at floor level and exhausts polluted warm air though the ceiling (Fig. 16.18e).

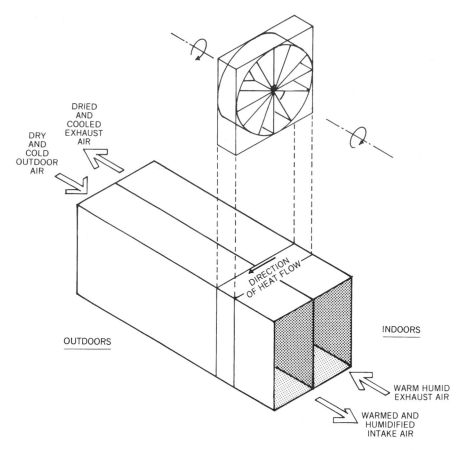

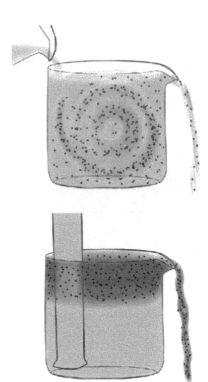

Figure 16.18c A heat-transfer wheel can recover both sensible and latent heat from exhaust air. Although the winter condition is shown, it works equally well in summer. (After Architectural Graphic Standards.)

Figure 16.18d When fresh, cool water is poured into a beaker of polluted water, the resulting water is a little less dirty and cooler. However, when fresh, cool water is carefully inserted at the bottom of a beaker, much more pollution is eliminated, and the bottom layer is clean and cool. When used with air, this method is called "displacement ventilation."

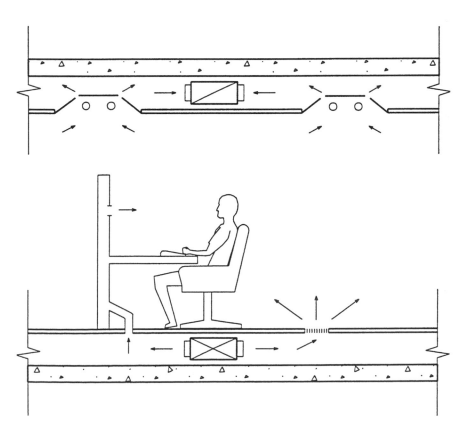

Figure 16.18e Displacement ventilation uses a raised floor to supply fresh air low in the room and sometimes directly to the occupants. The polluted warm air rises and is then exhausted at the ceiling and sometimes through the lighting, fixtures. This arrangement results in exceptionally clean air and is also more energy efficient.

16.19 AIR FILTRATION AND ODOR REMOVAL

Besides heating and cooling, the mechanical system must also clean the air. The amount of dust, pollen, bacteria, and odors in air has an effect on the health and comfort of the occupants, as well as the cleaning and redecorating costs of the building. Outdoor makeup air mixed with the return air should pass through filters first so that coils and fans can be kept free of the dirt that would reduce their efficiency. Among the many types of filters, the most popular are dry filters, electronic filters, water sprays, and carbon filters.

Dry filters are usually made of fiberglass and are thrown away when dirty. Although most dry filters remove only large dust and dirt particles, **high-efficiency particulate (HEPA)** dry filters that can remove microscopic particles, such as bacteria and pollen, are available. An efficient device for removing very small particles is the electronic air cleaner. Odors can be reduced by passing the air through a water spray or over activated carbon filters. The best solution for controlling odors is to prevent them, if possible, or use spot ventilation.

16.20 SPECIAL SYSTEMS

District Heating and Cooling

High efficiency is possible when a complex of buildings can be heated and cooled from a district plant. For example, on many college campuses, hot and chilled water is distributed through insulated pipes to all the buildings (Fig. 16.20a). The district plant contains large, efficient boilers, chillers, and cooling towers. Since the equipment is centralized and highly automated, a small staff can easily maintain it.

Combined Heat and Power

As first mentioned in Section 3.21, a **combined heat and power (CHP)** system can be an efficient method of supplying a building or a complex of buildings with electricity, hot water, and even chilled water. Through the generation of electricity on-site, the heat normally wasted can be used for space heating or domestic hot water. The waste heat can also be used to drive an absorption refrigeration machine to generate chilled water for summer cooling. Cogeneration can be used in installations as small as a fast-food restaurant or as large as a university campus.

With the restructuring of the electric power industry, it will be easier and more financially attractive to generate one's own electricity, with the "waste" heat being a bonus.

Thermal Energy Storage (TES)

The strategy of saving energy when an excess exists for a time when an energy shortage exists is rapidly gaining in popularity. We have seen this technique used for both passive heating and cooling where the mass of the building is usually used to store heat from day to night. Besides the heat storage of active solar hot-water systems, there are many other ways that active mechanical systems can store energy.

For example, since electric-power companies usually have excess capacity at night, they frequently offer substantially lower rates for electricity during night hours. In the winter, hot water can be generated at night and stored for space heating the next day. During the summer, chilled water can be produced at night for cooling the next day. Not only does the electricity cost much less, but the chillers operate much more efficiently during the cool nighttime hours.

The main additional cost for active thermal storage is the water tank required for holding the hot or chilled water. If the size of the chilled-water tank is limited, ice rather than water can be stored. Many high-rise office buildings now have swimming-pool-size water tanks in the basement for storing chilled water. Where open land is available, large, insulated tanks can be either partially buried or placed above ground to become part of the architecture (Fig. 16.20b).

Some people have realized that summer heat could be stored for use in the winter. A solar collector operating at peak efficiency in the summer or a condenser coil on an air-conditioning unit could heat water for the winter. In addition, the winter cold can be used to generate chilled water or ice to be stored for the following summer, much like the nineteenth-century New Englanders who harvested ice in the winter and sold it to the South in the summer. When seasonal ice is used, it should be stored in insulated tanks. When water is used, tanks tend to be too large and the water in the ground should be used. Waterproof liners and rigid insulation can isolate a section of earth with its groundwater. This concept is known as an **annual-cycle energy system (ACES)**. The geo-exchange, ground-coupled heat pumps described in Section 16.11 use this concept to a limited extent.

16.21 INTEGRATED AND EXPOSED MECHANICAL EQUIPMENT

Usually, mechanical equipment is a completely separate system hidden behind walls and above suspended ceilings. Perhaps it is time for the equipment to come out of the closet. This can happen either by integrating the mechanical equipment with other building systems, such as the structure, or by exposing the equipment to full view. Many successful buildings illustrate either approach.

One way to integrate the floor structure and mechanical equipment is illustrated by the Hoffmann-LaRoche Building in Nutley, New Jersey. The floor structure consists of an exposed waffle-slab. Lighting fixtures, air-supply outlets, and return grilles are designed to fit into the 2 × 2-ft × 18-in. (60 × 60 × 45 cm) deep coffers. All ducts, pipes, and wires run under a raised-floor system that rests on the waffle slab (Fig. 16.21a). The

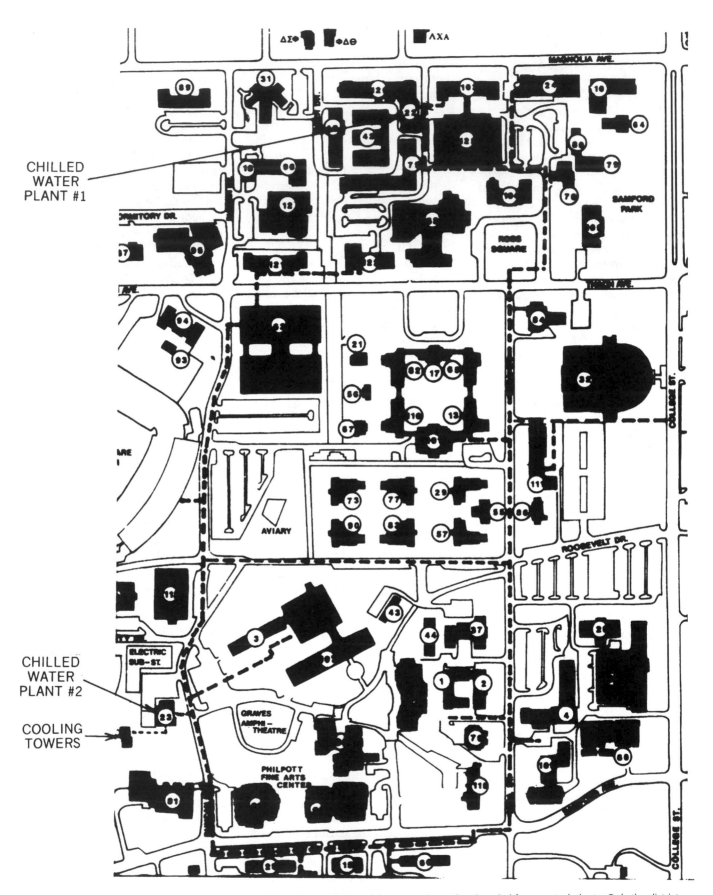

Figure 16.20a Most buildings on the Auburn University campus Auburn, Alabama, are heated and cooled from central plants. Only the district cooling system is shown. As time passes, more buildings, both new and old, are added to the district system.

Figure 16.20b This aboveground thermal/water storage tank is used as an aesthetic element. (Courtesy Chicago Bridge & Iron Company.)

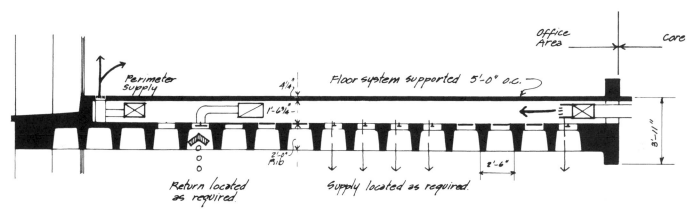

Figure 16.21a A section through the waffle slab of the Hoffman-La Roche Building, Nutley, New Jersey. (*After Design and Technology in Architecture* by D. Guise.)

plan in Fig. 16.21b shows how the supply and return ducts are connected to the core of the building.

Instead of separate systems, the integrated approach tries to make each construction element do as many jobs as possible. As Buckminster Fuller urged, "do more with less." Often there is synergy from the integration. For example, using the structure as ducts or plenums allows easy nighttime cooling of the structural mass to create a heat sink the next day. Although

the integrated approach promises great efficiency and cost reduction, it is a more sophisticated and difficult way to design and build. It requires much more cooperation among the various building professionals than does the existing approach of separate systems. The previous example was presented to illustrate the concept rather than any particular integrated design.

The most dramatic way to recognize the mechanical equipment as a legitimate part of architecture is to expose

it to view. Especially at a time when a more ornate and colorful style is replacing the simplicity and clean lines of modern architecture, the exposed mechanical equipment can add complexity and richness to a building.

An example of this approach is the Occupational Health Center in Columbus, Indiana, where all the pipes and ducts are exposed to view (Fig. 16.21c). Bright colors define and clarify the various systems of supply air, return air, hot-water heating, etc.

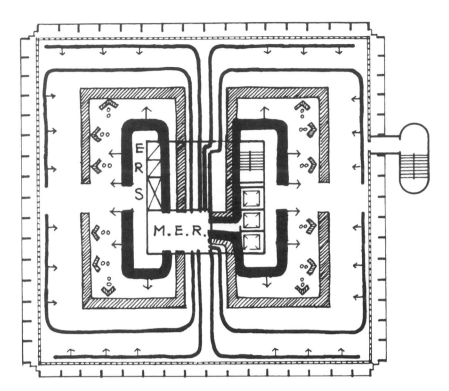

Figure 16.21b Plan of the Hoffmann-La Roche Building. S, supply-riser duct; R, return-riser duct; E, exhaust-riser duct. (After *Design and Technology in Architecture* by D. Guise.)

Figure 16.21c Exposing the mechanical equipment can add richness and complexity to architecture. Occupational Health Center, Columbus, Indiana, by Hardy, Holzman, Pfeiffer. (Courtesy of Cummins Corporation.)

Since exposed ducts must be made of better material and require higher-quality work, they cost more than conventional equipment. This higher cost can be offset by savings from the elimination of a suspended-ceiling system.

At the Centre Pompidou, in Paris, architects Richard Rogers and Renzo Piano exposed the mechanical equipment not only on the interior but also on the exterior (Fig. 16.21d). Any heat gain or loss to the ducts and pipes exposed on the interior is either helpful or not very harmful. For example, in the winter, any heat lost from ducts on pipes will help heat the interior. This is definitely not the case with exterior ducts or pipes, which are exposed to the harsh climate. It is worthwhile to note that in nature no creatures have their guts on the outside of their skin. Such creatures might be born, but they do not survive. The Centre Pompidou might be a great monument, but it should not be a prototype for more ordinary buildings, where most of the mechanical equipment should be on the inside of the building skin.

16.22 CONCLUSION

The architect determines the size, and to some extent the design, of the mechanical system during tiers one and two of the three-tier design approach. When the design of the building itself addresses heating, cooling, and lighting, the mechanical and electrical loads can be reduced as much as 80 percent. Even the remaining 20 percent can be further reduced when the architect works with the engineers. For example, short, straight, and large ducts require much less fan power than their opposites.

Now that society realizes the importance of sustainability, it is vital that we also recognize the responsibility and the opportunity for architects to reduce the energy appetite of buildings. No professionals other than politicians have as great an impact on the environment as architects.

Figure 16.21d The Centre Pompidou. Paris, France, by Richard Rogers and Renzo Piano. Much of the mechanical equipment is exposed on the exterior of the building. Biomimicry would suggest, however, that it is not a good idea to expose the guts to the outdoors. (Photograph by Clark Lundell.)

KEY IDEAS OF CHAPTER 16

1. Mechanical heating should supply only the small amount of heat still needed after a tight thermal envelope (tier one) and passive solar energy (tier two) have been fully utilized.

2. Fireplaces are highly inefficient unless they have a heat exchanger, outdoor combustion air, and doors. Stoves are much more efficient than even the best fireplaces.

3. All but the smallest buildings have more than one thermal zone.

4. The number of required zones has a great impact on the choice of a mechanical system

5. Heating systems
   a. Hot-water (hydronic) systems are efficient and comfortable but generally are not useful for cooling.
   b. Hot-air systems are appropriate when cooling is also required.
   c. Electric-resistance heating should be used as little as possible because it is most wasteful of energy.
   d. Heat pumps are an efficient way to heat with electricity. Earth-coupled heat pumps are more efficient than air-to-air heat pumps.
   e. **Combined heat and power (CHP)** systems can supply heat at low cost.

6. Mechanical cooling should supply only the small amount of cooling still required after all the heat avoidance (tier 1) and passive cooling (tier 2) techniques have been employed.

7. Cooling systems use refrigeration machines to pump heat from lower temperatures indoors to higher temperatures outdoors.

8. Although the compression refrigeration cycle is more efficient than the absorption refrigeration cycle, an inexpensive source of heat can make the absorption cycle attractive.

9. In the compression cycle, the refrigerant moves heat from the evaporator coil to the condenser coil.

10. Ground-coupled heat pumps are now called **geo-exchange** heat pumps. Four energy sources/sinks are possible: ponds, well water, vertical ground loops, and horizontal ground loops.

11. Chillers produce chilled water that is used in air-handling units and fan-coil units.

12. Large quantities of heat are more efficiently dumped into the atmosphere by evaporative coolers and cooling towers.

13. Package units allow a maximum of mechanical fabrication to be performed in the factory.

14. Split systems are, in effect, two-package systems.

15. Internal duct insulation and sections of flexible ducts control mechanical noise and vibration.

16. **Variable-air-volume (VAV) systems** are efficient but are limited to either heating or cooling a building at any one time.

17. Fan-coil systems provide many zones at modest cost, but they provide fresh air only if they are located on an outside wall.

18. **Mechanical-equipment rooms (MERs)** should be centrally located to minimize the quantity and complexity of the ductwork.

19. Round ducts are most efficient, but oblong rectangular ducts require less headroom. Flat, oval ducts are a compromise.

20. Diffusers and registers mix supply air and room air without causing drafts. Both have dampers to control the volume of air. Grilles might or might not direct the flow of air, and they do *not* contain dampers.

21. **Indoor-air quality (IAQ)** is the highest priority for health and productivity. Clean, healthy air is achieved by:
    a. Eliminating sources of pollution (e.g. volatile organic compounds [VOCs])
    b. Directly exhausting the source of pollutants
    c. Using ventilation to dilute pollutants
    d. Using living plants to clean air

22. Heat-recovery units are excellent devices for minimizing heat loss from ventilation. Both sensible and latent heat can be recovered from these air-to-air heat exchangers.

23. Displacement ventilation is more efficient than conventional ventilation in eliminating pollutants.

24. The economizer cycle uses cold outdoor air when available to cool a building.

25. Combined heat and power (CHP) systems, formerly known as **cogeneration systems**, can be more efficient than buying electricity and heating energy separately.

26. District heating and cooling systems are more efficient than smaller individual systems.

27. Thermal-storage systems can take advantage of low night electricity rates and the greater efficiency of running refrigeration machines in cool night air. The energy storage (heat sink) can be in the form of chilled water, ice, or the mass of the building itself.

28. Exposing mechanical equipment and ducts on the interior is efficient and has aesthetic potential. Exposing mechanical and equipment on the outside of the thermal envelope is very inefficient and should be avoided.

29. Ducts should be located inside the thermal envelope whenever possible.

Resources

FURTHER READING

(See the Bibliography in the back of the book for full citations.)

Allen, E. *How Buildings Work: The Natural Order of Architecture,* 2nd ed.

Allen, E., and J. Iano. *The Architect's Studio Companion: Technical Guidelines for Preliminary Design,* 3rd ed.

ASHRAE. *Air-Conditioning Systems Design Manual.*

ASHRAE. *Terminology of Heating, Ventilation, Air Conditioning, and Refrigeration,* 2nd ed.

Bachmann, L. *Integrated Buildings: The Systems Basis of Architecture.*

Baird, G. *The Architectural Expression of Environmental Control Systems.*

Banham, R. *The Architecture of the Well-Tempered Environment,* 2nd ed.

Bearg, D.W. *Indoor Air Quality and HVAC Systems.*

Bobenhausen, W. *Simplified Design of HVAC Systems.*

Bradshaw, V. *Building Control Systems,* 3rd ed.

Egan, M. D. *Concepts in Thermal Comfort.*

Flynn, J. E. *Architectural Interior Systems: Lighting, Acoustics, Air Conditioning,* 3rd ed.

Grumman, D. L., ed. *ASHRAE Green Guide.*

Guise, D. *Design and Technology in Architecture.*

Knight, P. A. *Mechanical Systems Retrofit Manual: A Guide for Residential Design.*

Lang, P. V. *Principles of Air Conditioning.*

Lyle, D. *The Book of Masonry Stoves: Rediscovering an Old Way of Warming.*

Reid, E. *Understanding Buildings: A Multidisciplinary Approach.*

Rush, R. D., ed. *The Building Systems Integration Handbook.*

Stein, B., S. Reynolds, W. T. Grondzik, and A. G. Kwok. *Mechanical and Electrical Equipment for Buildings,* 10th ed.

Trost, J. *Heating, Ventilating, and Air Conditioning.*

Wright, L. *Homefires Burning: The History of Domestic Heating and Cooking.*

ORGANIZATIONS

(See Appendix K for full citations.)
American Society of Heating, Refrigerating, and Air-Conditioning Engineers (ASHRAE) www.ashrae.org
GeoExchange www.geoexchange.org
The vital Signs Project www.ced.berkeley.edu/cedr/vs

CASE STUDIES

The fact is that our schools have now educated several generations of architects who depend exclusively on nonarchitectural means of environmental adaptation. The problems of this approach are now emerging, partly as an energy-consumption dilemma, but perhaps, more to my point, problems of architectural expression have appeared. A paucity of vocabulary has emerged as a professional and artistic dilemma: If all environmental problems can be handled by chemical and mechanical means, who needs the architect?

Ralph L. Knowles,
Sun Rhythm Form, *1981*

17.1 INTRODUCTION

Ralph Knowles answers the question he raises in the quote on the previous page. He argues that by responding to the energy and environmental problems, the designer enriches architecture. The following case studies were chosen in part to show how addressing environmental problems can create excellent architecture.

Up to this point, buildings have been used to illustrate the concept being discussed at the moment. However, since buildings must address many issues simultaneously, they must also incorporate many different design strategies. The successful integration of many environmental concepts is demonstrated in the following examples.

The buildings presented here as case studies are successful in part

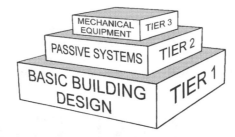

Figure 17.1 The heating, cooling, and lighting needs of buildings are best and most sustainably met by the three-tier design approach. The case studies presented in this chapter fully address the appropriate issues at each of the three tiers.

because their designers addressed environmental control issues at all three tiers: basic building design, passive systems, and mechanical equipment (Fig. 17.1). The case studies include a variety of building types, sizes, and styles.

17.2 THE REAL GOODS SOLAR LIVING CENTER

Retail store outside of Hopland, California

Architects: Van der Ryn Architects/ Ecological Design Institute and Arkin Tilt Architects

Landscape designers: Stephanie Kotin and Chris Tebbutt

Area: 5000 ft² (450 m²)

Built: 1996

The Real Goods Trading Company sells merchandise needed for a sustainable lifestyle and is a leading source of renewable-energy equipment. When new facilities were needed, its president and founder, John Schaeffer, decided it was time to "walk our talk."

A barren, blighted site was chosen in part because of its need for regeneration. The company wanted to demonstrate how to restore a rich ecology to land that had been ruined. Unlike the usual situation, the landscaping was started before the building construction so that the gardens and trees could start their long process of restoring life to this site. Plants were carefully chosen to return nitrates to the ground, thereby making chemical fertilizer unnecessary. Since the site was in a floodplain, ponds were excavated and the fill was used to raise the building above the 100-year flood level.

The landscaping was designed to delight visitors and customers and to engender the love of nature necessary for the restoration of the whole planet (see Chapter 7, Fig. 7.16c). The design of the landscape was based on the three themes of "inspiration, production (food gardens), and restoration." Part of the inspiration came from design elements that reflect the daily and seasonal cycles of our lives. Besides sundials of various sizes, shapes, and materials, there are fountains that rise and fall with the daily and seasonal cycles of the sun (Fig. 17.2a). The fountains and irrigation systems are powered by PV arrays whose output is proportional to the

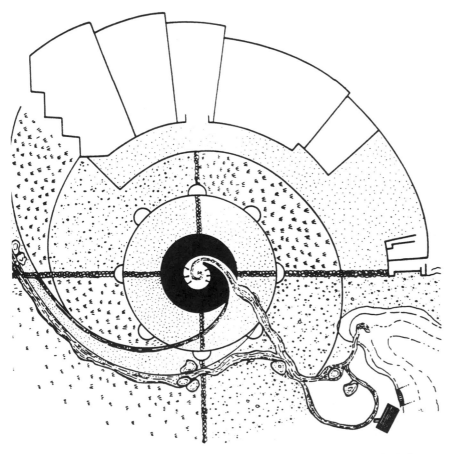

Figure 17.2a Water from a central fountain flows into the garden along several spiraling streams. The cardinal directions are clearly expressed in the landscaping design. The building protects the north side of the courtyard from the winter wind. (Courtesy Van der Ryn Architects ©.)

Figure 17.2b The all-glass south facade collects ample sunlight for winter heating and year-round daylighting. Large light shelves reflect much of the light off the ceiling to illuminate the far interior. (Illustration by David Arkin, A.I.A., Albany, CA.)

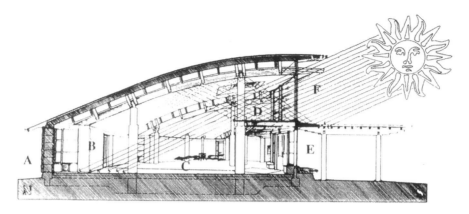

Cold Day Heating Mode

A. The mass of the highly insulated strawable and PISE™ walls produce a thermal "flywheel" effect, storing and releasing heat.

B. Stored heat in the thermal mass in the concrete floor and columns is also released to maintain comfort.

C. Efficient wood-burning stoves (working display models) are the only source of supplemental heat.

D. Light shelves control glare and direct gain, reflecting light on the curved ceiling.

E. Doors and windows can be opened to provide immediate cooling if the temperature indoors is too warm.

F. The low winter sun penetrates the building through substantial south-facing glazing.

Figure 17.2c On winter nights, the large light shelves rotate up to create additional insulation for the upper south-facing glazing. (Illustration by David Arkin, A.I.A., Albany, CA.)

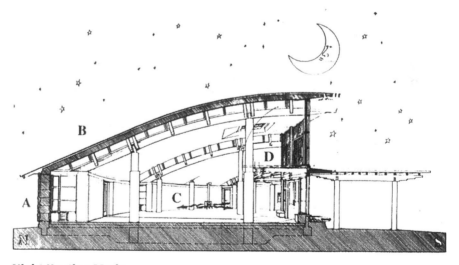

Night Heating Mode

A. The insulation in the straw bale and roof helps to retain the day's heat inside the building mass.

B. The 12 in. (30 cm) cellulose (recycled newspaper) insulation in the roof provides an R-value greater than 42 (8 SI).

C. The wood-burning stoves can be left on a slow burn on the coldest nights, balancing heat loss.

D. Light shelves are hinged and can be folded against the high glazing to reduce heat loss to the night sky.

amount of sunshine. Thus, the evaporative cooling from the fountains and irrigation systems rises to a maximum when the need is at a maximum, in the summer. All of the landscaping was carefully designed to moderate the intense summer heat through shading and evaporative cooling.

The Solar Living Center was designed to be energy-independent. Because of the energy-conscious architecture, it is possible for a small wind machine and seven PV-tracker arrays to generate most of the electricity needed on an annual basis. The building is connected to the power grid mainly to avoid the need for batteries. Power is bought at night, but during a typical sunny summer day, surplus electricity is generated and sold to the power company.

A sophisticated daylighting design enables the electric lighting to be on only about 200 hours instead of the more than 3000 hours per year of a standard retail or commercial building. Model studies showed that large south-facing windows with light shelves reflecting off a curved ceiling would create high-quality daylighting (see Fig. 17.2b). The light shelves are translucent so that the area underneath is not in darkness. On winter nights, the light shelves can be swung up to add additional insulation to the glazing (see Fig. 17.2c). Because the roofs were stepped up toward the west, a series of east-facing clerestories pick up additional daylighting. Automatic controls are used to turn off the electric lighting when sufficient daylight is present, and all lighting comes from fluorescent lamps—no incandescent lamps are used at all.

Heat transfer through the thermal envelope was kept to a minimum with generous insulation levels. The roof has 12 in. (30 cm) of loose cellulose with an R-value of about 42 (8 SI). There is also a 1½ in. (4 cm) air space with a radiant barrier that has an R-value of about 8 (1.4 SI) in summer and 2 (0.4 SI) in winter. The roofing membrane is made of white Hypalon,™ which reflects about 75 percent of the solar radiation.

The walls are made of 23-in.-thick rice straw-bales with an R-value of about 34 (6 SI) (see Fig. 17.2d). The bales are sprayed using gunite equipment, first with about 1 in. (25mm) of cement stucco and then with 3 in. (75 mm) more of Pise,™ a soil-cement mixture that gives the building a rich reddish-brown color (see Fig. 17.2e). The windows, most of which face south, are double-glazed with low-e for an R-value of about 2.8 (0.5 SI). Thus, little heat is lost in the winter, and very little heat is gained in the summer through the thermal envelope.

The main thermal load occurs in the summer, when temperatures are frequently higher than 100°F (38°C). The three-tier approach to cooling design was used. **Heat avoidance** was the first-tier strategy, utilizing high

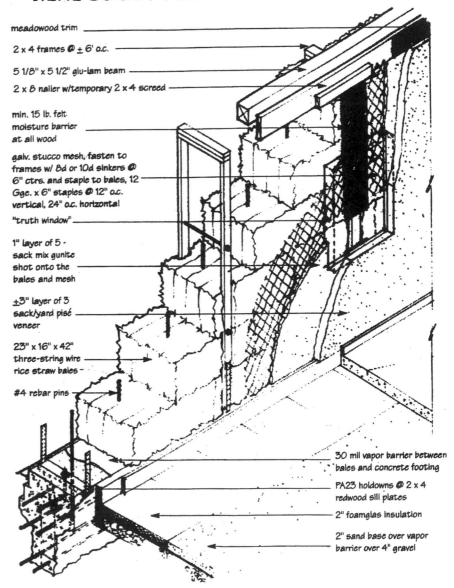

REAL GOODS STRAW BALE WALL SYSTEM

meadowood trim

2 x 4 frames @ ± 6' o.c.

5 1/8" x 5 1/2" glu-lam beam

2 x 8 nailer w/temporary 2 x 4 screed

min. 15 lb. felt moisture barrier at all wood

galv. stucco mesh, fasten to frames w/ 8d or 10d sinkers @ 6" ctrs. and staple to bales, 12 Gge. x 6" staples @ 12" o.c. vertical, 24" o.c. horizontal

"truth window"

1" layer of 5-sack mix gunite shot onto the bales and mesh

±3" layer of 3 sack/yard pisé veneer

23" x 16" x 42" three-string wire rice straw bales

#4 rebar pins

30 mil vapor barrier between bales and concrete footing

PA23 holdowns @ 2 x 4 redwood sill plates

2" foamglas insulation

2" sand base over vapor barrier over 4" gravel

Figure 17.2d The straw-bale walls were reinforced with steel rebar pins and wood frames. The walls are covered with a subcoat of cement stucco and finished with about 3 in. (75 mm) of a soil-cement mixture known as Pise. (Courtesy Van der Ryn Architects©.)

Figure 17.2e This view from the northwest shows the soil-cement finish on the straw-bale walls. (Courtesy Van der Ryn Architects©.)

when the outdoor temperature is higher than the indoor temperature. The top of the south glazing is shaded by overhangs, the middle section by awnings, and the lowest part by a trellis, which also shades the courtyard in front of the building to prevent reflected heat and glare (see Figs. 17.2h and 17.2i). The west wall has a sawtooth arrangement so that windows on the west facade all face south (see again Fig. 17.2e).

For the third tier, evaporative coolers were installed; however, they have never been turned on. Tiers one and two have been so effective that they are all that are needed. A customer once reprimanded the staff members for setting the air conditioning too low. She was astonished to learn that there was no air-conditioning equipment, only heat avoidance and passive cooling. Even on the hottest days, the indoor temperature stays in the 70s (°F) (21°–27°C).

In winter, the building is heated mainly by direct gain through the all-glass south wall. The large amount of mass is again useful for storing heat. On cold winter mornings, several wood stoves are used as auxiliary heaters, as demonstration items (one of the products for sale), and for ambiance.

To create such sustainable buildings, the architect Sim Van der Ryn uses a seven-part design process he calls "Eco-Logic" (Schaeffer, 1997):

1. Create program scenarios.
2. Analyze the site and ecological resources.
3. Investigate renewable and sustainable materials and systems.
4. Design the vision.
5. Develop and integrate systems.
6. Complete the detailed design.
7. Facilitate the construction.

Experience has shown that this design process results in buildings that have lower life-cycle costs, a high level of sustainability, a high satisfaction level for the owner and users, and higher productivity for the people working in the buildings.

levels of insulation, a very reflective roof membrane, no west windows (see Fig. 17.2f), few east windows, daylighting, and shading for all windows. The second-tier strategy involved night-flush cooling, because the dry climate has a large diurnal temperature range. At night, outdoor air drawn in through openings near the floor cools the massive floor, the walls, and the concrete columns, while the warm air leaves through the operable east clerestories (see Fig. 17.2g). Fans, wind, and the stack effect all help to ventilate the building. During summer days, the windows are closed

Figure 17.2f This view from the southwest shows that no windows face west. A sawtooth arrangement on the lower west wall has all glazing on the west facade facing south. (Courtesy Van der Ryn Architects©.)

Figure 17.2g Night-flush ventilation through the operable east clerestories enables the internal mass to cool down in preparation for the next hot day. (Illustration by David Arkin, A.I.A., Albany, CA.)

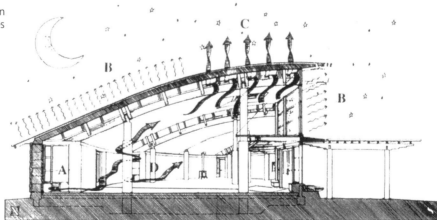

Night Cooling Mode

A. Fans in the evaporative coolers run after hot (100° F+ [38°C+]) days for additional air changes.

B. The roof and high windows radiate heat to the night sky.

C. A stack effect draws out warm air through clerestory windows and draws in cooler air through openings near the floor.

D. Night-sky radiation and cool night temperatures are used to "charge" the thermal mass of the building for the next day.

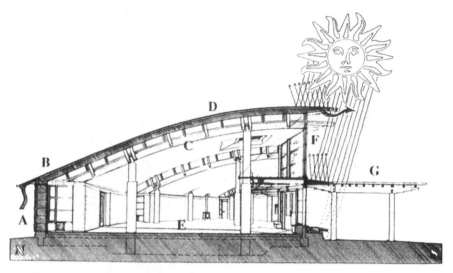

Figure 17.2h The impact of summer heat is prevented by high insulation levels, a very reflective roof membrane, and extensive shading. (Illustration by David Arkin, A.I.A., Albany, CA.)

Hot-Day Cooling Mode

A. The thermal mass and high insulation value of the straw-bale and PISE (sprayed soil-cement) wall protect against the thermal transfer of 1008°F+ (38°C+) outdoor summer temperatures.

B. The air space in the roof ventilates heat from the radiant barrier over 12 in. (30 cm) of cellulose insulation (R-50).

C. Clerestory windows are closed when the outside temperature exceeds the interior temperature.

D. The white Hypalon (synthetic rubber) roof membrane reflects gain from solar radiation.

E. The thermal mass of the concrete floor and columns absorbs heat from people and equipment; it is a heat sink due to the previous night flush.

F. Overhang and awnings shade windows, controlling solar gain. Light shelves and the curved white ceiling distribute daylight evenly, reducing the need for heat-producing lighting fixtures.

G. Trellis shades walls, windows, and the walkway in summer; allows gain in winter, and controls glare.

Van der Ryn has also developed five ecological principles that guide him in his design process (Schaeffer, 1997):

1. The best solution starts from paying attention to the unique qualities of the place.
2. Trace the direct and indirect environmental costs of design decisions: use ecological accounting, or **environomics**.
3. Mimic nature's processes in design so that your design fits nature.

The four key laws of ecological systems are:
a. Nature lives off solar income as captured in food webs.
b. All wastes are recycled as food for other processes.
c. Biodiversity promotes stability.
d. Networks of relationships are maintained through feedback.
4. Honor every voice in the design process (local residents and builders, building occupants, maintenance people, and skilled construction people).

5. Making nature visible through design transforms both makers and users.

Most of the information about the Solar Living Center comes from a book that the author highly recommends:

A Place in the Sun: The Evolution of the Real Goods Solar Living Center, Chelsea Green Publishing Co., White River Jct., Vermont, 1997, by John Schaeffer. (Also recommended is *Ecological Design*, Island Press, Washington, D.C., 1995, by Sim Van der Ryn and Stuart Cowan.)

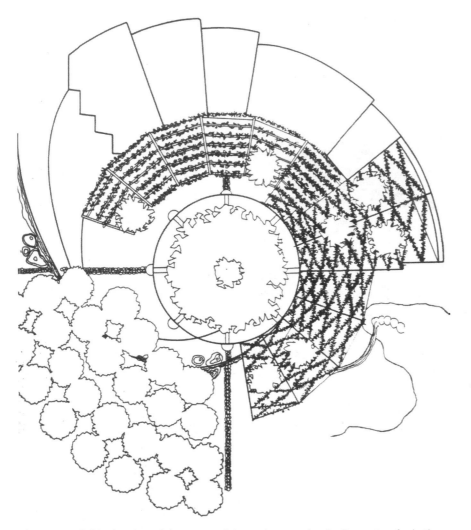

Figure 17.2i This plan view of the courtyard shows the extensive shading system for both the courtyard and the south windows of the building. Japanese grapevine was chosen for the trellis along the building. (North is up.) (Courtesy ©Van der Ryn Architects.)

17.3 THE URBAN VILLA

Apartment building in Amstelveen, the Netherlands, at 52° N latitude
Architect: Atelier Z, Zavrel Architecten BV, Rotterdam, Netherlands
Area: about 50,000 ft² (4500 m²)
Built: 1995

The Urban Villa project was built to prove that extreme energy savings are not an obstacle to good architecture in the predominantly cool and cloudy climate of the Netherlands, where the average maximum summer temperature is about 65°F (18°C) and the

average minimum winter temperature is about 35°F (2°C). The design takes advantage of a compact shape and many shared walls to greatly reduce the exterior exposure (see Chapter 7, Fig. 7.6h). The central atrium/sun space acts as an entrance vestibule, as well as a preheater for winter ventilation (Fig. 17.3a).

The design team decided to utilize passive solar heating and a superinsulated envelope to meet most of the winter-heating requirement. The superinsulated envelope has these R-values:

R-38 (6.8 SI) for the roof
R-33 (6 SI) for the walls
R-8 (1.4 SI) for the windows (very high for windows), and
R-1 (0.2 SI) for the sun-space glazing.

The concrete structure adds thermal mass, and the continuous exterior insulation reduces the number of heat bridges, which are minimized when they do occur. For example, the balconies have a separate structural system so that only a few small heat bridges are needed to tie the balconies to the main building.

Because of the low winter sun at 52° N latitude (Seattle is at only about 48° N latitude), even deep balconies allow much solar access on the south side for passive solar heating (Fig. 17.3b). Because 40 percent of the south facade is glass, the designers also decided that effective shading and ventilation would be needed to prevent summer overheating. In the summer, however, the balconies are not deep enough to fully shade the windows on hot days. Thus, an exterior roller shade was added at the outside edge of the balconies to descend automatically when indoor temperatures get too high (see again Fig. 17.3b). The sloped glazing of the atrium roof is also shaded on the inside during the summer (Fig. 17.3d bottom).

During the summer, both natural and forced ventilation are used for cooling. Cross-ventilation, high and low windows (Fig. 17.3c), and exhaust fans remove the hot indoor air. Besides the shading, the atrium is kept from overheating by opening high and low vents (Fig. 17.3d bottom). To maintain IAQ in the apartments in the winter, preheated air from the sunspace/atrium passes through heat-recovery units to ventilate each apartment with minimal energy losses (Fig. 17.3d top).

Domestic hot water is supplied primarily from active solar panels on the roof (Fig. 17.3d middle). The sun supplies about 60 percent of the hot water, and high-efficiency (90 percent) gas auxiliary boilers supply the rest, as well as provide space heating when necessary. Building monitoring has shown that energy consumption

1. living room
2. kitchen
3. bedroom
4. balcony
5. terrace
6. bridge
7. gallery
8. atrium

2nd   FLOOR   PLAN

Figure 17.3a The plan of the Urban Villa apartment building.

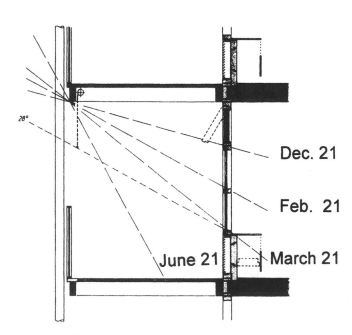

28°

Dec. 21

Feb. 21

June 21   March 21

Figure 17.3b A section through the balcony shows the summer and winter sun angles. Note the roll-down shade. (Courtesy Atelier Z, Zavrel Architecten, BV.)

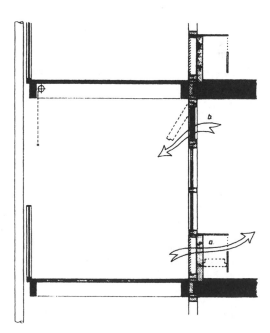

Figure 17.3c Summer ventilation is by means of high and low openings. The low openings are through heating convectors. (Courtesy Atelier Z, Zavrel Architecten BV.)

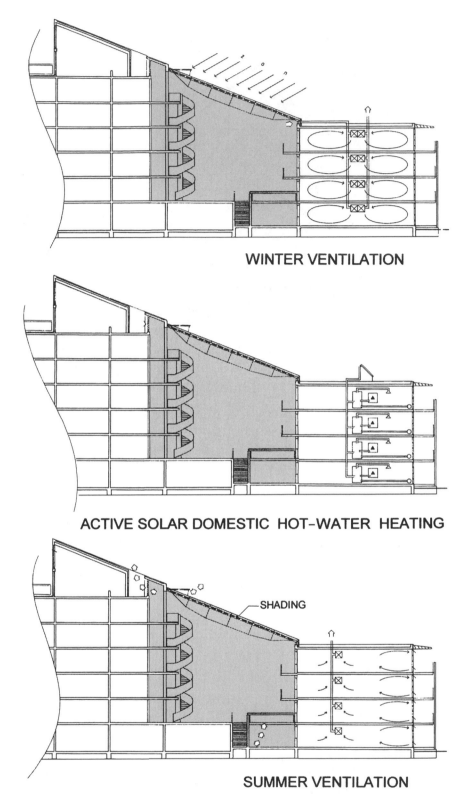

WINTER VENTILATION

ACTIVE SOLAR DOMESTIC HOT-WATER HEATING

SHADING

SUMMER VENTILATION

Figure 17.3d Top: Winter passive solar heating for the south facade and the atrium/sunspace that preheats the ventilation air for the apartments is shown. Additionally, heat exchangers recover much of the heat from the exhaust air. Middle: Active solar supplies most of the domestic hot water. Each apartment has its own storage tank and auxiliary gas boiler for both domestic hot water and space heating. Bottom: Summer shading and ventilation is shown. (Courtesy Atelier Z, Zavrel Architecten, BV.)

is 60 to 70 percent lower than that of conventional design, and the users are very satisfied with the buildings.

17.4 THE EMERALD PEOPLE'S UTILITY DISTRICT HEADQUARTERS

Office building near Eugene, Oregon
Architects: Equinox Design and
    WEGROUP, PC, Architects
Area: 24,000 ft² (2160 m²)
Built: 1987

This sophisticated design is a consequence of the collaboration between Equinox Design Inc., WEGROUP PC Architects, and an enlightened electric utility in need of a new headquarters complex, which includes the office building described here (Fig. 17.4a). The climate consists of cool winters, mild summers, and overcast days much of the year. The goal was to design a building that not only

created a pleasant and attractive work environment but also was energy-conscious.

With the building designed as a south-facing elongated rectangle, east–west windows were avoided and no point within the building is far from either north or south windows. All south windows, including the south-facing clerestory, have vine-covered trellises for protection from the high summer sun. In the winter, the deciduous vines lose their leaves and allow solar energy to heat the building (Fig 17.4b). Concrete-block exterior walls, concrete-block interior fin walls, and concrete ceiling planks provide ample thermal mass.

This same mass is used in the summer for night-flush cooling. The interior of the building is flushed with cool night air so that the mass can act as a heat sink the next day. To increase the efficiency of the thermal mass, air is blown through the cavities in the precast, hollow-core concrete slabs (Fig. 17.4c). Thus, at night

the slabs are thoroughly cooled with outdoor air, and during the day the slabs cool the circulating indoor air. Air is also blown through the hollow-core slabs on winter mornings to extract the heat stored in the concrete.

Numerous techniques were used to bring quality daylight to all parts of the building. Windows are T-shaped so that most of the glazing is placed high (Fig. 17.4d). Both north and south windows are supplied with interior light shelves. The view glazing, which is placed lower on the walls, is shaded by the vine-covered trellises. Venetian blinds provide additional protection from low sun angles. Sunlight entering through the clerestory windows is reflected off the ceiling. Glare from the clerestory windows is avoided by a large air-conditioning duct and by vine-covered trellises (Fig. 17.4b).

The electric lighting is a task/ambient system. Indirect fluorescent fixtures supply a very diffused ambient light ideal for offices, especially when computers are used. The fixtures are

Figure 17.4a The Emerald People's Utility District Headquarters (Courtesy of WEGROUP PC Architects and Planners, Solar Strategies by John Reynolds Equinox Design Inc.)

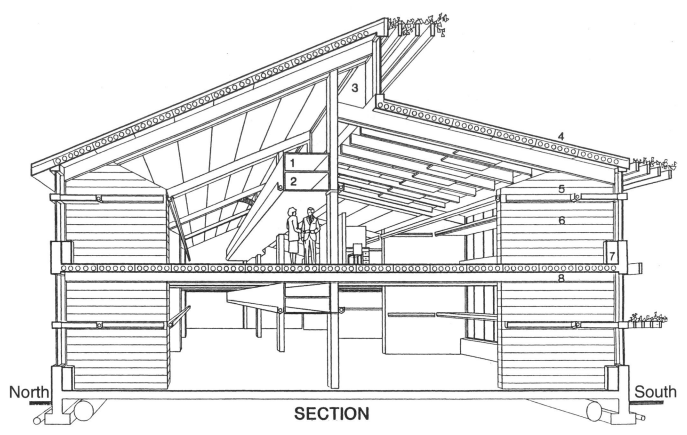

North   **SECTION**   South

Figure 17.4b A perspective section. 1, Night air flush cooling; 2, conditioned air supply; 3, clerestory windows; 4, core-slab roof; 5, indoor light shelves; 6, fin walls; 7, conditioned air return; 8, core-slab floor. (Courtesy of WEGROUP PC Architects and Planners, Solar Strategies by John Reynolds, Equinox Design Inc.)

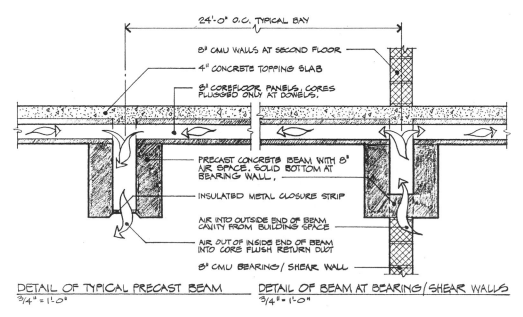

DETAIL OF TYPICAL PRECAST BEAM
3/4" = 1'-0"

DETAIL OF BEAM AT BEARING/SHEAR WALLS
3/4" = 1'-0"

Figure 17.4c Details of air flow through precast, hollow-core concrete slabs. (Courtesy of WEGROUP PC Architects and Planners, Solar Strategies by John Reynolds, Equinox Design Inc.)

Figure 17.4d T- shaped windows place most of the glazing up high for deep daylight penetration. The light shelf reflects the sunlight to the ceiling. (From Solar 88: 13th National Passive Conference. Proceedings. © American Solar Energy Society, 1988.)

arranged in rows parallel to the windows so that light sensors can progressively turn off rows as more daylight becomes available (Fig. 17.4b).

A variable-air-volume (VAV) system is supplemented by large exhaust fans for summer night-flush cooling and by electric-resistance heaters under the windows for auxiliary winter heating. An economizer cycle allows outside air to be used for cooling when the outdoor temperature is low enough. Windows that open also allow outdoor air to be used for cooling, especially during the spring and fall.

Because ceilings and walls are hard surfaces that reflect sound, floors are covered with carpets, and acoustical baffles hang from the ceiling. These baffles run perpendicular to the windows to avoid blocking the entering daylight.

The vine trellises on the south-facing windows deserve some extra comments (Fig. 17.4b). The vines add to both the commodity and delight of the building. They not only shade the windows but do it in phase with the thermal year. Much of the year, the vines also filter and soften the daylight. Because of the vines, the appearance of the building changes with the seasons. Even the view from the interior changes radically from the dense green leaves of summer to the colorful leaves of autumn to the leafless vines of winter.

Finally, another special feature of this building was the creation of a *User's Manual*. The owner realized that this building would function properly only with the cooperation of the users. The architect was asked to create a manual to explain the building to the employees working there. Figure 17.4d is one of the illustrations from that manual.

17.5 COLORADO MOUNTAIN COLLEGE

Blake Avenue College Center, Glenwood Springs, Colorado
Architect: Peter Dobrovolny, A.I.A., of Sunup Ltd.
Area: 32,000 ft² (2880 m²)
Built: 1981

This college and community building is located in Glenwood Springs, which lies in a sunny, arid region on the western slope of the Colorado Rockies (see Chapter 7, Fig. 7.9f). Winters are very cold, with a great deal of snow. Warm summer days and cool nights generate high diurnal temperature swings.

Although the climate suggests that the main concern is winter heating, the fairly large building is mainly an internally dominated type. Thus the cooling load from people and lights was more of a concern than originally expected. Through improvement of the daylighting, the cooling load was reduced sufficiently so that conventional air conditioning was not required.

This three-story building has community education facilities on the first two floors and offices on the third (Fig. 17.5a). The building has an atrium that acts not only as a central circulation and meeting space, but also as a source of solar heating and daylighting (Fig. 17.5b).

A combination of energy efficiency and solar energy furnishes most of the heating needs. The backup electric-resistance baseboard heaters are needed mainly in the morning until the warmth of the sun is felt. By building into the side of a south-facing hill, much of the building is earth-sheltered. Floors, walls, and roofs are very well insulated (R-17, R-26, and R-34, [3, 4.7, and 6.1 SI], respectively). In addition to the double or triple glazing, all windows are covered with movable insulation at night. All entries into the building are the air-lock vestibule type.

Much of the solar heating occurs via the central sunspace atrium (Figs. 17.5b and c). South-facing, stepped clerestory windows collect both the direct sun and the indirect sun off the highly reflective roof. The heat is then stored in the concrete floor, masonry walls, and exposed-steel structure. At night, automatic insulating curtains cover the clerestory windows (Fig. 17.5d). The otherwise unheated atrium can be shut off from the conditioned spaces by glass doors and movable walls. Antistratification ducts bring the warm air collecting near the ceiling of the atrium back down to the ground-floor level.

Solar Trombe walls make up most of the south facade that is not covered by windows. Automatic insulating curtains drop between the thermal wall and glazing to greatly reduce nighttime losses (Fig. 17.5e). The daycare center on the ground floor has a sunspace filled with water tubes to provide the required thermal mass. A series of skylights introduces heat and light to those parts of the building not facing south walls. Movable reflectors on the skylights increase winter collection while reducing summer overheating (Fig. 17.5f).

This college building (except the computer room) is cooled in summer only by passive means (Fig. 17.5g). The cooling load is minimized by a

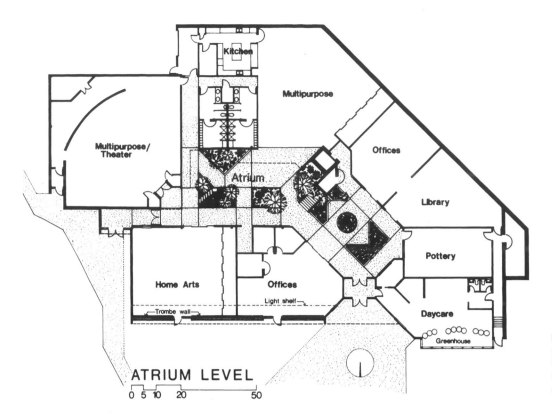

Figure 17.5a The first-floor plan of the Colorado Mountain College, Glenwood Springs, Colorado, is shown. (Courtesy of Peter Dobrovolny, A.I.A.)

Figure 17.5b A view of the atrium and clerestory windows. (Robert Benson, photographer.)

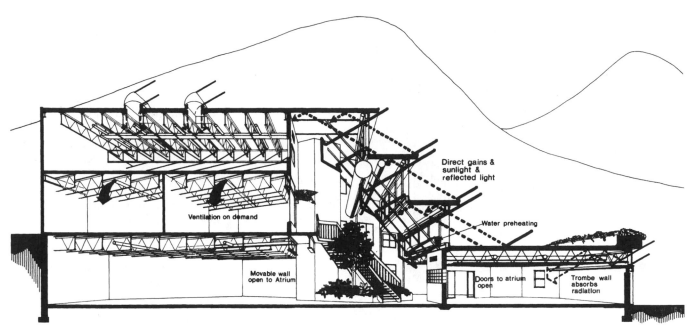

Figure 17.5c Winter-day solar collection. (Courtesy of Peter Dobrovolny, A.I.A.)

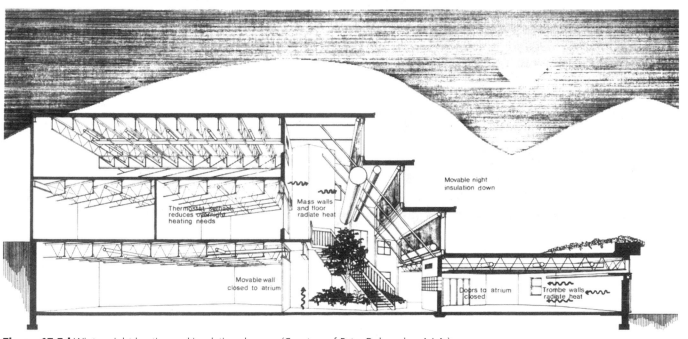

Figure 17.5d Winter-night heating and insulating closures. (Courtesy of Peter Dobrovolny, A.I.A.)

number of different strategies: daylighting, low electric-light levels, a highly reflective white roof surface, seasonal awnings over atrium windows, blinds on west windows, reflectors over skylights, and movable reflective insulation over the Trombe walls.

The modest cooling load that remains is handled mostly by night-flush cooling. Cool night air is brought into the building to cool the thermal mass to about 65°F (18°C) (Fig. 17.5h). The mass acts as a heat sink to hold the indoor temperature below 78°F (25°C) on most summer days. Fans and evaporative coolers come on as needed to handle any unusually high cooling loads.

To help minimize the cooling load, both daylighting and task/ambient lighting strategies were used. With the

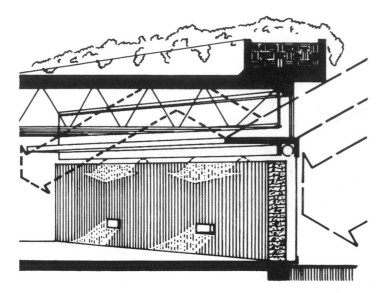

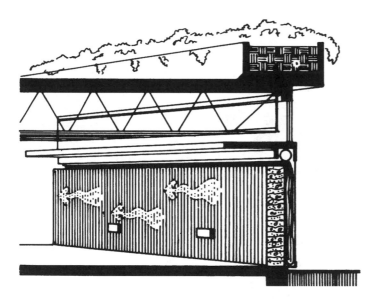

help of physical models, the building was designed so that most interior spaces receive their ambient light from natural sources. Additional task light is supplied as needed. The electric ambient lighting in all spaces can be set at two different levels: low for normal and high for special situations.

On south walls, light shelves introduce quality daylight. Automatic switches turn off the electric lighting when it is not necessary. The highly reflective surfaces on the stepped roofs over the atrium direct much of the light to the atrium ceiling. Adjacent spaces then "borrow" this light from the atrium. As mentioned before, the skylights, which have reversible reflectors, introduce controlled amounts of light.

Domestic hot water is preheated by the sun in a series of large tanks just inside the lower-atrium clerestory windows.

The energy consumption is only about one-fifth of that of a conventional building, and about 60 percent of that small amount comes from passive techniques.

Figure 17.5e Perspective sections illustrating the action of the Trombe walls during a winter day and night. The light shelf introduces both light and direct-gain heating during the day. Note the insulating curtain between the Trombe wall and the glazing during winter nights. (Courtesy of Peter Dobrovolny, A.I.A.)

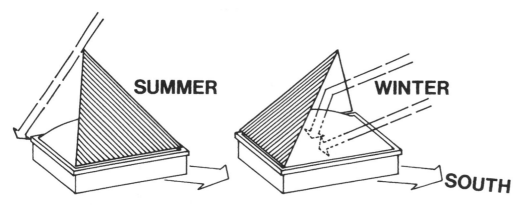

Figure 17.5f Movable reflectors on skylights for summer shade and increased winter solar collection. (Courtesy of Peter Dobrovolny, A.I.A.)

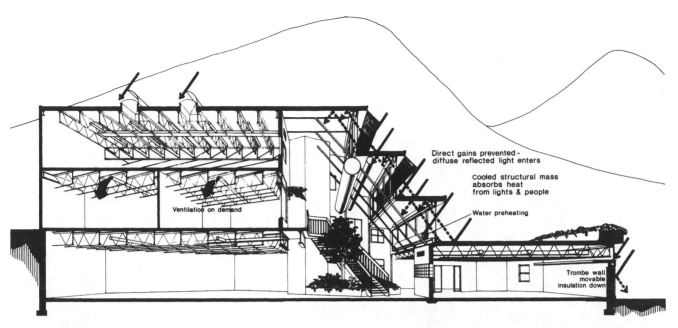

Figure 17.5g Summer-day heat rejection and passive cooling by the heat-sink action of the thermal mass is shown. (Courtesy of Peter Dobrovolny, A.I.A.)

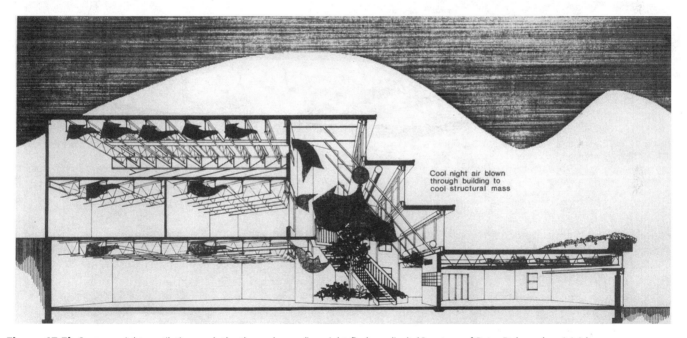

Figure 17.5h Summer-night ventilation cools the thermal mass (i.e. night-flush cooling). (Courtesy of Peter Dobrovolny, A.I.A.)

17.6 GREGORY BATESON BUILDING

State office building in Sacramento, California
Architect: Office of the State Architect for California
Area: 267,000 ft² (24,000 m²)
Built: 1981

It is no accident that this office building was named after the noted anthropologist Gregory Bateson. Although the program called for a building that would set an example for energy-conscious design, it also called for a building that would demonstrate the more humane values in architecture. Thus, this building is inviting to the public and friendly to its users. The aesthetic is not monumental but informal. Many indentations, setbacks, and terraces break up the facade of this rather large office building (Fig. 17.6a).

In the Bateson Building, architectural design and energy features are very well integrated. The rich, warm, articulated facades are largely consequences of the various shading

Figure 17.6a Each facade of the Bateson Building is somewhat different because the solar impact is different on each orientation of the building. Note the horizontal louvers in a horizontal plane on the south facade and the apparent lack of shading on the west facade in this morning photograph. In the afternoon, roll-down exterior shades protect the west windows, just as the east windows are protected in the morning (Fig. 17.6b). Architect: Office of the California State Architect. (Cathy Kelly, photographer.)

elements, and the appearance of the facades varies because the shading needs of different orientations vary (Fig. 17.6b).

Because of its large size and because of the mild climate of Sacramento, the Bateson Building is an internally dominated building. Consequently, cooling rather than heating is the main concern, and daylighting is important in reducing the cooling load. As in any good design, the first priority is to reduce the cooling load from the sun. A trellis system protects the south windows in the summer while allowing the winter sun to enter. Because the building covers a whole city block, east and west windows could not be avoided. Instead, movable exterior

roller shades block the sun on the east in the morning and in the west in the afternoon. These shades automatically glide up and down vertical exterior cables to give east and west windows a clear, sunless view for half of each day (Fig. 17.6c).

The atrium, which creates a conceptually clear circulation core and plaza for the workers and the public, also brings daylight to interior offices (Fig. 17.6d).

The atrium roof glazing is carefully designed to prevent unwanted sunlight from entering. Some of the glazing slopes to the north to capture year-round diffused skylight (Fig. 17.6e). The rest of the roof glazing faces south to capture the winter sun

(Fig. 17.6f). In the summer, this south glazing is protected by movable vertical louvers (Fig. 17.6g).

Although the atrium is not air-conditioned, it does act as a buffer space. Thus, much of the building is not exposed to hot or cold outdoor temperatures. The atrium also brings daylight to some of the interior spaces, thereby reducing the cooling load due to lighting (Fig. 17.6h).

Most of the cooling load that remains after the above-mentioned heat-avoidance techniques are employed is handled by night-flush cooling. Because Sacramento has a large diurnal temperature range (25° to 30°F [14° to 17°C]), cool night air is available to flush out the heat from the

Figure 17.6b Compare the north and east facades in this photograph with the west and south facades in Fig. 17.6a. Note how the east windows are protected from the morning sun.

Figure 17.6c The automated fabric roller shades on the exterior of east and west windows are guided by vertical support cables.

Figure 17.6d A large atrium with south-facing clerestories and north-facing skylights brings light to interior offices in the Bateson Building. The prominent stairs invite people to walk rather than use the elevators. Antistratification tubes hang from the atrium roof. (Courtesy of the Office of the California State Architect.)

thermal mass of the exposed-concrete frame. There are also two 700-ton (630,000 kg) rock beds under the atrium floor for additional thermal mass. During a summer day, this combined mass of rock beds and building structure can absorb enough heat to provide more than 90 percent of the building's cooling needs. The remaining cooling load is served by a conventional chilled-water VAV system. This air system also circulates the cool outdoor night air throughout the building, bringing it into close contact with the concrete structure to more fully recharge the "thermal batteries." Large exhaust fans are placed at the highest points in the atrium to exhaust the hottest air first (Fig. 17.6e).

The heating load in winter is small because of the climate, the small surface-area-to-volume ratio, and the heat produced by people, lights, and equipment. Most of this small heating load is handled by the solar energy received through the south windows and the south-facing atrium clerestories. Since the hot air will rise to the top of the atrium (good in summer but bad in winter), antistratification tubes are suspended from the ceiling of the atrium (Fig. 17.6d). These colorful fabric tubes have fans in their bottom ends that in the winter pull down the warm air collecting near the atrium's ceiling. Also, in winter the rock beds can be used to store excess afternoon heat for use early the following morning. Auxiliary heating comes from perimeter hot-water reheat coils.

By having an atrium, no point in the building is more than 40 ft (12 m) from a natural light source. The atrium receives diffused skylight from the north-facing skylights and direct sunlight from the south-facing clerestories. Banner-type screens are lowered in the winter to prevent glare and excessive brightness ratios from the direct sunlight entering the atrium. In the summer, the vertical louvers on the outside of the south-facing clerestories keep out the direct sun but allow a small amount of diffused light to enter. Windows are shielded from sun and glare by reflective venetian blinds.

Task/ambient lighting provides an efficient glare-free visual environment. Indirect fluorescent fixtures provide the soft ambient lighting, and each workstation has locally controlled task lights.

Figure 17.6e The steeply sloped clerestories face south (toward the right in the photograph) and the sloped skylights face north. Both the clerestories and skylights have exterior shading devices for solar control. The circles on the atrium roof gables are exhaust fans for night-flush cooling. (Courtesy of the Office of the California State Architect.)

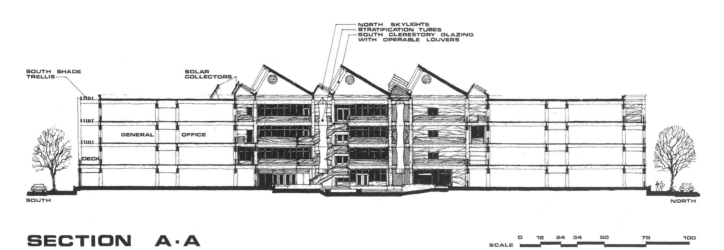

SECTION A·A

Figure 17.6f The north–south section illustrating the sloped south-facing clerestories that capture the winter sun. (Courtesy of the Office of the California State Architect.)

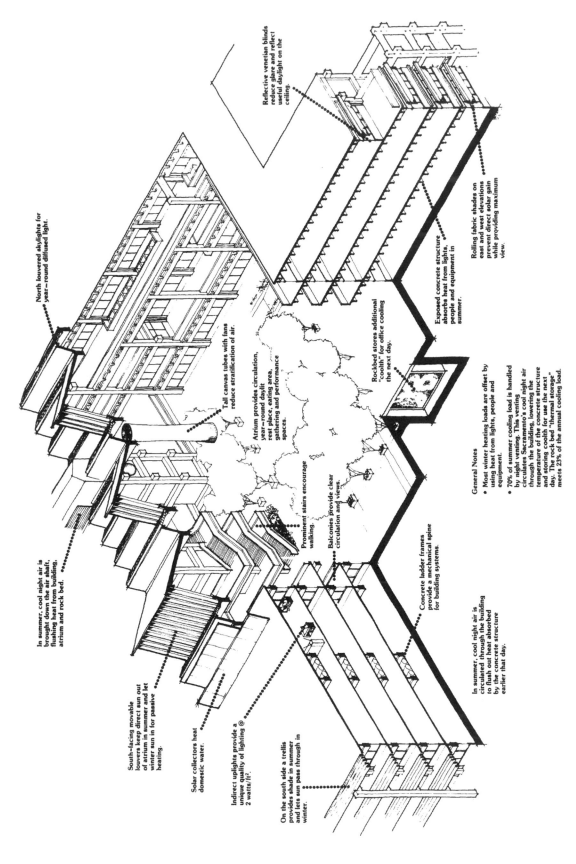

Reflective venetian blinds reduce glare and reflect useful daylight on the ceiling.

Rolling fabric shades on east and west elevations prevent direct solar gain while providing maximum view.

Exposed concrete structure absorbs heat from lights, people and equipment in summer.

Rockbed stores additional "coolth" for office cooling the next day.

North louvered skylights for year-round diffused light.

Tall canvas tubes with fans reduce stratification of air.

Atrium provides circulation, year-round daylit rest place, eating area, gathering and performance spaces.

Prominent stairs encourage walking.

Balconies provide clear circulation and views.

Concrete ladder frames provide a mechanical spine for building systems.

In summer, cool night air is brought down the air shaft, flushing heat from building, atrium and rock bed.

South-facing movable louvers keep direct sun out of atrium in summer and let winter sun in for passive heating.

Solar collectors heat domestic water.

Indirect uplights provide a unique quality of lighting @ 2 watts/ft².

On the south side a trellis provides shade in summer and lets sun pass through in winter.

In summer, cool night air is circulated through the building to flush out heat absorbed by the concrete structure earlier that day.

General Notes

• Most winter heating loads are offset by using heat from lights, people and equipment.

• 70% of summer cooling load is handled by night venting. This venting circulates Sacramento's cool night air through the building, lowering the temperature of the concrete structure and storing coolth for use the next day. The rock bed "thermal storage" meets 23% of the annual cooling load.

Figure 17.6g An isometric of the Bateson Building. (Courtesy of the Office of the California State Architect.)

576

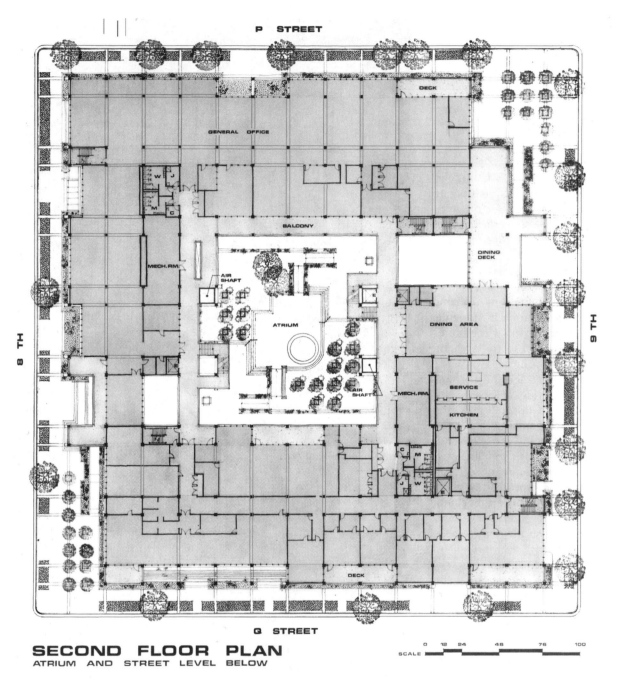

SECOND FLOOR PLAN
ATRIUM AND STREET LEVEL BELOW

Figure 17.6h The second-floor plan. (Courtesy of the Office of the California State Architect.)

The columns, beams, and floor slabs were left exposed so that they could function as thermal mass. However, the exposed concrete also creates acoustical problems. Carpeting on the floor and vertical white acoustical baffles hanging from the ceiling absorb excess office noise.

Domestic hot water is generated by 2000 ft² (180 m²) of active solar collectors located on the roof just south of the clerestories (Fig. 17.6f). The Bateson Building not only uses 70 percent less energy than a conventional building, but much of the electrical power is used during off-peak hours, when electricity is plentiful. Much of this efficiency is maintained by a computer-operated energy-management system that senses conditions throughout the building and then decides on the best mode of operation.

The Bateson Building is a valuable prototype because it addresses and successfully solves many of the important issues in architecture. It is a worthy destination for any pilgrim seeking great architecture, especially since it was built at almost the same cost as a conventional building.

17.7 COMMERZBANK

The Commerzbank Headquarters
Building in Frankfurt, Germany
Architects: Foster and Partners,
London, United Kingdom
Area: 62 stories: typical floor area is
about 8,530 ft² (776 m²)
Built: 1997

Frankfurt is at about 50° N latitude in a generally cold but still temperate climate similar to that of Boston. Even though the primary concern is winter heating, buildings also need protection from the summer sun.

One of the major goals in designing the Commerzbank was to reduce the need for fossil fuels by utilizing natural energies as much as possible. Also, it was important that the building's users have access to daylight, views, plants, and fresh air.

The design by Foster and Partners addressed these issues by using sky gardens that open around a central atrium forty-eight stories high (Fig. 17.7a). Because of the stack effect, a horizontal glass diaphragm separates the atrium into twelve-story sections, each of which is surrounded by three sky gardens in a spiral arrangement (Fig. 17.7b). Thus, each twelve-story section has one south-, one west-, and one east-facing sky garden, all open to the central atrium. The sky gardens facing west contain American plants, those facing east contain Asian plants, and those facing south contain Mediterranean plants. Each sky garden is an enclosed sunspace because of the four-story-high double-glazed curtain wall that separates it from the outdoor terrace. To reduce the number of confusing reflections, the curtain wall is canted outward (Fig. 17.7b). The sky gardens feel like outdoor public spaces and are used the same way: for meeting, relaxing, and lunch and coffee breaks.

The corner towers are for wind resistance, vertical support, vertical transportation, and services (Fig. 17.7c). Large riser ducts are not needed because of the extensive natural ventilation available via operable

Figure 17.7a The Commerzbank Headquarters Building in Frankfurt, Germany, was designed by Foster and Partners. (Courtesy Foster and Partners; Ian Lambot, photographer.)

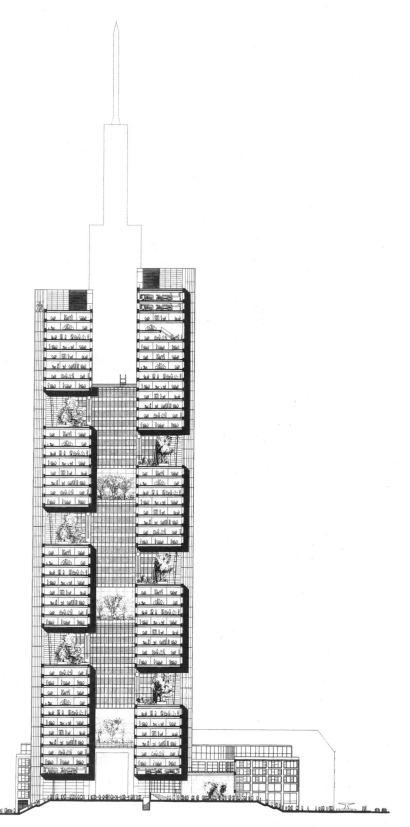

Figure 17.7b The four-story-high sky gardens spiral around the central atrium. Cross-ventilation is possible since the sky gardens have operable outside windows and are completely open to the atrium on the inside. The office areas have operable windows to the sky gardens, atrium, and outdoors. (Courtesy Foster and Partners.)

windows to the outdoors, atrium, and sky gardens. The top and a few bottom panels of the sky-garden curtain walls are also operable (Fig. 17.7d). Effective cross-ventilation is possible because all three sky gardens in each twelve-story section are open to each other via the atrium (Fig. 17.7e).

The outdoor windows of the office areas are part of the **climate facade** designed to prevent rain and high winds from entering open windows even on the highest floors (Fig. 17.7f). The climate facade consists of an outer fixed glass pane; a 7 in. (18 cm) air space; and an inner double-glazed, low-e movable sash that tilts in on top. Ventilation slots above and below the outer fixed glass allow controlled ventilation (Fig. 17.7g). Because of the aerodynamic profile of these openings, no air noise is generated. The operable windows allow for a high level of IAQ and, for the occupants, a degree of personal control over their environment.

Heating is achieved with conventional hot-water convectors under the windows, while cooling is achieved by chilled water passing through metal coils above the perforated metal ceiling panels (Fig. 17.7h). Since the water systems control most of the heat gain and heat loss, the mechanical system supplies only fresh air, and the ducts, therefore, are much smaller than those in a conventional office building. This mechanical ventilation system is needed only when the windows cannot be used: on very hot or very cold days, during storms, or when outdoor air pollution is very high.

Solar control is achieved via the venetian blinds located in the 7 in. (18 cm) cavity of the climate facade (Fig. 17.7f). Although the blinds can be controlled locally by the occupants, there is a central electronic **building management system (BMS)** that can override manual control when necessary. During the summer, the blinds are angled for solar rejection, while in the winter, maximum sunlight is collected and then reflected to the ceiling. Besides the blinds, the BMS also

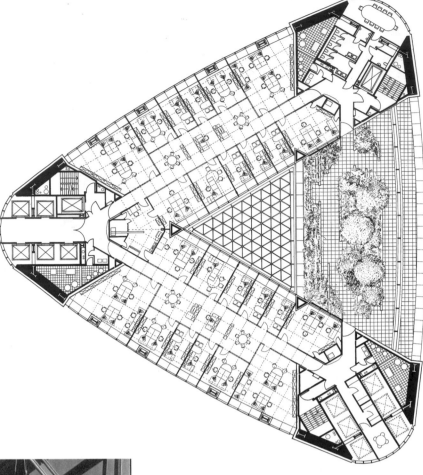

Figure 17.7c The plan of a typical office floor. The sky garden is open to the central atrium but separated from the outdoor terrace by the four-story glass curtain wall. (Courtesy Foster and Partners.)

Figure 17.7d The view from the sky garden to the exterior through the four-story, glass curtain wall. The top and bottom panels open for summer ventilation. (Courtesy Foster and Partners; Ian Lambot, photographer.)

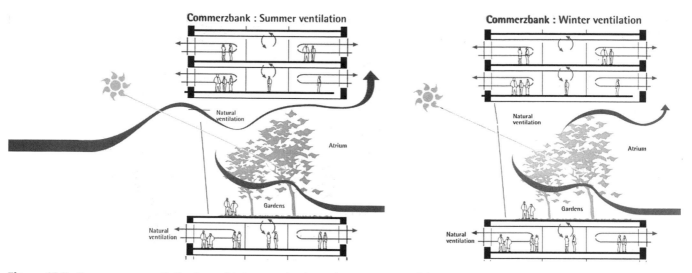

Figure 17.7e Summer cross-ventilation is possible because the sky gardens are connected through the atrium. (Courtesy Foster and Partners.)

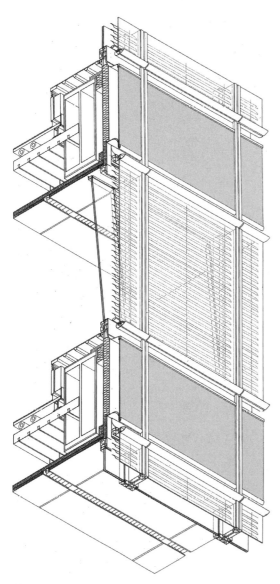

Figure 17.7f The climate facade controls both ventilation and sunlight. (Courtesy Foster and Partners.)

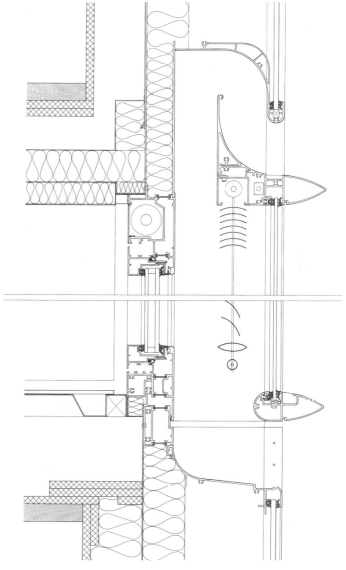

Figure 17.7g A detail of the climate facade. (Courtesy Foster and Partners.)

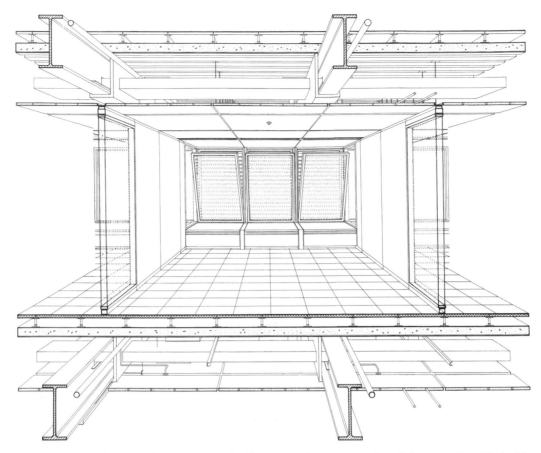

Figure 17.7h Chilled water passes through coils above the metal ceiling panels whenever natural ventilation cannot cool the building. Note the small rectangular ventilation ducts passing through the steel beams near midspan, where shear stresses are at a minimum. (Courtesy Foster and Partners.)

monitors and controls the electric lighting and air-conditioning systems. The BMS also turns on special indicator lights to let occupants know when windows can be opened.

The Commerzbank was the most "green" skyscraper when it was built in 1997 for more reasons than bringing gardens to the occupants. The building's management estimates that its energy use will be 25 to 30 percent less than the already strict German norms, mainly because of the reduced air-conditioning loads.

17.8 PHOENIX CENTRAL LIBRARY

A central library for Phoenix, Arizona
Architects: William P. Bruder and DWL
    Architects & Planners
Area: 280,000 ft² (25,200 m²)
Date: 1995

Arizona's Monument Valley, with its magnificent brown and red mesas, appears to be William P. Bruder's inspiration for the form and color of the Phoenix Central Library. His rational, flexible plan should serve the library well in the ever-changing future.

Because the climate of Phoenix consists of exceedingly hot summers with temperatures higher than 110°F (43°C) and very mild winters, heat rejection, shading, and daylighting are the primary passive strategies for this large, internally dominated library. Appropriately, the Phoenix Central Library has no east or west windows, and the all-glass north and south facades are carefully shaded.

The south facade is covered with movable, computer-controlled louvers to regulate both the quantity and quality of the daylighting (Fig. 17.8a). The outdoor louvers are about 3 ft

(90 cm) from the glazing to prevent hot air from being trapped next to the facade.

Because of the hot climate, even the north glazing is fully shaded with sail-like fins made of a Teflon-coated, perforated acrylic fabric (Fig. 17.8b). The deep but widely spaced fins allow great views of Phoenix and the surrounding mountains (Fig. 17.8c).

The east and west corrugated, copper-covered facades, known as "saddlebags," act as buffers against the intense summer sun (see again Fig. 17.8a). They contain the mechanical services, the wind-bracing structure, the fire stairs, and the restrooms (Fig. 17.8d). These service areas are separated from the library spaces by a 12 in. (30 cm) concrete wall whose eight-hour time lag significantly reduces heat gain. Although the copper facade effectively blocks the sun, tiny perforations let a small amount of daylight

Figure 17.8a The Phoenix Central Library as viewed from the southeast. Computer-operated exterior louvers cover the south facade. Copper-clad "saddlebags" shield the east and west walls from the intense sun. (Carl Walden Reiman, photographer.)

Figure 17.8c The sail-fins as seen from inside the north facade. (Courtesy William P. Bruder, Architects, Ltd.)

Figure 17.8b The north facade is shaded by the fabric sail-fins. (Courtesy William P. Bruder, Architects, Ltd.)

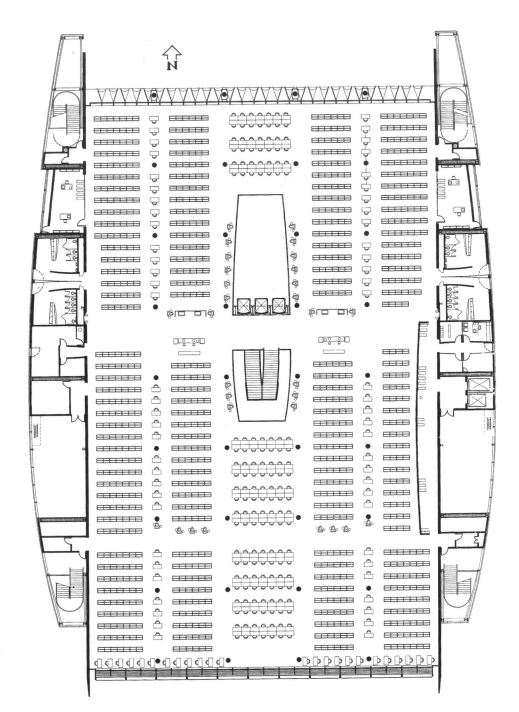

Figure 17.8d The fifth-floor plan. The large, "empty" spaces in each "saddlebag" are the mechanical-equipment rooms (MERs). All windows are on the north or south facades. (Courtesy William P. Bruder, Architects, Ltd.)

through, and at night, the perforated copper facade looks like a veil.

The fifth floor, which is the top level, houses the nonfiction collection and a grand reading room. Directly above the tall, tapered concrete columns are 6-ft-diameter skylights right where you would expect the roof structure to rest on the columns (Fig. 17.8e). This structural feat was made possible only because of the tensegrity structural system designed by the very

creative engineering firm of Ove Arup & Partners. Cables from the top of the columns support struts, which in turn support the slightly bowed roof.

The central five-story-high atrium is daylit by nine circular skylights 6 ft (1.8 m) in diameter (Fig. 17.8f). Computer-operated specular louvers on top of the skylights project light deep into this "crystal canyon" that contains the grand staircase and glass-enclosed elevators. The highlighted

atrium becomes an orientation focus for visitors to the library.

The (MERs) on each side of the building supply conditioned air to the main supply ducts running north–south just inside the 12 in. (30 cm) concrete wall that separates the library from the "saddlebag" service areas (Fig. 17.8e). These large ducts are located in dropped ceilings in order to clear the T-beams that span east–west (Fig. 17.8g). The supply

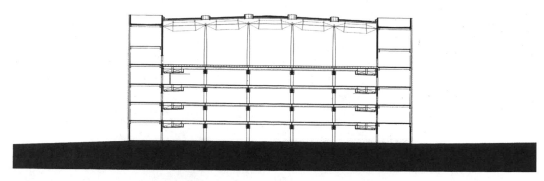

Figure 17.8e An east–west section. The (MERs) on either side supply the main ducts with conditioned air. The tensegrity structure allows the skylights to be placed directly over the columns. (Courtesy William P. Bruder, Architects, Ltd.)

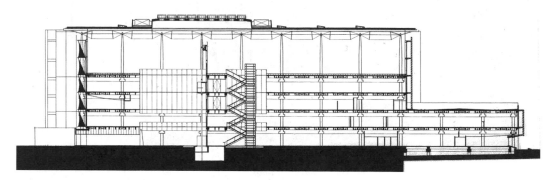

Figure 17.8f A north–south section. Nine skylights are located directly over the central circulation spine. Concrete T-beams function as the branch ducts. (Courtesy William P. Bruder, Architects, Ltd.)

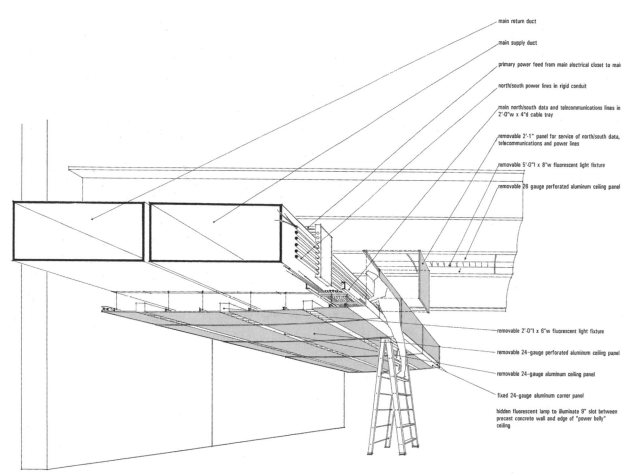

Figure 17.8g An east–west perspective section. The main north–south supply and return ducts are dropped below the east–west-spanning T-beams. Removable panels allow easy access to power and communication cables. (Courtesy William P. Bruder, Architects, Ltd.)

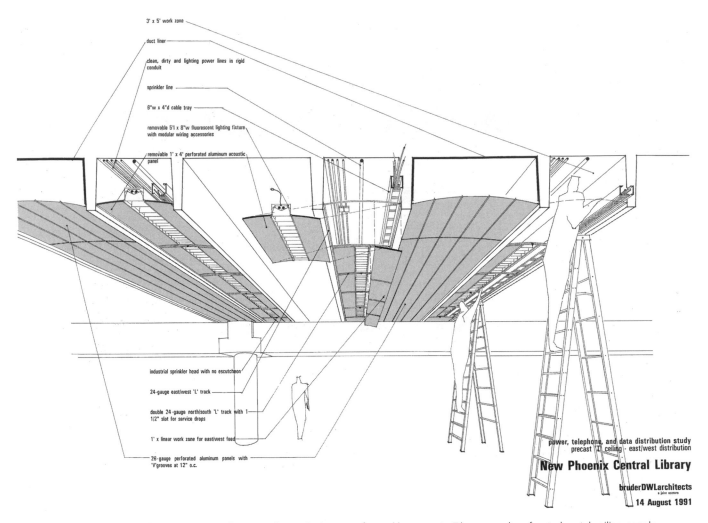

3' x 5' work zone

duct liner

clean, dirty and lighting power lines in rigid conduit

sprinkler line

8"w x 4"d cable tray

removable 5'l x 8"w fluorescent lighting fixture with modular wiring accessories

removable 1' x 4' perforated aluminum acoustic panel

industrial sprinkler head with no escutcheon

24-gauge east/west 'L' track

double 24-gauge north/south 'L' track with 1 1/2" slot for service drops

1' x linear work zone for east/west feed

26-gauge perforated aluminum panels with 'V'grooves at 12" o.c.

power, telephone, and data distribution study
precast T ceiling · east/west distribution

New Phoenix Central Library

bruderDWLarchitects
a joint venture

14 August 1991

Figure 17.8h A north–south-perspective section. Branch supply ducts are formed by concrete T-beams and perforated metal ceiling panels. (Courtesy William P. Bruder, Architects, Ltd.)

ducts feed the branch ducts above them, which are formed by the east–west spanning T-beams (Fig. 17.8h). Perforated metal panels cover the concrete channels as well as diffuse the air. The power and communication cables follow the same distribution logic. Only the top level has a raised floor for the distribution of air, power, and communication, because the ceiling is too high.

William P. Bruder designed the Phoenix Library as a simple rectangular solid in order to save on initial costs and operating costs. The compact design will forever minimize the surface area exposed to the hot Arizona sun and air. Instead of using complex masses, Bruder's design achieves aesthetic interest through the careful choice of color, texture, material, and shading systems.

Resources

FURTHER READING

(See the Bibliography in the back of the book for full citations.)

Davies, C., and I. Lambot. *Commerzbank Frankfurt: Prototype for an Ecological High-Rise.*

"Desert Illumination." *Architecture.*

"High Heat, High Tech." *Architecture.*

Pepchinski, M. "Commerzbank."

Schaeffer, J., 1997, *A Place in the Sun.*

Van der Ryn, S., 1995, *Ecological Design.*

Horizontal Sun-Path Diagrams

See Section 6.11 for a discussion of these horizontal sun-path diagrams.

For vertical sun-path diagrams see Appendix B, and for altitude and azimuth angles in tabular form see Appendix C.

All of these horizontal sun-path charts are for the Northern Hemisphere. However, it is easy to convert any of these charts for use in the Southern Hemisphere, as seen in Fig. A.1.

STEPS FOR CONVERTING SUN-PATH CHARTS FOR USE IN THE SOUTHERN HEMISPHERE

1. Choose the chart for the latitude desired, and then reverse N and S as well as E and W.
2. Reverse the order of the months (e.g., June 21 and December 21 are interchanged).
3. Reverse the hours of the day (e.g., 2 P.M. and 10 A.M. are interchanged).

The charts for 24° to 52° are from *Architectural Graphic Standards*, 11th ed., published by the American Institute of Architects (AIA), John Wiley and Sons, © 2007. Reprinted with permission of John Wiley & Sons, Inc.

36° S LATITUDE
A.21

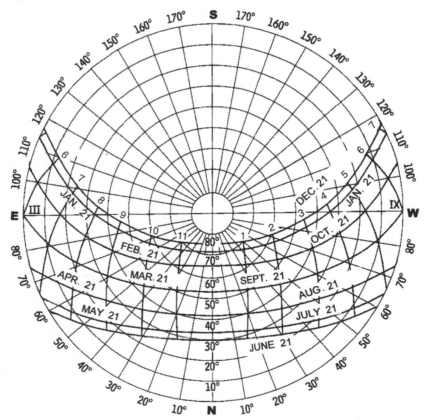

Figure A.1 This figure illustrates how to convert any of the Northern Hemisphere sun-path diagrams in this appendix into sun-path diagrams for the Southern Hemisphere.

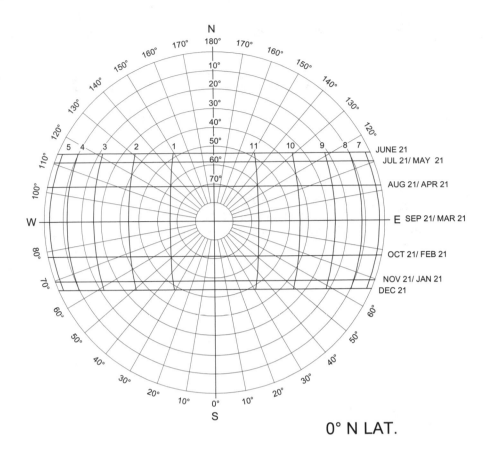

0° N LAT.

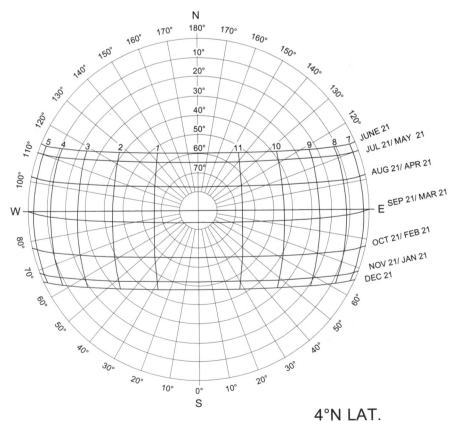

4°N LAT.

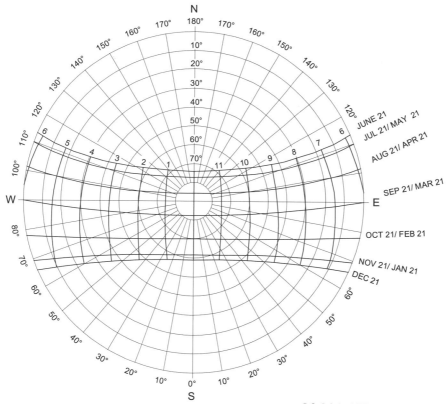

8° N LAT.

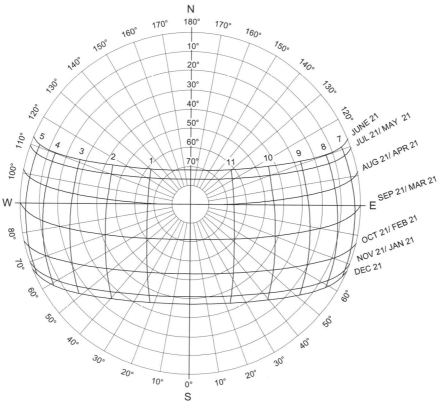

12° N LAT.

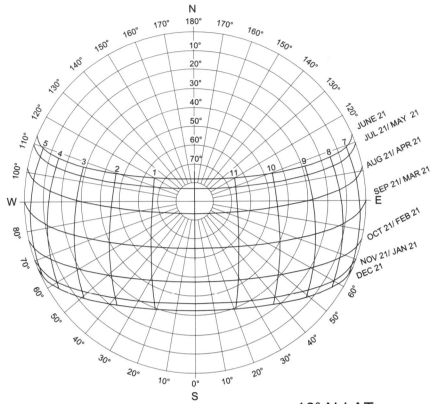

16° N LAT.

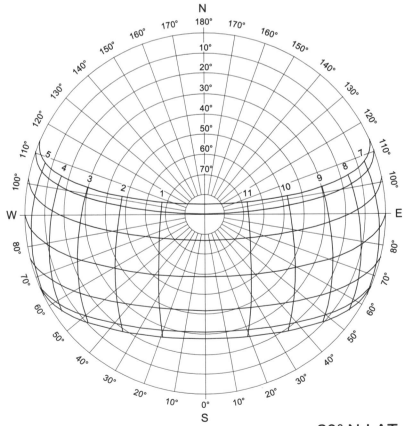

20° N LAT.

24° N LATITUDE
A.18

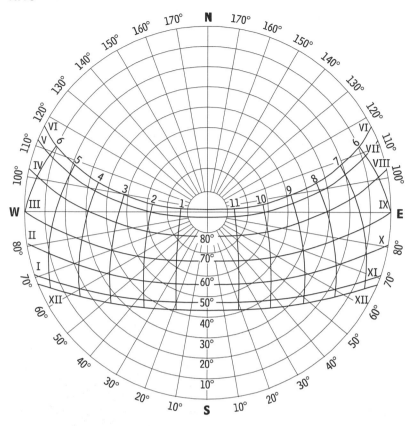

28° N LATITUDE
A.19

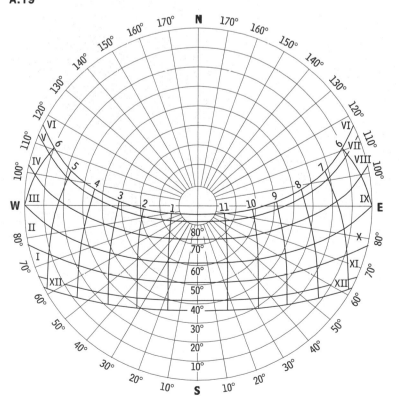

**32° N LATITUDE
A.20**

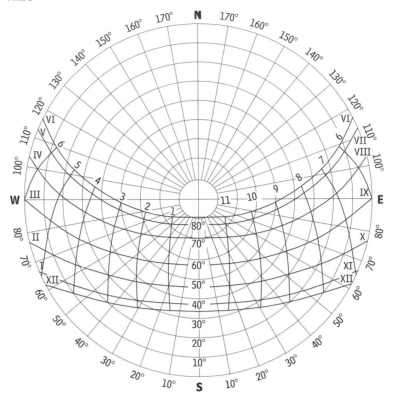

**36° N LATITUDE
A.21**

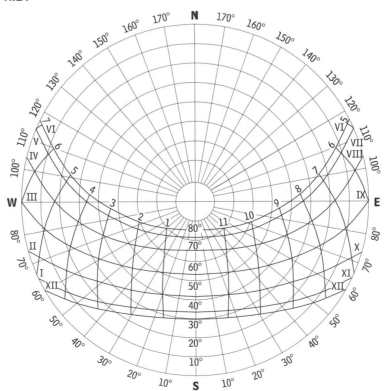

**40° N LATITUDE
A.22**

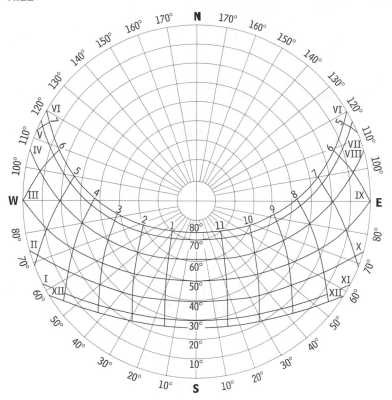

**44° N LATITUDE
A.23**

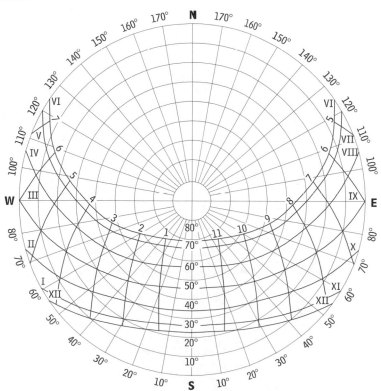

48° N LATITUDE
A.24

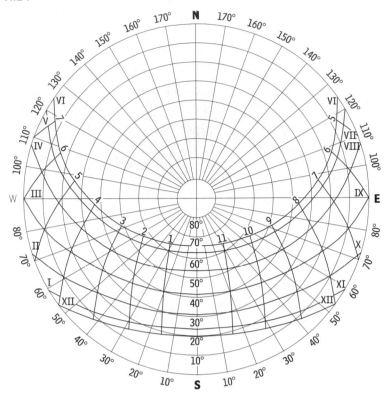

52° N LATITUDE
A.25

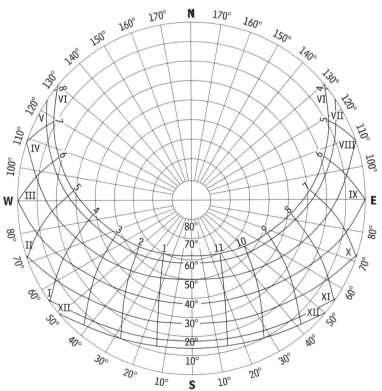

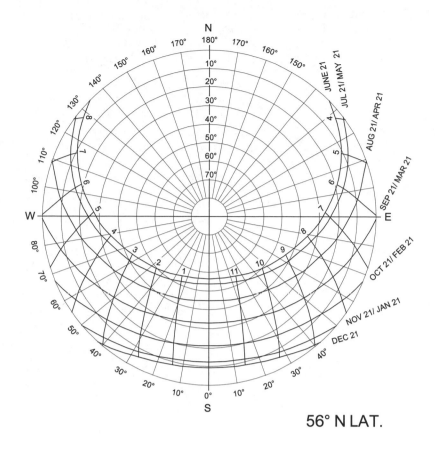

56° N LAT.

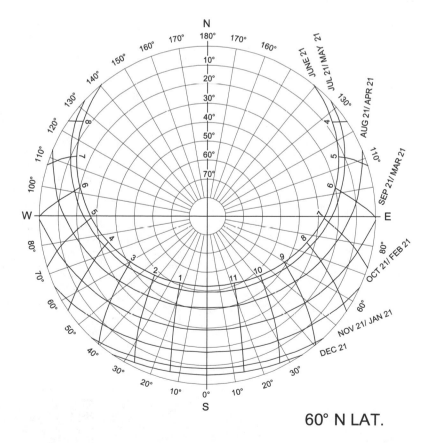

60° N LAT.

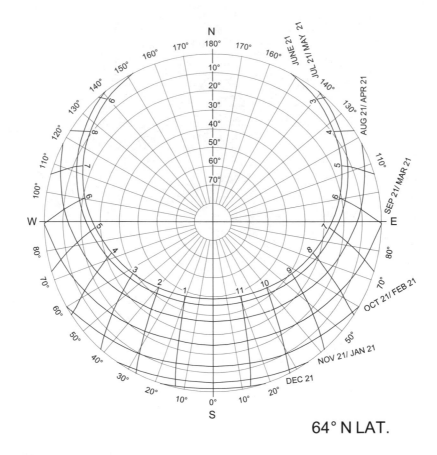

64° N LAT.

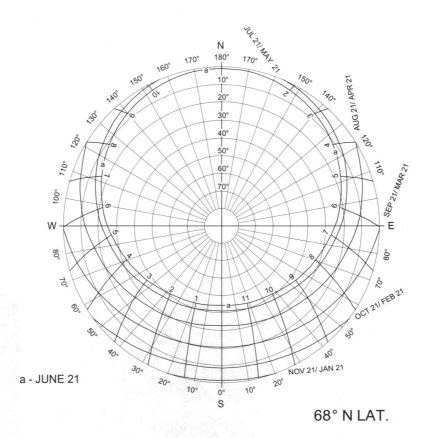

a - JUNE 21

68° N LAT.

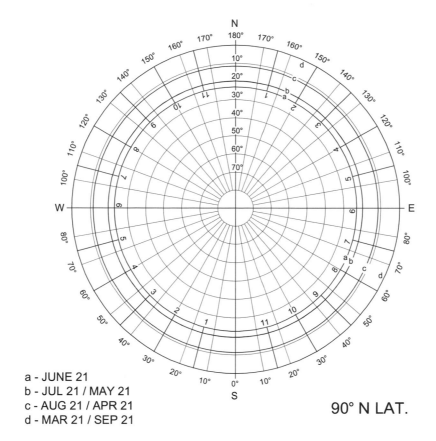

a - JUNE 21
b - JUL 21 / MAY 21
c - AUG 21 / APR 21
d - MAR 21 / SEP 21

90° N LAT.

APPENDIX B

Vertical Sun-Path Diagrams

See Section 6.12 for a discussion of these vertical sun-path diagrams. All of the charts are for the Northern Hemisphere. However, it is easy to convert any of these charts for use in the Southern Hemisphere, as seen in Fig. B.1.

STEPS FOR CONVERTING SUN-PATH CHARTS FOR USE IN THE SOUTHERN HEMISPHERE

1. Choose the chart for the latitude desired, and then reverse N and S as well as E and W.
2. Reverse the order of the months (e.g., June 21 and December 21 are interchanged).

3. Reverse the hours of the day (e.g., 2 P.M. and 10 A.M. are interchanged).

All of these vertical sun-path diagrams were generated with the Sun Path Chart Program created by the University of Oregon Solar Radiation Monitoring Laboratory (www.solardata.uoregon.edu/SunChartProgram).*

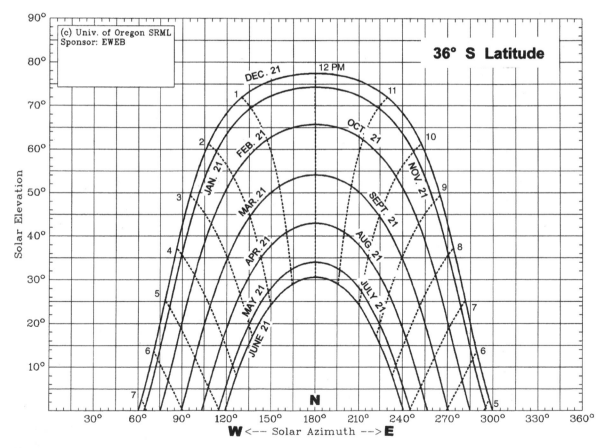

Figure B.1 This figure illustrates how to convert any of the Northern Hemisphere sun-path diagrams in this appendix into sun-path diagrams for the Southern Hemisphere.

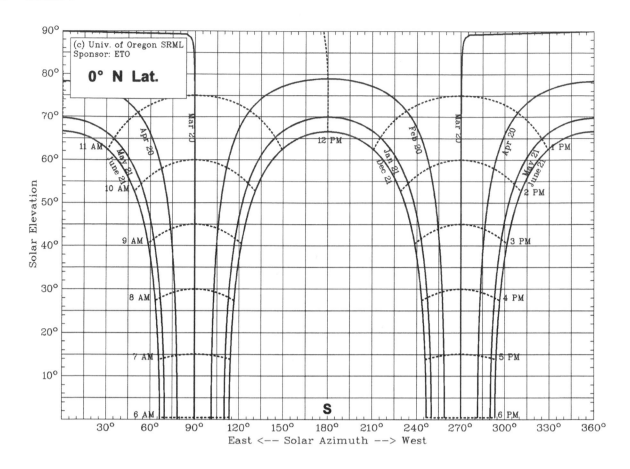

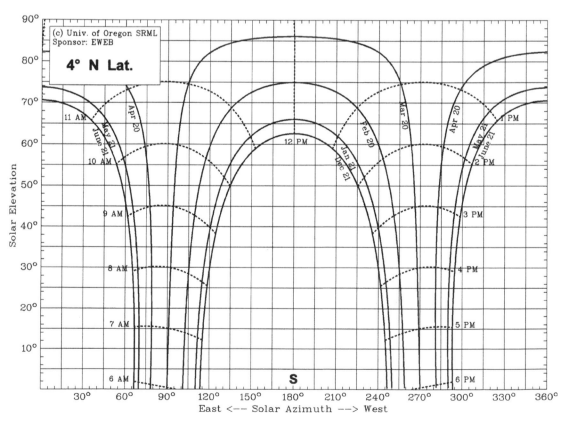

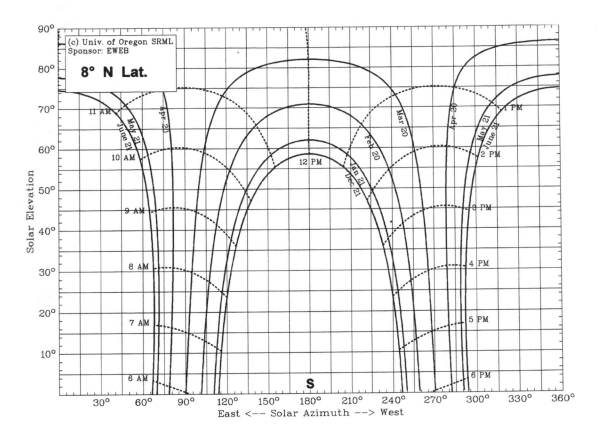

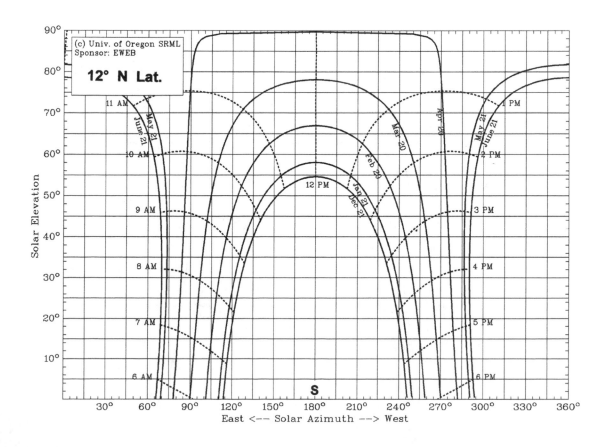

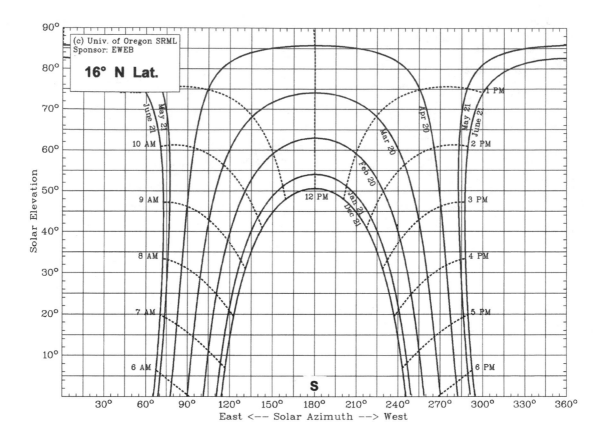

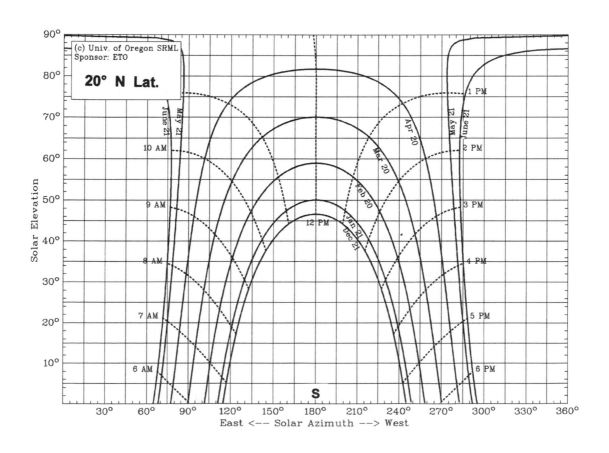

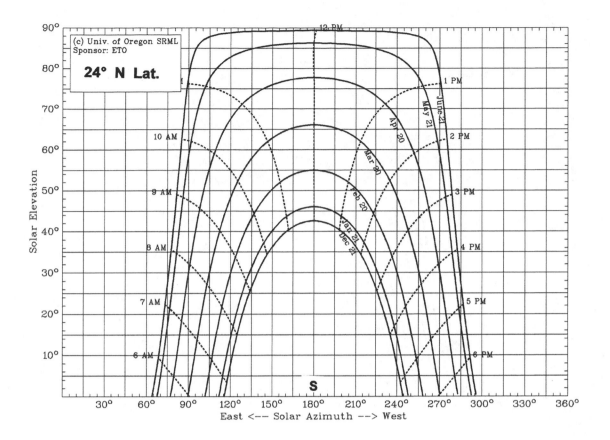

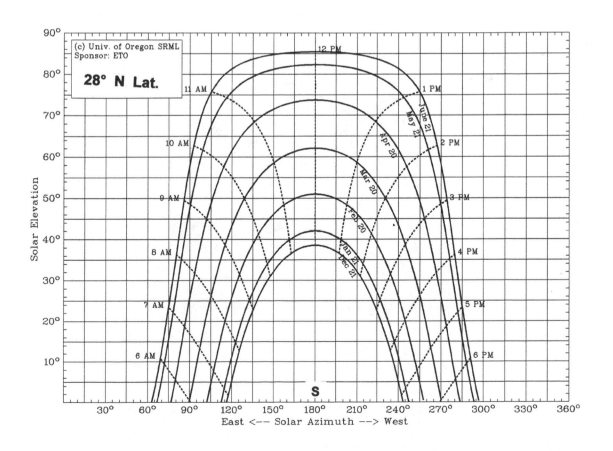

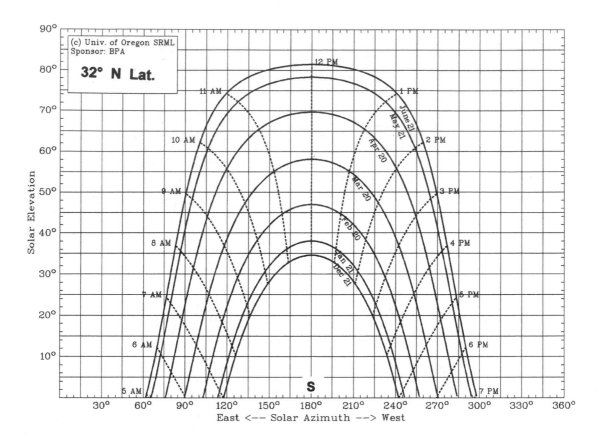

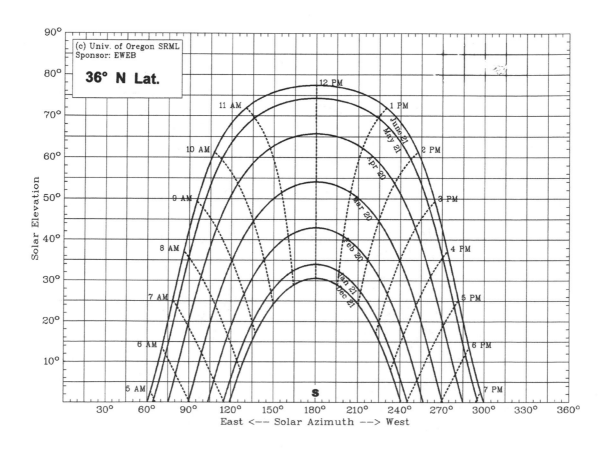

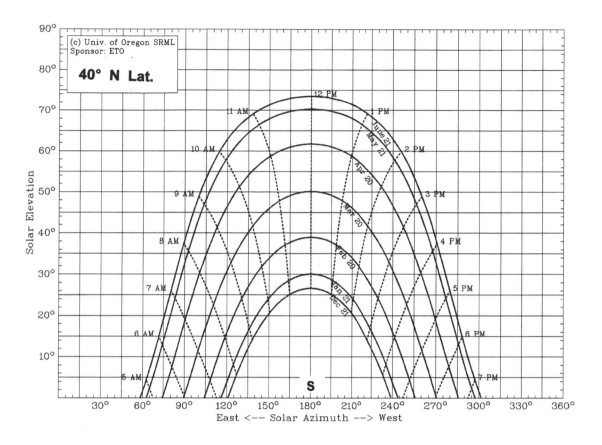

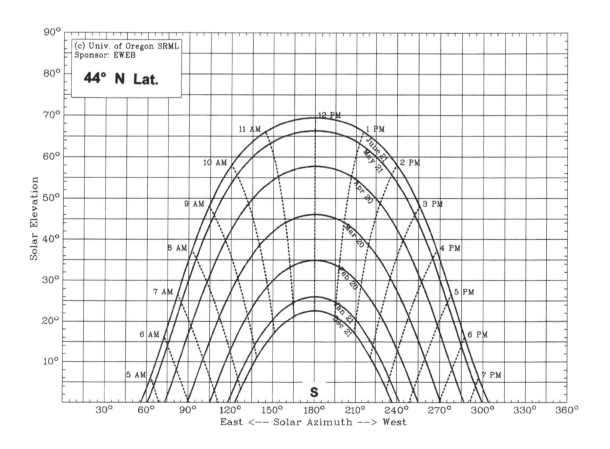

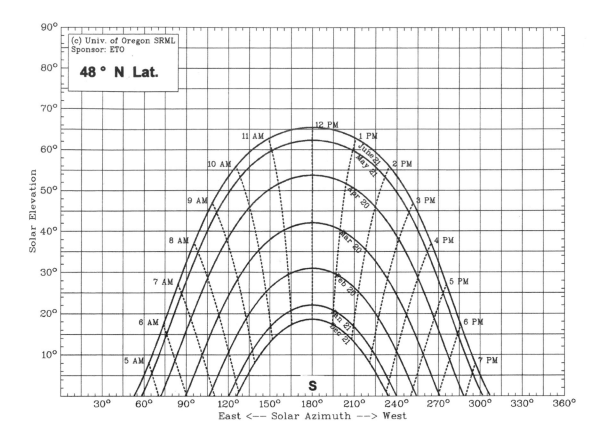

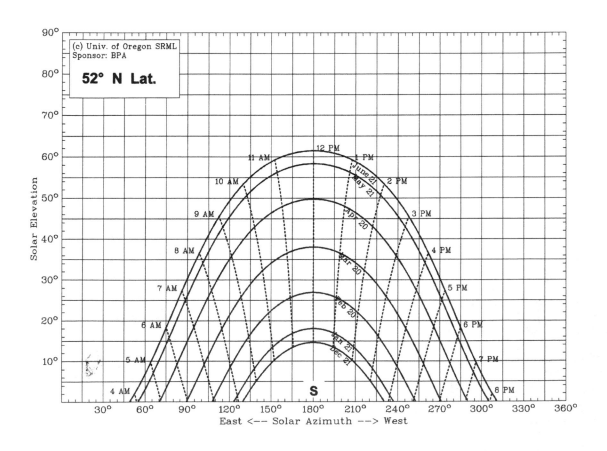

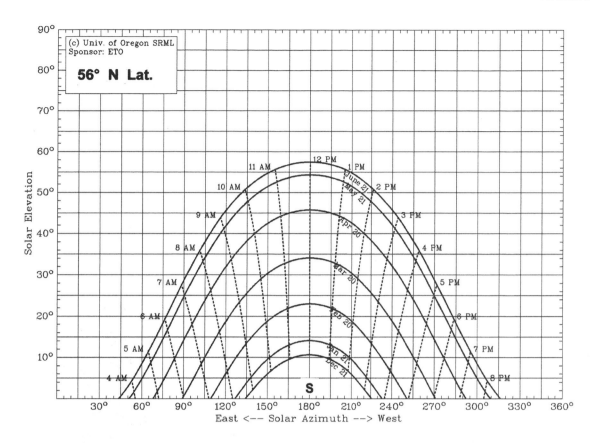

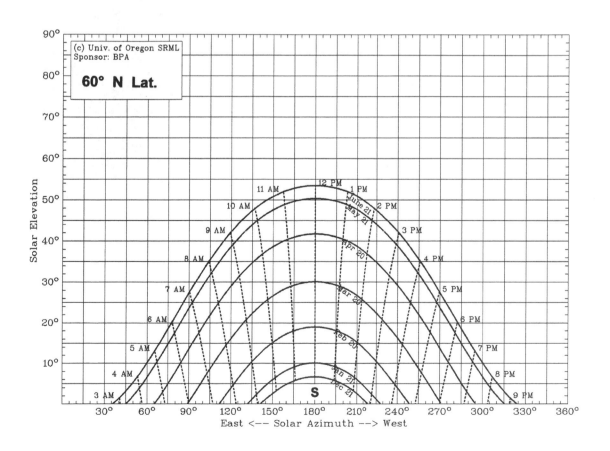

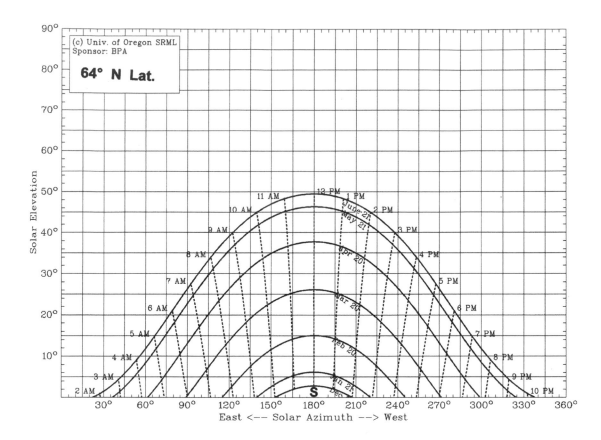

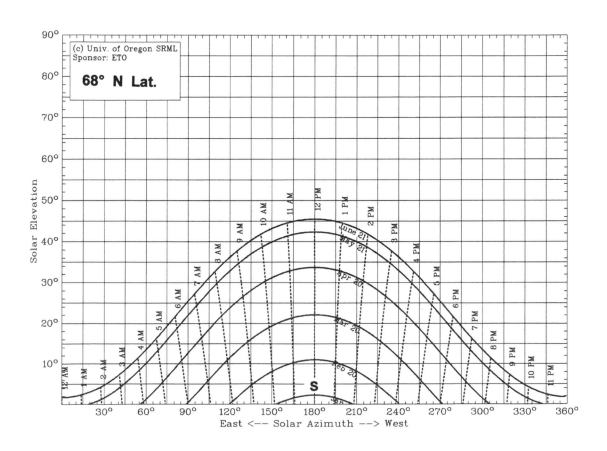

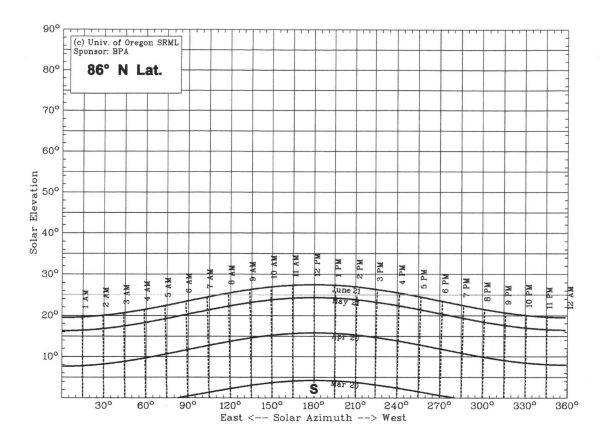

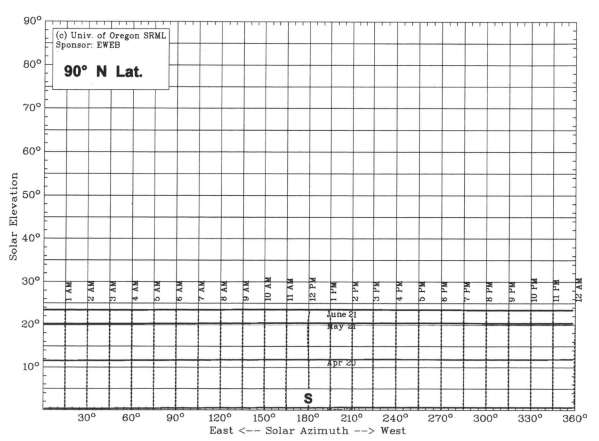

Solar Altitude and Azimuth Angles

The following tables of altitude and azimuth angles was obtained through the use of "Sun Angle," a Web-based calculation tool.

Sun Angle can also calculate additional data related to sun angles. It can be found at the Web site of Sustainable by Design, www.susdesign .com/sunangle.

Sustainable by Design is the consulting firm of Christopher Gronbeck, Seattle, Washington. The firm provides solar engineering, green building consulting, graphic design, and Web site design and programming services, primarily within the sustainable energy and architecture fields.

Date	Time (am/pm)	0 Lat alt	0 Lat azim	4 Lat alt	4 Lat azim	8 Lat alt	8 Lat azim	12 Lat alt	12 Lat azim	16 Lat alt	16 Lat azim	20 Lat alt	20 Lat azim
December 21	6/6	0	67										
	7/5	14	66	12	65	10	64	9	64	7	63	5	63
	8/4	27	63	25	62	23	60	21	59	19	57	17	46
	9/3	40	58	38	56	36	53	33	51	31	49	28	48
	10/2	53	49	50	45	46	42	44	40	41	37	38	35
	11/1	62	31	59	27	55	25	52	22	48	21	44	19
	12	67	0	63	0	59	0	55	0	51	0	47	0
Jan/Nov 21	6/6	0	70										
	7/5	14	69	13	68	11	68	10	67	8	66	6	65
	8/4	29	67	27	65	25	64	23	62	21	61	19	59
	9/3	42	63	40	60	38	57	35	55	33	52	30	50
	10/2	54	54	52	50	49	46	46	43	43	40	40	38
	11/1	65	35	62	31	58	28	55	25	51	23	47	21
	12	70	0	66	0	62	0	58	0	54	0	50	0
Feb/Oct 21	6/6	0	79										
	7/5	15	78	14	78	13	76	12	76	11	75	10	74
	8/4	29	77	28	75	27	73	26	71	25	69	23	68
	9/3	44	74	43	71	41	67	40	64	38	61	36	69
	10/2	58	69	57	63	55	58	52	53	50	49	47	46
	11/1	71	53	69	45	66	38	62	33	59	30	56	27
	12	79	0	75	0	71	0	67	0	63	0	59	0
Mar/Sep 21	6/6	0	90	0	90	0	90	0	90	0	90	0	90
	7/5	15	90	15	89	15	88	15	87	14	86	14	85
	8/4	30	90	30	88	30	85	29	83	29	81	28	79
	9/3	45	90	45	86	44	82	44	78	43	75	42	71
	10/2	60	90	60	83	59	76	58	70	56	65	54	59
	11/1	75	90	75	76	73	62	71	52	68	44	65	38
	12	90	0	86	0	82	0	78	0	74	0	70	0
Apr/Aug 21	6/6	0	101	1	101	2	101	2	101	3	101	4	101
	7/5	14	102	15	101	16	99	17	98	17	97	18	96
	8/4	29	103	30	101	31	98	31	96	32	94	32	91
	9/3	43	105	45	102	46	98	46	93	46	90	46	86
	10/2	58	112	59	106	60	99	60	91	60	85	60	78
	11/1	71	128	73	117	75	104	75	89	74	74	73	61
	12	79	180	83	180	87	180	89	0	85	0	81	0
May/Jul 21	6/6	0	110	1	110	3	110	4	110	5	109	7	109
	7/5	15	111	15	110	17	109	18	107	19	106	20	105
	8/4	28	113	30	111	31	109	32	106	33	104	34	101
	9/3	42	117	43	114	45	110	46	107	47	102	48	98
	10/2	54	126	57	121	59	116	60	110	61	103	62	95
	11/1	65	144	68	140	71	131	73	121	75	108	76	93
	12	70	180	74	180	78	180	82	180	86	180	90	180
21-June	6/6	0	113	2	113	3	113	5	113	6	113	8	112
	7/5	14	114	15	113	17	112	18	111	20	110	21	108
	8/4	27	117	29	115	31	113	32	110	33	108	35	105
	9/3	40	122	42	118	44	1115	46	111	47	107	48	103
	10/2	53	131	55	127	57	122	59	116	61	110	62	102
	11/1	62	149	66	145	69	139	71	131	74	120	86	106
	12	67	180	71	180	75	180	79	180	83	180	98	180

Date	Time (am/pm)	24 Lat alt	24 Lat azim	28 Lat alt	28 Lat azim	32 Lat alt	32 Lat azim	36 Lat alt	36 Lat azim	40 Lat alt	40 Lat azim	44 Lat alt	44 Lat azim
December 21	7/5	3	63	1	62								
	8/4	15	55	13	54	10	54	8	53	5	53	3	53
	9/3	35	46	23	45	20	44	17	43	14	42	11	41
	10/2	34	34	31	32	28	31	24	30	21	29	17	29
	11/1	40	18	37	17	33	16	29	16	25	15	21	15
	12	43	0	39	0	35	0	31	0	27	0	23	0
Jan/Nov 21	7/5	5	66	3	65	1	65						
	8/4	17	58	15	57	12	56	10	56	8	55	6	55
	9/3	28	49	25	47	22	46	20	45	17	44	14	43
	10/2	37	36	34	34	31	33	27	32	24	31	20	30
	11/1	44	20	40	18	36	17	32	17	28	16	24	15
	12	46	0	42	0	38	0	34	0	30	0	26	0
Feb/Oct 21	7/5	9	74	8	73	6	72	5	72	4	72	3	72
	8/4	22	66	20	65	18	63	16	62	15	61	13	61
	9/3	34	57	32	54	29	53	27	51	24	49	21	48
	10/2	44	43	41	41	38	39	35	37	32	35	28	34
	11/1	52	24	48	22	45	21	41	20	37	19	33	18
	12	55	0	51	0	47	0	43	0	39	0	35	0
Mar/Sep 21	6/6	0	90	0	90	0	90	0	90	0	90	0	90
	7/5	14	83	13	83	13	82	12	81	11	80	11	79
	8/4	27	77	26	75	25	73	23	71	22	70	21	68
	9/3	40	68	39	65	37	62	35	60	33	57	31	55
	10/2	52	55	50	51	47	47	44	44	42	42	38	48
	11/1	62	33	59	30	55	27	51	24	48	23	44	21
	12	66	0	62	0	58	0	54	0	50	0	46	0
Apr/Aug 21	6/6	5	100	5	100	6	100	7	99	7	99	8	98
	7/5	18	95	18	93	18	92	18	91	19	89	19	88
	8/4	32	89	32	86	31	84	31	81	30	79	29	77
	9/3	45	82	45	78	44	74	43	70	41	67	39	64
	10/2	59	71	57	65	55	60	53	55	51	51	48	48
	11/1	71	51	68	43	65	37	62	33	48	29	55	26
	12	77	0	73	0	69	0	65	0	61	0	57	0
May/Jul 21	5/7							0	115	2	115	4	115
	6/6	8	108	9	108	10	107	12	106	13	106	14	105
	7/5	21	103	22	102	23	100	23	98	24	97	24	95
	8/4	35	99	35	96	35	93	34	90	35	87	35	84
	9/3	48	94	48	89	48	85	48	80	47	76	46	72
	10/2	62	88	62	80	61	73	59	67	57	61	55	56
	11/1	76	77	74	63	72	52	69	44	66	37	63	32
	12	86	0	82	0	78	0	74	0	70	0	66	0
June 21	5/7					0	118	2	117	4	117	6	117
	6/6	9	112	11	111	12	110	13	107	15	108	16	107
	7/5	22	107	23	105	24	103	25	102	26	100	27	98
	8/4	35	102	36	100	37	97	37	94	37	91	37	88
	9/3	49	99	49	94	50	89	49	85	49	80	48	76
	10/2	63	95	63	87	62	80	61	72	60	66	58	60
	11/1	76	91	76	74	74	61	72	50	69	42	66	36
	12	89	0	85	0	81	0	77	0	73	0	69	0

Date	Time (am/pm)	48 Lat		52 Lat		56 Lat		60 Lat		64 Lat		68 Lat	
		alt	azim	alt	azim	alt	azim	alt	azim	alt	azim	alt	azim
December 21	8/4	1	53										
	9/3	8	41	5	41	2	40						
	10/2	14	28	10	28	7	27	3	27				
	11/1	17	14	13	14	10	14	6	14	2	14		
	12	19	0	15	0	11	0	7	0	3	0		
Jan/Nov 21	8/4	3	55	1	54								
	9/3	11	43	8	42	5	42	2	42				
	10/2	17	29	13	29	10	28	6	28	3	28		
	11/1	21	15	17	15	13	14	9	14	5	14	1	14
	12	22	0	18	0	14	0	10	0	6	0	2	0
Feb/Oct 21	7/5	1	71	0	71								
	8/4	11	60	9	59	7	59	4	58	2	58	0	58
	9/3	19	47	16	46	13	45	10	45	7	44	5	44
	10/2	25	33	22	32	18	31	15	30	11	30	8	30
	11/1	29	17	26	16	22	16	18	15	14	15	10	15
	12	31	0	27	0	23	0	19	0	15	0	11	0
	6/6	0	90	0	90	0	90	0	90	0	90	0	90
Mar/Sep 21	7/5	10	79	9	78	8	77	7	77	6	76	6	76
	8/4	20	67	18	65	16	64	14	63	13	63	11	62
	9/3	29	53	26	52	23	50	21	49	18	48	15	47
	10/2	35	38	32	36	29	35	26	34	22	33	19	32
	11/1	40	20	37	19	33	18	29	17	25	16	21	16
	12	42	0	38	0	34	0	30	0	26	0	22	0
Apr/Aug 21	5/7					1	109	2	108	4	108	5	108
	6/6	8	98	9	97	9	96	10	96	10	95	10	94
	7/5	18	86	18	85	18	84	17	83	17	81	16	80
	8/4	28	75	27	73	26	71	24	69	23	67	21	66
	9/3	38	61	36	58	33	56	31	54	29	52	26	51
	10/2	46	44	43	42	39	39	36	38	33	36	30	34
	11/1	51	24	48	22	44	21	40	19	36	18	32	17
	12	53	0	49	0	45	0	41	0	37	0	33	0
May/Jul 21	2/10											1	152
	3/9									1	138	4	138
	4/8					1	125	3	125	6	125	8	125
	5/7	5	114	7	114	8	113	10	113	12	112	13	111
	6/6	15	104	16	193	16	101	17	100	18	99	18	98
	7/5	25	93	25	91	25	89	25	87	24	86	24	84
	8/4	35	82	34	79	33	76	32	74	31	71	30	69
	9/3	44	68	43	65	41	61	39	59	37	56	35	54
	10/2	53	52	50	48	48	44	45	41	42	39	38	37
	11/1	60	29	56	26	52	23	49	22	45	20	41	19
	12	62	0	58	0	54	0	50	0	46	0	42	0
June 21	12 mid											1	180
	1/11											2	166
	2/10									0	153	4	153
	3/9							1	139	4	139	7	139
	4/8			2	127	4	127	7	127	9	126	11	126
	5/7	8	116	10	116	11	115	13	114	15	114	16	113
	6/6	17	106	18	105	19	104	20	102	21	101	22	99
	7/5	27	96	27	94	27	92	28	90	27	87	27	85
	8/4	37	85	37	82	36	79	35	76	34	73	33	71
	9/3	47	72	45	68	44	64	42	61	40	58	38	55
	10/2	56	55	53	50	51	46	48	43	45	40	42	38
	11/1	63	31	59	28	56	25	52	23	48	21	44	19
	12	65	0	61	0	57	0	53	0	49	0	45	0

Date	Time (am/pm)	72 Lat		77 Lat		82 Lat		86 Lat		90 Lat	
		alt	azim	alt	azim	alt	azim	alt	azim	alt	azim
December 21											
Jan/Nov 21											
Feb/Oct 21	9/3	2	44								
	10/2	5	29	0	29						
	11/1	6	15	1	15						
	12	7	0	2	0						
Mar/Sep 21	12 mid									0	180
	1/11									0	165
	2/10									0	150
	3/9									0	135
	4/8									0	120
	5/7									0	105
	6/6	0	90	0	90	0	90	0	90	0	90
	7/5	5	76	3	75	2	75	1	75	0	75
	8/4	9	61	6	61	4	60	2	60	0	60
	9/3	13	46	9	46	6	45	3	45	0	45
	10/2	16	31	11	31	6	30	3	30	0	30
	11/1	17	16	13	15	8	15	4	15	0	15
	12	18	0	13	0	8	0	4	0	0	0
Apr/Aug 21	12 mid					3	180	7	180	11	180
	1/11					3	165	7	165	11	165
	10/2					4	150	8	150	11	150
	3/9			2	136	6	136	8	135	11	135
	4/8	2	122	5	122	7	121	9	121	11	120
	5/7	6	108	8	107	9	106	10	106	11	105
	6/6	11	93	11	93	11	92	11	91	11	90
	7/5	15	79	14	78	13	77	12	76	11	75
	8/4	20	64	18	63	15	62	13	61	11	60
	9/3	24	49	20	48	17	46	14	46	11	45
	10/2	27	33	22	32	18	31	15	30	11	30
	11/1	29	17	24	16	19	16	15	15	11	15
	12	29	0	24	0	19	0	15	0	11	0
May / Jul 21	12 mid	2	180	7	180	12	180	16	180	20	180
	1/11	3	166	7	166	12	166	16	165	20	165
	2/10	4	152	9	152	13	151	16	151	20	150
	3/9	7	138	11	137	14	137	17	136	20	135
	4/8	10	124	13	123	16	122	18	121	20	120
	5/7	14	110	16	109	18	108	19	106	20	105
	6/6	19	96	19	95	20	93	20	91	20	90
	7/5	24	82	23	80	22	78	21	76	20	75
	8/4	28	67	26	65	24	63	22	61	20	60
	9/3	32	52	29	49	26	47	23	46	20	45
	10/2	35	35	31	33	27	32	23	31	20	30
	11/1	37	18	33	17	28	16	24	15	20	15
	12	38	0	33	0	28	0	24	0	20	0
June 21	12 mid	5	180	10	180	15	180	19	180	23.43	180
	1/11	6	166	11	166	16	166	20	165	23.43	165
	2/10	8	152	12	152	16	151	20	151	23.43	150
	3/9	10	139	14	138	18	137	21	136	23.43	135
	4/8	14	125	16	124	19	123	21	121	23.43	120
	5/7	18	111	19	110	21	108	22	107	23.43	105
	6/6	22	98	23	96	23	93	23	92	23.43	90
	7/5	27	83	26	81	25	78	24	77	23.43	75
	8/4	31	68	29	66	27	63	25	62	23.43	60
	9/3	35	53	32	50	29	48	26	46	23.43	45
	10/2	39	36	34	34	30	32	27	31	23.43	30
	11/1	41	18	36	17	31	16	27	15	23.43	15
	12	41	0	36	0	31	0	27	0	23.43	0

Methods for Estimating the Height of Trees, Buildings, etc.

To determine solar access and shading, one needs to know the approximate height of objects around the site being investigated. This is the case whether model studies, graphical analyses or computer analyses are used. Four methods are described below for finding the height of a tree; but, of course, these methods work equally well for buildings or other objects.

D.1 PROPORTIONAL-SHADOW METHOD

This method can be used only on sunny days during the hours when shadows are fairly long.

Set up a vertical stick so that you can measure its shadow at the same time the shadow of the tree is visible (Fig. D.1). Measure both shadows and the height of the stick. You can then determine the height of the tree by means of the following equation:

$$\frac{H}{S} = \frac{h}{s}$$

or

$$H = S \times \frac{h}{s}$$

D.2 SIMILAR-TRIANGLE METHOD

Although this method can be used whether the sun is shining or not, it is important to avoid looking directly into the sun on clear days. Hold a square with one leg horizontal and the other vertical. Use a small level on the horizontal leg or hang a weighted string from the top of the vertical arm to level the square. Sight along the square, and place a finger where the sight line intersects the vertical arm to find the height (h), as seen in Fig. D.2.

Then, by similar triangles:

$$\frac{H}{D} = \frac{h}{d}$$

or

$$H = D \times \frac{h}{d}$$

and the height of the object = $H + P$.

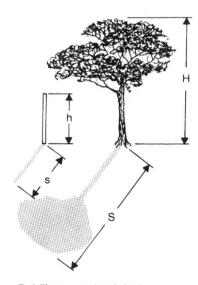

Figure D.1 The proportional-shadow method of finding the height of an object.

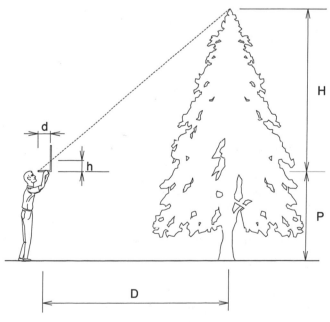

Figure D.2 The similar-triangle method of finding the height of an object.

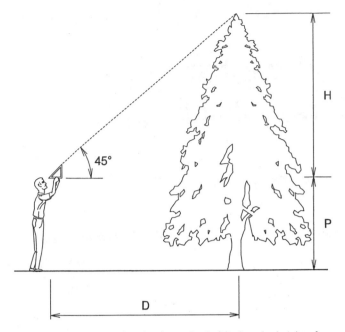

Figure D.3 The 45° right-triangle method of finding the height of an object.

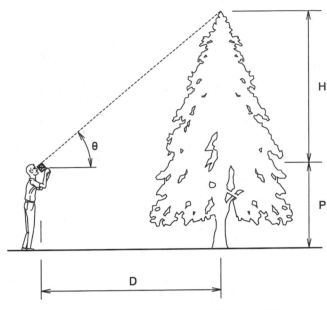

Figure D.4 The trigonometric method of finding the height of an object.

D.3 45° RIGHT-TRIANGLE METHOD

This method is a special case of the similar-triangle method. If the site allows one to sight along the hypotenuse of a 45° right triangle, the unknown height of the object above the triangle will simply be the horizontal distance to the sighting point (see Fig. D.3).

$$H = D$$

and the height of the object $= H + P$.

D.4 TRIGONOMETRIC METHOD

Use a transit or other device to measure the vertical angle θ (see Fig. D.4). Commercially available devices and a simple, inexpensive, do-it-yourself device to measure this angle are described in Section D.5.

Use the following equation to find (H):

$$H = D \tan \theta$$

and the height of the object $= H + P$.

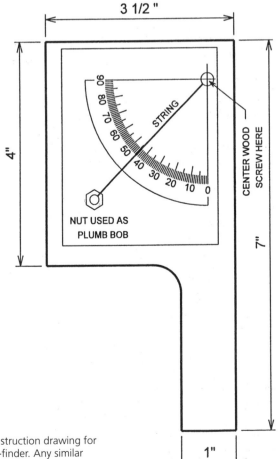

Figure D.5a Construction drawing for building the angle-finder. Any similar dimensions will work equally well.

D.5 TOOLS FOR MEASURING VERTICLE ANGLES

Of course, a professional transit can be used, but that tool is usually too expensive for this purpose. However, a much less expensive tool can still give precise results. A **clinometer** is a small pocket tool used for finding vertical angles, and it costs about $200 (see Fig. D.5b). It is widely used by foresters for finding the height of trees.*

Also available for about $15 is a special construction protractor, which is meant for finding the slope of pipes or structural members (Fig. D.5c). This tool is used much like the angle-finder described below.

The angle-finder is a simple and inexpensive do-it-yourself tool for measuring vertical angles, which can be cut from a 1 × 4 board about 7 in. (2 × 10 × 17 cm) long (see Fig. D.5a). The 90° scale can be photocopied from Fig. I.4f in Appendix I. Hang a plumb line from a screw inserted at the point shown in Fig. D.5a. A small machine nut can make a handy plumb bob.

To measure the altitude angle to the top of some object, hold the angle-finder in the vertical plane and sight along its top edge. After the plumb line has stopped swaying, place a finger on the line and measure the angle (Fig. D.5d).

Figure D.5b A commercially available clinometer is used for finding vertical angles.

Figure D.5c This construction protractor was purchased for about $15.

Figure D.5d Here, the angle-finder is being used to determine the height of an object.

*Clinometers can be obtained from Forestry Supplies, Inc., P.O. Box 8397, Jackson, MS 39284-8397, tel. 1-800-647-5368, www.forestry-supplies.com

Sundials, also known as "sun peg charts," can be used in conjunction with a heliodon to simulate sun angles. This application of sundials is explained in Appendix I and in Section 13.19.

Each sundial requires a peg (gnomon) of a particular height to cast the proper shadow. The length of the gnomon is indicated on each sundial so that enlargements or reductions of the sundials are convenient to make. Copy the sundial that comes closest to the latitude required and glue it on a piece of wood. Hammer a nail vertically into the wood at point A so that it projects a distance AB above the wood.

These charts were created from a freeware program called "Shadows" downloaded from the Web site www.shadowspro.com. The software was created by Francois Blateyron (copyright 1997–2006), who also makes available more sophisticated software for designing sundials. The above Web site can be used to create a sundial for any specific location on earth.

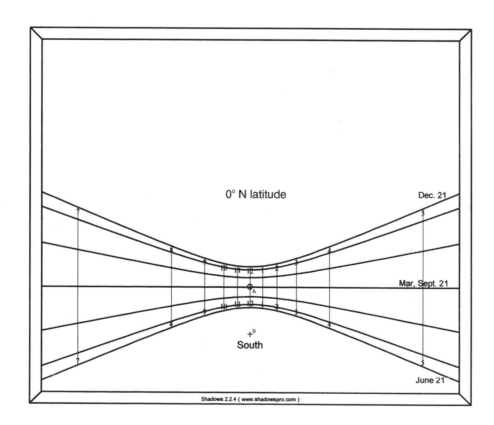

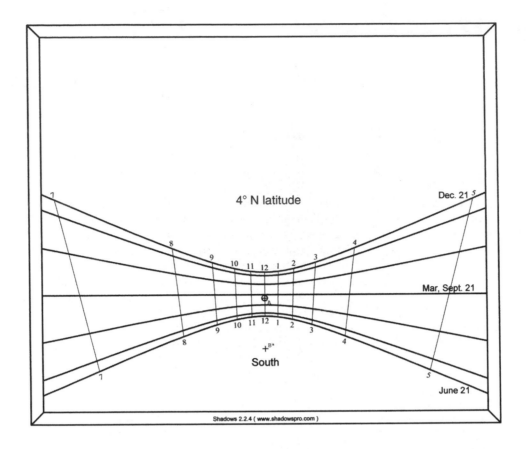

4° N latitude

Dec. 21

Mar, Sept. 21

South

June 21

Shadows 2.2.4 (www.shadowspro.com)

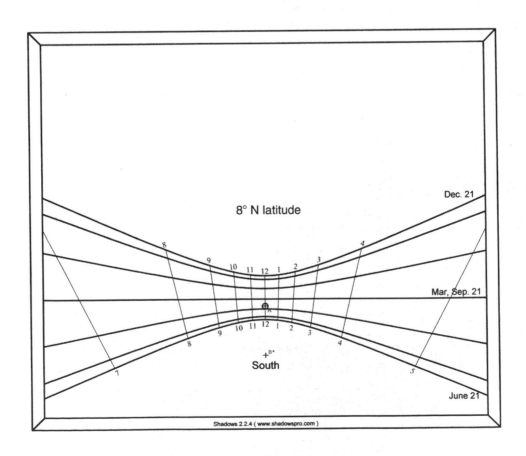

8° N latitude

Dec. 21

Mar, Sep. 21

South

June 21

Shadows 2.2.4 (www.shadowspro.com)

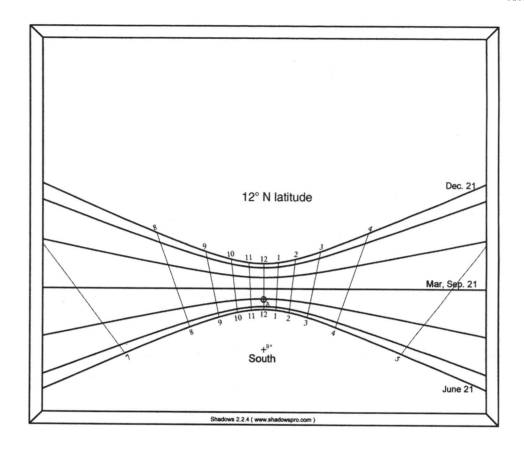

12° N latitude

Dec. 21

8 9 10 11 12 1 2 3 4

Mar, Sep. 21

⊕A

7 8 9 10 11 12 1 2 3 4 5

+B*
South

June 21

Shadows 2.2.4 (www.shadowspro.com)

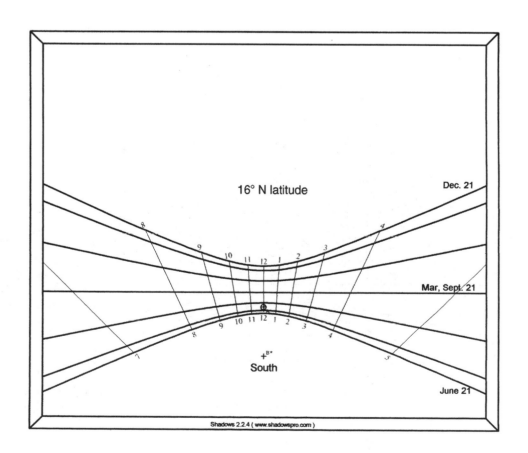

16° N latitude

Dec. 21

8 9 10 11 12 1 2 3 4

Mar, Sept. 21

⊕

7 8 9 10 11 12 1 2 3 4 5

+B*
South

June 21

Shadows 2.2.4 (www.shadowspro.com)

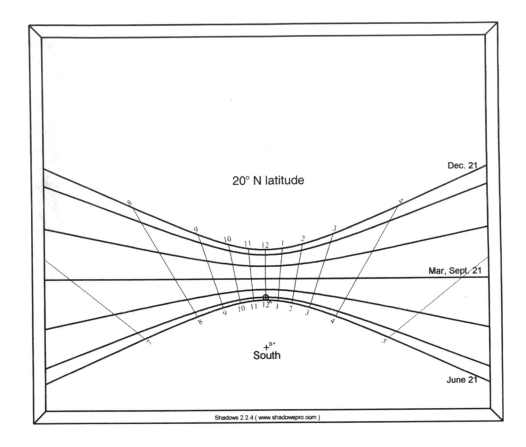

20° N latitude

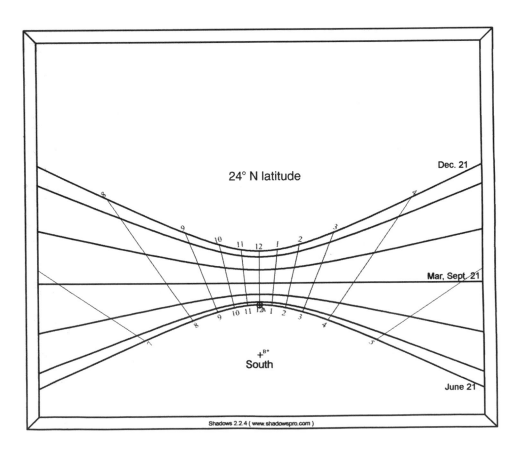

24° N latitude

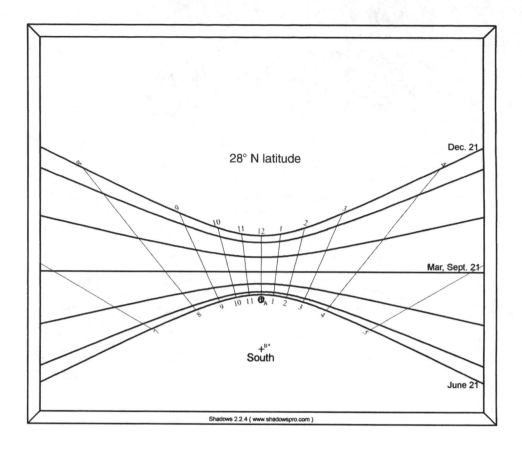

28° N latitude

Dec. 21

8
9
10 11 12 1 2
3
7

Mar, Sept. 21

8 9 10 11 ⊕ₐ 1 2 3 4
5

+ᴮ⁺
South

June 21

Shadows 2.2.4 (www.shadowspro.com)

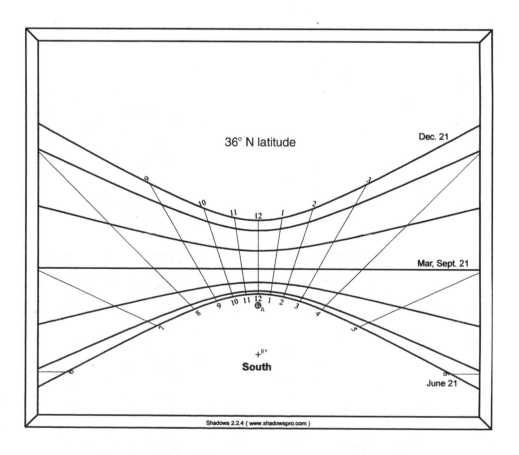

36° N latitude

Dec. 21

9
10 11 12 1 2
3

Mar, Sept. 21

8 9 10 11 12 1 2 3 4
5
7 ⊕ₐ
6

+ᴮ⁺
South

June 21

Shadows 2.2.4 (www.shadowspro.com)

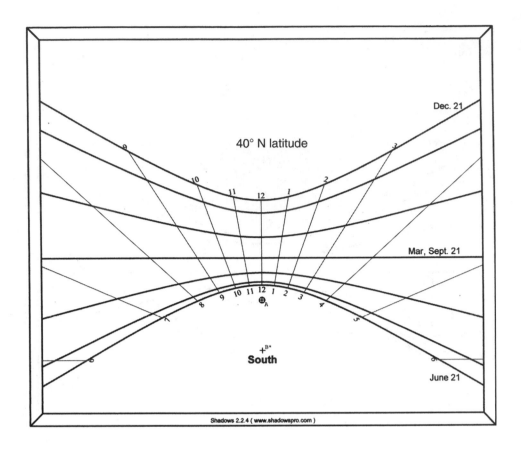

40° N latitude

Dec. 21

Mar, Sept. 21

South

June 21

Shadows 2.2.4 (www.shadowspro.com)

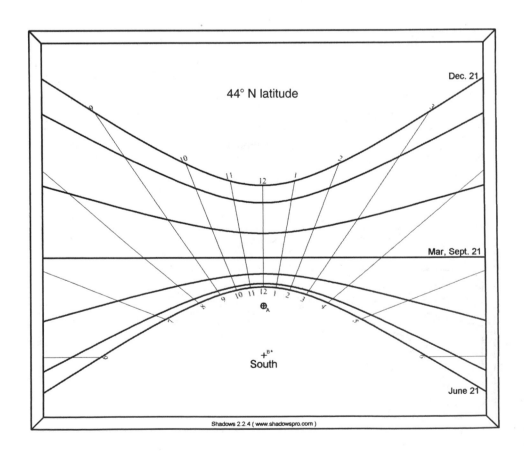

44° N latitude

Dec. 21

Mar, Sept. 21

South

June 21

Shadows 2.2.4 (www.shadowspro.com)

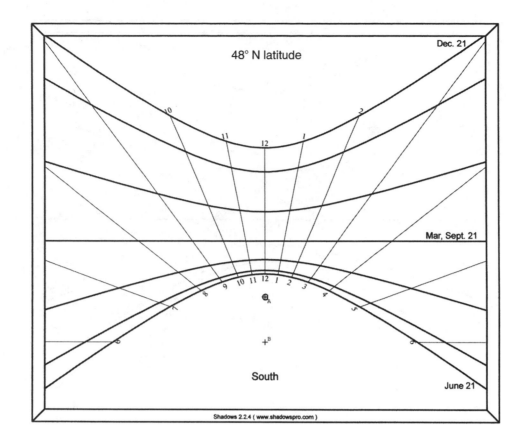

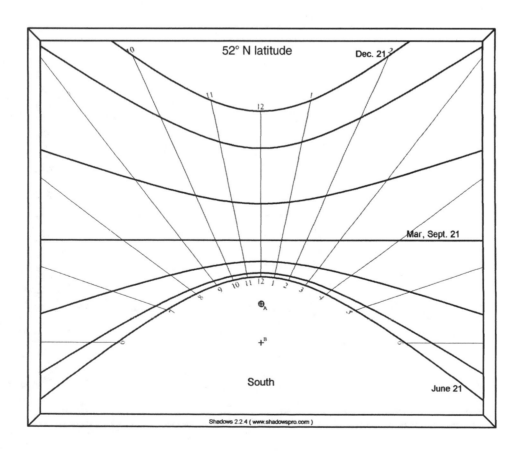

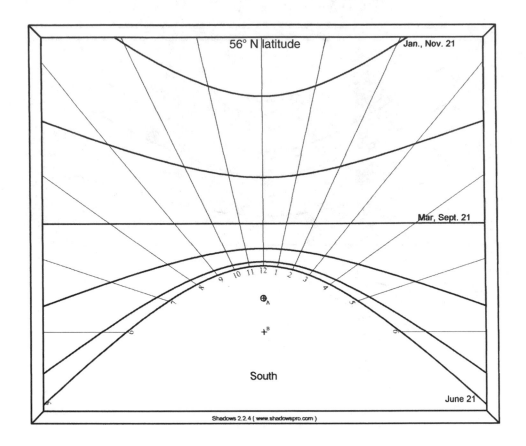

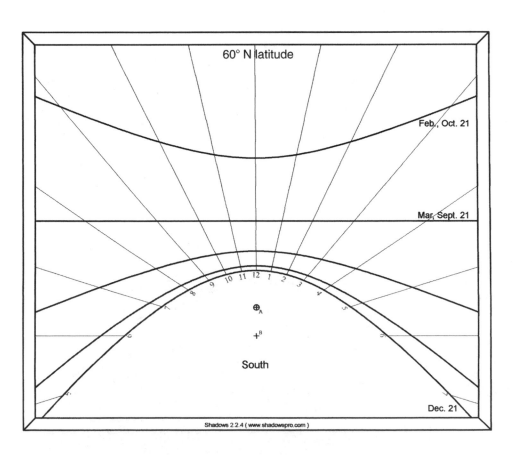

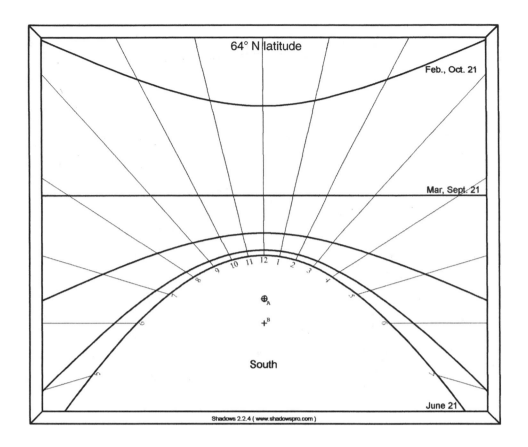

64° N latitude

Feb., Oct. 21

Mar, Sept. 21

9 10 11 12 1 2 3 4 5 6

⊕ A

+ B

South

June 21

Shadows 2.2.4 (www.shadowspro.com)

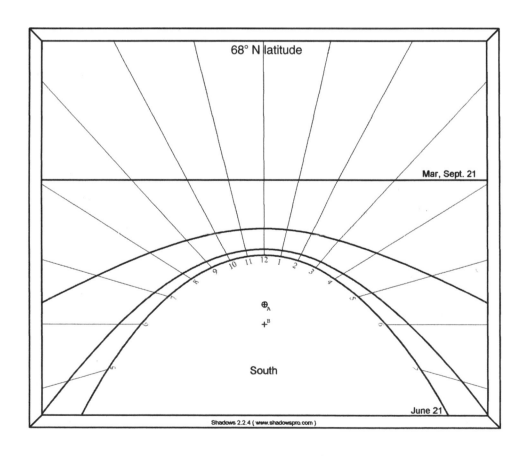

68° N latitude

Mar, Sept. 21

9 10 11 12 1 2 3 4 5 6

⊕ A

+ B

South

June 21

Shadows 2.2.4 (www.shadowspro.com)

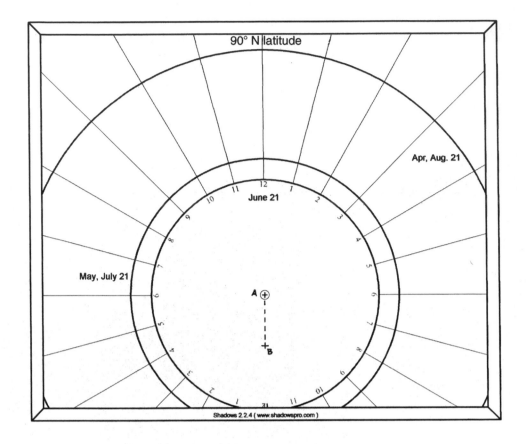

Sun-Path Models

F.1 INTRODUCTION

Sun-path models can be very useful in visualizing the complex motion of the sun. The following diagrams make it quite easy to construct a sun-path model for latitudes at 4° intervals. These diagrams are orthographic projections of a sky dome. Normal sun-path diagrams, as found in Appendix A, are not appropriate for this purpose. See Section 6.13 for an additional discussion of these sun-path models.

F.2 DIRECTIONS FOR CONSTRUCTING A SUN-PATH MODEL

Materials List

1. A piece of foam-core borad that is slightly larger than the horizontal projections found below. The board should be at least ¼ in. (65 mm) thick.
2. A piece of stiff, clear plastic film as large as the support quadrant. Acetate works well.
3. Pipe cleaners (three pieces), chenille (two pieces), which is available in hobby and craft stores, or thick soft wire, such as copper electrical wire.

Procedure

1. To make the base, photocopy the orthographic projection closest to the latitude of interest and glue it on a piece of foam board of the same size.

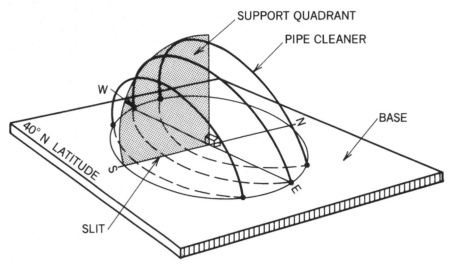

Figure F.2 A sun-path model.

2. Cut a deep slit where indicated on the projection (Fig. F.2).
3. Trace the support quadrant on a piece of fairly stiff, clear plastic film or photocopy onto clear film specified for copiers (absolutely do *not* use acetate in copiers).
4. Cut out the support quadrant and be sure to cut the three little notches where indicated.
5. Place the support quadrant in the slit so that marks A and B on the quadrant line up with marks A and B on the base (0 = south).
6. Use a pushpin or sharp pencil to make holes at the sunrise and sunset points for each of the three sun paths. The holes should pass all the way through the base and

be angled in the direction of the sun paths.
7. Insert one end of a pipe cleaner or wire in the sunrise hole for June 21. Bend it across the support quadrant and insert the other end in the sunset hole. Pull the pipe cleaner down until it rests in the top notch of the support quadrant. Repeat this procedure for the other two sun paths. Note that the three pipe cleaners should form segments of parallel circles.
8. Glue the pipe cleaners in place and trim off the excess from the bottom of the base.
9. Place a small balsa wood block (less than ¼ in. (65 mm) on a side) in the center to represent a building.

631

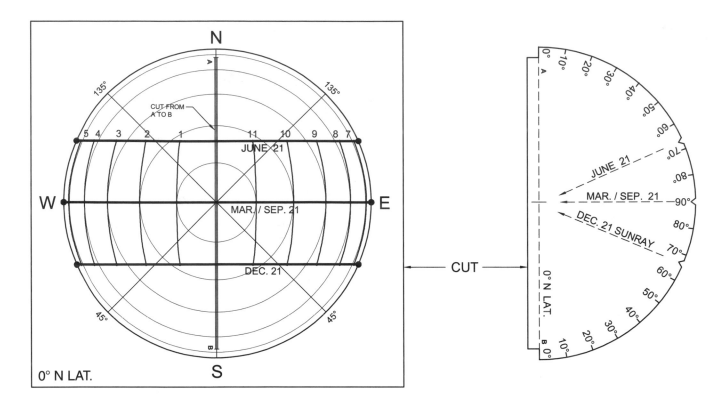

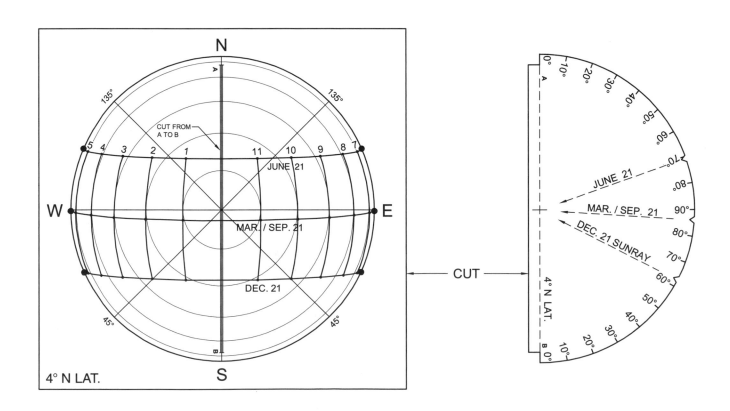

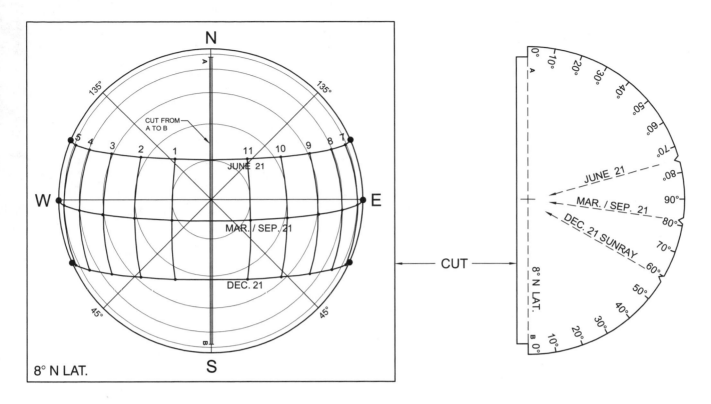

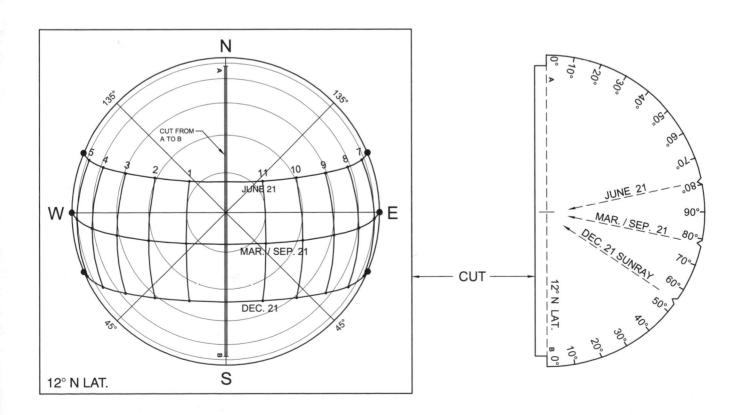

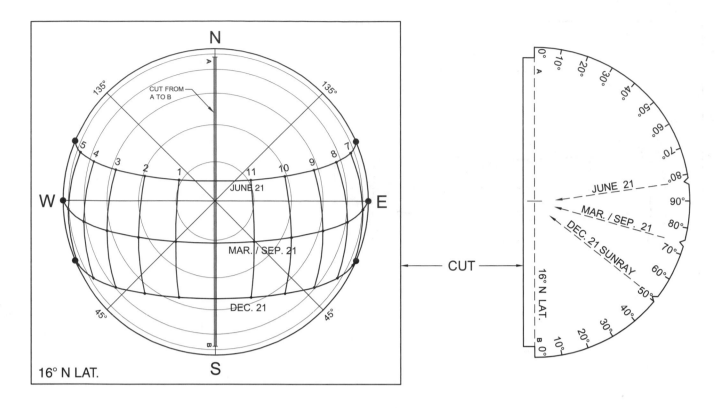

16° N LAT.

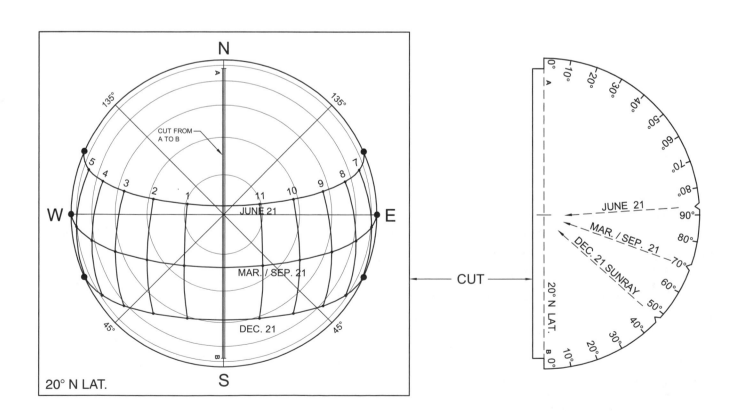

20° N LAT.

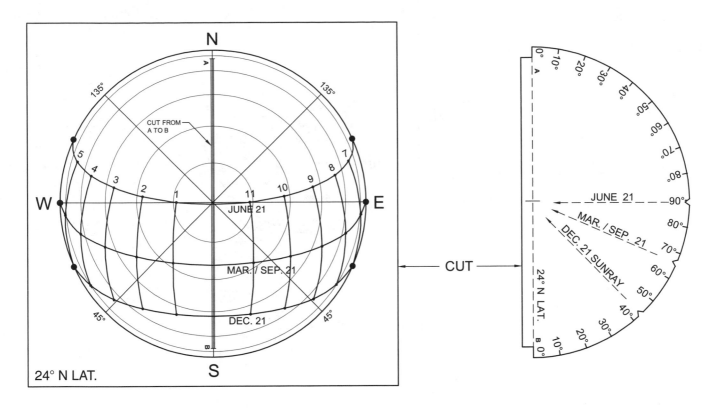

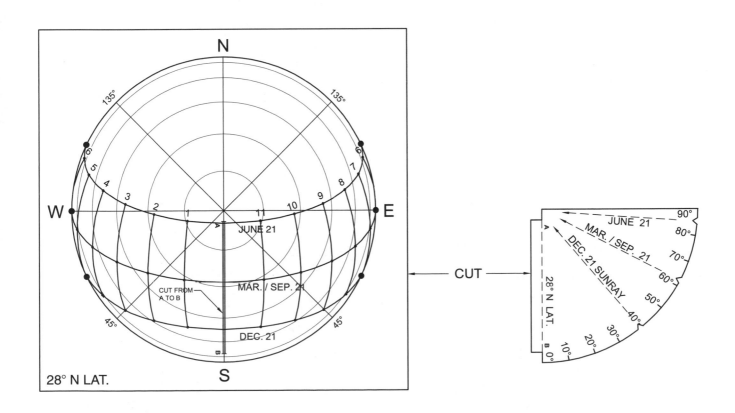

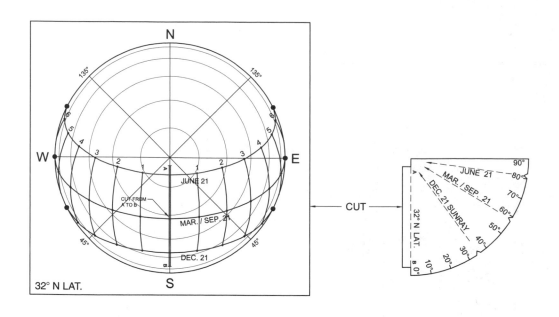

32° N LAT.

CUT

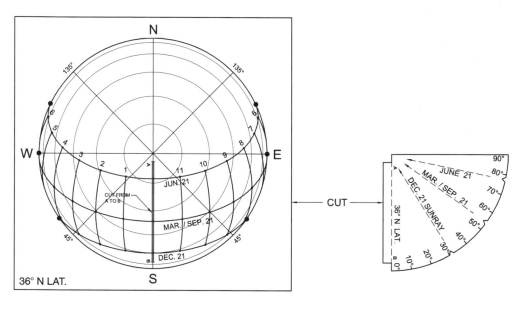

36° N LAT.

CUT

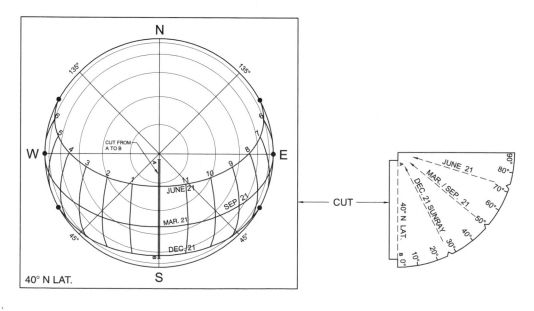

40° N LAT.

CUT

636

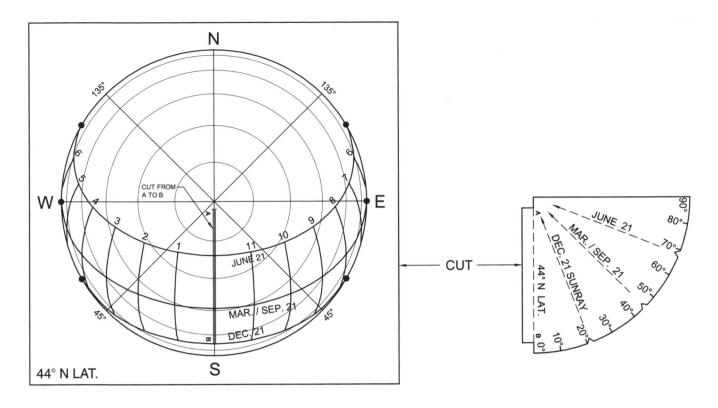

44° N LAT.

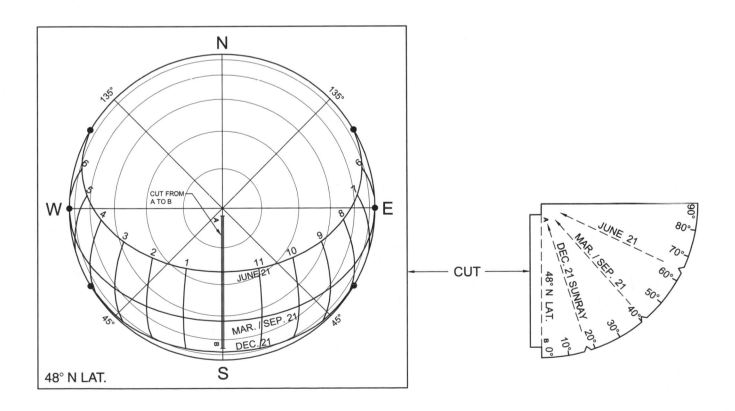

48° N LAT.

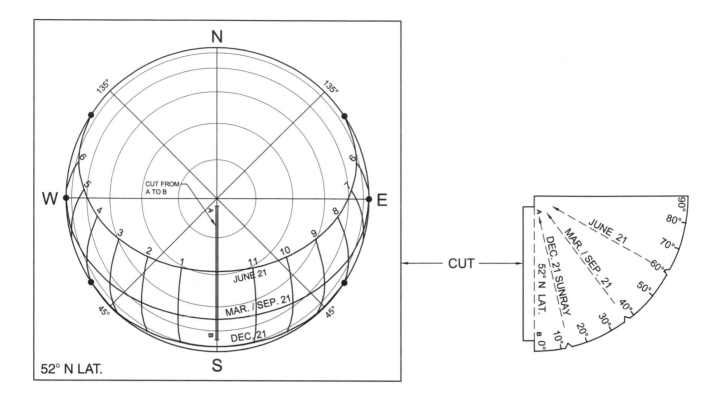

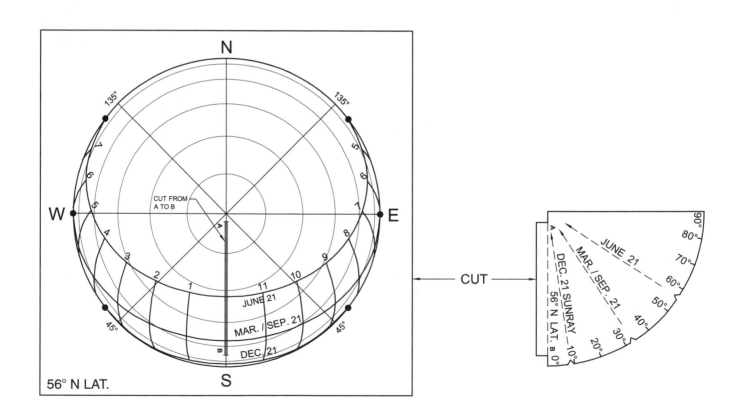

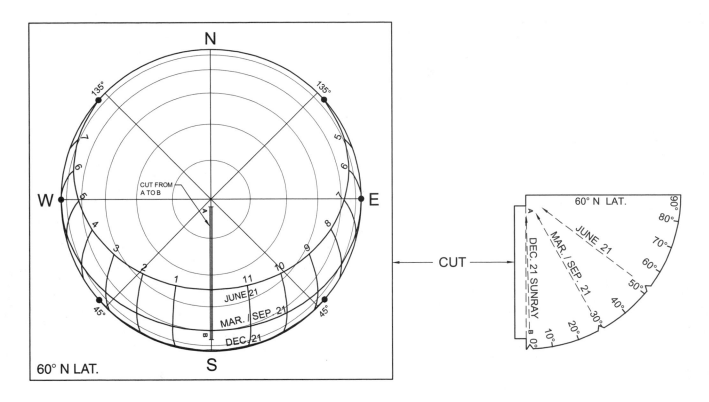

60° N LAT.

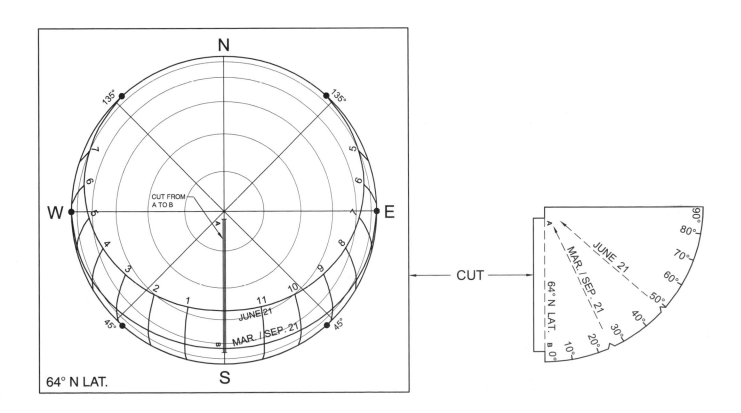

64° N LAT.

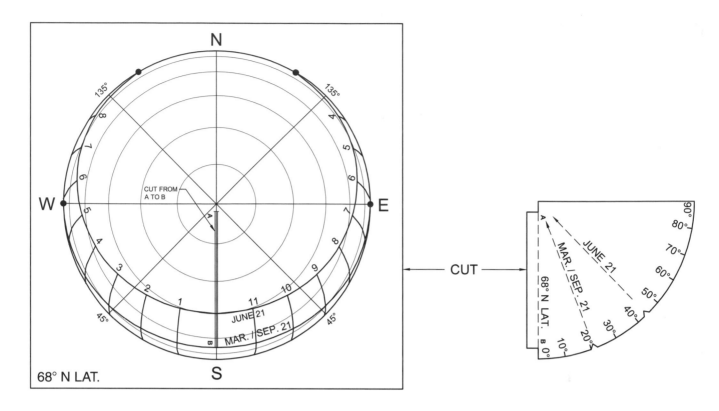

68° N LAT.

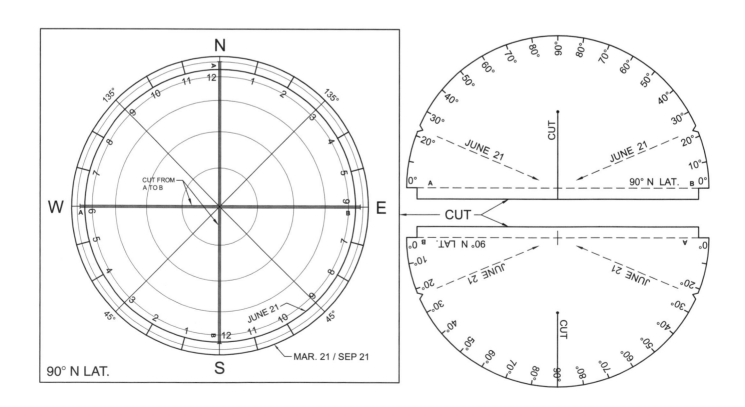

90° N LAT.

Computer Software Useful for the Schematic Design Stage

G.1 INTRODUCTION

A computer modeling tool for the schematic design stage must be easy to use, intuitive, and have clear graphical output. The following programs meet this criteria.

G.2 ECOTECT

Ecotect is a leading industry building analysis program that finally allows designers to work easily in three dimensions and apply all the tools necessary for creating an energy-efficient, sustainable future.

Ecotect is designed and written by architects and intended primarily for architects—although it is used extensively by engineers, local authorities, environmental consultants, and building designers, as well as owner-builders and environmental enthusiasts alike.

One of the greatest benefits of using Ecotect in the building design process is that you can analyze building at any level of simplicity (or complexity).

To foster this learning and investigation, Ecotect simulations are more visual and interactive than any other.

Encouraging designers to "play" with building performance is a key goal for Ecotect—with the ultimate aim of helping more and more designers easily integrate energy-efficient and sustainable design practices within their project workflows.

For more information, see www.ecotect.com.

G.3 ENERGY SCHEMING 3.0 (BY G. Z. BROWN, TOMOKO SEKIGUCHI, AND JEFFREY KLINE FOR MACINTOSH OR WINDOWS)

With Energy Scheming the designer thinks about building form and energy use together, right at the beginning stage of design, and gets expert advice while doing it. Energy Scheming is a design tool, not an analysis or evaluation tool. It helps the designer create an energy-efficient building rather than evaluate one already designed.

Take Off and Spec

All inputs are entirely graphic. No numbers! The design process using Energy Scheming starts with scanning in a drawing (cocktail napkins are fine), copying from another application, or drawing a building in the program. The building surfaces are then taken off with the tape measure cursor and associated with a specification.

Rule of Thumb

Energy Scheming gives you immediate feedback on window size for solar heating, ventilation, and daylighting for windows. You can simultaneously compose an elevation for appearance and size the windows for energy considerations.

Bar Graph

The building is evaluated and the results are shown in a bar graph. You can look at total loads for a whole day or just one hour. You can also get a detailed report on individual elements, such as windows or walls.

Thermographics

Energy Scheming's thermographic images illustrate your building's energy flow.

Advice

Expert advice is provided on how to improve the building's performance, redesign your building, and check performance.

Search for "Energy Scheming" on the Web or contact Terry Blomquist: (541) 346-5647, terryb@uoregon.edu.

G.4 ENERGY-10™

This is a powerful energy simulation tool for buildings and homes.

Advantages

- Allows you to integrate and assess dozens of energy-efficient design decisions quickly and accurately.
- Helps you and your clients understand and see the actual dollar savings that can be achieved through siting, materials selection, and integrated, energy-efficient design.
- Quantifies and clearly illustrates the impact of design decisions on first cost, operating costs, and pollution prevention.
- Helps you obtain energy credits under the U.S. Green Building Council LEED program. Output

reports for daylighting and total building energy use facilitate the LEED submission price.

Launch Energy-10 and within minutes, a detailed project simulation unfolds. The software performs hour-by-hour calculations and produces graphic reports depicting your building's thermal, HVAC, and daylighting performance over a full year of operation. Use actual energy and demand charges to track operating costs; evaluate hourly, monthly, or annual energy use; and track peak loads for your client's project.

For more information, go to www.sbicouncil.org/store.

G.5 UCLA ENERGY DESIGN TOOLS

All the software on the Energy Design Tools Web page (www.aud.ucla.edu/energy-design-tools) can be downloaded and used free. These tools were developed specifically for use at the very beginning of the architectural design process. This is the point where most of the decisions are made that will determine the building's final energy performance.

ClimateConsultant

At the beginning of a new project, an architect needs to understand the design implications of the local climate. Hourly climate data is available for more than 1000 stations. ClimateConsultant converts these files and displays dozens of different charts analyzing various aspects of the climate.

HEED (Home Energy Efficient Design)

This whole-building energy-analysis tool considers hundreds of different design variables. But at the very beginning of the design process, the architect knows only a few basic facts: the city, the building type, the square footage, and the number of stories. The expert system inside HEED uses these four facts to design a simple base-case, energy-efficient building. Then the architect's task is to mold and adapt this basic building to better meet the unique site, the program, and the aesthetic constraints. For each new scheme, the program shows graphically whether the building's energy performance is getting better or worse (Fig. G.5).

SOLAR-2 Window Sunshade Design Tool

This tool lets the architect fine-tune the shading of a window, whether it involves an overhang, fins, adjacent wings of the building, nearby walls, rows of trees, or even large buildings across the street.

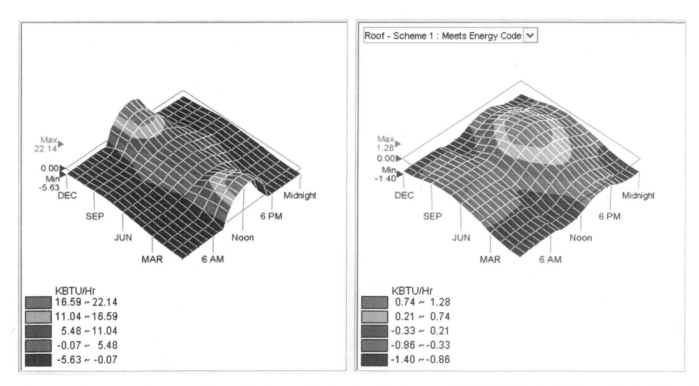

Figure G.5 These two graphs are part of the graphical output of HEED. The saddle shape on the left is desirable since it indicates that the design has the most heat gain in the winter (i.e., good solar design). The graph on the right shows that the alternative design is poor because it has the most heat gain in the summer. (Courtesy Prof. Murray Milne.)

OPAQUE Building Envelope Design Tool

Walls and roofs are an assembly of various materials, each with its own thermal properties. This design tool calculates many aspects of the envelope performance and produces dozens of charts and tables, including "Radiation on the Surface," "Surface Temperatures," "Heat Flow Through the Section," and "Solar Angles," plus the information for Form 3R required by the California Energy Code.

For more information, go to www.aud.ucla.edu/energy-design-tools.

Site Evaluation Tools

H.1 INTRODUCTION

As described in Section 6.14, site evaluation tools can describe how much solar access a specific site has. Four different tools are described below. The first two are commercially available, while the second two are do-it-yourself models. Make the Sun Locator (Fig. H.4) for a quick but approximate site evaluation tool, or make the Solar Site Evaluator (Fig. H.5a) for a much more precise site analysis tool. Just before publication, another fine site evaluation tool came on the market. The ASSET is a sight evaluation tool similar to the Sun Eye except that it uses vertical sun path diagrams rather than the horizontal sun-path diagrams of the Sun Eye. The ASSET is made by Wiley Electronics (www.wellc.com).

H.2 THE SOLAR PATHFINDER

All site evaluation tools superimpose the sun paths for that site (i.e., latitude) on top of a view of the actual site. By looking down onto the Solar Pathfinder, one can see a 360° panoramic image of the site reflected off the clear plastic dome (Fig. H.2). At the same time, one can see through the dome to view the sun-path mask placed under the dome. Thus, one sees the sun paths superimposed on a view of the site. The Solar Pathfinder comes with masks for various latitudes. Unlike the Solar Site Evaluator described in Section H.4, the Pathfinder is not affected much by wind. Software is also available to make this tool even more valuable. For more information, go to www.solarpathfinder.com or call (317) 501-2529.

H.3 THE SUNEYE™

The SunEye is a handheld electronic tool that instantly measures shading and solar access data for a particular location. With the press of a button, the user can see when and where shadows will occur throughout the day and year. The SunEye is used by solar panel installers to optimize the placement and orientation of solar panels and by green architects and landscape designers.

The integrated digital camera and fish-eye lens capture an image of the entire horizon in 360° (Fig. H.3).

Figure H.2 The Solar Pathfinder solar site evaluation tool. (Courtesy Solar Pathfinder, 3953 Marsh Greek Road, Linden, TN 37096; 317–501-2529.)

645

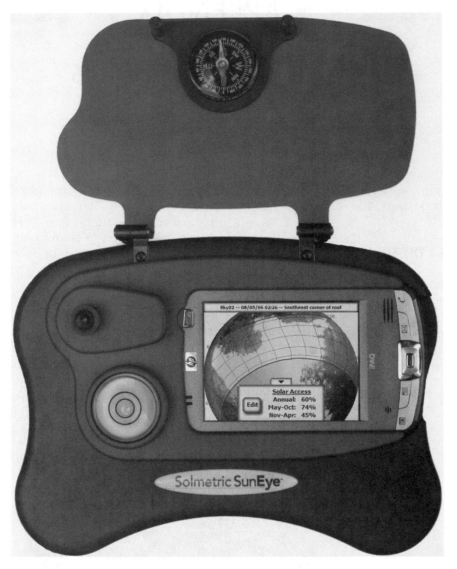

Figure H.3 The SunEye solar site evaluation tool. (Courtesy Solmetric.)

Onboard electronics do the following: superimpose the paths of the sun throughout the year based on latitude, detect shade-causing obstructions, and calculate the annual, monthly, daily, and hourly solar access. The SunEye can store more than fifty site readings, transfer data to a PC for further analysis, or export data into a printable report. The built-in edit tool can be used to easily simulate removal or trimming of shade-causing trees.

The SunEye is sustainably manufactured, incorporating a unique design that utilizes refurbished and recycled materials. For more information about Solmetric or the SunEye, go to www.solmetric.com.

H.4 THE SUN LOCATOR

Make an enlarged copy of the Sun Locator (Fig. H.4), and glue it to a cardboard backing. Trim along the line of the latitude nearest you. Place the locator in a level position at the area where the solar collectors are to be mounted. Align a compass along the correct magnetic declination line for true north and south (see Fig. H.5i). View from the corner over the top of the latitude line from 9 A.M. to 3 P.M. solar time. This is the path the sun will take in midwinter. If more than 5 percent of the path is blocked, the site might need closer evaluation. Even tree branches without leaves can block a considerable amount of winter sunlight. Consider trimming them if necessary.

H.5 DO-IT-YOURSELF SOLAR SITE EVALUATOR*

The Solar Site Evaluator consists of three parts: a semicircular wooden base, a clear plastic mask, and a removable wooden handle (see Fig. H.5a). The mask is held to the base via a Velcro™ strip for two reasons. The Velcro allows using different masks for different latitudes (4° intervals), and it makes the device easier to store and carry in a disassembled state. This Solar Site Evaluator is fairly easy and quick to build and costs only about $20 in materials.

The dimensions given in I-P are for convenience only—slightly larger or smaller site evaluators will work equally well. The only critical consideration is to match the length of the semicircle of the base to the length of the mask so that east is on one end, south in the middle, and west on the other end. Also, because it is desirable to use a photographic tripod to hold the site evaluator, the T nut should be for a ¼ in. screw, which is the standard on all cameras.

Parts List

- pine board, 1 × 8 × 15 (nominal dimensions)
- wooden dowel, ¾ in. diameter minimum and 6 in. long
- sheet clear acetate, 20 × 24 in., at least 0.005 in. thick
- compass (inexpensive kind)
- bull's-eye level

*Adapted from the design by Daniel K. Reif (www.homeplanner.com) from his book *Solar Retrofit: Adding Solar to Your Home*, Brick House Publishing Co., Amherst, NH, 1981.

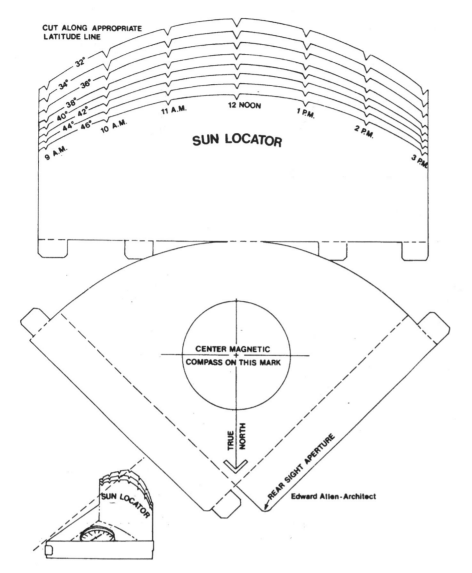

Figure H.4 The Sun Locator. (Courtesy Edward Allen and North Carolina Solar Center.)

ends. Finally, glue the compass and level to the top of the base, as shown in Fig. H.5a. Make sure that south on the compass is aligned with south on the mask.

Handle

Drill a $^{3}/_{16}$-in. hole in one end of the wood dowel, and insert the combination wood/machine screw in such a manner that about ¾ in. of the machine screw sticks out of the dowel.

Masks for Latitudes 26° to 46°

Drawings of masks for five different latitudes (28°, 32°, 36°, 40°, and 44°) have been prepared and are shown in Figs. H.5b to H.5f. Use the drawing that is less than 2° from the latitude desired. Enlarge it until the line marked 6 in. is full size or the length of the mask is the same as the semicircle of the wood base. Then transfer the lines onto a relatively stiff clear film, such as 0.005 in. (0.15 mm) thick acetate. Cut the film as shown, and apply along the bottom inside surface of the mask the ¾ in. self-adhesive Velcro strip that matches the one on the base. For extra strength, return the Velcro strip, as shown in the detail of Fig. H.5a.

Masks for Latitudes (Less Than 26° and More Than 46°)

To make a mask for latitudes not given, draw the winter sun paths for the required latitude on a **full-scale** version of the altitude/azimuth graph shown in Fig. H.5g. The altitude and azimuth angles for many latitudes are found in Appendix C of this book. Plot the points for each hour of the following sun paths: December 21, November/January 21, October/February 21, and March/September 21. Connect the points with solid lines to form the sun paths, and with dashed lines for the hours of the day to form a diagram like that in Fig. H.5e. Be sure to label the mask for the latitude of its sun paths. Then trace it onto a sheet of transparent film as described above for "Masks

- T nut, ¼ in. diameter and ¾ in. long (see fig. H.5a)
- combination wood/machine screw, ¼ in. diameter and 1½ in. long
- strip of self-adhesive Velcro about 28 in. long and ¾ in. wide
- cotton swab (e.g., Q-Tip™)

Construction Process

Base

Since a 1 × 8 board has an actual width of only 7¼ in., cut a semicircle with a 7¼ in. radius from the board.

Drill a hole 2 in. from the middle of the straight edge of the base for mounting the T nut as shown in Fig. H.5a. About ¼ in. from the middle of the straight edge, also drill a $^{3}/_{32}$ in. hole. Insert a cotton swab in this hole in such a manner that the top of the cotton tip is just above the base. The cotton swab is used as a sight in order to prevent potential damage to the eye. Next, glue a Velcro strip to the edge of the base. For better holding power, extend the Velcro around the base, as shown in the front view of Fig. H.5a, and staple the Velcro at both

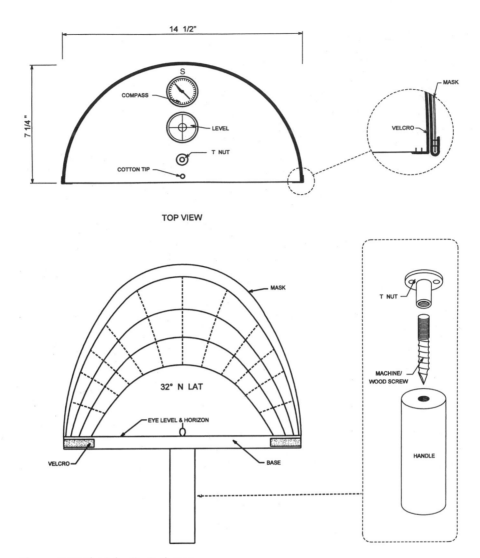

Figure H.5a The Solar Site Evaluator.

Using the Solar-Site Evaluator

This tool enables the user to determine when and how much a certain location will be shaded from the sun. This is possible because when one looks through the evaluator at the actual site, the sun-path diagrams are superimposed on the view of the site (see Figs. H.5h and 6.14). It is immediately obvious which

for Latitudes 26° to 46°." These masks can also be generated by the program ClimateConsultant, which is described in Appendix G, Section G.5.

trees or buildings are blocking the solar window and by how much. A record of the site condition can be traced on an overlay on the mask (see Fig.6.12c). This tool is best used on overcast days or on sunny winter days before 9 A.M. and after 3 P.M. so that it is not necessary to look directly into the sun.

Steps for Use

1. Attach the mask to the base by means of the Velcro strip.
2. Use a camera tripod to support the Solar Site Evaluator if at

all possible. The T nut will fit a camera tripod. Otherwise, use the handle.
3. At the specific place to be evaluated for solar access, set up the Solar Site Evaluator and level it by means of the bull's-eye level.
4. Orient the tool so that the 0° azimuth reference line faces true south. Use the Magnetic Declination Map in Fig. H.5i to determine how far true north is from magnetic north in your area. At the top of the map, two compasses illustrate the relative position

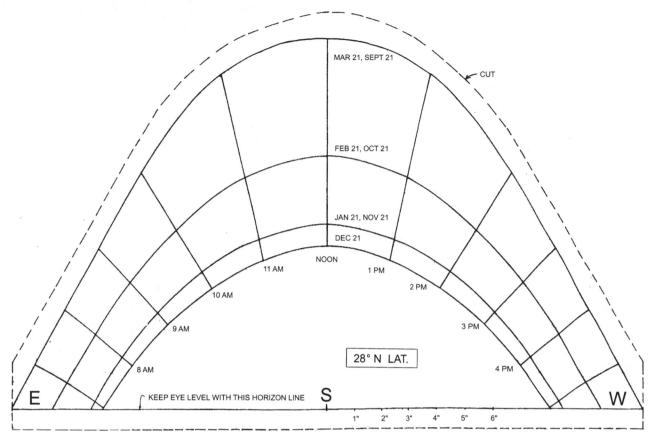

Figure H.5b The Solar Site Evaluator mask for 28° N latitude.

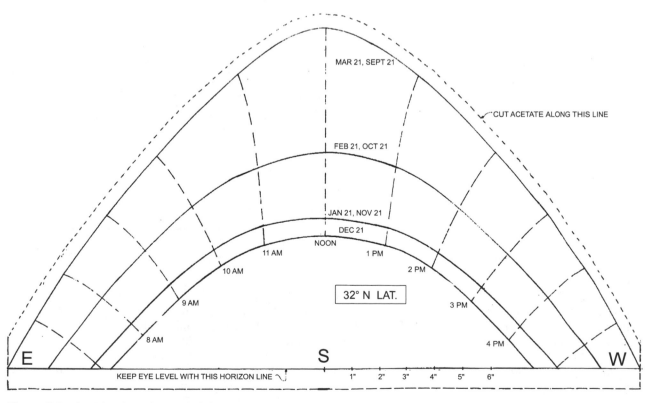

Figure H.5c The Solar Site Evaluator mask for 32° N latitude.

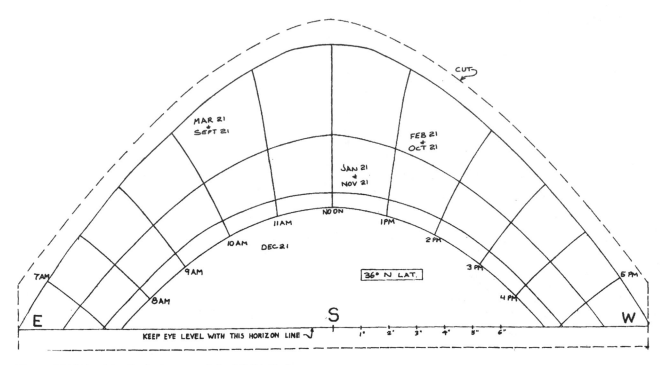

Figure H.5d The Solar Site Evaluator mask for 36° N latitude.

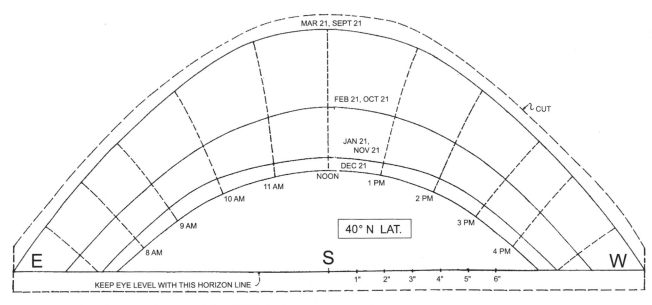

Figure H.5e The Solar Site Evaluator mask for 40° N latitude.

of true north and magnetic north on each side of the zero declination line in the United States. Use the following Web site for the exact declination in your area: www.ngdc.noaa.gov/seg/geomag/declination.

5. Bring your eye close to the top of the sight (cotton-swab tip), and look through the mask toward the south of the building site.

6. Evaluate the site by determining how much of the solar window is blocked.

7. If a record of the site is desired, draw on the acetate with a washable marker the outline of the objects viewed through the mask. By using clear acetate overlays, you can record any number of sites.

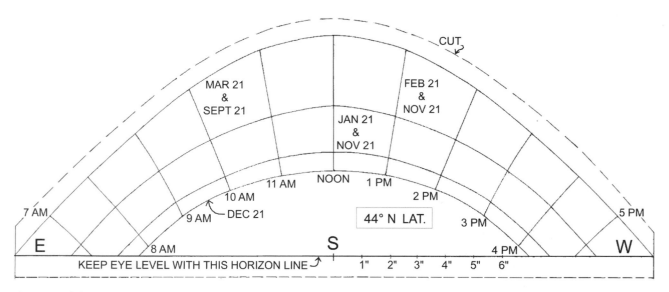

Figure H.5f The Solar Site Evaluator mask for 44° N latitude.

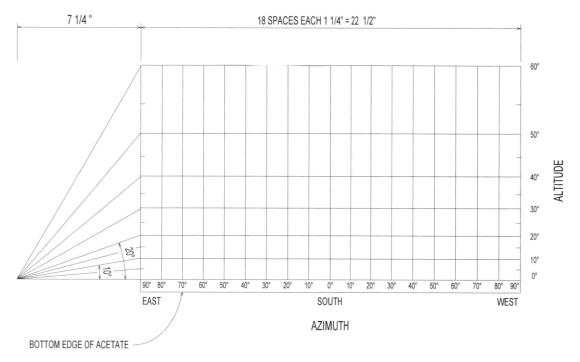

Figure H.5g The Solar Site Evaluator altitude/azimuth graph.

Figure H.5h Mounting the Solar Site Evaluator on a camera tripod is especially helpful when tracing a horizon profile.

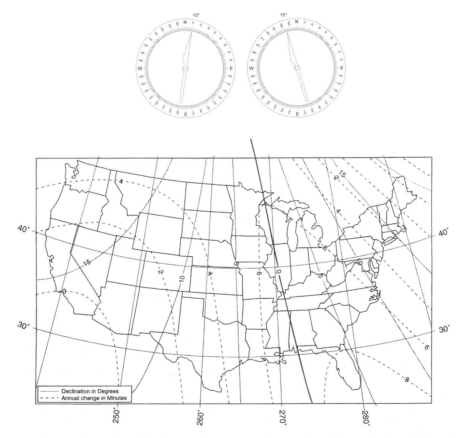

Figure H.5i The Magnetic Declination Map of the United States. True south and magnetic south are only aligned along the 0° declination line. Everywhere else, the compass must be rotated east or west according to the declination. For example, in the middle of Massachusetts, the compass must be rotated clockwise 15 degrees. Because the lines of magnetic declination shift with time, it is best to get the latest information from the Web site given in step 4 above. (Data from 1995 U.S. Geological Survey. Map courtesy of North Carolina Solar Center.)

Heliodons

I.1 INTRODUCTION

Heliodons, which were described in Section 6.15, are powerful design tools for generating solar-responsive architecture. For economy, most heliodons use one light to simulate the sun. However, by using many lights, it is possible to create conceptually clear heliodons, that are excellent teaching tools as well as good analysis tools. The type of heliodon chosen depends on the main purpose of the tool.

For schools of architecture, planning, and building, the author recommends one of two conceptually clear heliodons, of which the Sun Simulator is described in Section I.2 and the Sun Emulator in Section I.3. For low cost, compactness, and simplicity, the author recommends the Tabletop Heliodon described in Section I.4. That heliodon, however, is most appropriate for professionals who have a good understanding of solar geometry. Section I.5 describes how to make a Bowling Ball Heliodon, and Section I.6 lists some other commercial sources for heliodons.

Figure I.2 The author helped the faculty of architecture, at Chiang Mai University, Thailand, build this Sun Simulator Heliodon. For economy, it uses 50 W MR16 halogen lamps.

I.2 THE SUN SIMULATOR HELIODON

The Sun Simulator Heliodon is shown in Figs. 6.17a and in Fig. I.2. It has to be custom built for a specific latitude, although it can be adjusted for a range of latitudes plus or minus 5° from the constructed latitude. It is ideal for learning solar geometry and for generating enthusiasm for solar

design, because the device simulates our everyday experience. It is also extremely easy to use.

Although the Sun Simulator Heliodon can be built to any size, the author recommends a diameter over 10 ft (3 m), and larger is better. The author, who invented this heliodon, provides a complete set of computer-aided design drawings for free. Simply request an electronic copy by e-mail: lechnnm@auburn.edu.

I.3 THE SUN EMULATOR HELIODON

The Sun Emulator Heliodon (Fig. 6.17b) was developed by the author for those situations where the Sun Simulator Heliodon was not practical. The Sun Emulator is completely assembled in the factory and shipped to the site ready to go. It can be moved from room to room and requires a footprint of only 3 × 6 ft

653

Figure I.3 In its storage mode, the Sun Emulator table is rotated into the vertical position and the sun-path rings are placed at their 0° latitude position.

$(1 \times 2 \text{ m})$ (Fig. I.3). It can simulate all latitudes from the equator to the poles. However, because it is smaller than the Sun Simulator, smaller models must be used.

The Sun Emulator is made by High Precision Devices, located in Boulder, Colorado. They can be contacted at: www.hpd-online.com. The author has given the invention away and derives no income from it.

I.4 THE TABLETOP HELIODON

The heliodon shown in Fig. 6.15b and 6.16 consists of three parts:

1. a labeled ribbon, which is taped to the edge of a door
2. the clamp-on lighting fixture, which is supported by the edge of a door
3. the model stand, which rests on an ordinary table

In Fig. I.4a we see the precise spatial relationship of these three parts.

Ribbon

The cloth ribbon should be of a light color, about 2 in (5 cm). wide and 76 in (190 cm). long. The locations for the various months should be marked as indicated in Fig.I.4a (e.g., the top end should be labeled as June 21).

Light

Use a 50 W MR 16 or similar lamp in a clamp-on lighting fixture. The goal is to get a good quantity of light to shine on the model stand so that shadows are easy to see.

Model Stand: (see Fig.I.4b) Parts List

Size of Model Stand

Note that the heliodon model stand can be made to any size. The dimensions given here in the I-P system are for convenience only. Any size and thickness of material will work as long as the tilt table can tilt 90° from

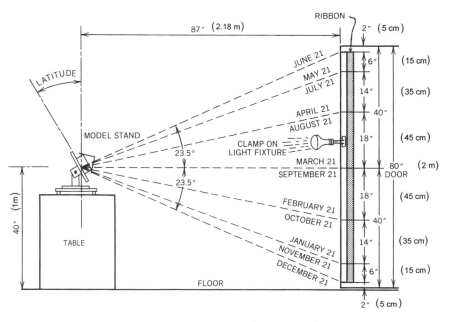

Figure I.4a These dimensions for the Tabletop Heliodon are critical.

horizontal to vertical and rotate 360° about the base.

- 2 pieces of ¾ in. plywood 12 × 12 in.
- 1 piece of ¾ in. plywood 12 × 10½ in.
- 2 pieces of wood ¾ × 1½ × 7 in. (Part A)
- 2 pieces of wood ¾ × 3½ × 7 in. (Part B)
- 3 carriage bolts ¼ in. diameter 2 in. long, with washers and winged nuts
- 6 wood screws 2 in. long, size #8
- 4 soft rubber no-slip feet (not gliders)
- 2 sheets of stiff plastic film about 8 × 8 in.
- 1 wood dowel ¼ in. dia., 1 ½ in. long

Construction Procedure

Drill a ¼ in.-diameter-hole in the center of the fixed base, in the corresponding location in the rotating base, and in Parts A and B (Fig. I.4c). Drill a ¾ in. hole in one part A as shown in Fig. I.4e. Also drill ³/₃₂ in. holes in the rotating base and the tilt table as indicated in Fig. I.4d. Drill all holes as accurately as possible.

Prepare both parts A by rounding one end of each. On the part A with the ¾ in. hole cut V groove as shown in Fig. I.4e. Glue a red thread into this groove to form a reference line across the hole. Make sure that no glue or thread protrudes above the surface. Screw parts A to the rotating base as shown in Fig. I.4c. Be sure to drill ³/₃₂ in. pilot holes to prevent splitting

of the wood. Part A with the ¾ in. hole should be on the west side and have the surface with the thread face inward.

Attach parts B to parts A with two carriage bolts. Then screw the tilt table to parts B as shown in Figures I.4c. Again drill ³/₁₆ in. pilot holes first in parts B to prevent splitting of the wood. Photocopy Fig. I.4f, cut along the dashed lines, and use a paper hole puncher to very carefully punch out the hole for the carriage bolt. Glue this latitude scale to the outside surface of part B on the west side. Make sure that the holes are aligned and that the zero line is parallel to the tilt table. Cover the scale with clear plastic or apply several coats of varnish for protection.

On the fixed base, label the hours of the day, and on the tilt table, label the cardinal directions of the compass (Fig. I.4d). Attach the four soft rubber feet to the bottom of the fixed base. Use the wood dowel to make a pointer on the rotating base (Fig. I.4d). From the stiff plastic film sheets, make two washers about 8 in. in diameter with a ¼ in. hole in the center. Assemble the tilt table with the acetate washers between the rotating base and the fixed base. However, there should be no washers between parts A and B.

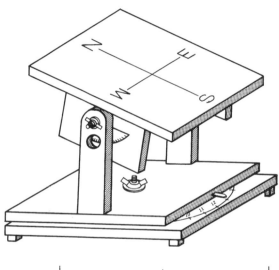

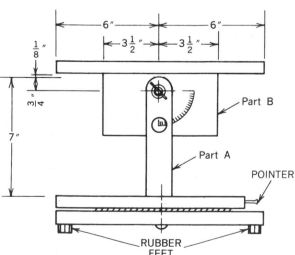

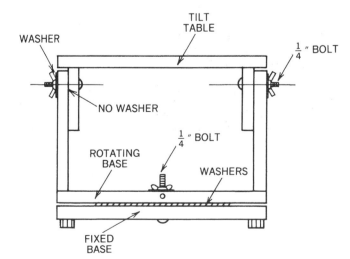

Figure I.4b Isometric view of the Tabletop Heliodon model stand.

Figure I.4c West side (left); south side (right). When working in SI units, use dimensions that are convenient, because actual size does not matter.

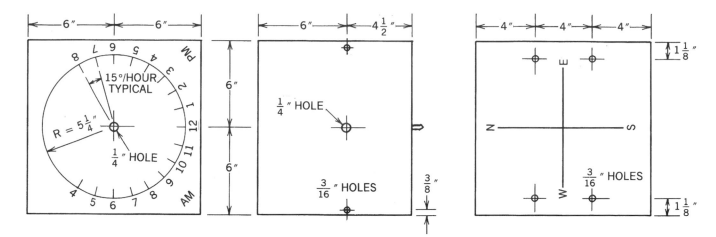

Figure I.4.d Fixed base (left); rotating base (center); tilt table (right).

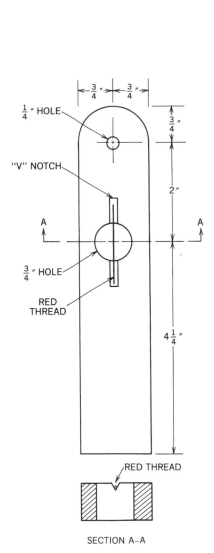

Figure I.4e Detail of part A for the west side.

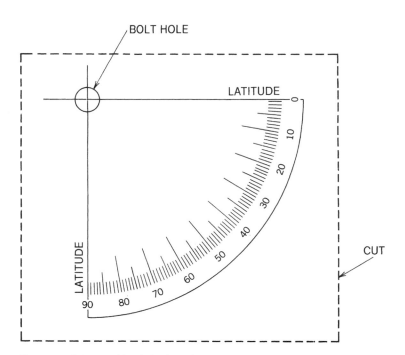

Figure I.4f Sun machine latitude scale.

Make sure that the rotating base can move very freely on the fixed base. It should, however, be possible to completely lock in place the tilt table when the winged nuts on the east and west sides are tightened. Check to make sure that the pointer, 12 noon, and south are all aligned. Also check to make sure that the latitude reads 90° for a horizontal tilt table and 0° when the tilt table is vertical.

Directions for Initial Setup

1. Tape the ribbon to the edge of a door as shown in Fig. I.4a.
2. Make sure that the clamp-on light fixture has a sufficiently long extension cord so that it can be placed anywhere along the vertical edge of the door.
3. Place the model stand on a table so that the center of the tilt table

is about 87 in. (218 cm) from the door edge and about 40 in. (100 cm) above the floor. Also make sure that 12 noon on the model stand faces the light on the door.

Directions for Use

1. Set and fix latitude by adjusting the angle of the tilt table.
2. Attach the model to the tilt table with pushpins or clamps. Align south of the model with south of the tilt table.
3. Set the clamp-on light to the desired month and aim the lamp at the model.
4. Turn the rotating base to the desired hour of the day.
5. The model will now exhibit the desired sun penetration and shading.

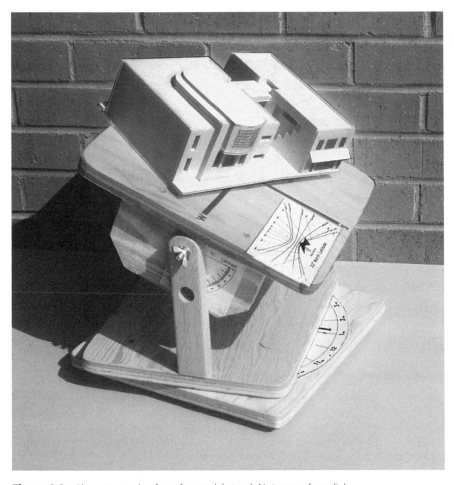

Figure I.4g Alternate mode of use for model stand. Note use of sundial.

Notes

1. Since the greatest accuracy occurs at the center of the tilt table, small models are more accurate than large models. However, many large models (e.g., site models) can be shifted around so that the part examined is always near the center of the tilt table.
2. The dynamics of sun motion can be easily simulated. Rotate the tilt table about its vertical axis to simulate the daily cycle. Move the light vertically along the edge of the door to simulate the annual cycle of the sun.
3. A correctly constructed heliodon will illuminate the east side of a model during morning hours. Check that the tilt table indicates 0° latitude when it is in a vertical

position. This would be the correct tilt for a model of a building located at the equator. Also make sure that the tilt table is horizontal when the latitude scale reads 90°(North Pole).

Alternate Mode of Use of The Heliodon

For greater accuracy, a source with more parallel light is required. Indoors, a slide projector at the far end of a corridor would give fairly parallel light rays. The best source of all, of course, is the sun. Since neither of these two sources of light can be moved up or down along the edge of a door, an alternate method of use for the model stand is required. Figure I.4g shows how a sundial is used in this alternate mode. Appendix E describes how sundials can easily be made for various latitudes.

Procedure for Alternate Mode of Use of the Heliodon

1. Attach the sundial of the appropriate latitude to the model in such a way that the base of the sundial is parallel to the floor plane of the model. Also align the south orientation of the model with that of the sundial.
2. Attach the model to the heliodon model stand. In this mode of use, the adjustments for latitude and time of day are ignored on the model stand.
3. Tilt and rotate the model stand until the gnomon of the sundial casts a shadow on the intersecting lines of the month and hour desired.
4. The model now exhibits with great accuracy the desired sun penetration and shadows (Fig. I.4g).

I.5 THE BOWLING BALL HELIODON

This bowling ball heliodon is simple to make and to use. However, it can only be used with sundials. it uses a

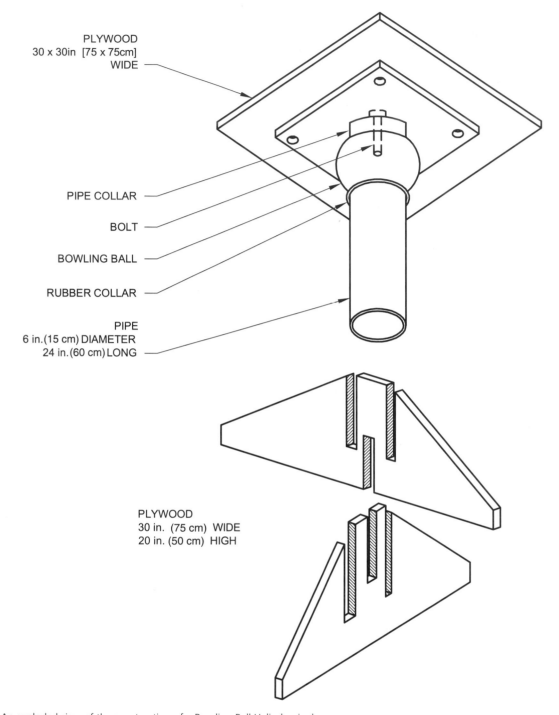

PLYWOOD
30 x 30in [75 x 75cm]
WIDE

PIPE COLLAR

BOLT

BOWLING BALL

RUBBER COLLAR

PIPE
6 in.(15 cm) DIAMETER
24 in.(60 cm) LONG

PLYWOOD
30 in. (75 cm) WIDE
20 in. (50 cm) HIGH

Figure I.5 An exploded view of the construction of a Bowling Ball Heliodon is shown.

bowling ball to allow easy adjustments in three axes, to simulate the sun angles for hours, months, and latitude (Fig. I.5). Because this heliodon can be readily disassembled, it is very portable and easily stored.

The heliodon base is made of two pieces of plywood that are approximately 20 × 30 in. (50 × 75 cm) and ¾ in. (2 cm) thick. Cut the plywood into the shapes shown in Figure I.5. The two pieces of plywood are then assembled into a cruciform shape. The top slits allow a pipe to be inserted. The top ring of this PVC pipe is then coated with rubber (e.g., plasti-dip) so that the tabletop mounted to the bowling ball can be set at a steep angle without slipping. The plywood tabletop is attached to the bowling ball with a 6 × ½ in. machine screw and a 2 in. (5 cm) collar made from the same PVC pipe that acts as a stand. Make sure that the screw head is countersunk so that the model has a flat surface to sit on. Used bowling balls are available at low cost at any bowling alley.

Caution: Users must be made aware of the danger of the bowling ball falling on their feet.

The Bowling Ball Heliodon was invented by Victor Olgyay, A.I.A., and Anna Maria R. Grune.

I.6 OTHER SOURCES OF HELIODONS

JT-11 Heliodon by the Beijing J-T Science Technology Co. Ltd. They also make the JT-1 Reflecting Dome Type Artificial Sky. www.bjsijt.com

Tabletop Heliodon (see Fig. I.6). l.c. This heliodon is similar to the one described in Section I.4. It is made by William Maffett, who can be contacted at Maffett and Associates, Cookeville, TN 38501; office: 931-526-7920; fax: 931-582-8430.

Sun Frost Heliodons. There are two kinds: the Sun Frost TT, which uses a remote light, and the Sun Frost MLS, with its own moving light source. www.sunfrost.com/heliodon.

Educational Opportunities in Energy-Conscious Design

Because of the rapid changes in architectural education, a Web page rather than the printed list of the Second Edition will provide the information on schools with programs of sustainability. The Society of Building Science Educators (SBSE) will continuously update this Web page, listing the schools that provide educational opportunities for students interested in sustainability and especially energy-responsive design: www.sbse.org/resources/index.htm

Another source of information on educational opportunities is the book *Ecological Design and Building Schools: Green Guide to Educational Opportunities in the U.S. and Canada*, by Sandra Leibowitz Early, New Village Press, 2005.

APPENDIX K

Resources

K.1 BOOKS

The following books are highly recommended. Because they cover the whole range of environmental-control topics, they are listed here. (See the Bibliography for full citations. The list includes valuable and out-of-print books.)

Anderson, B., ed. *Solar Building Architecture.*
Barnett, D. L., with W. D. Browning. *A Primer on Sustainable Building.*
Brown, G. Z., and M. DeKay. *Sun, Wind, and Light: Architectural Design Strategies*, 2nd ed.
Cofaigh, E. O., J. E. Olley, and J. O. Lewis. *The Climatic Dwelling: An Introduction to Climatic-Responsible Residential Architecture.*
Daniels, K. *The Technology of Ecological Building: Basic Principles and Measures, Examples and Ideas.*
Flynn, J. E., A. Stegal, G. T. Steffy, and G. R. Steffy, *Architectural Interior Systems.*
Givoni, B. *Climate Considerations in Building and Urban Design.*
Goulding, J. R., J. O. Lewis, and T. C. Steemers, eds. *Energy Conscious Design: A Primer for Architects.*
Lstiburek, J. W. *Builder's Guide—Hot-Dry and Mixed-Dry Climates; Builder's Guide—Cold Climates; Builder's Guide—Mixed Climates.*
Moore, F. *Environmental Control Systems.*
Olgay, V. *Design with Climate: A Bioclimatic Approach to Architectural Regionalism.*
Pearson, D. *The Natural House Catalog: Everything You Need to Create an Environmentally Friendly Home.*
Ramsey/Sleeper: Architectural Graphic Standards, 11th ed.
Stein, B., J. S. Reynolds, W. T. Grondzik, and A. G. Kwok. *Mechanical and Electrical Equipment for Buildings*, 10th ed.
Thomas, R., ed. *Environmental Design: An Introduction for Architects and Engineers.*
Tuluca, A. *Energy-Efficient Design and Construction for Commercial Buildings.*
Watson, D., and K. Labs, *Climatic Design: Energy-Efficient Building Principles and Practices.*

K.2 JOURNALS

Eco-Structure: Improving Environmental Performances of Buildings and Their Surroundings. www.eco-structure.com
Environmental Building News. 122 Birge Street, Suite 30, Brattleboro, VT 05301; 802-257-7300. www.buildinggreen.com
Environmental Design and Construction. 299 Market Street, Suite 320, Saddle Brook, NJ 07663-5312; 415-863-2614. www.edcmag.com
Green Source: The Magazine of Sustainable Design. www.GREENSOURCEMAG.com
Home Energy: The Magazine of Residential Energy Conservation. 2124 Kittredge Street, No. 95, Berkeley, CA 94704-9942; 510-524-5405.
Home Power: The Hands-on Journal of Home-made Power. Ashland, OR: Home Power, Inc. P.O. Box 5520, Ashland, OR 97520. 916-475-3179.
Renewable Energy World. James & James Ltd. 35-37 William Road, London, NW1 3ER U.K. +44 171 387 8558, +44 387 8998 (fax). rew@jxj.com, www.jxj.com.
Solar Industry Journal. Solar Energy Industries Association (SEIA), 122 C Street NW, Fourth Floor, Washington, DC 20001-2109. 202-383-2600.
Solar Today. The American Solar Energy Society. 2400 Central Avenue, Unit G-1, Boulder, CO 80301. 303-443-3130. (E-mail) ases@ases.org www.ases.org/solar

K.3 VIDEOS

Affluenza. Host, Scott Simon. Produced by KCTS/Seattle and Oregon Public Broadcasting (OPB). KCTS Television, 1997. Approximately 57 minutes. 1-800-937-5387. Discusses the environmental impact of a high standard of living.
An Inconvenient Truth www.CLIMATECRISIS.NET
Arithmetic, Population, and Energy. Dr. Albert A. Barlett. 1994. 65 minutes. University of Colorado ITS-Media Services Campus Box 379 Boulder, CO 80309-0379 303-492-1857 Fax: 303-492-7017 E-mail: Kathleen.Albers@colorado.edu
Keeping the Earth: Religious and Scientific perspectives on the Environment. 1996. 27 minutes. Publications Department Union of Concerned Scientists Two Brattle Square Cambridge, MA 02238-9105 617-547-5552 www.ucsusa.org
Kilowatt Ours www.KILOWATTOURS.ORG
World Population, Produced by Zero Population Growth (ZPG). ZPG 1400 16th Street NW, Suite 320 Washington, DC 20036 1-800-POP-1956 www.zpg.org

K.4 CD-ROMS

*E Build Library: Environmental Building
News on CD-ROM. Available from
Environmental Building News.*
Green Building Advisor.
   CREST Software Orders
   1200 18th Street NW, Suite 900
   Washington, DC 20036
   1-888-44CREST
   Fax: 202-887-0497
   www.crest.org/software-central

K.5 ORGANIZATIONS

American Institute of Architects,
   Committee on the Environment
   www.AIA.ORG/COTE
American Society of Heating,
   Refrigeration, and Air-Conditioning
   Engineers (ASHRAE) www.ashrae.org
   Works to educate members of the
   field and to set standards for the
   industry.
American Society of Landscape
   Architects (ASLA) www.asla.org
   A professional organization that,
   among other activities, provides
   training and advocates for livable
   communities and the environment.
American Solar Energy Society www
   .ases.org
   A nonprofit organization advocating
   the use of solar and other renewable
   energy sources, including through
   work with professionals.
American Wind Energy Association
   www.awea.org
   Advocates for and educates on the
   use of wind power.
Building Science Consulting
   www.buildingscience.com
   A Boston-based firm involved in
   building design, construction, and
   operation. It focuses on sustainable building in promoting energy
   efficiency and environmental
   protection.
Renewable Energy Policy Project and
   CREST Center for Renewable Energy
   and Sustainable Technology
   www.repp.org/efficiency/index
   Provides information about building
   energy efficiency.
EBuild
   www.ebuild.com

A builder's catalog collection published by Hanley Wood.
E Source Companies Ltd.
   www.esource.com
   Originally an offshoot of the
   Rocky Mountain Institute, E Source
   provides information to energy
   providers.
Energy and Environmental Building
   Association
   www.eeba.org
   Provides information to transform
   the residential design, development,
   and construction industries.
Florida Solar Energy Center
   www.fsec.ucf.edu
   The state's primary research facility
   on solar energy and other advanced
   fuels.
GeoExchange/Geothermal Heat Pump
   Consortium
   www.geoexchange.org
   Provides geothermal heat pumps in
   houses.
IESNA Illuminating Engineering Society
   www.iesna.org
   Publishes information on the latest
   knowledge in lighting.
International Association of Lighting
   Designers (IALD)
   www.iald.org
   Sets standards for lighting design
   and refers customers to lighting
   designers.
International Solar Energy Society
   www.ises.org
   Promotes and educates about solar
   energy and all other areas of renewable energy.
Iris Communications, Inc.
   www.irisinc.com
   Publisher of Oikos.com and Oikos
   Bookstore, which contains items on
   sustainability.
Lighting Design Lab
   www.lightingdesignlab.com
   Promotes quality lighting and sustainable lighting systems. It is a good
   source of information on lighting.
Lighting Resource Center
   www.lrc.rpi.edu
   A reliable source of objective information about lighting technologies,
   applications, and products. As part
   of Rensselaer Polytechnic Institute, it
   offers master's and Ph.D. programs
   in lighting. It provides training to
   people in the building professions.

National Association of Homebuilders
   Research Center (NAHBRC)
   www.nahbrc.org
   A resource for reliable, objective information and research on
   housing construction and development issues. Has published green
   building standards.
National Resources Defense Council
   www.nrdc.org
   The nation's most effective environmental action organization.
Negative Population Growth, Inc. (NPG)
   www.npg.org
   Provides information on the environmental impact of population
   growth.
North American Sundial Society
   www.sundials.org
   Dedicated to the study, development, history, and preservation of
   sundials.
North Carolina Solar Center
   www.ncsc.ncsu.edu
   Clearinghouse for solar and other
   renewable energy for citizens of
   North Carolina and beyond.
Northeast Sustainable Energy
   Association (NESEA)
   www.nesea.org
   The Northeast's leading organization of professionals and concerned
   citizens working in the areas of sustainable energy and whole systems
   thinking.
Oak Ridge National Laboratory
   www.ornl.gov
   Originally created to produce plutonium for the Manhattan Project, it is
   now a leading researcher in environmental and energy technologies.
Pacific Energy Center
   www.pge.com/pec
   Offers educational programs, design
   tools, advice, and support to create
   energy-efficient buildings and comfortable indoor environments.
The Population Connection
   www.populationconnection.org
   Explores issues involving connections between sustainability and
   population.
Rocky Mountain Institute
   www.rmi.org
   Founded by Hunter and Amory
   Lovins, the RMI is a source of
   information for sustainability in
   most areas.

Southface
> www.southface.org
> A nonprofit organization providing educational and outreach programs for both architects and the general public.

Sustainable Buildings Industry Council (SBIC)
> www.sbicouncil.org
> Promotes green building using a "whole building approach."

Union of Concerned Scientists
> www.ucsusa.org
> The leading science-based nonprofit organization working for a healthy environment and a safer world.

U.S. Environmental Protection Agency
> www.epa.gov
> The U.S. government's main regulatory agency for environmental matters.

U.S. Green Building Council
> www.usgbc.org
> Administers the LEED program, which certifies buildings as green.

Worldwatch Institute
> www.worldwatch.org
> Reports on sustainability issues worldwide.

Tables of R-Values

These technical tables are provided because the thermal resistance of building materials is a key aspect of sustainability. Table L.1 provides the thermal resistance of most common building materials. Table L.2 shows how the thermal resistance of an air space varies with orientation, direction of heat flow, and/or the reflectance/emittance of the air space surface. Table L.3 shows the resistances of common doors. For the thermal resistance of windows, see Fig. 15.9a.

Table L.1 R-Values for Typical Building Materials

	I-P System				Heat Capacity		SI System				Heat Capacity	
Material	Thickness in Inches	R per Inch*	R for thickness Listed†	Density (lb/ft³)	By Weight (Btu/lb.°F)	By Volume (Btu/ft³.°F)	Thickness in Meters	R per Meter‡	R for Thickness Listed§	Density (kg/m³)	By Weight (J/kg °C)	By Volume (J/m³.°C)
BRICK	4	0.1	0.5	120	0.19	22.8	0.1	0.7	0.09	1920	0.79	1525
CONCRETE BLOCKS												
Normal weight	4		0.7	69	0.22	15.18	0.1		0.13	1104	0.92	1015
	8		1.1	64	0.22	14.08	0.2		0.2	1024	0.92	942
	12		1.3	63	0.22	13.86	0.3		0.23	1008	0.92	927
Normal weight with insulated core	8		1.9	65	0.22	14.3	0.2		0.34	1040	0.92	9560
Lightweight with isulated core	8		5		0.21	0.21			0.9		0.88	1
STONE (lime or sand)	1	0.08		150	0.19	28.5	1	0.6		2400	0.79	1906
CONCRETE												
Normal weight	1	0.08		140	0.22	30.8	1	0.6		2240	0.92	2060
Lightweight	1	0.2→1.4					1	1.3→10				
WOOD												
Sheets of plywood, hardboard, particleboard, wood siding	1	1.2		34	0.29	9.86	1	8		544	1.21	659
Hardwoods	1	0.9		45	0.3	13.5	1	6		720	1.25	903
Softwoods	1	1.3		32	0.33	10.56	1	9		512	1.38	706
INSULATION												
Blankets												
Fiberglass	1	3.5					1	24				
Mineral wool	1	3.3					1	23				
Cotton fiber	1	3.9					1	27				
Loose fill												
Fiberglass	1	3					1	21				
Mineral wool	1	3.8					1	27				
Cellulosic fiber	1	3.5			0.33	0.33	1	25		16	1.38	22
Vermiculite–exfoliated	1	2.1		7	0.32	2.24	1	15		112	1.34	150
Perlite–expanded	1	2.7			0.26	0.26	1	19		16	1.09	17
Sawdust	1	2.2			0.33	0.33	1	14		16	1.38	22
Rigid boards												
Phenolic foam boad	1	8					1	56				
Polyurethane/ polyisocyanurate	1	6.5					1	46				
Polystyrene (extruded)	1	5					1	35				
Polystyrene (expanded-based board)	1	4					1	28				

Cellular glass	1	3		8.5	0.24	2.04	1	21		136	1	136
Glass fiber	1	4		9.5	0.23	2.185	1	28		152	0.96	146
Cork board	1	3.6					1	25				
Fiberboard	1	2.6					1	18				
Sprayed or Blown												
Polyurethane	1	6					1	48				
Cellulose	1	3.3										
Glass fiber	1	3.7										
Air-Krete	1	3.9		2.2				27				
Icynene	1	3.6		0.5				25				
Roofing												
Built-up roofing	0.38		0.3	70	0.35	24.5	0.0095		0.05	1120	1.46	1639
Asphalt shingles			0.4	70	0.3	21			0.07	1120	1.25	1404
Slate	0.5		0.1	201	0.3	60.3	0.0127		0.02	3216	1.25	4033
Wood shingles			0.9	40	0.31	12.4			0.16	640	1.3	829
Sheet metal			neg						neg			
GLASS	1		0.1						0.02			
GYPSUM OR PLASTER BOARD	0.38		0.3	50	0.26	13	0.009		0.05	800	1.09	869
	0.5		0.5	50	0.26	13	0.013		0.09	800	1.09	869
	0.62		0.6	50	0.26	13	0.016		0.1	800	1.09	869
FINISH FLOORING OR CEILING												
Hardwood	0.75		0.7	45		45	0.019		0.13	720	4.18	3010
Tile-asphalt, rubber, vinyl	0.13		neg	120	0.3	36	0.0032		neg	1920	1.25	2408
Tile-linoleum, ceramic, terrazzo	0.13		0.1	80	0.3	24	0.0032		0.02	1280	1.25	1605
Tile-cork	0.13		0.3	25	0.48	12	0.0032	15.4	0.05	400	2.01	803
Carpet	1		1					15	0.18			
Lay-in ceiling tile	0.5		1.3	18	0.14	2.52	0.0127	18	0.23	288	0.59	169
STRAW BALES	1	1.5→2.5						10→21				
EARTH												
Dry, loose	1	0.3						2.1				
Damp, packed	1	0.1						0.7				
METALS		neg						neg				
SAND	1	0.5		95	0.2	19		3.5		1520	0.84	1271
SNOW	1	0.2						1.4				

°F · ft² · h/Btu · in.
°F · ft² · h/Btu.
°C · m²/W.
°C · m²/W.

Table L.2 R-Values of Air Spaces

Surface or Space	Direction of Heat Flow	Nonreflective*		Bright Aluminimum Foil[†]	
		I-P[‡]	SI[§]	I-P[‡]	SI[§]
Surface Air Films					
Still air					
Horizontal	Up	0.6	0.10	1.3	0.22
Vertical	Horizontal	0.7	0.12	1.7	0.29
Horizontal	Down	0.9	0.15	4.6	0.78
Moving air (any position)		0.1–0.3	0.02–0.05		
Air Spaces					
Horizontal	Up	0.8	0.14	2.2	0.37
Vertical	Horizontal	0.9	0.15	3.2	0.54
Horizontal	Down				
¾ in. air space		1	0.17	3.4	0.58
3½ ft air space		1.1	0.19	8.7	1.48

*Any surface other than polished metal.
[†]Any polished metal–radiant barrier.
[‡]°F · ft^2 · h/Btu.
[§]°C · m^2/W.

Table L.3 Thermal Resistance for Slab Doors

Doors	I-P		SI	
	R*	U[†]	R[‡]	U[§]
Wood (solid)	2	0.5	0.36	2.8
w/storm door	3.3	0.3	0.59	1.7
Steel	1.6–5	0.2–0.6	.29–.89	3.4–1.12

*Total thermal resistance (°F · ft^2 · h/Btu)
[†]U-coefficient (Btu/°F · ft^2 · h).
[‡]total thermal resistance (°C · m^2/W).
[§]U-coefficient (W/°C · m^2).

Conversion Factors between the Inch-Pound (I-P) and System International (SI) systems

The SI (International System) of units is the modern version of the metric system. All major countries except the United States have switched to the SI system. When England switched to the SI system, it no longer made sense to call our system the "English System" Thus, we now call it the "Inch-Pound (I-P)" system of units. To speed up the switch to the SI system the U.S. federal government requires all construction documents for federal buildings to be drawn in SI units.

To convert	To	Multiply by
SI PREFIXES		
tera (T) = 1 trillion		
giga (G) = 1 billion		
mega (M) = 1 million		
kilo (k) = 1,000		
hecto (h) = 100		
deka (da) = 10		
deci (d) = 0.1		
centi (c) = 0.01		
milli (m) = 0.001		
micro (µ) = 1 millionth		
nano (n) = 1 billionth		
pico (p) = 1 trillionth		

To convert	To	Multiply by
Length		
inches (in.)	centimeters	2.54
inches	millimeters	25.4
feet (ft)	meters	0.305
yards (yd)	meters	0.914
miles (mi)	kilometers	1.61

(Continued)

To convert	To	Multiply by
centimeters (cm)	inches	0.394
meters (m)	feet	3.28
meters	yards	1.09
kilometers (km)	feet	3,280
kilometers	miles	0.621
Area		
square inches	square centimeters	6.45
square feet	square meters	0.0929
acres	hectares	0.405
square miles	square kilometers	2.59
square centimeters	square inches	0.155
square meters	square feet	10.8
hectares (ha)	acres	2.47
square kilometers	square miles	0.386
acres	square yards	4,840
acres	square feet	43,560
hectares	square meters	10,000
Energy (work, heat power)		
British thermal unit (Btu)	kilowatt hours	0.000293
therms	British thermal unit	100,000
kilowatt-hours (kwh)		
resistance per inch	resistance per meter	6.93
resistance (I-P)	resistance [SI]	
actual thickness	actual thickness	0.174
U-coefficient (I-P)	U-coefficient [SI]	5.73
Btu (energy)	kilocarlories	0.252
Btu (energy)	kilojoules	1.06
Btu/h (power)	watts	0.293
Btu/h ft^2 (energy transfer)	watts per square meter	3.16
Btu/°F (heat capacity)	kilojoules per kelvin	1.9
Btu/lb°F (specific heat)	kilojoules per kilogram per kelvin	4.18
Btu/h°F ft (thermal conductivity)	watts per kelvin per meter	1.73
Btu/h°F ft^2 (conductance)	watts per kelvin per square meter	5.67
watts	Btu per hour	3.41
watts per square meter	Btu per square foot	0.317
kilocalories	Btu	3.97
kilocalories	joules	4190
kilojoules	Btu	0.948
kilojoules per kilogram	Btu per pound	0.43
kilowatt-hours	megajoules	3.6
megajoules	kilowatt-hours	0.278
US horsepower (hp)	watts	746
horsepower	kilowatts	0.746
kilowatts	horsepower	1.34

To convert	To	Multiply by
Light		
footcandle	lux	10.8
Volume		
cubic inches	cubic centimeters	16.4
cubic feet	cubic meters	0.0283
cubic feet	gallons	7.48
cubic feet	liters	28.3
cubic yards	cubic meters	0.765
cubic centimeters	cubic inches	0.061
cubic meters	cubic feet	35.3
cubic meters	cubic yards	1.3
liters	cubic feet	0.0353
Liquids		
US gallons	liters	3.79
US gallons water	pounds water	8.35
liters (1)	fluid ounces (US)	33.8
liters	quarts	4.23
liters	gallons (US)	0.264
quarts	liters	0.946
barrels	US gallons	42
Weight		
ounces (oz)	grams	28.3
pounds (lb)	kilograms	0.454
pounds	grams	454
grams (g)	ounces	0.0353
kilograms (kg)	pounds	2.2
Density		
pounds per cubic foot	kilograms per cubic meter	16
pounds per square foot	kilograms per square meter	4.88
Speed		
feet per second (fps)	meters per second (mps)	0.305
meters per second	feet per minute	197
meters per second	miles per hour	2.24
miles per hour	kilometers per hour	1.61
miles per hour	meters per second	0.447
Temperature		
Celsius (°C)	Fahrenheit (°F)	multiply by 9, divide by 5, add 32
Fahrenheit (°F)	Celsius (°C)	subtract 32 multiply by 5 divide by 9
Celsius	Kelvin (K)	add 273.15

The Water Table for Ventilation Studies

N.1 INTRODUCTION

The water table illustrated in Fig. 10.7d can simulate air flowing through a building. Streams of colored water simulate in slow motion the smoke streams in a wind tunnel or in an actual building (Fig. N.1).

Water is allowed to flow evenly across the table on which a ¾ in. (2 cm) deep horizontal or vertical slice of a model is placed. Water will flow through openings in the model representing windows. After a steady-state flow has been achieved, dyed water is poured into the color tray to form parallel color streams. As these dye streams pass through the model, it is possible to determine where water is moving and where it is stagnant. A photo is then taken to document the ventilation pattern.

N.2 CONSTRUCTION OF A WATER TABLE

A sturdy table is necessary so that the water table surface can be completely flat. Also, adjustable legs allow the table to be leveled (Fig. N.2a) side by side and to have a slight slope in the long direction for the water to flow slowly.

The trough on one short end is filled with tap water, while the trough on the other short end is connected to a drain (Fig. N.2b). A valve allows the creation of a thin layer of water (about 2–3 mm) flowing across the table. A color tray spanning the short dimension of the water table is resting just above the water flowing across the table about 5 mm above the table (Fig. N.2c). At the appropriate time, colored water is poured into this tray. The colored water leaks out of tiny 1 mm equally spaced holes on the bottom of the tray (Fig. N.2d) so that parallel color streams are created in the flowing water.

The horizontal model slice of the building design to be tested consists of walls about 2 cm high glued to a thin sheet of plastic about 0.5 mm thick (Fig. N.2e).

Potassium permanganate makes a very good dye.

The information for this water table appendix was furnished by Prof. Ruht Tantachamroon of Chiang Mai University, Thailand.

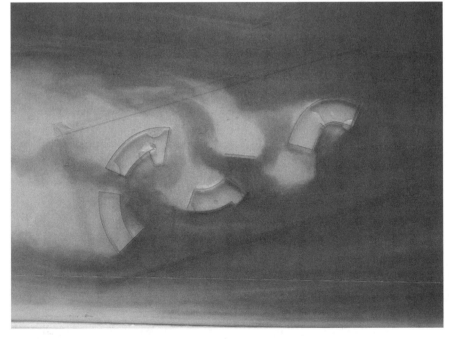

Figure N.1 Colored parallel streams of water flow through the shallow model of a building being tested on the water table at Chiang Mai University in Thailand. The water passing through the model closely simulates air flowing through a building. (Courtesy the 5th year project on Water Table Experiment, Chiang Mai University, Thailand.)

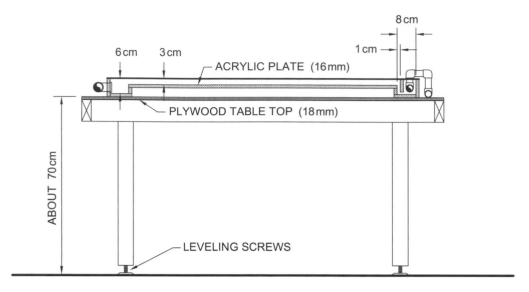

8 cm

6 cm 3 cm

1 cm

ACRYLIC PLATE (16 mm)

PLYWOOD TABLE TOP (18 mm)

ABOUT 70 cm

LEVELING SCREWS

LONGITUDINAL SECTION

Figure N.2a Longitudinal section.

Figure N.2b Plan view. Note how the color tray rests on the edges of the water table.

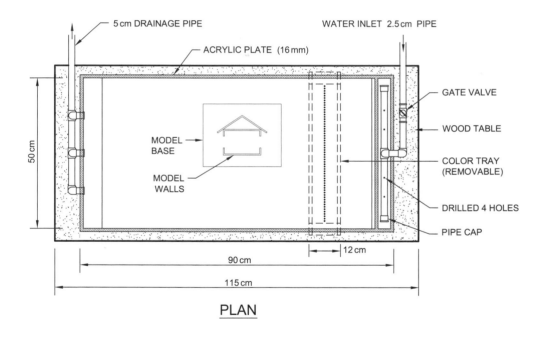

5 cm DRAINAGE PIPE

WATER INLET 2.5 cm PIPE

ACRYLIC PLATE (16 mm)

GATE VALVE

WOOD TABLE

50 cm

MODEL BASE

MODEL WALLS

COLOR TRAY (REMOVABLE)

DRILLED 4 HOLES

PIPE CAP

12 cm

90 cm

115 cm

PLAN

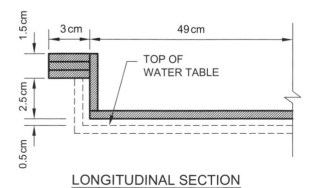

1.5 cm

3 cm

49 cm

TOP OF WATER TABLE

2.5 cm

0.5 cm

LONGITUDINAL SECTION

Figure N.2c Detail of color tray.

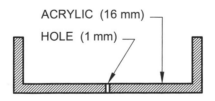

ACRYLIC (16 mm)

HOLE (1 mm)

CROSS SECTION

Figure N.2d The cross section of the color tray is shown. Drill 1 mm holes evenly along the center with a spacing of 10 mm.

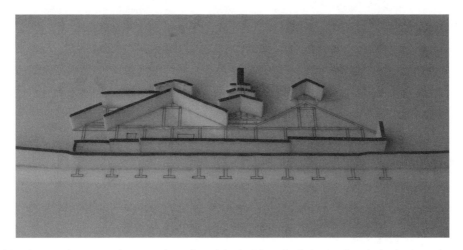

Figure. N.2e The model to be tested consists of a 2 cm deep slice of the building plan being analyzed. The horizontal or vertical slice is made where the critical windows are located.

Abrams, Donald W. *Low-Energy Cooling.* New York: Van Nostrand Reinhold, 1986.

AIA Research Corporation. *Solar Dwelling Design Concepts.* Washington, DC: U.S. Government Printing Office, 1976.

AIA Research Corporation. *Regional Guidelines for Building Passive Energy Conserving Homes.* Washington, DC: U.S. Government Printing Office, 1980.

Akbari, Hashem, J. S. Huang, and S. Davis. *Cooling Our Communities: A Guidebook on Tree Planting and Light-Colored Surfacing.* Washington, DC: EPA and DOE/Lawrence Berkeley Laboratory [LBL-31587], 1992.

Allard, Francis, ed. *Natural Ventilation in Buildings: A Design Handbook.* London: James & James, 1998.

Allen, Edward, drawings by David Swoboda and Edward Allen. *How Buildings Work: The Natural Order of Architecture*, 2nd ed. New York: Oxford University Press, 1995.

Allen, Edward, and Joseph Iano. *The Architect's Studio Companion: Technical Guidelines for Preliminary Design*, 3rd ed. New York: John Wiley & Sons, 2002.

American Wind Energy Association. *Permitting Small Wind Turbines: A Handbook.* Available at www.awea.org/smallwind/documents/permitting.pdf.

Ander, Gregg D. *Daylighting Performance and Design*, 2nd ed. Hoboken, NJ: John Wiley & Sons, 2003.

Anderson, Bruce. *Solar Energy: Fundamentals in Building Design.* New York: McGraw-Hill, 1977.

Anderson, Bruce, ed. *Solar Building Architecture.* Cambridge, MA: MIT Press, 1990.

Anderson, Bruce, and Malcolm Wells. *Passive Solar Energy.* Amherst, NH: Brick House Publishing, 1994.

Andrews, F. T. *Building Mechanical Systems.* New York: McGraw-Hill, 1977.

ASHRAE. *Passive Solar Heating Analysis: A Design Manual.* Atlanta: ASHRAE, 1984.

ASHRAE. *ASHRAE Terminology of Heating, Ventilation, Air Conditioning, and Refrigeration*, 2nd ed. Atlanta: ASHRAE, 1991.

ASHRAE. *Air-Conditioning Systems Design Manual.* Atlanta: ASHRAE, 1993.

ASHRAE. *ASHRAE Handbook Fundamentals.* Atlanta: ASHRAE, 1997.

ASHRAE Greenguide: The Design, Construction, and Operation of Sustainable Buildings. Atlanta: ASHRAE, 2006.

ASHRAE Handbook of Fundamentals. New York: American Society of Heating, Refrigerating, and Air-Conditioning Engineers.

Bachmann, Leonard. *Integrated Buildings: The Systems Basis of Architecture.* Hoboken, NJ: John Wiley & Sons, 2003.

Baird, George. *The Architectural Expression of Environmental Control Systems.* New York: Spon, 2001

Baker, Nick, and Koen Steemers. *Daylight Design of Buildings.* London: James & James, 2002.

Balcomb, J. Douglas. *Passive Solar Buildings.* Cambridge, MA: MIT Press, 1992.

Balcomb, J. Douglas, and Robert W. Jones. *Workbook for Workshop on Advanced Passive Solar Design*, July 12, 1987, Portland, Oregon. Sante Fe, NM: Balcomb Solar Association, 1987.

Banham, Reyner. *The Architecture of the Well-Tempered Environment*, 2nd ed. London: Architectural Press, 1984.

Barnett, Dianna Lopez, with William D. Browning. *A Primer on Sustainable Building.* Snowmass, CO: Rocky Mountain Institute, 1995.

Bartlett, Albert A. "Forgotten Fundamentals of the Energy Crisis."

American Journal of Physics, 46(9), September 1978.

Bearg, David W. *Indoor Air Quality and HVAC Systems.* Boca Raton, FL: Lewis Publishers/CRC Press, 1993.

Bell, James, and William Burt. *Designing Buildings for Daylight.* London: Construction Research Communications, 1995.

Bennett, Robert. *Sun Angles for Design.* Bala Cynwyd, PA: Robert Bennett, 1978.

Bobenhausen, William. *Simplified Design of HVAC Systems.* New York: John Wiley & Sons, 1994.

Boonstra, Chiel, ed. *Solar Energy in Building Renovation.* London: James & James, 1997.

Boutet, Terry S. *Controlling Air Movement: A Manual for Architects and Builders.* New York: McGraw-Hill, 1987.

Bowen, Arthur, Eugene Clark, and Kenneth Labs, eds. *Proceedings of the International Passive and Hybrid Cooling Conference*, Miami Beach, FL, Nov. 6–16, 1981. Newark, DE: American Section of the International Solar Energy Society, 1981.

Bowen, Arthur, and S. Gingras. "Wind Environments in Buildings and Urban Areas." Paper presented at the Sunbelt Conference, December, 1978.

Boyce, Peter. *Human Factors in Lighting*, 2nd ed. New York: Macmillan, 2003.

Boyce, P. R., N. H. Eklund, and S. N. Simpson. "Individual Lighting Control: Task Performance, Mood and Illuminance," *Journal of Illuminating Engineering Society.* 29: 131–142.

Boyer, Lester, and Walter Grondzik. *Earth Shelter Technology.* College Station, TX: Texas A&M University 1987.

Bradshaw, Vaughn. *Building Control Systems*, 3rd ed. New York: John Wiley & Sons, 2006.

Bradshaw, Vaughn. *The Building Environment: Active and Passive Control Systems.* Hoboken, NJ: Wiley, 2006. 3rd ed.

Brown, G. Z., and Mark DeKay. *Sun, Wind, and Light: Architectural Design Strategies*, 2nd ed. New York: John Wiley & Sons, 2000.

Brown, Robert D., and Terry J. Gillespie. *Microclimatic Landscape Design: Creating Thermal Comfort and Energy Efficiency.* New York: John Wiley & Sons, 1995.

Buckley, Shawn. *Sun Up to Sun Down.* New York: McGraw-Hill, 1979.

Butti, Ken, and John Perein. *A Golden Thread: 2500 Years of Solar Architecture.* New York: Van Nostrand Reinhold, 1980.

Campbell, C. J. *The Coming Oil Crisis.* Multi-Science Publishing Company & Petroconsultants S.A., 1988.

Campbell, C. J., and Jean H. Leherrére. "The End of Cheap Oil." *Scientific American, 278*(3). March 1998.

Carmody, John, and Raymond Sterling. *Earth Sheltered Housing Design*, 2nd ed. New York: Van Nostrand Reinhold, 1985.

Carmody, John, S. Selkowitz, E. S. Lee, D. Arasten, and T. Willmert, *Window Systems for High-Performance Buildings.* New York, Norton, 2004.

Carmody, John, Stephen Selkowitz, and Lisa Herschong. *Residential Windows: A Guide to New Technologies and Energy Performance*, 3rd ed. New York: Norton, 2007.

Carmody, John. *Builder's Foundation Handbook.* Oak Ridge National Laboratory, 1991. www.ornl.gov/sci/roofs+walls/foundation/ORNL_CON-295.pdf

Carver, Norman F., Jr. *Italian Hilltowns.* Kalamazoo, MI: Documan Press, 1993.

Clegg, Peter, and Derry Watkins. *Sunspaces: New Vistas for Living and Growing.* Charlotte, VT: Garden Way Publishing, Storey Communications, 1987.

Climate Atlas of the United States. Asheville, NC: U.S. Department of Commerce Environmental Science Services Administration, Environmental Data Service, 1983.

Climate Change: State of Knowledge. Washington, DC: Office of Science and Technology Policy, 1997.

Cofaigh, Eoin O., John A. Olley, and J. Owen Lewis. *The Climatic Dwelling: An Introduction to Climatic-Responsive Residential Architecture.* London: James & James, 1996.

Commission of the European Communities Directorate–General XII for Science Research and Development. *Daylighting in Architecture: A European Reference Book*, N. Baker, A. Fanchiotti, and K. Steemers, eds. London: James & James, 1993.

Commoner, Barry. *The Politics of Energy.* New York: Knopf, 1979.

Comparative Climatic Data for the United States/…/Prepared at the National Climatic Center. Asheville, NC: U.S. Department of Commerce, National Oceanic and Atmospheric Administration.

Cook, Jeffrey. "Cooling as the Absence of Heat: Strategies for the Prevention of Thermal Gain," *Proceedings of the International Passive and Hybrid Cooling Conference*, Miami Beach, FL, Nov, 6–16, 1981, ed. Arthur Bowen et al. Newark, DE: American Section of the International Solar Energy Society, 1981.

Cook, Jeffrey, ed. *Award Winning Passive Solar/House Designs.* New York: McGraw-Hill, 1984.

Cook, Jeffrey, ed. *Passive Cooling.* Cambridge, MA: MIT Press, 1989.

Cooling with Ventilation (SERI/SP-273-2966; DE96010701). Golden, CO: Solar Energy Research Institute, 1986.

Cooling Our Communities: A Guidebook on Tree Planting and Light Colored Surfacing. Washington, D.C.: U.S. Environmental Protection Agency, Office of Policy Analysis, Climate Change Division, 1992.

Crosbie, Michael J. *Green Architecture: A Guide to Sustainable Design.* Rockport, MA: Rockport Publications, 1994, Distributed by North Light Books, Cincinnati, OH.

Crowther, Richard L., ed. *Ecologic Architecture.* Butterworth Architecture, 1992.

Cuttle, Christopher. *Lighting by Design.* Burlington, MA: Architectural Press, 2003. "Desert Illumination." *Architecture.* October 1995, pp. 56–65.

Dagostino, Frank R. *Mechanical and Electrical Systems in Construction and Architecture.* Englewood Cliffs, NJ: Prentice Hall, 1995.

Daniels, Klaus. *The Technology of Ecological Building: Basic Principles and Measures, Examples and Ideas.* Trans. by Elizabeth Schwaiger. Basel, Switzerland: Birkhäuser, 1997.

Davidson, Joel. *The New Solar Electric Home: The Photovoltaics How-To Handbook.* Ann Arbor, MI: Aatec Publications, 1987.

Davies, Colin, and Ian Lambot. *Commerzbank Frankfurt: Prototype for an Ecological High-Rise.* Surrey, UIT Watermark, 1997.

DiLaura, David. *A History of Light and Lighting.* New York: Illuminating Engineering Society of North America, 2005.

Druse, Ken, with Margaret Roach. *The Natural Habitat Garden.* New York: Clarkson Potter, 1994.

Duly, Colin. *Houses of Mankind.* London: Thames and Hudson, 1979.

Duly, Colin. *The Houses of Mankind.* New York: Thames and Hudson, 1979.

Dunnett, Nigel, and Noël Kingsbury. *Planting Green Roofs and Living Walls.* Portland, OR: Timber Press, 2008.

Easton, David. *The Rammed Earth House.* White River Junction, VT: Chelsea Green Publishing, 1996.

Earth Pledge. *Green Roofs: Ecological Design and Construction.* Atglen, PA: Schiffer, 2005. "High Heat, High Tech." *Architecture.* October 1995. pp. 107–113.

Egan, M. David. *Concepts in Thermal Comfort.* Englewood Cliffs. NJ: Prentice-Hall, 1975.

Egan, M. David, and Victor W. Olgay *Architectural Lighting*, 2nd ed. Boston: McGraw-Hill, 2001.

Ehrlich, Paul R., and Anne H. Ehrlich. *The Population Explosion.* New York: Simon & Schuster Touchtone Books, 1991.

Energy Design Resources. *Skylighting Guidelines.* www.energydesign-resources.com/.

Environmental Protection Agency. *Cooling Our Communities.* Washington, DC: U.S. Environmental Protection Agency, Office of Policy Analysis, Climate Change Division, 1992.

Evans, Benjamin E. *Daylight in Architecture.* New York: McGraw-Hill, 1981.

Fathy, Hassan. *Natural Energy and Vernacular Architecture: Principles and Examples with Reference to Hot Arid Climates*. Chicago: University of Chicago Press, 1986.

Fitch, James Marston. *American Building: 1. The Historical Forces That Shaped It*, 2nd ed. New York: Schocken, 1973.

Fitch, James Marston, consulting ed. *Shelter: Models of Native Ingenuity: A Collection of Essays Published in Conjunction with an Exhibition of Katonah Gallery March 13–May 23, 1982*. The Katonah Galley, 1982.

Fitch, James Marston. *The Architecture of the American People*. New York: Oxford University Press, 2000.

Fitch, James M., with William Bobenhausen. *American Building: 2. The Environmental Forces That Shape It*. New York: Schocken, 1999.

Flynn, John E., J. A. Kremers, A. W. Segil, and G.Steffy. *Architectural Interior Systems: Lighting, Acoustics, Air Conditioning*, 3rd ed. New York: Van Nostrand Reinhold, 1992.

Fontoynont, Marc. *Daylighting Performance of Buildings*. London: James & James, 1999.

Ford, Robert M. *Mississippi Houses: Yesterday Toward Tomorrow*. Mississippi State University, 1982.

Foster, Ruth S., illustrations by James Lombardi. *Homeowner's Guide to Landscaping That Saves Energy Dollars*. New York: David McKay, 1978.

Francis, Mark. *Village Homes: A Community by Design: Case Studies in Land and Community Design*. Landscape Architecture Foundation, 2003.

Franta, Gregory, Kristine Anstead, and Gregg D. Ander. *Glazing Design Handbook for Energy Efficiency*. American Institute of Architects, 1997.

Futagawa, Yukio, ed. and photography. *Light and Space: Modern Architecture*. Tokyo: A.D.A. EDITA Tokyo Co., 1994.

Gelbspan, Ross. *The Heat Is On: The High Stakes Battle Over Earth's Threatened Climate*. Reading, MA: Addison-Wesley, 1997.

Gipe, Paul. *Wind Power for Home and Business: Renewable Energy for the 1990's and Beyond*. Post Mills, VT: Chelsea Green, 1993.

Gipe, Paul. *Wind Energy Comes of Age*. New York: John Wiley & Sons, 1995.

Givoni, Baruch. *Man, Climate and Architecture*, 2nd ed. New York: Van Nostrand Reinhold, 1976.

Givoni, Baruch. "Integrated-Passive Systems for Heating of Buildings by Solar Energy," *Architectural Science Review*, 24(2): 29–41, June 1981.

Givoni, Baruch. *Passive and Low Energy Cooling of Buildings*. New York: Van Nostrand Reinhold, 1994.

Giovoni, Baruch. *Climate Considerations in Building and Urban Design*. New York: Van Nostrand Reinhold, 1998.

Golany, Gideon, ed. *Housing in Arid Lands—Design and Planning*, New York: John Wiley & Sons, 1980.

Golany, Gideon. *Design and Thermal Performance: Below-Ground Dwellings in China*. Newark, DE: University of Delaware Press; London: Associated University Press, 1990.

Gordon, Gary and James L. Nuckolls. *Interior Lighting for Designers*, 4th ed. Hoboken, NJ: John Wiley & Sons, 2003.

Gordon, Gary, and James L. Nuckolls. *Interior Lighting for Designers*, 3rd ed. New York: John Wiley & Sons, 1995.

Gore, Al. *Earth in the Balance: Ecology and the Human Spirit*. Houghton Mifflin, 1992.

Goulding, John R., J. Owen Lewis, and Theo C. Steemers, eds. *Energy Conscious Design: A Primer for Architects*. London: Batsford, 1992.

Groesbeck, Wesley, and Jan Stiefel. *The Resource Guide to Sustainable Landscapes and Gardens*, 2nd ed. Environmental Resources, 1995.

Grosslight, Jane. *Lighting Kitchens and Baths*. Tallahassee, FL: Durwood, 1993.

Grosslight, Jane, *Light, Light, Light: Effective Use of Daylight and Electric Lighting in Residential and Commercial Spaces*. Tallahassee, FL: Durwood, 1998.

Grosslight, Jane. *Light, Light, Light, 3rd Ed*. Tallahassee, FL: Durwood, 1990.

Guiding Principles of Sustainable Design. Denver, CO: U.S. Department of the Interior, National Parks Service, Denver Center, 1993.

Guise, David. *Design and Technology in Architecture*, rev. ed. New York: Van Nostrand Reinhold, 1991.

Guzowski, Mary. *Daylighting for Sustainable Design*. New York: McGraw-Hill, 1999.

Hawken, Paul. *The Ecology of Commerce*. New York: HarperCollins, 1993.

Hawken, Paul, Amory Lovins, and L. Hunter Lovins. *Natural Capitalism: Creating the Next Industrial Revolution*. Boston: Little, Brown, 1999.

Heinz, Thomas A. "Frank Lloyd Wright's Jacobs II House," *Fine Home Building*, 20–27, June/July 1981.

Helms, Ronald N., and M. Clay Belcher. *Lighting for Energy-Efficient Luminous Environments*. New York: Prentice Hall, 1991.

Heschong, Lisa. *Thermal Delight in Architecture*. Cambridge, MA: MIT Press, 1979.

Hestnes, Anne Grete, Robert Hastings, and Bjarne Saxhof. *Solar Energy House: Strategies, Technologies, Examples*. London: James & James, 1997.

Highshoe, Gary L. *Native Trees, Shrubs, and Vines for Urban and Rural America: A Planting Design Manual for Environmental Designers*. New York: Van Nostrand Reinhold, 1988.

Hopkinson, Ralph Galbraith, P. Petherbridge, and James Longmore. *Daylighting*. London: Heinemann, 1966.

Hopkinson, R. G. *Architectural Physics: Lighting*. London: H. M. Stationery Office, 1963.

Hottes, Alfred C. *Climbers and Ground Covers, Including a Vast Array of Hardy and Subtropical Vines Which Climb or Creep*. New York: De La Mare, 1947.

Houben, Hugo, and Hubert Guillaud. *Earth Construction: A Comprehensive Guide*. London: Intermediate Technology Publications, 1994.

Humm, O. *[Photovoltaik und Architekture] Photovoltaics in Architecture: The Integration of Photovoltaic Cells in Building Envelopes*. Basel and Boston: Birkhaüser.

Hyde, Richard. *Climate Responsive Design: A Study of Buildings in Moderate and Hot Humid Climates*. London: Spon, 2000.

IESNA. *Lighting Handbook*. 2000

International Energy Agency. *Passive Solar Commercial and Institutional Buildings: A Sourcebook of Examples and Design Insights*. S. R. Hastings, ed. New York: John Wiley & Sons, 1994.

The IESNA Lighting Handbook: Reference and Application. 9th ed. New York: Illuminating Engineering Society of North America, 2000.

Jaffe, Martin S., and Duncan Erley, illustrated by Dava Lurie. *Protecting Solar Access for Residential Development: A Guidebook for Planning Officials.* Washington, DC: U.S. Department of Housing and Urban Development, Office of Policy Development and Research, 1979.

Jones, David Lloyd. *Architecture and the Environment: Bioclimatic Building Design.* Woodstock, NY: Overlook Press/Peter Mayer, 1998.

Jones, R. W., and R. D. McFarland. *The Sunspace Primer: A Guide to Passive Solar Heating.* New York: Van Nostrand Reinhold, 1984.

Kachadorian, James. *The Passive Solar House: Using Solar Design to Heat and Cool Your Home.* White River Junction, VT: Chelsea Green Publishing, 1997.

K. Cathcart Anders Architects. *Building Integrated Photovoltaics.* National Renewable Energy Laboratory, 1993. Available from NTIS, NTIS Order No. DE95004056.

Karlen, Mark, and James Benya. *Lighting Design Basics.* Hoboken, NJ: John Wiley & Sons, 2004.

Kellert, Stephen R., and Edward O. Wilson. *The Biophilia Hypothesis.* Washington, DC: Island Press, 1993.

King, Bruce. *Buildings of Earth and Straw: Structural Design for Rammed Earth and Straw-Bale Architecture.* Sausalito, CA: Ecological Design Press, 1996.

Knight, Paul A. *Mechanical Systems Retrofit Manual: A Guide for Residential Design.* New York: Van Nostrand Reinhold, 1987.

Knowles, Ralph L. *Energy and Form: An Ecological Approach to Urban Growth.* Cambridge, MA: MIT Press, 1974.

Knowles, Ralph L. *Sun Rhythm Form.* Cambridge, MA: MIT Press, 1981.

Knowles, Ralph L. "On Being the Right Size"; "The Ritual of Space"; "Rhythm and Ritual"; "The Solar Envelope." www.rcf.usc.edu/ ~rknowles.

Knowles, Ralph L. *Ritual House: Drawing on Nature's Rhythms for Architecture and Urban Design.* Washington, D.C.: Island Press, 2006.

Knowles, Ralph. *Rituals of Place.* Retrieved March 3, 2008 from www .rcf.usc.edu/~rknowles/rituals_place/ rituals_place.html

Kohlmaier, Georg, and Barna von Sartory. *Das Glashaus: Ein Bautypus des 19. Jahrhunderts.* Munich: Prestel-Verlag, 1981.

Komp, Richard J. *Practical Photovoltaics—Electricity from Solar Cells,* 3rd ed. Ann Arbor: Aatec, 1995.

Konya, Allan. *Design Primer for Hot Climates.* London: Architectural Press; New York: Whitney Library of Design, 1980.

Köster, Helmut. *Dynamic Daylighting Architecture Basics, Systems, Projects.* Basel: Birkhäuser, 2004.

Krigger, John. *Residential Energy: Cost Savings and Comfort for Existing Buildings.* Helena, MT: Saturn Resources Management, 1994.

Kukreja, C. P. *Tropical Architecture.* New Delhi: Tata McGraw-Hill, 1978.

Kwok, Alison G., and Walter T. Grondzik. *The Green Studio Handbook: Environmental Strategies for Schematic Design.* Burlington, MA: Oxford, 2007.

Lam, William M. C. *Sunlighting as Formgiver for Architecture.* New York: Van Nostrand Reinhold, 1986.

Lam, William M. C. *Perception and Lighting as Formgivers for Architecture.* Christopher Hugh Ripman, ed. New York: Van Nostrand Reinhold, 1992.

Lang, Paul V. *Principles of Air Conditioning,* 5th ed. Albany, NY: Delmar, 1995.

Leibowitz, Sandra. *Ecological Design and Building Schools.* New Village Press, 2005.

Leslie, Russell P., and Kathryn M. Conway. *The Lighting Pattern Book for Homes.* New York: McGraw-Hill, 1996.

Leslie, Russell P., and Paula A. Rodgers. *The Outdoor Lighting Pattern Book.* New York: McGraw-Hill, 1996.

Lewis, Jack. *Support Systems for Buildings.* Englewood Cliffs, NJ: Prentice Hall, 1986.

Lighting Handbook. Mark S. Rea. New York: Illuminating Engineering Society of North America, 1999.

Littlefair, P. J. *Designing Innovative Daylighting.* Watford, Hertfordshire, England: Construction Research Communications, 1996.

Los Alamos National Lab. *Passive Solar Heating Analysis—A Design Manual.* Atlanta: ASHRAE, 1984.

Lovins, Amory. "More Profit with Less Carbon." *Scientific American.* September 2005.

Lovins, Amory B. *Soft Energy Paths.* New York: Harper Colophon Books, 1977.

Lovins, Amory B., and L. Hunter Lovins. *Brittle Power: Energy Strategy for National Security.* Andover, MA: Brick House Publishing, 1982.

Lovins, Amory B. "More Profit with Less Carbon." *Scientific American,* September 2005, 74–82.

Lovins, Amory B. *Winning the Oil Endgame.* Snowmass, CO: Rocky Mountain Institute, 2004. Available at www.oilendgame.com.

Lstiburek, Joseph W. *Exemplary Home Builder's Field Guide.* Triangle Park, NC: North Carolina Alternative Energy Corporation, 1994.

Lstiburek, Joseph W. *Builder's Guide—Hot-Dry and Mixed-Dry Climates; Builder's Guide—Cold Climates; Builder's Guide—Mixed Climates: A Systems Approach to Designing and Building Homes That Are Healthy, Comfortable, Durable, Energy Efficient and Environmentally Responsible.* Building Science Corporation, 1998.

Lstiburek, Joseph W. *Builder's Guide to Cold Climates: Details for Design and Construction.* Newtown, CT: Taunton Press, 2000.

Lstiburek, Joseph W. *The Builder's Guide to Mixed Climates: Details for Design and Construction.* Newtown, CT: Taunton Press, 2000.

Lstiburek, Joseph W., and John Carmody. *Moisture Control Handbook.* New York: Van Nostrand Reinhold, 1993.

Lyle, David. *The Book of Masonry Stoves: Rediscovering an Old Way of Warming.* White River Junction, VT: Chelsea Green Publishing, 1984.

Lyle, John Tillman. *Regenerative Design for Sustainable Development.* New York: John Wiley & Sons, 1994.

Lyle, John Tillman. *Design for Human Ecosystems: Landscape, Land Use, and Natural Resources.* Washington, DC: Island Press, 1999.

Mann, Peter A. *Illustrated Residential and Commercial Construction.* Englewood Cliffs, NJ: Prentice Hall 1989.

Matus, Vladimir. *Design for Northern Climates: Cold-Climate Planning and*

Environmental Design. New York: Van Nostrand Reinhold, 1988.

Mazria, Edward. *The Passive Solar Energy Book: Expanded Professional Ed.* Emmaus, PA: Rodale Press, 1979.

McDonough, William and Michael Braungart. "The Next Industrial Revolution." *The Atlantic Monthly*. October 1998. Retrieved March 3, 2008 from www.theatlantic.com/doc/199810/environment

McHarg, Ian L. *Design with Nature*. New York: John Wiley & Sons, 1995.

McIntyre, Maureen, ed. *Solar Energy: Today's Technologies for a Sustainable Future*. Boulder, CO: ASES, 1997.

McPherson, E. Gregory, ed. *Energy Conserving Site Design*. Waldorf, MD: American Society of Landscape Architects, 1984.

Miller, Burke. *Buildings for a Sustainable America: Case Studies*. Boulder, CO: ASES, 1997.

Millet, Marietta S. *Light Revealing Architecture*. New York: Van Nostrand Reinhold, 1996.

Moffat, Anne Simon, and Marc Schiler, drawings by Dianne Zampino. *Landscape Design That Saves Energy*. New York: Morrow, 1981.

Moffat, Anne Simon, and Marc Schiler. *Energy-Efficient and Environmental Landscaping*. South Newfane, VT: Appropriate Solutions Press, 1993.

Moore, Fuller. *Concepts and Practice of Architectural Daylighting*. New York: Van Nostrand, 1985.

Moore, Fuller. *Environmental Control Systems*. New York: McGraw-Hill, 1993.

Nabokov, Peter, and Robert Easton. *Native American Architecture*. New York: Oxford University Press, 1989.

National Audubon Society and Croxton Collaborative, Architects. *Audubon House. Building the Environmentally Responsible, Energy-Efficient Office*. New York: John Wiley & Sons, 1994.

Neumann, Dietrich. *Architecture of the Night: The Illuminated Building*. Munich: Prestel, 2002.

Norton, John. *Building with Earth: A Handbook*. London: Intermediate Technology Publications, 1996.

Norwood, Ken, and Kathleen Smith. *Rebuilding Community in America:* *Housing for Ecological Living, Personal Empowerment, and the New Extended Family*. Berkeley, CA: Shared Living Resource Center, 1995.

Nuckolls, James L. *Interior Lighting*, 2nd ed. New York, John Wiley & Sons, 1983.

NY-Star Builder's Field Guide. Albany, NY: NY-Star, Inc., 1994.

Olgyay, Victor. *Design with Climate: A Bioclimatic Approach to Architectural Regionalism*. Princeton, NJ: Princeton University Press, 1953.

Olgyay, Aladar, and Victor Olgyay. *Solar Control and Shading Devices*. Princeton, NJ: Princeton University Press, 1957.

Olivieri, Joseph B. *How to Design Heating-Cooling Comfort Systems*, 4th ed. Troy, MI: Business News Publisher, 1987.

Ottesen, Carole. *The Native Plant Primer: Trees, Shrubs, and Wildflowers for Natural Gardens*. New York: Crown, 1995.

Panchyk, Katherine. *Solar Interior: Energy Efficient Spaces Designed for Comfort*. New York: Van Nostrand Reinhold, 1991.

Pearson, David. *The Natural House Catalog: Everything You Need to Create an Environmentally Friendly Home*. New York: Fireside, 1996.

Pearson, David. *The New Natural House Book-Creating a Healthy, Harmonious, and Ecologically Sound Home*. New York: Simon & Schuster, 2nd ed 1998.

Pepchinski, Mary. "Commerzbank." *Architectural Record*, January 1998.

Perlin, John. *From Space to Earth: The Story of Solar Electricity*. Ann Arbor, MI: Aatec, 1999.

Petit, Jack, Debra L. Bassert, and Cheryl Kollin. *Building Greener Neighborhoods: Trees as Part of the Plan*, 2nd ed. Washington, DC: American Forests: Home Builders Press, 1998.

Phillips, Derek. *Daylighting: Natural Light in Architecture*. Amsterdam: Elsevier, 2004.

Phillips, Derek. *Lighting Modern Buildings*.

Phillips, Derek. *Lighting Modern Buildings*. Oxford: Architectural Press, 2000.

Photovoltaics in the Building Environment. American Institute of Architects (AIA), 1996. Available from AIA Orders, 2 Winter Sport Lane, P.O. Box 60, Williston, VT 05495-0060.

Potts, Michael. *The New Independent Home: People and Houses That Harvest the Sun*. Rev. ed. White River Junction, VT: Chelsea Green Publishing, 1999.

Ramsey/Sleeper Architectural Graphic Standards, 11th ed. John R. Hoke, ed. New York: John Wiley & Sons, 2007. (American Institute of Architects).

Rapoport, Amos. *House Form and Culture* (Foundations of Cultural Geography Series). Englewood Cliffs, NJ: Prentice Hall, 1969.

Recommendations to the United Nations Commission on Sustainable Development: Final Report on the NGO Renewable Energy Initiative. Freiburg, Germany: ISES, 1995.

Reid, Esmond. *Understanding Buildings: A Multidisciplinary Approach*. Cambridge, MA: MIT Press, 1984.

Reif, D. K. *Solar Retrofit: Adding Solar to Your Home*. Amherst, NH: Brick House, 1981.

Roaf, Sue, David Chrichton, and Fergus Nicol. *Adapting Buildings and Cities for Climate Change: A 21st. Century Survival Guide*. Oxford, UK: Architectural Press, 2005.

Robbins, Claude. *Daylighting: Design and Analysis*. New York: Van Nostrand Reinhold, 1986.

Robinette, Gary O., ed. *Energy Efficient Site Design*. New York: Van Nostrand Reinhold, 1983.

Robinette, Gary O., and Charles McClenon. *Landscape Planning for Energy Conservation*. New York: Van Nostrand Reinhold, 1983.

Rocky Mountain Institute Staff. *Green Development: Integrating Ecology and Real Estate*. New York: John Wiley & Sons, 1998.

Rudofsky, Bernard. *Architecture without Architects: A Short Introduction to Non-Pedigreed Architecture*. New York: Museum of Modern Art; Garden City, NJ: Doubleday, 1965.

Rudofsky, Bernard. *The Prodigious Builders: Notes Toward a Natural History of Architecture*. London: Secker and Warburg, 1997.

Ruffner, James A., and Frank E. Bair. *The Weather Almanac*, 2nd ed. Detroit, MI: Gale Research, 1997.

Rush, Richard D., ed. *The Building Systems Integration Handbook.* New York: John Wiley & Sons, 1986.

Santamouris, Mat, and D. Asimakopoulos, eds. *Passive Cooling of Buildings.* London: James & James, 1996.

Schaeffer, J. *Eco-Logic: A Place in the Sun.* 1997.

Scheer, Hermann. *A Solar Manifesto: The Need for a Total Energy Supply—and How to Provide It.* London: James & James, 1994.

Schiler, Marc. *Simplified Design of Building Lighting.* New York: John Wiley & Sons, 1997.

Schiler, Marc, ed., *Simulating Daylight with Architectural Models.* Los Angeles. University of Southern California Press, 1985.

Sick, Friedrich, and Thomas Erge, eds. *Photovoltaics in Buildings: A Design Handbook for Architects.* London: James & James, 1996.

Singh, Madanjeet. *The Timeless Energy of the Sun for Life and Peace with Nature.* San Francisco: Sierra Club Books, 1998.

Solar Age [This periodical has been discontinued, but old issues are still very valuable]. Published by Solar Age Inc., 1976–1986; temporarily continued as *Progressive Builder*, published by International Solar Energy Society, 1986–1987.

Solar Today. American Solar Energy Society. Monthly.

Steffy, Gary R. *Time-Saver Standards for Architectural Lighting.* New York: McGraw-Hill, 2000.

Steffy, Gary R. *Architectural Lighting Design.* 2nd ed. New York: John Wiley & Sons, 2001.

Stein, Benjamin, John S. Reynolds, W. T. Grondzik, and A.G. Kwok. *Mechanical and Electrical Equipment for Buildings*, 10th ed. New York: John Wiley & Sons, 2006.

Stein, Richard G. *Architecture and Energy: Conserving Energy Through Rational Design.* New York: Anchor Books, 1977.

Sternberg, Guy, and Jim Wilson. *Landscaping with Native Trees.* Shelburne, VT: Chapters Publishers, 1995.

Steven Winter Associates. *The Passive Solar Design and Construction Handbook.* Ed. Michael J. Crosbie. New York: John Wiley & Sons, 1998.

Strong, Steven J., *The Solar Electric House: Energy for the Environmentally Responsive, Energy-Independent Home.* White River Junction, VT: Chelsea Green, 1993.

Strong, Steven J., with William G. Scheller. *The Solar Electric House: A Design Manual for Home-Scale Photovoltaic Power Systems.* Emmaus, PA: Rodale Press, 1987.

Susanka, Sarah. *The Not So Big House: A Blueprint for the Way We Really Live.* Newtown, CT: Taunton Press, 1998.

Szokolay, Steven V. *Environmental Science Handbook for Architects and Builders.* New York: John Wiley & Sons, 1980.

Szokolay, Steven V. *Introduction to Architectural Science: The Basis of Sustainable Design.* Oxford: Elsevier, 2004.

Tabb, Phillip. *Solar Energy Planning: A Guide to Residential Settlement.* New York: McGraw-Hill, 1984.

Tao, William K. Y. *Mechanical and Electrical Systems in Buildings,* 2nd ed. Upper Saddle River, NJ: Prentice Hall, 2000.

Taylor, John S. *Commonsense Architecture: A Cross-Cultural Survey of Practical Design Principles.* New York: Norton, 1983.

Thomas, Randall, ed. *Environmental Design: An Introduction for Architects and Engineers.* New York: E & FN Spon, 1999.

Traister, John E. *Residential Heating, Ventilating, and Air Conditioning: Design and Application.* Englewood Cliffs, NJ: Prentice Hall, 1990.

Trost, J. *Electrical and Lighting.* Upper Saddle River, NJ: Prentice Hall, 1999.

Trost, J. *Heating, Ventilating, and Air Conditioning.* Upper Saddle River, NJ: Prentice Hall, 1999.

Tuluca, Adrian. *Energy-Efficient Design and Construction for Commercial Buildings.* New York: McGraw-Hill, 1997.

Underground Space Center, University of Minnesota. *Earth Sheltered Housing Design. Guidelines, Examples, and References.* New York: Van Nostrand Reinhold, 1979.

U.S. Department of Energy, Office of Project and Facilities Management. *Site Development Planning for Energy Management.* 1985 DOE/MA-0129

U.S. Department of Housing and Urban Development. *Protecting Solar Access for Residential Development.* 1979 by Jaffe, M., and Erley, D. HVD-PDR-445.

U.S. Department of Housing and Urban Development. *Moisture-Resistant Homes: A Best Practice Guide and Plan Review Tool for Builders and Designers with a Supplemental Guide for Homeowners.* www.huduser.org.

Van der Ryn, Sim. *The Toilet Papers: Recycling Waste and Conserving Water.* Ecological Design Press, 1995.

Van der Ryn, Sim, and Peter Calthorpe. *Sustainable Communities: A New Design Synthesis for Cities, Suburbs, and Towns.* San Francisco: Sierra Club Books, 1986.

Van der Ryn, Sim, and Stuart Cowan. *Ecological Design.* Washington, DC: Island Press, 1995.

Vickery, Robert L. *Sharing Architecture.* Charlottesville: University Press of Virginia, 1983.

Watson, Donald. *Designing and Building a Solar House: Your Place in the Sun.* Rev. ed. Charlotte, VT: Garden Way Publishing, 1977.

Watson, Donald, and Kenneth Labs. *Climatic Design: Energy-Efficient Building Principles and Practices.* New York: McGraw-Hill, 1993.

Wendehack, Clifford C. *Golf and Country Clubs.* New York: William Helburn, 1929.

Wilson, Edward O. "Is Humanity Suicidal: We're Flirting with the Extinction of Our Species." *New York Times Magazine*, May 30, 1993.

Wirtz, Richard. *HVAC/R Terminology: a Quick Reference Guide.* Upper Saddle River, NJ: Prentice Hall, 1998.

World Commission on Environment and Development. *Our Common Future.* Oxford: Oxford University Press, 1987.

Wright, Lawrence. *Home Fires Burning: The History of Domestic Heating and Cooking.* London: Routledge & Kegan Paul, 1964.

Zeiher, Laura C. *The Ecology of Architecture: A Complete Guide to Creating the Environmentally Conscious Building.* New York: Whitney Library of Design, 1996.

Zweibel, K. *Harnessing Solar Power: The Photovoltaics Challenge.* New York: Plenum Press, 1990.

Trees, 221, 304, 324–327, 340. *See also* Plants
Trellis, 241–242, 325
Trigonometric method, 618
Trombe, Felix, 158, 325
Trombe walls, 153, 158–163, 567
  design guidelines, 163
Tropic of Cancer, 133
Tropic of Capricorn, 134
Trulli, Apulia, Italy, 261
Tuffa cones, 262–263
Tungsten filaments, 437
Tungsten halogen lamps, *see* Lamp, halogen
Turbines, 30–35, 182
Turning vanes, 276
Twain, Mark, 72
2030 Challenge, 11

U-coefficient, *see* Heat-flow coefficient
Ultraviolet radiation, *see* Radiation
Underground buildings, *see* Earth sheltering
Underhill, Michael, 311
Undershot wheel, *see* Hydropower
Unite d'Habitation at Marseilles, France, 278
United Nations Headquarters in New York City, 253, 255
United Nations World Commission on Environment and Development, 13
United States:
  energy consumption, 2, 25, 28, 38–39
  hydropower use, 34
  oil imports, 27, 30
  population, 38
  production of CO_2, 22, 39
United States climate regions, *see* Climate, regions (U.S.)
Unit heaters, 518
University of California at Davis, 253
Uranium, 29
Urban Villa, 155–156, 562–565
Urethane, *see* Insulation
U.S. Department of Energy (DOE), 471
U.S. Department of Housing and Urban Development (HUD), 315
U.S. Environmental Protection Agency (EPA), 251, 502
User's manual for The Emerald People's Utility District Headquarters, 567
U.S. Green Building Council (USGBC), 11, 386
U.S. Pavilion, Expo' 67, Montreal, 58, 238–239

Vacuum, 475
Vacuum bottles, 475
Vacuum-insulated panels (VIP), *see* Insulation
Vacuum insulation, *see* Insulation
Vacuum-tube solar collectors, 197. *See also* Active solar, system
Valence (bracket) lighting, *see* Lighting
Vancouver City Library, BC, Canada, 330
Van der Ryn, Sym, 556
Vapor barriers, 498–500
Vapor compression refrigeration, *see* Compression refrigeration cycle
Vapor diffusion, 498
Vaporization, 43
Variable-air-volume (VAV) systems, 532–533
VAV control boxes, 533
Vegetation, *see* Plants
Veiling reflections, 364–366, 369–370, 374, 394, 407, 448–449
Venetian architecture, 209
Venetian blinds, 223, 249, 404–405
Venice, Italy, 209
Vent, 500
  areas, 501
  ridge, 500
  soffits, 500
Ventilation, 464, 496–497, 543–546
  demand-controlled, 544
Ventilation systems, 543–546
Ventilators, 276–277
Ventura Coastal Corp. Administration Building, 402–403
Venturi effect, 500
Venturi passive ventilators, 270
Venturi tubes, 269
Veranda, 208, 265
Vernacular architecture, 3–7, 208–210, 258–266, 296–299
Vestibule doors, 497
Victorian architecture, 209
Village Homes in Davis, CA, 338–339
Vines, 221–222, 325, 328, 332, 567
VIP, *see* Vacuum-insulated panels
Visible radiation, *see* Radiation
Visible transmittance, 393
Vision, 353–354,
  peripheral, 354
Visitors Center at Zion National Park, UT, 159–160, 289–290
Visual comfort probability (VCP), 363
Visual light distribution, 451
Visual performance, *see* Task
Vitamin D deficiency (rickets), 373
Vitruvius, 71–72, 148

Volatile organic compounds (VOCs), 544
Voltage, *see* Low voltage
Volumetric heat capacity, *see* Heat storage materials
Vortec™, 499

Wall furnace, 516, 518
Wall illumination, *see* Lighting
Walls (as thermal envelopes), 476
Wallwasher, 447–448
"Waste equals food," 33
Water-resistant barriers, 499
Water table, 280–281, 675–677
Water tubes, 159
Waterwheels, *see* Hydropower
Watt-hours, *see* Electrical energy
Wattle-and-daub, 463
Watts per square feet, 436
Watts per square meter, 436
Wavelength, *see* Radiation, wavelength
Wave power, 35
Waverly Plantation, Columbus, MS, 265–266
Weather, 72
WEGROUP, 565
Well water temperatures, 291
West Point Pepperell factory, Lanett, AL, 527
Wet-bulb temperature, 62–63
Wilson, Alex, 10, 14
Wilson, E. O., 323
Wind, 82. *See also* Energy, wind
  barriers, 498
  power, 30–32, Color Plate 22
  resources, Color Plate 22
  roses, 81–85
  scoops, 258–259
  screens, *see* Windbreaks
  site-design, 317–323
  speed, 82, 88–121
  towers, 258–260
  turbines, 30–32
Windbreaks, 317–318, 320
Windchill factor, 60
Windmills, 30–31.
Windows, 370, 484–489. *See also* Daylighting; Glazing
  comparison of R-values, 406–407, 486
  and insect screens, 275–276
  location, 153, 394, 397–399
  operable, 578–582
  orientation, 394–395
  R-value, 484–489
  sizing, 156–158, 163, 166–167
  types, 273–274